Environmental History and the American South

environmental
history
and the
american
south

Environmental History and the American South

A Reader

Edited by
PAUL S. SUTTER
and
CHRISTOPHER J. MANGANIELLO

The University of Georgia Press

Athens & London

Copyrights and acknowledgments for previously published works appear on pages vii–ix, which constitute a continuation of the copyright page.

Printed digitally in the United States of America

Library of Congress Cataloging-in-Publication Data

Environmental history and the American South : a reader / edited by
Paul S. Sutter and Christopher J. Manganiello.
        p. cm. — (Environmental history and the American South)
    Includes bibliographical references and index.
    ISBN-13: 978-0-8203-3280-2 (hardcover : alk. paper)
    ISBN-10: 0-8203-3280-1 (hardcover : alk. paper)
    ISBN-13: 978-0-8203-3322-9 (pbk. : alk. paper)
    ISBN-10: 0-8203-3322-0 (pbk. : alk. paper)
    1. Southern States—Environmental conditions. 2. Ecology—Southern
States—History. 3. Agriculture—Environmental aspects—Southern States—
History. 4. Nature—Effect of human beings on—Southern States—History.
5. Natural history—Southern States. 6. Environmental protection—Southern
States—History. I. Sutter, Paul. II. Manganiello, Christopher J., 1973–
    GE155.S68E585 2009
    333.950975—dc22   2008037799

British Library Cataloging-in-Publication Data available

CONTENTS

ACKNOWLEDGMENTS AND EDITORS' NOTES

ASSEMBLING THIS VOLUME was a difficult task, and we have incurred some debts along the way. First, we would like to thank all of the authors who agreed to have their essays reprinted in this volume. Each patiently worked with us to edit and adapt their essays in small but important ways. All the authors had the opportunity to make small changes to their essays. Mostly these involved fixing errors from the original versions or polishing prose. Careful readers familiar with the originals will notice small changes to the text in some of these essays. Second, for reasons of length and copyright, we have omitted all photographs, maps, tables, and other illustrations that appeared in the original versions of these essays. In doing so, we also edited out explicit textual references to these visual materials. Finally, for almost every essay we have shortened the notes from the original journal versions, mostly by trimming discursive discussions. We thank the authors for countenancing these changes. *For those people interested in the full notes for any of these articles, please consult the original journal versions.* We also want to express our appreciation to Jack Temple Kirby, who agreed to write an original epilogue for this volume.

We are indebted to the editors of the journals in which these articles originally appeared, many of whom helped us to secure electronic versions of these pieces. We also want to thank the copyright holders who agreed to allow us to reprint these essays, in some cases at reduced permissions rates. We received two supportive and constructively critical outside reviews for this project, which made it better in important ways. Finally, we deeply appreciate the enthusiasm and assistance of Derek Krissoff, our acquisitions editor, and the entire production staff at the University of Georgia Press, who consistently make beautiful books.

Below are the original publication citations for the reprinted essays that appear in this volume:

Virginia DeJohn Anderson, "Animals into the Wilderness: The Development of Livestock Husbandry in the Seventeenth-Century Chesapeake," *William and Mary Quarterly* 59, no. 2 (2002): 377–408. Reprinted courtesy of the Omohundro Institute of Early American History and Culture.

James Taylor Carson, "Horses and the Economy and Culture of the Choctaw Indians, 1690–1840," *Ethnohistory* 42, no. 3 (1995): 495–513. Copyright 1995 The American Society for Ethnohistory. All rights reserved. Used by permission of the publisher.

Judith Carney, "Landscapes of Technology Transfer: Rice Cultivation and African Continuities," *Technology and Culture* 37, no. 1 (January 1996): 5–35. © Society for the History of Technology. Reprinted with permission of The John Hopkins University Press.

S. Max Edelson, "Clearing Swamps, Harvesting Forests: Trees and the Making of a Plantation Landscape in the Colonial South Carolina Lowcountry," *Agricultural History* (Summer 2007): 381–406. Reprinted courtesy of the Agricultural History Society.

Harry Watson, "'The Common Rights of Mankind': Subsistence, Shad, and Commerce in the Early Republican South," *Journal of American History* 83 (1996): 13–43. Reprinted courtesy of the Organization of American Historians.

Lisa Brady, "The Wilderness of War: Nature and Strategy in the American Civil War," *Environmental History* 10, no. 3 (July 2005): 421–47. Published by the American Society for Environmental History and the Forest History Society Durham, N.C.

Mart Stewart, "If John Muir Had Been an Agrarian: American Environmental History West and South," *Environment and History* 11 (2005): 139–62. Reprinted courtesy of The White Horse Press.

Claire Strom, "Texas Fever and the Dispossession of the Southern Yeoman Farmer," *Journal of Southern History* 66, no. 1 (February 2000): 49–74. Copyright 2000 by the Southern Historical Association. Reprinted by permission of the Editor.

Ralph H. Lutts, "Like Manna from God: The American Chestnut Trade in Southwestern Virginia," *Environmental History* 9, no. 3 (2004): 497–525. Published by the American Society for Environmental History and the Forest History Society Durham, N.C.

Albert G. Way, "Burned to Be Wild: Herbert Stoddard and the Roots of Ecological Conservation in the Southern Longleaf Pine Forest," *Environmental History*

11, no. 3 (July 2006): 500–526. Published by the American Society for
Environmental History and the Forest History Society Durham, N.C.

William Boyd, "Making Meat: Science, Technology, and American Poultry
Production," *Technology and Culture* 42, no. 4 (2001): 631–64. © Society for
the History of Technology. Reprinted with permission of The John Hopkins
University Press.

Joshua Blu Buhs, "The Fire Ant Wars: Nature and Science in the Pesticide
Controversies of the Late Twentieth Century," *Isis* 93 (2002): 377–400.
Reprinted courtesy of the University of Chicago Press.

Eileen Maura McGurty, "From NIMBY to Civil Rights: The Origins of the
Environmental Justice Movement," *Environmental History* 2, no. 3 (1997):
301–23. Published by the American Society for Environmental History and the
Forest History Society Durham, N.C.

Ted Steinberg, "Do It Yourself Deathscape: The Unnatural History of Natural
Disaster in South Florida," *Environmental History* 2, no. 4 (1997): 414–38.
Published by the American Society for Environmental History and the Forest
History Society Durham, N.C.

Craig E. Colten, "Reintroducing Nature to the City: Wetlands in New Orleans,"
Environmental History 7, no. 2 (2002): 226–46. Published by the American
Society for Environmental History and the Forest History Society Durham,
N.C.

Environmental History and the American South

PAUL S. SUTTER

Introduction

No More the Backward Region: Southern

Environmental History Comes of Age

IN THE SUMMER of 2000 *Southern Cultures* published an essay by Otis L. Graham titled "Again the Backward Region?: Environmental History in and of the American South." To the hardy few who had
been working in the field, it was an all-too-familiar call to action.[1] The
southeastern United States, despite a long and dramatic history of human-
environmental interactions and a growing contemporary assault on its
natural landscapes, remained at best a peripheral subject for environmental historians. There were, of course, some important exceptions, but they
were few enough to prove the rule.[2] American environmental history had
grown up in the West, and it had spent some time in New England and the
Midwest as well, but it had rarely ventured below the Mason-Dixon Line.[3]
The absence of a strong environmental history tradition, Graham feared,
was a sorry vestige of the benighted South.

When I accepted the editorship for a new book series on "Environmental History and the American South" a few years later, not a whole lot
seemed to have changed. While such a series was desperately needed, I had
to caution my editors that we might have to drum up business. And in the
presumed absence of acquirable manuscripts, I suggested we put together
a collection of articles in southern environmental history. My assumption
was that I could easily fit most of the quality article-length work into a
single volume, one that mixed classics with a sampling of recent work.
But several obstacles soon stood in the path toward the speedy assembly
of such a volume. Happily, I discovered that more people were working
on southern environmental history manuscripts than I had presumed, so

recruiting series authors and reading their work absorbed my attention. And when I was able to return to this idea of a collection, I realized, with Chris Manganiello's help, that the list of potential articles for inclusion in such a volume was much longer than either of us had imagined. Chris initially joined this project as a research assistant, and his first task was a thorough literature search to find candidate articles. He returned with a master list of almost one hundred possibilities, a list that has continued to grow, sometimes maddeningly, in the two years since he first generated it. It was at that point that Chris agreed to join me as a coeditor.

With a surprising wealth of articles from which to choose, we began furiously reading and winnowing. We also set some stricter parameters for inclusion. First, we decided to focus the collection on recent publications, settling on 1995 as a starting point. Second, we limited ourselves to peer-reviewed journal articles and privileged those from top journals where peer review was strongest. We also decided to avoid reprinting articles already anthologized in related collections, which cut several more top contenders.[4] Finally, we strove to provide the widest chronological, geographic, and topical coverage we could. And yet we still had several dozen articles worthy of inclusion, and thus some hard decisions to make. Perhaps, we realized, Graham's lament no longer held.

Environmental history in and of the American South is now a humming scholarly enterprise. And yet, to the extent that the field has arrived, it has done so quietly, disparately, and without much of a revisionist impetus. With the exception of Mart Stewart, the contributors to this volume do not proselytize for or devote much energy to situating their work within this emergent field. The heated debates over the New Western History that made western environmental history so compelling in the 1980s and 1990s do not have an analogue in southern environmental historiography. Instead, most of these essays read as studies that happen to be southern. Their authors certainly recognize the distinctive regional dimensions of their stories, but they often have other fish to fry. Moreover, the diversity of scholarly identities represented here is striking. There are several authors who see themselves as southern historians or environmental historians first and foremost, though only a handful would tell you that the confluence of those two fields is their primary research home. Harry Watson, for instance, is a distinguished southern historian who took a detour into environmental history, and the opposite might be said about Ted Steinberg, an accomplished environmental historian whose interest in disasters brought him south. Then there are those whose essays are informed by other fields of training or interest, such as agricultural history (Claire Strom), geography (Judith Carney and Craig E. Colten), the history of science (Joshua Blu Buhs), the history of technology (William Boyd), military history (Lisa Brady), colonial American history (Virginia DeJohn Anderson and S. Max Edelson), urban and regional planning history (Eileen Maura McGurty), and ethnohistory (James Taylor Carson). The arrival of southern environmental history has been unassuming in part because its key contributors have been converging from all directions instead of blazing a single path. The task of this volume, then, is to see how well this rendezvous has collectively defined the field and what it suggests about its neglected topics and future directions.

The late arrival of southern environmental history begs two important questions: Why have southern historians been slow to embrace environmental history, and why have environmental historians so rarely ventured south? The answers to each of these questions are complex, but their outlines can be quickly sketched. Contending with the first question, ironically, requires confronting an old, discredited southern historiography that made climate and environment central factors in explaining the rise of the southern plantation economy. Famously, U. B. Phillips began his landmark study, *Life and Labor in the Old South* (1929), by invoking the weather as "the chief agency in making the South distinctive."[5] His book is rightly criticized for how it fused environmental determinism with a contention that slavery was benign and paternalistic. When Kenneth Stampp came along in the 1950s and systematically repudiated Phillips's approach, insisting on the primacy of human agency in the making of the South's "peculiar institution," southern historians understandably shoved aside environmental analyses.[6] Indeed, southern historiography has been at the vanguard in making human agency the centerpiece of historical analyses, a process stimulated immeasurably by an African American freedom movement that embodied the power of agency from below. In the process, an interwar tradition of thinking about the environment's role in shaping the South—one whose practitioners were often more subtle and less deterministic in their approaches than Phillips was—has faded from view.[7] Here then is the "burden" of southern environmental history: to insist on the efficacy of environmental analyses while also confronting their past misuse.

To get the attention of other southern historians, we must offer causal arguments that suggest how environmental history can, in fact, offer richer and fuller accounts of human agency enmeshed in the natural world.[8]

Why environmental historians have been slow to give attention to the South is a question best approached by considering the original impetus for the field. While the environmental crises of the interwar years produced an early though abortive move toward southern environmental history, it was the postwar environmental movement that produced the field, and that movement was weak in the South. In a disproportionately poor and rural region renowned for being friendly to migrating industries and slow to regulate environmental impacts, southern environmentalists have had a hard time getting traction.[9] Moreover, for those whose environmental ideals were forged in and by the western wilderness, the South—a region so agrarian in its sensibilities, land use histories, and conservation traditions—has been an inscrutable place. However, recent trends in environmental historiography—a renewed emphasis on agricultural landscapes and their hybridity, attention to the social and racial histories of environmental thought and practice, and connections between health and the environment among them—have made the South newly attractive terrain. This volume suggests, then, that southern environmental history has not only arrived but also that it may prove an important space for the growth of the larger environmental history enterprise.

Like so much U.S. environmental history, this volume begins roughly at 1600, when the Old and New worlds came into sustained contact in North America. We hoped to include something on pre-Columbian environmental history, for there are few richer or more regionally coherent opportunities for doing so. The native societies of the Southeast—particularly the Mississippian peoples who were such formidable shapers of the natural world—need to be integrated into the narrative of southern environmental history, for they provide a compelling argument about just how inadequate it is to start our environmental histories at contact. Environmental historians are well aware of the perils of making 1491 an ecological baseline, but the moment of colonial contact still functions as a profound watershed, not only because it sent shockwaves through the region but also because it divides disciplines.[10] There is, of course, a substantial scholarship on the human and environmental histories of native peoples in the South-east before contact, mostly in anthropology, archaeology, ethnohistory, and historical ecology.[11] And one recent historical synthesis—Don Davis's *Southern United States: An Environmental History*—gives admirable cover-age to the precontact South (and the Spanish imperial South as well).[12] But the recent journal literature is less accommodating, with the best essays on Native American history focusing on the postcontact period.

Virginia DeJohn Anderson's essay makes Indians only a small part of the story, but hers is an argument built on an understanding that live-stock were crucial agents of ecological imperialism. As Anderson shows in *Creatures of Empire*, her larger comparative study, roaming livestock not only challenged Indians to make sense of property in animals, but they also forced cross-cultural negotiation and fomented disastrous conflict.[13] Livestock ownership was one of the critical features that separated English from Indian economies, ecologies, and cultures. As importantly, as An-derson's essay shows, livestock husbandry functioned as both a literal and a figurative model for the "civilized" control of nature. But a funny thing happened to English husbandry practices in the Chesapeake colonies. Just as colonists encouraged Indians to embrace livestock husbandry as a path to civilization, their own control over livestock grew tenuous. Indeed, the most important aspect of Anderson's essay for the field of southern envi-ronmental history is her explication of the origins of free-range husbandry in the Chesapeake, from which flowed many other distinctive aspects of southern agricultural practice—the extensiveness of agriculture in the re-gion, the development of the southern grazing commons, and the peculiar stock and fence laws that persisted into the twentieth century. The forces producing this system were both cultural and environmental, and the re-sult was a brand of livestock husbandry far removed from traditional Eng-lish practice. The tale Anderson tells is thus a foundational one in southern environmental history.

James Taylor Carson's essay comes at a similar theme from a different subject position. Focusing on the Choctaw, whose settlements were cen-tered in present-day Mississippi, Carson examines how horses, a Euro-pean import, transformed their lives and how the Choctaw in turn made horses part of their culture. The Choctaw were themselves a product of the collapse of the Mississippian cultures in the wake of Old World contact, and the horse was, across large swaths of North America, a transformative ingredient in the Columbian exchange. Perhaps most important, the horse helped to give rise to the bison-hunting Plains Indian cultures of the eighteenth and nineteenth centuries.[14] Carson takes a question more often applied to these Plains Indian groups and asks it of the woodland Indians of the Southeast: How did Choctaw men and women make sense, and use, of the horse? Carson shows how skillfully the Choctaw reoriented their economic activities around the horse. But they also worked horses into their language, games, and rituals, and horses became potent resources for maintaining traditional gender roles during a time of sustained crisis. A European import at the center of the dislocations Indian societies experienced, the horse also functioned to sustain cultural practices. The essays by both Anderson and Carson, then, suggest that ecological imperialism needs to be a suppler explanatory model.

The next two essays in this volume feature the colonial Lowcountry, that portion of the south Atlantic coast that was the geographic center of rice culture. We did not necessarily intend to have such a tight focus on the Lowcountry in this period, but we could not find comparable recent articles on, say, the spread of tobacco agriculture in the Chesapeake, another central and obvious topic for the colonial period. Avery O. Craven pioneered the study of this subject, and more recent scholarship by Tim Silver, Carville Earle, and Jack Temple Kirby has also attended to the colonial tobacco economy's environmental aspects. There is also some excellent work focusing on the environmental dimensions of tobacco farming in the nineteenth century.[15] But the article literature was again slight, and so we were left with the Lowcountry, the subject of a wealth of environmental history scholarship.

In a series of important articles, and then in her book, *Black Rice*, Judith Carney has made a sustained case for seeing the rice-growing techniques used by Lowcountry planters as the products of African technology transfer.[16] Scholars had long assumed that these complex systems of rice growing were the results of planter innovation and that African slaves had provided only brute labor. But several decades ago, Peter Wood and Daniel Littlefield challenged that thesis, suggesting that Africans contributed knowledge and skills to the evolution of these systems. Carney takes this black rice hypothesis to another level, though not without controversy. Her case is built more on a series of logical suppositions about transatlantic similarities than it is on indisputable archival evidence, of which there is an unfortunate paucity. As a result, her thesis has been contested, most recently by David Eltis, Philip Morgan, and David Richardson, who together challenge Carney's supposition that slaves from African rice-growing areas could have been the agents of this transfer (or, for that matter, that they would have willingly shared such knowledge under the circumstances).[17] And yet the basic point of her essay remains an important and provocative one: methods of rice cultivation in West Africa and the Lowcountry show remarkable affinities that make questions about African contributions unavoidable. Carney's work also suggests two other important lessons: that environmental historians need to take African American environmental knowledge and practices more seriously, and that we need to situate our studies in a broader Atlantic World context.

S. Max Edelson's essay asks its readers to divert their gaze from the complex engineering in the Lowcountry's rice fields to see the role that trees played in the region's settlement. For Edelson, trees were both central to a basic environmental reality of early settlement—that to create prosperous agricultural landscapes, settlers and slaves had to clear the land of its forest cover—and indicative of how settlers and slaves adapted themselves to new environmental realities. Trees provided natural resources, they were the subjects of natural histories, and, in their profusion, they marked New World landscapes as fertile and promising. Settlers also planted and cultivated trees to set apart refined spaces from those of raw production. Trees were not merely obstacles to agricultural colonization or commodities in a transatlantic economy; they were, Edelson suggests, the very stuff from which Old World peoples made their lives anew in North America.

Harry Watson's essay is an ideal one for pulling us out of the colonial and into the early national period, for it examines a transition that has long been a central concern among environmental historians: the transformation of rivers from commons to commercialized resources. As a number of historians have shown for New England, the appropriation of flowing water to power mills negatively affected agrarian users who relied on the services of natural rivers—from rich runs of anadromous fish to the seasonal flooding that maintained valuable meadowlands. The reorganization of nature required for industrial development was at the center of the social conflict caused by the transition to capitalism, for it favored a small group with economic power and hurt a larger group without such power.

Watson's story, then, is not necessarily a new one, but his essay is one of the first to examine the closing of a riparian commons in an antebellum South in the midst of its own version of the market revolution.[18]

As Watson notes, there are several distinctively southern characteristics to his story. First, the battle over the riparian commons in the South was not the agricultural-industrial contest that characterized the North. Rather, the fishing petitions he analyzes embodied conflict between two agricultural regimes, a yeoman Upcountry economy distant from markets and a decidedly commercial Lowcountry plantation economy. While mills and milldams were the central points of contention, as in New England, their supporters were almost always large planters, not industrialists. Challenging these entrenched plantation interests was a difficult task for southern yeomen, even though they were gaining a stronger political voice during this period. Beyond showing how shad were a source of contention between two agrarian classes, Watson also makes clear how ecological changes mattered to this story, as yeomen, seeing shad as providential, neglected their own impacts on streams that were critical to shad success. But it was the commercialization of fishing at the mouths of the region's rivers, more than milldams and Upcountry soil erosion, that undid the shad runs. Watson's essay beautifully illustrates the complex connections white southerners made during this period between nature and common rights in a slave society.

The dominant reality of the antebellum South was the westward expansion of slave-based plantation agriculture and, in particular, the growth of the cotton kingdom. We wanted to include an essay on the environmental dimensions of King Cotton, but again we were foiled by the absence of ideal candidates. Indeed, it is remarkable that environmental historians have yet to really tackle the antebellum cotton South. There have been some intriguing starts. Albert Cowdrey's survey, *This Land, This South*, contended with the history of soils and soil erosion produced during the expansion of cotton culture, while the geographer Stanley Trimble documented the extent of soil erosion in the Piedmont across the nineteenth and early twentieth centuries. Others have speculated on the connections between slavery and environmental stewardship. Gavin Wright, Steven Stoll, and others have looked at how planters' investments in slave property dissuaded them from investing time and energy in soil conservation, while Eugene Genovese provocatively connected environmental degradation to patterns of slave exploitation and resistance. The general consensus has been that the exploitation of labor and nature went hand in hand in the cotton South, a satisfying conclusion that has been more assumed than proven. Indeed, in a provocative recent article, the economic historians John Majewski and Viken Tchakerian used a statistical analysis to suggest that the southern practice of shifting cultivation was dictated more by environmental factors—climate, soil quality, and livestock diseases in particular—than it was by slavery or other cultural and economic forces peculiar to the region. Whether one finds their logic convincing or not, they challenge historians to take the southern environment seriously as a shaping force, or set of forces, in the development of antebellum southern agriculture.[19]

The South's slave society, and the working out of its fate within the larger nation, resulted in explosive sectional conflict, and while environmental historians have been slow to turn their attention to matters military, there is now a storm of interest gathering around the environmental dimensions of the Civil War. Scholars have taken, or are taking, a wide variety of approaches to the Civil War's environmental history. They are examining the role of weather and terrain in shaping warfare; the environmental dimensions of disease and death and the war's important place in the history of sanitation; the impacts the war had on the South's farmed, forested, and built landscapes; the environmental aspects of provisioning large armies; the ways in which the war was an ecological and economic watershed; and the history of battle site preservation.[20] Together, these approaches suggest just how much is to be gained from environmental histories of the Civil War and its legacies.

Lisa Brady's essay examines the intersection between ideas of nature and military strategy in the Civil War. More specifically, she looks at what happened in three critical campaigns—the siege of Vicksburg, the Shenandoah Valley campaign, and Sherman's March to the Sea—when the Union army exchanged its own supply lines for a strategy of *chevauchées*, or massive foraging raids, which aimed both to sustain Union troops and to undermine the capacity of Confederate forces to make war against them. This *chevauchée* strategy not only had a marked set of material environmental impacts but it also attacked the South's "view of itself" and southerners' relationships with their landscapes. The major psychological threat posed by these raids, as many a contemporary noted, was that the South would be reduced to a wilderness. That these raids remain at the forefront of white southern memory for their alleged indignities suggests their imaginative power. Brady's essay convincingly demonstrates that Union military leaders sought to connect Sherman's truism—that "war is hell"—to a landscape of conquest, one whose previously improved acres they transformed into a region-erasing wilderness.

In the years just after the Civil War, John Muir, a Wisconsin eccentric who would do much to reinvent wilderness as an affirmative concept, set out on an epic journey south. His "thousand mile walk to the Gulf" took him from the upper Midwest to Florida, where he hoped to catch a boat to South America to explore the wonders of tropical nature as he had imagined them. A case of malaria—a product, he thought, of the South's own tropical qualities—eventually shunted him to the mountains of California and the rest, as they say, is environmental history.[21] Mart Stewart uses Muir's journey to pose a powerful counterfactual question—what if John Muir had stopped in the South and become *its* environmental champion, rather than heading to the Sierras, where he made the protection of western wilderness a preeminent environmental concern? What might the broader American environmental tradition look like today if the southern, and not the western, landscape was at its center?

No one has done more to sketch out the parameters and possibilities of southern environmental history than Mart Stewart, and his essay in this volume functions as a pivot point between the early and modern environmental histories of the South. Stewart's basic point is a critical one: the South is an agrarian region, and while a substantial portion, a majority even, of the region's land base has almost always been in an uncultivated state, those "wilderness" margins have continually existed in a tight though tense relation to the cultivated core. The swamps, pine barrens, and successional "old fields" that resulted from the persistence of shifting cultivation served as a hunting, gathering, and grazing commons that supported agriculture—or, alternatively, as places to escape from the plantation core. As such, they have been human landscapes of meaning and power. The wilderness conceit—that there is a nature without humans—has never been comfortable in the South, just as Muir was not. Indeed, Stewart makes the sensible observation that the wilderness debate that has recently remade environmental history might have come earlier had the South been a touchstone region. Stewart's essay also suggests how tightly connected work and nature have been in the South's agrarian landscapes, and he charts an ambitious research agenda for using the region to think race and environment together. Finally, Stewart demonstrates how strongly the dominant agrarian themes of southern environmental history connect the United States to the global South.

The three essays that follow Stewart's, by Claire Strom, Ralph H. Lutts, and Albert G. Way, illustrate several of his central points. Strom's examination of the federal cattle tick eradication program and its effects on southern yeomen is a fascinating transect through the larger story of the closing of the southern range and the class conflict that surrounded it. At the heart of Strom's story are a parasitical protozoan—*Pyrosoma bigeminum*, which caused Texas fever in cattle—and a vector—*Boophilus bovis*, or the cattle tick, which spread protozoa among cattle. The climatic requirements for the vector tick limned the geographical bounds of the political and cultural South, and the region's free-range tradition meant that Texas fever easily spread among the region's backwoods herds. Here, then, is a perfect example of the coming together of ecology, economy, and culture to define the region. For those who used their cattle for subsistence and local trade, Texas fever was at best a minor annoyance. But for those interested in commercial cattle raising and in joining an increasingly nationalized livestock market in the late nineteenth and early twentieth centuries, Texas fever posed a major problem, and its control necessitated a coordinated effort that the states were incapable of launching. As with other agricultural pest problems during this period, such as the boll weevil, the cattle tick seemed to require a federal response and increased federal capacity. Indeed, as we will see in several of the essays that follow Strom's, one of the most important stories of twentieth-century southern environmental history has been the interaction between science and technology, federal and university agricultural expertise, and the modernizing southern agricultural sector. The federal tick eradication plan favored large-scale and market-oriented producers who had a stake in improving southern livestock and could afford the expense and labor involved against yeomen in marginal southern spaces who could not afford to comply and who rightly feared that tick eradication would transform their lives. Like Watson's essay, Strom's shows us not only how the privatization of commons resources led to social conflict—indeed, sometimes murder and the wanton destruction of property—but also how much the ecology behind these conflicts mattered.

Appalachia is a dominant southern subregion, and because it is mountainous, often wild, and home to a large percentage of the South's public lands it has received considerable attention from environmental historians.[22] It is perhaps surprising, then, that Ralph H. Lutts's essay on the chestnut trade is our only Appalachian entry. We certainly had other article-length options to choose from, by scholars such as Chad Montrie, Kathy Newfont, Sara Gregg, Dan Pierce, and Terry Young.[23] Indeed, two important themes stand out in this larger literature. The first is that, in southern Appalachia, removal of people often preceded protection of mountainous landscapes as national parks and forests—a lesson that environmental historians working in other regions have also taught us. But mountain residents have not merely rejected environmentalism as dispossessive, though they often have been skeptical of urban-based preservation efforts that threatened local land use traditions and interests. Rather—and here's the second lesson—they have embraced particular kinds of environmental activism while eschewing others. Kathy Newfont found in western North Carolina what she calls "commons environmentalism." While the residents she studied opposed wilderness designation for national forest lands whose resources they relied on, they also objected to the threats posed by industrial logging and mining operations. Their environmentalism accommodated commons resource use. And Chad Montrie has documented local opposition to the environmental effects of strip mining, an Appalachian environmentalism at once shaped and constrained by the positions of its key actors. Appalachia, in other words, has been a fascinating place to observe the dynamics of growing environmental concern among rural populations not traditionally associated with the movement.

Ralph H. Lutts's essay takes a different phenomenon as its focus. The chestnut blight, introduced into the United States in the early twentieth century, wiped from the eastern forest one of its most common trees. Scholars have long speculated that the disappearance of chestnuts, which were prodigious mast producers, had substantial social, economic, and cultural impacts on mountain communities. But Lutts is one of the few who has attempted to measure how important chestnuts were to Appalachian society. Looking at a variety of sources—oral histories, census reports, and

{ 12 } PAUL S. SUTTER

local store records among them—for a handful of southwestern Virginia counties, Lutts portrays a thriving commerce in chestnuts preceding the blight's arrival. Indeed, like shad, chestnuts were a providential resource that helped to anchor a semisubsistence economy, giving mountain residents access to small amounts of cash or sometimes serving in lieu of cash. The foraging commons in these counties was a complex one. Appalachian residents not only gathered wild chestnuts but also managed chestnut orchards, and chestnut mast was critical to the region's hog commons. The chestnut also linked southside Virginians with eastern urbanites who enjoyed roasted chestnuts as a seasonal treat. But unlike other commons stories, this "tragedy" is not one of unregulated resource overexploitation leading to collapse. Rather, it is the story of a nonhuman agent, *Cryphonectria parasitica*, undoing a local economy. Unlike in Watson's essay, where the commercial economy undermined subsistence fishing, the coming of the chestnut blight undermined a critical link between Appalachian residents and the commercial economy. The chestnut, then, was as much a path into the world of commerce as it was a hedge against it.

Albert G. Way's essay brings us to another distinctive southern subregion, the Coastal Plain, and the longleaf pine–grassland biome that historically covered an estimated 70 to 90 million acres of it. Today, remnant old growth longleaf hovers in the vicinity of 12,000 acres, making it one of the most endangered ecological communities in the United States. Concern over the fate of the longleaf forest dates to the turn of the twentieth century and an unusual confluence of people and events in the Red Hills, an area nestled between Thomasville, Georgia, and Tallahassee, Florida. Wealthy northerners came to the region for its supposed salubrious effects, and many stayed because of the superb quail hunting, consolidating a series of massive quail-hunting "plantations" that mixed longleaf-wiregrass savannas with patchy tenant farming. As Way shows, this was not a typical conservation landscape—it was certainly not a wilderness—and yet it gave birth to profoundly important ecological and conservation insights.

In the years after World War I, quail numbers seemed in decline and the wealthy preserve owners were at a loss. They called on the Bureau of Biological Survey (BBS), a federal agency, to examine the problem, and the BBS sent an unschooled but field-tested natural historian, Herbert Stoddard, to lead the effort. The result was a landmark study that not only helped lay the foundation for the profession of game management but also provoked a fierce discussion about the role fire played in the longleaf forest and other natural systems. Stoddard was in many respects the South's Aldo Leopold, and he helped give shape to what we would today call conservation biology. (In another recent study, Fritz Davis has claimed a similar mantle for the Floridian and sea-turtle specialist, Archie Carr.)[24] That such nationally and internationally important ecological insights came out of a distinctively southern agrarian landscape challenges our conservation history orthodoxies, not least in the ways that local knowledge came to inform professional practice in the Red Hills.

Way's explication of the rise of a particular kind of conservation science in the South meshes nicely with the following two stories of science and agriculture in the region. William Boyd examines the growth of the broiler industry over the course of the twentieth century and its increasing concentration in the South, where, as Monica Gisolfi has also noted, low wages and a history of contract farming made the transition from cotton to chickens a smooth one. But behind the promiscuous sprouting of rural poultry houses in places like the Delmarva Peninsula, northeast Georgia, and Arkansas were scientific and technological interventions that made the broiler into an industrial organism whose job was to transform grain into meat efficiently. That process of biological intensification, as Boyd shows, involved innovations in confinement and flow, nutrition, disease management, and genetics. From a small-scale husbandry practice, poultry production transmogrified into a modern agro-industry, with considerable help from both government and the poultry science programs of land-grant universities. Some of the intensification processes Boyd describes raise profound ethical questions, but his larger point is that modern poultry production is built on techno-scientific manipulations of nature that have purchased efficiency at the price of system vulnerability. The subordination of chicken biology to the logic of industrial production, to paraphrase Boyd, has produced new ecologies of instability. And while it is beyond the purview of Boyd's article, it is also worth noting that this agro-industrial transformation has had profound social, economic, and labor implications for the areas in which it has been most focused.[25]

Another important aspect of agricultural modernization in the South was the increasing reliance on chemical pesticides after World War II. As Pete Daniel has shown, few regions felt the impacts of those pesticides more poignantly than did the postwar South, where, along with fossil fuels and fertilizers, chemical pesticides facilitated the transition from labor-intensive to input-intensive agriculture. [26] In his essay, Joshua Blu Buhs examines the South's most distinctive contribution to the pesticide controversy—the U.S. Department of Agriculture's (USDA) futile efforts to eradicate the imported fire ant, an effort that Rachel Carson made infamous in *Silent Spring* (1962). But where previous students of this episode have followed Carson's line, Buhs has two other agendas. First, as a historian of science, he is interested in how the contending parties in debates over fire ant eradication constructed their scientific cases. As he suggests, environmental historians, eager to use science to animate nature as a character in their stories, have not paid enough attention to how science itself is a socially constructed activity. In the case of the fire ant wars, neither side had a corner on objective truth; both mixed facts with worldviews and rhetoric that simplified the complex and uncertain field of fire ant natural history. This leads us to Buhs's second goal in his essay: to show how the unpredictable nature of fire ants themselves continually deflected the story. Struggle as they did to figure out fire ant taxonomy and ecology, both sides were confounded when fire ants defied efforts to categorize them or explain their behavior. Neither the unmitigated disaster that the USDA control entomologists made them out to be nor the benign agents that the environmental camp insisted they were, fire ants were ambiguous and protean. For some, that may make for a less satisfying moral to the story, but it does make for better environmental history. Buhs's analysis also helps to explain the odd place that fire ants have come to occupy in the culture of the South. Indeed, few regions have so willingly embraced as icons of environmental identity their most troublesome invaders, from fire ants to boll weevils to kudzu.[27]

The very reasons that mainstream environmentalism has been relatively weak in the South also made the region a center of the environmental justice movement. The central charges of environmental justice activists are, first, that poor people, people of color, and others lacking political power bear the brunt of pollution and environmental degradation, and, second, that mainstream environmentalists—often white, urban or suburban, and affluent—have neglected the environmental issues critical to the poor and marginal. As a region with a permissive regulatory culture and substantial poverty as well as large populations of African Americans and, increasingly, Hispanics and other immigrant groups, the South is a fruitful region within which to study the environmentalism of the poor. Eileen Maura McGurty's essay focuses on a formative conflict in the creation of the movement: the fight over dumping soil contaminated with PCBs (polychlorinated biphenyls) in Warren County, North Carolina. This story is fascinating not merely because early environmental justice arguments flowed from the case but also because it produced an odd coalition of rural white landowners and black civil rights activists. Begun as a NIMBY ("Not in My Backyard") protest by county whites, who worked through traditional political channels and wielded rational scientific arguments, the fight changed course when formal appeals proved ineffective. Remarkably, rural whites sought the support of the civil rights movement establishment in Warren County, the members of which had extensive experience with direct action protest. In the process, African Americans steered the movement away from NIMBY appeals and toward arguments about environmental racism and justice. McGurty's essay shows how a problem distinct to the postwar era—the substantial increase in toxic chemicals being produced and then dumped into the environment—brought together in the South two of the era's defining movements: environmentalism and civil rights. While the biracial coalition was never an easy one, it served as a model for battles to follow.

The final two essays in this volume turn our attention to southern cities, which to date have been understudied by environmental historians. Ted Steinberg's essay looks at the intersection of urbanization and what are often called "natural disasters." Steinberg suggests that there is usually little that is natural about these disasters. Instead, the deaths and damage that result from them have been all too human, rooted in the political economy of urban development. While there is nothing particularly southern about the larger lessons Steinberg draws, the hurricanes on which he focuses have a particular disposition for making landfall in the South. Using Hurricane Andrew (1992) as his departure point, Steinberg takes his readers on a whirlwind tour of south Florida's agricultural and urban development and its predictable history of hurricanes. Rather than functioning as cautionary moments, many of these storms encouraged intensive redevelopment. Moreover, lulls in hurricane activity built a false sense of security among south Floridians, who relaxed building codes and countenanced the spread of vulnerable manufactured housing. To call Hurricane Andrew a natural disaster, Steinberg concludes, is to miss how a century of urbanization in south Florida contributed to the destructiveness of the storm.

Steinberg first published his indictment of south Florida's cavalier attitudes about hurricanes several years before Hurricane Katrina devastated another southern city, New Orleans. A similar story could easily be told about that city and its efforts to engineer its way out of hurricane danger. Both Craig E. Colten and Ari Kelman have written superb pre-Katrina environmental histories of New Orleans, a city that at once enjoys tremendous geographic advantages—it sits near the mouth of a river that drains a huge portion of the continent—and challenging environmental disadvantages—it was built initially on a natural levee, then pushed back into wetlands, and its continual subsidence has put much of the city below sea level.[28] The result is what Colten has called an "unnatural metropolis," one kept dry by an intricate and increasingly stressed system of levees, canals, pumps, and other engineering works. For some Katrina revealed the folly of living in such a vulnerable spot; for others the storm told a powerful tale of pernicious official neglect and environmental injustice. Either way, the history of Katrina (and Rita) will not be comprehensible without the tools environmental historians bring to the table.

One of the lessons we have learned in the wake of Katrina is the critical role that wetlands can serve in absorbing the force of storms. Craig E. Colten's essay, which rounds out this volume, tells the surprising story of a city slowly coming to appreciate its wetlands and incorporating them back into its urban fabric. No region has been more associated with wetlands than the South, and southern figures such as the ecologist Eugene Odum and the writer Marjory Stoneman Douglas have been crucial to getting Americans to rethink the roles and values of wetland environments.[29] That intellectual sea change is part of what Colten charts in his essay. But he is also interested in the constructedness of these wetlands and how they have served to put nature on display for urban residents. Indeed, two of the four wetlands Colten discusses were built from scratch and the other two bear the impressions of centuries of human activity. These areas have served, then, to connect urbanites to "nature" while also building a constituency for broader preservationist efforts. Colten's essay is a superb exploration of the cultural and spatial dimensions of growing urban environmental concern in a southern context.

The essays that we have collected in this volume are wide-ranging in space and time and cover much of the ground recently occupied by southern environmental historiography. But there are also plenty of areas that are underrepresented or where more work remains to be done. While several of the essays included here discuss African American environmental traditions and histories, there is a crying need for more scholarship on the African American environmental experience in the South and beyond. The field's core challenge will be to build a large literature on the environmental history of the plantation South and its legacies. Landscapes of leisure and tourism are also scantily covered in this volume, and while historians have done good work on southern national parks and forests, more attention to southern resort landscapes and the larger patterns of consumption that support them would be fruitful. Similarly, the environmental dimensions of southern suburbanization, a process that has often intersected with the history of resort landscapes, is also worthy of more attention. Indeed, a whole new sort of metropolitan environmental history could be crafted to make sense of southern places like Orlando, Florida, or Hilton Head, South Carolina.

Some of the most exciting recent environmental history examines the connections between health and environment, a theme that this volume barely touches on. Contending with disease and searching for health have been signature aspects of southern living, and environmental historians now have the tools to make these subjects their own.[30] Moreover, while climate, both natural and artificial, has been an important theme in southern environmental historiography thus far, this volume lacks an essay that represents that literature.[31]

Like the West, the South has been transformed over the last century by massive federal engineering projects and the footprint of the military-industrial complex. The federal government has expropriated large expanses of the southern landscape for military bases and other federal facilities, and while many of those landscapes suffer from pollution and other dire environmental problems, others have unintentionally preserved distinctive southern environments.[32] In other places, the siting of these facilities has gone hand in hand with the creation of conservation landscapes. Moreover, at places like the Savannah River Site and Oak Ridge National Laboratory, government scientific and military research helped give birth to modern ecological science.[33] The South is also a region that rivals the

West in the modern harnessing of its rivers and streams, though we have little scholarship on that outside of a vast Tennessee Valley Authority (TVA) literature.[34]

Although agrarian themes dominate this volume, there is plenty of farmland still to cover. The central role that soils have played in southern history is notable in its absence from this volume.[35] There also are whole agricultural commodity sectors missing, including sugar, citrus, peaches, pecans, and hogs, to say nothing of corn and soy. Moreover, the region's distinct foodways also deserve the attention of environmental historians. Finally, we also need to know more about the environmental dimensions of southern industrialization. These are but a few of the topics either poorly covered in this volume or in need of greater scholarly attention.

If the burden of southern environmental history is to consciously confront a past of dangerous environmental determinism, the challenge is to avoid a literature that becomes regionally parochial. Indeed, the great virtue of the essays in this volume is that they at once embody and transcend the region. It is perhaps unavoidable that southern environmental historians will ask how the region's environmental history has been distinctive. Indeed, I have emphasized regional distinctiveness in this introductory essay, and I hope it remains a part of the field's impetus. But to be truly innovative, southern environmental history must do two other things as well. First, it must situate the region in a larger world of connections and comparisons. Southern history has always been both defined and peripheralized by its comparative relation with the North. What is immediately refreshing about southern environmental history is how it tends to reorient regional comparisons westward. But southern environmental history cannot be merely sectional in its questions, comparisons, or chauvinisms. Instead, it must reach out to the rest of the world, particularly to the global south of the Caribbean, Africa, Latin America, and Asia. This expansive impulse must be matched by a second inward impulse, more modest if no less ambitious, for claims to regional distinctiveness can also obscure the stunning variety of histories and landscapes *within* the South. We need more studies that scale the analysis down to the local and that look at specific places in ways that will challenge our sense of regional coherence. Southern environmental history, then, need not be merely the search for a coherent regional narrative. At its best, it will be cacophonous mixing of these various agendas.

Notes

1. Otis Graham, "Again the Backward Region? Environmental History in and of the American South," *Southern Cultures* (Summer 2000): 50–72. See, for instance, Mart Stewart, "Southern Environmental History," in *A Companion to the American South*, ed. John B. Boles (Malden, Mass.: Blackwell, 2002), 409–23.

2. Albert Cowdrey, *This Land, This South: An Environmental History* (Lexington: University of Kentucky Press, 1983); Timothy Silver, *A New Face on the Countryside: Indians, Colonists, and Slaves in the South Atlantic Forests, 1500–1800* (New York: Cambridge University Press, 1990); Mart Stewart, *"What Nature Suffers to Groe": Life, Labor, and Landscape on the Georgia Coast, 1680–1920* (Athens: University of Georgia Press, 1996); Jack Temple Kirby, *Poquosin: A Study of Rural Landscape and Society* (Chapel Hill: University of North Carolina Press, 1995).

3. Here I echo Mart Stewart's essay in this volume.

4. For instance, see Jack Davis, "'Conservation is Now a Dead Word': Marjory Stoneman Douglas and the Transformation of American Environmentalism," *Environmental History* 8, no. 1 (January 2003): 53–76, reprinted in *Paradise Lost: The Environmental History of Florida*, ed. Ray Arsenault and Jack Davis (Gainesville: University of Florida Press, 2005); Dianne D. Glave, "'A Garden So Brilliant with Colors, So Original in Its Design': Rural African American Women, Gardening, Progressive Reform, and the Foundation of an African American Environmental Perspective," *Environmental History* 8, no. 3 (July 2003): 395–411, reprinted in Dianne Glave and Mark Stoll, *To Love the Wind and Rain: African Americans and Environmental History* (Pittsburgh: University of Pittsburgh Press, 2006).

5. U. B. Philips, *Life and Labor in the Old South* (Boston: Little, Brown, and Company, 1929), 3.

6. Kenneth Stampp, *The Peculiar Institution: Slavery in the Ante-bellum South* (New York: Knopf, 1956).

7. I am thinking of figures such as Avery Craven, Arthur Ryker Hall, Rupert Vance, Arthur Raper, Lewis Gray, and Hugh Hammond Bennett. For a discussion of this cohort, see Lynn Nelson, *Pharsalia: An Environmental Biography of a Southern Plantation* (Athens: University of Georgia Press, 2007), 1–28.

8. Stewart's *"What Nature Suffers to Groe"* is a model for this sort of approach to agency.

9. James Cobb, *Industrialization and Southern Society, 1877–1984* (Lexington: University of Kentucky Press, 1984), 121–35.

10. See Charles Mann, *1491: New Revelations of the Americas Before Columbus* (New York: Knopf, 2005).

11. See, for instance, Hudson's *Knights of Spain, Warriors of the Sun: Hernando de Soto and the South's Ancient Chiefdoms* (Athens: University of Georgia Press, 1997); Paul A. Delcourt and Hazel R. Delcourt, *Prehistoric Native Americans and Ecological Change: Human Ecosystems in Eastern North America since the Pleistocene* (New York:

Cambridge University Press, 2004). There are a number of environmental histories of Indian-settler interactions in the Southeast. See, for example, Silver, *New Face on the Countryside*; Richard White, *Roots of Dependency: Subsistence, Environment, and Social Change among the Choctaws, Pawnees, and Navajos* (Lincoln: University of Nebraska Press, 1983); Shepard Krech III, *The Ecological Indian: Myth and History* (New York: Norton, 1999); Robbie Ethridge, *Creek Country: The Creek Indians and their World* (Chapel Hill: University of North Carolina Press, 2003); and Kathryn Braund, *Deerskins and Duffels: The Creek Indian Trade with Anglo-America, 1685–1815* (Lincoln: University of Nebraska Press, 1993).

12. Don Davis, ed., *Southern United States: An Environmental History* (Santa Barbara, Calif.: ABC-CLIO, 2006).

13. Anderson, *Creatures of Empire: How Domestic Animals Transformed Early America* (New York: Oxford University Press, 2004).

14. See, for instance, Andrew Isenberg, *The Destruction of the Bison* (New York: Cambridge University Press, 2000).

15. See Silver, *New Face on the Countryside*; Nelson, *Pharsalia*; Avery O. Craven, *Soil Exhaustion as a Factor in the Agricultural History of Virginia and Maryland, 1606–1860* (Urbana: University of Illinois Press, 1926).

16. Judith Carney, *Black Rice: The African Origins of Rice Cultivation in the Americas* (Cambridge, Mass.: Harvard University Press, 2001); "From Hands to Tutors: African Expertise in the South Carolina Rice Economy," *Agricultural History* 67, no. 3 (1993): 1–30; "Rice Milling, Gender and Slave Labour in Colonial South Carolina," *Past and Present* 153 (1996): 108–34; and "The African Antecedents of Uncle Ben in U.S. Rice History," *Journal of Historical Geography* 29, no. 1 (2003): 1–21.

17. David Eltis, Philip Morgan, and David Richardson, "Agency and Diaspora in Atlantic History: Reassessing the African Contribution to Rice Cultivation in the Americas," *American Historical Review* 112, no. 5 (December 2007): 1329–58.

18. See Ted Steinberg, *Nature Incorporated: Industrialization and the Waters of New England* (New York: Cambridge University Press, 1991) and "Down to Earth: Nature, Agency, and Power in World History," *American Historical Review* 107, no. 3 (June 2002): 798–820; Brain Donahue, "'Damned at Both Ends and Cursed in the Middle': The 'Flowage' of the Concord River Meadows, 1798–1862," in *Out of the Woods: Essays in Environmental History*, ed. Char Miller and Hal Rothman (Pittsburgh: University of Pittsburgh Press, 1997), 227–42; Daniel Vickers, *Farmers and Fishermen: Two Centuries of Work in Essex County, Massachusetts, 1630–1850* (Chapel Hill: University of North Carolina Press, 1994); Vickers, "Those Dammed Shad: Would the River Fisheries of New England Have Survived in the Absence of Industrialization?" *William and Mary Quarterly* 61, no. 4 (October 2004): 685–712; and John Cumbler, *Reasonable Use: The People, the Environment, and the State: New England, 1790–1930* (New York: Oxford University Press, 2001).

19. Cowdrey, *This Land, This South*; Gavin Wright, *Old South, New South: Revolutions in the Southern Economy since the Civil War* (New York: Basic Books, 1986); Steven

Stoll, *Larding the Lean Earth: Soil and Society in Nineteenth-Century America* (New York: Hill and Wang, 2002); Eugene Genovese, *The Political Economy of Slavery: Studies in the Economy and Society of the Slave South* (New York: Pantheon, 1965); John Majewski and Viken Tchakerian, "The Environmental Origins of Shifting Cultivation: Climate, Soils, and Disease in the Nineteenth-Century South," *Agricultural History* 81, no. 4 (Fall 2007): 522–49.

20. On connections between environmental history and war, see Edmund Russell, *War and Nature: Fighting Humans and Insects with Chemicals from World War I to Silent Spring* (New York: Cambridge University Press, 2001); and Edmund Russell and Richard Tucker, eds., *Natural Enemy, Natural Ally: Toward an Environmental History of Warfare* (Corvallis: Oregon State University Press, 2004). On the Civil War, see Mark Fiege, "Gettysburg and the Organic Nature of the American Civil War," in *Natural Enemy, Natural All*, 93–109; Ted Steinberg, "The Great Food Fight," in *Down to Earth: Nature's Role in American History* (New York: Oxford University Press, 2002); and Jack Temple Kirby, "The American Civil War: An Environmental View," National Humanities Center Online Essay: http://www.nationalhumanitiescenter.org/tserve/nattrans/ntuseland/essays/amcwar.htm.

21. John Muir, *A Thousand-Mile Walk to the Gulf* (Boston: Houghton Mifflin, 1916); Natalie Ring, "Inventing the Tropical South: Race, Region, and the Colonial Model," *Mississippi Quarterly* 56 (Fall 2003): 619–31.

22. See, for instance, Margaret Lynn Brown, *The Wild East: A Biography of the Great Smoky Mountains* (Gainesville: University of Florida Press, 2000); Daniel S. Pierce, *The Great Smokies: From Natural Habitat to National Park* (Knoxville: University of Tennessee Press, 2000); and Don Davis, *Where There are Mountains: An Environmental History of the Southern Appalachians* (Athens: University of Georgia Press, 2000).

23. Chad Montrie, "Expedient Environmentalism: Opposition to Surface Coal-Mining in Appalachia and the United Mine Workers of America, 1945–1975," *Environmental History* 5, no. 1 (2000): 75–98; Sara Gregg, "Uncovering the Subsistence Economy in the Twentieth Century South: Blue Ridge Mountain Farms," *Agricultural History* 78, no. 4 (2004): 417–37; Kathy Newfont, "Grassroots Environmentalism: Origins of the Western North Carolina Alliance," *Appalachian Journal* 27, no. 1 (Fall 1999): 46–61; Dan Pierce, "The Barbarism of the Huns: Family and Community Removal in the Establishment of the Great Smoky Mountains National Park," *Tennessee Historical Quarterly* 57, no. 1 (1998): 62–79; Justin Reich, "Re-creating the Wilderness: Shaping Narratives and Landscapes in Shenandoah National Park," *Environmental History* 6, no. 1 (January 2001): 95–117; and Terry Young, "False, Cheap and Degraded: When History, Economy and Environment Collided at Cades Cove, Great Smoky Mountains National Park," *Journal of Historical Geography* 32, no. 1 (2006): 169–89.

24. Frederick Rowe Davis, *The Man Who Saved Sea Turtles: Archie Carr and the Origins of Conservation Biology* (New York: Oxford University Press, 2007).

25. Monica Richmond Gisolfi, "From Crop Lien to Contract Farming: The Roots

of Agribusiness in the American South, 1929–1939," *Agricultural History* 80, no. 2 (2006): 167–89.

26. Pete Daniel, *Toxic Drift: Pesticides and Health in the Post–World War II South* (Baton Rouge: LSU Press, 2005); Daniel, *Lost Revolutions: The South in the 1950s* (Chapel Hill: University of North Carolina Press, 2000), 7–90. See also James Giesen, *Boll Weevil Blues: Cotton, Myth, and Power in the American South* (Chicago: University of Chicago Press, forthcoming); Margaret Humphreys, "Kicking a Dying Dog: DDT and the Demise of Malaria in the American South, 1942–50," *Isis* 87 (1996): 1–17.

27. See Joshua Blu Buhs, *The Fire Ant Wars: Nature, Science, and Public Policy in Twentieth-Century America* (Chicago: University of Chicago Press, 2004); Derek H. Alderman and Donna G'Segner Alderman, "Kudzu: A Tale of Two Vines," *Southern Cultures* 7, no. 3 (2001): 49–64; Mart Stewart, "Cultivating Kudzu: The Soil Conservation Program and the Kudzu Distribution Program," *Georgia Historical Quarterly* 81, no. 1 (Spring 1997): 151–67; and Giesen, *Boll Weevil Blues.*

28. Ari Kelman, *A River and Its City: The Nature of Landscape in New Orleans* (Berkeley: University of California Press, 2003); Craig E. Colten, *An Unnatural Metropolis: Wresting New Orleans from Nature* (Baton Rouge: LSU Press, 2005).

29. On wetlands in general, see Ann Vileisis, *Discovering the Unknown Landscape: A History of America's Wetlands* (Washington, D.C.: Islands Press, 1997); David C. Miller, *Dark Eden: The Swamp in 19th Century American Culture* (New York: Cambridge University Press, 1989); and Jeffrey Stine, *America's Forested Wetlands: From Wasteland to Valued Resource* (Durham, N.C.: Forest History Society, 2008). On Odum, see Betty Jean Craige, *Eugene Odum: Ecosystem Ecologist* (Athens: University of Georgia Press, 2001). On Douglas, see Jack Davis, *An Everglades Providence: Marjory Stoneman Douglas and the American Environmental Century* (Athens: University of Georgia Press, 2009).

30. For an introduction to this literature, see Gregg Mitman, "In Search of Health: Landscape and Disease in American Environmental History," *Environmental History* 10 (April 2005): 184–210; for an analysis that straddles South and West, see Conevery Bolton Valenčius, *The Health of the Country: How Settlers Understood Themselves and Their Land* (New York: Basic Books, 2002).

31. See, for instance, Raymond Arsenault, "The End of the Long Hot Summer: Air Conditioning and Southern Culture," *Journal of Southern History* 50 (November 1984): 597–628; Karen Kupperman, "Fear of Hot Climates in the Anglo-American Colonial Experience," *William and Mary Quarterly* 16 (April 1984): 213–40; and Mart Stewart, "'Let US Begin with the Weather': Climate, Race, and Cultural Distinctiveness in the American South," in *Nature and Society in Historical Context*, ed. Mikulas Teich, Roy Porter, and Bo Gustafsson (New York: Cambridge University Press, 1997), 240–56.

32. Neil Maher is working on an environmental history of the National Aeronautics and Space Administration (NASA), tentatively titled *Ground Control*, which will examine these issues.

33. See Frank Golley, *The Origins of the Ecosystem Concept in Ecology: More than the Sum of Its Parts* (New Haven, Conn.: Yale University Press, 1996).

34. An important exception is Jeffrey Stine, *Mixing the Waters: Environment, Politics, and the Mixing of the Tennessee-Tombigbee Waterway* (Akron, Ohio: University of Akron Press, 1993).

35. Several scholars have made a start. See Stanley Trimble, "Perspectives on the History of Soil Erosion in the Eastern United States," *Agricultural History* 59, no. 2 (April 1985): 162–80; Doug Helms, "Soil and Southern History," *Agricultural History* 74 (2000): 723–58.

VIRGINIA DEJOHN ANDERSON

Animals into the Wilderness

The Development of Livestock Husbandry
in the Seventeenth-Century Chesapeake

IN THE MIDDLE of the seventeenth century, any English colonist in Virginia who killed a wolf earned a bounty of one hundred pounds of tobacco. Indians who performed the same service received a rather different reward. According to the terms of a 1656 statute, for every eight wolves' heads brought to the county commissioner, the native hunters' "King or Great Man" would be presented with a cow. This reward, Virginia's burgesses insisted, would "be a step to civilizing" the Indians "and to making them Christians." It would also dissuade them from attacking their English neighbors, since cattle-owning sachems would have "something to hazard & loose besides their lives" in any ensuing conflict. Each cow bestowed on Indians in this way thus served not just as a bounty but also as an emissary of English-ness. The burgesses' confidence in the civilizing power of cattle, however, reflected their general belief in English cultural superiority more clearly than their actual experience as livestock owners in the New World.[1]

Embedded in the 1656 statute was a bundle of assumptions about the ways in which English behavior offered a model for Indian improvement. Foremost among these was the firm belief that civility—the adoption of an English mode of living—went hand in hand with conversion to Christianity. (Another provision of the 1656 law outlined a plan whereby Indians could leave their children with colonists to be brought up "in Christianity, civillity and the knowledge of necessary trades.") In addition, the burgesses assumed that property ownership would instill in native leaders a sense of responsibility they currently lacked because they had no private estates. But why animal property? Why a cow?[2]

The burgesses felt no need to spell out their meaning, for they presumed that everyone—at least every civilized person—knew what it meant to keep a cow and thus how cow-keeping could reform Indians. The possession of domestic animals fulfilled the scriptural injunction that humans exercise dominion over the creatures of the earth, a responsibility that Indians largely ignored. People who combined livestock-keeping with arable farming enjoyed a more sedentary way of life than those who merely chased game through the woods.[3] Keeping cattle (rather than more self-sufficient creatures such as pigs and goats) encouraged steady habits: the animals needed careful management, and their keepers in turn needed to rise early, work hard, and plan for the future. Since properly managed cattle grazed in fenced pastures, their presence improved the land and reinforced their owners' property rights. Raising livestock, then, was integral to civilized living.[4]

But if English-style livestock husbandry was a measure of civility, Chesapeake colonists themselves fell short of the mark. The same practices the burgesses wanted the Indians to adopt were under siege in the English plantations, a development that was certainly apparent by 1656. Chesapeake farmers had adapted their animal husbandry to conserve scarce labor and minimize "improving" alterations to the land and in the process strayed far from English methods. Because European visitors, and not the colonists themselves, commented most extensively on the nature of these changes, settlers may have been unaware of how far they had diverged from "civilized" husbandry. What the consequences of that divergence might be—and how, in particular, it might affect the colonists' legal control over their animal property—only emerged when Chesapeake practices were compared to English standards. Confronted by the unorthodox nature of their husbandry, Chesapeake planters had to defend their own civility in ways they could scarcely have anticipated.

Whatever visions of gold or other riches inflamed their imaginations, the first English colonists in the Chesapeake celebrated the discovery of a very different resource: hay. George Percy, who arrived in Virginia in 1607, enthusiastically reported: "I have seene many great and large medowes having excellent good pasture for any Cattle." A year later, Francis Perkins spied land near Jamestown that promised "an abundance of [fresh] fodder for any kind of live stock, especially pigs and goats, even if there were a million of them." The proliferation of livestock, Governor

Francis Wyatt insisted, would assure Virginia's success. The "healthfull and prosperous estate of this Colony," he announced in 1623, "depends upon nothing more, then the plentifull encreasing and preserving of all sorts of Beasts and birds of domesticall or tame nature." Colonists had little reason to expect anything other than the easy transfer of animal husbandry to the Chesapeake, for the region appeared to be nothing less than an earthly paradise for livestock.[5]

The Virginia Company aimed to supply its fledgling colony with all the "domesticall" beasts it needed. Two years after the first ships landed, the colony had "6 mares and a horse, 5 or 600 swine, as many hens and chickens; some goates, [and] some sheep." By 1619, company officials estimated that 20 "young Heifers" were needed to support every 100 men.[6] They sent 112 head of cattle and 4 mares that year and expected in 1620 to ship a further 200 cattle, 400 goats, 20 mares, and "fourescore Asses, to be procured from France."[7] These animals arrived in a land with seemingly limitless amounts of natural meadow and a temperate climate roughly similar to England's, but their survival was not assured.[8]

English colonization of the Chesapeake took place just as the region's climate experienced severe fluctuations that imposed unexpected hardships on animals weakened by lengthy voyages. A "little ice age," lasting from 1550 to 1700, brought unusually cold weather to the area. Bitter winters occurred during the first decade of the seventeenth century and again in the 1640s. Cattle and swine—the most numerous livestock species brought to the Chesapeake—can endure frigid temperatures, but only briefly. Unfortunately, animals faced harsh conditions before they had fully recovered from their journeys and before harried colonists could build shelter for them.[9] To make matters worse, the area around Jamestown suffered a terrible drought between 1606 and 1612. This placed a particular strain on cattle, which require substantial amounts of fresh water in order to thrive. Animals debilitated by climatic fluctuations subsequently fell prey to various New World parasites, including cattle ticks and kidney worms.[10]

Colonists, however, worried far more about losing livestock to wolves—predators that no English farmer (or English animal) had had to worry about since the fifteenth century. In 1632, Virginia's House of Burgesses passed the first of many acts authorizing the payment of bounties to encourage the killing of wolves. Maryland's legislature followed suit, permitting Indians to be hired and armed for the job. Wolf populations possibly increased because of the introduction of new and unwary species of prey, although calves and newborn livestock rather than full-grown beasts would have been most at risk. Moreover, wolves may have become convenient targets for the wrath of colonists who actually lost livestock to straying or negligence. Even if reports of predation were somewhat exaggerated, the frequent renewal of wolf bounty acts indicates that the colonists' concern persisted over time. A half-century after colonization began, the House of Burgesses still received complaints about "the frequent and many injuries done by wolves to the cattell and hoggs of severall inhabitants."[11]

The most dangerous predators, at least at first, turned out to be the colonists themselves. Lacking adequate supplies from England, unwilling or unable to produce sufficient food on their own, and unsuccessful in their attempts to seize enough from the Indians, starving colonists declared open season on what was supposed to have been Virginia's breeding stock. By the end of the winter of 1609–1610, according to John Smith, "our commanders and officers" had eaten up "our hogs, hens, goats, sheep, horse, or what lived," leaving only "some small proportions (sometimes)" for everybody else. Virginia's deputy governor, Sir Thomas Gates, sent to salvage the failing colony in 1612, found it necessary to impose martial law, making it a capital crime to kill "any Bull, Cow, Calfe, Mare, Horse, Colt, Goate, Swine, Cocke, Henne, Chicken, Dogge, Turkie, or any tame Cattel, or Poultry, of what condition soever" without permission, whether the animal was privately owned or company property.[12]

Such extreme measures (which coincided with the end of the drought) probably turned the tide, although a report stating that livestock were "plentifully increasing and thriuing" as early as 1615 may have demonstrated wishful thinking on the part of observers desperate to cast a failing commercial enterprise in the best possible light. By 1620, however, the livestock population had begun to recover. A census made in that year recorded more than 300 head of cattle, about the same number of "tame" swine (excluding hogs running wild in the woods), more than 200 goats, and 11 horses. Just two years later, Edward Waterhouse counted, perhaps a bit optimistically, nearly 1,500 cattle in Virginia, or just about one beast for every colonist.[13]

But once again man-made and natural disasters struck the animal population. When Powhatan Indians launched a surprise attack in March 1622, they killed 347 colonists as well as untold numbers of cattle. Following hard on the heels of this crisis, a mysterious "generall death of men and Cattle" descended on the beleaguered colony during the winter of 1622–1623. One distressed survivor informed his brother in England that "he that had 40 hoggs about his house hath one or two: and a hundredth henns hath now 3 or 4." As for "tame Cattle," there were "no more to be had." By early 1625, Virginia's livestock population had barely recovered to 1620 levels. Another census of animals conducted in the waning months of 1624 reported 365 neat cattle, 518 swine, 215 goats, and just one horse—although this count surely omits animals that had run off into the woods for good.[14]

Swine, which can produce two litters a year, probably rebounded quickly from these setbacks, but cattle and horses only established a secure foothold in the Chesapeake in the second half of the seventeenth century. With the demise in 1624 of the Virginia Company—the principal source for imported livestock—colonists relied almost exclusively on animal reproduction to increase their herds. Stepping into the breach, the House of Burgesses encouraged livestock population growth with such measures as a 1630 statute that required colonists to preserve "with all care and diligence" their female cattle, prohibiting any to be killed unless they "are eyther past breedinge, or are likely to dye by some infirmity." Such expedients evidently worked: by 1649, one Virginian could boast that the colony had 20,000 head of cattle, 200 horses, 50 asses, 3,000 sheep, 5,000 goats, "innumerable" swine, and poultry "without number." Planters had even begun shipping surplus animals to Barbados and New England.[15]

The expansion of livestock populations still could not be taken for granted. Reproductive rates remained low throughout the century, particularly for cattle; perhaps fewer than half of all cows survived to produce offspring. Sows as young as one year old could bear litters, but it is likely that half of the piglets died before reproducing.[16] And disasters continued to strike intermittently. The 1644 Powhatan attack in Virginia once again killed many animals. In Maryland in 1694–1695, the "Excessive sharpness" of the winter carried off more than 25,000 cattle and 60,000 swine, creating an unprecedented health hazard from mounds of rotting carcasses once temperatures rose above freezing.[17] Despite these setbacks, conditions in general were certainly improving.

The measure of that success can be seen in the ubiquity of livestock ownership in the Chesapeake after mid-century. Virtually everyone kept cattle and pigs, which meant that even the poorest planters enjoyed an advantage over English farm laborers, who were less likely to own live-stock. As the supply of domestic creatures increased, their cost diminished, which further encouraged investment in animal property—and the occasional donation of cows to worthy Indians.[18] The eventual proliferation of livestock in the Chesapeake, however, owed more to the animals' adaptation to their environment and to the availability of land than it did to the exertions of their owners. The colonists may have been successful in transferring English livestock to the Chesapeake, but not in replicating "civilized" methods of husbandry.

If Gervase Markham, a prominent agricultural writer, can be believed, seventeenth-century English farmers devoted the vast majority of each working day—as many as fourteen of seventeen waking hours during plowing season—to laboring with and caring for their animals.[19] No European country, with the possible exception of the Netherlands, depended so heavily on domestic animals for food and labor as England. Even if its farmers did not regularly spend more time with their livestock than with their families, they dedicated many hours each day to regulating their animals' lives. English farmers monitored their creatures' diet, kept track of their location, controlled the timing of their breeding, and determined how long they would live.[20] Early Chesapeake planters did not have the luxury of following their example. Workers were far scarcer and more expensive in Virginia and Maryland than in England, and virtually all available labor was devoted to tobacco production.[21] For livestock husbandry to succeed in the Chesapeake, it had to operate in tandem with tobacco, absorbing as little labor as possible. The result was an approach to animal husbandry that stretched the meaning of the term and undermined the qualities that made it a hallmark of civility.

Colonists initially imported the entire array of English domestic animals, but the mix of livestock species on Chesapeake plantations eventually came to reflect local needs more than English experience. In England, sheep supplied wool and mutton, oxen and horses provided muscle power, cows produced milk and beef, and pigs furnished meat. On seventeenth-century Chesapeake farms, however, sheep all but disappeared, largely because the "humility of their nature," as one observer put it, made them easy prey for wolves. Thus wool and mutton remained scarce, at least until the last quarter of the seventeenth century, when most predators in the longest-settled areas had been eliminated.[22] Few oxen were needed to pull plows since Chesapeake colonists, following Indian practice, used hoes to cultivate tobacco and corn, the region's two principal crops. Ralph Hamor announced in 1615 that Virginians soon hoped to have all of "three or foure Ploughes going"; by mid-century, there were only about 150 plows at work in a colony with a white population approaching 12,000. A census reporting in 1620 that one out of three "horned cattle" in Virginia was an ox probably represented a high point, occurring as it did before tobacco cultivation was in full swing. In the latter part of the century, as the character of colonial-style agriculture became clear, fewer than one in ten Marylanders owned plows and—presumably—oxen. Durand of Dauphiné, a visiting Frenchman, observed as late as 1686 that Virginians "do not know what it is to work the land with cattle."[23]

They did not work the land with horses either, which may account for that species' scarcity in the Chesapeake during most of the seventeenth century. One account has just 200 horses in all of Virginia in 1649. This shortage surely affected colonists' social lives as well as their agricultural activities, since plantations lay widely dispersed along rivers and creeks in order to facilitate the shipping of tobacco. Virginia's House of Burgesses was sufficiently concerned about the continuing dearth of horses in 1662 that it prohibited their export from the colony. Horse ownership in Maryland was more common, but only in the 1670s did the horse population of the Chesapeake as a whole really expand.[24]

Dairying, so important in the English countryside, diminished in significance in the Chesapeake colonies. Few women were available to carry on what was assumed to be a quintessentially female occupation. In 1639, a Maryland official explained his colony's neglect of this enterprise by noting that "the dairy will require a woman" and no suitable candidates could be found.[25] Part of the problem also lay with Chesapeake cows. Because of the poor quality of natural forage and the animals' sensitivity to summertime heat, cows produced only a quart or two of milk a day (usually low in butterfat), hardly enough to warrant the making of butter or cheese. Even in winter, according to John Clayton, Virginians refrained from milking their cows, "having a Notion that it would kill them." The combination of warm summer temperatures and a scarcity of cold streams in which to chill dairy products also rendered them susceptible to quick spoilage. Most observers agreed that Chesapeake butter was edible enough, but the limited supply of cheese was "nothing to boast of." Maryland's governor went so far as to report to the colony's proprietor in 1672 that "the Cheeses Generally made here are soe Ranke and soe full of Eyes, that your Lordshipp would be angry with mee should I send such."[26]

Although Chesapeake colonists bent their backs to their hoes instead of leading oxen to the plow, spread their butter thinly, and learned to ignore the "Eyes" in their cheese, they at least enjoyed a diet rich in meat. In early Virginia and Maryland, the many uses that livestock fulfilled in England were essentially reduced to this single function. Depending on their age, gender, and economic status, colonists ate an estimated annual average of 45 to 200 pounds of meat each. This protein-rich diet—to which fish and game were occasionally added—surpassed that of many inhabitants of England, where, at least according to one seventeenth-century observer, a quarter of the population was lucky to taste meat just once a week. Moreover, meat supplied a necessary supplement to the colonists' corn-based diet, which otherwise would have left them vulnerable to pellagra and other ailments caused by nutritional deficiencies.[27]

Livestock used for draft or dairying needed to be kept nearby and carefully tended: all English agricultural writers agreed on this point.[28] Since few Chesapeake animals performed these functions, however, their owners had little incentive to keep close track of them. This result perfectly suited a region with little labor to spare for animal husbandry. Adopting what can only be called a *laissez-faire* approach to livestock care, Chesapeake colonists largely abandoned English practices and made a virtue of necessity by letting their animals roam freely.

The resort to free-range husbandry did not occur immediately. In 1609, the Virginia Company, clearly anticipating an easy transfer of English practices, instructed Deputy Governor Gates to "giue order that yor Catle be kept in heards waited and attended on by some small watch." Early Jamestown hired a keeper to mind the town's cattle, although his main job was to protect the animals from two threats unknown in England: wolves and Indians.[29] Following English precedent, colonial officials tried to create fenced pastures or at least to fence in natural meadows. In 1611, Gates ordered a palisade to be built to protect hogs. By the 1630s, colonists had erected a six-mile-long fence between the James and York Rivers, boasting that they had produced a safe cattle range as large as the English county of Kent. Rochdale Hundred, up the James River, reportedly had a fenced range of twenty circuit miles. Using water as a natural barrier, colonists also deposited animals on offshore islands that had been emptied of wolves. By 1609, there was already an "Ile of Hogges" in Chesapeake Bay. Maryland's governor, Leonard Calvert, informed the colony's proprietor in 1638 that Palmer's Island had been fortified and stocked with thirteen head of cattle. The following year, Father Andrew White advised Lord Baltimore to "choose some large Iland for a breede of Swine" and also "a heard of goates and yong calfes" where they could soon "grow upp into great flocks without any farther cost att all."[30] English experience guided these efforts to control domestic animals, but the creation of such enormous ranges reflected a distinctly American adaptation to the availability of land.

Few colonists kept penned animals on their farms. Only toward the end of the seventeenth century, according to Durand of Dauphiné, did Virginians temporarily pen calves as a way to lure dairy cows back to the plantation; having milked the cows, planters would "only then permit the calves to suck." There was an even greater incentive to confine swine, which damaged fields with their rooting. In 1640, the Virginia assembly required colonists to pen their hogs at night and hire keepers during the day. The inhabitants of St. Mary's City in Maryland likewise urged the province's council in 1685 to require owners to restrain their swine.[31] Penning livestock, despite such injunctions, proved to be more trouble than it was worth. John Lewger's ambitious plan to "plant corne for the swine, and . . . build sties and necessary penns for them, & . . . lead them out to their places of feeding" on his Maryland plantation almost certainly came to naught once he realized how much labor it would entail.[32] Besides building the pens, planters would have to assign workers either to lead animals "to their places of feeding" (and presumably keep an eye on them there) or to bring food to them. Even animals penned only at night needed to be fed. Cattle and swine feed mostly during the day, but in hot weather prefer to eat in the cooler evenings. And the amount of food they require is substantial. Modern beef cattle consume about 2 percent of their weight in hay each day—20 pounds of hay for a 1,000-pound cow—and each one can drink as much as 12 gallons of water daily. A modern 1,000-pound working horse requires a daily ration of about 22 pounds of food, and because horses digest hay less efficiently than cattle, they need oats or some other supplemental grain. The native grasses on which Chesapeake cattle and horses grazed were less nutritious than the cultivated grasses and small grains raised by English farmers, which meant that colonial livestock needed a great volume of fodder in order to put on weight. Even adult swine eat 5 to 6 pounds of food a day—a considerable amount of grain and table scraps to carry to troughs for penned hogs each morning and evening.[33]

Faced with these unacceptable labor requirements, which would have diverted workers from tending tobacco, Chesapeake planters eventually let their animals forage for themselves. Free-range livestock husbandry gained legal sanction in Virginia in 1643, when the assembly ruled that colonists had to fence in their crops, not their animals, a decision that effectively gave livestock the run of the land. Farmers who neglected to build fences and then sustained damage from roaming livestock had no legal grounds for redress. In 1646, the assembly defined a "sufficient" fence as being four and a half feet high and "substantiall close downe to the bottome"—tall enough to thwart leaping cattle and low enough to discourage rooting swine. Only an aggrieved farmer who had such a fence and kept it in good repair could sue the owner of trespassing animals for damages. A livestock owner could also gain protection from charges of trespass: so long as he gave notice to his neighbors, every planter had the right to "seake or fetch his owne cattle and hoggs from off any mans land." Maryland's legislature passed similar measures, although it eventually called for five-foot-high fences to discourage horses as well as cattle.[34]

When Chesapeake lawmakers required planters to protect their fields, they reversed common English practice, which, by the seventeenth century, placed a greater burden on livestock owners to control their animals.[35] Together colonists and their domestic animals created a landscape thoroughly unlike England itself, a place where fenced islands of tobacco and corn dotted a sea of open meadows and woodlands reserved, in effect, as an enormous commons for animals grazing beyond the bounds of human supervision. As European visitors to the Chesapeake were quick to point out, this was not the proper way to exercise dominion over God's creatures, and the results were plain for all to see.

If there was anything cavalier about Chesapeake colonists, it was their approach to their livestock. In 1613, the Reverend Alexander Whitaker, minister of Henrico, offered an early example of what became a litany of complaints about the colonists' husbandry practices. Writing at a time when the survival of domestic animals in Virginia remained uncertain, the minister argued that they would do fine "if they might bee prouided for." Conditions had scarcely improved sixty years later when Thomas Glover similarly asserted that Virginia's cattle "might be much larger than they are, were the Inhabitants as careful in looking after them and providing fodder for them as they in *England* are." The only supplemental feeding the animals got in winter was "the husks of their *Indian* Corn," which was not enough to keep hungry animals from foraging in "Marshy grounds and swamps . . . where very many are lost."[36]

Durand of Dauphiné further expounded on the deficiencies of Chesapeake husbandry during his visit in 1686. Because "nothing was given them to drink," Virginian hogs invaded peach orchards and "kept drunk on the fruit." The colonists did "not know what it is to save hay" and instead made livestock forage in the woods in all seasons. At times, carelessness merged into cruelty. Virginians "had no mercy upon their cattle," the Frenchman complained after a severe January snowstorm. "I saw the poor beasts of a morning all covered with snow and trembling with the cold, but no forage was provided for them. They eat the bark of the trees because the grass was covered." He went on to note with obvious astonishment that "despite this treatment, I saw no dead cattle." The gentlemen whom Durand visited were not yet as enamored of horse-racing as their eighteenth-century descendants would be, and this may explain why they often gave "little more care to their horses than to their cattle." Offering a decidedly mixed compliment, Durand observed that "I do not believe that there are better horses in the world, or worse treated."[37]

The English-born John Clayton, rector of Jamestown parish from 1684 to 1686, likewise faulted colonists for failing to shelter cattle and horses, even in winter, and for refusing to provide sufficient fodder. Drawing on his knowledge of superior English practices, the minister urged one woman in his neighborhood—doubtless in vain—to "sow her Wheat as early as possible" so that by spring "she might turn thereon her weak Cattle"; he also suggested she grow sainfoin, a nutritious forage crop that many English farmers cultivated. Matters had not improved by the turn of the eighteenth century, however, for one of Virginia's native sons, Robert Beverley, felt compelled similarly to upbraid his neighbors for their "exceeding Ill-husbandry" in refusing to provide fodder for their animals. Though swine flourished in spite of planters' negligence, Beverley's comments scarcely suggested approbation of Chesapeake husbandry methods. "Hogs swarm like Vermine upon the Earth," he observed, "find[ing] their own Support in the Woods, without any Care of the Owner."[38]

One result of these practices was a continual uncertainty about how many animals one actually possessed, which undermined the principle of ownership that marked livestock-keeping as a civilized endeavor. Such a careless approach to property evidently perturbed Beverley more than it did his neighbors. In Virginia, he reported, "when an Inventory of any considerable Man's Estate is taken by the Executors, the Hogs are left out, and not listed in the Appraisement," presumably because no one knew their number or whereabouts. Beverley was hardly exaggerating. In 1643, Robert Smith admitted to Maryland's Provincial Court that he "hath some hogs in the woods but how many he knoweth not." When Robert Cole made a detailed account of his property in 1662 prior to a voyage to England, he acknowledged that the "number of my hoggs is uncertaine butt of them that come home I thinke there is twenty nine of them and four young piggs." A decade later, when Luke Gardiner rendered an account of the deceased Cole's estate, of which he was guardian, he similarly noted that the number of "horses mares & Colts in the woods" was "uncertaine."[39]

Livestock owners regularly plastered courthouse doors with notices of lost animals, including elaborate descriptions in hopes that the beasts might turn up on someone else's property. Yet it was common knowledge that many animals that wandered off into the woods and swamps were as good as gone forever. A weary familiarity with the potential consequences of straying may explain why one Virginian saw fit to name his cow "brooken leggs." According to Clayton, "several Persons lose ten, twenty or thirty Head of Cattle in a Year" in the marshes—surely an exaggeration, but one that nonetheless drew attention to one of the principal costs of free-range husbandry.[40]

Even more disturbing was the fact that English animals appeared to decrease in size under Chesapeake conditions. Notwithstanding a few early reports that livestock transported to the region "doe become much bigger of body then the breed from whence they came," the descendants of immigrant animals were more likely to be smaller than their forebears.[41] Full-grown hogs, for instance, probably weighed little more than 100 to 150 pounds. Beverley believed that the colonists' failure to provide winter fodder for their cattle "stint[ed] their Growth; so that they seldom or never grow so large as they would do, if they were well manag'd." By the 1680s,

Maryland legislators worried about "the small stature of Stallions" in their colony, fearing that eventually all horses would diminish in size.[42]

Observers of this development took care to attribute it to poor husbandry rather than to any intrinsic deficiencies in the Chesapeake environment, lest the experience of English animals in any way call into question the suitability of the region for English people.[43] And in good part, they were right; uncontrolled breeding and insufficient diet probably contributed more than anything else to smaller livestock. Studies of modern free-range ponies on the Chesapeake island of Assateague (probably descendants of seventeenth-century horses) suggest that a diet made up exclusively of natural forage supplies inadequate protein to ensure proper growth.[44] Only swine, though small in size, seem to have prospered in the Chesapeake woods. Even Beverley grudgingly admitted that, when it came to the quality of their meat, colonial pigs "must be allowed to have very much the advantage . . . of those in *England*."[45]

The Chesapeake approach to livestock husbandry also encouraged colonists to modify or abandon certain practices associated with English-style arable farming in ways that attracted the scorn of outsiders. Tobacco and corn exhausted the soil after several years of cultivation but, as Glover observed, colonists "never manure it to bring it to heart again" for that would require gathering dung in the woods. Planters instead adopted a long-fallow method of husbandry, moving on to new lands and allowing exhausted plots to rest for as long as twenty years before returning them to cultivation. Only near the end of the seventeenth century did some colonists pen livestock temporarily on land that needed improvement. Durand of Dauphiné described a sort of field rotation system in Virginia in the 1680s whereby farmers worked a quarter of their acreage, let cattle graze on another quarter, and left the remaining half in woodland. After four years, they rearranged fences to confine cattle on the exhausted cropland, and tilled the former pasture. Only cornfields were fertilized this way, for Chesapeake farmers believed that tobacco suffered from the application of manure. According to Clayton, "Smoakers say they can plainly taste the fulsomness of the Dung."[46]

Together long-fallow agriculture and free-range animal husbandry compelled colonists to spread out across the land more widely and quickly than they would have done had they simply replicated English farming practices. The needs of livestock may have been paramount in encouraging population dispersal, although tobacco has typically been regarded as the main cause.[47] According to a modern estimate, just one free-ranging cow requires as much as five acres of pinewoods to sustain itself in summer and fifteen acres in winter; in deciduous forest, it needs even more land in winter. Moreover, grazing animals alter the composition of the forests, reducing the land's ability to support them. Cattle browsing in pine forest initially consume the scarcer undergrowth of oak and other hardwoods, while swine dig up roots of smaller pine trees. Thus animals could not feed in the same places for long. Because colonists' animals foraged for themselves, their owners had to reserve vast tracts for open grazing. This, in turn, led European visitors to reprove lazy colonists for their slowness in converting wilderness into a civilized landscape. Even at the end of the seventeenth century, one observer complained, "not the hundredth Part of the Country is yet clear'd from the Woods."[48]

Woodlands, even more than the open meadows that so entranced the first colonists, proved essential to the survival of livestock, thus preserving some forests—as much as removing others—characterized seventeenth-century Chesapeake agriculture. Clayton recognized that most plantation owners tried to strike a balance between cleared and forested land on their estates. Ambitious planters, he reported, acquired a mix of lands so "that they may be sure to have enough to plant, and for their Stocks and Herds of Cattle to range and feed in." In the 1680s, fully two-thirds of Ralph Wormeley's plantation at Rosegill, which extended four miles along the Rappahannock River, remained forested as grazing for his livestock. At the time of his death in 1701, Wormeley had amassed more than 6,000 acres, much of which remained undeveloped in order to sustain his 439 cattle, 86 sheep, an unknown number of horses, and too many pigs to count.[49]

Poorer planters rarely had the luxury of supporting their animals solely on their own lands. With an average of perhaps ten cows and as many swine—which would have required 50–150 acres of woods to support them, depending on the season and the composition of the forest—these colonists relied on ready access to unpatented lands.[50] Dick Willan of Maryland, whose cattle and hogs ran at large on the aptly named "Pork Hall neck," testified to the importance of such public range. Hearing rumors that Pork Hall neck was about to be granted, Willan protested that "if any body did seate that land it would ruin him in his stock."[51] The legal sanctioning of free-range animal husbandry implicitly recognized the legitimacy of such protests insofar as it could only function if public access to sufficient land was maintained.

Far from encouraging responsibility and steady habits, then, Chesapeake-style livestock husbandry gave every appearance of undermining them. In a place where land was easier to come by than labor and where tobacco was more profitable than forage crops, the exercise of human dominion over domestic creatures was compromised in ways that hardly set an example of civility. Give a cow to a Christian (never mind an Indian), visitors to the region might have scoffed, and he would most likely starve it, let it run wild, and probably lose track of it altogether. Yet while colonists abandoned most of the finer points of good husbandry in the interests of adapting to local conditions, they would not surrender their firm belief that livestock—no matter how they were cared for—remained private property. Throughout most of the seventeenth century, the animals' status as property served as the single most important marker of their domestication. Colonists did not immediately recognize, however, how much their distinctive style of animal husbandry complicated the task of assigning a fixed right to a moveable beast.

No experienced Chesapeake livestock owner would have agreed with the naive visitor who blithely asserted that the "only robbers the planters fear . . . are the wolves."[52] On the contrary, colonists knew all too well that their fellow settlers were just as likely to be at fault whenever an animal went missing. Free-range husbandry only emboldened unscrupulous colonists to prey on the property of others. Following the 1622 Powhatan uprising, for instance, starving colonists appropriated any livestock they could find. Virginia's governor Francis Wyatt and his council responded in 1623 by proclaiming that anyone convicted of stealing any "Beasts or Birds of Domesticall or tame nature" worth more than twelve pence would be put to death; stealing creatures of lesser value earned the offender a whipping. Lest anyone complain that "in England the vallue of some of these tame things is farr lesse" and thus subjected a thief to a charge of petty larceny rather than felony, Wyatt countered that "here they are of farr higher rates, by reason of theire scarscitie, and therefore wilbe found punishable with no lesse than Death."[53]

As livestock populations rebounded, the penalty for theft diminished. A first offense for hog stealing ceased to be prosecuted as a felony in Virginia in 1647. The result—surely not coincidentally—was a veritable epidemic of that crime. Hogs, no doubt because of their ubiquity, inspired more mischief than any other animal. The legislatures of both Chesapeake colonies tried to stem the problem—there were more laws about pilfering hogs than stealing any other kind of livestock—but to little avail. Such laws were frequently renewed, often with escalating penalties, yet hog stealing remained "a generall crime usually comitted and seldom or never detected or prosecuted."[54]

Nevertheless, lawmakers did their best. In the 1640s, the assemblies of both Virginia and Maryland stipulated stiff fines for convicted hog stealers, and in Virginia an indigent thief could be forced into two years of servitude. When incorrigible offenders were not deterred, legislators added humiliation, pain, and disfigurement to the financial toll. A statute passed in 1679 gave Virginian courts a colonial version of the "three strikes" rule. A first-time offender paid a fine; for a second conviction, the thief had his ears nailed to the pillory for two hours and then "cut loose from the nailes." A third offense was tried as a felony, with a penalty of death. In 1662, Maryland legislators decreed that a two-time hog stealer "be burned in the Shoulder with a Letter H with a red hott iron." This was still not enough to deter malefactors, so four years later they agreed that, in addition to paying a heavy fine, a second offender would be branded with an H in the forehead, permanently identifying him in a place he could not so easily cover with clothing. A third offense brought a charge of felony and potential execution. Similar measures reappeared in both colonies for the rest of the century, suggesting that compliance remained a problem.[55]

Even under the best of circumstances, enforcement of the law was difficult. This may explain why formal prosecution for theft and the illicit killing of livestock was relatively rare in the Chesapeake, in contrast to much higher rates of indictment for similar offenses in England. It was not enough simply to report that one's hogs were missing—a claim that in itself might be hard to sustain given the colonists' general uncertainty about the size of their herds. A plaintiff also needed a culprit, a witness if possible, and evidence—which, given its edibility, was usually difficult to find. As often as not, trials degenerated into rancorous exchanges of charges and counter-charges. In Maryland in 1658, for instance, accusations of hog stealing flew during a night of "merry drinking & dancing" but could not be adjudicated for lack of evidence. Kent County residents John and Jane Salter and William Price ended up in court because their neighbors began losing hogs "very strangly of a suden," and "pork [was] offten seene" in the Salters' house although they "had no hogs of theire owne to kill." Thomas Baker came under suspicion in Charles County for telling John Wood that "hee was sory thear was no meat in the hows but it shoold not bee so long" before there was some. Sure enough, Baker soon showed up with a dead hog. This testimony actually emerged in a case where *Baker* was plaintiff—charging his neighbors with hog stealing and defamation because they had labeled him a common hog stealer. Seth Forster similarly dragged his neighbor Robert Knapp into Talbot County court for saying "hee was A hogg stealing fellow from his Cradle."[56]

Cattle and horses disappeared, too, driven away by "evil minded people." Marylanders stole cattle from the proprietor's herds and from each other with equal nonchalance. Virginia authorities suspected that debtors who moved to the frontier—and away from their creditors—stocked their new farms with stolen cattle. In 1658, the House of Burgesses decreed that, before their departure, such people had to give notice of their plans, satisfy all debts, and have four neighbors certify that they actually owned any cattle they intended to take with them. Residents of Cecil County, Maryland, similarly attributed an upsurge in cattle rustling to the founding of Pennsylvania, accusing "diverse wicked persons inhabiting in Delaware precincts" of driving off their livestock and seeking refuge in the new colony.[57]

By making servitude one of the punishments for convicted hog thieves, Virginia legislators revealed their assumption that servants, or recently freed servants, were the biggest offenders. If true, this probably reflected their preponderance in the colony's population rather than an innate propensity for theft. Servants and debtors had no monopoly on larceny. In 1617, Virginia's governor Samuel Argall was suspected of diverting company property—including livestock—to his own use. Just over a decade later, another governor, John Potts, allegedly appropriated other men's animals to build up his own herds.[58] Toward the end of the seventeenth century, some Maryland men appointed as rangers—mounted patrols charged with rounding up wild horses that damaged property—stood accused of driving their neighbors' animals into the woods "in hope of having Pay for Bringing them up againe" and perhaps keeping a few on the side.[59]

Fully as bad as outright theft was the practice of taking up—and keeping—stray animals. Roughly following English common law, the Virginia legislature ruled in 1656 that anyone who found a stray animal had to report within a month to the county court and state where the creature had been found and what it looked like. In England, an unclaimed animal was forfeit to the crown or the crown's grantee; in Virginia, the finder could keep the animal if no owner came forward within a year and a day.[60] English law—the guarantor of property rights—was predicated on the assumption that most livestock were either confined or supervised: a stray animal was an anomaly. With Chesapeake free-range husbandry, however, "stray" animals were the rule, which made their appropriation by unscrupulous colonists hard to stop.

In the colonies, as in England, livestock owners could protect their rights to mobile property by marking their animals, and in the Chesapeake this expedient became more important than ever. Few colonists branded their animals; earmarks were the preferred method of identification during the seventeenth century. Colonists described their earmarks to the secretary of their county court, who recorded the information to help in returning stray animals to their rightful owners.[61] Accused livestock thieves had to show the ears of dead animals in order to prove that they had killed their own beasts. Enterprising malefactors tried to evade the law by "Cutting and mangling" the ears of filched creatures to disguise the mark, or by cutting the ears off altogether. This ploy only landed them in deeper trouble if they were caught. For instance, when Thomas Hebden failed to produce the ears of two hogs that he had allegedly stolen and killed, his excuse that the ears "were at home" did not wash with magistrates, who fined him a thousand pounds of tobacco. Aggrieved livestock owners may have considered the cropped ears and branded foreheads of convicted hog thieves to be unusually fitting punishments, marking them like the animals they had stolen with the emblems of a state authority that would not be flouted.[62]

Marking animals also addressed another difficulty with free-range livestock husbandry as it developed in the early Chesapeake. There was a risk that livestock would cease to be domesticated in any meaningful sense since their owners exercised so little supervision over them. The best candidates for domestication in the first place were social animals, however, and Chesapeake planters could exploit this trait to maintain at least some control.[63] The sociability of swine, for instance, made them easier to find in the woods. Beverley repeated the common observation that it was best "if the Proprietor can find and catch the Pigs . . . when they are young, to mark them; for if there be any markt in a Gang of Hogs, they determine the Property of the rest, because they seldom miss their Gangs; but as they are bred in Company, so they continue to the End." This was clearly the assumption of Henry Potter, Edward Hall, and Martin Kirke, who combed the Maryland woods in 1650 "to looke for Sowes that had pigs." Once one of the men found a sow with his earmark, he could mark any piglets found with her, confident that they were her offspring and his property. A 1671 Maryland law confirmed this understanding by casting suspicion on anyone carrying off unmarked pigs, unless they had been found on the person's own land or had been "in Company with his owne Hoggs."[64]

Marking animals also introduced a young creature to its owner. Every time a colonist handled a piglet, examining it for size or vigor before clipping its ears and perhaps soothing it afterward, he began to domesticate it, imprinting the animal with a human connection. Piglets that are gently stroked during the first month or two of life develop less fear of humans, are willing to be in their company, and so are easier to catch later on. Young calves likewise respond to gentle handling by acting less skittishly around humans. Thus the process of earmarking, and not just the result, initiated a connection between livestock and their owners.[65]

One brief encounter was not enough and had to be reinforced by sporadic contact between animals and their owners. This surely explains the colonists' practice of setting out small amounts of corn or husks for their livestock. They were not deliberately starving them (as critics maintained) but training them to come home now and then and renew their acquaintance with their owners.[66] Clayton admitted that Virginia planters' practice of offering corn to their cattle each morning and evening made the animals "linger about the Houses for more." Jasper Danckaerts, a Dutch visitor to Maryland in 1680, described a similar habit among that colony's planters.[67] By the late seventeenth century, planters sometimes lured their animals home in this way and then penned them in empty tobacco barns to fatten them for slaughter. They may also have begun to confine pregnant cows and farrowing swine, which simplified the job of marking newborn animals and imprinting them with a human connection.[68]

These expedients reveal how thinly the ties of domestication—and the concomitant claims to animal ownership—were stretched in the seventeenth-century Chesapeake. Only a slit or notch in the ear, unaccompanied by any pretense at close supervision and care, identified an animal as property. The ingenuity of thieves repeatedly demonstrated to colonists how easily their property rights could be subverted. Yet the law still offered a measure of protection to owners who managed to mark their wandering creatures. Legal precedent, however, provided little help in dealing with feral livestock—animals that had slipped the bonds of domestication altogether. It did not take long for these creatures to populate the woods in alarming numbers—witness the Virginia census that as early as 1620 declined to enumerate the "Swine of the fforest."[69] Were these animals property, too, and if so, to whom did they belong?

Colonists tended to call both truly feral animals and unretrievable strays "wild" livestock, but the two were different. Stray animals had been born tame, while feral ones—descendants of lost strays—were born wild and remained so. The behavioral characteristics that identified both sets of creatures as "wild" were more apparent in feral animals. Feral livestock had been naturally selected for hardiness and wariness, and these attributes manifested themselves in aggressiveness toward people who confronted them. The animals might also act aggressively around their own kind. Wild stallions and bulls contended with other males in their herds for dominance and control of breeding females. After breeding season, wild cows and calves and feral sows and piglets roamed the woods in "gangs," which colonists approached at their peril, for the mothers responded to any perceived threat to their young by taking the offensive against an intruder.[70]

Feral livestock do not just behave differently from tame animals: they look different. Feral creatures tend to be smaller and thinner than domesticated livestock, owing mainly to poor diet and unregulated breeding. Feral hogs develop a smaller and somewhat flatter skull shape than domesticated swine, and they often have a dense coat of curly underfur not seen on "home hogs."[71] It might take a few generations for these morphological changes to become fully visible, but the span of a pig generation is all of two or three years (the age at which wild pigs will begin to breed). The same is roughly true for wild cattle, and for wild horses a generation lasts about three to four years.[72]

Feral livestock, in short, were leaner and meaner versions of domesticated animals, and as their numbers swelled, Chesapeake colonists had to figure out what to do with them. English experience offered little guide, for only in northernmost England or Wales could a few wild cattle or horses be found in the seventeenth century.[73] Moreover, feral animals rarely let people get close to them. Clayton attributed the evasiveness of wild cattle to their "great Acuteness of Smelling," which alerted them to the approach of humans. Beverley reported that "wild Horses are so swift, that 'tis difficult to catch them; and when they are taken, . . . they are so sullen, that they can't be tam'd." He likened wild hogs to bears and wildcats in their propensity "ever [to] fly from the Face of Man."[74]

Had feral animals and "wild" strays avoided the English settlements, they could have been ignored. They were not so obliging, however, and their occasional appearance near plantations loosened colonists' already tenuous hold over their animal property. The abundance of wild pigs, for instance, gave accused hog thieves like William Price and John and Jane Salter a perfect alibi. Yes, they had killed a hog, they admitted to a Maryland court on New Year's Day 1656, but it was a "wild small hog" and not one from William Eliot's herd. Because the pig's ears were gone—dogs ate them, or so the defendants claimed—and most of the beast had been eaten, there was no evidence to prove the charge of theft.[75]

There were other instances when colonists blamed feral animals themselves for the disappearance of tame livestock. In 1650, Marylanders approached their governor and his council for help in addressing the problem of "having theire tame Cattell carried away and spoiled by Wild Bulls," which were following their instincts in accumulating a harem of breeding females to take into the woods. The petitioners wanted the offending animals rounded up and distributed among themselves, but the magistrates refrained from doing so, at least until possible owners of the bulls could be found.[76] Wild horses could be just as bad, for they too either lured breeding mares away to the forest or mated with them on the plantation, which, colonists complained, "doth both Lessen & spoyle the whole breed and Streyne of all horses." They also wreaked havoc on corn and tobacco fields and pastures when they galloped through them.[77]

The most direct solution to the problem of feral livestock was to kill them. The Maryland assembly periodically authorized group hunts to eliminate wild horses and cattle after fair warning had been given to possible owners. By the turn of the eighteenth century, according to Beverley, "the Hunting of wild Horses . . . sometimes with Dogs, and sometimes without," had become the sport of Virginia gentlemen.[78] Yet colonists always felt uneasy about killing feral creatures because the practice subverted deeply held beliefs about livestock. No matter how wild they looked or behaved, feral hogs, horses, and cattle were still livestock species, and livestock by definition belonged to people. The word "cattle" shares etymological roots both with "chattel" and "capital," and the link between livestock and property had existed, as far as the colonists were concerned, from time out of mind. In order to countenance the destruction of wild livestock, the colonists had to find a way around their essential condition as property.[79]

A potential solution lay in English common law. The colonists might have designated the animals as *ferae naturae* (wild in nature), which would have erased their status as private property because they had no owner.[80] This was the thrust of one Virginian's claim as early as 1623 that as far as wild hogs were concerned, "wee accounte of them as of the Deare in Virginia things belonginge to noe man."[81] It turned out that this was an idea that few colonists would accept. In the end, colonists in both Virginia and Maryland came to recognize an implicit royal right to feral animals. Still, they were careful to insist that the right was based not on the principle of *ferae naturae* but on the king's customary claim to waifs and strays. To protect their rights to their own free-range animals, the colonists contended that the royal prerogative applied only to unmarked feral animals for which no other owner could be found. The roundabout way in which the crown's right was eventually asserted suggests how difficult it was to reconcile English notions of property with the *laissez-faire* livestock husbandry of the Chesapeake.

In the case of Virginia, the joint-stock company that founded the colony assumed that all livestock not claimed by individual planters were by default company property because it had paid to bring the animals from England in the first place. This assumption surfaced in a dispute sparked by Captain John Martin in June 1623. Martin and several other malcontents concocted a story, which they presented as a petition to King James I, claiming that years earlier a large tract of land had been acquired from the Powhatan Indians and designated "the Kings fforest." In it roamed many "Deare and wild Swine" that were, perforce, royal property but were not being properly cared for. The petitioners humbly requested that His Majesty appoint some men to do the job, without going quite so far as to nominate themselves. When Virginia Company officials got wind of Martin's scheme, they informed the king that the "Kings fforest" was "a name happily knowne to Capt.: Martin and his Associates but not to the Company" and the land on which it supposedly sat encompassed Jamestown as well as several private plantations. Moreover, the wild swine of Virginia were "no other then ye breed of such as haue bin transported thither by the Companie" and thus belonged to it as well.[82]

Within a year the Virginia Company went bankrupt, and the crown took direct control of the colony. Now—with no other obvious contender in sight—most colonists appeared willing to grant the monarch a tacit prerogative right to wild unmarked livestock. The royally appointed governor asserted the claim on the king's behalf, and colonists acceded to this convenient solution to the vexing question of ownership. Once they did so, they could not presume to hunt feral livestock at will but first had to obtain licenses from the governor. Permission could be gained in other ways, too. In 1632, the earliest act establishing a wolf bounty allowed any colonist who killed a wolf "to kill also one wild hogg and take the same for his owne use." Colonists, however, did not need licenses to hunt deer or "other wild beasts or fowle in the common woods, forests, or rivers," although such a case for royal prerogative could presumably have been made. Instead, only wild livestock—animals that the English could not see as anything but property—belonged to what was in effect a new category of creature: wild but owned, if only in the most limited sense.[83]

In Maryland, the fate of wild livestock became entangled in the perpetual confrontation between the proprietor and the colonists. From the start, the Lords Baltimore claimed a prerogative right to the animals, which they believed King Charles I had transferred to them through the colony's charter. The governor, as the proprietor's representative, issued licenses to hunt the creatures. Often these licenses stipulated that the hides and tallow of dead animals had to be reserved "for his lordships use," a purely symbolic gesture that could only have been added to remind colonists to whom they owed fealty. Toward the end of the seventeenth century, the Provincial Council (appointed by the governor) also issued commissions to rangers to eliminate troublesome feral livestock.[84]

Not all Marylanders obtained licenses as required, but it is impossible to discern if their defiance stemmed from self-interest or a principled rejection of proprietary claims. The authorities, to be sure, suspected that sedition, not principle, lay at the heart of the matter. In 1653, the Provincial Council denounced the "bould Contemptious unwarrantable" acts of several unlicensed hunters whose misdeeds not only deprived the proprietor of his rightful property but demonstrated "Contempt of the Government here Settled under him"—language that implied that their actions smacked more of petit treason than petty larceny. As late as the 1690s, the Provincial Council made proclamations deploring the unlicensed hunting of wild livestock.[85]

Maryland's proprietor was not the only person whose rights could be trampled by illegal hunters. The original plan for the colony allowed the Lords Baltimore to grant manors to prominent individuals who would in turn recruit English tenants to work them. Thomas Gerard, the lord of St. Clement's Manor (one of the few such estates to be laid out), insisted on a prerogative right to wild livestock within the bounds of his estate. Often when Gerard sold or leased land, he expressly retained his lordly right to any wild hogs on the transferred property. In 1659, one of his tenants, Luke Gardiner, appeared before the St. Clement's manorial court "for catching two wilt hoggs & not restoringe the one half" to Gerard, "which hee ought to haue done." Gardiner was fined 1,000 pounds of tobacco (later reduced to 200 pounds) not only for his unsanctioned hunting but also "for his contempt therein."[86]

Gerard's right to feral animals rested on shaky legal grounds, for when Lord Baltimore made the manorial grant in 1639, he did not know that such creatures even existed. But the proprietor's own, more expansive claim to stray and feral creatures generated the greatest controversy. Matters came to a head after the Glorious Revolution as officials on both sides of the Atlantic sorted out the proprietor's new role now that Maryland had become a royal colony. Most of the transatlantic debate swirled around such crucial issues as the nature of the proprietor's political authority and the fate of Catholicism in a colony that had originally been conceived as a Catholic refuge. Given the gravity of these questions, it might seem surprising that the comparatively inconsequential issue of rights to stray and feral animals even came up. From the colonists' perspective, however, this controversy was anything but insignificant. Marylanders' precarious sense of themselves as a civilized people had become thoroughly entangled in the fate of the "wild gangs" of the Chesapeake.

The debate commenced in the Maryland assembly in May 1692 and dragged on for three years in response to the beleaguered proprietor's reassertion of his right to "Wafts [waifs]"—property found ownerless and left unclaimed—and "Strays." His claim rested on his reading of the provision in the 1632 charter that gave his family the same rights and privileges in Maryland as belonged to "any Bishop of Durham"—ancient legal short-hand indicating rights tantamount to those of a sovereign. The assembly-men's vehement opposition to this particular proprietary privilege included a startlingly frank acknowledgment that livestock husbandry in the Chesa-peake in no way corresponded to the English practices that informed the charter's language. Lord Baltimore's claim, the legislators argued, simply did not "Suit with the Nature and Constitution of this Province" because "the whole Stock of the Country run promisc[u]ously one amongst the other . . . Some Mens Stocks wandering Ten or Twenty Miles from their Plantation" as the "Law of Necessity" required. Should Baltimore's claim be upheld, "his Lordship would Entitle himself and Engross into his hands the whole Stock of the Province, and destroy every Mans property in the Same"—an utterly unacceptable proposition. The assembly insisted that marked animals, no matter how far they strayed, remained the property of their owners. As for unmarked feral livestock, legislators countered the proprietor's demand with an audacious claim of their own. Up to this point, they asserted, the assembly had freely given the proprietor rights to "unmarked wild Cattle Horses and Hogs" in order "to avoid the Con-tentions that happened about the Property having no Mark" to identify an owner. Now that Maryland was a royal colony, however, the assem-bly transferred "all the Title his Lordship can pretend to such Unmarked Cattle" to King William and Queen Mary.[87]

Nine months later, the Provincial Council received a message from the Lords of Trade and Plantations that provided only partial satisfaction. The king's advisory body supported the colonists' rights to their marked stray livestock and ruled that neither the Maryland charter nor the colony's as-sembly had the legal authority to give unmarked feral animals to the pro-prietor. Feral livestock properly belonged to the crown. So far so good; Marylanders found little to object to here. What they contested, however, were the proposed grounds by which the crown staked its claim to wild livestock. The Lords of Trade informed Marylanders that the royal right derived from the animals' status "as being fferae Naturâ"—a designation that colonists could not abide.[88]

Marylanders' objection to feral livestock being called "wild in nature" provoked a debate that had little practical significance. The animals, after all, possessed minimal economic value. Colonists readily granted the crown's right to the creatures, so their recognition of royal prerogative was not at issue. English settlers who hunted down troublesome wild hogs or horses without first obtaining a license had little to fear from officials who hardly had the means to stop them. The Marylanders' protest clearly had less to do with the animals themselves than with their identification as *ferae naturae,* a legal term that—if it were accepted—raised the ominous possibility that English creatures transplanted to the New World could become something quite different from what they once had been.

On learning in the spring of 1695 that Sir Thomas Laurence, the king's solicitor general, had upheld this designation, the Maryland assembly objected that he "was not well informed" on the matter. Laurence obviously did not know "that there were no horses, Beeves or hoggs in this Country" prior to colonization. These were all imported English animals, and as such they could by no stretch of the imagination—no matter how they looked or behaved—be considered "wild in nature." The legislators would only go so far as to "conceive" that feral livestock "are in the nature of Waifes and Strayes." This infinitely more acceptable proposal acknowledged a royal claim to the creatures but in no way compromised the animals' essential English-ness.[89]

The colonists' extraordinary sensitivity regarding the legal status of feral animals was surely heightened by the circumstances in which this debate occurred. The transatlantic exchange about proprietary privilege not only compelled Marylanders to recognize how their husbandry practices had diverged from those of England, but also forced them to defend their methods before an audience of England's highest officials. The proprietor's claim to strays struck an especially raw nerve because it threatened colonists' already tenuous hold on their animal property. The abandonment of most of the practices that characterized good husbandry made property ties all the more important. Livestock may have fended for themselves in the woods much like deer, but in the eyes of colonial owners, their status as chattel permanently distinguished them from indigenous animals.

So, too, did their identity as immigrant English creatures. The notion that livestock might become "wild in nature" in America undermined their status as emblems of civility and implied that a profound transformation in their essential character could result from moving to the New World. No wonder Marylanders objected so strenuously. If such a change could happen to English animals, might it not affect English people too? The consequences for the colonizing enterprise as a whole were too alarming even to contemplate. Livestock could no more become *ferae naturae* than colonists could become Indians.

As it turned out, the anxieties of many Tidewater farmers diminished in the eighteenth century when the shift from servants to slaves and an improving international market for grain allowed them to adopt more "civilized" livestock husbandry practices. Planters with sizable estates and numerous slaves converted tobacco lands to fields of wheat and maize. Because these crops required plowing, planters made greater use of draft animals and compelled their slaves to increase production in order to provide corn and fodder for livestock as well as grain for sale. Now domestic animals could be penned on the plantation and their manure used for fertilizer. Confident that a century of English settlement had eliminated the problem of wolves, some farmers turned to sheep-raising. At least on larger plantations, the lax practices that so disturbed European visitors like Durand of Dauphiné were on the wane.[90]

Free-range husbandry had not disappeared so much as it had been displaced to newer-settled areas, where scarce labor and abundant land prompted farmers to make the same adaptations that early Chesapeake planters had made. This turn of events allowed Tidewater elites to direct toward western settlers the same complaints that had once been lodged at their own fathers and grandfathers. Thus William Byrd II haughtily dismissed the "Indolent Wretches" of the North Carolina frontier who allowed their livestock to "ramble in the Neighbouring Marshes and Swamps" and lost the advantage of their animals' milk and manure because of such "ill Management." For elite planters like Byrd, whose domestic animals were presumably kept within bounds and used to the fullest, the deficient practices of North Carolinians offered the perfect foil for their own superior behavior. The lazy men who lived "just like the Indians" on the frontier might invite suspicion, but Byrd and other Tidewater planters no longer had any reason to doubt that their own status as civilized English farmers was secure.[91]

Notes

1. William Waller Hening, ed., *The Statutes at Large; Being a Collection of All the Laws of Virginia . . .* , 13 vols. (Richmond, Va.: R. & W. & G. Bartow, 1819–1823), 1:328, 393–96 (hereafter cited as *Statutes of Virginia*).

2. Ibid., 1:396.

3. Livestock-rearing without arable farming was not considered sufficient. As Edmund Spenser noted of the Irish, the "keping of cowes is of it self a verie idle lyfe and a fitt nurserie for a theif"; quoted in Wesley N. Laing, "Cattle in Seventeenth-Century Virginia," *Virginia Magazine of History and Biography*, 67 (1959), 144.

4. Leonard Mascal, *The Government of Cattell. Divided into Three Books . . .* (London, England: Thomas Harper for Martha Harrison, 1653); Allan B. Forbes et al., eds., *Winthrop Papers, 1498–1654*, 6 vols. (Boston, Mass.: Massachusetts Historical Society, 1929–1992), 2:120.

5. "Observations by Master George Percy, 1607," in Lyon Gardiner Tyler, ed., *Narratives of Early Virginia, 1606–1625* (New York, N.Y.: C. Scribner's Sons, 1907), 18; Philip L. Barbour, ed., *The Jamestown Voyages under the First Charter 1606–1609*, 2 vols., Hakluyt Society, 2d ser., I, no. 136 (London, England: The Hakluyt Society, Cambridge University Press, 1969), 161; Susan Myra Kingsbury, ed., *The Records of the Virginia Company of London*, 4 vols. (Washington, D.C.: G.P.O., 1906–1935), 4:283.

6. John Smith, *The Proceedings of the English Colonie in Virginia, [1606–1612] . . .* , in Barbour, ed., *The Complete Works of Captain John Smith (1580–1631)*, 3 vols. (Chapel Hill: University of North Carolina Press, 1986), 1:273; Kingsbury, ed., *Records of the Virginia Company*, 1:257.

7. *A Declaration of the state of the Colonie and Affaires in Virginia . . .* (London, England: Snodham, 1620), in Peter Force, ed., *Tracts and Other Papers, Relating Principally to the Origin, Settlement, and Progress of the Colonies in North America, From the Discovery of the Country to the Year 1776*, 4 vols. (Washington, D.C., 1836–1844; rpt. Gloucester, Mass.: P. Smith, 1963), 3:§§5, 9, 15.

8. Timothy Silver, *A New Face on the Countryside: Indians, Colonists, and Slaves in South Atlantic Forests, 1500–1800* (New York, N.Y.: Cambridge University Press, 1990), 14–15, 61–62.

9. Karen Ordahl Kupperman, "The Puzzle of the American Climate in the Early Colonial Period," *American Historical Review*, 87 (1982), 1264–65; E. S. E. Hafez, ed., *Adaptation of Domestic Animals* (Philadelphia, Pa.: Lea & Febiger, 1968), 107, 117, 183, 187, 242, 289; L. E. Mount, *The Climatic Physiology of the Pig* (Baltimore, Md.: Williams & Wilkins, 1968), 120–21, 123.

10. David W. Stahle et al., "The Lost Colony and Jamestown Droughts," *Science*, 280 (1998), 564–67; Hafez, ed., *Adaptation of Domestic Animals*, 175–76; Frederick F. Siegel, *The Roots of Southern Distinctiveness: Tobacco and Society in Danville, Virginia, 1780–1865* (Chapel Hill: University of North Carolina Press, 1987), 71.

11. Frederick Zeuner, *A History of Domesticated Animals* (London, England: Hutchinson, 1963), 82; Hening, ed., *Statutes of Virginia*, 1:199, 395, 456, 2:87; Warren M.

Billings, ed., "Some Acts Not in Hening's *Statutes:* The Acts of Assembly, April 1652, November 1652, and July 1653," *Virginia Magazine of History and Biography*, 83 (1975), 68, 69; William Hand Browne, ed., *Archives of Maryland . . .* , 72 vols. (Baltimore: Maryland Historical Society, 1883–1972), 1:362–63; Silver, *New Face on the Countryside*, 176; Silver, "A Useful Arcadia: European Colonists as Biotic Factors in Chesapeake Forests," in Philip D. Curtin, Grace S. Brush, and George W. Fisher, eds., *Discovering the Chesapeake: The History of an Ecosystem* (Baltimore, Md.: Johns Hopkins University Press, 2001), 160–61.

12. Smith, *Proceedings of the English Colonie in Virginia*, 275; *For The Colony in Virginea Britannia. Lavves Diuine, Morall and Martiall, &c.* (1612) in Force, ed., *Tracts and Other Papers*, 3:§§2, 15; Edmund S. Morgan, *American Slavery, American Freedom: The Ordeal of Colonial Virginia* (New York, N.Y.: Norton, 1975), chap. 4, esp. 72–73, and Kupperman, "Apathy and Death in Early Jamestown," *Journal of American History*, 66 (1979), 24–40.

13. Ralph Hamor, *A True Discourse of the Present State of Virginia* (1615) (Richmond, Va.: Virginia State Library, 1957), 23; Martha W. McCartney, "An Early Virginia Census Reprised," *Quarterly Bulletin of the Archaeological Society of Virginia*, 54 (1999), 179, 181; Waterhouse, "A Declaration of the State of the Colony . . . ," in Kingsbury, ed., *Records of the Virginia Company*, 3:545. Morgan estimates that Virginia's English population in 1625 stood at about 1,300 in *American Slavery, American Freedom*, 404.

14. Kingsbury, ed., *Records of the Virginia Company*, 3:612, 4:228–29, 235, 476. For an account of the 1622 attack, see Morgan, *American Slavery, American Freedom*, 98–99, 104. The muster of 1624–1625 is reprinted in Annie Lash Jester and Martha Woodroof Hiden, eds., *Adventurers of Purse and Person: Virginia, 1607–1625*, 2d ed. (Richmond, Va.: Order of First Families of Virginia, 1964), 5–69.

15. Hening, ed., *Statutes of Virginia*, 1:153; "A Perfect Description of Virginia . . ." (London, 1649), in Force, ed., *Tracts and Other Papers*, 2: §§ 8, 3, 12; Morgan, *American Slavery, American Freedom*, 139–40.

16. Lois Green Carr, Russell R. Menard, and Lorena S. Walsh, *Robert Cole's World: Agriculture and Society in Early Maryland* (Chapel Hill: University of North Carolina Press, 1991), 223, 228.

17. "Perfect Description of Virginia," 11; Browne, ed., *Archives of Maryland*, 20:191–92, 269–70.

18. James Horn, *Adapting to a New World: English Society in the Seventeenth-Century Chesapeake* (Chapel Hill: University of North Carolina Press, 1994), 277; Gloria Main, *Tobacco Colony: Life in Early Maryland, 1650–1720* (Princeton, N.J.: Princeton University Press, 1982), 61–62, 67–68.

19. Markham, *Markham's Farewel to Husbandry: Or, the Enriching of All Sorts of Barren and Sterile Grounds in our Nation . . .* , 10th ed. (London, England: George Sawbridge, 1676), 115–16.

20. Keith Thomas, *Man and the Natural World: A History of the Modern Sensibility* (New York, N.Y.: Pantheon Books, 1983), 26; Markham, *Cheape and Good Husbandry*, 11th ed. (London, England: W. Wilson, 1664); Mascal, *Government of Cattell;* Thomas

Tusser, *Five Hundred Points of Good Husbandry* (London, England: J.M. for Company of Stationers, 1663); John Worlidge, *Systema Agriculturae; The Mystery of Husbandry Discovered*, 4th ed. (London, England: Thomas Dring, 1687). See also G. E. Fussell, *The English Dairy Farmer, 1500–1900* (London, England: F. Cass, 1966).

21. On the labor demands of tobacco, see Morgan, *American Slavery, American Freedom*, 108–13, 141–42.

22. "Perfect Description of Virginia," 3; John Hammond, *Leah and Rachel, or, The Two Fruitfull Sisters Virginia and Mary-Land* (1656), in Clayton Colman Hall, ed., *Narratives of Early Maryland, 1633–1684* (New York, N.Y.: Charles Scribner's Sons, 1910), 291; George Alsop, *A Character of the Province of Maryland* (1666), in ibid., 347; Thomas Glover, *An Account of Virginia* . . . , reprinted from *Philosophical Transactions of the Royal Society*, June 20, 1676 (Oxford, 1904), 19; "A Letter from Mr. John Clayton . . . to the Royal Society, May 12, 1688," in Force, ed., *Tracts and Other Papers*, 3:§§12, 35; Carr et al., *Robert Cole's World*, 51; Main, *Tobacco Colony*, 62; Lewis Cecil Gray, *History of Agriculture in the Southern United States to 1860*, 2 vols. (Washington, D.C.: Carnegie Institution of Washington, 1933), 1:207–8; Philip Alexander Bruce, *Economic History of Virginia in the Seventeenth Century* . . . , 2 vols. (New York, N.Y.: P. Smith, 1895), 1:298–99, 376–77.

23. Hamor, *True Discourse of the Present State of Virginia*, 23; Bruce, *Economic History of Virginia*, 1:200, 223–24; McCartney, "Early Virginia Census," 181; Main, *Tobacco Colony*, 76; [Durand of Dauphiné], *A Frenchman in Virginia: Being the Memoirs of a Huguenot Refugee in 1681* (Richmond, Va.: n.p., 1923), 108. For the white population of Virginia in 1650, see John J. McCusker and Russell R. Menard, *The Economy of British America, 1607–1789* (Chapel Hill: University of North Carolina Press, 1985), 136. For conditions in Maryland, see also Carr et al., *Robert Cole's World*, 35. The scarcity of plows persisted into the eighteenth century; see Gray, *History of Agriculture in the Southern United States*, 1:194–95.

24. Bruce, *Economic History of Virginia*, 1:298, 335, 374, 375; Main, *Tobacco Colony*, 45, 67; Morgan, *American Slavery, American Freedom*, 137; David O. Percy, *Of Fast Horses, Black Cattle, Woods Hogs, and Rat-Tailed Sheep: Animal Husbandry Along the Colonial Potomac*, National Colonial Farm Research Report No. 4 (Accokeek, Md.: n.p., 1979), 5–6; Carr et al., *Robert Cole's World*, 137; "Perfect Description of Virginia," 3; Gray, *History of Agriculture in the Southern United States*, 1:38, 202; Carr and Menard, "Immigration and Opportunity: The Freedman in Early Colonial Maryland," in Thad W. Tate and David L. Ammerman, eds., *The Chesapeake in the Seventeenth Century: Essays on Anglo-American Society* (Chapel Hill: University of North Carolina Press, 1979), 218; Kevin P. Kelly, "'In dispers'd Country Plantations': Settlement Patterns in Seventeenth-Century Surry County, Virginia," in ibid., 183–205; [Durand of Dauphiné], *Frenchman in Virginia*, 23.

25. Morgan, *American Slavery, American Freedom*, 336; Julia Cherry Spruill, *Women's Life and Work in the Southern Colonies* (New York, N.Y.: Norton, 1998; orig. pub. 1938), 3–19; Calvert Papers, *Maryland Historical Society Fund-Publications*, 3 vols. (Baltimore, Md.: J. Murphy & Co., 1889–1899), I (no. 28), 196.

26. Percy, *Fast Horses*, 22, 30–33; Main, *Tobacco Colony*, 200; Carr et al., *Robert Cole's World*, 38, 69, 72, 73–74, 95–96; Siegel, *Roots of Southern Distinctiveness*, 71; Joanne Bowen, "A Comparative Analysis of the New England and Chesapeake Herding Systems," in Paul A. Shackel and Barbara J. Little, eds., *Historical Archaeology of the Chesapeake* (Washington, D.C.: Smithsonian Institution Press, 1994), 161; Laing, "Cattle in Seventeenth-Century Virginia," 154–55. See also "Relation of the Lord Dela-ware" (1611), in Tyler, ed., *Narratives of Early Virginia*, 213, and "Perfect Description of Virginia," 14–15. According to John Worlidge, *Systema Agriculturae*, 172, "Dutch" cows, available in England, produced two gallons of milk at each milking. For quotations, see "Letter from Mr. John Clayton," 25; [Durand of Dauphiné], *Frenchman in Virginia*, 116–17; and Calvert Papers, *Maryland Historical Society Fund-Publications*, I (no. 28), 263.

27. Henry M. Miller, "An Archaeological Perspective on the Evolution of Diet in the Colonial Chesapeake, 1620–1745," in Lois Green Carr, Philip D. Morgan, and Jean B. Russo, eds., *Colonial Chesapeake Society* (Chapel Hill: University of North Carolina Press, 1988), 176–99; Carr et al., *Robert Cole's World*, 97, 217–18; Main, *Tobacco Colony*, 204; Kupperman, "Apathy and Death in Early Jamestown," 32–33. The English commentator was Gregory King, cited in Thomas, *Man and the Natural World*, 26.

28. Markham, *Cheape and Good Husbandry*, 11th ed., 2–73; Mascal, *Government of Cattell*, 2–166; Markham, *Markham's Farewel to Husbandry*, 10th ed., 115–18.

29. Kingsbury, ed., *Records of the Virginia Company*, 3:18, 221; see also Laing, "Cattle in Seventeenth-Century Virginia," 160; Morgan, *American Slavery, American Freedom*, 137; and Carr et al., *Robert Cole's World*, 46.

30. Robert Beverley, *The History and Present State of Virginia*, ed. Louis B. Wright (Charlottesville, Va.: Dominion Books, 1968; orig. pub. 1947), 37; Bruce, *Economic History of Virginia*, 1:209–10, 300, 312; Morgan, *American Slavery, American Freedom*, 136–37; Kingsbury, ed., *Records of the Virginia Company*, 3:473; Barbour, ed., *Complete Works of Capt. John Smith*, 2:242; Hamor, *True Discourse of the Present State of Virginia*, 30–31; Lorena S. Walsh, Ann Smart Martin, and Joanne Bowen, "Provisioning Early American Towns; The Chesapeake: A Multidisciplinary Study," Final Performance Report, NEH Grant RO-22643-93 (1997), 32. For the use of islands, see "Letter of Governor Leonard Calvert to Lord Baltimore, 1638," in Hall, ed., *Narratives of Early Maryland*, 154; *A True Declaration of the estate of the Colonie in Virginia . . .* (London, 1610), in Force, *Tracts and Other Papers*, 3:§1; Barbour, ed., *Complete Works of Capt. John Smith*, 1:254; and Calvert Papers, *Maryland Historical Society Fund-Publications*, I (no. 28), 208.

31. [Durand of Dauphiné], *Frenchman in Virginia*, 116–17. For occasional nighttime penning of cattle, see "Letter from Mr. John Clayton," 26, and Edmund Berkeley and Dorothy S. Berkeley, eds., "Another 'Account of Virginia' by the Reverend John Clayton," *Virginia Magazine of History and Biography*, 76 (1968), 419; Morgan, *American Slavery, American Freedom*, 137. On the penning of swine, see Hening, ed., *Statutes of Virginia*, 1:228; Bruce, *Economic History of Virginia*, 1:315; Browne, ed., *Archives of Maryland*, 17:422–23; and Walsh et al., "Provisioning Early American Towns," 30. For

court cases involving errant swine, see Accomack County Records, Virginia State Library, microfilm, reel 4, fol. 226, and Browne, ed., *Archives of Maryland*, 4:412–13.

32. Calvert Papers, *Maryland Historical Society Fund-Publications*, I (no. 28), 196. On the cost of feeding penned animals, see Main, *Tobacco Colony*, 63–64.

33. James Blakely and David H. Bade, *The Science of Animal Husbandry*, 4th ed. (Reston, Va.: Reston Pub. Co., 1985), 106, 125, 394, 586, 587; Katherine A. Houpt, *Domestic Animal Behavior for Veterinarians and Animal Scientists*, 3d ed. (Ames: Iowa State University Press, 1998), 100, 289–90, 319; Siegel, *Roots of Southern Distinctiveness*, 70–71.

34. Hening, *Statutes of Virginia*, 1:244–45, 332, 2:96–97, 100–101; Billings, "Some Acts Not in Hening's *Statutes*," 58; Browne, ed., *Archives of Maryland*, 1:96, 344, 413–14, 2:350, 398–99, 13:472–73, 487, 22:477–78. On Virginia fences, see Berkeley and Berkeley, eds., "Another 'Account of Virginia,'" 426.

35. William Holdsworth, *A History of English Law*, 5th ed., 16 vols. (London, England: Methuen, 1942), 3:378–79; Peter Karsten, "Cows in the Corn, Pigs in the Garden, and 'the Problem of Social Costs': 'High' and 'Low' Legal Cultures of the British Diaspora Lands in the 17th, 18th, and 19th Centuries," *Law and Society Review*, 32 (1998), 66–67; Bruce, *Economic History of Virginia*, 1:313–15.

36. [Whitaker], *Good Newes from Virginia . . .* (London, 1613; facsimile, New York, n.d.), 41; Glover, *Account of Virginia*, 19. For similar observations, see Nathaniel Shrigley, *A True Relation of Virginia and Mary-Land . . .* (1669), in Force, ed., *Tracts and Other Papers*, 3:§5; Joseph and Nesta Ewan, eds., *John Banister and His Natural History of Virginia, 1678–1692* (Urbana: University of Illinois Press, 1970), 356.

37. [Durand of Dauphiné], *Frenchman in Virginia*, 54, 59, 60, 115–17. On horse-racing in colonial Virginia, see T. H. Breen, "Horses and Gentlemen: The Cultural Significance of Gambling Among the Gentry of Virginia," *William and Mary Quarterly*, 3d Ser., 34 (1977), 239–57; Rhys Isaac, *The Transformation of Virginia, 1740–1790* (Chapel Hill: University of North Carolina Press, 1982), 98–101; and Jane Carson, *Colonial Virginians at Play* (Charlottesville, Va.: University Press of Virginia, 1965), 102–32, 257–60.

38. "Letter from Mr. John Clayton," 25–26, 35; Beverley, *History and Present State of Virginia*, ed. Wright, 291, 314, 318. On English farmers' use of sainfoin, see Eric Kerridge, *The Agricultural Revolution* (New York, N.Y.: Allen and Unwin, 1967), 278–80.

39. Beverley, *History and Present State of Virginia*, ed. Wright, 318; Browne, ed., *Archives of Maryland*, 4:168; Carr et al., *Robert Cole's World*, 177, 187.

40. For examples of notices of lost animals, see Accomack Co. Records, reel 2, fols. 95, 96, 123, 135–36, 142, 149, 151, 152, 172, 182. On the particular dangers of marshes, see Glover, *Account of Virginia*, 18–19; "Letter from Mr. John Clayton," 20, 25–26 (quotation). The cow "brooken leggs" is mentioned in H. R. McIlwaine, ed., *Minutes of the Council and General Court of Colonial Virginia*, 2d ed. (Richmond, Va.: Virginia State Library, 1979), 129.

41. Waterhouse, "Declaration of the State of the Colony . . ." (1622), 545; see also the letter from John Pory in Kingsbury, ed., *Records of the Virginia Company*, 3:221.

42. Main, *Tobacco Colony*, 65; Beverley, *History and Present State of Virginia*, ed. Wright, 291; Browne, ed., *Archives of Maryland*, 38:11; see also Walsh et al., "Provisioning Early American Towns," 39–41.

43. Joyce Chaplin, *Subject Matter: Technology, the Body, and Science on the Anglo-American Frontier, 1500–1676* (Cambridge, Mass.: Harvard University Press, 2001), chap. 4.

44. Ronald R. Keiper, *The Assateague Ponies* (Centreville, Md.: Tidewater Publishers, 1985), 15–16. Modern free-ranging feral cattle also tend to be small; H. Epstein and I. L. Mason, "Cattle," in Ian L. Mason, ed., *Evolution of Domesticated Animals* (London and New York: Longman, 1984), 25.

45. Beverley, *History and Present State of Virginia*, ed. Wright, 291; "A Relation of Maryland, 1635," in Hall, ed., *Narratives of Early Maryland*, 78–79; see also "Letter from Mr. John Clayton," 36; Shrigley, *True Relation of Virginia and Mary-Land*, 5; and "Perfect Description of Virginia," 3.

46. Glover, *Account of Virginia*, 12–13; Alsop, *Character of the Province of Maryland*, 348; Henry Hartwell, James Blair, and Edward Chilton, *The Present State of Virginia, and the College* (1727), ed. Hunter Dickinson Farish (Williamsburg, Va.: Colonial Williamsburg, 1940), 9; [Durand of Dauphiné], *Frenchman in Virginia*, 109; "Letter from Mr. John Clayton," 20–21; Jones, *Present State of Virginia*, ed. Morton, 77; Carr and Menard, "Land, Labor, and Economies of Scale in Early Maryland: Some Limits to Growth in the Chesapeake System of Husbandry," *Journal of Economic History*, 49 (1989), 407–18; Morgan, *American Slavery, American Freedom*, 141; Carr et al., *Robert Cole's World*, 52; Carville V. Earle, *The Evolution of a Tidewater Settlement System: All Hallow's Parish, Maryland, 1650–1783* (Chicago: University of Chicago Press, 1975), 24–30; Bruce, *Economic History of Virginia*, 1:322; Gray, *History of Agriculture in the Southern United States*, 1:198; Richard L. Bushman, "Opening the American Countryside," in James A. Henretta, Michael Kammen, and Stanley N. Katz, eds., *The Transformation of Early American History: Society, Authority, and Ideology* (New York, N.Y.: Random House, 1991), 242–43.

47. Kelly, "'In dispers'd Country Plantations,'" 183–205; Earle, *Evolution of a Tidewater Settlement System*, 138–40; Main, *Tobacco Colony*, 30–31.

48. Sam B. Hilliard, *Hog Meat and Hoecake: Food Supply in the Old South, 1840–1860* (Carbondale: Southern Illinois University Press, 1972), 136; Silver, *New Face on the Countryside*, 179; Hartwell et al., *Present State of Virginia, and the College*, ed. Farish, 8; Silver, "Useful Arcadia," 155, 161.

49. "Letter from Mr. John Clayton," 21; [Durand of Dauphiné], *Frenchman in Virginia*, 59; Darrett B. Rutman and Anita H. Rutman, *A Place in Time: Middlesex County, Virginia, 1650–1750* (New York, N.Y.: Norton, 1984), 153; Main, *Tobacco Colony*, 128.

50. Main, *Tobacco Colony*, 62. Horn, *Adapting to a New World*, 169, calculates that just over 40 percent of landholders in mid-seventeenth-century Lower Norfolk County, Va., owned fewer than 300 acres.

51. Calvert Papers, *Maryland Historical Society Fund-Publications*, I (no. 28), 238–39.

52. [Durand of Dauphiné], *Frenchman in Virginia*, 114.

53. Kingsbury, ed., *Records of the Virginia Company*, 4:283–84.

54. Hammond, *Leah and Rachel*, 295; Hening, ed., *Statutes of Virginia*, 1:350.

55. Hening, ed., *Statutes of Virginia*, 1:350–51, 2:129, 440–41; Billings, ed., "Some Acts Not in Hening's *Statutes*," 62, 83; Beverley, *History and Present State of Virginia*, ed. Wright, 259; Browne, ed., *Archives of Maryland*, 1:251, 455, 2:140–42, 277–79, 7: 201–3, 13:477–78.

56. Browne, ed., *Archives of Maryland*, 41:161, 53:234–37, 54:42–43, 384; for similar cases, see 10:233–34, 53:206, 237–39, 544–48, 54:369–70; Accomack Co. Records, reel 4, fols. 130–31, 137, 158, 223–28. See also Raphael Semmes, *Crime and Punishment in Early Maryland* (Baltimore, Md.: Johns Hopkins Press, 1938), chap. 3, and Horn, *Adapting to a New World*, 352, 360–61. On slander and defamation in early America, see Helena M. Wall, *Fierce Communion: Family and Community in Early America* (Cambridge, Mass.: Harvard University Press, 1990), chap. 2, and Mary Beth Norton, *Founding Mothers and Fathers: Gendered Power and the Forming of American Society* (New York, N.Y.: Knopf, 1996), 211–17, 269–74.

57. Browne, ed., *Archives of Maryland*, 1:253, 17:135–36, 38:77–78; Hening, ed., *Statutes of Virginia*, 1:465–66. On theft of livestock, see also Gray, *History of Agriculture in the Southern United States,* 1:143–45, and Bruce, *Economic History of Virginia*, 1:371–72, 379.

58. Hening, ed., *Statutes of Virginia*, 1:145–46; Gray, *History of Agriculture in the Southern United States*, 1:143; Morgan, *American Slavery, American Freedom*, 122.

59. Browne, ed., *Archives of Maryland*, 2:346–47, 5:568–69, 8:36–37, 15:155–56; Semmes, *Crime and Punishment in Early Maryland*, 76.

60. Hening, ed., *Statutes of Virginia*, 1:420–21; Billings, ed., "Some Acts Not in Hening's *Statutes*," 67–68. On English practice, see Charles M. Andrews, *The Colonial Period of American History*, 4 vols. (New Haven, Conn.: n.p., 1936), 2:208.

61. For scattered references to branding, see Billings, ed., *The Old Dominion in the Seventeenth Century: A Documentary History of Virginia, 1606–1689* (Chapel Hill: University of North Carolina Press, 1975), 90; Barton H. Wise, ed., "Northampton County Records in the 17th Century," *Virginia Magazine of History and Biography*, 4 (1897), 406; Gray, *History of Agriculture in the Southern United States*, 1:144–45; and Carr et al., *Robert Cole's World*, 176–77. For earmarking, see Browne, ed., *Archives of Maryland*, 1:295; Wise, ed., "Northampton Co. Recs.," 404; Gray, *History of Agriculture in the Southern United States*, 1:144–45; and Laing, "Cattle in Seventeenth-Century Virginia," 159–60. For examples of earmarks, see Accomack Co. Records, reel 2, fol. 142, reel 4, fols. 267–70; Susie M. Ames, ed., *County Court Records of Accomack-Northampton, Virginia, 1640–1645* (Charlottesville: University Press of Virginia, 1973), 30; and Carr et al., *Robert Cole's World*, 176–77.

62. Browne, ed., *Archives of Maryland*, 4:207, 22:554–55, 41:20–21, 523; Hening, ed., *Statutes of Virginia*, 1:244.

63. Zeuner, *History of Domesticated Animals*, 37, and Juliet Clutton-Brock, *Domesticated Animals from Early Times* (Austin: University of Texas Press, 1981), 15–16.

64. Beverley, *History and Present State of Virginia*, ed. Wright, 318; Browne, ed., *Archives of Maryland*, 10:236, 2:277–79; see also Browne, ed., *Archives of Maryland*, 53:545.

65. Clutton-Brock, *Domesticated Animals*, 15; Hafez, ed., *Behaviour of Domestic Animals*, 16–17, 112; Houpt, *Domestic Animal Behavior for Veterinarians and Animal Scientists*, 242, 248; Caroline Grigson, "Porridge and Pannage: Pig Husbandry in Neolithic England," in Martin Bell and Susan Limbrey, eds., *Archaeological Aspects of Woodland Ecology*, British Archaeological Reports International Series 146 (Oxford, England: B.A.R., 1982), 303; H. B. Graves, "Behavior and Ecology of Wild and Feral Swine (Sus Scrofa)," *Journal of Animal Science*, 58 (1984), 483.

66. See Sytze Bottema, "Some Observations on Modern Domestication Processes," in Clutton-Brock, ed., *The Walking Larder: Patterns of Domestication, Pastoralism, and Predation* (London, England: Unwin Hyman, 1989), 44, and Grigson, "Porridge and Pannage," 302, 303.

67. "Letter from Mr. John Clayton," 26; Bartlett Burleigh James and J. Franklin Jameson, eds., *Journal of Jasper Danckaerts, 1679–1680* (New York, N.Y.: Charles Scribner's Sons, 1913), 134. This practice continued into the nineteenth century; see Hilliard, *Hog Meat and Hoecake*, 99.

68. Bruce, *Economic History of Virginia*, 1:379; for examples of penned animals, see Browne, ed., *Archives of Maryland*, 4:412–13, 54:396. On the utility of penning farrowing swine as a method of domestication, see Grigson, "Porridge and Pannage," 305.

69. McCartney, "Early Virginia Census Reprised," 178.

70. Houpt, *Domestic Animal Behavior for Veterinarians and Animal Scientists*, 38, 46–47, 55–56, 173; Hafez, ed., *Adaptation of Domestic Animals*, 43; Tom McKnight, *Feral Livestock in Anglo-America*, University of California Publications in Geography, vol. 16 (Berkeley: University of California Press, 1964), 19, 28, 41, 43; Keiper, *Assateague Ponies*, 39; John J. Mayer and I. Lehr Brisbin Jr., *Wild Pigs of the United States: Their History, Morphology, and Current Status* (Athens: University of Georgia Press, 1991), 8–9; G. W. Arnold and M. L. Dudzinski, *Ethology of Free-Ranging Domestic Animals* (New York, N.Y.: Elsevier Scientific Pub. Co., 1978), 125; Hilliard, *Hog Meat and Hoecake*, 95; Graves, "Behavior and Ecology of Wild and Feral Swine," 483–90. See also Alfred W. Crosby, *Ecological Imperialism: The Biological Expansion of Europe, 900–1900* (New York, N.Y.: Cambridge University Press, 1986), 174–87.

71. H. Epstein and I. L. Mason, "Cattle," in Mason, ed., *Evolution of Domesticated Animals*, 25; McKnight, *Feral Livestock in Anglo-America*, 41; Mayer and Brisbin, *Wild Pigs*, 124, 127, 134, 139, 147; Graves, "Behavior and Ecology of Wild and Feral Swine," 484; Keiper, *Assateague Ponies*, 16.

72. Epstein and M. Bichard, "Pig," in Mason, ed., *Evolution of Domesticated Animals*, 146; Epstein and Mason, "Cattle," 7; Keiper, *Assateague Ponies*, 58–59.

73. Joan Thirsk, ed., *The Agrarian History of England and Wales*, vol. 4: *1500–1640* (Cambridge, England: Cambridge University Press, 1967), 19, 138, 160, 187.

74. "Letter from Mr. John Clayton," 35; Beverley, *History and Present State of Virginia*, ed. Wright, 153–54; 312.

75. Browne, ed., *Archives of Maryland*, 54:42–43.

76. McKnight, *Feral Livestock in Anglo-America*, 31, and Browne, ed., *Archives of Maryland*, 10:48–49.

77. McKnight, *Feral Livestock in Anglo-America*, 17; Browne, ed., *Archives of Maryland*, 38:11–13.

78. Browne, ed., *Archives of Maryland*, 1:418–19, 10:109–10; Beverley, *History and Present State of Virginia*, ed. Wright, 312.

79. *Oxford English Dictionary*, s.v. "cattle"; see also Gary L. Francione, *Animals, Property, and the Law* (Philadelphia, Pa.: Temple University Press, 1995), 34.

80. On the legal concept of *ferae naturae*, see Francione, *Animals, Property, and the Law*, 41, and Holdsworth, *History of English Law*, 3:367–68.

81. "An answere to a Declaracion of the present state of Virginia . . ." (attributed to Alderman Johnson), in Kingsbury, ed., *Records of the Virginia Company*, 4:138.

82. "An answere to a Declaracion of the present state of Virginia . . ." (attributed to Alderman Johnson), in Kingsbury, ed., *Records of the Virginia Company*, 4:138.

83. Hening, ed., *Statutes of Virginia*, 1:199, 244.

84. Browne, ed., *Archives of Maryland*, 1:418–19, 8:392–93, 17:233, 241–42, 41:441, 57:115. See also Susan Rosenfeld Falb, *Advice and Ascent: The Development of the Maryland Assembly 1635–1689* (New York, N.Y.: Garland Pub., 1986).

85. Browne, ed., *Archives of Maryland*, 3:295, 4:142–43, 10:149–50, 20:294.

86. Andrews, *Colonial Period of American History*, 2:294–97; Carr et al., *Robert Cole's World*, 5–9; Browne, ed., *Archives of Maryland*, 41:188–89, 49:575, 586–87, 53:628.

87. See Carr and David William Jordan, *Maryland's Revolution of Government, 1689–1692* (Ithaca, N.Y.: Cornell University Press, 1974).

88. Browne, ed., *Archives of Maryland*, 20:26.

89. Ibid., 19:184.

90. Carr and Menard, "Land, Labor, and Economies of Scale in Early Maryland," 413–18; Walsh, "Plantation Management in the Chesapeake, 1620–1820," *Journal of Economic History*, 49 (1989), 393–406; Walsh, "Land Use, Settlement Patterns, and the Impact of European Agriculture, 1620–1820," in Curtin et al., eds., *Discovering the Chesapeake*, 237, 240–41; Main, *Tobacco Colony*, 73–74; Bruce, *Economic History of Virginia*, 1:481–83.

91. William K. Boyd, ed., *William Byrd's Histories of the Dividing Line Betwixt Virginia and North Carolina* (New York, N.Y.: Dover Publications, 1967), 54, 92.

JAMES TAYLOR CARSON

Horses and the Economy and Culture of the Choctaw Indians, 1690–1840

IN THE COURSE of a generation, horses revolutionized life among many of the Plains tribes. Many agricultural peoples were able to drop their hoes and pick up and follow the buffalo herds in a nomadic hunting lifestyle. Unlike the Plains Indians' experience, however, horses did not suddenly transform Choctaw society. Lacking expansive flat plains and roving buffalo herds, the dense woodlands of Mississippi precluded the innovative use of horses in nomadic hunting and predatory warfare. Nevertheless, among the Choctaws, horses proved to be an equally influential, if less dramatic, social, economic, and symbolic innovation that stimulated an evolution, rather than a revolution, of lifestyle. From the 1690s, when the Choctaws first acquired horses, to the 1830s, when the United States removed the Choctaws to Indian Territory, horses allowed the Choctaws to alter substantially their economic life and simultaneously to preserve much of their social values and traditions.[1]

In traditional Choctaw society, men and women performed distinct socioeconomic tasks. Women directed domestic life and enjoyed a special relationship with the plant world. Among their many duties, they fabricated utensils and earthen containers, prepared food, drew water, and sowed and harvested crops. Their wide fields of corn, beans, pumpkins, and squash provided two-thirds of the Choctaw diet and made the Choctaws what Bernard Romans termed a "nation of farmers."[2] In addition to their household and farming duties, women accompanied men on long hunting expeditions to prepare the men's meals because cultural taboos forbade males from doing so. Women also transported the game killed by the men, which contributed the remaining one-third of the Choctaw diet, from the forest back to the villages, where they processed the animals' skins, meat, and bones into clothing, food, and tools.

Men also performed certain functions in Choctaw society. They directed the external affairs of the village or nation, and they shared a unique relationship with the animal world. They performed rituals, oversaw relations with surrounding peoples, and, above all, waged war and hunted. One common ritual activity that combined the strength and endurance of warfare and the close relationship to animals characterized by hunting was the ball game. In the mid-eighteenth century Frenchman Jean-Bernard Bossu visited the Choctaw Nation and observed such a game between two rival villages. Commenting on the fast-paced action and furious contact between opposing players, Bossu noted that many Choctaw players had affixed wildcat tails and white bird feathers to their ballsticks and breech-clouts. For the Choctaws, such decoration imbued the ballplayer with the wildcat's spirit and ferocity and the bird's swiftness. The ball game, or the "little brother of war," provided entertainment for women and men alike and allowed men to test the skills that would be essential in hunting and warfare.[3]

Hunting and warfare were the Choctaw male's greatest social responsibilities, and his importance in society often depended on his success in these endeavors. During the fall and winter hunting season, Choctaw males, often accompanied by women and children, set up in winter hunting camps far from their villages or relied on their knowledge of the Choctaw borderlands to locate white-tailed deer closer to home. More than any other wild animal, deer provided Choctaw families with meat for food, skins for clothing, and antlers and bones for tools. If Choctaw men could control its timing, they preferred to make war after the hunting season during the spring and summer months. Exhorted by their wives who followed them on distant forays "to die like real men," Choctaws used warfare to defend their hunting grounds and to still the "crying blood" of kinsmen who had lost their lives at the hands of outsiders. Warfare provided an arena for young men to gain adulthood and for warriors to demonstrate the judgment and expertise that society esteemed. Exploits on the battle-field led to civic responsibilities, and leaders often introduced themselves to assemblies and diplomatic delegations with "a recital of [their] feats in war." Such success permitted gradual advancement up the social hierarchy, but advancement and prominence came with risk. If a chief failed in war, he could lose his position. Although Choctaw males served a variety of important functions in their society, warfare and hunting were the cornerstones of their lives, and without these activities Choctaw males would have lost much of their social, economic, and political significance.[4]

Hunting, fighting, and trading carried Choctaws far and wide, put them into contact with tribes west of the Mississippi River, and exposed them to a vast and ancient trade network that stretched as far as New Mexico. By the 1690s the Choctaws had encountered horses as trade goods. Acquired originally in New Mexico, horses were traded across the Great Plains and distributed among several tribes that bordered the western reaches of the Choctaw Nation. By 1690, the Caddo Indians as well as the neighboring Osage, Wichita, and Avoyello tribes had acquired horses. The Caddo in particular had been carrying on a substantial trade in horses with the Spanish and other Indian groups but had not integrated horses into their culture. Their name for horses, *cauali*, derived from the Spanish *caballo*, suggests the regional trade of horses in conformity with Spanish conceptions of trade and alliance. Consequently, horses served these tribes as an important exchangeable commodity in the trade with Europeans for guns, cloth, and other manufactured items.[5]

Unlike the Caddo, the Choctaws developed an indigenous term for the new animal. Jesuit priest Jacques Gravier recorded in 1701 that Choctaws called horses *isuba*, which derived from *isi holba*, or deer-resembler. As a four-footed grass-eating animal, the horse fit into the same category as deer and would have also been considered to be edible. Like most tribes unfamiliar with horses and their utility, the Choctaw hunting parties who initially encountered the animals most likely shot the horses and ate them, a practice they continued well into the eighteenth century. Initially integrated into the Choctaw diet, horses were soon a part of Choctaw culture, for the trade network among the Spanish, Caddos, Wichitas, and Avoyellos introduced enormous numbers of horses into the native Southeast.[6]

By the 1730s horses had become a fixture among the Choctaws and other Southeastern Indians. Moreover, the animals played a crucial role in the development of the growing deerskin trade with the French and the British. Indeed, the incorporation of horses into Choctaw culture is virtually inseparable from the deerskin trade, for horses provided the wherewithal to rapidly expand the scope and intensity of Choctaw hunting expeditions.

Choctaw men learned to ride horses to reach distant hunting grounds, and women began to use horses to fetch the game. Women also drove horse trains laden with provisions when they accompanied their husbands on long hunting journeys and returned with horse trains weighted down by the skins procured by their husbands and processed by hand. A Spanish ship captain traveling in January 1793 on the Mississippi River just north of its confluence with the Yazoo River observed such a party. Twenty-five men, their wives, and their children were leading a train of fifteen horses laden with skins and pelts.[7]

The rise of the deerskin trade and the importance of horses in that trade dramatically imprinted the Choctaw landscape. Footpaths became horse-paths, and routes previously used for intervillage and intertribal communication expanded to serve the burgeoning deerskin trade. Consequently, Choctaws began to incorporate isuba into their toponymic system and horses into their functional conception of the landscape. Traveling from Mobile into the Choctaw Nation in the early 1730s, Regis du Roullet reported two such toponyms. The first, *conchak ou soubaille* (canebrake where a horse drowned), commemorated perhaps the personal loss of a Choctaw man or woman. The second, *Bouk ite tchuie souba* (the bayou where there is a tree that marks a horsepath), indicated the regular passage of horses along the route from the Choctaw Nation to Mobile and bore testimony to the substantial horse traffic between the two.[8]

Despite the instrumental role horses played in the deerskin trade, Choctaws did not just use them for their labor. The animals also entered into Choctaw ritual life, as Louis Leclerc de Milford observed in a Choctaw funeral. Choctaws placed the bodies of the dead on open air scaffolds until they had decayed sufficiently for bonepickers to remove the flesh. The bones were then bundled for presentation to the deceased's clan and interment in the village bonehouse. After the bonepickers completed their task, they slaughtered the deceased's horse(s) and roasted the carcass(es) for a feast. Sharing the feast with kinfolk or the community, the deceased's relatives celebrated his or her passage and reaffirmed the bonds of community and kinship that bound Choctaws together.[9]

Such scattered observations of the impact of horses on Choctaw life point to a broad acceptance of the animals in a number of functions. The growing need for more horses, for trade or personal use, further influenced Choctaw behavior. Choctaw warriors quickly became embroiled in a regional pattern of horse raiding and herding. Sometime before 1763 a band of Choctaws settled permanently among the Caddo Indians along the Red River, close to the French trading post at Natchitoches. These Choctaws participated in slave, cattle, and horse raids against the Osage and Wichita Indians. To capture horses, Choctaws used the same guns with which they hunted the deer. They would train their aim on the horse's mane and fire so as to graze the animal's neck. Stunned, the horse would collapse, and the hunter would run up and secure the animal. By the 1780s the areas around the Sabine, Red, and Arkansas Rivers had become thriving centers for such activities. In 1807 John Sibley, United States Indian Agent at the Natchitoches post, reported several groups of Indians passing both eastward and westward through his district with enormous herds of horses.[10] The same economic imperatives that motivated Choctaws to range across the Mississippi River in quest of more horses were part of the deerskin trade, but the fate of the latter did not determine the fate of horses among the Choctaws, for horses had become essential to Choctaw daily life and culture independent of market fluctuations.

The French who had settled the lower Mississippi River valley at the end of the seventeenth century had inaugurated the trade in deerskins, but the trade intensified after the French ceded control of the eastern lower Mississippi River valley to the British in 1763. By the 1780s, after two decades of British trade, the Choctaws' demand for European goods had exceeded their ability to pay British prices. To compensate for this unfavorable balance of trade, the Choctaws overhunted the white-tailed deer for their valuable skins. As the deer became scarce in the immediate vicinity, the Choctaws ventured beyond the borderlands surrounding their towns and crossed the Mississippi River, where they had already found horses, to find more deer.[11] Because deer hunting was essential to traditional Choctaw male and female life and material culture, the disappearance of the deer meant the potential disappearance of a substantial part of their culture. By the late eighteenth century, deer were harder to come by, and the deerskin trade had taken a permanent downward turn. Coinciding roughly with the collapse of the deer economy in Mississippi, Choctaw warfare suffered a similar fate.

Traditional forms of warfare and colonial client warfare largely ceased after the United States had asserted a tenuous sovereignty over the southern frontier with treaties negotiated at Hopewell, South Carolina, in the

1780s. The treaties established peaceful relations between the United States and the Choctaws, Chickasaws, and Cherokees and opened the way for increasing American intervention and interference in Choctaw affairs. In 1798 the federal government organized the area surrounding the Choctaws into the Mississippi Territory with the expectation of settling the region.[12] Because of the chronic overhunting of deer, the collapse of the deerskin trade, and the diplomatic efforts of the United States to suppress hostilities, deer hunting and warfare had declined substantially by 1800. This state of affairs imperiled the roles and responsibilities of Choctaw males in their society and affected women as well.

Other factors further contributed to a sense of crisis among the Choctaws during the late 1700s. Natchez, formerly a French colonial town that had produced tobacco and cattle, burgeoned with an influx of Loyalist settlers from the East after the American Revolution. Cotton soon supplanted tobacco as Natchez's most profitable staple crop, and the town's population grew from 1,926 in 1788 to 4,436 in 1792. Consequently, plantation agriculture began to expand along several large creeks, and settlers crept inland along these creeks into the Choctaw borderlands. Moreover, droughts had ruined the Choctaw corn crops of 1792 and 1793, exacerbating the difficulties brought on by an epidemic that struck the Choctaws in 1790 and killed most of their horses. Many observers commented on the Choctaws' lack of food and resources, and their imminent starvation. Holding American settlers responsible for these catastrophic events, Choctaw warriors sought to drive the settlers away from their villages and borderlands by raiding their property, burning what they could, and stealing the settlers' horses. Consequently, Choctaw males transferred techniques perfected in the trans-Mississippi horse raids and brought them to bear on American settlers.[13]

Choctaw horse raids combined an aggressive territorial defense with strategies for economic gain into an innovative form of warfare that perpetuated male values and traditions in the absence of deer hunting and traditional warfare. Choctaw warriors commenced their horse raids on American settlers during the traditional hunting season, between late August and late April, perhaps because they considered horses as deer-resemblers. However, the horse raiders also displayed certain warlike characteristics, for, by raiding frontier farms, they both defended their territorial boundaries and punished a threatening foe.[14] The location of horse raids in relation to the marked boundaries between the Choctaws and the United States cannot be determined precisely, but the Choctaws most likely targeted illegal squatters who had crossed the surveyed borders onto Choctaw land. In a confrontation with such squatters, Choctaw leaders threatened: "You are all Americans and usurpers of these lands, and as such I warn you to leave them with all your property within the next two weeks. Then I shall return with my warriors . . . to compel all of your people to evacuate this territory."[15] Anxious to protect their borders, Choctaw headmen constantly reiterated to federal and territorial officials a desire to have their national boundaries clearly marked to prevent trespassing by Americans. In an attempt to clarify the boundaries between the Choctaws and the United States, the two nations negotiated three treaties: Fort Adams (1801), Fort Confederation (1802), and Hoe Buckintoopa (1803). During the 1801 Treaty of Fort Adams negotiations Choctaw headmen specifically asked the federal commissioners to remove Americans and their livestock from the Choctaw side of the boundary. Governor Winthrop Sargent supported the Choctaw claim, fearing that as long as the United States refused to accommodate their wishes the Choctaws would continue to steal horses and destroy farmsteads.[16]

The Choctaws possessed a legal right to protect their territory in such a manner. The Treaty of Hopewell reserved for them the right to punish illegal squatters "as they please," and they employed the horse raid to fulfill this stipulation. The raids frequently forced settlers to abandon their farmsteads, but the complaints lodged by settlers never mentioned fatalities. According to the Hopewell Treaty, if any Choctaw murdered an American citizen, Choctaw leaders had to deliver the perpetrator to the appropriate authorities who would punish the offender according to United States law. By not harming American citizens, the Choctaws avoided potentially dangerous conflicts with settlers and the federal government but still accomplished their ultimate goal.[17]

American settlers and officials equated horse raids with stealing, an antisocial and illegal appropriation of another person's private property. Historian William McLoughlin has concurred with this assessment, arguing that horse stealing among the Cherokees indicated a breakdown of their culture. However, like their Plains Indian counterparts, the Choctaws incorporated horse theft into their war complex. Consequently, raiding the enemy and taking his horses became perfectly legitimate and even desirable activities.[18] The Choctaw warriors' determination to perpetuate their hunting and warring ways through the theft of horses, and their underlying motivations for such behavior, surfaced secondhand in a letter penned by the governor of Mississippi Territory, Winthrop Sargent, that demanded the return of some stolen horses:

> In a case of some horses demanded from them . . . they have declared
> their determination sooner to shoot and take them for food than make the
> surrender. Observing that their Country, once affording abundance, had
> become desolate by the hands of a People who knew not but to increase
> their Wretchedness . . . they were determined in future to Consider our
> Domestic Animals as fit Objects for the chase.[19]

Choctaw males fully appreciated the impact American settlement had had on their hunting and warfare traditions, and "roguish young men," growing to maturity in a society where the traditional means of social and political advancement were no longer present, provided eager levies for the horse raids.[20] For these young men the horse raid and horse stealing affirmed and perpetuated male cultural values and traditions, defended the integrity of the Choctaw Nation against settlers—"the plague of locusts"—and dissuaded settlers from venturing too far from what the Choctaws perceived as an acceptable frontier between the two peoples.[21]

The 1790s and 1800s, the era of the horse raids, culminated the Choctaws' ascendancy on the frontier. During this time the Choctaws enjoyed a great measure of power and independence from the United States. Ruefully admitting the strength of the Choctaw Nation, Mississippi Territory Governor William Claiborne lamented that American settlers had suffered great "inconvenience" at the hands of the Choctaws, but counseled them to acquiesce to Choctaw aggression in the broader interests of diplomacy. In his instructions to the commissioners who negotiated the 1801 Treaty of Fort Adams, Secretary of War Henry Dearborn cautioned them to regard the Choctaws as "the most powerful Nation of Indians within the limits of the United States."[22]

However, Choctaw political power in relation to the United States began deteriorating in 1803 and was decisively broken with the negotiation of the Treaty of Mount Dexter in 1805. In 1803 Governor William Claiborne charged recently appointed Choctaw Agent Silas Dinsmoor with reclaiming the Choctaws from "a State of Savage ignorance."[23] The agent's presence and broadly conceived mission of "civilization" allowed the United States to affect directly Choctaw culture, politics, and factionalism. Besides the arrival of Agent Dinsmoor, the firm of Panton, Leslie, and Company, based in Spanish Pensacola, began to demand from the Choctaws repayment of substantial debts incurred by their purchase of bullets, guns, and powder on credit. Unable to repay these debts, the credit trap ensnared the Choctaws. With Choctaw debts totaling over forty-six thousand dollars in 1803, the firm demanded a land cession by the Choctaws to retire the debt.[24] Opposed to the cession of Indian land to private individuals, the federal government held treaty talks with the Choctaws. Negotiated in 1805, the Treaty of Mount Dexter ceded a substantial portion of southeastern Mississippi to the United States for fifty thousand dollars, and the federal government used the cash settlement to liquidate the Choctaw debt owed to Panton, Leslie, and Company. Perhaps more significantly, however, the treaty invalidated the right conferred by the Treaty of Hopewell to allow the Choctaws to defend their territorial integrity. What proceeds remained after paying the debt owed to Panton, Leslie, and Company were earmarked to compensate citizens who had suffered depredations committed "on stock, and other property by evil disposed persons of said Choctaw nation."[25] This stipulation successfully discouraged further horse raiding, for shortly after the conclusion of the treaty horse raids disappeared from the historical record.

The aftermath of the Creek Civil War accelerated the decline of Choctaw power that had begun in 1803. The 1814 Treaty of Fort Jackson, negotiated with the Creeks, opened central Alabama to American settlement, and, consequently, settlement pressures on the Choctaws in Mississippi greatly increased. Thousands of settlers came to Mississippi; the population soared from just over thirty thousand in 1810 to seventy-five thousand in 1820. Immigrants typically claimed the cheap undeveloped land on the Choctaw frontier and had no compunctions about crossing the surveyed lines and squatting on the Choctaws' remaining land.[26] As the American population grew to outnumber the Choctaws, the shift in the balance of power was completed. The decline of Choctaw political power and increased pressure from encroaching settlers signaled the beginning of a new era of Choctaw history, one marked by instability and doubt about their future in Mississippi. But the horse continued to play an integral role in the historical evolution of Choctaw society.

Many of the substantive ways Choctaws exploited horses in the eighteenth century extended well into the nineteenth century, but there were significant alterations of earlier practices. Choctaws still used horses to carry goods for trade with Americans, but the saddlepacks were loaded primarily with beeswax, honey, chestnuts, and tallow, not with deerskins. Choctaws still traveled on horseback throughout the nation and beyond, but they also hired themselves out as guides to travelers for a cash fee. Women also probably used horses, rather than manual labor, to plow fields. One Choctaw word for the plow, *isuba inchahe*, suggests the intimate association between the animal and the implement. Furthermore, Choctaw leaders occasionally requested fancy saddles, saddlebags, bridles, and spurs for themselves and their wives as part of the annual annuity distributed by the federal government.[27]

Although such finery separated the leaders from the common Choctaws, who used wooden bits and rags to outfit their horses, horses still functioned to bind the society and to reinforce the Choctaws' sense of community and place in the world. In an attempt to interdict the alcohol trade, to check frontier violence, and to defend the nation's borders, the Choctaws organized a national police force in 1823. This "first instance of the organization of a civil power among the Choctaws" proved somewhat successful in controlling the flow of rum into the nation.[28] Significantly, the force consisted of mounted men, and the light horse patrols thus allowed Choctaw males, who could no longer rely on deer hunting, traditional warfare, or even horse raids, to maintain a martial function in their society.[29]

The conservative function of horses in Choctaw traditions found further expression in other activities, especially in the evolution of the ball game and funerary rituals. Visiting the Choctaws in 1820, Adam Hodgson, an Englishman who traveled through Mississippi while visiting the Choctaw missionary stations, noted that males wore long white horsetails, rather than wildcat tails and white bird feathers, as part of their game dress. The shift from the association of masculinity with wild animals, witnessed by Bossu in the mid-eighteenth century, to one with domesticated animals reveals not only a transformation of the regional animal ecology over a century but the creation and acceptance of new symbols of power and manhood. Hodgson also noted a change in the funerary practices seen by Louis Leclerc de Milford during his visits with the Choctaws over forty years earlier. By the late eighteenth century they had begun to bury their dead men with their guns, tomahawks, and favorite horses, so that they would have something to ride to the afterlife. Horses had thus attained a significance inseparable from the hunting and warfare traditions and essential to the passage from life to death. Unfortunately, Hodgson did not record how the funeral rituals for women changed or persisted.[30]

By the 1820s, however, rather than kill the valuable animals and eat them in a communal feast as was done in the early 1700s, or bury them as in the late 1700s, Choctaws instead preferred to believe that the horse's spirit accompanied the deceased into the afterworld while its body remained to render useful live service on earth to the deceased's kinfolk or community.[31] As men and women came to depend on horses for much of their livelihood, eating or burying horses no longer made sense, and funeral traditions changed to reflect this new sensibility.

Horses had been an important part of the Choctaw economy since contact with Europeans, but when the deerskin trade collapsed, horses passed from an economic means to an economic end. In the early nineteenth century a Choctaw horse economy developed in response to the broader emergence of the market economy, and it encompassed an external trade in horses overseen by men and an internal trade involving horse-related products overseen by women.

The external horse economy involved the exchange of horses with Americans, a transaction fraught with theft and violence. Attracted to the large numbers of horses in the Choctaw Nation, Americans increasingly filtered into the nation to steal, to trade, or to purchase horses and drive them to markets in surrounding towns. A Choctaw woman named Nancy Gillett complained to Choctaw Agent William Ward that some white men had stolen one of her horses, valued at fifty dollars, while it grazed in her front yard. Quickly borrowing a neighbor's horse, Gillett pursued the rustlers to the Tombigbee River at the Choctaw Nation border—a journey of thirty-six miles. Revealing a commonplace acceptance of Americans visiting the nation to trade for horses, two Choctaw men who had seen the fleeing whites thought nothing of the matter, just as Gillett thought nothing of jumping on a horse and galloping over thirty miles in pursuit of the thieves.[32]

Nancy Gillett's story was typical. Little Leader, a Choctaw headman, also lost a bay mare, a stud colt, and a brown mare and her colt to rustlers.

Having branded his horses, Little Leader hoped for several years to reclaim them. One wandered back to his house, but he never located the remaining horses. Other Choctaws accused a ring of American rustlers of coordinating the horse thefts. One prominent Choctaw leader, David Folsom, charged that "there are some white men who sit near the edges of our country, who steal our horses . . . [and] who lay whiskey there."[33]

Choctaw leaders had good reason to be alarmed at the vulnerability of the nation's horse stocks. Estimates based on a missionary census taken in 1829 indicated that the Choctaw herd was worth just under half a million dollars. To squander such a resource on alcohol drew the ire of several headmen. Of particular concern to leaders were Choctaw men who received rum from American traders, traded it to Choctaws for their horses and other items, and then traded the horses to the American traders for more alcohol and other supplies. One leader from the Six Towns district, Hwoolatahoomah, declared that he would destroy any whiskey brought into the nation by Choctaw warriors to trade for the "blankets, guns, and horses" of the nation.[34] Hwoolatahoomah's efforts suggest that the external trade of horses was exerting an enormously disruptive influence on the internal state of the nation. Men, who had traditionally overseen the external affairs of their villages, oversaw the nineteenth-century external horse economy, but they were unable to fully control its more pernicious aspects.[35]

Women, who had also used horses since the eighteenth century, drew on their traditional prerogatives to create an internal horse economy that rivaled the external economy and seems to have had a much less deleterious impact on the nation. Horses required food, and Choctaw women exploited their traditional links to the plant world to profit from this need. The amount of corn and fodder sold to other Choctaws cannot be ascertained, but American travelers were beholden to the women for essential provisions. Although the cash transactions between Americans and Choctaw women were small—seventy-five cents for pumpkins for a horse or a dollar for some corn and fodder—the women set the prices, and this hard currency exchange enabled them to purchase goods from factors and traders without resorting to the barter of furs and skins procured by males.[36]

Women had made the Choctaws what Bernard Romans had termed in the mid-eighteenth century a "nation of farmers." However, in the early nineteenth century the Choctaws were a nation of horsemen and horsewomen. They owned approximately fifteen thousand horses in 1829, a ratio of .7 horse per capita. (The state of Mississippi in 1840 had a ratio of .8 horse per capita.) Further attesting to the widespread ownership of horses, the American Board missionaries reported that even most Choctaw children possessed "some of these animals."[37] Because horse ownership was undifferentiated by gender or age, most Choctaws were able to profit and perhaps prosper within the horse economy. However, the prosperity would not last in Mississippi because settlers and politicians from that state in collusion with the administration of Andrew Jackson pressured the Choctaws to remove to Indian Territory in 1830.[38]

The 1830 Choctaw removal treaty made no provision for the transportation of the Choctaw horses to Indian Territory and did not, as it did with cattle, set up a program whereby the federal government agreed to valuate and pay for animals left behind in Mississippi. To accommodate the Choctaw herd, William Armstrong, the agent supervising removal, recommended to Secretary of War Lewis Cass that the United States construct a special ferryboat for the exclusive transport of Choctaw horses over the Mississippi River.[39]

The federal government never built such a boat, and after 3 years of removal to Indian Territory, Agent Armstrong estimated that the Choctaws had lost 2,000 horses to death, disease, and theft. David Folsom, one of the Choctaws' principal leaders, lost 7 horses valued at $235, and his archrival Nittakechi lost 12 valued at $310. Women also suffered. Unnohoka claimed $140 for the 5 horses she lost, and Nancy Gillett, who had earlier been victimized by horse thieves, suffered even more. She lost 6 horses worth $230. Altogether, hundreds of Choctaws requested compensation in Indian Territory for the loss of over 2,000 horses worth almost $80,000.[40]

Despite the enormous numbers of horses lost during removal, the animals assumed a critical importance in Indian Territory. The environment of Indian Territory was conducive to large-scale cattle raising, and Choctaw cowboys bought new stocks of horses to help them control their vast herds. Horses were so essential that for most Choctaws "to ride on horseback was the first lesson ever learned."[41] Rivaling the herds of the Texas cattle barons, the Choctaw cattle economy thrived until their herds were decimated in the Civil War. Nevertheless, the horse-driven cattle economy drew the Choctaws further into the nineteenth-century market economy and undermined the traditions and values that had characterized Choctaw society before contact with Europeans. However, certain traditions did remain intact.

One old tradition that survived the rough journey from Mississippi to Indian Territory was the ball game. Visiting the Choctaws in Indian Territory some years after removal, George Catlin witnessed a game and recorded his impressions in ink on paper and in oils on canvas. Those who played the ball game no longer wore wildcat tails or white bird feathers. Like their counterparts in the 1820s, Choctaw ballplayers continued to attach tails made of white horsehair to their backsides and draped colored manes of horsehair around their necks.[42] Their dress transformed them into horses, a vital part of their contemporary economy and life, but it also symbolically transformed them into deer-resemblers, thus linking the players and spectators to a lifestyle and culture far removed in time and space. Horses had prompted substantial changes in the Choctaws' culture and economy over a century and a half, but their power as symbols enabled equally important continuities that underlay the first one hundred fifty years of tumultuous contact with Europeans and Americans.

Notes

1. See Everett M. Rogers, *Diffusion of Innovations* (New York, N.Y.: Free Press, 1962), 77–124; Robert L. Rands and Carol L. Riley, "Diffusion and Discontinuous Distribution," *American Anthropologist* 60 (1958): 247–97; and Lawrence P. Brown, *Innovation Diffusion: A New Perspective* (London, England: Methuen, 1981). On horses among the Plains Indians, see John C. Ewers, *The Horse in Blackfoot Indian Culture*, Bureau of American Ethnology Bulletin 159 (Washington, D.C., 1955); Gilbert L. Wilson, "The Horse and the Dog in Hidatsa Culture," *Anthropological Papers of the American Museum of Natural History*, vol. 15, pt. 2 (New York, 1924), 125–310; Clark Wissler, "Material Culture of the Blackfoot Indians," *Anthropological Papers of the American Museum of Natural History*, vol. 5, pt. 2 (New York, 1910), 1–177; David G. Mandelbaum, "The Plains Cree," *Anthropological Papers of the American Museum of Natural History*, vol. 37, pt. 2 (New York, 1940); Frank Gilbert Roe, *The Indian and the Horse* (Norman: University of Oklahoma Press, 1955); and Willard H. Rollings, *The Osage: An Ethnohistorical Study of Hegemony on the Prairie-Plains* (Columbia: University of Missouri Press, 1992).

2. Bernard Romans, *A Concise Natural History of East and West Florida; a Facsimile Reproduction of the 1775 Ed.* (Gainesville: University of Florida Press, 1962), 71. For those who have accepted Romans's judgment, see John R. Swanton, *Source Material for the Social and Ceremonial Life of the Choctaw Indians*, Bureau of American Ethnology

Bulletin 103 (Washington, D.C., 1931), 46; and Carolyn Keller Reeves, ed., *The Choctaw Before Removal* (Jackson: University Press of Mississippi, 1985), 31–34. William Willis has critically examined Romans's claims in "The Nation of Bread," *Ethnohistory* 4 (1957): 126–41. For the most extensive treatment of Choctaw subsistence, see Richard White, *The Roots of Dependency: Subsistence, Environment, and Social Change among the Choctaws, Pawnees, and Navajos* (Lincoln: University of Nebraska Press, 1983), chaps. 2, 4.

3. Jean-Bernard Bossu, *Travels in the Interior of North America, 1751–1762*, trans. and ed. Seymour Feiler (Norman: University of Oklahoma Press, 1962), 169–70; Swanton, *Source Material*, 44; and Mary Haas, "Creek Inter-town Relations," *American Anthropologist* 42 (1940): 483.

4. Romans, *Concise History*, 76; John McKee to Choctaw Headmen, 11 December 1815, United States, War Department, Letters Received by the Secretary of War Relating to Indian Affairs, 1800–1823, M271, hereafter cited as U.S., WD, M271; Bossu, *Travels*, 164–65.

5. Antoine Le Page du Pratz, *The History of Louisiana*, ed. Joseph G. Tragle Jr. (Baton Rouge: LSU Press, 1975), 71–72, 166; Dunbar Rowland, A. G. Sanders, and Patricia Galloway, eds., *Mississippi Provincial Archives: French Dominion, 1729–1748* (Baton Rouge: LSU Press, 1984), 4:32; William Bartram, *The Travels of William Bartram*, ed. Mark Van Doren (New York, N.Y.: Dover, 1940), 185; and Timothy K. Perttula, *The Caddo Nation: Archaeological and Ethnohistoric Perspectives* (Austin: University of Texas Press, 1992), 11, 29. Francis Haines, "Where Did the Plains Indians Get Their Horses?" *American Anthropologist* 40 (1938): 112–17, counters anthropologist Clark Wissler's theory that the Plains Indians' horses originated from lost or stolen horses from the De Soto expedition. See also "A Narrative of the Expedition of Hernando De Soto into Florida. By a Gentleman of Elvas"; and Luis Fernandez de Biedma, "A Narrative of the Expedition of Hernando DeSoto," in *Historical Collections of Louisiana*, pt. 2, ed. Benjamin F. French (Philadelphia, 1850), 97, 104, 122, 163. In "The Northward Spread of Horses among the Plains Indians," *American Anthropologist* 40 (1938): 429–37, Haines maps the diffusion of the Plains horse trade and examines exchange patterns. The trade network that introduced the horse to the Choctaws probably originated long before the seventeenth century. See Patricia Galloway, ed., *The Southeastern Cultural Complex: Artifacts and Analysis* (Lincoln: University of Nebraska Press, 1989); Duane C. Anderson and Joseph A. Tiffany, "A Caddoan Trade Vessel from Northwestern Iowa," *Plains Anthropologist* 32 (1976): 93–96; James Howard, "The Southern Cult in the Northern Plains," *American Antiquity* 19 (1953): 130–38; Perttula, *Caddo Nation*, 199; and Pierre Margry, *Découvertes et établissements des Français dans l'ouest et dans le sud de l'Amerique septentrionale, 1614–1754* (Paris, 1888), 6:230.

6. Gravier transcribed the term as *su'ba*; Marc de Villiers, "Notes sur les Chactas d'apres les Journaux de Voyage de Regis du Roullet (1729–1732)," *Journal de la Societe des Americanistes de Paris* 15 (1923): 234; and Cyrus Byington, *A Dictionary of the Choctaw Language*, Bureau of American Ethnology Bulletin 46, ed. John R. Swanton and Henry S. Halbert (Washington, D.C., 1915), 197.

7. Rowland, Sanders, and Galloway, *French Dominion*, 4:151; Horatio B. Cushman, *History of the Choctaw, Chickasaw, and Natchez Indians* (Greenville, Tex.: Headlight, 1899), 180, 235; Lawrence Kinnaird, ed., "Spain in the Mississippi Valley, 1765–1794," *Annual Report of the American Historical Association* (Washington, D.C., 1949), 4:114; and James Adair, *Adair's History of the American Indian*, ed. Samuel Cole Williams (Johnson City, Tenn.: The Watauga Press, 1930; rpt. Nashville, Tenn., 1953), 139, 142, 242, 340, 457.

8. Villiers, "Notes," 236–37; and P. L. Rainwater, ed., "The Autobiography of Benjamin Grubb Humphreys, August 26, 1808–December 20, 1882," *Mississippi Valley Historical Review* 21 (1934): 232.

9. Louis Leclerc de Milford, *Memoir or a Cursory Glance at My Different Travels and My Sojourn in the Creek Nation*, ed. John Francis McDermott, trans. Geraldine de Courcy (Chicago, Ill.: The Lakeside Press, 1956), 204.

10. Glover, "A History of the Caddo Indians," 888, and John Sibley, "Historical Sketches of the Several Indian Tribes in Louisiana," in *The Southern Caddo: An Anthology*, ed. H. F. Gregory (New York, N.Y.: Garland, 1986), 721–23; Gilbert C. Din and Abraham P. Nasatir, *The Imperial Osages: Spanish-Indian Diplomacy in the Mississippi Valley* (Norman: University of Oklahoma Press, 1983), 31, 97, 162–63, 222, 263, 279–81, 307, 342; Dunbar Rowland and A. G. Sanders, eds., *The Mississippi Provincial Archives: French Dominion* (Jackson: Press of the Mississippi Department of Archives and History, 1927, 1932), 1:100, 3:529–32; John Sibley to Henry Dearborn, 8 August 1807, U.S., WD, M271; and Milford, *Memoir*, 64.

11. White, *Roots*, chaps. 2, 4.

12. United States, Bureau of Indian Affairs, Ratified Indian Treaties, 1722–1869, M668 (hereafter cited as U.S., BIA, M668); and Clarence Edwin Carter, comp., ed., *The Territorial Papers of the United States: The Territory of Mississippi, 1798–1817* (Washington, D.C.: G.P.O., 1937), 5:16–18.

13. Jack D. L. Holmes, "Law and Order in Spanish Natchez, 1781–1798," *Journal of Mississippi History* 25 (1963): 192–95; D. Clayton James, *Antebellum Natchez* (Baton Rouge: LSU Press, 1968), 5–46; Kinnaird, "Spain in the Mississippi Valley," 4:77; White, *Roots*, 28, 101; and Cecil Johnson, *British West Florida, 1763–1783* (New Haven, Conn.: Yale University Press, 1943), 39–40.

14. Dunbar Rowland, ed., *The Mississippi Territorial Archives, 1798–1803* (Nashville, Tenn.: Press of Brandon Printing Co., 1905), 1:33, 45–46, 148, 350, 393, 402, 405, 460; Rowland, *Official Letter Books of W. C. C. Claiborne, 1801–1816* (Jackson, Miss.: State Department of Archives and History, 1917), 2:67, 193, 203, 6:138, 151; and Kinnaird, "Spain in the Mississippi Valley," 3:72, 4:100, 265, 281.

15. Kinnaird, "Spain in the Mississippi Valley," 3:38.

16. Henry Dearborn to Benjamin Hawkins, 24 January 1803, United States, War Department, Letters Sent by the Secretary of War Relating to Indian Affairs, 1800–1824, M15 (hereafter cited as U.S., WD, M15); James Wilkinson and Benjamin Hawkins to Henry Dearborn, 18 December 1802, U.S., WD, M271; Treaty of Fort Adams, 17 December 1801, U.S., Bureau of Indian Affairs, Documents Relating to the Negotiation

of Ratified and Unratified Treaties, 1801–1869, T494; Rowland, *Letter Books*, 1:193; and Rowland, *Territorial Archives*, 1:46.

17. Treaty of Hopewell, 3 January 1786, Articles 4 and 5, U.S., BIA, M668; and Rowland, *Letter Books*, 6:138, 234. In the African chiefdom of Ukaguru, Thomas Biedelman has found patterns of behavior similar to those of the Choctaws between the Kaguru and Baraguyu of Tanzania ("Beer Drinking and Cattle Theft in Ukaguru: Intertribal Relations in a Tanganyika Chiefdom," *American Anthropologist* 63 [1961]: 534–44), and Louise Sweet has identified striking similarities to this process among the Bedouin ("Camel Raiding of North Arabian Bedouin: A Mechanism of Ecological Adaptation," *American Anthropologist* 67 [1965]: 1132–45). See also R. Brian Ferguson, ed., *Warfare, Culture, and Environment* (Orlando, Fla.: Academic Press, 1984), 17, 24, 37, 41.

18. The horse raid demonstrates ethnocentricity as described by William Sumner, whose theories have come under much criticism. Nevertheless, Sumner's schematic use of "in-groups" and "out-groups" provides the most plausible explanation of Choctaw group behavior. See Robert A. LeVine and Donald T. Campbell, *Ethnocentrism: Theories of Conflict, Ethnic Attitudes, and Group Behavior* (New York, N.Y.: Wiley, 1972), 1–68. See also William G. McLoughlin, *The Cherokee Ghost Dance* (Macon, Ga.: Mercer University Press, 1984), 30–36; Ewers, *Blackfoot Culture*, 173–77; and Mandelbaum, "Plains Cree," 195.

19. Rowland, *Territorial Archives*, 1:148.

20. John McKee to Choctaw Headmen, 11 December 1815, U.S., WD, M271.

21. Kinnaird, "Spain in the Mississippi Valley," 3:117.

22. Rowland, *Letter Books*, 1:25; Henry Dearborn to William Davie, James Wilkinson, and Benjamin Hawkins, 24 June 1801, U.S., WD, M15.

23. William Claiborne to Silas Dinsmoor, 28 January 1803, Proceedings of the Governor of the Mississippi Territory as Superintendent of Indian Affairs, Territorial Governor's Papers, Alabama Department of Archives and History, Montgomery.

24. William Simpson, Abstract of Debts Owed to Panton, Leslie, and Company, 20 August 1803, U.S., WD, M271.

25. Treaty of Mount Dexter, 16 November 1805, Article 2, U.S., BIA, M668.

26. Bureau of the Census, *The Statistical History of the United States, from Colonial Times to the Present* (New York, N.Y.: Basic Books, 1976), 30; and James Taylor Carson, "Frontier Development and Indian Removal: Mississippi and the Choctaws, 1788–1833" (M.A. thesis, Tulane University, 1992), chap. 2.

27. Choctaw Agent John McKee's Journal, 2 November 1817, and James Wilkinson to Silas Dinsmoor, 19 August 1805, U.S., BIA, M271; William Ward to Thomas McKenney, 12 December 1825, Estimated Travel Expenses of Choctaw Delegation Traveling from Washington to the Choctaw Nation, 1825, Memorandum of Goods for the Annuity for Tapanahooma's District for the Year 1826, 16 July 1825, Memorandum of Goods for Mushulatubbee's District for the Year 1826, 27 August 1825, Abstract of Articles Delivered to Choctaw Leaders . . . for the Year 1828, and William Ward to Thomas McKenney, 26 March 1825, U.S., BIA, M234; John Hersey to Thomas McKenney, 25 June 1821, and Eden Brashears to Thomas McKenney, 26 April 1820, U.S.,

BIA, Letters Received by the Superintendent of Indian Trade, 1806–1824, T58; Henry Dearborn to Silas Dinsmoor, 9 January 1804, U.S., BIA, M15; Adam Hodgson, *Remarks During a Journey through North America in the Years 1819, 1820, and 1821, in a Series of Letters* . . . (New York, 1824), 272; and Byington, *Choctaw Dictionary*, 520.

28. Cushman, *History*, 393.

29. *Missionary Herald* 19 (January 1823): 8; William Ward to Thomas McKenney, 26 March 1825, U.S., BIA, M234.

30. As part of their horse complex, the Choctaws learned rudimentary veterinary skills, probably from Europeans or Americans. See Adam Hodgson, *Letters from North America Written During a Tour in the United States and Canada* (London, 1824), 1:214, 220; Hodgson, *Remarks*, 271; Cushman, *History*, 363; *Panoplist and Missionary Herald* 15 (October 1819): 461; and Leonard Pearson et al., *Special Report on Diseases of the Horse* (Washington, D.C., 1903), 57.

31. Hodgson, *Remarks*, 271.

32. William Ward to Thomas McKenney, 4 November 1825 and 14 September 1826; and Iahocautubbee and Tishohuabbee Testimony, 14 September 1826, U.S., BIA, M234.

33. George Gaines to William Ward, 24 January 1824; Middleton Mackey Deposition, 4 July 1826; William Ward to James Barbour, 11 July 1826, U.S., BIA, M234; and *Missionary Herald* 25 (December 1829): 378.

34. *Missionary Herald* 19 (January 1823): 10.

35. Horse values fluctuated between twenty-five and seventy-five dollars. I have used sixty dollars as an average price because it was the standard price of a horse according to the missionaries in the Choctaw nation (*Missionary Herald* 17 [April 1821]: 110; 25 [February 1829]: 62; and 25 [May 1829]: 62, 153).

36. *Panoplist and Missionary Herald* 15 (October 1819): 460; and various lists of sundry travel expenses, Records of the Choctaw Trading House, Under the Office of Indian Trade, 1803–1824, Miscellaneous Accounts, 1811–1815, T500; Eron Opha Rowland, "Peter Chester, Third Governor of the Province of West Florida under British Dominion, 1770–1781," *Publications of the Mississippi Historical Society*, Centenary Series (Oxford, M.S.: The Society, 1925), 5:83–84.

37. *Missionary Herald* 25 (February 1829): 61.

38. Romans, *Concise History*, 71; *Missionary Herald* 25 (May 1829): 153; Document 27, *Senate Documents*, 20th Cong., 2d sess. (Washington, D.C., 1829), 1:6; Bureau of the Census, *Statistical History*, 30; Lewis Cecil Gray, *History of Agriculture in the Southeastern United States to 1860* (Washington, D.C.: Carnegie Institution, 1933), 2:1042; and Schedule of horses alleged to have been lost during removal, 8 October 1837, U.S., BIA, Choctaw Agency West, 1825–1838, M234. The Choctaw horse population of .7 horse per capita contrasts with various Plains Indian horse populations, which had the following per capita ratios: Apache (1871) 3.3, Comanche (1786) 2.7, Osage (1850) 2.2, Crow (1833) 2, Flathead (1805) 1.2, Cheyenne (1864) 1.2, Navahos (1786) .3 or .4, Hidatsa (1833) .2, Pawnee (1820) .7. See Ewers, *Blackfoot Culture*, 21–27.

39. William Armstrong to Lewis Cass, 20 April 1832, U.S., BIA, M234.

40. Jonathan Coleman to Lewis Cass, 10 February 1833; William Armstrong to Elbert Herring, 25 April 1834, 12 May 1834, and 25 May 1834; and Schedule of horses alleged to have been lost during removal, 8 October 1837, U.S., BIA, M234. The schedule corroborates Armstrong's estimate. The figure of twelve thousand five hundred removed Choctaws left a remaining population of six thousand to eight thousand Choctaws in Mississippi (see Arthur H. DeRosier Jr., *The Removal of the Choctaw Indians* [Knoxville: University of Tennessee Press, 1970], 147, 153, 162).

41. Michael Doran, "Antebellum Cattle Herding: Indian Territory," *Geographical Review* 66 (January 1976): 48–58; and Henry Clark Benson, *Life Among the Choctaw Indians* . . .(Cincinnati, Ohio, 1860), 55.

42. George Catlin, *North American Indians* (Edinburgh, Scotland: J. Grant, 1926), 2:142. Calvin Brown witnessed the use of horsehair manes in a ball play among the Mississippi Choctaws in 1923 as well (*Archaeology of Mississippi* [Jackson, Miss., 1926], 363).

JUDITH CARNEY

Landscapes of Technology Transfer

Rice Cultivation and African Continuities

BY THE MID-1700S a distinct cultivation system, based on rice, rimmed the Atlantic basin. The eastern locus of rice cultivation extended inland from West Africa's upper Guinea coast. To the west the system flourished in the southeastern United States, principally along the coastal plain of South Carolina and Georgia. On both sides of the Atlantic, rice growing depended on African labor. West African farmers planted rice as a subsistence crop on smallholdings, with surpluses occasionally marketed, while the southeastern United States depended on a plantation system and West African slaves to produce a crop destined for international markets.

While rice cultivation continues in West Africa today, its demise in South Carolina and Georgia swiftly followed the abolition of slavery. The year 1860 marked the apogee of the antebellum rice economy. Total U.S. production reached 187.2 million pounds, with South Carolina accounting for 63.6 percent of the total and Georgia an additional 28 percent.[1] Abolition doomed this rice plantation system by liberating some 125,000 slaves who grew rice along nearly 100,000 acres of coastal plain, the property of about 550 planters.[2]

The South's most lucrative plantation economy continued to inspire nostalgia well into the twentieth century, when the crop and the princely fortunes it delivered remained no more than a vestige of the coastal landscape. Numerous commentaries documented the lifeways of the planters, their achievements, as well as their ingenuity in shaping a profitable landscape from malarial swamps.[3] These accounts never presented African slaves as having contributed anything but their unskilled labor. The 1970s witnessed a critical shift in perspective, as historians Converse Clowse and Peter Wood drew attention to the skills of slaves in the evolution of the

South Carolina economy. Clowse, writing in 1971, revealed the importance of skilled African labor in ranching and forest extractive activities during the early colonial period. Wood's careful examination of the role of slaves in the Carolina rice plantation system during the same period, published in 1974, challenged the prevailing planter-biased rendition of the rice story. His scholarship recast the prevalent view of slaves as mere field hands and showed that they contributed agronomic expertise as well as skilled labor to the emergent plantation economy.

Wood's evidence rested on the presence of slaves in South Carolina from the onset of settlement in 1670, early accounts suggesting that slaves produced their own subsistence crops, and the contrast between a lack of prior rice farming knowledge among the English and the French Huguenot planters and the knowledge and skill of their African slave workforce.[4] Daniel Littlefield later built on Wood's path-breaking thesis by discussing the antiquity of African rice farming practices and by revealing that more than 40 percent of South Carolina's slaves during the colonial period originated in West Africa's rice cultivation zone.[5]

While this scholarship has resulted in a revised view of the rice plantation economy as one of both European and African cultures, the agency of African slaves in its evolution is still debated. Current formulations question whether planters recruited slaves from West Africa's rice coast to help them develop a crop whose potential they discovered independently or whether African-born slaves initiated rice planting in South Carolina by teaching planters to grow a preferred food crop. The absence of archival materials that would document a tutorial role for African slaves is not surprising given the paucity of records available in general for the early colonial period, and because racism over time institutionalized white denial of the intellectual capacity of bondsmen. An understanding of the potential role of slaves requires other forms of historical inquiry.

This article combines geographical and historical perspectives to examine the likely contributions of African-born slaves to the colonial rice economy. A spatial approach is used to focus attention on the principal microenvironments planted to rice on both sides of the Atlantic, as well as on the techniques developed for soil and water management during the colonial period. The century 1670–1770 is crucial for examining these issues since it spans the initial settlement of South Carolina by planters and slaves as well as the expansion of tidal (tidewater) rice cultivation into

Georgia. By analyzing the spatial and agronomic (i.e., land management) parameters of rice cropping systems, this cross-cultural analysis emphasizes linkages between culture, technology, and the environment that traversed the Middle Passage with slaves.

The discussion has four parts. The first section examines the geographical and historical context for rice cultivation in the Atlantic basin, while the water- and soil-management principles underlying the three major West African rice systems are discussed in greater detail in the second part. The discussion shifts in the third section to South Carolina and Georgia, where the rice economy unfolded over time from rain-fed to inland swamp production and culminated in the tidal system. The concluding section raises several questions about the issue of technology development and transfer while suggesting a lingering Eurocentric bias in historical reconstructions of the agricultural development of the Americas.

The Geographical and Historical Context of Rice Cultivation along the Atlantic Basin

Some 3,500 years ago West Africans domesticated rice (*Oryza glaberrima*), independently of the Asian cultivar (*Oryza sativa*), along the floodplain and inland delta of the upper and middle Niger River in Mali.[6] The rice-growing area of West Africa extends along the coast from Senegal to the Ivory Coast and into the interior through the savanna along river banks, inland swamps, and lake margins. Within this climatically and geographically diverse setting, two secondary centers of rice domestication emerged: a floodplain system located along river tributaries north and south of the Gambia River (bounded on the north by the river Sine and on the south by the river Casamance, both in Senegal); and another, rain-fed system found farther south in the forested Guinea highlands where rainfall reaches 2,000 mm per year. By the end of the seventeenth century rice had crossed the Atlantic basin to the United States, appearing first as a rain-fed crop in South Carolina before its diffusion along river floodplains and into Georgia from the 1750s.

Many similarities characterized rice production on both sides of the Atlantic basin. The most productive system in South Carolina developed along floodplains, as in West Africa. Precipitation in each region follows a marked seasonal pattern, with rains generally occurring during the months from May/June to September/October. Rice cultivation flourished in South Carolina and Georgia under annual precipitation averages of 1,100–1,400 mm, figures that represent the midrange of a more varied rainfall pattern influencing West African rice cultivation. In the West African production zone, precipitation increases dramatically over short distances in a north-to-south direction, with much less variation occurring over greater distances from east to west. Thus, in the Gambian secondary center of domestication, semiarid (900 mm annual precipitation) conditions prevail, as in the Malian primary center, while farther south in Guinea-Bissau and Sierra Leone precipitation exceeds 1,500 mm per year.[7]

The topography of the rice-growing region on both sides of the Atlantic presents a similar visual field. The coastline is irregularly shaped and formed from alluvial deposits that also create estuarine islands. Rivers carry freshwater downstream on their way to the sea, resulting in tidal flows over the floodplain. The steeper descent from the piedmont in South Carolina and Georgia delivers freshwater tidal flows to floodplains just 10 miles from the Atlantic coast. But the less-pronounced gradient of West Africa's rice rivers means that freshwater tides meet marine water much farther upstream from the coast. Saltwater constantly menaces the downstream reaches of rivers like the Gambia, where salinity permanently affects the lower 80 km but seasonally intrudes more than 200 km upstream.[8] The advance of saltwater in coastal estuaries, however, failed to discourage West Africans from adapting rice cultivation to this environment. Farther south of the Gambia River, where rainfall exceeds 1,500 mm, rice planting occurs in an even more challenging environment—on tidal floodplains formed under marine water influence. The underlying potential acid-sulfate soils depend on water saturation to prevent them from oxidizing and developing the acidic condition that would preclude continued planting.[9] West African rice farmers avoid this problem by constructing an elaborate network of embankments, dikes, canals, and sluice gates to bar marine water while capturing rainfall for cultivation.

Rice cultivation continues throughout West Africa today under conditions similar to those that prevailed at the onset of the Atlantic slave trade. When Islamic scholars followed preexisting overland trade routes to the Malian empire in the fourteenth century, they arrived in the heart of West African rice domestication, where food surpluses had sustained empire formation from the ninth century.[10] Their earliest commentaries mention the crop's widespread cultivation.[11] Description of West African rice systems came later, with the arrival of European vessels along the Atlantic coast from 1453. Dependence on marine navigation brought the Portuguese into early contact with the rice cultivation systems developed along coastal estuaries (mangrove rice) and tidal rivers.[12]

As the Atlantic slave trade gained momentum in the region over the next century, rice cultivation on the littoral drew repeated interest and comment. In 1594, long before the permanent settlement of South Carolina, André Alvares de Almada provided the first detailed description of the mangrove rice system that continues to characterize coastal estuary production south of the Gambia River. He noted the use of dikes to impound rainwater for seedling submergence and desalination, ridging to improve soil aeration, and transplanting.[13] De Almada's description leaves no doubt as to the existence of sophisticated water- and soil-management techniques from the earliest period of contact with Europeans. One eighteenth-century slaver captain, Sam Gamble, found this system so elaborate that he provided a diagram of the field layout in conjunction with his description of water-management techniques.[14]

Discussion of the upland and inland swamp cultivation systems away from coastal and riverine access routes first appeared around 1640 in a manuscript published by an Amsterdam geographer, Olfert Dapper. Relying on information supplied by Dutch merchants operating during the early seventeenth century in the region currently known as Sierra Leone and Liberia, Dapper described a rice farming system where cultivation occurred in distinct microenvironments along a lowland-to-upland landscape gradient which included inland swamps as well as uplands: "Those who are hard-working can cultivate three rice-fields in one summer: they sow the first rice on low ground, the second a little higher and the third . . . on the high ground, each a month after the previous one, in order not to have all the rice ripe at the same time. This is the commonest practice throughout the country . . . The first or early rice, sown in low and damp areas . . . the second, sown on somewhat higher ground . . . the third, sown on the high ground."[15]

Additional observations of these systems came later, during the mid-eighteenth century, when Europeans financed overland expeditions for exploration, trade, and science.[16] The growing dispersal of Europeans into

the West African interior during the nineteenth century brought more detailed commentaries on forest clearance for planting rain-fed rice and the
field's subsequent rotation for cattle grazing, as well as the use of earthen
reservoirs in inland swamps for water impoundment against drought.[17]

The Agronomic and Technological Basis of
West African Rice System

Even though higher-yielding Asian rice (*O. sativa*) varieties and pump-ir-
rigation systems now dominate throughout the West African rice zone, the
production systems that predate the Atlantic slave trade persevere in the
region today. Several researchers have favorably compared the diversity of
the West African rice systems to those in Asia, especially noting the African crop's production under quite different rainfall patterns, soils, farming systems, and land types.[18] A recent study underscored the diversity of
microenvironments and land-management practices characteristic of the
African systems by identifying eighteen different environments planted in
the West African rice zone.[19] This article emphasizes the main features of
African production systems that potentially bear on the evolution of the
rice plantation economy in South Carolina and Georgia.[20] Prioritized for
discussion are the type of water regime(s) utilized for production, the underlying agronomic techniques, and each system's relationship to yield and
labor availability.

The three principal water regimes influence West African rice planting:
rainfall, groundwater, and tides. The resultant rice systems are respectively
known as upland, inland swamp, and tidal production.[21] The source of
water for rice planting also reflects the cropping system's position along
a lowland-to-upland landscape gradient. West African rice systems occur
along a continuum of changing ecological conditions where one or more
moisture regimes are manipulated for production.[22]

The long-standing practice of planting rice sequentially along a landscape continuum from low to high ground confers several advantages, as
Dapper noted in the early seventeenth century.[23] By manipulating several
water regimes, farmers initiate and extend rice growing beyond the confines of a precipitation cycle. In so doing they even out potential labor
bottlenecks, since cropping demands (sowing, transplanting, weeding, and

harvesting) are staggered through different periods of the agricultural season. By relying on several sources of water and several cropping environments, farmers enhance subsistence security by minimizing the risk of the rice crop completely failing in any given year.

Of the three forms of rice cultivation, the upland system depends strictly on precipitation; for this reason it is usually planted last in a rice farming system. The designation "upland rice" derives from planting the crop at the top of the landscape gradient, which may rest a mere 100 feet above sea level. Where rainfall reaches at least 1,000 mm, West African farmers commonly plant the crop in rotation with cattle grazing. Once cleared of vegetation, and with surface debris burned off, fields are planted to upland rice. Following harvest, the rice field converts to cattle grazing. The animals feed on the crop residues, their manure fertilizing the soil. The variability of rainfall patterns both within and between agricultural seasons results in generally lower yields (often below 1 ton per hectare) with upland rice cultivation than in the other two systems. Despite this risk and the initial effort expended for land clearance, upland rice demands less labor than the other West African production systems.

The second system, cultivation in inland swamps, overcomes the precipitation constraints of upland production by capturing groundwater from artesian springs, perched water tables, or catchment runoff. "Inland swamps" actually refers to a diverse array of microenvironments which include valley bottoms, low-lying depressions, and areas of moisture-holding clay soils. The broad range of inland swamps sown to rice reflects farmers' sophisticated knowledge of soils, particularly moisture-retention properties, and their effective methods to impound water for supplemental irrigation. Where high groundwater tables keep inland swamps saturated, rice planting may begin before the rains, continue beyond the wet season, and take place under low rainfall conditions (below 900 mm per year).

But planting rice in inland swamps requires careful observance of topography and water flow. Farmers often construct bunds, small earthen embankments, around the plot to form a reservoir for capturing rainfall or stream runoff. The practice keeps soils saturated through short-duration dry cycles of the cropping season. This form of supplemental irrigation drew the interest of the French explorer René Caillié, who in 1830 noted: "As the country is flat, they take care to form channels to drain off the water. When the inundation is very great, they take advantage of it and fill their little reservoirs, that they may provide against the drought and supply the rice with the moisture it requires."[24] If excess flooding threatens the rice crop, the plot can be quickly drained by puncturing the bund.

Farmers sometimes improve drainage and aeration in inland swamp plots by ridging the soil. Rice seedlings are then either sown directly atop the ridges or transplanted, the latter method being favored when waterlogging poses a risk to seedling development. In such cases, the young plants are established near the village and transplanted to the inland swamp about three weeks later. Though more labor-intensive, transplanting increases the plot's productivity. The process of pulling up the seedlings strengthens the root system and promotes tillering, which can increase rice yields by as much as 40 percent over direct-seeded plots.[25] Such practices and the use of supplemental groundwater resources combine in inland swamp rice production to improve subsistence security and increase rice yields, which generally exceed 1 ton per hectare.

The remaining African production system, tidal rice, occurs on floodplains of rivers and estuaries. Dependent on tides to flood and/or drain the fields, cultivation involves a range of techniques from those requiring little or no environmental manipulation (planting on freshwater floodplains) to ones demanding considerable landscape modification cultivation along coastal estuaries (known as mangrove rice). Tidal rice cultivation embodies complex hydrological and land-management principles that prove especially pertinent for examining the issue of African agency in the transfer of rice cultivation to the Americas.

Tidal rice cultivation occurs in three distinct floodplain environments: along freshwater rivers, along seasonally saline rivers, and along coastal estuaries with permanent marine water influence. The first two involve similar methods of production—letting river tides irrigate the rice fields— while the third system combines principles of each major rice system for planting under problematic soil and water conditions.

The riverine floodplain in the first two systems actually includes two microenvironments: the area alongside a river irrigated by diurnal tides, and its inner margin, reached only during full moon tides, where the landscape gradient begins to rise. The inner floodplain's position along this gradient means that the crop relies in part on rainfall for water requirements. As the inner floodplain receives only occasional tidal flooding, rice varieties are frequently directly sown. But the floodplain flooded daily requires transplanting so that seedlings first reach sufficient height to withstand tidal surges. Both floodplain crops mature from moisture reserves captured in the alluvium during flood recession.

Similar topographic distinctions and agronomic techniques apply in the second type of riverine floodplain cultivation, which involves careful observation of saltwater and freshwater dynamics in order to plant areas under the seasonal influence of marine water. As rains discharge freshwater into West African rivers after the onset of the wet season, the saltwater interface retreats downstream. Rice cultivation takes place along riverine stretches that experience at least three months of freshwater (the maturation time of the fastest-growing seed varieties). This second type of tidal system requires less labor than the freshwater one, since seasonal saltwater conditions depress weed growth, but yields are similar, averaging between 1 and 2 tons per hectare, with the lower range found on the inner floodplains.[26]

Mangrove rice, the third form of tidal cultivation, takes place along coastal estuaries and represents the most sophisticated West African production environment. The principles underlying this system have not been sufficiently conceptualized by historians of rice development in South Carolina who have looked to West Africa for potential influences.[27] Their comparisons of rice production on both sides of the Atlantic basin understandably focus on the tidal freshwater system that sustained the lucrative antebellum economy of South Carolina and Georgia. But an emphasis on one production environment misses Dapper's seventeenth-century insight that rice planting occurs in distinct production environments along a landscape gradient. By separating out for analysis just one among the multiple environments that typically characterize a rice farming system, scholars only glimpse a fraction of the agronomic techniques and specialized knowledge that inform West African cultivation.

Thus, in emphasizing freshwater floodplain production, Littlefield correctly concludes that the African system involves minimal landscape manipulation.[28] However, rice production in tidal estuaries, on the other hand, demands considerable landscape modification and, sometimes, inter-village cooperation to manage the extensive water control system.[29] One important outcome of this emphasis on the West African tidal river system in cross-cultural comparison is to leave unquestioned the assumption that Europeans provided the technological basis to the South Carolina tidewater system.[30] The case for African agency in introducing the sophisticated soil- and water-management infrastructure to South Carolina floodplains dramatically improves by detailing the mangrove rice system.

West African rice production in tidal estuaries occurs south of the Gambia River in areas of permanently saline water conditions where annual rainfall generally exceeds 1,500 mm. These are environments mantled by extensive stretches of mangroves whose aerial roots trap fertile alluvium swept over the littoral by marine tides. The organic matter deposited on these soils makes them among the most fertile of the West African rice zone, but they require considerable care to prevent oxidation and their transformation into acid-sulfate soils. By manipulating several water regimes and developing the infrastructure for its control, a highly productive rice system results.

Preparation of a tidal rice field begins with site selection and the construction of an earthen embankment parallel with the coast or riverine arm of the sea. Frequently more than a meter's height and width (the dimensions needed to block the entry of marine tides onto the rice field), the embankment stretches for several kilometers, sometimes threading together rice fields of different villages. A stand of mangroves often is left in place between the estuary and the embankment to reduce tidal force. The void left by soil removal for the embankment establishes the location of the principal drainage canal. A series of secondary embankments (dikes) are then formed perpendicular to the main one in order to divide the perimeter into the individual rice fields.

The mangrove rice system achieves a dual purpose with water control. It captures rainfall for irrigation while storing water for the controlled floodings that drown unwanted weeds. Sluices built into the dikes facilitate water control through the canals for either irrigation or drainage. Fitted with valves made from hollow tree trunks and plugged with palm thatch, the dike sluices drain into a more substantial one located in the principal embankment. The principal sluice is sometimes fashioned from an old canoe with a board vertically positioned like a rudder to control water flow.[31] Once enclosed, the field is flooded by impounding rainwater and evacuating it from the field at low tide. Rainfall (and sometimes seasonal freshwater springs) leaches out the salts, which low tides help evacuate into the estuary.[32] It takes years to desalinate a mangrove field before cultivation can ensue. Each season, as farmers await the rains that will rinse away residual dry season salts, they establish rice in nurseries near the village where the plants can be hand watered.

After about a month's growth the seedlings are transplanted atop the rice field's ridges, a practice that promotes protection from residual salinity. At this point, the mangrove rice field reverts to rain-fed cultivation. Harvest occurs about four months later, the crop ripening from accumulated moisture reserves after the rains cease. Farmers annually renew soil fertility during the dry season by periodically opening the sluices to tidal marine water. This action prevents the soil acidification that leads to acid-sulfate formation and permits deposit of organic matter. In the month or so preceding cultivation, the sluices once again remain closed to block the entry of saltwater. Farmers prepare the plot for the new cultivation cycle by layering the ridges with accumulated deposits of swamp mud.

The creation of a mangrove rice system demands considerable labor for perimeter construction and desalination over a period of several years, as well as much effort annually to maintain the system's earthworks. But the reward for such monumental labor is yields that frequently exceed 2 tons per hectare. Besides displaying the range of soil- and water-management techniques developed for rice cultivation, the mangrove system illustrates a preexisting West African familiarity with the sophisticated earthworks infrastructure long associated with the South Carolina and Georgia tidal rice plantation.

The complex soil- and water-management principles embodied in planting rice along a landscape gradient in interconnected environments illustrate the ingenuity that characterized West African rice production. Numerous affinities exist with the rice systems of South Carolina and the process of technology development in tidewater rice, the antebellum era's quintessential production system.

The Temporal and Spatial Discontinuities of Rice Cultivation in South Carolina and Georgia

By 1860 rice cultivation extended over 100,000 acres along the eastern seaboard from North Carolina's Cape Fear River to the St. Johns River in Florida and inland for some 35 miles along tidal waterways.[33] The antecedents of the rice plantation economy date to the first century of South Carolina's settlement (1670–1770), and especially to the decades prior to the 1739 Stono slave rebellion. Rice cultivation systems analogous to those in West Africa, using identical principles and devices for water control, were already evident in this period. Dramatic increases in slave imports during the eighteenth century facilitated the evolution and commoditization of the South Carolina rice economy. The process of technology development, moreover, occurred in tandem with the emergence of the task labor system that distinguished coastal rice cultivation. Colonial rice production shifted respectively from reliance on rainfall to inland swamps and, from mid-century, to the tidal (tidewater) cultivation system that characterized the antebellum era.

This section presents an overview of the material conditions and historical circumstances within which rice production developed in South Carolina. The technical changes marking the evolution of the colonial rice economy illuminate three issues that bear on comparative studies of technology and culture: first, the need in cross-cultural analysis to examine the technical components of production as part of integrated systems of knowledge and not merely as isolated elements; second, the extent to which superior social status coincides with a superiority in knowledge; and third, the relationship between technical expertise, patterns of labor utilization, and technological change.

Slaves accompanied the first settlers to South Carolina in 1670; within two years they formed one-fourth of the colony's population, their numbers surpassing those of whites as early as 1708.[34] Rice cultivation appears early in the colonial period, with planting occurring in numerous environments. The earliest reference to the cereal's cultivation dates to 1690, when plantation manager John Stewart claimed to have successfully sown rice in twenty-two different locations.[35] Just five years later cultivation efforts culminated in South Carolina's first recorded rice exports: one and one-fourth barrels shipped to Jamaica.[36] In 1699 exports reached 330 tons, and during the 1720s rice emerged as the colony's leading trade item.[37] Years later, in 1748, Governor James Glen drew attention to the significance of rice experimentation during the 1690s for the subsequent unfolding of the South Carolina economy.[38]

The growing emphasis on rice exports from the turn of the century resulted by the 1740s in the documented presence of all three principal

West African production systems: upland, inland swamp, and tidal.[39] Each dominated a specific phase in the South Carolina rice economy. As rice was gradually commodified during the eighteenth century, the numerous production environments mentioned by Stewart no longer characterized the pattern of rice cultivation. Instead, planting occurred in specific environments selected for emphasis at different moments in the crop's evolution as a commodity.

Upland rice production received initial emphasis in the eighteenth century for its complementarity with the colony's early economic emphasis on stock raising and forest-product extraction. Slave labor underpinned this agro-pastoral system, which involved clearing forests, the production of naval stores (pine pitch, tar, and resin), cattle herding, and subsistence farming.[40] The export of salted beef, deerskins, and naval stores generated the capital for additional slaves. With the dramatic increase in slave imports (from 3,000 in 1703 to nearly 12,000 by 1720) rice cultivation shifted to the inland swamp system.[41]

The higher-yielding inland swamp system represented the first attempt at water control in South Carolina's rice fields but demanded considerable labor for clearing the cypress and gum trees and developing the network of bunds and sluices necessary for converting a plot into a reservoir. Like its counterpart in West Africa, the inland swamp system impounded water from rainfall, subterranean springs, high water tables, or creeks for soil saturation. Rice cultivation in South Carolina's inland swamps eventually evolved to the point where reserve water could be released on demand for controlled flooding at critical stages of the cropping cycle.[42] The objective of systematic plot irrigation was to drown unwanted weeds and thereby reduce the labor spent weeding. The principle of controlled field flooding was analogous to the one found in the West African mangrove rice system.

Field flooding for irrigation and weed control occurred in a variety of inland swamp settings. For instance, swamps located within reach of streams or creeks often used the landscape gradient for supplemental water delivery. Placement of an embankment at the low end of an undulating terrain kept water on the field while the upper embankment dammed the stream for occasional release. Sluices positioned in each earthen embankment facilitated field drainage and irrigation.[43]

Similar principles sometimes permitted rice planting in coastal marshes near the ocean.[44] Under special circumstances—where a saltwater marsh was located near the terminus of a freshwater stream, for example—rice planting occurred in soils influenced by the Atlantic Ocean. The conversion of a saline marsh to a rice field depended on soil desalination, a result not so quickly achieved under South Carolina's lower annual precipitation (1,100–1,200 mm) as in West Africa, where rainfall in tidal rice-growing areas generally exceeds 1,500 mm per year. Often a creek or stream served the purpose of rinsing salts from the field. Once again the water control system relied on proper placement of embankments and sluices. The lower embankment permanently blocked the inflow of saltwater at high tide, while opening the sluice at low tide enabled water discharge from the plot. A sluice positioned in the upper embankment delivered stream water as needed for desalination, irrigation, and weed control. This type of inland swamp system functioned in the vicinity of the embouchure of the Cooper River, where "rice marshes tempted planters as far down the river as Marshlands [Plantation], nearly within sight of the ocean. Here they had to depend entirely on 'reserve' waters formed by damming up local streams."[45]

The principle of canalizing water for controlled flooding also extended to settings where subterranean springs flowed near the soil surface. Edmund Ravenel described one system that continued to function until the Civil War: "The water here issues from the marl which is about two or three feet below the surface at this spot. This water passes South and is carried under the Santee Canal in a Brick Aqueduct, to be used on the Rice-Fields of Wantoot Plantation."[46]

During the antebellum period another inland swamp system functioned alongside tidewater rice cultivation. While its colonial antecedents remain uncertain, this system flourished where a landscape gradient sloped from rain-fed farming to the inner edge of a tidal swamp.[47] Enclosing a tract of land with earthen embankments on high ground created a reservoir for storing rainwater, the system's principal water source. The reservoir fed water by gravity flow to the inland rice field through a sluice gate and canal. Excess water flowed out of the plot through a drainage canal and sluice, placed along the lower end of the rice field. The water then drained into a nearby stream, creek, or river.[48] Many techniques of this inland swamp system suggest a West African origin, among them employing a landscape gradient for rice farming, converting a swamp into a reservoir with earthen embankments, and using sluices and canals for water delivery. However, the development of a separate reservoir for water storage perhaps reveals a South Carolina innovation. Only further research can determine whether the creation of a supplementary reservoir for irrigating a swamp field is West African, European-American, or the hybridized contribution of both cultures.

By the mid-eighteenth century rice production was steadily shifting from inland swamp systems to tidal river floodplains in South Carolina and into Georgia, just prior to repeal of Georgia's antislavery law in 1750.[49] The swelling number of slaves entering South Carolina from the 1730s to 1770s, plus the fact that these slaves came from West Africa, proved crucial for the transition, and perhaps also to the concomitant emergence of the distinctive task labor system that characterized tidal rice cultivation. Some 35,000 slaves were imported into the colony during the first half of the century and over 58,000 between 1750 and 1775, making South Carolina the largest importer of slaves on the North American mainland between 1706 and 1775.[50] The share of slaves brought directly from the West African rice coast grew during these crucial decades of tidewater rice development from 12 percent in the 1730s to 54 percent (1749–65) and then to 64 percent between 1769 and 1774.[51]

One of the earliest references to the existence of the tidal floodplain system appeared in 1738 with notice of a land sale by William Swinton of Winyah Bay, South Carolina: "that each [field] contains as much River Swamp, as will make two Fields for 20 Negroes, which is overflow'd with fresh Water, every high Tide, and of Consequence not subject to the Droughts."[52] By 1752 rich Carolina planters were converting inland swamps and tidal marshes along Georgia's Savannah and Ogeechee rivers to rice fields, a process actively under way during the 1772 visit by naturalist William Bartram.[53] The shift to tidal production accelerated after the American Revolution, and tidal rice remained the basis of the region's economic prominence until the demise of rice cultivation during the 1920s.[54]

Tidewater cultivation occurred on floodplains along a tidal river where the diurnal variation in sea level resulted in flooding or draining a rice field.[55] Three factors determined the siting of tidewater rice fields: tidal amplitude, saltwater encroachment, and estuary size and shape. A location too near the ocean faced saltwater incursion, while one too far upstream removed a plantation from tidal influence. Like the West African mangrove rice system, a rising tide flooded the fields while a falling tide facilitated field drainage. Along South Carolina rivers tidal pitch generally varied between 1 and 3 feet.[56] These conditions usually prevailed along riverine stretches 10–35 miles upstream from the river's mouth.[57]

Estuary size and shape also proved important for the location of tidewater plantations since these factors affected degree of water mixing and thus salinity. The downstream extension of tidal rice cultivation in South Carolina and Georgia reflected differences in freshwater dynamics between rivers draining the uplands and those flowing inland from the sea. As rivers of piedmont origin deliver freshwater within miles of the coast, tidal cultivation often occurred within a short distance from the ocean. But other coastal rivers are arms of the sea and must reach farther inland for freshwater flows. Along such rivers the freshwater stream flow forms a pronounced layer on top of the heavier saltwater, thereby enabling tapping of the former for tidal irrigation.[58] Success under these conditions depended on knowledgeable observation of tidal flows and the manipulation of saltwater-freshwater interactions to achieve high productivity levels in the rice field—skills already belonging to West African tidal rice farmers.

Preparation of a tidal floodplain for rice cultivation followed principles remarkably similar to those of the mangrove rice system. The rice field was embanked at sufficient height to prevent tidal spillover, the process leaving a canal adjacent to the embankment. Sluices built into the embankment and field sections operated as valves for flooding and drainage much as they do in Africa's mangrove rice system. The next step involved dividing the area into quarter sections of 10–30 acres, with river water delivered to these sections through secondary ditches. This elaborate system of water control enabled slaves to directly sow rice along the floodplain.

Tidewater cultivation required considerable landscape modification and even greater numbers of laborers than the rice-growing systems that first featured prominently in the South Carolina economy. The labor in transforming tidal swamps to rice fields proved staggering, as vividly described by historical archaeologist Leland Ferguson:

> These fields are surrounded by more than a mile of earthen dikes or
> "banks" as they were called. Built by slaves, these banks . . . were taller

than a person and up to 15 feet wide. By the turn of the eighteenth century, rice banks on the 12 1/2 mile stretch of the East Branch of Cooper River measured more than 55 miles long and contained more than 6.4 million cubic feet of earth. . . . This means that . . . working in the water and muck with no more than shovels, hoes, and baskets . . . by 1850 Carolina slaves . . . on [tidal] plantations like Middleburg throughout the rice growing district had built a system of banks and canals . . . nearly three times the volume of Cheops, the world's largest pyramid.[59]

The earthen infrastructure continued to make considerable demands on slave labor for maintenance even as it reduced labor spent weeding rice plots.[60] With full water control from an adjacent tidal river, the rice crop could be flooded on demand for irrigation and weeding, and the field renewed annually by alluvial deposits. Historian Lewis Gray underscored the significance of tidal flow for irrigation as well as weeding in explaining the shift from the inland swamp rice system to tidewater cultivation: "Only two flowings were employed [inland swamp] as contrasted with the later period when systematic flowings [tidal] came to be largely employed for destroying weeds, a process which is said to have doubled the average area cultivated per laborer. . . . The later introduction of water culture [tidal] consisted in the development of methods making possible a greater degree of reliance than formerly on systematic raising and lowering of the water."[61] A slave consequently could manage 5 acres instead of the 2 typically assigned with inland rice cultivation.[62]

The systematic lifting and lowering of water noted by Gray was achieved by the sluices located in the embankment and secondary dikes. These crucial devices for water control had assumed the form of hanging floodgates by the late colonial period.[63] As this type of sluice is not traditionally found in West Africa, the hanging gate probably is of European-American origin. Even when this gate replaced earlier forms, the sluices maintained the appellation "trunk" by Carolina planters. The continued use of this term throughout the antebellum period suggests that the technological expertise of Africans indeed proved significant for establishing rice cultivation in the earlier colonial era. During the antebellum period trunks evolved into large floodgates, anchored into the embankment at a level above the usual low tide mark. Doors (gates) placed at both ends would swing when pulled up or loosened. The inner doors opened in response to river pressure as the water flowed through the raised outer door and then closed when the tide receded. Field draining reversed the arrangement, with the inner door raised and the outer door allowed to swing while water pressure in the field forced the door open at low tide.[64]

Curiosity over the origin of the term "trunk" for sluices or floodgates led planter descendant David Doar to unwittingly stumble on likely technology transfer from West Africa:

> For years the origin of this name bothered me. I asked every old planter
> I knew, but no one could enlighten me. One day a friend of mine who
> planted on one of the lowest places . . . said to me with a smiling face:
> "I have solved that little trunk question. In putting down another one, I
> unearthed the granddaddy of plug trunks made long before I was born."
> It was simply a hollow cypress log with a large hole from top to bottom.
> When it was to be stopped up a large plug was put in tightly and it acted
> on the same principle as a wooden spigot to a beer keg.[65]

The earliest sluice systems in South Carolina looked and functioned exactly like their African counterparts.

Tidewater cultivation led South Carolina to economic prominence in the antebellum era. Its appearance in the colony from the 1730s, and rapid diffusion from mid-century, occurred during a period of escalating slave imports from Africa's rice coast. The evidence presented here concurs with Wood's original claim that Africans tutored planters in developing South Carolina's rice economy. The African experience with planting a whole range of interconnected environments along a landscape gradient likely permitted the sequence of adaptations that marked the growth of the South Carolina rice industry. While the overview of rice cultivation in South Carolina suggests that planters indeed reaped the benefits of a rice farming system perfected by West Africans over millennia, an important question remains: Why would West African slaves transfer a sophisticated technology of rice cultivation to the planters when the result harnessed them to brutal toil in malarial swamps?

The answer is perhaps revealed in the appearance of an innovative form of labor organization, the task system, that characterized coastal rice plantations from the mid-eighteenth century. Task labor differed sharply from the more typical "gang" form of work organization, as Gray explains: "Under the task system the slave was assigned a certain amount of work for the day, and after completing the task he could use his time as he pleased." In the gang system "the laborer was compelled to work the entire day."[66] Without overstating the differences in workload between gang and task labor, the task system did set normative limits to the number of hours demanded of slave labor. Such seemingly minor differences, however, could deliver tangible improvements in slave nutrition and health, as Johan Bolzius implied in 1751 with his observation: "If the Negroes are Skilful and industrious, they plant something for themselves after the day's work."[67]

The emergence of the task labor system in South Carolina during the same historical period as accelerating slave imports from West Africa's rice coast and tidewater development is perhaps significant. This form of labor organization may have represented the outcome of negotiation and struggle between master and slave over agronomic knowledge and the labor process. By providing the crucial technological basis for plantation profits, slaves perhaps discovered a mechanism to negotiate improved conditions of bondage. Additional research on the task labor system, whose origins may be African, promises to illuminate the complex relationship between patterns of labor utilization and technical expertise in slave-based plantation systems.[68]

Conclusion

"What skill they displayed and engineering ability they showed when they laid out these thousands of fields and tens of thousands of banks and ditches in order to suit their purpose and attain their ends! As one views this vast hydraulic work, he is amazed to learn that all of this was accomplished in face of seemingly insuperable difficulties by every-day planters who had as tools only the axe, the spade, and the hoe, in the hands of intractable negro men and women, but lately brought from the jungles of Africa."[69] When Doar echoed in 1936 the prevailing view that slaves contributed little besides labor to the evolution of the South Carolina rice economy, no historical research suggested otherwise. While more recent research challenges such assumptions, a bias nonetheless endures against considering the prior rice cultivation experience of African slaves in the context of the crop's appearance during the eighteenth century in several areas of the Americas.

In his classic book on global rice cultivation, now in multiple editions, D. H. Grist describes the mangrove system when he writes about empoldering as "a method of restricting floods and thus securing adjacent areas from submergence."[70] He is referring to a type of paddy rice cultivation found in British Guiana (now Guyana) and in the neighboring former Dutch colony of Surinam. On its origins he hypothesizes: "The Dutch are probably responsible for introducing this system into British Guiana in the eighteenth century. Today, all the land developed for paddy cultivation and in the adjacent Dutch colony of Surinam is protected by this means."[71]

This area of northern South America in the late seventeenth through early eighteenth centuries, however, was a plantation society with one of the highest ratios of Africans to Europeans in the Americas (65:1 in Surinam's plantation districts, compared to Jamaica's 10:1).[72] Slave imports continued well into the eighteenth century, with a high percentage originating from the West African rice area discussed by Dutch geographer Dapper in the previous century.[73] Grist's perfunctory treatment of *Oryza glaberrima* in his book (due to the species being "confined to small areas in West Africa . . . [and thus] . . . relatively unimportant") is emblematic of a more pervasive scholarly view toward Africa and its peoples as having contributed little across geographic space besides labor.[74]

This view, however, is giving way as new evidence comes to light from several academic disciplines informed by multicultural and cross-cultural perspectives. Recent studies suggest that Europeans and people of European descent can no longer be viewed as the sole masters of technology development and innovation.[75] Yet research on the origins of the rice plantation economy in South Carolina and Georgia displays a lingering Eurocentric bias, granting slaves an initial role in the inland swamp rice system but attributing to planters the crucial technological development of water control that led to tidewater rice cultivation: "Slaves who had experience growing rice in West Africa were probably instrumental in the successful creation of early rice plantations. . . . Some prescient innovators realized that the system would eventually yield diminishing returns and looked for an alternative way to irrigate their crops. The diurnal rising and falling of coastal rivers, caused by the flow and ebb of ocean tides, seemed a likely source of irrigation water. . . . As early as the 1730s, planters noted tidal flow in rivers and, gingerly, began to flow estuarial water over their fields."[76]

The cross-cultural and historical perspective on two important rice-growing regions of the Atlantic basin presented here suggests otherwise. Evidence from the first fifty years of settlement in South Carolina supports the view that technological development and innovation in the rice economy began as an African knowledge system but eventually bore the imprimatur of both African and European influence.[77] By the American Revolution the technological and agronomic heritage of each knowledge system had combined in new ways to shape rice cultivation along the south Atlantic coast of the United States, a process that Paul Richards terms "agrarian creolization."[78] By way of analogy with its linguistic namesake, Richards is referring to the convergence of different knowledge systems (e.g., germ plasm resources and cultivation strategies—in this example, African and Asian germ plasm and African cultivation strategies) and their recombination into new hybridized forms. The outcome of this convergence in South Carolina was a rice production system fashioned from an indigenous African crop that came to bear the distinctive signature of European as well as African culture. Thus, as Africans and Europeans faced each other in new territory under dramatically altered and unequal power relations, the outcome was diffusion, technological innovation, and novel forms of labor organization.

Notes

1. *Agriculture of the U.S., United States Census Office 1860*, 8th census (Washington, D.C.: U.S. Government Printing Office, 1864).
2. Douglas C. Wilms, "The Development of Rice Culture in 18th Century Georgia," *Southeastern Geographer* 12 (1972): 45–57; Julia Floyd Smith, *Slavery and Plantation Growth in Antebellum Florida, 1821–1860* (Gainesville: University of Florida Press, 1973), and *Slavery and Rice Culture in Low Country Georgia, 1750–1860* (Knoxville: University of Tennessee Press, 1985); Pat Morgan, "A Study of Tide Lands and Impoundments within a Three River Delta System—the South Edisto, Ashepoo, and Cumbahee Rivers of South Carolina" (M.A. thesis, University of Georgia, 1974); James Clifton, *Life and Labor on Argyle Island* (Savannah, Ga., 1978), viii–ix, and "The Rice Industry in Colonial America," *Agricultural History* 55 (1981): 266–83; Charles A. Gresham and Donal D. Hook, "Rice Fields of South Carolina: A Resource Inventory and Management Policy Evaluation," *Coastal Zone Management Journal* 9 (1982): 183–203.
3. Ulrich B. Phillips, *American Negro Slavery* (New York, N.Y.: D. Appleton and Company, 1918); A. S. Salley, *The Introduction Of Rice Culture into South Carolina*

(Columbia, S.C.: Printed for the Commission by the State Company, 1919); Ralph Betts Flanders, *Plantation Slavery in Georgia* (Chapel Hill: University of North Carolina Press, 1933); David Doar, *Rice and Rice Planting in the South Carolina Low Country* (1936; reprint, Charleston, S.C.: Charleston Museum, 1970); Alice Huger Smith, *A Carolina Plantation of the Fifties* (New York, N.Y.: W. Morrow and Company, 1936); Norman Hawley, "The Old Plantations In and Around the Santee Experimental Forest," *Agricultural History* 23 (1949): 86–91; Duncan Heyward, *Seed from Madagascar* (Chapel Hill: University of North Carolina Press, 1937).

4. Converse Clowse, *Economic Beginnings in Colonial South Carolina* (Columbia: University of South Carolina Press, 1971); Peter Wood, *Black Majority* (New York, N.Y.: Knopf, 1974), 57–64.

5. Daniel Littlefield, *Rice and Slaves* (Baton Rouge: Louisiana State University Press, 1981). Betty Wood, *Slavery in Colonial Georgia* (Athens: University of Georgia Press, 1984), 103, indicates a similar trend for Georgia.

6. Roland Portères, "Primary Cradles of Agriculture in the African Continent," in *Papers in African Prehistory*, ed. J. D. Fage and R. A. Oliver (Cambridge, England: Cambridge University Press, 1970), 43–58; Jack Harlan, J. De Wet, and A. Stemler, *Origins of African Plant Domestication* (Chicago, Ill.: Aldine, 1976); R. Charbolin, "Rice in West Africa," in *Food Crops of the Lowland Tropics*, ed. C. L. A. Leakey and J. B. Wills (Oxford, England: Oxford University Press, 1977), 7–25.

7. Charles Kovacik and John Winberry, *South Carolina: A Geography* (Boulder, Colo.: Westview Press, 1987); Timothy Silver, *A New Face on the Countryside* (New York, N.Y.: Cambridge University Press, 1990); Judith Carney, "The Social History of Gambian Rice Production: An Analysis of Food Security Strategies (PhD diss., University of California, Berkeley, 1986).

8. Carney, "The Social History of Gambian Rice Production," 23; George Brooks, *Landlords and Strangers: Ecology, Society, and Trade in Western Africa, 1000–1630* (Boulder, Colo.: Westview Press, 1993), 9–13.

9. F. R. Moorman and W. J. Veldkamp, "Land and Rice in Africa: Constraints and Potentials," in *Rice in Africa*, ed. I. Buddenhagen and J. Persely (London, England: Academic Press, 1978), 29–43; West African Rice Development Association, *Types of Rice Cultivation in West Africa*, Occasional Paper no. 2 (Monrovia, Liberia, 1980); Carney, "Social History of Gambian Rice."

10. H. A. R. Gibb, *Ibn Battuta: Travels in Asia and Africa, 1325–1354* (London, England: Routledge & K. Paul, 1969); Graham Connah, *African Civilizations* (New York, N.Y.: Cambridge University Press, 1987).

11. Tadeusz Lewicki, *West African Food in the Middle Ages* (New York, N.Y.: Cambridge University Press, 1974).

12. See, e.g., Paul Pélissier, *Les paysans du Sénégal: Les civilisations agraires du Cayor à la Casamance* (Saint-Yrieix, France: Fabregue, 1966), 711–12. See also Gomes Eannes de Azurara, *The Chronicle of the Discovery and Conquest of Guinea*, vol. 2 (London, England: Hakluyt Society, 1899); G. R. Crone, *The Voyages of Cadamosto* (London,

England: Hakluyt Society, 1937); A. Donelha, *An Account of Sierra Leone and the Rivers of Guinea and Cape Verde* (Lisbon, Portugal: Junta de Investigacoes Cientificas do Ultramar, 1977).

13. Valentim Fernandes, *Description de la Côte Occidentale d'Afrique* (Bissau, Guinea-Bissau: n.p., 1951); Walter Rodney, *A History of the Upper Guinea Coast, 1545–1800* (New York, N.Y.: Clarendon Press, 1970).

14. See Judith Carney, "From Hands to Tutors: African Expertise in the South Carolina Rice Economy," *Agricultural History* 67 (1993): 1–30.

15. Translation and excerpt drawn from Olfert Dapper, *New Description of Africa*, by Paul Richards, in "Culture and Community Values in the Selection and Maintenance of African Rice" (paper presented at the Conference on Intellectual Property Rights and Indigenous Knowledge, Lake Tahoe, Calif., October 5–10, 1993). On Dapper, see also Adam Jones, *From Slaves to Palm Kernels* (Wiesbaden: F. Steiner, 1983), and "Decompiling Dapper: A Preliminary Search for Evidence," *History in Africa* 17 (1990): 171–209.

16. M. Adanson, *A Voyage to Sénégal, the Isle of Gorée and the River Gambia* (London, England: n.p., 1759); Francis Moore, *Travels into the Inland Parts of Africa* (London, England: E. Cave, 1738); G. Mollien, *Travels in Africa* (London, England: Sir R. Phillips and Co., 1820); Mungo Park, *Travels into the Interior of Africa* (1799; reprint, London, England: Dutton, 1954); Pélissier.

17. Rodney; Thomas Winterbottom, *An Account of the Native Africans in the Neighbourhood of Sierra Leone* (London, England: C. Whittingham, 1803); René Caillié, *Travels through Central Africa to Timbuctoo, and across the Great Desert, to Morocco, Peqomd in the Years 1824–1828* (London, England: H. Colburn and R. Bentley, 1830).

18. Pierre Viguier, *La riziculture indigène au Soudan Français* (Paris, France: n.p., 1939); Littlefield; Paul Richards, *Indigenous Agricultural Revolution* (London, England: Hutchinson, 1985), and *Coping with Hunger* (London, England: Allen & Unwin, 1986).

19. W. Andriesse and L. O. Fresco, "A Characterization of Rice-growing Environments in West Africa," *Agriculture, Ecosystems and Environment* 33 (1991): 377–95.

20. The discussion is based on fieldwork by Judith Carney in Senegambia over a ten-year period, as well as on research in Casamance, Senegal, by Olga F. Linares, and in Sierra Leone by Paul Richards; see, e.g., Olga F. Linares, "From Tidal Swamp to Inland Valley: On the Social Organization of Wet Rice Cultivation among the Diola of Senegal," *Africa* 5 (1981): 557–94, and *Power, Prayer and Production* (New York, N.Y.: Cambridge University Press, 1992); Richards, *Indigenous Agricultural Revolution and Coping with Hunger*.

21. F. R. Moorman and N. Van Breeman, *Rice: Soil, Water, Land* (Los Banos, Philippines: International River Research Institute, 1978).

22. Richards, *Coping with Hunger;* Andriesse and Fresco, "Characterization of Rice-growing Environments."

23. Richards, "Culture and Community Values." See also C. Fyfe, *A History of Sierra Leone* (Oxford, England: Oxford University Press, 1962), 4.

24. Caillié, 162.

25. Francesca Bray, "Patterns of Evolution in Rice Growing Societies," *Journal of Peasant Societies* 11 (1983): 3–33.

26. Food and Agriculture Organization, *Rice Mission Report to the Gambia* (Rome [Italy]: Food and Agriculture Organization of the United Nations, 1983).

27. Littlefield; Joyce Chaplin, *An Anxious Pursuit: Agricultural Innovation and Modernity in the Lower South, 1730–1815* (Chapel Hill: University of North Carolina Press, 1993).

28. See, for instance, Littlefield, 86.

29. Pélissier; Linares, "From Tidal Swamp" and *Power, Prayer and Production*.

30. Heyward; Doar; Chaplin.

31. Rodney.

32. Linares, "From Tidal Swamp," and *Power, Prayer and Production*.

33. Albert Virgil House, *Planter Management and Capitalism in Ante-Bellum Georgia* (New York, N.Y.: Columbia University Press, 1954); James Clifton, "Golden Grains of White: Rice Planting on the Lower Cape Fear," *North Carolina Historical Review* 50 (1973): 365–93; and Clifton, "Rice Industry."

34. P. Wood, 25–26, 36, 143–45.

35. Ibid., 57–58.

36. Clifton, "Rice Industry," 269.

37. P. Wood, 55.

38. Ibid., 57–58. See Clifton, "Rice Industry," 270, for the earliest indirect evidence for rice growing in South Carolina.

39. Doar; Kovacik and Winberry; Judith Carney and Richard Porcher, "Geographies of the Past: Rice, Slaves and Technological Transfer in South Carolina," *Southeastern Geographer* 33 (1993): 127–47.

40. John S. Otto, *The Southern Frontiers, 1607–1860* (New York, N.Y.: Greenwood Press 1989); P. Wood, 30–32, 105–14; Terry Jordan, *Trails to Texas: Southern Roots of Western Cattle Ranching* (Lincoln: University of Nebraska Press, 1981), 14, 29, 33.

41. On numbers of imported slaves, see Clowse, 252; P. Wood, 143–45; Peter Coclanis, *The Shadow of a Dream* (New York, N.Y.: Oxford University Press, 1989), 64. For descriptions and periodization of the rain-fed and inland swamp systems, see Thomas Nairne, "A Letter from South Carolina," in *Selling a New World: Two Colonial South Carolina Promotional Pamphlets*, ed. Jack Greene (1710; reprint, Columbia: University of South Carolina Press, 1989), 33–73; Lewis Gray, *History of Agriculture in the Southern U.S. to 1860* (Gloucester, Mass.: n.p., 1958), 1:279; Clifton, *Life and Labor*; Clarence Ver Steeg, *Origins of a Southern Mosaic* (Athens, Ga.: n.p., 1984); Otto.

42. Heyward; Sam B. Hilliard, "Antebellum Tidewater Rice Culture in South Carolina and Georgia," in *European Settlement and Development in North America: Essays on Geographical Change in Honour and Memory of Andrew Hill Clark*, ed. James Gibson (Toronto, Canada: University of Toronto Press, 1978), 91–115; Richard Porcher, "Rice Culture in South Carolina: A Brief History, the Role of the Huguenots, and the Preservation of Its Legacy," *Transactions of the Huguenot Society of South Carolina* 92

(1987): 11–22; David Whitten, "American Rice Cultivation, 1680–1980: A Tercentenary Critique," *Southern Studies* 21 (1982): 5–26.

43. Clifton, "Rice Industry," 275.

44. Hawley.

45. John B. Irving, *A Day on the Cooper River* (Charleston, S.C.: Press of the R.L. Bryan Co., 1969), 154.

46. Edmund Ravenel, "The Limestone Springs of St. John's, and their probable Availability for increasing the quantity of Fresh Water in Cooper River," *Proceedings of the Elliott Society of Science and Art, of Charleston, South Carolina* 2 (October 1860): 28–31, quote on 29.

47. See Hilliard, 99.

48. Porcher, "Rice Culture in South Carolina."

49. Wilms; Smith, *Slavery and Rice Culture.*

50. David Richardson, "The British Slave Trade to Colonial South Carolina," *Slavery and Abolition* 12 (1991): 125–72, esp. 127–28.

51. Ibid., 135–36.

52. *South Carolina Gazette*, January 19, 1738; Clifton, "Rice Industry," 275–76.

53. Wilms, 49.

54. Clifton, "Rice Industry," 276.

55. Hilliard, 100.

56. Chaplin.

57. John Drayton, *View of South Carolina* (1802; reprint, Spartanburg, S.C.: Reprint Co., 1972), 36; Chaplin, 231.

58. Hilliard.

59. Leland Ferguson, *Uncommon Ground: Archaeology and Early African America, 1650–1800* (Washington, D.C.: Smithsonian Institution, 1992), xxiv–xxv, 147.

60. See, e.g., Amelia Wallace Vernon, *African Americans at Mars Bluff, South Carolina* (Baton Rouge: Louisiana State University Press, 1993). Vernon documents the survival of rice cultivation among African Americans as a response to blacks' restricted access to farmland following Reconstruction.

61. Gray, 281.

62. R. F. W. Allston, "Essay on Sea Coast Crops," *De Bow's Review* 16 (1854): 589–615; James Glen, "A Description of South Carolina: Containing Many Curious and Interesting Particulars Relating to the Civil, Natural and Commercial History of That Colony," in *Colonial South Carolina: Two Contemporary Descriptions*, ed. Chapman J. Milling (Columbia: University of South Carolina Press, 1951), 15; Clifton, "Rice Industry", 275; Whitten, 9–15.

63. Richard Porcher, *A Teacher's Field Guide to the Bluff Plantation* (New Orleans, La.: Kathleen O'Brian Foundation, 1985), 26–27.

64. House, 25.

65. Doar, 12.

66. Gray, 550–51; Philip Morgan, "Work and Culture: The Task System and the World of Low Country Blacks, 1700 to 1880," *William and Mary Quarterly*, 3d ser., 39 (1982): 563–99; Smith, *Slavery and Rice Culture*, 61.

67. Bolzius quoted in Morgan, 565. The entire document appears in "Johan Bolzius Answers a Questionnaire on Carolina and Georgia," ed. and trans. Klaus G. Loewald, Beverly Starika, and Paul Taylor, *William and Mary Quarterly*, 3d ser., 14 (1957): 218–61.

68. Carney, "From Hands to Tutors," 26–28.

69. Doar, 8.

70. D. H., Grist, *Rice*, 4th ed. (London, 1968), 45.

71. Ibid.

72. See, e.g., Richard Price and Sally Price, *Stedman's Surinam: Life in an Eighteenth-Century Slave Society* (Baltimore, Md.: Johns Hopkins University Press, 1992), xii, 208–19.

73. Ibid.

74. Grist, 56.

75. Doar, 20. Work countering the attribution of European political-economic hegemony to technological superiority over other cultures is presented in Michael Adas, *Machines as the Measure of Men* (Ithaca, N.Y.: Cornell University Press, 1989); and Jim Blaut, "On the Significance of 1492," *Political Geography* 11 (1992): 355–85.

76. See Chaplin, 228–36; quotes are from 228, 231, 232.

77. See, e.g., ibid., 147–50.

78. Richards, "Culture and Community Values," 2. Several decades ago, Melville Herskovits drew attention to the significance of the idea of cultural "creoliziation" for research in *The New World Negro: Selected Papers in Afroamerican Studies*, ed. Frances Herskovits (Bloomington, Ind.: Indiana University Press, 1966), 36–37.

S. MAX EDELSON

Clearing Swamps, Harvesting Forests

Trees and the Making of a Plantation Landscape in the Colonial South Carolina Lowcountry

ENGLISH LAND SCOUTS sent to reconnoiter the Carolina Low-country in the 1660s "ranged through very spacious tracts of rich Oake land" before declaring the region fit for colonial occupation. Alongside these commonplace European hardwoods, the scents and sights of peach, fig, and cedar trees stirred the first settlers' imaginations about its extraordinary potential. Over the next century planters and slaves developed this vast coastal plain, clearing forests and swamps of their trees to produce one of the most prosperous and repressive plantation economies in the Western Hemisphere. Trees stood for the land the English came to inhabit. With their roots anchored in the soil, the girth of trunks and the reach of canopies testified to the land's underlying fertility. They represented the tension between the exotic and the familiar that was at the center of conceptions of early American nature. Trees demonstrated the land's remarkable powers of generation, but also held out the promise that some version of European farming—and some version of European life—could be practiced on it with success. As South Carolina colonists established their political independence from Britain in the 1770s, they adopted a unique local species, the cabbage palmetto, as their corporate symbol.[1]

Paying attention to this intense engagement with trees emphasizes two dynamic features of agricultural experience in the colonial Southeast. First, colonists carved fields out of swamps and forests, transforming the landscape they found into one geared for market agriculture. Migrants came to colonial British America to claim their share of abundant North American land. Land was the key credential that made a settler a stakeholder in provincial governments. Men who owned land could secure a family's subsistence and engage in production for local and transatlantic markets of consumption. With the exception of the "old fields" that Native Americans had once cultivated and settlers claimed, this land was encumbered by trees. The first object of agriculture in early America was clearing terrain in preparation for planting.

Second, planters exploited land and labor more effectively over the course of the eighteenth century. How they used and thought about trees reveals a dynamic process of adaptation behind the colonization of the Lowcountry. Environmental historians have focused on the disruptions and displacements caused by settling plantations and producing commodities for export. Production, however, was only one side of the encounter between the Europeans and Africans who colonized the Lowcountry and the people, plants, animals, soils, and climate they found already there. Although historians more often note the thousands of barrels of rice and casks of indigo shipped eastward that defined South Carolina's place within the Atlantic economy, settlers and slaves made meals, built houses, and reconstructed material lives in a new world. Colonists worked to create a viable domestic economy in the Lowcountry, devoting enormous cultural and economic energies to the task of implanting a self-sustaining British society. We should understand planters as environmental agents who were creative as well as destructive, rather than as interlopers who imposed an external order on the land. To this end, it is impossible to understand how settlers colonized the Carolina Lowcountry without taking stock of what happened to its trees.

Environmental historians describe the creation of plantation societies in the Americas as a destructive invasion characterized by the external imposition of European market agriculture. In *A New Face on the Countryside*, Timothy Silver catalogues the depopulation, deforestation, and habitat disturbance that came with establishing plantations in mainland America. The arrival of Europeans in Florida, Virginia, Carolina, and elsewhere along the coast put an end to the sustainable patterns of development initiated by Native Americans. Europeans left an indelible mark on southeastern landscapes, whether measured by the smoke pouring from burning woodlands or the dilating swath of cleared farmland that always followed.

Planters believed that the market crops their slaves cultivated "brought new order and stability to the South Atlantic landscape," but in this conviction they were mistaken. As it impoverished the land, Silver argues, staple agriculture encouraged a potent mix of pests, weeds, and diseases that made early modern colonial life especially precarious. As "resources became commodities," planters left behind a trail of destruction.[2]

Recent regional studies have added to this picture of widespread destruction in plantation America. Mart A. Stewart's examination of rice cultivation in early Georgia argues that establishing this plantation landscape came with high ecological costs. Converting swamps into rice fields was an artificial imposition on a diversified natural zone that resulted in long-term instability. Rice plantations simplified the hydrography of the coastal plain in ways that made it more prone to unpredictable and destructive flooding. Deforestation on tropical islands in the East and West Indies was so severe that imperial officials adopted a prescient preservationist stance simply to secure their ongoing possession of these strategic territories. The history of Portuguese Brazil can be summarized by the sounds of forests succumbing to the ax and the sights of hillsides washed away by erosion. As Virginia DeJohn Anderson has shown, the destructive presence of cows and pigs let loose in the woods destabilized the Anglo-Indian frontier. Ranging far beyond the pale of English outposts, livestock served as the shock troops of colonization in eastern North America.[3]

As Stewart observes, American environmental history has privileged the frontier or wilderness encounter and the North American West as a place for analysis. Investigating the environmental history of American plantation societies requires a model for analysis that privileges agricultural change. If the study of people and nature in the South must be steeped in the particularities of race and commercial farming in general, the environmental dimensions of the colonial experience in the Chesapeake, Lowcountry, and Caribbean need to be focused in a more particular fashion still. The idea that nineteenth-century plantations were inefficient economic entities that impeded innovation is one that historians continue to debate, but as instruments of colonization these early plantations secured an "adaptation to the difficult environment that the first colonist encountered." Instead of hewing to a single, immovable form, colonists took the common ingredients of the plantation complex—African slavery, specialization in one (or a few) crops, and integration within the Atlantic economy—and tailored their plantations to fit particular soils, climates, and topographies. Colonists built these adaptive American plantations around the ecological demands of plants that became staple commodities, namely sugar in the Caribbean, tobacco in the Chesapeake, and rice in the Carolina Lowcountry.[4]

Agricultural historians stress adaptation more than degradation as part of the process of implanting early American economies. Although clearing and grazing New England lands contributed to "destabilizing the forest environment," argues E. L. Jones, colonists' responses to new weeds and pests solved many of the farming challenges such intrusions triggered. In his recent study of farming in and around Concord, Massachusetts, Brian Donahue shows that instead of wearing out supposedly poor soils, agriculture in the colonial Northeast was an "ecologically sustainable adaptation of English mixed husbandry to a new, challenging environment." Studies of plantation agriculture in the colonial Chesapeake have demonstrated how effectively settlers accumulated capital by clearing land and raising livestock, applied new modes of cultivation and processing to grow tobacco, and shifted land and slave labor to wheat in response to changes in market conditions. Although not slighting the economic drag caused by the exhaustion of tidewater fields, economic historians of tobacco's development tend to view plantations as successful adaptations to New World conditions. Modeled on the example of the "improved" English farm, plantations imported a focus on new crops geared for the market. Wealthy planters saw themselves as elites in the English mold. As Joyce E. Chaplin's history of South Carolina and Georgia planters' restless experimentation with rice, indigo, and cotton reveals, colonists attempted to establish their credentials as gentlemen farmers by adopting the most advanced agricultural techniques available to them.[5]

Understanding colonists as responsive environmental actors rather than primarily as agents of ecological disruption sheds new light on the origins of plantation agriculture in the Carolina Lowcountry. Extending some five hundred miles along the coast from North Carolina's Lower Cape Fear into East Florida, the Lowcountry was one of colonial British America's primary centers of seventeenth-century settlement and eighteenth-century development. Like colonists everywhere, Lowcountry planters transformed the land and secured it for colonial occupation through agricultural enterprise. These changes were particularly dramatic on the South Carolina and

Georgia coasts, where slaves cleared freshwater swamps and riverside flood plains to grow rice, the region's dominant staple commodity. Commercial rice growing began in small wetland plots within thirty miles of Charlestown during the 1690s. As exports of South Carolina rice accelerated in the early eighteenth century, colonists adapted English agricultural precedents to initiate technical advances in field embankment, reservoir construction, mechanized processing, and tidal irrigation. These innovations increased productivity and sheltered rice from the fluctuations of a volatile climate, especially by securing supplies of water for this moisture-dependent plant during extended droughts.[6]

As they learned to grow rice in cleared swamps, planters changed the criteria by which good agricultural land was valued. After first settling on arable uplands—hardwood soils much like those prized in England for cereal cultivation—they acquired new tracts of wetlands after 1700, fusing swamps, bottomlands, savannas, and woodlands into large rice plantations. These settlements clustered along waterways, taking in the diversity of soil types that typically characterize areas located along a landscape gradient that drain into adjacent marshes and rivers. In an ongoing internal process of colonization marked by the constant clearing of new land, planters deployed their slaves within these large holdings to grow provisions, saw lumber, and bring new swamplands into cultivation.

Colonists began using the ebb and flow of tidal rivers to irrigate their rice fields around 1750. By this time they had already extended their plantation landscape into new zones of settlement more than fifty miles beyond Charlestown, the colony's Atlantic port as well as its political, cultural, and social capital. The wealthiest among them deployed slaves by the hundreds to colonize South Carolina's vast coastal frontiers with the most advanced irrigation technologies. As they developed the Carolina Lowcountry between 1670 and 1785, colonists were not only far more responsive to the natural world's complexity than historians suspected, but this process of engagement with nature was also the critical factor that shaped their distinctive mode of agriculture. How British planters adapted swamps and forests for commercial agriculture defined the Carolina Lowcountry as one of colonial British America's principal areas of settlement and made it into a bellwether region in the formation of the United States South.[7]

Seventeenth-century promotional writers focused on trees to fix the promise of the Carolina Lowcountry in the minds of prospective settlers.

During Carolina's first three decades as an English colony, the region's extensive forests contrasted with the scarcity of wood, timber, and trees in England and the English West Indies. Against the backdrop of England's own romance with the oak as a national symbol, the exotic mulberry represented the Carolina colony as it began. When the first settlers fortified their Ashley River compound against attack in 1670, they "fasten[ed] the Gate of their Pallisado" to a huge mulberry tree. Because this tree's leaves were the silkworm's only food, finding mulberries growing wild "every where amidst the Woods" convinced seventeenth-century colonists, like Scottish agricultural "projector" John Stewart, that Carolina would "undowbtedly be a silk country." Those who returned from this fortified outpost reported that "they never saw any Oak in *England* bigger" than the tree to which the colonists entrusted their security. Caught up by the craze for sericulture that promised to make them rich, the first planters lined the "Rows and Walks" of their plantations with mulberry trees that, once planted for "Pleasure," could be defoliated for profit.[8]

Native Americans inhabited a different landscape in which this tree had other meanings. Lowcountry Indians looked to the fruit of the mulberry, not its leaves, to stand for their country's bounty. So "abundantly stored with Mulberries" were its "rich and fertill" lands and "pleasant vallies" that cakes made from the berries became a signature food that Indian travelers took with them on their journeys. When De Soto reached what would become the South Carolina interior in 1540, his party was greeted by "twenty Indians all loaded with baskets of Mulberries." For Carolina's first colonists these abundant mulberries promised a bright commercial future for a colony that seemed destined by nature to produce silk as a staple commodity. The tree around which they built their fortified compound was also a token of the landscape they sought to create out of the one they found.[9]

Instead of forbidding forests, the colony's promoters described a country so open to occupation that "a man may ride his horse a hunting." Promotional writer Samuel Wilson found its terrain similar to "pleasant parks in England" in 1666. Some of Carolina's first settlers compared this landscape "to a Bowling ally full of dainty brooks." Such idealized points of reference imagined Carolina as a natural pleasure ground of the sort that wealthy English landowners reserved for their enjoyment. Although coastal Indians had in fact created this park-like landscape by firing forests around their villages to enrich the soils and create deer habitat, colonists did not credit

Native American ingenuity when they admired such altered woodlands. Instead, they understood them as scarce natural resources dense with Old World associations of privation and social demarcation.[10]

Unregulated stands of trees were rare sights in the early modern English countryside, where woods not managed for their timber, pasture, or game signified infertile lands not worth the trouble to clear or preserve. Early medieval law introduced the term "forest" into the language as a regulated royal domain. By the seventeenth century England was among Europe's least wooded countries. Rising urban and rural populations and the expansion of rural industries consumed more wood for fuel and building, further stripping England of its woodlands. Although commonplace features of the rural landscape, where groves stood beside villages and served as windbreaks around fields, trees became an increasingly contested resource. Even these scarce trees, whose boughs curved after a lifetime of buffeting by the wind, were increasingly harvested to make the hulls of ships that plied the routes of Britain's transatlantic empire. As subjects found their access to woods restricted by the enclosure of common lands and manorial wastes, elites demonstrated their growing power by planting groves and orchards on their estates. With the passage of the Black Act of 1723—which made every conceivable popular use of forests a capital offense—the contest over trees became a flashpoint for class conflict in early eighteenth-century Britain.[11]

South Carolina's promotional writers made trees objects of the desire to own land. Against this backdrop of scarce woods, colonists were invited to "make a handsome Retreat from the World" in Carolina. For those who sought "Solitude, Contemplation, Gardening, Groves, Woods, and the like innocent Delights of plain simple Nature," promised Thomas Nairne in 1710, "there can scarce any Place in the *British* Dominions be found, that will better answer their Expectation." Thwarted at home with every legal and physical boundary that cut prospective settlers off from access to the woods, land overgrown with trees could be had almost for the taking in Carolina. In the profusion of fruits that appeared to "grow without Culture," hanging from the boughs of trees for anyone to pick, Carolina's promoters found a potent image with which to market the new colony. Grapes, limes, apricots, and strawberries grew wild "up and down the Woods" along with "tenn thousand more plants, herbs, fruits then I know," wrote an early official. Acquiring land came with a rise in rank, marked with new pleasures of consumption.[12]

Invited by the descriptions of the trees, explorers scoured the Carolina landscape for signs that English agriculture might be practiced in the Lowcountry. "Gallant Groves of Pines," "Delightfull forrests of Oake," and "Cypress trees innumerable, very tall and large" all "preclaimed the richnes of the soyle" beneath them. During their brief expeditions scouts in the service of the colony's Lords Proprietors scanned the land for stands of hardwood trees that they called, without hesitation, by their English common names. The stature of these trees made manifest the two invisible processes that combined to generate life: the subterranean strata of soils that nourished vegetation from below and the wind, rain, and heat that encouraged growth from above. In the vicinity of Port Royal, on the colony's southern coast, the "Lands are laden with large tall Oaks" and there was plenty of "good Soyl, covered with black Mold," reported William Hilton in 1664. Land that was "burthened exceedingly" by trees demonstrated powers of generation.[13]

While England's improving farmers struggled to enhance the productivity of marginal lands, Carolina's settlers could take advantage of "good land enough for millions of people to live & worke on" already perfected by nature. "Mellow" in appearance and "soapy" to the touch, these deep deposits of "black Earth" scattered "generally all over the Countery" were "just like the fine Mould of our well order'd Gardens." So "satisfied" was Robert Sandford "by the sorts of woods" he saw on his 1666 expedition that he felt no need to venture onto shore at every opportunity. He was confident that the trees he observed from afar captured the promise of the land he failed to examine. A great tree marked a spot on the land where moisture, sunlight, and nourishment combined to support robust vegetable life. It represented decades of undocumented ecological history, summarizing the living product of growing seasons—harsh and benign—and its "incredible magnitude" testified to the land's fertility and the climate's temperateness.[14]

"A soil so productive," noted planter and politician John Drayton in 1802, "sufficiently denotes its riches." In writing that brought early Carolina into focus as a physical place for European readers in the seventeenth century, the colony's trees filled in for the environmental experience that they lacked. Before colonists inhabited the land, they looked to trees to value the Lowcountry as a place to settle, cultivate, and claim. A century later Lowcountry planters still scrutinized trees, but they did so with a far more precise and detailed understanding of what they indicated about the land's value for commercial agriculture.[15]

Long-term use of the land bred familiarity with it and a more specialized knowledge of it. South Carolina planters continued to use trees as edaphic markers that revealed the qualities of the soil on which they stood. George Olgilvie's 1776 georgic poem "Carolina; Or, the Planter," began with the declaration that trees were the signs by which "virgin nature's indicating hand, / Unerring marks the quality of land." Eighteenth-century land descriptions made use of the same rule of thumb employed before 1700, that visible vegetation indicated underlying soil quality. What differed in these later assessments was their exhaustive catalogues of plant life. Royal Surveyor William Gerard De Brahm listed thirty-six different plants and trees that reflected swamp fertility, seventeen common to sandy lands, and forty-one common on high land. Infertile "bay" swamps could be detected, and avoided, by the sight of numerous bay trees and low-growing ferns and briars. More productive swamps supported "tupelo, cypress, ash, maple, water oak, bay, gum, elm, and white oak" trees "in proportion to the greater or less strength of the land, and the higher or lower the situation may be, on which they grow."[16]

As soon as colonists settled in the Lowcountry they began to relieve the land of its "burthens," turning trees into commodities. As they searched for a viable transatlantic export, trees yielded profits in the form of tar and lumber, including "divers sorts of lasting Timber that England hath not" and trunks "big enough to Mast the greatest Ships." Settlers from Barbados, where sugar production had all but deforested the island by the 1660s, knew firsthand the value of woodlands to provide food, fuel, and building materials for West Indian consumers. As multiplying herds of cattle and hogs gathered "their Food in the Woods," even the poorest landowners, recently freed indentured servants, found a way to raise cash and join the ranks of South Carolina's slave-owning planters. Raising cattle in open pastures provided a stepping stone to slave purchases, financing more labor-intensive ventures in lumber and naval stores production and, after 1700, in rice cultivation. One of the colony's most important early exports, deerskins obtained in trade with Native American hunters, were likewise commodities drawn from southeastern forests. Before planters were able to cultivate this landscape in rice, they extracted wealth from its woods.[17]

Before agricultural production began in earnest, surveyors traipsed across the land, marking corner trees to indicate the boundaries of an intended plantation. Trees cut down to clear fields became materials with which to mark the land off for human use and habitation. Planters and slaves took up residence in houses constructed on-site from timbers, rafters, and shingles hewn from the land's trees. Slaves on early South Carolina plantations fashioned barrels, made ship masts out of pine trunks, sawed lumber to build houses and barns, and chopped cord after cord of firewood. Wood and lumber, the byproducts of field clearing, served a new settlement's consumption needs first, but a surplus could also be sold to Charlestown artisans, shipbuilders, vessels anchored in the harbor, and the Caribbean planters whose demands for every sort of wood product kept pace with their increasing sugar production.[18]

Once they had cleared a new swamp field for rice planting, slaves fired the downed limbs and underbrush and then turned to the "vast dismember'd trunks that load the ground." They selected the largest swamp trees to saw into planks of the kind of "lasting wood" that planters favored for their rural residences and split smaller oaks into the zig-zag, or "worm," fences that kept cattle out of the corn fields. Planters cleared trees with a sense of their marketable uses; carpenters favored watertight cypress for shingles, coopers used white oak for barrel staves, and cabinetmakers valued cedar for its fine grain. Before he made a name for himself as a naturalist, William Bartram settled an East Florida rice plantation in 1766. He was advised to order his slaves to harvest the cypress in his swamp to "convert into shingles and ready money." Because trees could be cut down, processed, and sold at any point in the season, lumber production provided income between harvests. After tasks in the rice, corn, and indigo fields, planters sent slaves to cut trees and saw wood. When agricultural activity slowed in winter, commercial lumber production drew laborers from field to forest. Taking advantage of their abundant woods and finding "severall wayes to rais monys" from them, planters never entirely tied their fortunes to the price of rice.[19]

Despite a longstanding English preference for hardwoods over conifers, South Carolina plantations secured an early foothold in the Atlantic economy by rendering naval stores out of longleaf pine. "To those that has Plenty of that Wood," distilling tree gum into turpentine and firing tar kilns filled with the lightwood that littered the sandy uplands was a profitable way of converting forests into income. The "custom of burning the woods" to clear new fields and make tar enveloped the settled Low-country in a "continual smoke" as thick as fog. That it made economic sense to burn vast quantities of pine to extract its resins revealed both the Lowcountry's natural abundance and colonists' willingness to exploit it. However wasteful such use of trees could seem, South Carolina's naval stores industry supplied British vessels with a vital strategic commodity. When war in northern Europe interrupted Britain's supplies of Baltic tar, pitch, and turpentine in the early eighteenth century, Parliament granted a bounty for American naval stores that stimulated exports, lowered prices, and demonstrated the value of the mainland plantation colonies to em-pire. During the early 1720s some observers attributed the growth of slave imports not to rice, but rather to the "Pitch, and tarr Trade prodigiously encreasing."[20]

When Parliament let the bounty lapse in 1724, in part because of com-plaints of low-quality Carolina tar, small planters who specialized in naval stores found themselves unable to produce the high-bulk, low-cost goods profitably. To planters who survived the short-lived naval stores boom, this abrupt shift in policy seemed to stigmatize their crude use of Caro-lina trees. The loss of mercantilist support triggered a spate of bankrupt-cies, driving many to migrate to North Carolina, where the naval stores industry continued to transform longleaf pine forests into vital products for Britain's military and merchant fleets. In North Carolina's Lower Cape Fear region, as Bradford J. Wood shows, forest products as a group were so dominant that they assumed the role of a staple commodity throughout the colonial period. Although British agricultural critics denigrated sandy forests as a kind of wasteland, the Lowcountry's northernmost area became a place in which "Tar Heels" saw their vast stands of trees as a valuable storehouse for empire.[21]

Few slaves were allowed to set aside their axes, saws, and wedges for long as rice, which they planted in cleared swamps along the Lowcountry's coastal plain, emerged as the region's most successful staple commodity. South Carolina plantations encompassed, on average, about five hundred acres. Reserves of swamps and woods allowed for internal expansion within a tract's boundaries. Despite claims that rice swamps were inexhaustibly fertile, long use invited competing grass species into the fields, decreasing productivity and frustrating slaves as their tasks grew more difficult. For every new field worker added to the labor force, slaves cleared five acres of swamp for rice and up to ten acres of high land for provisions. Long after a plantation was first settled, slaves continued to colonize lands within the perimeter of the original grant. Only after years of cultivation did some land finally play out. In 1777 Richard Hutson offered his lands along Wappoo Creek, one of the colony's earliest places of settlement, for sale "because they are old and full of grass and have little good timber left."[22]

For field slaves the ongoing expansion of plantations into new lands imposed heavier work burdens. When rice fields became too grassy to work, slaves were sent to "clear new ground of its woods," working by day to cut down trees and, after an hour's rest, returning at night to finish the task of "lopping and burning of the limbs." The work of making timber and fuel from the "bodies of the trees" was added to slaves' daily tasks "as they have leasure." After they "set about sawing, splitting, cutting, and piling" wood at the edges of newly cleared fields, "they dare never return from their fields with out bringing a load of fire wood on their shoulders." Because the basic material infrastructure of plantations—their outbuildings, furniture, machines, dwellings, wagons, and watercraft—was made from wood, those slaves who learned to do more with trees than turn them into firewood and fence rails became indispensable.[23]

No plantation labor force was said to be "complete" without black carpenters to construct houses, barns, boats, and processing machinery; sawyers to turn trees into boards and building timber; and coopers who fashioned rice barrels and indigo casks in which commodities were packed for market. After a few weeks working with hired artisans, black workers with no previous training became "good carpenters enough to raise a shed, or build any plain outhouse, such as you see common in England in little farmyards." Such informal apprenticeships created a corps of workers who replaced expensive white artisans and could be hired out to bring in a new stream of income. Enslaved woodworkers took advantage of unique opportunities to move across the countryside, accumulate cash, and turn specialized knowledge into a measure of material security.[24]

As they settled plantations alongside Lowcountry rivers and swamps, planters in the throes of clearing land for agriculture often left trees to rot if they were "too far from navigation" to transport economically to market.

As early as 1682, only twelve years after colonization began, land in the immediate vicinity of Charlestown had been "pillaged of all its valuable Timber." Rising demand for wood combined with the increasing "Scarcity of Timber Trees Convenient to the Landing Places" to raise firewood prices to extravagant rates. By 1764 merchant and planter Henry Laurens suggested that, with firewood so "very scarce & dear in this Country," coal might be imported from England at a profit to supply Charlestown's hearths. One of his plantations, Mepkin, made more money from selling firewood in town than from rice and indigo combined. Despite the market opportunity this pattern of exploitation created, the careless use of woods rankled Laurens. Because "every Man cuts down & wastes" South Carolina had little ship timber, once a valuable export, left to sell. He predicted that

> the day is not far distant in the long tract of Time, when we shall be stripped of that essential article. The Europeans will laugh at us, our Children will rue the folly of their Fathers. For every Live Oak you cut down you ought to Plant out ten young Trees, prune & attend them as carefully as you clean your Rice field . . . but few of us Southern Americans have patience to look forty Years forward, we are for grasping all the golden Eggs at once. I hope the ensuing Winter to add to my Stock an hundred young Live Oak & as many black Walnut Trees, from which I can only expect to reap the blessings of posterity when I have finished planting & reaping.

The post-Independence scarcity of these valuable trees, once so abundant, seemed to indict its planters for their reckless exploitation of Lowcountry woodlands. As South Carolina left behind its colonial past as provider of strategic materials to an empire, Laurens criticized his fellow citizens for their failure to preserve the resources required to secure the economic independence of their new state.[25]

Despite these signs of a ravaged landscape, deforestation posed no threat to South Carolina's plantation economy. Planters failed to keep an accessible stock of the strong, curved trees that shipwrights needed to form the hulls of boats. They denuded the banks of rivers and creeks where it was easiest to load wood for market. Far from suffering a wood shortage at the end of the colonial period, however, more and more plantations entered into the "wood business" as a lucrative sideline to rice and indigo production. Plantations advertised for sale in the *South-Carolina Gazette* often included a list of suggested productions to which the land was suited. By this measure wood products were always an important part of plantation production. As the economy as a whole moved from extractive to agricultural enterprises, the proportion of plantations promoted in this way declined, reaching a low of 15 percent in the 1740s. As the Lowcountry economy extended its territorial reach after mid-century, however, the lumber industry surged. Large-scale saw-milling ventures took orders for thousands of feet of board, and planters close to Charlestown loaded schooners with hundreds of cords of firewood. As ax-wielding slaves cleared more swamps for rice fields, planters continued to send more wood to market. By the end of the colonial period, lumber had "become a very profitable, quick saleable, and ready-money Article." One in four plantations was advertised with a capacity to produce planks, staves, boards, scantling, hoop poles, shingles, bark, firewood, and many other tree products.[26]

Colonial planters understood that their wealth depended on transforming a landscape of trees into ordered fields. Their slaves were more than just chattel property in this enterprise. From within the plantation looking out into a surrounding wilderness, planters saw the enslaved "hands" who wielded axes as the most compelling emblems of motive force in an expanding colonial landscape. So ingrained was this image of slave-with-ax that one planter compared the destruction wrought by a hurricane to the work of "a thousand negroes . . . employed for a whole day in cutting down . . . trees." Although images of cutting down trees loomed large in the colonial imagination, the application of so much labor and the extraction of so many commodities had not deforested the Lowcountry at the end of the eighteenth century. Its length and breadth was still "covered with wood except small spots where Plantations are settled." So tall and dense was this tree cover that the openings made by plantations seemed "small in comparison with the immence woods." A glance across this landscape revealed only "Boundless forest."[27]

Around the residences of their showplace plantations elite planters in the late eighteenth century established "pleasure grounds" that featured trees for their ornamental beauty. Members of the Manigault family sought advice from London on how to turn their 1,870-acre Amelia Plantation, newly seated in the interior neighborhood known as the High Hills of Santee, into a "beautifull place." Along slopes of the river bank leading to Santee River they were advised to plant "Lombardy Poplars, Birch, sweet scented & other flowering shrubs interspersed with fruit trees" that produced "all kinds of European fruit both great & small." An "Avenue of Life-Oaks" lined the road to some plantation mansions. These were designed to impress those who passed beneath their canopies, making the journey from the road to the residence a procession that displayed the planter's dominion over the land. Massive trees aligned in orderly rows suggested that an ancient patriarch had planted them generations before, giving the plantation owner claims to family authority rooted deep in time. The oak alley's illusion of occupation from time immemorial was in fact the product of selective cutting and landscaping to make plantations seem, like the trees, "almost coeval with the alluvial soil in which they had vegetated."[28]

South Carolina's trees—a mixed array of exotic and familiar species domesticated through gardening—became mementos of a natural world in which colonists found their bearings and could take comfort. In 1735 William Bohun, a colonist who had returned to settle an English country estate known as "The Beeches," asked his nieces in South Carolina to send him an elaborate token by which he could remember the Lowcountry. He asked them to construct a painted canoe and to "send in her some Young trees with matts about the roots to preserve them." To complete this "whimsicall" request, they were to include specimens of persimmons, chikapin, mulberry, tulip, locust, and other distinctive Carolina trees, each identified with a name plate made of wood. Once this shipment reached Britain, Bohun intended to plant the trees and take the boat out fishing. He was not the only metropolitan resident to import Carolina trees. British commentators in the seventeenth century tended to focus on what exotic crops might be transplanted to plantation America to be grown for a profit. During the eighteenth century, as naturalist Mark Catesby observed, subtropical and tropical colonies became sources for new tree species, supplying Britain in the span of half a century a "greater variety of trees than has been procured from all the other parts of the world for more than a thousand years past."[29]

From the first moments that English land scouts used trees to reveal the fertility of Carolina soil, how to describe American trees became a problem of analogy. Colonists found ready correspondences between Old and New World poplars, elms, and ashes, but they mislabeled swamp conifers as cypresses and mistakenly called the eastern juniper a red kind of cedar. Among the many sorts of the most important English tree, the oak, they found one that bested the original. The live oak's "Leaves continue green thereon all the Winter," and its wood was valued as highly for its "Toughness, and the Goodness of its Grain." When colonists throughout mainland British America anointed liberty trees as sites of extra-legal protest during the 1760s, they avoided the oak as a traditional symbol of England and a specific emblem of the restored House of Stuart. In Carolina, however, patriot gatherings took place below a "most noble LIVE-OAK Tree, in Mr. Mazyck's pasture, which they formally dedicated to LIBERTY" in 1768. This tree, located in a suburban neighborhood of tenements and merchant compounds close to the Cooper River's Atlantic wharves, proclaimed the American quest for liberty as an inextinguishable desire, rooted in British traditions, but as "ever green" as the tree's foliage.[30]

White Carolinians associated themselves with another distinctive tree species—the palmetto (*Sabal palmetto*)—that they claimed as their own as they defined themselves separately from the British nation. That a tree that "grows from twenty to forty feet high without branches, and then terminates in something resembling the head of a cabbage," became an enduring patriotic emblem bears some explanation. Palmetto logs formed the walls of a hastily constructed fort on strategic Sullivan's Island, which commanded a view of the city from within its harbor and withstood intense bombardment by British forces in 1776. During this initial, aborted invasion, "Hardly a hut or tree on the island escaped," but by a seeming miracle, the shots that "struck the fort were ineffectually buried in its soft wood." As British cannonballs "lodged in the logs as in a sponge," South Carolina forces repulsed the invasion, forcing a British withdrawal at the cost of several ships and heavy casualties. The almanac for 1777 recognized June 28 as the day of the "PALMETTO." In 1778 South Carolina's pro-independence whites prepared to celebrate the second anniversary of their successful defense of the province. Their boats, loaded with "Palmetto Trees and Boughs" cut in the countryside, converged on Charlestown. The state's revolutionary seal featured a palmetto tree looming above "an English oak fallen, its root above the ground, and its branches lopt." First a "symbol of the novel landscape for arriving Europeans," whites embraced the cabbage palmetto over the oak to declare allegiance to South Carolina in no uncertain terms. Like the tree, however outlandish it appeared to English eyes, they too were products of its soil and claimed identities shaped by life and work in its low-lying, subtropical environment.[31]

For slaves the palmetto was an American exotic that could be domesticated and brought into the service of reconstituting Old World forms of material culture in the New. African slaves made coiled baskets out of sea grasses and palmetto fronds. The tree provided material for thatching clay dwellings, with which early slaves refashioned a basic West African house form on the plantations. In the specific context of building the fort on Sullivan's Island, the palmetto also became a symbol of the violence whites used to maintain their hold on slave labor during the disruptions of the Revolutionary Era. In 1776 the "negroes ordered down from the country" to construct the fort might have viewed their labors with irony, if not anguish. Those who came to South Carolina on slave ships would have remembered the purgatory of "performing quarantine" on the island's "pest house" before being transported to Charlestown for sale.[32]

Not only was Sullivan's Island known to the slaves for its pest house, but as they chopped and hauled palmetto trunks for the fort's construction, none could have forgotten the recent violence that had taken place there. By December 1775 several hundred runaways had fled to Sullivan's Island, "Induced, 'tis Thought," by promise of freedom held out by the commanders of British men-of-war anchored offshore. Under cover of darkness, a force of more than fifty colonists raided their camp, set fire to the pest house where they took shelter, killed five slaves, and took most of the rest prisoner to be returned to their masters. Fewer than twenty escaped to the safety of British boats dispatched to the beach to rescue them. Just as contrasting English and Indian uses for mulberry trees represented different modes of exploiting natural resources at South Carolina's inception, African-American and European-American perspectives on the palmetto revealed a divided view of this landscape at the end of the colonial period.[33]

Overseers tasked slaves with chopping down trees at the rate of about one acre per slave per week. A team of eight slaves, over the course of a day, might clear a single acre of land of its largest timber. Multiplied over more than a century of territorial expansion—by 1770 nearly 130,000 acres were devoted to growing rice and indigo—chopping down trees amounted to a staggering application of human labor to prepare the land for planting. That Lowcountry swamp stands, woodland outcrops, and pine forests played a supporting role in the plantation economy should not diminish their standing as vital indicators of how colonists remade the region in the late seventeenth and eighteenth centuries. The planters' landscape always centered on trees and their evocative capacity to bring into view what was otherwise hidden.[34]

Environmental historians have viewed the creation of a plantation landscape in the American subtropics as an imposition of European mastery bent on exploiting the land, and rightly so. Disruptive transformations accompanied advancing plantation settlement at every turn. This view of planter and plantation as agents of environmental destruction has done a good job of tallying the costs of colonization, but in doing so historians have mischaracterized the nature of colonial interactions between European settlers and the landscapes they invaded. Europeans arrived to claim the swamps and forests of the Carolina Lowcountry, but their ability to do so rested as much on their capacity to adapt to the environment as it did on a willingness to exploit it for profit.

Planting rice was the focus of South Carolina's economy, but trees grew and fell at the center of its economic culture. Because trees were involved in every economic activity colonists undertook, from building a shelter to creating a field, they serve as sensitive indicators of this process at work. At every stage of South Carolina's development colonists imagined, observed, harvested, and planted trees. Trees documented the land's historic productivity, stood for social desires, marked off refined from uncultivated spaces, demonstrated the environmental agency of slave workers, and served as emblems of collective identity. Planters were effective colonizers because they tailored production and subsistence to the specificities of this environment.

A peculiar desire lurked in the heart of these interactions with North American trees. Settlers were lured to Carolina to claim land and sell commodities, but also by the promise that a more conventional British material culture could be transplanted intact to the New World. In this they were mistaken and misled. Slaves working in waterlogged rice fields, bowls of maize mush, and cattle ranging in unclaimed woodland wastes defined South Carolina's emerging eighteenth-century plantation society. To critical British eyes this slovenly agricultural landscape was an inferior version of an ideal countryside made up of tidy farmsteads. Colonists embraced the distinctive advantages of South Carolina's natural endowment for agriculture and, at the same time, worked to reconcile the discrepancies between British standards and American practice that this exotic environment introduced into life and landscape.

Setting their sights on "planting themselves in America and breeding there," Joyce E. Chaplin argues, British colonists came to the New World to transform it, adapting commercial farming to its varied climates and terrains, and making it into a place that could support transplanted British people, culture, and society. There is much to be gained by following Alfred Crosby and seeing European settler societies in the Americas as "neo-Europes," places that featured climates and soils into which European animal husbandry and cereal agriculture could be transplanted. Plantation colonies, like colonies established in the Northeast, followed this pattern of replicating Old World agriculture, but with strains and departures that sometimes make it difficult to see where European influences ended and American discrepancies began. Warmer weather and longer growing seasons made possible the extensive cultivation of market crops that were impossible to grow in colder climes. Settlers in Carolina, who craved beer and wheat bread as essential nourishment, made do with imported wines and maize when it proved difficult to make these staples of the English diet in a humid, hot climate. Plantation America was a "neo-Europe," but one in which analogues were substituted for Old World plants and animals that failed to thrive in new environmental conditions. The persistent white belief that only black bodies could endure the rigors of cutting cane and planting rice likewise changed the racial character of agricultural labor.[35]

So rich with emotive associations, trees were capable of providing, as Keith Thomas has put it, a "visible symbol of human society." As colonists staked out independent identities as citizens they embraced the palmetto, a native tree that was no longer perceived as exotic, but rather symbolized their entrenched place within the Lowcountry. Trees offered planters metaphors for generation, providing a language with which to anticipate the transformation of nature through agriculture. Trees stood in the way of cultivation and provided the essential material by which people made the land habitable. Finding oaks, elms, and hickories held out the prospect that this rough landscape land might someday resemble the countryside they left behind. In a colony of dispersed plantation sites, where it seemed as if everyone lived "almost in a private forest," views of American nature changed as colonists adapted agriculture to the Lowcountry environment and struggled to reconstitute a viable material life from its resources. Trees served as the matter with which colonists imagined nature in relation to

culture. The sheer range of perceptions and uses they found—and the v
these changed over time—reveals a dynamic, adaptive relationship
the environment.[36]

Notes

1. Robert Sandford, "A Relation of a Voyage on the Coast of the Province of Carolina, 1666," in *Narratives of Early Carolina, 1650–1708*, ed. Alexander Salley Jr. (New
York, N.Y.: Barnes & Noble, Inc., 1939), 89; Nicholas Carteret, "Mr. Carteret's Relations of their Planting at Ashley River '70," in *Narratives of Early Carolina*, 119–20.

2. Timothy Silver, *A New Face on the Countryside: Indians, Colonists, and Slaves in
the South Atlantic Forests, 1500–1800* (New York, N.Y.: Cambridge University Press,
1990), 147, 189, 197.

3. Mart A. Stewart, *"What Nature Suffers to Groe": Life, Labor, and Landscape on
the Georgia Coast, 1680–1920* (Athens: University of Georgia Press, 1996); Richard H.
Grove, *Green Imperialism: Colonial Expansion, Tropical Island Edens, and the Origins
of Environmentalism, 1600–1860* (New York, N.Y.: Cambridge University Press, 1995);
Warren Dean, *With Broadax and Firebrand: The Destruction of the Brazilian Atlan-
tic Forest* (Berkeley: University of California Press, 1995); Virginia DeJohn Anderson,
Creatures of Empire: How Domestic Animals Transformed Early America (New York,
N.Y.: Oxford University Press, 2004).

4. Mart A. Stewart, "If John Muir Had Been an Agrarian: American Environmental
History West and South," *Environment and History* 11 (May 2005): 139–62, quotation
on 141.

5. E. L. Jones, "Creative Disruptions in American Agriculture, 1620–1820," *Agricultural History* 48 (Oct. 1974): 510; Brian Donahue, *The Great Meadow: Farmers and the
Land in Colonial Concord* (New Haven, Conn.: Yale University Press, 2004), xv; Lois
Green Carr, Russell R. Menard, and Lorena S. Walsh, *Robert Cole's World: Agriculture
and Society in Early Maryland* (Chapel Hill: University of North Carolina Press, 1991);
T. H. Breen, *Tobacco Culture: The Mentality of the Great Tidewater Planters on the Eve
of Revolution* (Princeton, N.J.: Princeton University Press, 1985); James Horn, *Adapting to a New World: English Society in the Seventeenth-Century Chesapeake* (Chapel Hill:
University of North Carolina Press, 1994); Paul G. E. Clemens, *The Atlantic Economy
and Colonial Maryland's Eastern Shore: From Tobacco to Grain* (Ithaca, N.Y.: Cornell
University Press, 1980); Joyce E. Chaplin, *An Anxious Pursuit: Agricultural Innovation
and Modernity in the Lower South, 1730–1815* (Chapel Hill: University of North Carolina Press, 1993).

6. S. Max Edelson, *Plantation Enterprise in Colonial South Carolina* (Cambridge,
Mass.: Harvard University Press, 2006).

7. Ibid. On "culture hearths" and the Carolina Lowcountry, see D. W. Meinig,
The Shaping of America: A Geographic Perspective on 500 Years of History, vol. 1: *Atlantic
America, 1492–1800* (New Haven, Conn.: Yale University Press, 1986), 52–53, 172–90.

8. On oaks in early modern English culture, see Simon Schama, *Landscape and Memory* (New York, N.Y.: A. A. Knopf, 1995), 153–74; see also Keith Thomas, *Man and the Natural World: Changing Attitudes in England, 1500–1800* (London, England: Allen Lane, 1983), chap. 5; John Ogilby, *America: Being the Latest, and Most Accurate Description of the New World* (London, England: John Ogilby, 1671), 205–6 at Early English Books Online, http://eebo.chadwyck.com (hereafter cited as EEBO); T. A., "Carolina; or a Description of the Present State of that Country, and the Natural Excellencies Thereof" (1682), in *Historical Collections of South Carolina*, ed. B. R. Carroll, 2 vols. (New York, N.Y.: Harper & Brothers, 1836), 2:65; John Stewart, "Letters from John Stewart to William Dunlop," *South Carolina Historical and Genealogical Magazine* 32 (Apr. 1931): 86–87.

9. William Owen to Lord Ashley, Sept. 15, 1670, in *The Shaftesbury Papers and Other Records Relating to Carolina* (Charleston, S.C.: Tempus, 2000), 201; Gentleman of Elvas, *A Relation of the Invasion and Conquest of Florida by the Spaniards Under the Command of Fernando de Soto* (London, England: John Lawrence, 1686), 71, at "Early Encounters in North America," http://www.alexanderstreet2.com/EENA/.

10. "An Old Letter" (c. 1671), in *Shaftesbury Papers*, 308–9; Samuel Wilson, "An Account of the Province of Carolina, in America" (1682), in *Historical Collections of South Carolina*, 2:27–28; Silver, *A New Face on the Countryside*, 61.

11. Joan Thirsk, ed., *The English Rural Landscape* (Oxford, England: Oxford University Press, 2000), 27, 52, 74, 123, 133–34, 148–49; Nuala Zahedieh, "New World Resources and the Expansion of England's Merchant Marine, 1660–1775," paper presented at the Tenth Anniversary Conference on Atlantic History, Cambridge, Mass., Aug. 8–13, 2005; E. P. Thompson, *Whigs and Hunters: The Origin of the Black Act* (New York, N.Y.: Pantheon Books, 1975).

12. Thomas Nairne, "Letter from South Carolina," in *Selling a New World: Two Colonial South Carolina Promotional Pamphlets*, ed. Jack P. Greene (Columbia: University of South Carolina Press, 1989), 66; Wm. Dunlop to James Montgomerie, n.d. (c. 1687), Letters from William Dunlop, Papers of the Lords Proprietors in the Malmsbury Collection, South Carolina Department of Archives and History, Columbia, S.C.; "Proposals by Mr. Peter Purry, of Newfchatel," in *Historical Collections of South Carolina*, 2:131; Richard Blome, *A Description of the Island of Jamaica with the Other Isles and Territories in America to which the English are Related . . .* (London, England: J. B. for D. Newman, 1678), 69, EEBO; T. A., "Carolina," 2:69; Ogilby, *America*, 205, EEBO; "An Old Letter," 308; Maurice Mathews to Lord Ashley, Aug. 30, 1671, in *Shaftesbury Papers*, 333.

13. "An Old Letter," 308; Maurice Mathews to Lord Ashley, Aug. 30, 1671, 335; Sandford, "Relation of a Voyage," 100, 102–3; William Hilton, "Relation of a Discovery," in *Narratives of Early Carolina*, 44; Carteret, "Mr. Carteret's Relations," 119–20.

14. William Sayle and Council to Lords Proprietors, 1670, in *Shaftesbury Papers*, 175; Ogilby, *America*, 207, EEBO; Sandford, "Relation of a Voyage," 102–3; Robert Ferguson, *The Present State of Carolina with Advice to the Settlers Present State* (London, England: John Bringhurst, 1682), 11, EEBO.

15. John Bartram, "Diary of a Journey through the Carolinas, Georgia, and Florida from July 1, 1765, to April 10, 1766," in *Transactions of the American Philosophical Society*, vol. 33:1 (Philadelphia, Pa.: American Philosophical Society, 1942), 15n; John Drayton, *A View of South Carolina As Respects her Natural and Civil Concerns* (Charleston, S.C.: W. P. Young, 1802), 7n, 8–9.

16. George Ogilvie, *Carolina; Or, the Planter* (1776), reprinted in *The Southern Literary Journal* (1986): 7; William Gerard De Brahm, "Philosophico-Historico-Hydrogeography of South Carolina, Georgia, and East Florida" (c. 1772), in *Documents Connected with the History of South Carolina*, ed. Plowden Charles Jennett Weston (London, England: n.p., 1856), 173–76.

17. Wilson, "Account of the Province," 2:28; Grove, *Green Imperialism*, 276–77; John Norris, "Profitable Advice for Rice and Poor" (1712), in *Selling a New World*, 90–91, 102; Aaron M. Shatzman, *Servants into Planters: The Origin of an American Image: Land Acquisition and Status Mobility in Seventeenth-Century South Carolina* (New York, N.Y.: Garland Publishing, Inc., 1989), 45, 51–52, 115, 131; John Solomon Otto, "Livestock-Raising in Early South Carolina, 1670–1700: Prelude to the Rice Plantation Economy," *Agricultural History* 61 (Fall 1987): 21; and see Peter A. Coclanis, *Shadow of a Dream: Economic Life and Death in the South Carolina Low Country, 1670–1920* (New York, N.Y.: Oxford University Press, 1989), 58–63.

18. Nairne, "A Letter from South Carolina," 62–63; Norris, "Profitable Advice," 96–97.

19. Ogilvie, *Carolina; Or, the Planter*, 59–60; Henry Laurens to John Bartram, Charleston, S.C., Aug. 9, 1766, in *The Correspondence of John Bartram, 1734–1777*, ed. Edmund Berkeley and Dorothy Smith Berkeley (Gainesville: University Press of Florida, 1992), 671; James Glen, "A Description of South Carolina" (1761), in *Colonial South Carolina: Two Contemporary Descriptions*, ed. Chapman J. Milling (Columbia: University of South Carolina Press, 1951), 17–18; Elizabeth Hyrne to Burrell Massingberd, c. 1702, "Hyrne Family Letters, 1701–10," in *The Colonial South Carolina Scene: Contemporary Views, 1697–1774*, ed. H. Roy Merrens (Columbia: University of South Carolina Press, 1977), 19.

20. Stephen Daniels, "The Political Iconography of Woodland in Later Georgian England," in *The Iconography of Landscape: Essays on the Symbolic Representation, Design and Use of Past Environments*, ed. Denis Cosgrove and Stephen Daniels (New York, N.Y.: Cambridge University Press, 1988), 51; Norris, "Profitable Advice," 105; Mark Catesby, *The Natural History of Carolina, Florida, and the Bahama Islands . . .*, 2 vols. (London, 1771), 1:ii, Eighteenth-Century Collections Online, http://www.gale.com/EighteenthCentury/ (hereafter cited as ECCO).

21. Queries from the Lords of Trade About Carolina, Aug. 10, 1720 (typescript), William R. Coe Papers, Folder 2, South Carolina Historical Society (hereafter cited as SCHS); H. Roy Merrens, *Colonial North Carolina in the Eighteenth Century: A Study in Historical Geography* (Chapel Hill: University of North Carolina Press, 1964), 85–90; M. Eugene Sirmans, *Colonial South Carolina: A Political History, 1663–1763* (Chapel Hill: University of North Carolina Press, 1966), 155, 162; Lawrence Lee, *The Lower*

Cape Fear in Colonial Days (Chapel Hill: University of North Carolina Press, 1965), 97–99; Alexander Hewit, "An Historical Account of the Rise and Progress of the Colonies of South Carolina and Georgia" (1779), in *Historical Collections*, 1:172–74. See also Silver, *Face on the Countryside*, 120–26; Bradford J. Wood, *This Remote Part of the World: Regional Formation in Lower Cape Fear, North Carolina, 1725–1775* (Columbia: University of South Carolina Press, 2004), 179–82, 186–87; Robert B. Outland III, *Tapping the Pines: The Naval Stores Industry in the American South* (Baton Rouge: Louisiana State University Press, 2004), chap. 1.

22. Johann Martin Bolzius, "Reliable Answer to Some Submitted Questions Concerning the Land Carolina," ed. and trans. Klaus G. Loewald et al., *William and Mary Quarterly*, 3d ser., vol. 14 (Apr. 1957): 233, 247, 257; Hutson to James Hamilton, May 1, 1777, Richard Hutson Letterbook, SCHS.

23. De Brahm, "Philosophico-Historico-Hydrogeography," 197–98; see also Peter H. Wood, *Black Majority: Negroes in Colonial South Carolina from 1670 through the Stono Rebellion* (New York, N.Y.: Norton, 1974), 108–14.

24. Joseph Clay? to ———, Dec. 6, 1785?, Edward Telfair Papers, William R. Perkins Library, Special Collections, Duke University, Durham, N.C.; Jean Pierre Purry, "Memorial of . . . Carolina" (1731), in *Tracts and Other Papers, Relating Principally to the Origin, Settlement, and Progress of the Colonies in North America . . .*, comp. Peter Force (Washington, D.C.: P. Force, 1836), 1:§11:7; Harry J. Carman, ed., *American Husbandry* (1775; repr., New York, N.Y.: Columbia University Press, 1939), 343–44; S. Max Edelson, "Affiliation Without Affinity: Skilled Slaves in Eighteenth-Century South Carolina," in *Money, Trade, and Power: The Evolution of South Carolina's Plantation Society*, ed. Jack P. Greene, Rosemary Brana-Shute, and Randy J. Sparks (Columbia: University of South Carolina Press, 2001), 217–55.

25. Bolzius, "Reliable Answer to Some Submitted Questions," 244, 258; J. F. D. Smyth, *A Tour of the United States of America*, 2 vols. (Dublin: n.p., 1784), 2:49; Wilson, "Account of the Province," 2:24; Josiah Smith Jr. to John Smith Jr., Jan. 12, 1773, Josiah Smith Letterbook, Southern Historical Collection, University of North Carolina, Chapel Hill, N.C.; Laurens to John Knight and Thomas Mears, Feb. 24, 1764, in *The Papers of Henry Laurens*, ed. Philip M. Hamer et al., 16 vols. (Columbia: University of South Carolina Press, 1968–2003), 4:184. See also Martha Zierden, "The Urban Landscape in South Carolina," in *Carolina's Historical Landscapes: Archaeological Perspectives*, ed. Linda F. Stine (Knoxville: University of Tennessee Press, 1997), 168; Henry Laurens to John McQueen, Charleston, S.C., Sept. 10, 1785, in *Laurens Papers*, 16:593.

26. *South-Carolina Gazette*, Mar. 20, 1762; Nov. 15, 1735; Feb. 7, 1771, in South Carolina Newspapers Microfilm Series, 1732–1782 (Charleston, S.C.: Charleston Library Society, 1956); Bolzius, "Reliable Answer to Some Submitted Questions," 258; Laurens to Benjamin Smith, Nov. 30, 1762, *Laurens Papers*, 3:177–78; Laurens to Stephen Miller, Feb. 24, 1763, *Laurens Papers*, 3:268.

27. S. Max Edelson, "The Nature of Slavery: Environmental Disorder and Slave Agency in Colonial South Carolina," in *Cultures and Identities in Colonial British*

America, ed. Robert Olwell and Alan Tully (Baltimore, Md.: Johns Hopkins University Press, 2006), chap. 1; Drayton, *View of South-Carolina*, 20; George Ogilvie to Pegie Ogilvie, June 25, 1774, in "The Letters of George Ogilvie," ed. David S. Shields, *The Southern Literary Journal*, special issue (1986): 118–19.

28. John Farquharson to Gabriel Manigault, June 24, 1789, Manigualt Family Papers, South Carolina Library, University of South Carolina, Columbia, S.C.; Advertisement of Stephen Carter, *South-Carolina Gazette*, Feb. 28, 1774, 11; Dell Upton, *Holy Things and Profane: Anglican Parish Churches in Colonial Virginia* (New Haven, Conn.: Yale University Press, 1997), 206–7; G. S. S., "Sketches of the South Santee," in *The Old South*, ed. Mark M. Smith (Malden, Mass.: Blackwell, 2001), 20. On English precedents for the oak alley, see Thomas, *Man and the Natural World*, 207–8, 217–18. On antebellum transplanting, see William P. Baldwin Jr., ed., *Plantations of the Low Country: South Carolina 1697–1865* (Greensboro, N.C.: Legacy Publications, 1985), 12, 77; see also Leland Ferguson, *Uncommon Ground: Archaeology and Early African America, 1650–1800* (Washington, D.C.: Smithsonian Institution Press, 1992), xxiii.

29. William Bohun to Mary Bohun Baker and Elizabeth Bohun Garandeau, Aug. 9, 1735, Baker Family Correspondence, Folder 3, Record No. 11/537/3, SCHS; Joyce E. Chaplin, "Mark Catesby, A Skeptical Newtonian in America," in *Empire's Nature: Mark Catesby's New World Vision*, ed. Amy R. W. Meyers and Margaret Beck Pritchard (Chapel Hill: University of North Carolina Press, 1998), 81–82.

30. Carl Sauer, "The Settlement of the Humid East," in *Climate and Man: Yearbook of Agriculture, 1941*, USDA (Washington, D.C.: G.P.O., 1941), 159; Norris, "Profitable Advice," 89; Gent, "Carolina," 2:66; Alfred F. Young, "Liberty Tree: Made in America?" paper presented to the Newberry Library Seminar in Early American History, Chicago, Ill., Sept. 25, 2003; *Laurens Papers*, 6:123.

31. Louisa Susannah Wells, *The Journal of a Voyage from Charlestown, S.C., to London* (1779; repr., New York, N.Y.: New York Historical Society, 1906), 2; David Ramsay, *The History of the Revolution of South-Carolina . . .*, 2 vols. (Trenton, N.J.: Isaac Collins, 1785), 1:141, 148, Early American Imprints Series I, Archive of Americana, Readex Digital, infoweb.newsbank.com (hereafter Early American Imprint Series I); John S. Pancake, *This Destructive War: The British Campaign in the Carolinas, 1780–1782* (Tuscaloosa: University of Alabama Press, 1985), 20–24; John Tobler, *The South-Carolina and Georgia Almanack, For the Year of our Lord 1778 . . .* (Charlestown, S.C.: Robert Wells and Son, 1777), Early American Imprints Series I; *The Annual Register, or a View of the History, Politics, and Literature, for the Year 1778*, 2d ed. (London, England: J. Dodsley, 1781), 169, ECCO. The palmetto was added to the South Carolina state flag in 1861. Peter H. Wood, "'It was a Negro Taught Them,' a New Look at African Labor in Early South Carolina," *Journal of Asian and African Studies* 9 (1974): 164.

32. Wood, "'It was a Negro Taught Them,'" 162, 164; Ferguson, *Uncommon Ground*, 66, 74–75, 80; Ramsay, *Revolution in South Carolina*, 1:143; Pelatiah Webster, "Journal of a Visit to Charleston, 1765," in *Colonial South Carolina Scene*, 224.

33. Walter Edgar, *South Carolina: A History* (Columbia: University of South Carolina Press, 1998), 231; Josiah Smith Jr. to James Poyas, Jan. 10, 1776, Josiah Smith Jr.

Letterbook. On this raid, see Robert Olwell, *Masters, Slaves, and Subjects: The Culture of Power in the South Carolina Low Country, 1740–1790* (Ithaca, N.Y.: Cornell University Press, 1998), 239n.

34. De Brahm, "Philosophico-Historico-Hydrogeography," 197–98. On the pace of land clearing, see also Carr, Menard, and Walsh, *Robert Cole's World*, 37. This conservative estimate of non-corn acreage under cultivation is from Robert M. Weir, *Colonial South Carolina: A History* (Millwood, N.Y.: KTO Press, 1983), 172.

35. Joyce E. Chaplin, *Subject Matter: Technology, the Body, and Science on the Anglo-American Frontier, 1500–1676* (Cambridge, Mass.: Harvard University Press, 2001), 117; Alfred W. Crosby, *Ecological Imperialism: The Biological Expansion of Europe, 900–1900*, 2d ed. (New York, N.Y.: Cambridge University Press, 2004).

36. Thomas, *Man and the Natural World*, 219; Bolzius, "Reliable Answer to Some Submitted Questions," 246.

HARRY WATSON

"The Common Rights of Mankind"

Subsistence, Shad, and Commerce

in the Early Republican South

IN THE SUMMER of 1787, while delegates to the federal convention in Philadelphia struggled in the arena of high politics to balance conflicting demands for public liberty and the common good, the free inhabitants of Orangeburg District, South Carolina, were angry about a more local version of that perennial problem. "No individual has a Right to Arrogate or Assume to himself an exclusive & partial Right," they fumed, "whereby he may deprive the People in its vicinage of those just Rights & Privileges which as Citizens of a free & independent State they are entitled to." The specific problem was a dam, which stretched across the Edisto River and created a fall of water to power Ferguson's Mills, incidentally blocking the movement of rafts and fish on the river. As a result of this dam, petitioners from the upstream neighborhoods bitterly protested, "they are totally cut off from availing themselves of the common Rights of Mankind."[1]

By some lights, the dam for Ferguson's Mills was essential to the rural economy, as much a part of the pastoral landscape as cornfields or framed houses. Its water-powered saws cut logs into lumber for sale to local customers, to downstream owners of Sea Island plantations, and perhaps to more distant consumers. In addition, mills such as Ferguson's often supplied local families with cornmeal for their daily bread, and they also ground wheat flour, an article that southern farmers were more likely to export than to eat themselves.

Many of Ferguson's neighbors saw the matter differently. Most obviously, the dam prevented other sawmill operators, located upstream, from floating their products to market. Petitioners complained to the legislature that the Edisto dam deprived them of something even more important, "the Benefits and Emoluments arising from a Fishery." Expanding on this theme, residents a few years later declared that the offending dam even deprived them "of *a necessary of life*, which their fellow citizens living upon other water courses 200 miles above the said Mills enjoy in the Greatest plenty."[2]

The "necessary of life" that the Orangeburg petitioners demanded was the American shad, *Alosa sapidissima*, a species of Atlantic Ocean fish that ascends rivers every spring, from Florida to Canada, in order to spawn. Still prized in regional cooking as a bony but succulent delicacy, shad were extremely abundant before the nineteenth century and fed Indians, pioneers, and slaves alike. Together with their cousins the alewives *(Alosa pseudoharengus)* and the blueback herring *(Alosa aestivalis)*, shad penetrated eastern rivers in massive spawning runs and were freely available to anyone who could operate a fish trap, cast a hook and line, or wield a hand-held dip net. The itinerant artist David Hunter Strother captured the likeness of one such happy fisherman in his illustrated account of a trip to North Carolina published in 1857. Salted shad and herring were regarded as cheap food for the laboring poor as late as the mid-nineteenth century, when a leading commercial fisherman of North Carolina declared them "cheaper than bacon." Judging from the controversy they generated in early republican state legislatures, shad and herring played a much more important role in the southern semisubsistence economy than most historians have realized.[3]

Complaints against the Edisto Sawmills were not isolated incidents, but manifestations of a widespread regional controversy over milldams and fishing rights that produced hundreds of angry petitions to legislatures in the South Atlantic area between 1750 and 1850. Some aspects of the dispute surfaced in almost every southeastern state at almost every legislative session in this period, leading each state to erect complex thickets of special legislative acts to regulate the competing claims of fishermen and millers.[4] The issue demonstrated the place of fish in southern diets, but the controversy also had a deeper meaning. The damming of southeastern creeks and rivers and the campaign to keep them open reflected a major transition in social and economic history, as the backcountry South shifted from an economy based on pioneer subsistence to one based on slavery and the market. Voluminous petition campaigns reveal that this transition was heavily contested by southern yeomen who feared and resented the threat mills posed to their independence and livelihoods. They fought back with some success, using petitions and the languages of republican virtue and liberal rights bequeathed them by the American Revolution. But their petitions of protest had diminishing effects, as the power and ideology of the "market revolution" undermined their appeals and the full ecological dimensions of the shad problem escaped them. In other words, petitions against enterprises such as the Edisto Sawmills represented more than the pique of frustrated sportsmen; they were eloquent testimony to the interaction of nature, politics, and market forces in the transformation of early republican society.

Historians have not always recognized the complexity of that transformation, which may explain why the numerous fishing petitions in southern legislative archives have not received much scholarly attention. Writing about antebellum economic development, scholars have sometimes assumed that nothing but physical barriers to the production and transportation of staple crops stood between upcountry southern farmers and the enthusiastic embrace of commercial agriculture and the system of slave labor that powered it. This assumption has guided numerous accounts of antebellum campaigns for "internal improvements," and it inspired W. J. Cash's unforgettable anecdote of "the stout young Irishman"—who bore an uncanny resemblance to the father of Margaret Mitchell's Scarlet O'Hara—who rose to "aristocracy" on a path opened by the cotton gin.[5]

More recently, however, scholars have questioned whether the move from semisubsistence farming to plantations and markets was quite so simple as Cash had implied. In his pathbreaking study of the Georgia upcountry, Steven Hahn has found that small farmers of the antebellum period, fearing that commercial fluctuations could snare them in debt and deprive them of their lands and independence, hesitated to commit themselves to full-scale production for the market. Gavin Wright's account of "safety-first" agriculture plausibly explains why small southern farmers chose to limit their risky ventures into commercial agriculture in order to preserve the security of their households. Concentrating on the production of corn, pork, and other provisions that were used mostly for family consumption, yeoman households traded a small surplus to pay for what they could not make and treasured their independence from merchants, creditors, and landlords. Often calling themselves "poor," these families nevertheless sustained a standard of living that enabled the household head to defend his standing as a free and equal member of the larger community of white citizens.[6] Other explorations of the Old South's "dual economy" of semisubsistence farms and slave plantations (and the gradual shift of dominance from one to the other) have increased in number in recent years, as scholars of all parts of the United States pay increasing attention to the transforming power of the market revolution in the lives of early nineteenth-century Americans.[7]

Current literature does not fully establish who brought about the shift from one form of economic organization to another in the backcountry, nor the motives that lay behind their actions. Did upland southern farmers actively long for economic specialization, commercial exchange, and the opportunities available in a cash and credit economy? Or did they prefer the security and independence they found by raising and gathering food for their own consumption, relegating commercial dealings to the disposition of a marginal "surplus"? If the latter, how did plantations, stores, and railroads find customers for their ultimately successful entry into the backcountry? Were these engines of economic development welcomed by the great body of the white population or imposed by the power of an aspiring elite? To ask the question another way, what combination of imposition and invitation brought market society to the southern interior? What were the social, economic, political, and ecological ramifications of the shift from a mostly subsistence economy to a more commercialized one? How can we portray resistance to market transformation while exploring the reasons for the ultimate success of the market?

The story of the Edisto fishermen and of other upcountry shad lovers may help us answer those questions. The fishermen's complaints were directly tied to the advancing market because the mills they protested made flour and lumber for export and ground meal to feed large forces of slaves. The petitions and political rhetoric that upland southerners used to defend their communal access to fish, moreover, were direct legacies of the American Revolution, and the relative success or failure of these methods gives us an unusual measure of the significance of democratic politics in the lives of ordinary people of the early republic. Finally, since long-standing traditions of riparian law put the disposition of streams and fishing grounds squarely within the legislature's purview, the fishery disputes had a public, political dimension (and a paper trail in the public archives) that some market-related changes did not have.

The conflict between millers and fishermen forced southern lawmakers to locate "the common Rights of Mankind." Did "rights" belong to property holders as individuals, protecting them in the unrestricted use of their privately owned lands and machinery? Or were there "common Rights," the collective property of a community, that gave inhabitants a collective claim on flowing streams and protected their access to traditional forms of subsistence? English law had placed strict limits on private rights over flowing water, but how far would these restrictions apply in a growing American economy? Unlike the judges of this era, who aggressively supported the cause of increased economic development, elected politicians were reluctant to impose tidy solutions to difficult questions; they preferred to find a middle ground that offered something valuable to all the voters involved.[8] In the ensuing compromises, the only clear losers (besides the shad) were the farmer-fishermen, who were frustrated by an ineffective legal and political struggle for their "rights," outmaneuvered by commercial predation on the fish, and overwhelmed by an ecological crisis to which they themselves had unwittingly contributed.

In its widest context, the quarrel over mills and shad in the early republican South is more than a simple fish story. The persistence, ingenuity, and initial success of yeoman petitioners in protecting their access to migratory fish are significant testimonials to the limited power of market-based society and to the contested character of its rise. The ultimate failure of the fishermen to protect the fish, however, is an equally powerful clue to the weaknesses that beset their communities, and to the sources of the slave owners' strength. Struggling to protect their independence and their food supplies, southern farmers were not the only Americans who disputed the use of streams and rivers in legislatures of the early republic. Gary Kulik has documented the efforts of eighteenth-century Rhode Island farmers to protect their own access to fish and to resist the damming of rivers to power gristmills, iron forges, and early textile mills.[9] Kulik's Rhode Islanders were like their southern counterparts in many ways. They harvested the annual spawning runs of salmon, shad, and herring to feed themselves and their families, not for sale or sport. They spiced their streamside work with hard drinking and disorderly play, much to the annoyance of their more straitlaced neighbors. They defended their "rights" by petitioning state authorities, and they often met with partial success. In the end, they lost their fight when the devices they used to help the fish cope with dams proved ineffective and when downstream commercial fishermen used superior technology to monopolize the fish before they could reach the inland fishing sites.

Beneath superficial differences the transition to a more commercialized economy shared many common features in the North and the South. New England fishermen and southern yeomen both lost ground to rival systems of production that used water mills to process exports for distant markets. Whether "capitalist" or "quasi-seigneurial" (as competing schools of interpretation contend), the millers and slaveholders who led the attack on traditional southern fishing practices pursued their interests vigorously and showed no complaisant paternalism to those who stood in their way. Nor were the protesting fishermen crippled by deference, but defended themselves with vigor and some success.[10]

Despite these similarities, however, the transformation of southern fishing was not a simple replication of the New England experience. Plantation slavery was a key feature of the commercialized agriculture that threatened the yeomen's pursuit of subsistence, and slavery had a powerful impact on the choices they faced in the changing economy. Unlike the growing mills of New England, expanding plantations offered little in the way of employment or market outlets for displaced yeomen and thus laid a correspondingly heavier burden on the families they affected. As historians have long noted, articulate protests against the plantation system and the institution of slavery that sustained it were nearly impossible in the antebellum backcountry. The system of racial privilege and cultural hegemony that stifled objections to the peculiar institution kept yeomen's complaints against the loss of their fishing rights limited to narrowly focused petitions that never fully confronted the roots of their problems. The effect of encroaching milldams on southern yeoman households, in other words, was arguably more severe and more difficult to protest than corresponding changes in the free states. Contrasts between fishing controversies in New England and the South thus cast significant light on the power of the South's institutions, and on the resulting regional differences in the nature of the market revolution and its impact on American social development. In the late eighteenth- and early nineteenth-century South, disputes over dams and fish typically erupted in yeoman communities above the fall line, where local producers faced a transition from semisubsistence to market-oriented agriculture. Since the beginnings of European settlement in the mid-eighteenth century, families in those communities had grown food crops for their own consumption, and many of them had eschewed the purchase of slaves. Most shipped no more than a small surplus to seaboard markets. Residing in tight-knit, often densely interrelated communities and relying on what Steven Hahn called "habits of mutuality" for common survival, white yeoman families of the upper South's backcountry tended to work, vote, pray, marry, and fight together as late as the mid-nineteenth century. Their way of life encouraged intense clan loyalties and strong community attachments. For the first several generations of settlement, life-styles in these frontier regions reminded sophisticated visitors such as William Byrd and Charles Woodmason of the customs of "savage" Native Americans. In fact, these backcountry settlers did adopt important elements of the Indians' economy, including the use of slash-and-burn techniques for the culture of maize, the regular hunting of wild game, and the annual harvest of migratory fish.[11]

Along with the culture of maize, pioneers apparently borrowed Indian techniques for grinding it into meal. "There are no Wind-Mills in this Province at present, and not above two or three Water-Mills," wrote John Brickell in 1737, referring to North Carolina, "but the common method that the Planters use to grind their Corn is with Hand-Mills, which almost every one of them has." These "mills" were made from locally quarried stone, Brickell added, suggesting a connection to Native American grinding technology. The exorbitant price of water milling reflected the scarcity of alternatives to hand grinding, even when allowances are made for Brickell's propensity for exaggerating. "The Proprietors of these Mills take most commonly every other Barrel as Toll, for grinding," he declared, "but the Laws of the Country allow only every sixth."[12] Other sources imply that slaves sometimes used mortars and pestles to pound cornmeal, a technique that may have derived from the African devices used to hull rice.[13] Water mills were not inevitable features of the rural landscape. They normally followed white settlers into an area, and there could be a long interval between the establishment of European settlement and the stream blockages associated with milldams. Alternative uses for inland rivers continued to flourish in this interval.

Like maize, shad and herring were also part of the Indian legacy to European settlers, and they inspired the conflict between fishing rights and dams. Both species are *anadromous*, that is, the adults spend most of their lives in remote parts of the ocean but swim up freshwater streams in spring to lay their eggs and fertilize them. Shad are larger than herring; modern specimens range between three and four pounds, but early accounts reported individuals as heavy as fourteen pounds. Shad also travel farther up the rivers, giving them greater importance to the inhabitants of the eighteenth- and nineteenth-century Piedmont. Their natural range extends from the St. Johns River in Florida to the Gulf of St. Lawrence. In the twentieth and twenty-first centuries, most shad are netted in protected coastal waters such as those of Chesapeake Bay or Albemarle Sound, but eighteenth- and nineteenth-century observers reported shad runs as far inland as Wilkesboro, North Carolina, 451 miles up the Great Pee Dee and Yadkin rivers from the Atlantic Ocean. Shad were also recorded more than 250 miles inland on the St. Johns, the Altamaha, the Edisto, the Santee, the Neuse, and the James rivers. The various species of herring, including alewives and blueback, or glut, herring, did not travel nearly so far but rose in vast shoals to just beyond the limit of tidewater.[14]

Native Americans were the first to harvest the annual bounty of these migrating fish, and they transmitted their skills to the English colonists who displaced them. In 1585, the English artist John White depicted Algonquian Indians of the Albemarle Sound region using traps and spears to capture a canoeful of shad and preserving their catch by "brovvyllinge" it on a wooden frame. Over a century later, the explorer John Lawson reported the purchase of two dozen "ready barbaku'd" shad from a passing Indian and foretold the development of a large herring fishery in the waters of North Carolina. "The Herrings in *March* and *April* run a great way up the Rivers and fresh Streams to spawn," he explained, "where the Savages make great Wares, with Hedges that hinder their passage only in the middle, where an artificial Pound is made to take them in; so that they cannot return." After another generation of settlement, Brickell reported that "the civilized *Indians*" were teaching their skills to English colonists, "making Weares to catch Fish for a small consideration . . . , after a method peculiar to the *Indians* only."[15]

By the middle of the eighteenth century, migratory fish were recognized as an important source of food for white families who had established themselves in the upper country of Virginia and the Carolinas. Still relying heavily on what they could gather directly from the forests and streams, these families sought government protection for their access to the annual migrations. Other households fought these efforts and embraced the superior efficiency of water-powered machinery. Eliminating the onerous chore of hand grinding corn, gristmills offered a convenience to those who owned pack animals for the journey to and from the mill and whose crops were large enough to spare the miller's toll. Mills could also grind wheat into flour or, as in the case of Ferguson's Mills, saw logs into lumber. Water-ground cornmeal was normally eaten locally, but wheat flour was an export product that gained popularity in the late eighteenth century as planters grew disenchanted with tobacco.[16] Milldams were therefore more than simple elements of the pastoral landscape; they were crucial advance engines of the market economy.

The dams came in all shapes and sizes. Normally constructed of stone and timber, they might be tall where rivers ran through steep, narrow banks, impounding a long, narrow backwater that did not overflow the existing streambed. Producing at least a ten-foot fall of water, these dams were tall enough to utilize the more efficient overshot waterwheels. Dams might also be long and low, like Shaler Hillyer's dam, which crossed the Broad River in Wilkes County, Georgia, at a height of four feet. Using a millrace, or elevated channel, to carry flowing water over a further declivity in the terrain, millers like Hillyer could create a six- to ten-foot fall of water to operate a breast mill, in which the falling stream struck the waterwheel about halfway up its height. Some "dams" did not even cross the full width of a river, but merely narrowed it, raising the level of the stream a sufficient distance for a millrace, while leaving an open sluice for a deepened main channel. Skilled millwrights naturally insisted that each mill-site required a distinctive dam design. But less expert observers who noted the range of successful dams might freely assume that there was never an irreconcilable conflict between millers and other users of a stream since dams could be modified to satisfy the other legitimate users.[17]

An important trend in southern state government had a major bearing on the battle over dams and fish. The American Revolution had seen a significant shift of political power in the South, downward in the social structure and westward into the region's isolated backcountry. In North Carolina, constitution writers moderated the landholding requirement for suffrage, while legislators created seventeen new counties between 1775 and 1790, lifting western representation in the legislature closer to parity with that of the more conservative eastern section. In South Carolina, gentry leaders extended the right to vote to all white men and conceded control of the lower house of the legislature to the upcountry in the famous Compromise of 1808. In Georgia, leaders revised the state constitution repeatedly to accommodate the expansion of white population into each successive area acquired from the Indians. Worried by the presence of a large non-slaveholding population in Virginia's western mountains, the state's leaders resisted the trend toward a wider franchise but protected their legitimacy by remaining responsive to other popular demands. These changes were all consistent with a larger movement toward more democratized politics for white men throughout the United States.[18]

As egalitarian political culture took shape, white yeomen used their enhanced political standing to pursue personal and public goals. Petitions demanding special action by a state legislature were a favorite tactic. In requests supported by one to several hundred signatures, citizens asked lawmakers to pass private bills to authorize payment for wartime damages, or to emancipate favored slaves, or to legitimize out-of-wedlock children, or to pardon popular felons, or to grant divorces. Beyond these personal objectives, yeoman communities also used petitions to demand protection for their collective autonomy and material security. Backwoods communities petitioned for strengthened fence laws, for example, or measures against hog thieves, or protection of deer from attacks by dogs.[19]

The petition campaign for southern shad, which began in the mid-eighteenth century, was a central part of this larger political effort. A Virginia statute of 1752 complained that "the upper part of the rivers Appomattox and Pamunkey are become useless to the inhabitants of this colony, by means of mill-dams, fish hedges, and other obstructions" and appointed a clutch of Randolphs, Nelsons, Wormeleys, and related gentlemen as trustees responsible for clearing the rivers and opening passages in the dams. Similar statutes of 1759, 1761, 1769, and 1772 addressed the same problem on the Rapidan, Meherrin, Nottoway, Rivanna, and Hedgman rivers.[20]

As settlement extended southward, comparable legislation appeared on the statute books of the Carolinas and Georgia, often becoming law about a generation after the beginnings of permanent white settlement in an area. A 1782 statute in North Carolina, entitled "An Act to amend the several Acts passed within this State, to prevent the stoppage of the passage of Fish up the Several Rivers therein mentioned," stiffened the penalties for blocking streams to correct for the effects of revolutionary inflation. A South Carolina law of 1796 responded to petitions from Chesterfield, Darlington, Kershaw, and Lancaster counties and imposed a penalty of eight pounds per day on anyone blocking Big Lynches Creek "by fish dams, mill dams, hedges, and other obstructions" between February 15 and April 1 of every year. Similar legislation in 1796 and 1800 mentioned further petitions from the districts of Lexington, Chesterfield, Pendleton, and Greenville and dealt with fishing problems along Chinquepin and Thomason's creeks and the Saluda, Enoree, Broad, Catawba, Keowee, and Reedy rivers. In Georgia, a typical provision from 1802 echoed the twin concerns of the Edisto River petitioners of South Carolina when it declared that "the keeping open the River Savannah, is of the greatest importance to the citizens of the back country, as well in consequence of navigation, as the advantages resulting to the citizens generally, by having an annual supply of fish therefrom," and imposed fines and jail terms on those who might block the river from the city of Augusta north to the junction of the Tugaloo and Keowee rivers (a distance of some eighty miles) and, beyond there, to Hattan's Ford.[21]

The language of fish petitions makes clear that the signers regarded themselves as poor people who intended to eat their fish, not to sell them. An appeal from Lunenburg and Mecklenburg counties in Virginia described "the great benefit and advantage" of fish to everyone along the banks of the Meherrin River, "but more Especially, the poorer Sort, whose families were chiefly supported thereby." Petitions from North Carolina told a similar story. A memorial of 1771 referred to the "many poor familys" on Deep River in Guilford County "who Depended on said fishing for a great part of their living, it being well known that No River of its Size in this provence afforded greater Quantity of Exelant Shad and other fish." Twenty years later, a Moore County petition likewise insisted that the spring fishing season on Deep River was "not only a matter of Convenience but of real Necessity . . . to many poor families in more western Counties up Sd. River." By 1830, the supply of fish had evidently thinned, but the plain folk of Edgecombe County reminded the legislature that the fish were no less esteemed for their scarcity. "Residing at a distance from any regular market," the petitioners explained, "they have found it pleasant heretofore to enjoy the variety and luxury [of] a fresh shad or rock[fish] upon their tables as well as their wealthy and more influential neighbour."[22]

By contrast, the defenders of milldams identified themselves as large planters and other participants in marketplace prosperity who needed the assistance of mill machinery far more than they hungered for a mess of fish. In 1778, for example, Virginia planters in Orange and Culpeper counties protested that if onerous restrictions on Rappahannock milldams were reinstated, "the Proprietors are Ruin'd, and Five Hundred Families put to the Outmost distress, many of which have Eighty, and a Hundred Souls under their Charge. O Horrid Arrogancy!" the counterpetitioners continued, using an argument intended to enlist the sympathies of their fellow planters in the House of Delegates, "to compel yr. Petitrs. to Imploy three, or Four, of their best Hands, to pound Corn in a Mortar, to gratify a few individuals."[23]

Two sets of North Carolina petitions from the year 1810 allow us to measure the relative economic standing of fish supporters and mill supporters. One set pertained to a sizable dam at the Great Falls of the Tar River, located on the boundary between Edgecombe and Nash counties. The second addressed the presence of mills on Little River, a tributary of the Neuse that crossed part of Wayne County and extended into Johnston County. Both sets of documents came from the western edge of North Carolina's coastal plain, a region of sandy loam soils and gently sloping terrain, where the introduction of large-scale cotton production by slave labor was beginning to put pressure on an earlier economy based on family farming. The documents are unusual because texts and numerous signatures survive from participants on both sides of the controversy, while an indication of the signers' wealth is readily available in the manuscript returns of the United States Census.

The Great Falls of the Tar River was such an important waterpower site that the Battle family of Nash and Edgecombe counties later used it to drive a successful early cotton mill, laying the basis for the modern town of Rocky Mount adjacent to the site. In 1807, at least a decade before the construction of the cotton mill, investors built a sizable dam at the falls, which replaced an earlier structure and provided energy to a pair of gristmills, one on each side of the river. The dam was equipped with a "slope," a wide, ramplike chute or spillway that fish could use to cross dams with safety. In 1810, however, a massive petition from 405 inhabitants of upstream Nash County complained that the new slope was ineffective and demanded that the General Assembly require that the dam be opened entirely every spring, "that fish may have a free pasage up and down the said River during the Run of fish in said River, which your petitioners Humble Conceve would Tend to the Conveance of Your petitioners to Receve apart of the fish." An identically worded petition from Franklin County, still farther upstream, added 135 names to the list of aggrieved citizens.[24]

A counterpetition from Nash and Edgecombe counties rejected the arguments of the foregoing protests. The 459 signers declared that authorized commissioners had duly approved the slope's design when the dam was rebuilt in 1807. "For General usefulness," they claimed, the mills at the Great Falls of the Tar were "excelled by few if any in the State," and they applied an elementary form of cost-benefit analysis to judge the relative merits of mills and fish. "Were the whole dam removed," they reasoned, "the numbers of fish that would pass up, would not . . . be Sufficient to remunerate the persons who should attempt to take them—Whereas by any regulation . . . having a tendency to injure the aforesaid Mills, hundreds of people would be either intirely deprived or put to Considerable difficulty in Getting their Corn or wheat Ground." An accompanying certificate signed by 14 persons affirmed that fish could indeed pass the existing slope, even in times of low water.[25]

The dam at the Great Falls clearly had friends as well as enemies. Surviving tax lists are too fragmentary to specify the total property holdings of the rival groups of signers, but the federal census of 1810 listed the number of slaves owned by each free household, and slave ownership may be taken as a proxy for other forms of wealth and as an indicator of commitment to staple-crop production.[26]

Edgecombe and Nash counties contained nearly identical proportions of slaves in 1810—41.1 and 39.8 percent, respectively—and slaveholders and nonslaveholders could be found on both sides of the dispute. Milldam supporters, however, were far more likely to own human property than were their opponents. Of the 225 signers of the petition in favor of the mill (from Edgecombe and Nash counties) who could be located in the 1810 census, 62.7 percent were slaveholders. But of the 247 signers of the petition against the mill (from Nash County only) who could be located in that census, only 35.7 percent were slaveholders. The two groups likewise differed in the mean number of slaves held: mill supporters owned an average of 5.9 slaves each, while fish supporters (including the signers from Franklin County) owned an average of 2.9. Evidently, wealthy farmers saw the advantages of good gristmills far more clearly than their poorer neighbors. Legislators were likewise more sympathetic to millers than to fishermen; they rejected all three petitions on technicalities, a solution that left the existing dam and slope in place.[27]

A similar situation prevailed in nearby Wayne and Johnston counties. Wayne contained a higher proportion of slaves in 1810 (31.7 percent as opposed to Johnston's 22.2 percent), but the counties were otherwise very similar in soil and suitability for staple-crop agriculture. In that year, Johnston County residents along the banks of the Little River complained of "great disadvantage owing to several Mills being erected a cross said river which entirely Prevents fish from runing up said River for many Miles, where they formerly did in a bundance." The 138 signers of this petition also pointed out that high waters often made the mills on the main channel useless "in the time of runing of shads" and suggested that residents could use other mills on smaller tributaries during the shoaling season. In reply, 55 residents of downstream Wayne County reminded the legislature of "the advantage and Benifit of good and useful Mills to their Inhabitance, Perticular in Dry Seasons" and alleged "that the fish taken up the Said River Can in no wise be as much Benifit to the Inhabitance as but few fish Come up said River of late years."[28]

Of the 138 signers of the Johnston County pro-fish petition, 80 could be identified in the manuscript returns of 1810. Of these, fully 63.3 percent were nonslaveholders. Of the 55 signers of the Wayne County pro-mill petition, 43 could be located in the census, and 69.8 percent were slaveholders. Moreover, the Johnston County signers owned an average of 1.8 slaves each, while the Wayne County petitioners owned an average of 5.3.[29]

Defenders of the Little River mills warned the legislature that the petitioners who sought fishing opportunities were only "a few Intrusted Indeviduals with their Influenc'd Subscribers," and at least one of the Johnston County signers appears to have been an owner of one of those smaller mills, located on tributaries that could expect more business if the mainstream mills were closed for the fishing season. The census evidence shows, however, that the majority of fish supporters from Johnston County were a tight-knit group of neighbors. The 138 signers shared only 64 surnames among them; they included 10 Oneals, 8 Bayleys, 5 Richardsons, and 5 Stancells. Of the 80 identified names, 74 appeared on 7 adjacent pages of the census manuscript, while their 43 Wayne County antagonists were scattered across 44 pages. Finally, the disparity of wealth between the two groups is striking. As in Edgecombe, Nash, and Franklin counties, a large majority of the shad-fishing kinsmen on Little River were nonslaveholders who still counted on their hooks, lines, and nets to meet their families' needs for protein.[30]

The language used by petitioners to defend their access to the shad runs stressed that the community's rights to its food supply were superior to the private property rights of millowners. Many petitions declared that fish were a gift from God or "Nature" to humanity in general. In 1776, 236 petitioners from Sussex County, Virginia, described the shad runs as "this great blessing & advantage which kind providence intended bountifully to bestow on all such as should live on or near the [Nottoway] river." The North Carolina petitioners from Nash and Franklin counties likewise referred to "the fish that the allmity intended for all man kind." An 1805 petition from citizens residing near the Uwharrie River in Montgomery County, North Carolina, complained that milldams "deprived [them] of the benefits that providence by nature has bestowed upon us," while an 1830 missive from the Yadkin and Pee Dee basins agreed "that the fish was made for the people at large." In South Carolina, citizens on the Broad and Saluda rivers complained that milldams deprived them of "the Bounty of Providence," while those on the Broad and Pacolet rivers asked that "every person have an equal chance [for fish] as intended by the god of nature." Quoting the language of a petition that is no longer extant, a Georgia statute declared that "a great number of the citizens of the counties of Wilkes, Oglethorpe, Elbert, Jackson, and Franklin, are improperly and unjustly restrained from partaking of the advantages and benefits which nature has ordained and granted them."[31]

Petitioners likewise demanded protection in the name of republican equality. "We are rougued out of a part of our rights," cried residents of North Carolina's Yadkin and Pee Dee river valley in 1830, as they demanded an amended fish law "Such as will give Every free person equal Justice." Remonstrating against the operator of a seine, or massive commercial fishing net, who cut off their customary access to shad, Edgecombe County fishermen "deem[ed] it unjust that they should be denied this great blessing and their neighbor be permitted in violation of the spirit of the Constitution to enjoy a monopoly." An 1825 protest against a milldam in Surry County, North Carolina, likewise demanded that the legislature "consider the many in prefferance of one Individual."[32]

South Carolina grievants were even more adamant in their claims of republican equality. In 1792, the inhabitants along Big Lynches Creek called themselves "Justly Entituled to an Equal Distribution of Justice with Other Men" and insisted "on the goodness & wisdom of the Legislature to Devise some method of Redress which shall be Permanent & lasting." Almost two decades later, 95 residents of the Union and Spartanburg districts combined religious and republican themes, calling for

> a law to open . . . tiger River for the free passage of boats and fish as both
> are our natural Rights the free gift of god and we as free men natural
> born citizens and Republicans in spirit and princible plead for our natural
> Rights as both are profitable and Desirable.[33]

No matter how much state legislators may have sympathized with the interests of commercial mill operators, they were normally reluctant to offend such large numbers of complaining constituents. Their preferred solution was to require the installation of slopes, thus preserving the interests of millers and fishermen alike. Alternatively, millers could agree to open sluices or gates in their dams to allow the passage of boats and fish in season. Legislators took pains to bar fishermen from operating too close to the slopes and sluices, fully aware that use of these bottlenecks as de facto fish traps would defeat the purpose of the regulations. Virginia adopted a general law to this effect as early as 1769 and refined it in 1772, 1785, and 1792. In 1787 North Carolina enacted a general statute that authorized counties to appoint commissioners to inspect streams and to keep the deepest quarter of all major riverbeds open for the passage of fish during a specified season in the spring. South Carolina passed a similar law in 1827. In addition, all the southeastern states continued to pass local and private laws to regulate fishing and milling on particular rivers and streams, with Georgia relying exclusively on such measures.[34]

The only problem with these political compromises was that they did not work. Stubbornly, the fish proved much less responsive to petitions than were the legislators. As population rose in the South Atlantic states and a rising level of commercial activity increased pressure on the region's river systems, petitioners on both sides of the issue agreed that the number of shad was steadily declining, regardless of the slopes and sluices in the existing milldams. As in the controversy at the Great Falls of the Tar, fishermen often explained the problem by insisting that the slopes were not working properly and ought to be redesigned or that the dams ought to be completely opened in fishing season.[35] As early as 1776, Virginians mourned "that your petitioners were once bless'd with great plenty of fine fish which were maynely catch'd as they came up Nottoway River." Despite the passage of two laws to require openings for the fish to pass, petitioners complained that millowners had evaded the requirements and the shad had ceased to run. In Winton County, South Carolina, settlers on the upper branches of the Savannah River recalled in 1794 that "a great plenty of Fish came up said Waters yearly," until John Rutledge built his sawmill downstream. Four years later, complainants along the Saluda River in South Carolina declared that the current was too strong over local slopes and asked that milldams be opened "to the mud sill" for the duration of every fishing season. "Of late years," agreed petitioners from Little River in Fairfield district in 1811, "It has become a rare thing for a Shad to be caught in that river except within a few miles of its mouth." Instead of blaming milldams, however, they pointed to the practice of felling timber into streams and the excessive use of fish traps where the Little River joined the Broad.[36]

Millowners seized upon uncertainty over the cause of dwindling shoals to argue that dams were not to blame for the problem and that mills were more important to the region than the few fish that might still penetrate the backcountry. "We do not know the laws that determine the migration of fish," admitted mill supporters living between the Tyger and Enoree rivers in upper South Carolina, "but their rout is of late entirely diverted from these two rivers." Darlington County millowners claimed that in 1797 they had gone to great expense to build locks in their dams, but "very few fish run up the same." By 1828, supporters of a mill at Grendol Shoals on the Pacolet River near Spartanburg, South Carolina, assured themselves that other downstream dams had ended the local shad fishery long ago. "I do not consider the passage of fish of any importance since the erection of the 'Columbia Dam,'" wrote one. "It is very seldom we hear of a Shad being caught."[37]

Balancing the profits from mills against the presumed lack of profits from fish, mill supporters applied a balance-sheet logic that ignored the use value of shad to impoverished local fishermen, as well as the intangible rewards they derived from the camaraderie of the fishing experience. In 1783, led by Richard Bennehan, founder of one of North Carolina's most opulent mercantile and planter dynasties, mill supporters from the upper Neuse River valley defended their proposal for a new mill on the site of "Daniels fish camp" by remarking that the "mill will be much more profit then the fish that come up said river." More than four decades later, defenders of the mill at Grendol Shoals averred that "the few fish that would pass that high . . . would not pay for in twenty years the value of the loss that would be sustained by the country adjacent in one year on account of the destruction of the mills."[38]

Another clue to the unpopularity of shad fishing among some local leaders appeared in an 1825 statute from Maryland, which required the clerk of a county court to issue retail liquor licenses to all operators of shad and herring fisheries during the annual runs. If the annual fishing season had become the occasion for heavy drinking and a carnival atmosphere, it is easy to see why the guardians of public order viewed it with suspicion. As early as 1808, mill supporters from upper South Carolina gave hints of this attitude. Their language associated fishing with the survival among poor men of a collective culture in which the gathering of free food from the rivers doubtless mixed with generous indulgence in liquor, boasting, and horseplay, possibly followed by outbursts of fighting and other violations of public order. "Was there not a single obstruction on said rivers," declared mill supporters on the Tyger and Enoree rivers, "there would not come up as many fish as would be an inducement to an *industrious* planter to neglect his farm & attend a fishery even if he had the monopoly of them all." State protection of the shad runs, they claimed, "affords an inducement to idleness, by tempting the attendance of numbers, at the fisheries, for days together, whose attention at that season is greatly needed in their farms, and who are, perhaps, not rewarded with a half a dozen of fish." Clearly indicating their moral disapproval, these signers believed that public policy should discourage behavior they regarded as lazy and irresponsible and prompt a more enterprising spirit of industry and individualism among the poor. The artist David Hunter Strother strongly reinforced this view of fishing with his depiction of shad fishing in late antebellum North Carolina, which contrasted the somnolence of the individual fisherman with the industrial efficiency of the commercial operation based on slave labor.[39]

These arguments touched the heart of the quarrel over mills and fish, for a deep clash of values lay beneath the surface dispute between rival claimants for the benefits of public policy. The emergent culture of the marketplace stood on one side, celebrating hard work and personal advancement. The culture of an older subsistence community, long disparaged as "Lubberland" by elite observers, took the other side, depending on natural abundance, the rhythms of nature, and the consumption needs of its members to regulate its work life.[40]

In the decades between the American Revolution and the age of Jackson, the culture of subsistence clearly persisted in the southern backcountry, but the culture of the marketplace just as clearly grew stronger. The trend appeared earliest in Virginia, where late eighteenth-century demands for open rivers began to treat the needs of fishermen as secondary to the draft requirements of boat traffic. By the 1790s, petitions from Southside counties drained by tributaries of the James and the Roanoke commonly asked for roads, ferries, town charters, and inspection stations for tobacco and flour, rather than protection for migrating shad. By 1796, tobacco plantations were expanding in the upper Roanoke Valley, and most petitioners ignored the fishing issue as they begged the assembly "to lessen if possible the expense & difficulty of transporting the produce of their lands to market." Similar requests appeared in neighboring capitals. In 1797, residents of Cheraw District in South Carolina boasted of the two stores and numerous saw and gristmills that adorned the banks of Black Creek. Like the Orangeburg residents who protested the dam of the Edisto Sawmills, the Cheraw petitioners mentioned a need for fish slopes, but their principal demand was that all milldams be required to provide locks for the passage of boats and floating timber. Other South Carolina documents mentioned the need for mills to process wheat into flour, not for family consumption, but for export. In 1795, for example, defenders of a Tyger River mill in the Newberry District rebutted complaints by insisting that "there are not Creeks suitable to Erect other Mills not even to grind meal for Bread for the Inhabitants of these parts, much less to manufacture Flour for market which your Memorialists expect will soon become a Staple of their Produce." Contemporary Georgia statutes gave equal stress to fishing and navigation on the Savannah and other rivers, and they declared that "the erection and establishment of merchant mills [for grinding flour] are objects of utility, and the first importance to the citizens of this state."[41]

Intensified agriculture in the backcountry also had an unintended effect on stream ecology that few petitioners remarked on, though it undoubtedly affected the behavior of the shad. Edward Wood, an experienced commercial fisherman on Albemarle Sound, reported in 1871 that "the fish . . . always avoid . . . muddy water." According to Wood, "the freshets of the Roanoke river frequently prove disastrous to the success of the fishermen, pouring large quantities of muddy water into the Sound, which color the water for forty miles below its mouth." Long before 1871, however, petitions casually complained of "the frequent freshes" and sometimes blamed the absence of fish on the development of large sandbars at the mouths of tributaries.[42]

Floods and sandbars resulted from the stripping of forest cover in the southern watersheds, which led to increased storm runoff, soil erosion, and torrents of muddy water. By the early nineteenth century, the extensive clearing of southern forests by farmers searching for "new ground" to replace "old fields" had led to complaints of timber shortage in such widely scattered places as Lunenburg County, Virginia, and McIntosh County, Georgia. According to later investigations, nothing could be worse for the shad. "During heavy rains the plowed soil upon the hillsides is easily washed into gullies," one early fish scientist observed, "filling them beyond their capacity and bringing into them masses of earth and other debris, thus covering the spawning-grounds. The freshets are soon over, and the flow of water in the streams becomes so small that shad are not induced to proceed so far up as formerly."[43] Obviously, the yeoman farmers of the backcountry shared responsibility for the destruction of the southern forest with their more commercially minded neighbors, unwittingly contributing to the ecological crisis they so earnestly deplored. It is possible, indeed, that farmers who lost access to shad responded by clearing more land and cultivating more crops to make up the difference either to exchange for the salted, or "pickled," products of commercial fishermen or to feed to hogs in final preparation for slaughter. In doing so, they would have made the problems of erosion and runoff even worse.[44]

The commercialization of fishing itself, however, was the most glaring and probably the most important factor in the decline of the shad population. Though most yeoman fishermen intended to eat their catches at home, some ambitious settlers had quickly realized that the annual shoals of shad could become the basis for a thriving business in pickled fish. Several Virginia petitioners admitted that they "were induced to purchase their Lands at a very high price Through Motives of Deriveing grate Advantages from the Fish," and an 1812 Georgia statute mentioned the "very exorbitant prices" given for lands along the Oconee River, which had been "considerably enhanced by certain shad fisheries which were said to be attached thereto." The construction of elaborate and expensive stone fish traps in South Carolina rivers likewise reflected the efforts of some inland entrepreneurs to develop a profitable fishing industry.[45]

The most extensive shad fisheries did not develop on inland rivers, however, but in the protected coastal sounds and estuaries that the shad and herring entered to begin their lengthy journey to the branch heads. Chesapeake Bay and the large rivers, such as the Potomac, that emptied into it as well as Albemarle and Pamlico sounds in North Carolina were ideal spots for commercial shad and herring fisheries, for wide expanses of relatively shallow water made it easy to manipulate large seines there, and broad sandy beaches offered suitable locations for landing and cleaning the catch. As early as 1807, Albemarle Sound became the center of a major business. By 1840, the United States census reported the production of 73,359 barrels of pickled fish in North Carolina, chiefly in the counties on the sounds. Virginians added 30,315 more barrels, while South Carolina and Georgia reported no more than 425 and 14 barrels, respectively. Wholesale distributors in Baltimore and the ports of Virginia marketed the salted catch to customers throughout the upper South, many of them planters seeking inexpensive rations for their slaves.[46]

The methods used by commercial fishermen to collect such vast stocks of fish differed considerably from the hand-held "dip nets" of subsistence fishermen in the interior. Early producers set "wares, dams, or stoppages" across stream channels to trap entire shoals of fish. Later operators preferred to "shoot" a massive seine across the main channel of a given stream or estuary, thereby capturing virtually everything that swam in it. In the practice known as "double seining," workers used windlasses to haul in one net while others shot out a second net, thereby preventing the passage of more fish while the first seine was unloaded. Working around the clock in the shoaling season, big operators at favored landing sites near the mouths of rivers could thus monopolize the bounty of the waters. A large force of male and female slaves to set and haul the nets and clean, salt, and pack the catch for sale was an essential part of such large-scale operations.[47]

Commercial fishing had a dramatic impact on the sound region and the lower reaches of the rivers that fed the sounds. In contrast to the picture of idle yeomen frolicking on inland riverbanks, waiting days for a half a dozen shad, the scene at major fisheries was intense and overpowering. As early as 1807, the youthful James Cathcart Johnston, heir to the stately Hayes plantation outside Edenton wrote his cousin James Iredell Jr., about the latter's anticipated return from college. "You will see Roanoke in all its glory—cover'd with Seines—its bank strewed with fish carts—fish & fish guts—more fragrant than the roses & lilies with which poets & romance writers have decorated their streams & rivulets." The offal that Johnston joked about, however, would soon be highly prized by Albemarle planters, who purchased it to restore the fertility of their depleted fields. Leases for prime fishing beaches were occasionally offered in exchange for the offal that a fishery produced, a practice that occasionally gave rise to litigation, which the adult James Iredell Jr. later recorded faithfully in his compilation of the decisions of North Carolina's Supreme Court.[48]

Generally speaking, North Carolina legislators recognized the injustice of monopolistic fishing practices and sought to limit them when prodded by petitions. As early as 1764, the colonial assembly banned the use of double seines in fishing season by "avaricious persons" in the waters of the Meherrin, Pee Dee, and Catawba rivers. William Tryon, the same royal governor who crushed the North Carolina Regulators, shared the commercial values of leading coastal fishermen. He thus vetoed a bill to restrict the operation of seines, "esteeming it prejudicial to the general interest of the country and destructive of that spirit of industry and commerce so much wanted to be encouraged in this colony."[49]

Following independence, and well into the nineteenth century, the North Carolina General Assembly sought to balance the needs of commerce and subsistence by protecting customary practices that allowed all watermen an equal chance at catching fish, while it condemned the greed that inspired persistent efforts to obtain a monopoly. An 1820 preamble thus denounced "many evil-minded persons [who] . . . increase their own profits and injure others" and firmly forbade certain methods of placing nets that petitioners had denounced as unfair. A crazy quilt of private acts proliferated to regulate fishing on each major river, generally restricting the use of double seines and seines that extended more than three-quarters of the way across a main channel (especially at the mouths of streams) from late February to mid-May. Legislation also commonly banned the operation of seines on Sunday during the same period, not only to honor the sabbath but also to allow some shoals to escape upstream for other fishermen. Like their counterparts in other states, North Carolina legislators were normally willing to require millowners either to open sluices in their milldams during the spring fishing season or to furnish the dams with slopes to accommodate the upstream migrations.[50]

Despite the legislature's efforts to ensure a fair distribution of the catch, sound fishermen were increasingly successful in monopolizing the annual run of shad and herring. An 1840 report to the legislature claimed that the seventeen fisheries of Albemarle Sound had employed 765 hands to pack 25,500 barrels of fish in the previous season, at a cost of $102,000. Six years later, more than 1,000 slaves were employed, while the number of seines in Albemarle Sound reached seventy by 1852. Choice fishing sites traded hands for steep prices, and the cost of a single seine was quoted at $3,000. The industry had become concentrated in the hands of the largest planters of the shoreline, proprietors of graceful mansions known by such names as Belvidere, Montpelier, and Mulberry Hill. In the face of such competition, upstream yeomen stood little chance.[51]

The results of this business were quickly apparent. The Select Committee on Fisheries reported in 1852 that the rivers that had once overflowed with shad, rockfish, and herring were now virtually empty. Seining had been abandoned in the principal rivers and now took place in the estuary of the Chowan River and in Albemarle Sound alone, "where seins are used of more than a mile in length and thousands of drag and set nets dot over the waters in every direction." Even so, the size of the catch had radically declined, and the price of salted fish had doubled from an unstated level "but a few years ago." Though commercial fishermen maintained that fish still constituted "a necessary article of food . . . [for] the most indigent of our citizens," the power to obtain these fish directly from streams had disappeared.[52] For all practical purposes, shad were now available solely through the market economy.

Observers of the late antebellum fishing industry agreed with earlier petitioners that "the annual periodical supply of shad and herring in our waters is . . . one of the most highly prized benefactions bestowed by the Great Creator, on mankind." Legislators also feared the political consequences of any interference with the people's access to fish. "They indulge an habitual attachment to this kind of food," lawmakers admitted, "and would probably rather be subjected to almost any other privation than to be deprived of this highly prized enjoyment."[53] Perhaps because they thought the fish had come from "heaven," however, no one stopped to ask if the declining catch had anything to do with a massive assault on the animals' reproductive cycle. Legislators of 1852 simply agreed that the remaining fish should be equally shared and asked how this goal might be accomplished.

The committee charged with devising a solution acknowledged that fishing regulations had been intended to benefit poor people who lived along the shore. They noted, however, that regulations did nothing for poor people who lived elsewhere and sententiously declined to condone any special privileges for the former over the latter. Applying the logic of Victorian laissez-faire, they concluded that the best way to ensure an equal share of fish for everyone was to suspend *all* regulation of the fishing industry, except for a ban on the use of nets and seines between sundown on Saturday and midnight on Sunday. This reform would protect the sabbath and make the catch as large as possible, giving all inhabitants of the state an equal chance to buy whatever fish they could afford. Needless to say, this recommendation closely followed the suggestions of the fishing industry's own lobbyist.[54]

The Select Committee on Fisheries swathed the new policy in sentimental rhetoric and suggested that it only coincided with long-established realities.

Such is the anxious desire of the people to secure a supply of fish in the spring of the year that a stranger to their habits would be astonished to see the innumerable wagons and carts wending their toilsome way from one hundred to one hundred and fifty miles, to the fisheries in quest of their accustomed supply. . . . The owner of the wagon, and the poor man with his horse and cart, constituting nearly the whole of his wealth, find their way to the fisheries, and with their hard earnings, purchase their loads of fish, and go their way rejoicing. It is true, they pay dearly for this indulgence, and it is difficult to understand how those who travel the greater distances can afford it, but they meet the disadvantages cheerfully, and come and go apparently joyous and happy.[55]

So far as state policy on fishing was concerned, this report marked an end to the independence and empowerment that had once been established by republican government and the subsistence economy. Well into Reconstruction, state lawmakers indulged popular hopes by adopting more measures to promote the passage of fish up inland rivers, but laws alone could not restore what earlier generations had called "the common Rights of mankind."[56] As the legislators acknowledged, poor North Carolinians who bought fish instead of catching them were themselves hooked on the need for a cash income and the "hard earnings" that market dependency entailed. Despite a long history of protest, the evolution of commercial fishing had left them no choice, and those who looked cheerful were undoubtedly making the best of a painful situation. What the American Revolution had granted, the market revolution was taking away.

The transformation of Tarheel fishing found its echo in other patterns of state life. As petitions for pardons, divorces, and the erection of fish ladders declined, the number of requests for turnpike roads and bank charters went up. Yeomen occasionally protested when such "privileged monopolies" trod excessively on popular liberties, and resentment of their inroads stimulated the growth of Andrew Jackson's Democratic Party. For the most part, however, North Carolina yeomen found that relations with their more privileged neighbors were increasingly mediated through the institutions of the market. Their republican traditions had ill prepared them for the shift, and they had no ready means of answering when legislators applied the rhetoric of equality to guarantee the monopolies of planter-fishermen and other representatives of commercial privilege.

It was probably no coincidence that the end of the inland shad fishery coincided with the heyday of the South's second party system, though direct connections remain elusive. Political parties drew their energy from a reaction against large enterprises such as the commercial fisheries of Albemarle Sound. They also co-opted the popular anger that had once fueled petition campaigns and turned it to electoral purposes. Perhaps as a consequence, petitions against local social and economic conditions are rare after 1830.

The success of inland shad fishermen in protecting "the common Rights of mankind" should not be underestimated, however. From the middle of the eighteenth century to the middle of the nineteenth, southern colonial assemblies and legislatures had met the demand for protection of their rivers with a welter of local legislation requiring fish slopes, fish sluices, fishing seasons, fish commissioners, limits on seining, and seemingly endless similar measures. The campaign at the Edisto Sawmills was among these victories; South Carolina legislators insisted that a channel around the offending dam be available for both boats and fish, specified its hours of operation, and appointed commissioners to enforce the regulation.[57] But such victories held little meaning in the long run. Eventually, the shad stopped coming despite the sluices, and upstream fishermen found no means to coax them back.

The yeomanry's emphasis on "common rights" to take fish that were assumed to come in unlimited numbers "from God" had been a creative and successful appropriation of republican political principles. Though rewarded with political success, this strategy could not address the fundamentally biological issues of fish reproduction and stream health that would ultimately control the presence of fish in southern rivers. The fish, after all, did not come directly "from God." They came instead from fish eggs, which had to be deposited and fertilized in appropriate spawning beds and had to be allowed to mature for a return trip to the sea before any new generation of shad could be brought to southern rivers. Milldam petitions were normally silent on the subject of fish reproduction, and neither yeomen nor commercial fishermen showed more than a foggy awareness of the biological reasons for the shad migrations. Consequently, neither group was intellectually or culturally prepared to devise solutions that would take into account the shad's needs along with their own. Not until the end of the nineteenth century would a shad-fishing industry in the Albemarle and the Chesapeake revive, based on the culture of young shad in fish hatcheries. Today, hatchery efforts continue, and sports fishermen are excited by the chance to take a few shad from choice rivers, but the massive inland spawning runs of the past are probably gone forever.[58]

More immediately, the yeomanry's emphasis on common rights proved vulnerable to economic reasoning that glorified markets as the most appropriate means for distributing the resources of nature. If the "public" should be the ultimate beneficiary of the fish, it was easy to argue that the marketplace served a much wider public than the inhabitants of any particular stream bank; the market should therefore have privileged access to the fish that God had sent to men in general. This was essentially the unanswered argument of the North Carolina Select Committee on Fisheries in 1852.

The fishermen's ultimate inability to fend off the milldams that interfered with their catches likewise reflected their difficulty in opposing the system of agriculture of which milldams were part. Machine-ground corn and "merchant's mills" for grinding wheat were aspects of an expanding and more commercialized farming complex that yeomen did not fully resist. The new system had its undeniable advantages. Women who were spared the backbreaking labor of grinding corn by hand must have been especially grateful for the relief afforded by a water-powered mill. Many successful male farmers, who began to patronize the new mills and substituted pork or store-bought fish for the shad that used to appear in the river, undoubtedly shared similar views. For poor men, however, the end of the shad runs brought a corresponding loss of personal dignity and independence. "The poorest Planter has as much Right to the delicaccies of this Country, as the richest," John Brickell had boasted in 1737, "nay the very Labourer is intituled to the Same Privilege."[59] With the shad gone, the ability of antebellum poor whites to make the same claim was diminished, though not destroyed.

Human bondage stood at the center of the agricultural system that displaced the shad. As analysis of the Tar River and Little River petitioners of 1810 demonstrates, slaveholders were far more likely to favor milldams than nonslaveholders. When the shad stopped coming inland to feed the white poor, moreover, they were caught at the coast by slaves to feed more slaves throughout the region. Yet slavery was scarcely mentioned in the petition wars over fish and milldams. In facing threats to their customary chance to fish for subsistence, as in so many other aspects of antebellum life, yeomen protested the impact of slavery on their lives, but only in muted terms. The importance of slavery to the outcomes of southern fishing disputes highlights the underlying differences between the protests of South Atlantic fishermen and their New England counterparts. The expansion of northern textile mills threatened the independence of yeoman households, but it also offered jobs and markets to farm families who reconciled themselves to the change. Aside from marginal opportunities as overseers and day laborers, the expanding plantation offered few equivalents to the yeoman families in its path. In the South, the frustrated yeoman could make the transition from fish and hand-ground cornmeal to cotton and wheat flour, or he could make his retreat to the beckoning West, hoping to re-create in Trans-Appalachia the world of independence that had eluded him near the seaboard. If he chose to remain, the purchase of slaves and increasing sensitivity to the power of the marketplace would be indispensable to his success. Alternately, he might remain as a yeoman inside an expanding plantation belt, struggling to maintain his sense of white male equality while acknowledging the actual superiority of others, in a complex set of rituals and relationships we are only beginning to understand.[60]

To ascribe the coming of factories and the coming of plantations to the same "market revolution" expresses an important truth about the common processes affecting the experience of most antebellum Americans. The term will obscure more than it explains, however, if we forget that the kinds of markets and the things being marketed varied significantly from section to section, and even from neighborhood to neighborhood. So far as the shad were concerned, a dam was a dam, whether North or South, and the effect on reproduction and migration patterns was the same. For the fishermen who sought the shad, however, the purposes of the dam and the social and economic system it represented could make a profound difference. In the North, the closing of a stream might be balanced against the opening of job opportunities. In the South, a similar dam might open the way for domestic conveniences, marketing advances, and a network of paternal dependency upon the miller (and the slaveholder who stood behind him) that could not easily be calculated.

Whether he joined the culture of the milldam or rejected it, the southern yeoman would probably keep a love of hunting and fishing alive as an emblematic reminder of his cherished independence. Throughout the nineteenth and twentieth centuries, observers have called attention to the importance of outdoor sports, especially hunting and fishing, to a southern male ethos. In antebellum days, elite outdoorsmen such as South Carolina's

William Elliott emphasized the class differences between gentlemen who hunted and fished for sport and lesser sorts who took to the woods and waters in search of food.[61] While provisioning the family table never disappeared as a significant aspect of outdoor sports in the South, the decline of wildlife populations increasingly made food gathering secondary to the experience of male independence and camaraderie. For yeomen and gentry alike, fishing became a pastime expressing virility and "mastery," and thus a form of male bonding across classes, where it had once been an arena of class contention. An account of the transformation of fishing from its origins in food gathering to its development as a sport or leisure activity is beyond the scope of this essay, but it is clear that the early southern fascination with fish contributed to regional social culture long after the shad stopped running in vast numbers. Slavery, then, left its irresistible imprint on southern fishing. Like the mills themselves and their convenient products, slaves were an alluring menace to the yeoman way of life. They might undermine a traditional economy, but they offered obvious advantages to any free person who successfully exploited them. It would not be fair or accurate to say that yeoman fishermen ultimately chose slavery over shad, for the choice was never that simple. The petition campaigns demonstrate that the expansion of slave-based commercial agriculture was strongly contested in its day. But when the biological obstacles to the fishes' reproduction combined with the attractiveness of slave-based "progress," disappearance of the shad, and so much else, was the unavoidable consequence. To put it another way, the early republican period saw a critical moment of negotiation between the South's slaveholders and nonslaveholders. In the decades that immediately followed the American Revolution, the implied promises of republicanism clashed sharply with received traditions of deference and emerging patterns of commercial enterprise. In the ensuing confusion, petitioning became a favored political instrument for plain folk seeking to protect their independence from wealthier challengers. The outcome of these decades of negotiation saw the yeomanry's political equality increasingly secure, while their economic independence remained a hostage to the vagaries of the market. Implied support for slavery was an integral part of this development. The modest evidence of dams and fish testifies to the fragility of such an outcome, but the plain folk could obtain little better in the remaining years before secession.

Notes

1. Petition from the Orangeburg District, on the Edisto River, General Assembly Petition 1787-08-01 (South Carolina Department of Archives and History, Columbia).

2. Ibid.; "The humble Petition of the Inhabitants of Orangeburgh District living above the Edisto Saw Mills," General Assembly Petition 1792-87-01, ibid. Emphasis added.

3. Porte Crayon [David Hunter Strother], "North Carolina Illustrated. I—The Fisheries," *Harper's New Monthly Magazine*, 14 (March 1857), 438–47; Edward Wood, *To the President of the State Agricultural Society of North Carolina* (Edenton, 1871) (broadside, North Carolina Collection, Wilson Library, University of North Carolina, Chapel Hill). On fish in the southern food supply, see Sam Bowers Hilliard, *Hog Meat and Hoecake: Food Supply in the Old South, 1840–1860* (Carbondale, Ill.: Southern Illinois University Press, 1972), 85–87; Charles H. Stevenson, "Fisheries in the Ante-Bellum South," in *The South in the Building of the Nation*, vol. V: *Southern Economic History, 1607–1865*, ed. James C. Ballagh (Richmond, Va.: Southern Historical Publication Society, 1909), 267–71; and Joyce E. Chaplin, *An Anxious Pursuit: Agricultural Innovation and Modernity in the Lower South, 1730–1815* (Chapel Hill: University of North Carolina Press, 1993), 351–53.

4. William Waller M. Hening, comp., *The Statutes at Large; Being a Collection of All the Laws in Virginia, from the first Session of the Legislature in the Year 1619* (13 vols., Richmond, 1820–1823); William L. Saunders and Walter Clark, comps., *The Colonial and State Record of North Carolina* (30 vols., Raleigh, 1886–1914); Thomas Cooper and David J. McCord, comps., *The Statutes at Large of South Carolina* (10 vols., Columbia, 1836–1841); Augustin Smith Clayton, comp., *A Compilation of the Laws of Georgia, Passed by the Legislature Since the Political Year 1800, to the Year 1810, Inclusive* (Augusta, 1813); Oliver H. Prince, comp., *A Digest of the Laws of the State of Georgia* (Milledgeville, 1822); Henry Potter, J. L. Taylor, and Bartlet Yancey, comps., *Laws of the State of North Carolina* (2 vols., Raleigh, 1821); Samuel Shepherd, comp., *The Statutes at Large of Virginia from October Session 1792 to December Session 1806, Inclusive* (3 vols., Richmond, 1835–1836); and Lucius Q. C. Lamar, comp., *A Compilation of the Laws of the State of Georgia* (Augusta, 1821).

5. W. J. Cash, *The Mind of the South* (New York, N.Y.: Knopf, 1941), 14–16. See also Lewis Cecil Gray, *History of Agriculture in the Southern United States to 1860* (2 vols., Washington, D.C.: Carnegie Institution, 1932), I, 437–61; Ulrich Bonnell Phillips, *History of Transportation in the Eastern Cotton States to 1860* (New York, N.Y.: Columbia University Press, 1908); George Rogers Taylor, *The Transportation Revolution, 1811–1860* (New York, N.Y.: Rinehart, 1951); and Cecil K. Brown, *A State Movement in Railroad Development: The Story of North Carolina's First Effort to Establish an East and West Trunk Line Railroad* (Chapel Hill: University of North Carolina Press, 1928).

6. Steven Hahn, *The Roots of Southern Populism: Yeoman Farmers and the Transformation of the Georgia Upcountry, 1850–1890* (New York, N.Y.: Oxford University Press,

1983); Steven Hahn, "The Yeomanry of the Nonplantation South: Upper Piedmont Georgia, 1850–1860," in *Class, Conflict, and Consensus: Antebellum Southern Community Studies*, ed. Orville Vernon Burton and Robert C. McMath Jr. (Westport, Conn.: Greenwood Press, 1982), 29–56; Steven Hahn, "Hunting, Fishing, and Foraging: Common Rights and Class Relations in the Postbellum South," *Radical History Review*, 26 (1982), 37–64; Gavin Wright, *Political Economy of the Cotton South: Households, Markets, and Wealth in the Nineteenth Century* (New York, N.Y.: Norton, 1978); Gavin Wright and Howard Kunreuther, "Cotton, Corn, and Risk in the Nineteenth Century," *Journal of Economic History*, 35 (Sept. 1974), 526–51; Gavin Wright and Howard Kunreuther, "Cotton, Corn, and Risk in the Nineteenth Century: A Reply," *Explorations in Economic History*, 14 (April 1977), 183–95. On yeoman "independence" and its implications for class, race, and gender relations, see Stephanie McCurry, *Masters of Small Worlds: Yeoman Households, Gender Relations, and the Political Culture of the Antebellum South Carolina Low Country* (New York, N.Y.: Oxford University Press, 1995).

7. Charles Sellers, *The Market Revolution: Jacksonian America, 1815–1846* (New York, N.Y.: Oxford University Press, 1991); Morton Rothstein, "The Antebellum South as a Dual Economy: A Tentative Hypothesis," *Agricultural History*, 41 (Oct. 1967), 373–83; Lacy K. Ford Jr., *Origins of Southern Radicalism: The South Carolina Upcountry, 1800–1860* (New York, N.Y.: Oxford University Press, 1988); Rachel N. Klein, *Unification of a Slave State: The Rise of the Planter Class in the South Carolina Backcountry, 1760–1800* (Chapel Hill: University of North Carolina Press, 1990); David F. Weiman, "The Economic Emancipation of the Non-Slaveholding Class: Upcountry Farmers in the Georgia Cotton Economy," *Journal of Economic History*, 45 (March 1985), 71–93; David F. Weiman, "Farmers and the Market in Antebellum America: A View from the Georgia Upcountry," *Journal of Economic History*, 47 (Sept. 1987), 627–47; David F. Weiman, "Families, Farms, and Rural Society in Preindustrial America," *Research in Economic History*, suppl. 5 (1989), 255–77; Allan Kulikoff, "The Transition to Capitalism in Rural America," *William and Mary Quarterly*, 46 (Jan. 1989), 120–44; Harry L. Watson, "Conflict and Collaboration: Yeomen, Slaveholders, and Politics in the Antebellum South," *Social History*, 10 (Oct. 1985), 277–85.

8. Morton Horwitz, *The Transformation of American Law, 1780–1860* (Cambridge, Mass.: Harvard University Press, 1977), 34–53; Gordon Wood, *The Radicalism of the American Revolution* (New York, N.Y.: Knopf, 1992), 188–89, 324–25.

9. Gary Kulik, "Dams, Fish, and Farmers: Defense of Public Rights in Eighteenth-Century Rhode Island," in *The Countryside in the Age of Capitalist Transformation: Essays in the Social History of Rural America*, ed. Steven Hahn and Jonathan Prude (Chapel Hill: University of North Carolina Press, 1985), 25–50.

10. For the debate over the taxonomy of slavery, see Eugene D. Genovese, *The Political Economy of Slavery: Studies in the Economy and Society of the Slave South* (New York, N.Y.: Pantheon, 1965); Eugene D. Genovese, *Roll, Jordan, Roll: The World the Slaves Made* (New York, N.Y.: Pantheon, 1974); Robert William Fogel and Stanley L. Engerman, *Time on the Cross: The Economics of American Negro Slavery* (Boston, Mass.:

Little, Brown, 1974); Robert William Fogel, *Without Consent or Contract: The Rise and Fall of American Slavery* (New York, N.Y.: Norton, 1989); and James Oakes, *The Ruling Race: A History of American Slaveholders* (New York, N.Y.: Knopf, 1982); Steven Hahn and Jonathan Prude, "Introduction," in *Countryside in the Age of Capitalist Transformation*, ed. Hahn and Prude, 11–12.

11. See notes 6 and 7, above, for the literature on yeoman farming communities in eighteenth- and nineteenth-century America. On Piedmont yeoman communities, see Robert C. Kenzer, *Kinship and Neighborhood in a Southern Community: Orange County, North Carolina, 1849–1881* (Knoxville: University of Tennessee Press, 1987); William Byrd, "History of the Dividing Line," in *The Prose Works of William Byrd of Westover: Narratives of a Colonial Virginian*, ed. Louis B. Wright (Cambridge, Mass.: Belknap Press, 1966), 184; Charles Woodmason, *The Carolina Backcountry on the Eve of the Revolution*, ed. Richard J. Hooker (Chapel Hill: University of North Carolina Press, 1953), 15; Timothy Silver, *A New Face on the Countryside: Indians, Colonists, and Slaves in South Atlantic Forests, 1500–1800* (New York, N.Y.: Cambridge University Press, 1990), 96–97, 104–7, 135.

12. John Brickell, *The Natural History of North Carolina* (1737; Raleigh, N.C.: Reprinted by authority of the Trustees of the public libraries, 1911), 263–64. For nineteenth-century acts regulating the tolls of public mills, see Prince, *Digest of the Laws of the State of Georgia*, 339; Potter, Taylor, and Yancey, *Laws of the State of North Carolina*, I, 345; and Shepherd, *Statutes at Large of Virginia*, I, 137.

13. "To His Honor the Speaker, and Gent. of the House of Delegates," petition from Orange and Culpeper counties, Oct. 19, 1778, Culpeper County Legislative Petitions, 1776–1790 (Library of Virginia, Richmond); Peter Wood, *Black Majority: Negroes in Colonial South Carolina from 1670 through the Stono Rebellion* (New York, N.Y.: Knopf, 1975), 61–62.

14. *North Carolina Geological and Economic Survey, 1891–1921*, vol. 11; Hugh M. Smith, *The Fishes of North Carolina* (Raleigh, N.C.: E. M. Uzzell & Co., 1907), 122–29; Charles H. Stevenson, "The Restricted Inland Range of Shad due to Artificial Obstructions and Its Effects on Natural Reproduction," *Bulletin of the United States Fish Commission*, 17 (1897), 265–71.

15. Paul Hulton, *America, 1585: The Complete Drawings of John White* (Chapel Hill: University of North Carolina Press, 1984), 73, 75, 181; John Lawson, *A New Voyage to Carolina*, ed. Hugh Talmage Lefler (Chapel Hill: University of North Carolina Press, 1967), 66, 93, 160, 163, 218; Brickell, *Natural History of North Carolina*, 42.

16. Harry Roy Merrens, *Colonial North Carolina in the Eighteenth Century: A Study in Historical Geography* (Chapel Hill: University of North Carolina Press, 1964), 111–19.

17. "The Memorial of Sundry Citizens residing at and near Tiger River," Nov. 2, 1795, General Assembly Petition 1795-139-01 (South Carolina Department of Archives and History); "An Act to authorize Shaler Hillyer . . . to build a mill-dam across Broad River. . . ." (1815), in *Compilation of the Laws of the State of Georgia*, comp. Lamar, 494–98; Deposition of Archibald Boling, Dec. 1, 1828, General Assembly Petition ND-

1030-09 (South Carolina Department of Archives and History); "Petition of the Citizens of Union District," c. 1828, General Assembly Petition ND-1030-13, ibid.; Charles Howell, "Colonial Watermills in the Wooden Age," in *America's Wooden Age: Aspects of Its Early Technology*, ed. Brooke Hindle (Tarrytown, N.Y.: Sleepy Hollow Restorations, 1975), 120–59; "Mill," in *The Cyclopedia; Or, Universal Dictionary of Arts, Sciences, and Literature*, comp. Abraham Rees (41 vols., Philadelphia, 1810–1824), XXIV, n.p.

18. Fletcher M. Green, *Constitutional Development in the South Atlantic States, 1776–1860* (Chapel Hill: University of North Carolina Press, 1930); Jackson Turner Main, "Government by the People: The American Revolution and the Democratization of the Legislatures," *William and Mary Quarterly*, 23 (July 1966), 391–407.

19. Ruth Bogin, "Petitioning and the New Moral Economy of Post-Revolutionary America," *William and Mary Quarterly*, 45 (July 1988), 391–425. For examples of petitions relating to communal food supplies, see "The Petition of sundry inhabitants of the County of New Hanover," H. Dec. 13, 1791, box 3, Petitions (Miscellaneous), session of Dec. 1791–Jan. 1792, General Assembly Session Records (State Archives, North Carolina Division of Archives and History, Raleigh; the H. preceding a date indicates that a petition was originally introduced in the North Carolina House of Commons); "The petition of the Subscribers. . . . ," Sept. 1792, H. Nov. 24, 1792, box 4, Petitions, session of Nov. 1792–Jan. 1793, ibid.; and "To the Honourable the Genl. Assembly of the State of No. Carolina now Siting," H. Nov. 27, 1792, ibid.

20. Hening, *Statutes at Large*, VI, 291–93, VII, 321–22, 409–10, VIII, 581–83.

21. Saunders and Clark, *Colonial and State Records of North Carolina*, XXIV, 460; Cooper and McCord, comps., *Statutes at Large of South Carolina*, V, 217--18, 278–79, 383, 508–9, 647–48, 700–701; Clayton, *Compilation of the Laws of Georgia*, 80–81.

22. "The Petition of the freeholders and inhabitants of the Counties of Lunenburg and Mecklenburg," Oct. 31, 1776, Lunenburg County Legislative Petitions, 1776–1806 (Library of Virginia); "To his Excellency Josiah Martin . . . " [1771], in *Colonial and State Records of North Carolina*, comp. Saunders and Clark, IX, 87–88; "The Petition of the Inhabitants of moore and other Counties . . . ," Petitions, session of Nov. 1792–Jan. 1793, General Assembly Session Records; "Your memorialists citizens of the county of Edgecombe . . . ," Petitions (Miscellaneous), box 6, session of Nov. 1830–Jan. 1831, ibid.

23. "To His Honor the Speaker, and Gent. of the House of Delegates," petition from Orange and Culpeper counties, Oct. 19, 1778, Culpeper County Legislative Petitions, 1776–1790.

24. Kemp Plumer Battle, "A History of the Rocky Mount Mills," in Herbert Bemerton Battle, *The Battle Book: A Genealogy of the Battle Family in America* (Montgomery, Ala.: Paragon Press, 1930), 177–82; "The Petition of Sundry the Inhabetants of Nash County," Dec. 4, 1810, General Assembly Session Records; "The petition of Sundry Inhebitents of Franklin County," Dec. 4, 1810, ibid.

25. "To the Honorable the Genel Assembly of the State of North Carolina" [1810], box 3, session of Nov.–Dec. 1810, General Assembly Session Records; "We the inhabitants of the Counties of Nash & Edgecombe," ibid.

26. Wright, *Political Economy of the Cotton South*, 43–88.

27. Manuscript Population Schedules, Edgecombe County, North Carolina, Third Census of the United States, 1810 (microfilm: reel 40, M 252), Records of the Bureau of the Census, RG 29 (National Archives, Washington, D.C.); Manuscript Population Schedules, Nash County, North Carolina, Third Census of the United States (reel 41, M 252), ibid.

28. Manuscript Population Schedules, Johnston County, North Carolina, Third Census of the United States (reel 40, M 252), ibid.; Manuscript Population Schedules, Wayne County, North Carolina, Third Census of the United States (reel 42), ibid.; "The Petition of the undersigned Inhabitants of Johnston County," [1810], Petitions, box 3, session of Nov.–Dec. 1810, General Assembly Session Records; "Whereas We the Inhabitance of the County of Wayne. . . . ," Nov. 20, 1810, ibid.

29. The value of *t* for these distributions was 3.2, which confirms a significant difference of means at the .0023 level. Manuscript Population Schedules, Johnston County, North Carolina, Third Census of the United States (reel 40, M 252), Records of the Bureau of the Census; Manuscript Population Schedules, Wayne County, North Carolina, Third Census of the United States (reel 43), ibid.

30. In 1806, Freeman Killingsworth, owner of eight slaves, asked the Nash County court for a license to build a mill on Mocoson Creek, on the boundary of Nash and Johnston counties. See Nash County Mill Records, CR 069.928.3 (State Archives, North Carolina Division of Archives and History). Manuscript Population Schedules, Johnston County, North Carolina, Third Census of the United States, pp. 233–40 (reel 40, M 252), Records of the Bureau of the Census; Manuscript Population Schedules, Wayne County, North Carolina, Third Census of the United States, pp. 802–46 (reel 43), ibid.

31. "The Petition of the inhabitants of Sussex County," Oct. 31, 1776, Sussex County Legislative Petitions (Library of Virginia); "The Petition of Sundry the Inhabetants of Nash County," Dec. 4, 1810, General Assembly Session Records; "The petition of the inhabitants of Montgomery County," Petitions (Miscellaneous), box 3, session of Nov.–Dec. 1805, General Assembly Session Records; "To the Honorable The General Assembly of North Carolina," Nov. 1830, Petitions (Miscellaneous), box 6, session of Dec. 1830–Jan. 1831, ibid.; "The petition and Remonstrance of the citizens Inhabiting the Fork, between the Broad and Saluda Rivers," Feb. 21, 1784, General Assembly Petition 1784-47 (South Carolina Department of Archives and History); "The Petition of the Commissioners of Navigation on Broad and Pacolet Rivers and other citizens," Nov. 29, 1810, General Assembly Petition 1810-140, ibid.; Clayton, Compilation of the Laws of Georgia, 459–60.

32. "To the Honorable the General Assembly of North Carolina," Nov. 1830, Petitions (Miscellaneous), box 6, session of Dec. 1830–Jan. 1831, General Assembly Session Records; "Your memorialists citizens of the county of Edgecombe . . . ," ibid.; "The Remonstrance and petition of Sundry of the Inhabitants of Surry County," House Committee Reports (Propositions and Grievances—Miscellaneous), box 4, session of Nov. 1825–Jan. 1826, ibid.

33. "The Petition of the Inhabitants of Big Lynches Creek," Dec. 4, 1792, General Assembly Petition 1792-215-01 (South Carolina Department of Archives and History); "To the honourable Senate and house of Representatives," Oct. 12, 1811, General Assembly Petition 1811-112, ibid.

34. Hening, *Statutes at Large*, VIII, 361–62, 581–83, XII, 187–90; Shepherd, *Statutes at Large of Virginia*, I, 136–39; Saunders and Clark, *Colonial and State Records of North Carolina*, XXIV, 902–3; Cooper and McCord, *Statutes at Large of South Carolina*, VI, 340–41; Lamar, *Compilation of the Laws of the State of Georgia*, 487–90.

35. On fishway designs, see Stevenson, "Restricted Inland Range of Shad," 268.

36. "The petition of the inhabitants of Sussex County," Oct. 31. 1776, Sussex County Legislative Petitions 1776; "Petition of Sundry Inhabitants of Winton county," General Assembly Petition 1794-157-01 (South Carolina Department of Archives and History); Petition of the Inhabitants of Abbeville and Laurens districts, n.d., General Assembly Petition 1800-137, ibid.; Petition of the Inhabitants of Fairfield district, Nov. 10, 1811, General Assembly Petition 1811-116, ibid.

37. Petition from Union, Newberry, and Laurens districts, Nov. 20, 1808, General Assembly Petition 1808-3 (South Carolina Department of Archives and History); Petition of Robert Ellison and others of Darlington County, General Assembly Petition 1797-13, ibid.; Samuel M. Gowdey to John H. Farnandis, Jan. 16, 1828, attached to General Assembly Petition ND-1030, ibid.

38. "Petition from Wake county and adjoining parts of Orange & Granville," box 1, Miscellaneous Petitions, session of April–May 1783, General Assembly Session Records. For Richard Bennehan, see Jean Anderson, *Piedmont Plantation: The Bennehan-Cameron Family and Lands in North Carolina* (Durham, N.C.: Historic Preservation Society of Durham, 1985), 1–14. Petition of the Union district, General Assembly Petition ND-1030-27 (South Carolina Department of Archives and History).

39. *Laws Made and Passed by the General Assembly of the State of Maryland . . . 1825* (Annapolis, 1826), 83; Petition of the Union, Newberry, and Laurens districts, Nov. 20, 1808, General Assembly Petition 1808-30 (South Carolina Department of Archives and History), emphasis added; Strother, "North Carolina Illustrated," 435, 437.

40. Byrd, "History of the Dividing Line," 204–5. Cf. Sellers, *Market Revolution*, 3–33; and Chaplin, *Anxious Pursuit*, 131–84.

41. "The petision of sundry inhabetants of the County of Halifax," Nov. 7, 1791, Halifax County Legislative Petitions, 1792–1796 (Library of Virginia); "Petition of the inhabitants of Halifax county, Va. and Caswell county, N.C.," Nov. 15, 1796, ibid. See also Halifax County Legislative Petitions, 1776–1791, 1792–1796, 1797–1805, ibid.; Mecklenburg County Legislative Petitions, 1792, ibid.; and Pittsylvania County Legislative Petitions, 1776–1793, ibid. "Humble Petition of Sundry Inhabitants of Cheraw District residing on and near the Stream of Black Creek," Dec. 9, 1797, General Assembly Petition 1797-014 (South Carolina Department of Archives and History); "The Memorial of Sundry Citizens residing at and near Tiger River," Nov. 2, 1795, General Assembly Petition 1795-139-01, ibid.; Clayton, comp., *Compilation of the Laws of Georgia*, 80–81; Lamar, comp., *Compilation of the Laws of the State of Georgia*, 483.

42. Wood, *To the President of the State Agricultural Society of North Carolina*, n.p.; Petition from the residents of Little River in Fairfield District, General Assembly Petition 1811-116 (South Carolina Department of Archives and History). See also petition from the Orangeburg District, on the Edisto River, General Assembly Petition 1787-08-01, ibid.

43. Silver, *New Face on the Countryside*, 114–15; Petition from Lunenburg County, Dec. 14, 1811, in Lunenburg County Legislative Petitions, 1807–1821 (Library of Virginia); Clayton, comp., *Compilation of the Laws of Georgia*, 521; Stevenson, "Restricted Inland Range of Shad," 268.

44. I am indebted to David Weiman for this observation.

45. "The Petition of Sundray Inhabetents Freholders in the County of Pittsylvany," Oct. 21, 1791, Pittsylvania County Legislative Petitions, 1776–1793. See also "The petition of the inhabitants of Sussex County," Oct. 31, 1776, Sussex County Legislative Petitions, 1776; and "The petition of the Inhabitants of the County Halifax," Oct. 10, 1791, Halifax County Legislative Petitions, 1776–1791. Lamar, comp., *Compilation of the Laws of the State of Georgia*, 487; *Boatwright v. Bookman*, 24 S.C.L. (Rice) 447–48 (1839).

46. U.S. Department of State, *Compendium of the Enumeration of the Inhabitants and Statistics of the United States, as Obtained at the Department of State, From the Returns of the Sixth Census* (Washington, 1841), 158, 170, 182, 194, 206. See also Mark T. Taylor, "Seiners and Tongers: North Carolina Fisheries in the Old and New South," *North Carolina Historical Review* 69 (Jan. 1992), 1–36.

47. For the techniques of small fishermen, see "The Petition of Thomas Mercer & Others of the County of Camden," Petitions, box 3, session of Nov. 1810–Jan. 1811, General Assembly Session Records. For commercial fishing practices, see the acts that sought to regulate them. *Laws of North Carolina*, 1764, ch. XIII; ibid., 1766, ch. XXI; ibid., 1770, ch. XXI. For examples in the early republican period, see ibid., 1819, ch. XCVIII, ch. XCIV, ch. CIII; ibid., 1820, ch. LIII, ch. CV, ch. CXXII; ibid., 1821, ch. LVIII, LXIII. For the late antebellum period, see Jos. B. Skinner, *Letter on the Subject of the Albemarle Fisheries* (n.p., 1846); North Carolina General Assembly, "Report of the Select Committee on Fisheries," Senate Document no. 22 (Raleigh, 1852); and Strother, "North Carolina Illustrated," 438–47.

48. James Cathcart Johnston to James Iredell Jr., April 12, 1807, Charles E. Johnston Collection, Private Collections (State Archives, North Carolina Division of Archives and History); *Read v. Granbeny*, 30 N.C. (8 Ired.) 109 (1847); *Capeheart v. Jones' Executor*, ibid., 383.

49. *Laws of North Carolina*, 1764, ch. XIII; William Tryon to Lord Hillsborough, Nov. 30, 1769, in *Colonial and State Records*, comp. Saunders and Clark, VIII, 153–54.

50. See *Laws of North Carolina, 1764–1860*, and General Assembly Session Records, passim.

51. "To the Honbl the General Assembly of the State of North Carolina," Nov. 17, 1840, Petitions, box 5, session of Nov. 1840–Jan. 1841, General Assembly Session

Records; Skinner, "Letter on the Subject of the Albemarle Fisheries," 7; North Carolina General Assembly, "Report of the Select Committee on Fisheries," 182.

52. North Carolina General Assembly, "Report of the Select Committee on Fisheries," 182.

53. Ibid., 181.

54. Ibid., 183–84.

55. Ibid., 181–82.

56. See, for example, "An Act to Remove Obstructions in the Pedee, Yadkin, and Wharie Rivers for the Purpose of Allowing Shad and Other Fish Free Passage Up the Same," *Public Laws of the State of North Carolina . . . , 1870–'71* (Raleigh, 1871), ch. 262, 418–20.

57. General Assembly Report 1792–3 (South Carolina Department of Archives and History).

58. Stevenson, "Restricted Inland Range of Shad," 270; Charles Epes, "Officials Begin Restocking Shad," *Richmond Times-Dispatch*, July 21, 1992; Louis D. Rubin Jr., "On Catching Shad Fever at Fishing Creek," *Southern Living*, 13 (March 1978), 52–56.

59. Brickell, *Natural History of North Carolina*, 46.

60. McCurry, *Masters of Small Worlds*.

61. Ted Ownby, *Subduing Satan: Religion, Recreation, and Manhood in the Rural South, 1865–1920* (Chapel Hill: University of North Carolina Press, 1990); Stuart A. Marks, *Southern Hunting in Black and White: Nature, History, and Ritual in a Carolina Community* (Princeton, N.J.: Princeton University Press, 1991); William Elliott, *Carolina Sports by Land and Water; Including Incidents of Devil-Fishing, Wild-Cat, Deer and Bear Hunting, Etc.* (1846; Columbia: University of South Carolina Press, 1994); McCurry, *Masters of Small Worlds*.

LISA BRADY

The Wilderness of War

Nature and Strategy in the
American Civil War

IN 1865, the scars on the land wrought by the American Civil War were painfully evident and, for some, took on an ominous countenance. Union Major George Ward Nichols described the war-torn countryside in northern Georgia after William Tecumseh Sherman's Federal and Joe Johnston's Confederate armies clashed there in late 1864: "The soil which formerly was devoted to the peaceful labors of the agriculturalist has leaped up, as it were, into frowning parapets, supported and surmounted by logs, and guarded in front by tangled abattis, palisades, and *chevaux de frise.*" These fortifications were "reflected in quiet, rippling streams," still guarded by abandoned *tetes du pont.*[1] If at times the transformation of the earth appeared an active process to Nichols, at others it seemed as though "some giant plowshare had passed through the land, marring with gigantic and unsightly furrows the rolling plains, laying waste the fields and gardens, and passing onto the abodes of men, upturning their very hearths, and razing even towns and cities." Nor were hills and mountains immune: Nichols imagined what a future traveler might see—Kennesaw Mountain rising before him, "with its grandeur of 'everlasting hill' intensified by the mute records of human warfare—with its impregnable front furrowed and crowned with the marks of war."[2] Subject and object both, nature bore silent testimony to the awesome conflict of the Civil War.

Across the South and in a few places in the North, massive armies collided, leaving trenches and rifle pits gaping like open sores; pits from the explosions of underground mines pock marked the ground, and where thick woods once stood, little but broken trunks and shattered limbs remained. In the most heavily contested areas, the effects of the Civil War were akin to a natural disaster, a comparison often made by those who witnessed its destructive power. Major Henry Hitchcock, a staff officer under Sherman, likened the random devastation of war to the damage done by thunderstorms. Indeed, he believed that the "outrages of war" were "as much a part of the inscrutable and all-wise providence of God, and as necessary and ultimately as beneficial, as the terror which His wisdom has made part of the visible phenomena of Nature."[3]

Hitchcock's analogy was an appropriate one, for like a violent storm, war does not discriminate when meting out its awful destruction: urban or rural, human or not, nothing is immune from war's ruinous power. War can turn cities into piles of rubble and farmland into wasteland. War's power is not absolute, however; it is, after all, a human endeavor, constrained by the technologies and the ideologies brought to the conflict by those involved. The wartime relationship between humans and nature is a complex arrangement, characterized at times by collaboration, at others by adversarial competition. In the Civil War, both Union and Confederate forces continually negotiated the terms of this relationship, attempting to overcome nature's obstacles as they fought to defeat their human foes.

The landscape was not simply a backdrop to the events of the war—a place where battles took place—but a powerful military resource and an important factor in military decision making. The material exigencies of nature certainly were foremost in military strategists' minds throughout the war, but three of the most successful Union operations—Ulysses S. Grant's relentless attempts to capture Vicksburg, Mississippi, Philip H. Sheridan's campaign in the Shenandoah Valley of Virginia, and Sherman's marches through Georgia and the Carolinas—focused not on overcoming nature as object, but on destroying the enemy's primary relationship with the natural world. During these campaigns, Federal forces attacked the foundations of southern agriculture, exposed the tenuous nature of southerners' control over the landscape, and exploited a deep-seated American fear of wilderness.

Though the success of these campaigns is well known, the part nature played in them has not been explained clearly. Nature—as material object and as intellectual idea—takes an active role in war, though historians have only recently begun to examine its importance. To be sure, military historians always have analyzed how issues such as weather, terrain, and disease affected operations and troop morale. Indeed, analyses of specific battles or larger campaigns must incorporate discussion of topography, geography, vegetation cover, and weather in order to explain why one opponent bested the other on the field of battle. Military geographer Harold Winters' book, *Battling the Elements: Weather and Terrain in the Conduct of War*, is an excellent analysis of the "potent and omnipresent synergy between the environment, or physical geography, and battle."[4] Likewise, Russell Weigley frequently acknowledged in his book *A Great Civil War* the importance of environmental factors in the outcome of battle; he noted that Vicksburg's greatest defense was its rugged, broken terrain and suggested that South Carolina's best protection against Sherman's advancing troops in 1865 was not the Confederate army, but "geography and weather."[5] Geographer Warren E. Grabau's monumental study, *Ninety-eight Days*, also focused on the fundamental importance of terrain and geography to the defense and ultimate capture of Vicksburg.[6] These examples are merely representative of the wealth of information military histories provide about the natural obstacles officers and soldiers in the field—and those responsible for keeping them supplied—had to overcome in order to win a battle or capture important ground.[7]

Though campaign or battle histories typically include both geographic analysis and graphic descriptions of war's destructive nature, nature's agency is largely missing from more traditional military studies of the Civil War. As environmental historian Jack Temple Kirby explained, "Military historians preoccupied with combat on specific landscapes *almost* do environmental history, and environmentally-minded readers may deduce from conventional texts ecological aspects of warfare," but the military and environmental historiographies of war—any war—are "parallel; that is, they do not intersect."[8] This failure to connect is all the more curious because scholars in both fields have bemoaned their marginalized positions within the broader discipline. Military and environmental historians alike urge their colleagues to make their work more accessible to non-specialists; ironically, neither, until very recently, has looked to the other as a possible avenue for bridging the gap and widening their audience.[9]

Kirby's own contribution to narrowing the gap between military and environmental history was significant. His essay, "The American Civil War: An Environmental View," was the first to examine the Civil War (or any war) from a strictly environmental point of view. His purpose was not to provide a definitive history of that conflict, but rather to suggest a variety of issues in need of study. Edmund Russell's path-breaking work, *War and Nature: Fighting Humans and Insects with Chemicals from World War I to Silent Spring*, further connected military and environmental histories when it appeared in 2001. Since then, a growing number of scholars have started to draw the two fields closer together.[10] Ted Steinberg addressed issues of war and environment in *Down to Earth: Nature's Role in American History*, including a thought-provoking chapter on the Civil War entitled "The Great Food Fight."[11] In 2004, *Natural Enemy, Natural Ally* hit the shelves; edited by Richard Tucker and Edmund Russell, the volume collected ten essays on topics ranging from pre-modern warfare in India and Africa to the two World Wars to "argue for the importance of understanding war as a major and distinctive force in environmental change, as well as the environment as a force in shaping warfare."[12]

Natural Enemy, Natural Ally included Mark Fiege's excellent study, "Gettysburg and the Organic Nature of the American Civil War," which suggested that the Gettysburg campaign "exemplified the environmental conditions that motivated and influenced the larger conflict." Fiege contended that the war was a conflict over "the fate of the American West. The two regions [North and South] had opposing visions of western social development" and these "competing land ideologies . . . impelled the two sections into war." He further suggested that "much of the struggle between North and South was over geographic space," and that the side "that dominated and defined space, either in the West or in actual theaters of combat, was the side that would prevail."[13]

Fiege set a high standard for future environmental analyses of the Civil War: he clearly demonstrated that military and environmental histories are inextricably linked. Fiege accomplished what Ellen Stroud urged all environmental historians to do—he brought "to light connections, transformations, and expressions of power" that otherwise would have remained obscure.[14] Fiege's emphasis on the material realities of waging war exposed the power—military and social—that the physical control of nature offered. War is not fought only on the ground, however; it also is fought in the hearts and minds of those involved. It is here, in the realm of ideas, where environmental history can contribute most to our understanding of the Civil War and to military history more generally. Nature is not just a material reality; it also has intellectual and psychological importance to human societies. When Grant, Sheridan, and Sherman planned their campaigns against the southern landscape, they did not simply set out to gain physical control over the rebellious territories, they developed a specific strategy that exploited one of the oldest relationships Americans had with the natural world: a fear of wilderness. Faced with a return to chaos, and paired with physical destruction of once productive landscapes, southern support for the Confederacy weakened and Union victory was attained.

The Wilderness of War

In 1861, when eleven states voted to secede from the Union, the majority of Americans, north and south of the Mason-Dixon line, were farmers who cultivated intimate connections with the land they worked. In the North, small family farms predominated, with wheat, corn, and livestock comprising the main agricultural pursuits. The primary source of labor was the family itself, supplemented with hired hands during planting and harvesting seasons. In the South, the region's human and material resources were funneled—directly or indirectly—into the plantation system of cash crop monoculture. By the middle of the nineteenth century, "King Cotton" reigned throughout the South, encroaching even upon lands once devoted solely to indigo, rice, sugar, and tobacco.[15]

Although the South was less industrialized than the North—if factories are the standard by which a society is deemed industrial—it was no less tied to the industrial capitalist impulse. The cotton grown throughout the South fed the textile mills of the North and England. Thus, when war broke out on 12 April 1861, the conflict was not between an "industrial" society and an "agricultural" one, but, rather, it was a clash between a society that relied on "free" wage labor and one that depended on the labor of enslaved African Americans. Guiding both societies was the belief that humans controlled nature, an assumption seemingly supported by a variety of technological advances including steam engines, mechanical reapers, and railroads. Paradoxically, though perhaps not surprisingly, even as they attempted to subdue the natural world, Americans perceived a latent power in the landscape. Harnessing that potential promised other kinds of power.[16]

Agriculture was one method Americans used to rein in the landscape. Premised on a particular view of the land and its products as commodities, private ownership of land formed the basis of nineteenth-century American agricultural practices. Americans in this period prided themselves in carving civilization out of the continent's vast wilderness, supplanting unmanaged landscapes and unmanageable species with fenced-off tracts of land cultivated with domesticated plants and animals. Agriculture was a symbol of human control over nature and a material safeguard against the perils of wilderness.

The fear of wilderness, or uncontrolled landscapes, has a long history in America. As historian Roderick Nash argued in his pioneering work *Wilderness and the American Mind*, the concept of wilderness was a crucial factor in the ways European colonizers approached the North American landscape. According to Nash, they "recognized that the control and order their civilization imposed on the natural world was absent and that man was an alien presence."[17] Landscapes perceived as wild—that is, devoid of human influence—"constituted a formidable threat" to survival and "acquired significance as a dark and sinister symbol."[18] This version of wilderness, though not always a guide to conduct, continued to dominate American ideas about nature through the Civil War era. When war began to tear through the American landscape, reducing large areas of it to what observers at the time called "barren wastes" and "wilderness," many Americans had to contend with what those war-changed landscapes meant.

Early in the war, Union Captain Thaddeus Minshall of the 33rd Ohio Volunteers wrote home, exhorting a friend to "thank your stars that you live in a state untrod by the foot of the invader. No one can form an idea of the evils of war but one who has been in the vicinity of an army."[19] Several months later he declared, "war is a terrible thing. In its tread it desolates the fair face of nature—all the works of the husbandman, and tramples out all the divine parts of human nature."[20] Minshall did take some comfort that nature's seasons continued "coming on apace" despite the horrors of war; he described the beautiful sight of peach and plum trees in bloom, relieved that spring brought signs of life to a landscape dominated by death and destruction. The obvious juxtaposition caused the philosophical Minshall to ponder its larger meaning: "I can but reflect how nature and man are at war," he wrote. "Nature is strugling to give every thing a renewed appearance, but the grim monster, war, stalks on in the same unvaried course of desolation and ruin," Minshall predicted. "Terrible will be the condition of the South this season; nothing but the spontaneous effort of nature to indicate that the pursuit of agriculture is possible in the country."[21]

Minshall's descriptions of the war-torn landscape in Tennessee support historian Jack Temple Kirby's argument that few "can conceive of war without environmental danger if not disaster."[22] Some of the worst damage during the Civil War occurred in heavily wooded areas. Stray bullets, cannon shot, and the occasional saber pounded into the trunks and limbs of trees. Captain Theodore F. Allen of the 7th Ohio Cavalry recalled the fate of "a small grove of about 200 locust trees," most of them "about the size of a common bed-post," after the battle of Franklin, Tennessee: "These little trees were literally cut to pieces by the bullets. Some of them not as large as a man's body had 50 and 60 bullet marks. A reward of [$25.00] has been offered by Several officers to any person who will find in that grove a Tree or Limb 5 feet long which has not been struck by a bullet."[23] John Tilford, second assistant surgeon for the 79th Indiana Infantry, described a similar scene near Atlanta: "The trees in the wood was riddled to splinters by the leaden hail."[24]

Cities as well as cultivated fields and gardens suffered extensive damage not only from heated battles, but also simply from armies passing through. To describe the effects, countless chroniclers of the Civil War relied upon images of wilderness reflecting a centuries-old American fear of disordered landscapes. Describing a stretch of northern Georgia, an article published in the *Natchez Weekly Courier* noted how "the utter loneliness, the want of human life, strikes one with a feeling of desolation." Citing the lack of all signs of human improvements in the region—fences, livestock, working mills—the author wrote, "So startling is the utter silence, that even when the wild bird of the forest carols a note, you look around surprised that amid such loneliness any living being should be happy. This is the result of war, stern desolating war!"[25]

On a beautiful spring morning in 1865, noted diarist Mary Boykin Chesnut similarly awoke to the scent of violets placed in her room by her thoughtful hostess. For a brief moment, the flowers' perfume allowed Chesnut to forget the horrible events taking place around her, and evoked memories of a part of her life when the "Sweet south wind that blew in that Garden of Paradise." Her reverie was cut short, however, when "it all came back, the dread unspeakable that lies behind every thought now."[26]

Chesnut referred, of course, to the vicious war tearing through her beloved southern home, transforming it into "a howling wilderness, the land laid waste, all dust and ashes."[27]

The comparisons between a war-ravaged southern landscape and a "howling wilderness" were not made lightly, especially when the destruction was the result of deliberate strategy, rather than simply being an unintended casualty of war.[28] Descriptions of such scenes reflected a painful recognition by southerners toward the end of the war that they no longer controlled their environment and that their power to transform the southern landscape into a reflection of southern society was ephemeral. Indeed, a strategy used by General Grant in early 1863, and later by his lieutenants Sheridan and Sherman, which targeted southern agricultural practices and threatened to turn the southern landscape into a "barren waste" and a "wilderness," had symbolic as well as material import.

One of the Union's most effective means of attacking the South's view of itself was the *chevauchée*, or massive foraging raid. The *chevauchée* was meant to be a dramatic demonstration of power, and transformed the destruction of the landscape from a consequence into a weapon of war. These raids, in both their ancient and modern emanations, were intended to disrupt the daily lives of noncombatants and gain resources for the invading forces while denying them to the enemy.[29] In a modern war such as the Civil War, the raids reached epic proportions. Called "hard war" by some and "total war" by others, the strategy was a complex mix of operational and tactical maneuverings premised on new ideas about warfare.[30] It deviated from previously accepted rules of war that attempted to spare noncombatants, and made southern citizens, through attacks on their economic and natural resources, a prime target.

The strategy also was premised on particular ideas about nature. The South's agricultural wealth was its greatest military asset, providing food and forage for its men at arms, but it was also its most vulnerable resource. According to historian Russell Weigley, a "strike against war resources suggested an indirect means of accomplishing the destruction of the enemy armies. If the enemy were deprived of the economic means to maintain armies, then the armies obviously would collapse."[31] Although railroads, armories, iron works, and cotton stores were primary targets of the new strategy, the vast acres of fertile farmland that grew crops for human and livestock consumption were more important to southern economic, social, and cultural systems. In targeting the South's agricultural sector, the Union strategy undermined the region's most basic relationship to the natural world, destroyed the Confederacy's ecological foundations, and assured Federal victory.

A region's ecological foundations—the constantly evolving interaction between social, economic, and ecological systems—are the means through which human communities transform material nature into a "system that produces resources for their consumption."[32] In transforming nature, though, humans and human systems (economic, social, cultural, and political) are transformed, too. Thus, an attack against an enemy's resources goes beyond the simple destruction of material products toward the destruction of the enemy's social and economic systems as well.[33]

Under the capable leadership of Grant and through the remorseless execution of Sheridan and Sherman, the *chevauchées* successfully undermined the relationships between southerners and their landscapes, eliciting a profound change in the region's ecological foundations and requiring the local population to negotiate a new relationship to the land. These demonstrations of power used widespread, visible devastation as proof of Union might, achieving psychological victory over the southern populace sympathetic to the Confederate cause and logistical victory over the Confederate army. Grant's revival of a strategy deemed both militarily and economically unfeasible and ethically unacceptable since the eighteenth century led to a broader American strategic tradition of attacking an enemy's ecological foundations. The tactical use of such an attack was employed many times during the war, but its viability as a strategy on the operational level only became clear in the Union's actions against Vicksburg, Mississippi.[34]

The campaign against Vicksburg was crucial to Union success in the war. Called the "Gibraltar of the South," Vicksburg was an important port through which the Confederacy transported cattle and other goods from the Southwest and Mexico to its troops throughout the South. It also was surrounded by rich agricultural land. Situated nearly two hundred feet above the Mississippi River, on bluffs formed by the swift currents of the eastern side of a hairpin curve in the river's path, Vicksburg benefited from holding the high ground over any Union approaches from the west by land or water. A series of wide, gently sloping, natural levees or ridges created by the river's yearly floods composed a deceptively flat landscape to the west of the city; rising ten to fifteen feet above the water level, and ranging from one hundred yards to miles wide, these ridges provided the rich, dry land that made cotton production in the area possible. They also formed the edges of the area's nearly impassable swamps. Likewise, the eastern approach to Vicksburg was riddled with narrow streams and swamplands fed by the Big Black River and its tributaries. Located in the heart of bayou territory, these numerous streams created a large system of twisting ridges in the loess soil, and formed a nearly impenetrable fortress around Vicksburg. Each of these natural features would play an important role in the various Union attempts to capture the rebel fortress.

In August 1862 Grant took command of the Army of the Tennessee with orders to gain control over the entire Mississippi River. Vicksburg was the last obstacle to that goal, and Grant planned on marching south toward the city through northwestern Mississippi. Following standard military practice, he established a stationary base behind his army from which supplies easily could be transported to the moving column. Leaving a garrison to guard the supplies, Grant marched toward Vicksburg. However, General Earl Van Dorn of the Confederate cavalry sneaked to Grant's rear and destroyed the supply depot at Holly Springs, leaving Grant and his army in hostile country with no provisions. Grant recalled the Mississippians' reaction to the news: "They came with broad smiles on their faces, indicating intense joy, to ask what I was going to do now without anything for my soldiers to eat." Grant informed the gloaters that he was taking care of the problem by collecting all food and forage to be found in a fifteen-mile area. "Countenances soon changed," Grant wrote, "and so did the inquiry. The next was, 'What are *we* to do?'" Grant told them: "We had endeavored to feed ourselves from our own northern resources while visiting them; but their friends in gray had been uncivil enough to destroy what we had brought along, and it could not be expected that men, with arms in their hands, would starve in the midst of plenty."[35] This was a lesson not soon forgotten by Grant, and one that he and others taught the southern populace time and again during the remainder of the war.

During a long and fruitless winter encampment on Young's Point, Louisiana—the spit of land made by the horseshoe bend in the Mississippi River across from Vicksburg—Grant planned another attack on the city.[36] Beginning in April 1863, Grant aimed at creating wilderness through the revival of the ancient practice of the *chevauchée*. He initiated this plan largely out of necessity; once on the Mississippi's eastern bank, Grant was in hostile territory. Mississippi's population was staunchly Confederate in its sentiments, and Confederate President Jefferson Davis sent massive reinforcements to defend his home state. Steep ridges and precipitous ravines characterized western Mississippi's landscape, making the movement of a large army with all its supplies nearly impossible. In light of these natural obstacles, Grant decided to cut loose from his supply line and live off the country—implementing the very strategy that would eventually win the war.

Grant's foraging operations in Mississippi uncovered the Confederacy's Achilles' heel—its rich, fertile landscape. In commandeering the stores local residents produced for themselves and for the Confederacy, Grant struck not only a military blow to the rebel forces, but a psychological one against civilian Confederate sympathizers as well. Grant's orders stated, "It is our duty to use every means to weaken the enemy, by destroying their means of subsistence, withdrawing their means of cultivating their fields, and in every other way possible."[37] The results of this policy were not lost on those who suffered from it, nor on those who implemented it. As one female Vicksburg resident wrote in her diary toward the end of the siege, "provisions [were] so nearly gone, except the hogshead of sugar, that a few more days will bring us to starvation indeed. Martha says rats are hanging dressed in the market for sale with mule meat: there is nothing else."[38]

Separated from its hinterland, Vicksburg could not long survive. But the hinterland, too, suffered at the hands of Grant's nearly seventy-five thousand troops. Agriculture was the cornerstone of the region's relationship with the natural world, its success the result of constant and delicate negotiation between humans and their environment. Grant's revival of the *chevauchée* preyed on the tenuous nature of this arrangement. Sherman, who served under Grant during the Vicksburg campaign, predicted, "We have ravaged the Land and have sent away half a million negros so that this country is paralyzed and cannot recover its lost strength in twenty years."[39] Despite its obvious hyperbole, Sherman's assessment was based in truth. In targeting everything southerners employed in pursuit of agricultural productivity—tools, storage buildings, animals, and slaves—Grant's army attacked the ecological foundations of the Confederacy. What had begun as a measure of simple expedience proved to be such a powerful weapon that Grant integrated it into his arsenal upon taking command of all Union forces in late July 1863. As historian Edward Phillips explained, foraging, "converted now into a weapon, would serve henceforth the same ends as devastation."[40]

The first real test of the new strategy was Sheridan's assignment to "end the [Shenandoah] Valley's days as the 'Breadbasket of the Confederacy.'" Grant told Sheridan and his cavalry to "eat out Virginia clear and clean as far as they go, so that crows flying over it for the balance of the season will have to carry their provender with them."[41] More specifically, Grant's orders explicitly instructed Sheridan's army of nearly fifty thousand men to destroy existing agricultural goods and any possibility of producing such goods in the area for the remainder of that season. Put another way, Grant ordered Sheridan to take control of the landscape away from the local residents.

The historian Gary Gallagher has described the Shenandoah Valley as "a landscape of breathtaking beauty and agricultural bounty." It was one of the most productive regions of Virginia prior to the outbreak of the war. Three railroads served the region, moving the vast agricultural stores from the valley to Virginia's urban areas in the east. Staunton was the main railroad depot, and the macadamized Valley Turnpike "provided all-weather service" between that city and Martinsburg to the north.[42] The valley's numerous mills transformed wheat into flour, wool into textiles, skins into leather, and trees into lumber.[43] With the outbreak of armed conflict in 1861, the resources of the Shenandoah Valley made it one of the most important and contested areas in the country. Often referred to as the "granary of the Confederacy," the valley became a "lynchpin of the Southern Cause and a primary target of the Northern war machine."[44]

From the outset of the war until its final six months, however, the valley remained an elusive goal for the Union forces. First under the legendary Thomas "Stonewall" Jackson, then under the irascible Jubal Early, the Confederate Army of the Valley protected the fertile Shenandoah from all Union incursions. In concert with its Confederate defenders, according to historian Jeffry Wert, the "Valley itself contributed significantly to Union frustration and defeat in the region." Federal forces had to subdue "a huge corridor" guarded on the west by the "formidable sentries" of the Alleghenies and on the east by the Blue Ridge Mountains, which in one soldier's estimation resembled breastworks thrown up by "a race of titans [that] had been at war."[45] Although employing much more utilitarian language, a Union officer similarly attributed Federal difficulties to the geography and terrain of the valley; he noted that the lay of the land favored Confederate movements on Washington, Maryland, and Pennsylvania. For the Union armies, however, the "Valley led away from the objective, Richmond," and "exposed [them] to flank attacks through the gaps from vantage ground and perfect cover" firmly under Confederate control. The same officer noted that until "the summer of 1864 the Shenandoah Valley had not been to the Union armies a fortunate place either for battle or for strategy."[46]

Grant, recognizing the importance of the Shenandoah for the Confederates as both a storehouse and a secure transportation route, noted that it was "well known that they would make a desperate struggle to maintain it."[47] And indeed they did, plowing through two Union commanders in less than three months. Grant's first attempt to dislodge the Confederates from the valley ended in disaster. Franz Sigel, charged with tearing up the valley's railroads, moved tentatively up the valley toward Harrisonburg until he met with resistance at the town of New Market on 15 May. A lovely pastoral town, New Market nestled against the massive Massanuttens, orchards skirted the village, and green meadows lay between Sigel's men and his enemy. Former U.S. Vice President John C. Breckenridge led the rebel forces, which included 247 eager cadets from the nearby Virginia Military Institute.[48] The young rebels routed Sigel, who quickly retreated down the valley.

After Sigel's ignominious defeat, Grant realized that aggressive operations in the valley were of no use to him and decided instead that the best alternative was to make the region "untenable for either army." Far from a counterintuitive decision, Grant's plan to destroy the valley's resources had a solid basis in logic. Wesley Merritt, Major General of U.S. Volunteers, explained: Grant "reasoned that the advantage would be with us, who did not want it as a source of supplies, nor as a place of arms, and against the Confederates, who wanted it for both."[49] Furthermore, Grant had successfully implemented such a plan the year before in Mississippi. Undermining an area's ability to support its military forces—psychologically or materially—was a proven method for Grant, and he determined that the Shenandoah Valley posed an excellent opportunity to deploy the strategy once again.

Under Grant, the Shenandoah would no longer be for Union forces a "green and golden deathtrap"—in the words of historian Jeffry Wert—

standing defiantly "unconquered." Drawing on his experiences in Mississippi the previous year, Grant implemented a new strategy that virtually eliminated obstacles posed by the valley and its rebel defenders. He "finally determined to change the past, with a weapon created for the task and with instructions that meant a new, grim-visaged war."[50] Grant's plan "aimed at both the destruction of rebel armies and the destruction of rebel war-making capabilities." As Mark Grimsley noted in *The Hard Hand of War*, under P. H. Sheridan's command, Union forces would "launch expeditions against Southern croplands, railroads, and war resources."[51] In other words, they were to attack the valley's ecological foundations.

Sheridan's campaign in the valley began slowly, but after several battles against Jubal Early's Confederates, he gained unstoppable momentum. Pursuing Early's retreating forces, Sheridan marched three columns of his army up the Valley Turnpike, passing farms like Robert Barton's "Springdale" along the way. Barton recalled that two columns flanked the road skirting his property, marching in the fields and "destroying everything before them. Hogs, sheep, cattle &c. were shot down and left to rot and horses were taken and carried away, whether needed by the army or not. Springdale was left like a wilderness, almost every living animal on the place either being driven off or else killed and left in sheer deviltry and wickedness."[52] With equal venom and disdain, rebel General John Gordon claimed that after the third battle of Winchester, Sheridan "decided upon a season of burning, instead of battling; of assaults with matches and torches upon barns and haystacks, instead of upon armed men who were lined up in front of him."[53]

In a report to Grant, Sheridan noted that "the whole country from the Blue Ridge to the North Mountains has been made untenable for a rebel army." He then proceeded to inventory what his army had destroyed or confiscated in the Luray, Little Fork, and Main valleys: "I have destroyed over 2,000 barns filled with wheat, hay and farming implements; over seventy mills filled with flour and wheat; have driven in front of the army over 4,000 head of stock, and have killed and issued to the troops not less than 3,000 sheep . . . A large number of horses have been obtained, a proper estimate of which I cannot now make." He reported that the "people here are getting sick of the War, heretofore they have had no reason to complain because they had been living in great abundance." Sheridan concluded with a promise to Grant: "Tomorrow I will continue the destruction of wheat forage &c. down to Fisher's Hill. When this is completed, the valley from Winchester up to Staunton (ninety-two miles) will have but little in it for man or beast."[54]

Four years of armed conflict did indeed take its toll on the lovely valley. As the *New York Herald* reported on 13 March 1865, just a week after Early suffered his final defeat at the hands of the brash General George Custer at Waynesboro, "Between Sheridan and Early, the fertile Shenandoah valley has been thoroughly cleaned out; the country east of the Blue Ridge, from Leesburg to Richmond, has been left exhausted and desolate by the spoils of both armies."[55] In the valley proper, retreating rebel cavalry "encountered scenes of utter desolation: smoking ruins, the carcasses of animals in various stages of decomposition, horses killed in earlier battles and skirmishes, and farm animals recently slaughtered. Thousands of buzzards—with lice, one of the few breeds of living things which had prospered and multiplied during this war—circled overhead to gorge on putrescent flesh."[56]

As Gallagher stated, "Sheridan and his men left a legacy of blackened ruin that served as graphic counterpoint to the storied lushness of the area."[57] Likewise, Margaretta Barton Colt, Robert Barton's descendant, noted that the soldiers from the valley "came home to a wasteland—no trees, no fences, no barns, no mills. One Scottish visitor compared it to a moor."[58] In his official report at the end of the campaign, Sheridan accounted for everything his men had appropriated or destroyed.[59]

In Gallagher's view, without "an appreciation of why the Shenandoah Valley became first a battle ground and then a wasteland, it is impossible to understand fully the last year of the war."[60] By laying waste to the valley's most visible and material source of strength, Sheridan's campaign furthered the Union cause more than almost any campaign up to that time. It was a strategic, logistic, political, and psychological success. Sheridan's *chevauchée* through the fertile valley "constituted the first large-scale demonstration that the strategy of exhaustion could accomplish the psychological and logistical damage envisioned by Grant."[61] It would not be the last, however. As Sheridan was wrapping up his campaign in the Shenandoah, another of Grant's commanders was beginning his own farther south. On 16 November 1864, Sherman cut loose his supply lines and set out on his infamous "March to the Sea."

Sherman's marches through Georgia and the Carolinas grew from the same premise: undermine local control over the landscape and victory is assured. "We have devoured the land," Sherman wrote to his wife. "All the people retire before us, and desolation is behind. To realize what war is, one must follow our tracks."[62] The ability to wreak such havoc was a symbol of power in Sherman's estimation, and he consciously transformed his southern campaign into a demonstration of that power. Using foraging as a weapon, he cut a swath of destruction up to sixty miles wide along his path from Atlanta to Savannah and through the Carolinas to Raleigh. He lived up to his promise to Grant to do "irreparable damage" to the Confederacy.[63]

What became one of the most celebrated and condemned campaigns of the war was both a military triumph and a psychological one. Sherman recognized this fact, claiming in a letter to Grant that the march would be "a demonstration to the World, foreign and domestic, that we have a power which [Jefferson] Davis cannot resist." The *chevauchées* through Georgia and the Carolinas illustrated quite clearly that southerners' attempts to manipulate the landscape were futile in the face of Federal might. Sherman's campaigns were the culmination of the achievements and insights gained in Grant's maneuvers against Vicksburg in 1863 and Sheridan's rampage through the Shenandoah Valley in the autumn of 1864. "This may not be war, but rather Statesmanship," Sherman proclaimed, "proof positive that the North can prevail."[64] Sherman's final campaigns made tangible the authority of the Federal government and confirmed the broadly held assumption that power over the environment was inextricably linked to other kinds of power.

According to the *New York Herald*, "Sherman had discovered from his foraging expeditions around Atlanta that Central Georgia was filled with supplies; that her endless cottonfields of 1860 had become her inviting corn fields of 1864, for the subsistence of rebel armies."[65] "They don't know what war means," Sherman wrote to Chief of Staff Henry Wager Halleck, "but when the rich planters of the Oconee and Savannah [rivers] see their fences and corn and hogs and sheep vanish before their eyes they will have something more than a mean opinion of the 'Yanks.' Even now our poor mules laugh at the fine corn-fields, and our soldiers riot on chestnuts, sweet potatoes, pigs, chickens, &c."[66] Confident of ample provisions for his men and animals, Sherman set fire to the railroad depot, cotton warehouses, and armory in Atlanta and moved out with sixty thousand men on 15 November 1864.

The stated goal of Sherman's campaign was to dismantle the military infrastructure of the Confederacy. Railroads, factories, and armories comprised the Federal forces' main targets. Sherman's men set fire to any building, warehouse, or structure that could be used for military purposes; they pried up the railroads, set the ties ablaze, and melted the rails, twisting them into "Sherman neckties." Cotton stores, too, were burned, with the purpose of undermining the Confederacy's ability to finance its war effort. Fire was one of Sherman's greatest tools, providing him the means to literally reduce the Confederacy's military assets to ashes.

The obliteration of the Confederacy's military infrastructure was only part of the battle, however, as a surgeon in the Union army intimated in a letter home: "It seems now we will hold no interior point between Chattanooga and the Gulf, as all railways, foundries, and other public works will be destroyed before this campaign shall end, and much of the country effectually eaten up and desolated."[67] Sherman believed that he was fighting not only "hostile armies, but a hostile people," and that the war could not be won until the southern people were conquered.[68] His secondary goal, therefore, was to demonstrate the futility of civilian resistance to the overwhelming power of the Union army. His method was ingenious, though not unprecedented. Like Grant in Mississippi and Sheridan in the Shenandoah Valley, Sherman would march his army through the heart of Secessia, living off the land, leaving the local residents little except food for thought.

Georgia provided well for the Union army. Sherman recalled that between Covington and Milledgeville they found "an abundance of corn, molasses, meal, bacon, and sweet potatoes" in addition to "a good many cows and oxen, and a large number of mules." He attributed this wealth to the state "never before having been visited by a hostile army; the recent crop had been excellent, had just been gathered and laid by for winter."[69] The riches of Georgia, however, were quickly depleted; Sherman's army of sixty thousand had to move continuously or risk the same fate as those left starving in its wake.[70] This danger increased as the army neared its final objective in Georgia—the city of Savannah. With the rich cornfields of central Georgia behind them, the foragers had to rely on the rice fields of the coastal lowlands. Although Sherman noted that Savannah's rice plantations contained ample food and forage, it was only a short while before his army depleted those supplies. Within a week, however, the Federal forces moved into the city. On the morning of 21 December Sherman telegraphed President Abraham Lincoln, presenting Savannah to him "as a Christmas-gift."[71] Sherman's nearly bloodless campaign—his "demonstration to the world"—ended a grand success.

Sherman and his men were well aware of the effects, both military and psychological, of their recent campaign. Union Major Henry Hitchcock wrote in his diary that the campaign proved "that a large army can march with impunity through the heart of the richest rebel state, after boldly cutting loose from all its bases, and subsisting on the country." Hitchcock concluded that the campaign was a "great and important success, full of significance for the future."[72] Another soldier predicted that the campaign "will be one of the really historical campaigns of the war, much more so than some where vastly more fighting was done. It was brilliant in conception and well executed, but practically one of the easiest campaigns we have had."[73]

Brilliant, significant, easy—each word accurately described the March to the Sea. In less than one month, Sherman had marched an army sixty thousand strong through the heart of enemy territory with little resistance. The Military Division of the Mississippi left the foothills of Atlanta on 15 November 1864, traversed the rolling country near Milledgeville, crossed the swampy lowlands to the seacoast, "foraging liberally" along the way, and captured Savannah on 21 December. Sherman understood that taking or destroying everything associated with agricultural production would bring the Confederacy to its knees. "I know my Enemy," he wrote to his brother Philemon Ewing, "and think I have made him feel the Effects of war, that he did not expect, and he now Sees how the Power of the United States can reach him in his innermost recesses."[74] The Confederacy's strength as well as its weakness stemmed from its power to transform the environment into a productive landscape; by trumping that power, Sherman's March to the Sea struck a powerful blow to the rebellion.

Daniel Oakey, Captain of the 2nd Massachusetts Volunteers, remarked that the Georgia campaign was seen as "a grand military promenade, all novelty and excitement." He believed it had a deeper significance, though: Its "moral effect on friend and foe was immense. It proved our ability to lay open the heart of the Confederacy, and left the question of what we might do next a matter of doubt and terror."[75] Emma LeConte, a young woman living in Columbia, South Carolina, certainly wondered what lay in store for her native state. "Yes, the year that is dying has brought us more trouble than any of the other three long dreary years of this fearful struggle," she wrote in her diary on New Year's Eve, 1864. "Georgia has been desolated. The resistless flood has swept through that state, leaving but a desert to mark its track." LeConte had heard that Sherman's men were "preparing to hurl destruction upon the State they hate most of all, and Sherman the brute avows his intention of converting South Carolina into a wilderness."[76] Indeed, exhilarated by his success in Georgia, Sherman wrote to Grant in late December exclaiming, "I could go on and smash South Carolina all to pieces."[77]

Sherman set out from Savannah on 19 January 1865, and was on the coast of South Carolina four days later. Daniel Oakey described the impending campaign as "formidable," one that would involve "exposure and indefatigable exertion." Sherman's plan for the Carolinas mirrored his actions in Georgia, with four corps organized into two wings marching north along nearly parallel lines from the coast toward Columbia. From there he would march to Goldsboro, North Carolina, and end his "demonstration" at Raleigh.

Oakey noted that the campaign's success depended on continuous forward movement, "for even the most productive regions would soon be exhausted by our 60,000 men and more, and 13,000 animals." He further remarked that, despite being fully prepared for "a pitched battle, our mission was not to fight, but to consume and destroy."[78] Special Field Orders No. 120, issued at the beginning of the Georgia campaign and remaining in effect for the entire campaign, included demands for restraint and order in their implementation. Geographic and political differences between Georgia and the Carolinas, however, made the enforcement of such limitations ineffective in the present campaign.

Sherman's campaigns through Georgia and the Carolinas left behind an awesome vista of destruction. For some of Sherman's men, like Oakey, these scenes verged on the sublime. Describing the army's advance into "the wild regions of North Carolina," he wrote: "The scene before us was very striking; the resin pits were on fire, and great columns of black smoke rose high into the air, spreading and mingling together in gray clouds, and suggesting the roof and pillars of a vast temple." Despite the scene's allure, however, Oakey concluded that the "wanton" destruction was "sad to see," all the more so because the "country was necessarily left to take care of itself, and became a 'howling waste.'"[79]

The campaigns successfully destroyed the last sources of supplies available to the dwindling rebel armies and sent a powerful message to the Confederate populace about the reach of Federal power. The March to the Sea and the Carolinas campaigns demonstrated that the Federal government ultimately controlled how the American landscape and its resources would be used and by whom. The strategy was at once subtle and overt, but its message was inescapable: Sherman's *chevauchées* through the Deep South proved Federal power to determine one face of the American landscape. The campaign delivered the fatal blow to the rebellion.

The nature of Sherman's strategy—to "forage liberally off the land"—targeted the South's agricultural landscape, its most important resource and the basis of its economy, society, and identity. Union troops destroyed or confiscated cotton, food, forage, crops, livestock, and agricultural implements. The immediate effects of the campaigns were obvious. Alexander Lawson, a Confederate prisoner for part of the march through Georgia, vividly recalled "the davastations that [Sherman's] army committed." Lawson recalled that Sherman "made brags that he would make a black mark to the sea. He certainly did." Lawson escaped just outside of Savannah, and turned back on Sherman's path: "I found nothing, no hogs, cattle, sheep, chicken or anything else to eat. I saw a number of the very finest ladies in Georgia in the camps picking up grains of corn for the purpose of sustaining life, who a week before that did not know what it was to want for anything. I finally crossed the Savannah River into South Carolina, where his army hadn't been, and it was the first food that I had for about eighteen days." For these depredations, Lawson believed that Sherman had earned a "warm spot in Hell."[80]

Sherman did not destroy the land; what was laid waste, however, was the ecological foundation of the Confederacy. Agriculture based on slavery was the cornerstone of the southern relationship to the natural environment. Its success relied on a precarious system of power premised on the oppression of black Americans and on constant and delicate negotiations with nature. Sherman's *chevauchées* through Georgia and the Carolinas capitalized on the nature of this relationship, shifting the balance of power just enough to cause the Confederacy to topple in upon itself.

An Enduring Legacy

"It is difficult to condense into a few pages, and yet to render my tale interesting but not wearisome, the harrowing sight of ruin and destruction, the incontrovertible accounts of hardships encountered and to be endured, which met me at every turn."[81] The challenge that postwar traveler Henry Deedes faced in writing about the destruction of the South is the same one that historians of the conflict also must overcome. Tales of the devastation to the southern economy and its landscape—that is, to its ecological foundations—abound, as do commentaries on its immediate consequences and long-term repercussions.

As early as February 1865, witnesses to the strategy's agricultural devastation predicted a dark future for the South, marked by barren fields and abandoned farms. After campaigning through Georgia and the Carolinas with Sherman, Thomas Osborn remarked, "Unless the war closes within the year, the people of Georgia, South Carolina and North Carolina will do no producing this year, positively from an inability to do it, and partially from actual discouragement. People the world over raise crops for their support and making money, but if it yields them neither, they will not do much at it. This certainly has been the case in these three states, as well as in a considerable portion of Mississippi that last year."[82] He also anticipated that the devastation to agricultural regions would unhinge southern society and prompt its citizens to desert their homes. "Our Army has travelled over thousands of miles of territory which will be abandoned by the inhabitants who will never return, and these sections will grow up to a wilderness."[83]

The degeneration of a once populated and "civilized" landscape into a state of wilderness—devoid of people and basic amenities—was a dismal prospect, and southerners' attempts to recover from the war and re-establish agricultural productivity appeared unsuccessful to many visitors immediately after the war. The most common indicator that the South was in danger of returning to a state of wilderness was the lack of even the most basic symbols of "improvement": fences and well-tended, cultivated fields, both of which were primary targets of the *chevauchées*. Their absence provided visible and tangible evidence of the strategy's success. In targeting southern agriculture, Grant, Sherman, and Sheridan undermined southerners' control over their own landscapes. In destroying barns, tools, crops, and fences, the Union generals and their troops effectively obliterated the artifacts that once served as evidence of human influence over the environment. If left to its own devices, in other words, the landscape soon would return to the wilderness previous generations of southerners had worked so hard to eradicate.

The war did not literally destroy the southern landscape, however; historian Mart Stewart clearly demonstrated this in his study of coastal Georgia. What was devastated, though, were the means by which the antebellum southern landscape was maintained.[84] As Thomas Clark and Albert Kirwan suggested in their study *The South Since Appomattox*, in "an agrarian society like that of the ante-bellum South, ravages of war are erased from the land more quickly than in urban, industrialized countries." Fields covered in clover instead of cotton remain fields, but buildings destroyed by cannon fire are not so easily disguised. "Even so," Clark and Kirwan noted, "it would be long years before physical reminders of the devastation disappeared from the southern countryside."[85]

It would be even longer before the psychological scars would begin to heal. Tales of Sherman's marches still resound through the South, evidence of the continuing legacy that campaign—and its focus on transforming civilization into wilderness—had on the region. Though postwar descriptions and memories of the "waste lands" Sherman left behind far outstrip the actual devastation, that exaggeration demonstrates the psychological power of the military strategies based on fear of wilderness.

The consequences of the Union's shift in military policy extended well beyond the surrender of Robert E. Lee and Johnston in April 1865. The three commanders most responsible for the new policy—Grant, Sherman, and Sheridan—maintained control over Federal military policy for the next three decades. As Lance Janda argued in "Shutting the Gates of Mercy," the Civil War set an important precedent in American strategy making. Janda argued that the "application of force against an enemy's noncombatants and resources" in the Civil War led directly to the strategies employed against Native Americans later in that century. As the primary executor of the *chevauchée* in the Shenandoah Valley, Sheridan learned a powerful lesson, and applied his knowledge and experience in the Indian campaigns of the following decade. On becoming General-in-Chief, Sheridan proposed to destroy the buffalo herds upon which the Plains peoples depended. He knew from his Civil War experience that attacking the enemy's resources could be an effective strategy; he believed that he would defeat the American Indians if he could destroy their means of survival.[86]

Sheridan's determination to follow through on his threat is debatable. The herds had already declined significantly by the 1870s as a result of sport hunting by curious travelers moving west and a vigorous trade in buffalo hides in America and abroad. What is important, however, are the implications Sheridan's words had for his contemporaries as well as his successors. That Sheridan believed that he and his army—much reduced in size after the late conflict—had the power to accomplish such an enormous task is the most significant aspect of his statement. Words, in this instance, spoke louder than actions. Sheridan's threat provided a terrible template for future contests by American armed forces. The belief that humans had undeniable power over nature, and that they could destroy it at will to defeat an enemy, took on awesome proportions in the twentieth century. Chemical and biological weapons, atomic bombs, defoliation agents, and attempts to control the weather for military purposes are all products of the deep-seated belief that humans control nature.[87]

Thus, the lasting changes wrought by the war were not the physical transformations of the natural environment, but rather the ways in which Americans thought about war and interacted with their landscapes. As Edmund Russell demonstrated in *War and Nature*, American military strategies often mirrored American attempts to control the natural environments closer to home. That presumption did not originate in World War I, but rather in the Civil War, when the triumvirate of generals—Grant, Sheridan, and Sherman—demonstrated their power over the Confederacy's armies and its territory through the destruction of the southerners' control of their domestic landscapes.

Notes

1. *Chevaux de frise* ("horses of Holland," named after where they were first used) are defensive, fence-like structures composed of long, sharply pointed stakes (often small

tree trunks) set at angles intended to obstruct cavalry movements. *Tetes du pont* (bridge-heads) are defensive works in front of bridges to prevent enemy access to the span.

2. George Ward Nichols, *The Story of the Great March from the Diary of a Staff Officer* (New York, N.Y.: Harper & Brothers, 1865), 16. See also Theodore F. Upson, *With Sherman to the Sea: The Wartime Diaries of Theodore F. Upson*, ed. Oscar Osburn Winther (Bloomington, Ind.: Indiana University Press, 1958), 114–15.

3. Henry Hitchcock to Mary Collier Hitchcock, 29 January 1865, in *Marching with Sherman: Passages from the Letters and Campaign Diaries of Henry Hitchcock*, ed. M. A. DeWolfe Howe (New Haven, Conn.: Yale University Press, 1927), 217.

4. Harold A. Winters et al., *Battling the Elements: Weather and Terrain in the Conduct of War* (Baltimore, Md.: Johns Hopkins University Press, 1998), 1.

5. Russell F. Weigley, *A Great Civil War: A Military and Political History, 1861–1865* (Bloomington, Ind.: Indiana University Press, 2000), 268, 418.

6. Warren E. Grabau, *Ninety-eight Days: A Geographer's View of the Vicksburg Campaign* (Knoxville: University of Tennessee Press, 2000).

7. In addition to those mentioned in the text, a particularly useful study is Earl B. McElfresh, *Maps and Mapmakers of the Civil War* (New York, N.Y.: Harry N. Abrams, 1999). For general histories of the war, see James M. McPherson, *Battle Cry of Freedom* (New York, N.Y.: Oxford University Press, 1988), and Bruce Catton, *The Coming Fury, Terrible Swift Sword, and Never Call Retreat* (New York, N.Y.: Doubleday, 1961, 1963, and 1965).

8. Jack Temple Kirby, "The American Civil War: An Environmental View," on the National Humanities Center website, *Nature Transformed: The Environment in American History*: http://www.nhc.rtp.nc.us/tserve/nattrans/ntuseland/essays/amcwar.htm. Other studies that mention environmental aspects of the Civil War include Thomas D. Clark and Albert D. Kirwan, *The South Since Appomattox: A Century of Regional Change* (New York, N.Y.: Oxford University Press, 1967); Paul Wallace Gates, *Agriculture and the Civil War* (New York, N.Y.: Knopf, 1965); John Solomon Otto, *Southern Agriculture during the Civil War Era, 1860–1880* (Westport, Conn.: Greenwood Press, 1994); and Mart Stewart, *"What Nature Suffers to Groe": Life, Labor, and Landscape on the Georgia Coast, 1680–1920* (Athens: University of Georgia Press, 1996).

9. See John Lynn, "The Embattled Future of Academic Military History," *Journal of Military History* 61 (October 1997): 777–89. On the future of environmental history, see Adam Rome, "What Really Matters in History?: Environmental Perspectives on Modern America," *Environmental History* 7 (April 2002): 303–18; Ted Steinberg, "Down to Earth: Nature, Agency, and Power in History," *American Historical Review* 107 (June 2002): 798–820; Ellen Stroud, "Does Nature Always Matter?: Following Dirt through History," in *History and Theory*, Theme Issue 42 (December 2003): 75–81.

10. Edmund Russell, *War and Nature: Fighting Humans and Insects with Chemicals from World War I to Silent Spring* (New York, N.Y.: Cambridge University Press, 2001).

11. Ted Steinberg, *Down to Earth: Nature's Role in American History* (New York, N.Y.: Oxford University Press, 2002).

12. Richard P. Tucker and Edmund Russell, eds., *Natural Enemy, Natural Ally: Toward an Environmental History of Warfare* (Corvallis: Oregon State University Press, 2004), 2. See also J. R. McNeill, "Woods and Warfare in World History," *Environmental History* 9 (June 2004), 388–410, quotation on 406.

13. Mark Fiege, "Gettysburg and the Organic Nature of the American Civil War," in *Natural Enemy, Natural Ally*, 93–109. Quotes from 93–95.

14. Stroud, "Does Nature Always Matter?" 80.

15. For excellent overall studies of the agriculture of the South, see works cited in note 8.

16. Leo Marx, *The Machine in the Garden: Technology and the Pastoral Ideal in America* (New York, N.Y.: Oxford University Press, 1964), 157.

17. Roderick Nash, *Wilderness and the American Mind*, 3d ed. (New Haven, Conn.: Yale University Press, 1982), 7.

18. Ibid., 24.

19. Thaddeus Minshall to Friend, 2 January 1861 [1862], Papers of Judge Thaddeus A. Minshall, Filson Historical Society, Louisville, Ky. (hereafter FHS).

20. Minshall to Friend, 26 November 1862, FHS. All spellings are original.

21. Minshall to Friend, 26 March 1863, Camp Near Murfreesboro, Tenn., FHS.

22. Kirby, introduction to "The American Civil War: An Environmental Perspective."

23. Theodore Allen, Diary, 12 January [1865], uncataloged collection, FHS.

24. John H. Tilford, Diary, 16 May 1864, FHS.

25. *Natchez Weekly Courier*, 15 November 1864 (originally published in the *Indianapolis Journal*), Newspapers and Periodicals Division, Library of Congress (hereafter NPD, LOC).

26. Mary Boykin Chesnut, 29 March 1865, in *A Diary from Dixie*, ed. Ben Ames Williams (1905; reprint, Boston, Mass.: Houghton Mifflin, 1961), 510.

27. Chesnut, 26 February 1865, *Diary*, ed. Williams, 489.

28. Although an appreciation for wilderness began to develop in the first quarter of the nineteenth century, Nash rightly pointed out that "it was seldom unqualified. Romanticism, including deism and the aesthetics of the wild, had cleared away enough of the old assumptions to permit a favorable attitude toward wilderness without entirely eliminating the instinctive fear and hostility a wilderness condition had produced." Nash, *Wilderness and the American Mind*, 66.

29. See Mark Grimsley, *The Hard Hand of War: Union Military Policy toward Southern Civilians, 1861–1865* (New York, N.Y.: Cambridge University Press, 1997), 190–91.

30. Mark Grimsley prefers the first term; more common are the historians who describe the Civil War as "total war." See, for example, Stig Förster and Jörg Nagler, eds., *On the Road to Total War: The American Civil War and the German Wars of Unification, 1861–1871* (Washington, D.C., and Cambridge, England: German Historical Institute and Cambridge University Press, 1997); Daniel Sutherland, "Abraham Lincoln, John Pope, and the Origins of Total War," *Journal of Military History* 56 (October 1992):

567–86; Lance Janda, "Shutting the Gates of Mercy: The American Origins of Total War, 1860–1880," *Journal of Military History* 59 (January 1995): 7–26; McPherson, *Battle Cry of Freedom*; and Phillip Shaw Paludan, *"A People's Contest": The Union and Civil War, 1861–1865*, 2d ed. (Lawrence: University Press of Kansas, 1996). For an opposing opinion, see Mark E. Neely Jr., "Was the Civil War a Total War?" *Civil War History* 37 (1991): 5–28.

31. Russell Weigley, *The American Way of War: A History of United States Military Strategy and Policy* (Bloomington, Ind.: Indiana University Press, 1973), 145.

32. Donald Worster, "Transformations of the Earth: Toward an Agroecological Perspective in History," *Journal of American History* 76 (March 1990): 1090.

33. My argument here is influenced by William Cronon, *Changes in the Land: Indians, Colonists, and the Ecology of New England* (New York, N.Y.: Hill & Wang, 1983), 1 and 165; and Worster, "Transformations of the Earth," 1087–1106.

34. See Weigley, *The American Way of War*, 128–52; Weigley, "American Strategy from Its Beginnings through the First World War," in *Makers of Modern Strategy: From Machiavelli to the Nuclear Age*, ed. Peter Paret (Princeton, N.J.: Princeton University Press, 1986), 408–43; and Janda, "Shutting the Gates of Mercy." On Napoleon's use of foraging, see Gunther E. Rothenberg, *The Art of Warfare in the Age of Napoleon* (Bloomington, Ind.: Indiana University Press, 1980). General John Pope used the massive foraging raid earlier in the war than did Grant, but he was condemned for doing so. See Sutherland, "Abraham Lincoln, John Pope, and the Origins of Total War," 567–86.

35. Ulysses S. Grant, *Memoirs and Selected Letters*, ed. Mary Drake McFeely and William S. McFeely (New York, N.Y.: Library of America, 1990), 290. Emphasis in the original.

36. Young's Point was the location of a proposed canal that attempted to bypass the city of Vicksburg and open the Mississippi River to Union control and navigation. For a postwar reaction to the place, see Henry Deedes, *Sketches of the South and West, or Ten Months' Residence in the United States* (Edinburgh and London: William Blackwood and Sons, 1869), 100–101. For a military analysis of the endeavor, see David F. Bastian, *Grant's Canal: The Union's Attempt to Bypass Vicksburg* (Shippensburg, Pa.: The Burd Street Press, 1995). For earlier, similar efforts, see Lisa M. Brady, "War Upon the Land: Nature and Warfare in the American Civil War" (PhD dissertation, University of Kansas, 2003), 27–28.

37. Ulysses S. Grant to Frederick Steele, 11 April 1863, *Official Records of the War of the Rebellion* Ser. 1, vol. XXIV/3 (s38) (Washington, D.C.: Government Printing Office, 1880), 186–87.

38. "A Union Woman Suffers through the Siege of Vicksburg," in *The Blue and the Gray: The Story of the Civil War as Told by Participants*, ed. Henry Steele Commager (New York, N.Y.: Wings Books, 1991), 667.

39. W. T. Sherman to Ellen Sherman, 5 July 1863, in *Sherman's Civil War: Selected Correspondence of William Tecumseh Sherman, 1861–1865*, ed. Brooks D. Simpson and Jean V. Berlin (Chapel Hill: University of North Carolina Press, 1999), 500.

40. Edward H. Phillips, *The Shenandoah Valley in 1864: An Episode in the History of Warfare*, The Citadel Monograph Series, No. 5 (Charleston, S.C.: The Citadel, 1965), 18–19.

41. Quoted in Grimsley, *Hard Hand of War*, 167.

42. Gary W. Gallagher, "The Shenandoah Valley in 1864," in *Struggle for the Shenandoah: Essays on the 1864 Valley Campaign*, ed. Gary Gallagher (Kent, Ohio: Kent State University Press, 1991), 1–3.

43. See Phillips, *Shenandoah Valley*, 22–23; Gallagher, "Shenandoah Valley," 2.

44. Thomas A. Lewis, *The Guns of Cedar Creek* (New York, N.Y.: Harper & Row, 1988), 5.

45. Jeffry D. Wert, *From Winchester to Cedar Creek: The Shenandoah Campaign of 1864* (Mechanicsburg, Pa.: Stackpole Books, 1997), 27. Wert quotes George T. Stevens, *Three Years in the Sixth Corps: A Concise Narrative of Events in the Army of the Potomac, From 1861 to the Close of the Rebellion, April, 1865* (Albany, N.Y.: S. R. Gray, 1866), 390.

46. Wesley Merritt, "Sheridan in the Shenandoah Valley," in *The Way to Appomattox*, ed. Robert Underwood Johnson and Clarence Clough Buel (1887; reprint, New York, N.Y.: Castle Books, 1956), 500.

47. Grant, *Memoirs*, 614.

48. For a first-hand account of the battle, see John Wise, "V.M.I. Boys Fight at New Market," in *The Blue and the Gray*, ed. Commager, 1031–36.

49. Merritt, "Sheridan in the Shenandoah Valley," 500.

50. Wert, *From Winchester to Cedar Creek*, 28.

51. Grimsley, *Hard Hand of War*, 163. Grimsley applies this argument to the entire "strategy of raids" instituted under Grant's command in 1864–1865. For Wert quote, see note 50.

52. Robert Barton memoir excerpt in Margaretta Barton Colt, *Defend the Valley: A Shenandoah Valley Family in the Civil War* (New York, N.Y.: Orion Books, 1994), 340.

53. John B. Gordon, *Reminiscences of the Civil War* (New York, N.Y.: Charles Scribner's Sons, 1903), 327.

54. Sheridan to Grant, 7 October 1864, 9, P. M. Sheridan Papers (Microfilm Edition), Library of Congress.

55. *New York Herald*, 13 March 1865, NPD, LOC.

56. Phillips, *Shenandoah Valley*, 21.

57. Gallagher, "Shenandoah Valley," 1.

58. Colt, *Defend the Valley*, 19.

59. Phillips, *Shenandoah Valley*, 22–23.

60. Gallagher, "Shenandoah Valley," 18.

61. Ibid., 16.

62. William T. Sherman to Ellen Sherman, 26 June 1864, in *Sherman's Civil War*, ed. Brooks and Berlin, 657.

63. Sherman to Ellen Sherman, 1 October 1864, in ibid., 727.

64. Sherman to Grant, 6 November 1864, in ibid., 751.

65. *New York Herald*, 28 November 1864, reprinted in *Natchez Weekly Courier*, 9 December 1864, NPD, LOC.

66. Sherman to Halleck, 19 October 1864, in *Sherman's Civil War*, ed. Brooks and Berlin, 736.

67. *Natchez Weekly Courier*, 2 December 1864, NPD, LOC.

68. Sherman to Halleck, 25 December 1864, in Sherman, *Memoirs*, 705.

69. Sherman, *Memoirs*, 658.

70. Jacob D. Cox, *Sherman's March to the Sea*, Campaigns of the Civil War, vol. 12 (1882; reprint New York, N.Y.: Da Capo Press, 1994), 22.

71. Sherman, *Memoirs*, 711.

72. Hitchcock Diary, 10 December 1864, in *Marching with Sherman*, ed. M. A. DeWolfe Howe, 167.

73. Thomas Osborn to S. C. Osborn, 31 December 1864, in *The Fiery Trail: A Union Officer's Account of Sherman's Last Campaigns*, ed. Richard Harwell and Philip N. Racine (Knoxville: University of Tennessee Press, 1986), 80.

74. Sherman to Philemon B. Ewing, 29 January 1865, in *Sherman's Civil War*, ed. Brooks and Berlin, 810.

75. Daniel Oakey, "Marching Through Georgia and the Carolinas," in *The Way to Appomattox*, ed. Johnson and Buel, 674.

76. Emma LeConte, *When the World Ended: The Diary of Emma LeConte*, ed. Earl Schenck Miers (New York, N.Y.: Oxford University Press, 1957), 3–4. Entry dated 31 December 1864, Columbia, S.C.

77. Sherman to Grant, 22 December 1864, in *Sherman's Civil War*, ed. Brooks and Berlin, 722.

78. Oakey, "Marching Through Georgia," 675.

79. Ibid., 677–78.

80. Alex Lawson to Mr. S. A. Cunningham, 12 December 1910, FHS.

81. Deedes, *Sketches*, 77.

82. Thomas Ward Osborn, 27 February 1865, in *The Fiery Trail*, ed. Harwell and Racine, 154.

83. Osborn, 22 March 1865, in ibid., 201.

84. Stewart, *"What Nature Suffers to Groe,"* 4.

85. Clark and Kirwan, *The South Since Appomattox*, 23.

86. Ibid..

87. For an overview of such efforts, see Arthur Westing, ed., *Environmental Warfare: A Technical, Legal, and Policy Appraisal* (London, England: Taylor & Francis, 1984).

MART STEWART

If John Muir Had Been an Agrarian

American Environmental History

West and South

IMAGINE IF JOHN MUIR, during his thousand-mile trek through
southeastern North America to the Gulf of Mexico two years after the end
of the Civil War, had developed more than a passing infatuation with the
landscapes of "happy negroes" and "dark mysterious Savannah cypress forests" of Georgia or the palmetto "hummocks" of Florida, and had decided
to stay and live in the South.[1] If he had met up with Sidney Lanier and Joel
Chandler Harris and imbibed from them the sensibilities of the southern
Arcadian tradition. If he had, late in life, learned enough about history and
social justice from W. E. B. Du Bois and his student fieldworkers at Atlanta
University to become, like Du Bois, one of the pioneers of environmental
justice in America. And if he had written a series of essays about a nature
pastoralized and had become a cantankerous inspiration to the Vanderbilt
Agrarians as they took their stand. If this Muir, like the other one, had also
been one of the founding fathers of American environmentalism, what
kind of Sierra—or Appalachian, rather—Club would have been founded?
What landscapes would have been venerated and called up for protection
if Muir had been agrarian and pastoral, rather than wilderness and biocentric, in his sensibilities? Would he have proclaimed, "In the *agrarian* is the
preservation of the world"?[2]

Of course, Muir was no southerner and his passage through the Kentucky, Tennessee, Georgia, and Florida countrysides, though on foot, was
ultimately feverish in pace. Muir remained blind throughout the trip to
the social turmoil and changes on the land that were occurring—in the
parts of Georgia he visited, especially—because of Emancipation and

realignments of land and labor in the post–Civil War South. And he never returned. But conducting this thought-exercise might tell us something about an ongoing issue in American environmental history. Why has environmental history, a growing and now well-established field, developed more slowly and much differently in the American South? And by what measure should we judge this? At the same time, historians of this region have often talked about the land, and southern history has a deep tradition of agricultural history and human geography that can be described as "environmental"—yet American environmental historians in general scarcely know about this literature and this tradition. The huge literature that considers the history of agrarian strife, the struggle of agricultural laborers against masters, landlords, lenders, and their supporters in local and state governments over access and control of resources, is akin to the literature, some of it by environmental historians, about agrarian struggle in places not American and some historians of the South are quite aware of this kinship. But this awareness has yet to have much of an impact on American environmental history in general. What, indeed, kind of environmental history would have developed if John Muir had stayed in the South and become an agrarian?

Muir, of course, was not the only, and probably not even the most important, source or intellectual influence in the development of American environmentalism and environmental history in the United States. The importance of an agrarian sensibility as well as an agrarian experience—and the hopes for a republic of yeoman citizens—in shaping the early history of American relationships to the land, too, has certainly had its historians. But much of the strongest founding work in American environmental history was written by historians of the West and shaped by sensibilities akin to Muir's: with an interest in "wild" places and in the preservation of them, a concern with capitalist despoliations of pristine environments, the assumption that nature has fundamental value apart from what we ascribe to it, and an engagement with the politics of conservation and environmental protection—all out on the frontier bee meadows and sequoia margins of American settlement, and under a very big sky.[3]

The history of humans and nature in the South, however, has more often assumed a different measure of the "natural," one that does not take humans out of nature, and that is more informed by an agricultural experience than a wilderness one. The South has been an agricultural region, and more profoundly an agricultural region than other parts of the United States where agriculture was important but not so woven into both sense and sensibility as in the South. Every attempt by scholars to understand, as pioneering agricultural historian Lewis Gray explained his mission, "the way of life of a great section of a country which was almost entirely agricultural" has required a close look at the interaction of cultivators and the cultivated—and at perceptions of and ideas about this interaction. Agricultural history, as Donald Worster has both observed and demonstrated, can provide a lens for examining environmental history itself.[4] For most of the history of the South, further, significant social and political relationships cannot be separated from the agricultural landscapes in which they are embedded without a loss of meaning and understanding. In parts of the South these relationships have persisted well beyond the demise of the original form of agriculture that gave rise to them.

America was generally a rural nation with most Americans engaged in the work of agriculture until the early twentieth century. But the imprint of agriculture was deeper in the South, lasted longer, and almost from the beginning (at least after Europeans arrived) was driven by a set of relationships that gave landowners control over both land and labor. Agriculture in many parts of the South evolved within or in relationship to a distinctive form, the plantation. Plantations where staple crops were worked by unfree labor emerged very soon after the first southern British colonies were founded in the Chesapeake and the Carolina Lowcountry. And the social and economic effects of plantation agriculture have lasted in the South long after the demise of plantation agriculture in the mid-twentieth century—sometimes with profound environmental consequences as well, in old cotton belt communities blighted by poverty that became the sites (or proposed sites) of toxic waste dumps.[5]

The plantation itself was an adaptation to the difficult environments that the first colonists encountered—but also one that allowed them to transfer to North America a form of agricultural production that had worked in kindred climates and soils in the Caribbean. Long growing seasons and ample moisture, and a good river system for transporting cash crops, made commodity crop production possible at the same time that poor soils and the conditions of slavery forced mobility in both land and labor. By the nineteenth century, plantations were the backbone of nineteenth-century southern agriculture and drove the economy of the region.

Cotton agriculture moved from Georgia and South Carolina to Texas; the significant frontier in southern history is the cotton frontier—and slavery moved along with it. How the South as a region—given its geographical diversity and that a large percentage of landowners did not own slaves—can be identified has been an issue of perennial debate for historians of the South. But that the planter class held most of the wealth and the power in the region and that southern society was from the beginning at least biracial is beyond question.[6]

By reorganizing agricultural labor, landowners were able to re-invent plantation agriculture after Emancipation. The Civil War had been the first "total war," in which armies warred not only against other armies but against the societies that sustained them and even against the very landscape itself. The scorched earth tactics practiced in Georgia and other places by Union troops gave the South a distinctive regional history, unique in the United States, of defeat and subjugation by occupying troops. Union troops cut a swath through both the cultivated and uncultivated environments of the South. Making Georgia howl, for example, meant the destruction of seed and livestock and agricultural infrastructure, and the confirmation of emancipation at the same time. Large amounts of land in the South were temporarily abandoned after the war was over, farm animals that had been drafted into military service were gone and so were many that had not. In those places where Union foragers had extracted harvests and sometimes everything else, residents, both black and white, were forced to rely more extensively on wild resources, intensifying a relationship between the cultivated and uncultivated portions of the South that already had a long history. Five years after the war less than half the formerly improved land in the South was in use.[7]

Southerners set to work at reviving regional agricultural regimens, and improved land stabilized at about one-third of the total area after 1880. The agricultural economy that postbellum southerners put together had far more farm units and laborers were dispersed in separate households and worked smaller fields instead of living in quarters and working in gangs on large fields—but the same class of southerners owned the land and the same class worked the land after the war as before. The agricultural culture of the South was shaken to its foundations by the war, but the struggle to recover what had been lost dug it even deeper into the region. Long after the South began to modernize through infusions of capital by

New Deal programs and the invention of the mechanical cotton picker, the geography of plantations continued to shape the southern economy and southern culture, and the bustling Sunbelt has a shadow landscape of exhausted soils, pine (and marijuana) plantations, and impoverished rural communities in its stead.[8]

Those who worked the land and the understandings they developed and employed as agricultural workers were as important to the environmental history of the South as was the structure of agriculture and of crop regimens. Much of the South was shaped by the production of a very few staple crops on plantations, but more directly by the laborers who grew these crops. As Philip Morgan and Ira Berlin have pointed out, cultivation and culture were always linked in the plantation South and Caribbean; how people *worked* tells us a great deal about their cultures. Morgan and Berlin emphasize labor much more than land and the work culture of slaves more than the complex set of relationships they had with the environment. The work that these scholars have collected and themselves done has made the hands that shaped southern landscapes more visible, but for them and for other historians who have studied southern labor land continues to be little more than abstraction or scene of action. But the hands that shaped plantation agriculture also shaped countervailing and sometimes competing landscapes at the same time, because of and by way of the work that they did.[9]

Competing landscapes, too, were important expressions of cultural and especially environmental perceptions and power relations. Plantation landscapes were thoroughly racialized; what used to be called "race" bound up or split apart just about everything else in the region as well. American environmental historians discovered race only about a decade ago; southern historians have seldom been able to avoid it, and have created a superb and complex literature about race relations and constructions of both whiteness and blackness.

Slavery and racism, as it was articulated by way of plantation agriculture, structured the cultivated landscape in the South, but also drove perceptions and uses of the uncultivated landscape as well. The South has had its own kind of "wilderness." Indeed, Muir noticed it, but a much different and much more inhabited one than the realm of alpine glaciers and water ouzels he later explored in the Sierras. About 80 percent of the region in

1860 was uncultivated before the Civil War, and when Muir strolled to the Gulf Coast after the war much more had been added around the edges by way of abandoned fields and destroyed farms.

The forests, wetlands, and savannahs of the wild places in the South were uncultivated, but were linked to cultivated ones through a complex of uses—some of them also agricultural. Small farmers and hill folk ranged cattle on wiregrass savannahs and in canebrakes, and hogs in mast-bearing deciduous woods—the enormous canebrakes of the South were vital to the large cattle industry of the region. Hunting and gathering were important components of the subsistence strategies to the more than 80 percent of southerners who did not own slaves—and for some of those who did. Southerners routinely burned the woods in some areas in an early spring ritual to destroy insects and improve understory and savannah browse for their free-ranging cattle.

More importantly, this wilderness South was as structured by social and cultural categories as the cultivated one; and the cultivated and uncultivated were inhabited and used in tandem by southerners. If one of the questions American environmental historians have been asking in the last decade is "what wilderness should we get back to?" the answer for the South is that wild lands were always the terrain of an array of purposes and of social and cultural differences—so much so, that they were hardly "wilderness" at all. In plantation districts, both the cultivated and uncultivated environments were often better known by slaves than by their masters. The work slaves did accustomed them to a closer view of the cultivated environment. They were aware, from row to row, of the progress of the plants during the growing season. They put seeds in the ground and covered them with their feet, stirred and tilled the earth when hoeing, and bent down over rice stalks or moved slowly down rows of cotton during harvest. The hands experienced crop cultures from the ground up. Masters sometimes even depended on the first-hand—and often more tangible—perceptions of leading slaves to make decisions about crop regimens. At the same time, when a storm came up slaves went in the fields or out on the levees or rice banks to do repairs and salvage crops. They endured suffocating summer heat—especially in the Lowcountry rice swamps or in the damp thickets of Lower Mississippi sugar plantations—while doing the heavy labor of tending and harvesting the crops. Masters and overseers rode or strolled along the borders of the fields and sometimes down the rows, but the slaves who turned the soil, tended the plants, and harvested the crops acquired a first-hand knowledge of the cultivated landscape on the plantation.[10]

Slaves knew the woods and swamps that were not cultivated, too, and often as intimately. The conduits and seams of significance in slave landscapes were marked out not by the boundaries of the fields they were forced to work, but by the pathways and waterways along which they acquired opportunities for small measures of autonomy beyond the fields. They met in the "holler" for worship, and many depended in part on the local environments for sustenance, oak or seagrass for baskets, roots and herbs for medicine or other purposes—even quilt patterns.[11] Hunting and fishing in the surrounding woods and waterways were an important source of food for slaves. Not all slaves hunted—some plantation surroundings were not rich enough in game to yield much to hunters, and going off the plantation without a pass was too risky in some neighborhoods. But many did, if not with the rare guns they were able to use as hunters for their masters or that they owned themselves, with an ingenious array of snares, set traps, and turkey pens. Or whatever else was at their disposal: Georgian Aunt Harriet Miller reported to a WPA interviewer that when she was a slave, she and other slaves used blow guns made out of sugar cane and burned out at the joints to "kill squirrels and catch fish."[12] With sometimes nothing more than motivation, opportunity, and a good stick, slaves sought something of their own by way of hunting. Slaves hunted everything, but the most common animals that found their way into pots in the quarters were opossums, raccoons, and rabbits. Rabbits were plentiful and had savory meat, roasted raccoon was meat with character, and the meat of the opossum, when scalded, rubbed in hot ashes, and roasted, and then eaten with roasted sweet potatoes and coffee, was prized most of all by slaves who hunted.[13] But whatever the animal, slaves had to be doubly stealthy and more knowledgeable than common for white hunters: they had to avoid stepping into their masters' landscapes of control and domination at the same time that they had to be closely attentive—especially if they were hunting merely with sticks and smarts and at night—to the nuances of the behavior and environment of their prey. Hunting put meat in the pot: on the Georgia and South Carolina coasts, for example, slaves may have procured nearly half the meat in their diets from wild sources—a crucial margin that added substantially to nutrition and sustenance.[14] At the same time, hunting was one more way that slaves acquired knowledge about the physical environment in their neighborhoods and annotated their surroundings with meanings that were both subversive of the totality of white power and positive expressions of an African American environmental ethos.

Again, what happened in the woods was linked to the interstices of agricultural regimens—and the history of plantation agriculture in the South. Most slaves devised ways to carve out some of their "own" time to expand their exploitation of local resources beyond the fields or apply specialized skills off task to cultivate, hunt, or gather after their work in the fields was done. Slaves were not only able to supplement rations and feed their families and neighbors. The food that slaves procured from the wild environment became imbued with cultural value when slaves developed a cuisine and tastes for certain wild foods, and used gifts of meat and other foods to reinforce community bonds. They also used what they raised and procured in the wild places to trade for goods and property of their own. Cattle and hogs that ranged in the woods were, indeed, capital on the hoof, which increased by way of the browse that could be found there. Like their masters, slaves extracted commodities from the environment in which they lived and worked, and indeed masters often encouraged some property ownership by slaves—they believed it would make them less likely to run away, and sometimes slave property substantially supplemented plantation rations. Whatever property they could acquire had more than simple economic value, however. In a relationship with other humans and larger institutions that defined them as human property, outside civil society and subject to the almost absolute domination of their masters, small bits of property represented considerable increments of independence and autonomy, even when they also served the goals of masters. Property was not simply wealth, but represented a small measure of security and something that was slaves' own, and more slaves than not had some.[15]

At the same time, "wilderness" resources and the property made from them were used not merely to strengthen individual positions of power, but were important in consolidating family bonds. Wild resources and the process of procuring them did not produce family, but were often the medium of kinship. Cooperative arrangements that freed some slaves to cultivate their own plots, fish, hunt, or gather and then trade or sell, were usually kin arrangements. Slaves worked with relatives to extract resources, relatives took care of property when the owner was absent, and some slaves got their start—a few chickens or a shoat or a calf—by way of a gift or a loan from a relative. When slaves disputed ownership of something, they negotiated a resolution by way of kinship networks—relatives or reliable neighbors were witnesses and trusted ones were arbiters. When slaves died, their children inherited what they had. The resources enslaved African Americans were able to gather or the small property they were able to procure because of these arrangements reinforced and further strengthened kinship ties. Property ownership was so interrelated with kinship for slaves that the making of property and the making of family often went hand in hand. Slaves metabolized resources from the fields, forests, and swamps of plantation neighborhoods in their social arrangements as well as adding to their food supply and nutrition. They crafted expressions of culture and values, and also quite literally claimed family ties with what they extracted—in both the process and the product—from the environment.[16]

Uncultivated environments had another important social link to cultivated ones among slaves who ran "away" from one to the other. Though relatively few African Americans, like Frederick Douglass, "stole themselves" to the North and away from slavery altogether, many of them ran away, to visit family on other plantations, or simply to "lay out" in the local swamps for a spell. For these, the wild places were quite literally havens, or crucial highways to family reunions. Slaves who sought either to escape—even if just for awhile—the harsh constraints of plantation life and agricultural regimens, or who traveled to other plantations to visit family, traveled or hid out off the roads. The *petit marronage* engaged in by slaves who sought either to escape for awhile a particularly repressive master or overseer or who wanted to visit with family on other plantations was common on every plantation and was an important form of resistance that was also shaped by close observation of geography and the weather. Slaves made their way from plantation to plantation, usually at night and with both short and extended periods of truancy, to visit kinfolks and to improve the quality of their family relations. When they "layed out" to avoid punishment or work, or when they traveled from one plantation to another to visit relatives, they also depended upon the support of slaves who stayed home. The physical environment off the plantation, then, was hardly "marginal" to plantation laborers, but an intricate part of the elaborate geography of kinship and social connection.[17]

Though maroon communities were relatively rare in the South, they were not unknown. Such communities existed, at least, on Georgia's Savannah River in colonial Georgia and in colonial Louisiana between the mouth of the Mississippi River and New Orleans, but also in mountainous, forested, or swampy regions throughout the South. Gwendolyn Hall has explained how groups of runaway creole slaves in Louisiana built huts in the cypress swamps on and behind the estates of French settlers, with secret paths leading to them (sometimes covered with woven mats that were noisy when someone walked on them), grew corn, squash, and rice on small high places in the swamps, gathered berries, dwarf palmetto roots, China-smilax roots (which they pounded into flour and cooked) and sassafras, and hunted and fished. In other words, they created communities in the swamps, raised their own food, and sometimes sold cypress logs to sawmill owners to procure cash for small commodities they could not make or obtain in the "wild." Sometimes entire families fled together—and those who did not run away provided support for those who did. Africans in the swamps had a symbiotic relationship with slaves on the plantation. When Cajuns and Canary Islanders came to these swamps in the late eighteenth century, they learned how to live in them from those who were already there—the debt of these fiercely independent people to maroon communities, Hall explains, is engraved on the language they still speak today—most often by men, when they are fishing and hunting. Hall does not fully enough explain the history of maroons in this region, and the extent of what she credits as a maroon culture in Louisiana has been contested, but the notion that Afro-Creole traditions that had their origins in the maroon communities in the eighteenth century have left cultural tracks in the vernacular of those who move along similar pathways in the swamps even today suggests the strength of this kind of "wilderness" tradition at the same time that it illuminates its origin in an agricultural one.[18]

Though more land was brought into cultivation in the South after the Civil War, open land continued to be important to the sustenance of poor whites and blacks—Steven Hahn and several other scholars have explained the social and political turbulence that occurred when influential southerners began to expand their control of "wild" lands through legislation that made it illegal to run hogs and cattle on unenclosed private lands or "trespass" to hunt. The struggle between tenants or small farmers and wealthier landholders in the South over access to resources on unenclosed lands differed only on the face of it from kindred agrarian struggles elsewhere. It was a contest over access to lands that in terms of current property law was private property owned by individuals rather than public lands that the state sought to control, conserve, manage, or otherwise make more "legible" as an extension also of state policy initiatives. But the "state"—in this case, state and county governments—was a part of the process by which lands were enclosed in the South. Local-option stock laws that were passed by state assemblies and then adopted at the county level and which required owners of livestock to fence them in on their own lands were the medium for the enclosure of uncultivated land. Further, the meaning of private property laws was conditioned by long traditions of use that defined unenclosed and uncultivated lands, whatever their legal status, as a kind of "commons." This commons, once again, was for poor whites and blacks either an outfield where they ranged hogs or cattle or a hunting ground where they could procure provisions and other necessities to supplement what they could grow closer to home. Traditions for the use of uncultivated lands in the South, in other words, survived the Civil War and began to disappear not because they were absorbed and diminished by a wilderness ethic or because they were subdued by state conservation measures, but because landlords and local officials sought to expand the cotton-producing agricultural landscape that was dominated by large landowners and to extend control over all.[19]

Simply, the environmental history of the American South has largely been an agrarian one. It has not produced an indigenous notion of "wilderness" as unoccupied or relatively undisturbed nature, nor have historians of the South had to argue against a historiographical tradition that takes such a wilderness for granted. Even the attempt of modern environmentalists to re-create wilderness in protected areas in the South has had to import the idea from outside the region. Margaret Brown, in her study of the Great Smoky Mountains and the Great Smoky Mountains National Park, *The Wild East*, explains how notions of what a wild park should look like were imported from the West and then integrated into the development and management policies of this lodestar national park in the South.[20] For African Americans, wild land was often a source of sustenance and community survival, and for slaves the place beyond the plantation bounds was a place of potential deliverance as well as a region where family and community values could be affirmed.[21]

Uncultivated land never acquired the meaning of "wilderness" in the South. Even William Faulkner, a reference to whom is an obligation for those who wish to speak about the South, saw uninhabited nature not in biocentric terms or apart from humans. In his paean to the southern wilderness, "The Bear," the wilderness is not a place where one goes for salvation, for transcendence, but to discover the darkest part of one's being and also to put oneself into contact with manliness and with other men—it's another, perhaps the supreme, southern hunting story. The wilderness of "The Bear" is not a redwood cathedral but a "not farm," "unaxed," and the home of an animal who earned his reputation through "corn-cribs broken down and rifled, of shoats and grown pigs and even calves carried bodily into the woods and devoured and traps and deadfalls overthrown and dogs mangled and slain and shotgun and even rifle shots delivered at point-blank range yet with no more effect than so many peas blown through a tube by a child."[22] In the South, nature and humans were never unhitched.

The beginnings of conservation in the South—until recently largely ignored by American environmental historians, who have favored the kinds of environmentalism created by the real John Muir and by liberal moments and leaders who have focused on more open places in America—was also thoroughly enmeshed in the culture of slavery, the history of the plantation, and the agricultural history of the South. In the 1820s and 1830s, when many southerners began to feel their region was in the grip of a cultural and economic crisis and also began to chafe against the attacks against slavery from outside the region, they sought solutions through agricultural reform and conservation practices. Leading planters, especially in the older parts of the South where soil exhaustion most profoundly challenged the continued vitality of plantation society, advocated more beneficent management practices for both slaves and soils. They exchanged and promoted ideas about better ways to grow rice, cotton, sugar, tobacco, and other crops, about crop rotation and fertilizing, about machines that would make agricultural practices more efficient, all with the goal of diversifying southern agriculture and making it more efficient and restoring depleted lands. An ethic of stewardship emerged in the abundant discussions of agricultural improvement that showed up in addresses to agricultural societies and in the pages of new agricultural journals.

Some of the practices advocated by planters followed what modern environmentalists might recognize as ecological principles. One of the Georgia Lowcountry's most progressive planters, James Hamilton Couper, for example, sought not only the salvation of tired soils, but agricultural practices that would harmonize with "the principles of vegetation." In a contribution to the *Southern Agriculturist* in 1833, he described an elaborate soil and crop management program that went further than the usual laments about soil exhaustion in its recognition of the basic unsoundness of monoculture and the implications for plantation agriculture. "Where nature is allowed to sow her own seeds and reap her own harvest," he wrote, "the earth, instead of being impoverished by her vegetable productions, seems at each new effort but to augment that fertility, which is ever presenting to the eye a varied aspect of beauty and fruitfulness." When the earth is instead controlled by humans for specific agricultural productions, though, the effects have been markedly different: "Their exhaustion generally follows production, and utter impoverishment would succeed to teeming fertility, were not resort made to benign nature, or to expensive manures, to restore the lost fertility." Once soil was used for agriculture, planters should carefully follow crop rotation schemes that "harmonized" with nature, Couper explained, if they wished to ensure perennial fertility. In the second part of the article he laid out such a scheme, one that he had worked out on the highlands and tidal swamplands of his Georgia plantation.[23]

Many planters merely talked about reform and did not dirty their hands with the attentive management and hard work that was required to carry reform ideas into practice. But even armchair agricultural reform constituted an early source of conservation ideas that has only recently been examined by scholars who have studied the history of conservation and environmental ideas and politics. These conservation ideas, though they had much in common with a larger movement among reform farmers throughout the older regions of the United States in antebellum America to stay and improve rather than skim and move, took shape in a distinctive form within the context of slavery and regional consciousness. This, too, is part of the deeply social content of southern environmental history.[24]

Planters went further than the advocacy of new methods when they developed ideas about the relationship between nature, agriculture, and culture—not just with ideas about how to improve nature through proper cultivation as the foundation of a regional counter-revolution and as a way to develop a path to southern economic strength. They also used nature as part of an argument to justify agriculture and slavery and to defend what they believed to be distinctive about southern society. In the mid-nineteenth century, the South was not just a region or a section, but for four years also a nation that leading southerners justified partly by a defense from nature. In the 1850s, some influential southerners developed a pro-slavery argument that *naturalized* staple crop production, slavery, and southern society. The argument went like this: because of the climate, staple crop agriculture was the best adapted to the region (and as the defensive fever of the 1850s intensified, southerners ignored variations in climate within what became the solid South); because of this agriculture, the plantation was the best unit of organization for growing staple crops; because of plantations, slavery was the best labor system; because Africans had been imported as plantation laborers and, according to prominent variants of the argument, were better suited for labor in the long, hot summers; because of all three, the South possessed an economic and cultural uniqueness. Pro-slavery ideologues more often defended the peculiar institution and the culture that depended upon it in arguments derived from Scripture rather than nature, but by the end of the 1850s, "the sunny South" and the "peculiar climate" had become a fundamental point in an ideological defense, a note in a common chord struck to reinforce the commitment of leading southerners to slavery and to southern society. The South, especially after secession, was also Nature's Nation, but with a consistently agrarian content.[25]

Black southerners who knew how to extract resources discretely and who occupied a natural landscape that was leavened with strategies for strengthening kin and community had the makings of a different environmental ethos that also operated in tension with the conservation ethos of their masters. But it was this very experience with the conservation ethic and other demands of elite southerners—those who owned them but to whom they were partly invisible—that contributed the crucial element to African American environmentalism (even as it has bloomed in more recent times). Slaves were required to negotiate for everything, either directly or indirectly, with masters and with the systems of control they devised. They had to bargain with both words and behavior for access to resources, to move around on the plantation and beyond the bounds of the cultivated fields, to manipulate adjustments to the burden of labor that was placed upon them, and to do all in the interest of kin and community. Anything they did for themselves was potentially and sometimes quite overtly an act of resistance, and had to be negotiated carefully. Even the medicine they sought to apply to treat illness, even if it brought back a slave's health and his or her capacity to be a productive worker, was usually regarded by planters, who sought to control the bodies of slaves as well as what those bodies could do, as an act of subversion. Reformers and Freedmen's Bureau officials who worked with freedmen in the South just after Emancipation were often surprised—stunned, even—by the speed and deftness and with what collective force freedmen laborers negotiated with landowners or managers to mark out better terms for themselves. They remarked often about the rapidity with which freedmen and freedwomen organized churches—usually with denominational lines that followed kinship and neighborhood ones—that also became homes to community political activities and expressions. What they were witnessing and experiencing was not something new, but a political behavior with deep roots in the conditions of American slavery and in the relationship of African Americans to the land.[26]

This history left twentieth-century black southerners with a double-edged inheritance. Those who lived in the old plantation districts were more likely, at the end of the century, to live in poverty than their urban African American counterparts. Again, poor, underdeveloped counties in the South with large black populations have also been more likely to be locations or proposed locations of hazardous waste sites or factories that spew noxious pollutants. But slavery and emancipation and the political culture that came out of them—both in the countryside and in the urban places to which rural southern blacks migrated—have produced a positive response to injustices—environmental ones included. Relationships with the environment have always been social and collective for African Americans, and always in process of negotiation.[27]

Nature provided resources not just for profit but often to consolidate community—moving into nature and through nature was usually a collective matter, as was negotiating either individual or group spaces from masters using environmental knowledge or by way of spaces in the fields and the surrounding forests and swamps. For African Americans, "wilderness" was not a place in which the preservation of the world could be found, but a site of healing, a trail to kinship, a place where a decisive edge of resources could be added to meager plantation rations, a place where salvation could be gained—either through worship in the "holler" or through stealing oneself away permanently. Slave experiences with the environment were profoundly social ones—they moved into nature to enact social meanings, at the same time that they did not make the sharp distinction between the human and nonhuman worlds that were common for whites. For African Americans in the South, nature was negotiated, it was kin, and it was community. And for both black and white Southerners, nature was *inhabited*.

So what about the question at the outset of this essay: Why has environmental history of the South appeared to lag in development behind the field elsewhere—or why is, as one observer has explained about southern environmental history, the South "again the backward region"?[28] And what kind of environmental history would we have had if the field had first emerged in the South and been shaped by deep traditions of southern history? Historians of the South have themselves been preoccupied with their region as Region, and have often written about the relationship of the South to the rest of the nation by asking questions about how the South became like the rest of America, how it became "Northernized" or "Americanized." They have also made legitimate claims as well as wry and deliberately tongue-in-cheek ones about how the South has also transformed America, how Dixie has "Southernized" America—or, at least, how the rest of America, after cracks in its progressive façade were opened up in the 1960s and 1970s by urban race riots, defeat in Vietnam, and the political corruption revealed by Watergate, has become more like the South. Reflecting on identity is an old preoccupation in the South that dates at least back to the antebellum planters who attempted to claim a special status for slavery by proclaiming southern cultural distinctiveness. And it has usually been done in the same way that the South has been observed from outside, by comparing it to a yardstick of something better, usually in terms of "the North." Historians have often either pronounced the South as special, blighted, or "distinctive," or have asked "why not?" instead of "why?"[29]

The venerable C. Vann Woodward, in a classic and widely read essay published a half century ago, on the other hand, noted that the complex history of struggle and defeat that has been the South's is not so distinctive nor so blighted when viewed in a global context instead of by way of comparison to the North.[30] Indeed, comparative history of the richest and most revealing dimensions has been done by historians of the South who have compared slavery, emancipation, and segregation there with slavery and emancipation in Brazil and elsewhere in the Americas, the emancipation of the serfs in Prussia or Russia, and racism and apartheid in South Africa. Even some of the spare environmental literature on the plantation South or on the disease environments of the South has pointed to the importance of at least a transnational view of the South. This scholarship, as Woodward recommended, has found its rewards not by measuring the history of the South against the history of the rest of the United States, but by looking at it in comparison to places elsewhere on the globe.[31]

These two historiographical trends suggest that any assessment of environmental history of the South needs to take into account how southerners themselves conceive of environmental values and politics and the practice of environmental history as well as compare this practice not with the American environmental history Ur-region, the American West, but with environmental history elsewhere in the world. The environmental history of the American South may have more in common with environmental history that has emerged in other parts of the world, which has had to come to terms with landscapes that have been continuously occupied and cultivated, with a history of interactions between humans and nature that have been structured more by agriculture and urban spaces rather than wilderness ones, with a history that has not worried itself so much with locating the boundary between culture and nature (and finding or erasing "frontiers"), and in which Frederick Jackson Turner and his long and doggedly persistent train of interpreters and refuters are nigh alien. Like most of the hemispheric "South," the American South was a colonial economy until well into the twentieth century and has had to confront the problems of how to solve environmental problems and at the same time resolve countryside poverty. The history of disease and how it has shaped the geography of the South, the agriculture of the region, and even concepts of race, has a profound kindred literature in African environmental history, and also connects with a growing literature on the shaping influence of disease regimens on colonial enterprises as well as ideas of "whiteness" in Asia. Southern planters exercised their own kind of imperial action on the environment and on ideas about nature that can be illuminated by looking at the rich literature of the relationship between imperialism and the environment elsewhere in the world. And unlike all of the rest of relatively isolated North America, the South has experienced the environmental ravages of modern war—and the history of this, much of it not yet written, will connect the South with other parts of the world in yet another important way.

What about the "wilderness" in which the preservation of the world can be found? The South was quite simply a different place, come time for "wilderness" and all the questions associated with it. The struggle in the South over uncultivated places could more often be characterized as an agrarian struggle, and one that reflected racial and social divisions that have an old history in the South. This history indeed may have more in common with agrarian struggles in other parts of the world, which has its own literature, than with the environmental history of wild places elsewhere in the United States. This connection has not gone unnoticed by historians of the South, who have recognized that the struggle over access to resources by a disenfranchised southern "peasantry" has much in common with kindred struggles elsewhere in the world, at the same time that they have not fully greened their understanding of "resources"—and especially in the terms in which the "peasants" they study may have understood them. The very recent discovery by historians of the West that the "pristine" natural areas that were enclosed by the National Park system were not so pristine after all, but human landscapes from which the original inhabitants were removed, or the study of agrarian struggles against state conservation efforts elsewhere in the United States—including the West—is not so much an innovation as an environmental take on a subject that has a deep literature in southern history (at the same time that these studies largely ignore the South).[32]

If John Muir had been an agrarian, then, the history of environmental history might not have been so eccentric—so shaped by that peculiarly American obsession with the frontier and wilderness and everything that goes along with it. It might not have taken environmental historians so long to have discovered that landscapes are always riven by what we used to call "race"—as well as by gender, ethnicity, and class. The history of other variants of environmentalism and conservation might not have taken so long for American environmental historians to acknowledge, and might not have taken so much instruction from abroad, if they had looked more closely at the deeply conservative and paternalistic conservation ideas of antebellum improving planters as well as the environmental sensibilities and politics of the African American slaves upon whose labor these planters were utterly dependent. Several deep seams in the history of the South might have provided riches that could have saved a whole generation of New Enviro-Western historians a great deal of labor. Indeed, as environmental history continues to develop in the South, we may discover that the South is not so "backward" after all, but way out ahead, and at the same time a window to the rest of the world and a less provincial practice of environmental history in America.[33]

Notes

1. John Muir, *A Thousand Mile Walk to the Gulf* (Boston and New York: Houghton Mifflin Company, 1916), 58, 69, 115–17.

2. "Agrarian" is meant to be taken broadly in this essay, as designating a way of life, a set of practices, values, and environmental behaviors, as well as the ideas about them, connected to the general practice of agriculture. The term is also deployed here in the same sense that it is used by scholars of agrarian culture outside the United States, to refer to farmers and others who live off the land who often function on the margins of commercial economies and practice mixed subsistence strategies—who are often called by scholars "peasants." On the pastoral tradition in southern literature, see Lucinda Hardwick McKethan's *The Dream of Arcady: Place and Time in Southern Literature* (Baton Rouge: Louisiana State University Press, 1980). For the agrarian tradition in southern political thought, see Paul V. Murphy, *The Rebuke of History: The Southern Agrarians and American Conservative Thought* (Chapel Hill: University of North Carolina Press, 2001).

3. Few of the many historiographical essays written by environmental historians have engaged the southern literature. Environmental history textbooks also slight the South; only Theodore Steinberg's *Down to Earth: Nature's Role in American History* (New York, N.Y.: Oxford University Press, 2002) attends to the South. On the New Western History, see Patricia Nelson Limerick, Clyde A. Milner II, and Charles E. Rankin, eds., *Trails: Toward a New Western History* (Lawrence: University Press of Kansas, 1991).

4. Lewis Cecil Gray, *History of Agriculture in the Southern United States to 1860* (Gloucester, Mass.: Peter Smith, 1958; repr. of 1932 ed.), vol. 1: xi; though Worster has focused almost exclusively on capitalist agriculture, see Donald Worster, "Transformations of the Earth: Toward an Agroecological Perspective in History," *Journal of American History* 76 (March 1990): 1087–1106.

5. On the persistence of plantation geography in the old cotton belt, see Charles S. Aiken, *The Cotton Plantation South since the Civil War* (Baltimore, Md.: Johns Hopkins University Press, 1998). On the placement of toxic waste dumps in the vicinity of poor rural black communities in the old cotton belt, see ibid., 360–61, and Robert D. Bullard, *Dumping in Dixie: Race, Class, and Environmental Equality* (Boulder, Colo.: Westview Press, 1990).

6. Even though commentators exaggerate the homogeneity of the South as a way to identify it, investigators have found a high level of consensus among black and white residents of "the South" that their region has cultural integrity. At the same time, as Edward L. Ayers concludes, "The South is continually coming into being, continually being remade, continually struggling with its pasts." See Edward L. Ayers, Patricia Nelson Limerick, Stephen Nissenbaum, and Peter S. Onuf, *All Over the Map: Rethinking American Regions* (Baltimore, Md.: Johns Hopkins University Press, 1996), 82.

7. On the environmental damage of the Civil War in the South, see David De Laubenfels, "Where Sherman Passed By," *Geographical Review* 47 (1957): 381–95; Jack Temple Kirby, "The American Civil War: An Environmental View," on TeacherServe, http://www.nhc.rtp.nc.us:8080/tserve; and the essay by Lisa Brady in this volume.

8. The literature on the reorganization of land and labor after the Civil War and Emancipation is huge—for a summary, see two essays in John Boles, ed., *A Companion to the American South* (Malden, Mass.: Blackwell, 2002); Laura F. Edwards, "Emancipation and Its Consequences," 269–83; and Joseph P. Reidy, "Economic Consequences of the Civil War and Reconstruction," 303–20.

9. On the central place of agricultural work in the history of early America, see T. H. Breen, "Back to Sweat and Toil: Suggestions for the Study of Agricultural Work in Early America," *Pennsylvania History* 49 (October 1982): 241–58. For an analysis of how labor was the nexus of culture and cultivation in slave societies, see the essays in Ira Berlin and Philip D. Morgan, eds., *Cultivation and Culture: Labor and the Shaping of Slave Life in the Americas* (Charlottesville: University Press of Virginia, 1993); for an analysis of how environment was also important in this nexus, see Mart Stewart, *"What Nature Suffers to Groe": Life, Labor, and Landscape on the Georgia Coast, 1680–1920* (Athens: University of Georgia Press, 1996). See also Stewart, "Rice, Water, and Power: Domination and Resistance in the Low Country, 1790–1900," *Environmental History Review* 15 (Fall 1991): 47–64.

10. For an influential critique of the wilderness idea, see William Cronon, "The Trouble with Wilderness; or, Getting Back to the Wrong Nature," in *Uncommon Ground: The Reinvention of Nature*, ed. William Cronon (New York, N.Y.: Norton, 1996), 24–37. On slave perceptions of agricultural work, see Stewart, *"What Nature Suffers to Groe,"* 98–102, 135, 146–48.

11. Though they must be used carefully, the WPA Slave Narratives, published in George P. Rawick, ed., *The American Slave: A Composite Autobiography*, 23 vols. (Westport, Conn.: Greenwood Publishing Co., 1972–79), are rich accounts about what slaves grew, hunted, gathered, or made from their surrounding landscapes. See also

Elizabeth D. Blum, "Power, Danger, and Control: Slave Women's Perceptions of Wilderness in the Nineteenth Century," *Women's Studies* 31 (2002): 247–65.

12. Rawick, *The American Slave*, Georgia, vol. 13, part 3, 130.

13. Nicolas Proctor, *Bathed in Blood: Hunting and Mastery in the Old South* (Charlottesville: University Press of Virginia, 2002), 144–68. Notes on the value of various animals for food can be found in Rawick, *The American Slave*, ser. 2, vol. 12, Georgia, part 1, 3–4; and supplement 1, Miss., vol. 8, part 3, 1293. See also Stuart A. Marks, *Southern Hunting in Black and White: Nature, History, and Ritual in a Carolina Community* (Princeton, N.J.: Princeton University Press, 1991).

14. Tyson Gibbs, Kathleen Cargill, Leslie Sue Lieberman, and Elizabeth Reitz, "Nutrition in a Slave Plantation: An Anthropological Examination," *Medical Anthropology* 4 (Spring 1980): 175–262.

15. On the cultural meanings of slave food, see Charles W. Joyner, "Soul Food and the Sambo Stereotype: Foodlore from the Slave Narrative Collection," *Keystone Folklore Quarterly* 16 (1971): 171–78; Stacy Gibbons Moore, "'Established and Well Cultivated': Afro-American Foodways in Early Virginia," *Virginia Cavalcade* 39 (1989): 70–83; Philip D. Morgan, *Slave Counterpoint: Black Culture in the Eighteenth-Century Chesapeake and Lowcountry* (Chapel Hill: University of North Carolina Press, 1998), 134–45. On slave property, see Dylan C. Penningroth, *The Claims of Kinfolk: African American Property and Community in the Nineteenth-Century South* (Chapel Hill: University of North Carolina Press, 2003), 45–78.

16. Penningroth, *The Claims of Kinfolk*, 79–109. For slaves and later for freedmen, property was always connected to family, Penningroth argues, and "was less an institution or a legal right than a social process." He connects this insight to scholarship in African Studies that argues that access to resources is connected to social identity and that property ownership is more an ongoing social process than a matter of having something to the exclusion of the claims of others: 191–92. African Americans also developed a strong sense of place, which wove together networks of kin and their close understanding of local environments. See Herbert G. Gutman, *The Black Family in Slavery and Freedom, 1750–1925* (New York, N.Y.: Pantheon Books, 1976), 208–11; Drew Gilpin Faust, "Culture, Conflict, and Community: The Meaning of Power on an Ante-Bellum Plantation," *Journal of Social History* 14 (Fall 1980): 93–94; Patricia Guthrie, "Catching Sense: The Meaning of Plantation Membership Among Blacks on St. Helena Island, South Carolina" (PhD dissertation, University of Rochester, 1977), 114–29; Hahn, *A Nation Under Our Feet: Black Political Struggles in the Rural South from Slavery to the Great Migration* (Cambridge, Mass.: Harvard University Press, 2003), 139–40.

17. See Morgan, *Slave Counterpoint*, 524–30; Stephanie M. H. Camp, "'I Could Not Stay There': Enslaved Women, Truancy and the Geography of Everyday Forms of Resistance in the Antebellum Plantation South," *Slavery and Abolition* 23 (December 2002): 1–20.

18. Minutes of the Governor and Council, July 7, 1772, *Colonial Records of Georgia*, 14:292–93; Gwendolyn Midlo Hall, *Africans in Colonial Louisiana: The Development of*

Afro-Creole Culture in the Eighteenth Century (Baton Rouge: Louisiana State University Press, 1992), 201–36. Gilbert C. Din claims Hall overestimates the extent of *grand maroonage* in colonial Louisiana, but does not deny that it happened: *Spaniards, Planters, and Slaves: The Spanish Regulation of Slavery in Louisiana, 1763–1803* (College Station: Texas A & M University Press,), 19–34. Herbert Aptheker, in a classic essay about maroon communities, identified about fifty in that part of North America within the present-day limits of the United States: "Maroons Within the Present Limits of the United States," in *Maroon Societies: Rebel Slave Communities in the Americas*, ed. Richard Price (Baltimore, Md.: Johns Hopkins University Press, 1996), 151–67.

19. Steven Hahn, "Hunting, Fishing, and Foraging: Common Rights and Class Relations in the Postbellum South," *Radical History Review* 26 (1982): 37–64; Hahn, *The Roots of Southern Populism: Yeoman Farmers and the Transformation of the Georgia Upcountry, 1850–1890* (New York, N.Y.: Oxford University Press, 1983), esp. chapter 7; and chapter 3 of Jack Temple Kirby's *Countercultural South* (Athens: University of Georgia Press, 1995). On how "the State" sees and makes legible resources and public lands, see John C. Scott, *Seeing Like a State: How Certain Schemes to Improve the Human Condition Have Failed* (New Haven, Conn.: Yale University Press, 1998), esp. chapter 1, but *passim*.

20. Margaret Lynn Brown, *The Wild East: A Biography of the Great Smoky Mountains* (Gainesville: University Press of Florida, 2000).

21. Melvin Dixon discusses how this notion of wilderness as a place of deliverance was accentuated in slave spirituals and was meant to be taken literally as well as in the Biblical sense. See *Ride Out the Wilderness: Geography and Identity in Afro-American Literature* (Urbana: University of Illinois Press, 1987), 1–28.

22. "The Bear" (*Go Down, Moses* version), in *Bear, Man, and God: Seven Approaches to William Faulkner's "The Bear,"* ed. Francis Lee Utley, Lynn Z. Bloom, and Arthur F. Kinney (New York: Random House, 1964), 5–114, quotation on 7. For another interpretation, see Louise H. Westling, *The Green Breast of the New World: Landscape, Gender, and American Fiction* (Athens: University of Georgia Press, 1996), 101–24.

23. James Hamilton Couper, "Essay on Rotation of Crops," *Southern Agriculturist* 6 (February–March 1833): 57–66, 113–20. For a full discussion of Couper, planter conservation ideas, and "green paternalism," see Stewart, *"What Nature Suffers to Groe,"* 182–88, 323–45, n74.

24. For other discussions of the emergence of ecological sensibilities among southern planters, see Joan E. Cashin, "Landscape and Memory in Antebellum Virginia," *Virginia Magazine of History and Biography* 102 (October 1994): 477–500; Jack Temple Kirby, *Poquosin: A Study of Rural Landscape and Society* (Chapel Hill: University of North Carolina Press, 1995), 61–94; introduction to Kirby, *Nature's Manager: Writings on Landscape and Reform by Edmund Ruffin* (Athens: University of Georgia Press, 2000); and Steven Stoll, *Larding the Lean Earth: Soil and Society in Nineteenth-Century America* (New York, N.Y.: Hill and Wang, 2002). Richard Grove recognized the antecedents to conservation thought among slave-holding planters in the seventeenth and eighteenth century in Dutch, French, and English colonies—island colonies

especially. See *Green Imperialism: Colonial Expansion, Tropical Island Edens and the Origins of Environmentalism, 1600–1860* (New York, N.Y.: Cambridge University Press, 1995), esp. 2–15.

25. See Mart A. Stewart, "'Let Us Begin with the Weather?': Climate, Race, and Cultural Distinctiveness in the American South," in *Nature and Society in Historical Context*, ed. Mikuláš Teich and Roy Porter (New York, N.Y.: Cambridge University Press, 1997), 240–56.

26. See Hahn, *A Nation Under Our Feet*, 2, 128; Kirby, *The Countercultural South*, 8–32. Kirby argues that deep traditions of negotiation and collective action have given African Americans more political power, once segregation was demolished, than poor whites—who have tended to withdraw into isolation or into individual acts of subversion.

27. Aiken, *The Cotton Plantation South*, 360–61. Steven Hahn explains how rural black southern culture was transported to urban places during the Great Migration, and there became the foundation for Garveyism and other important expressions of collective action and black nationalism: Hahn, *A Nation Under Our Feet*, 465–78. For a review of the origins of African American environmentalism, see Mart Stewart, "Nature, Negotiation, and Community: Slavery and the Origins of African American Environmentalism," in *"To Love the Wind and the Rain": Essays in African American Environmental History*, ed. Dianne Glave and Mark Stoll (Pittsburgh, Pa.: University of Pittsburgh Press, 2006).

28. Otis Graham, "Again the Backward Region: Environmental History In and Of the American South," *Southern Cultures* 6 (Summer 2000): 50–72. See also Mart A. Stewart, "Southern Environmental History," in Boles, *Companion to the American South*.

29. Some of the extensive scholarship that reflects on the place of the South in the United States is discussed in James C. Cobb, *Redefining Southern Culture: Mind and Identity in the Modern South* (Athens: University of Georgia Press, 1999).

30. C. Vann Woodward, "The Irony of Southern History," *Journal of Southern History* 19 (February 1953): 3–6.

31. Peter Kolchin has reviewed as well as amplified the rich literature that has compared the South with "Un-souths," kindred Souths, and other Souths in *A Sphinx on the American Land: The Nineteenth-Century South in Comparative Perspective* (Baton Rouge: Louisiana State University Press, 2003). For studies that argue the importance of comparing or connecting transnational environments, see Daniel Littlefield, *Rice and Slaves* (Baton Rouge: Louisiana State University Press, 1981), 84–92; Stewart, *"What Nature Suffers to Groe,"* 93, 102; and Judith Carney, *Black Rice: The African Origins of Rice Cultivation in the Americas* (Cambridge, Mass.: Harvard University Press, 2001).

32. On agrarian revolt as struggle over access to resources, see Hahn, *The Roots of Southern Populism*. The tenant farmers union movements in Alabama and Arkansas in the 1930s are other examples of agrarian revolt. See Theodore Rosengarten, *All God's Dangers: The Life of Nate Shaw* (New York, N.Y.: Alfred A. Knopf, 1974), 296–375;

Robin Kelly, *Hammer and Hoe: Alabama Communists During the Great Depression* (Chapel Hill: University of North Carolina Press, 1990); and Howard Kester, *Revolt Among the Sharecroppers* (Knoxville: University of Tennessee Press, 1997). For Native Americans and de-populating the National Parks, see Mark David Spence, *Dispossessing the Wilderness: Indian Removal and the Making of National Parks* (New York, N.Y.: Oxford University Press, 2000). For struggles between rural residents and state conservation efforts, see Louis Warren, *The Hunter's Game: Poachers and Conservationists in Twentieth Century America* (New Haven, Conn.: Yale University Press, 1999); and Karl Jacoby, *Crimes Against Nature: Squatters, Poachers, Thieves, and the Hidden History of American Conservation* (Berkeley: University of California Press, 2001). Jack Temple Kirby's *Mockingbird Song: Ecological Landscapes of the South* (Chapel Hill: University of North Carolina Press, 2006) includes the first full consideration of the resistance of rural southerners to state conservation initiatives, especially to fire control regimes.

33. For a reassessment of environmental history of another important American region, New England, in terms that are more home-grown and less shaped by the agenda of environmental historians of the West, see Richard W. Judd, "Writing Environmental History from East to West," in *Reconstructing Conservation: Finding Common Ground*, ed. Ben A. Minteer and Robert E. Manning (Washington, D.C.: Island Press, 2003).

CLAIRE STROM

Texas Fever and the Dispossession of the Southern Yeoman Farmer

> "Well, the guy that come aroun' talked nice as pie.
> 'You got to get off. It ain't my fault.'
> 'Well,' I says, 'whose fault is it? I'll go an' I'll nut the fella.'
> 'It's the Shawnee Lan' an' Cattle Company. I jus' got orders.'
> 'Who's the Shawnee Lan' an' Cattle Company?'
> 'It ain't nobody. It's a company.'"
> STEINBECK, *The Grapes of Wrath* (1939)

IN HIS CLASSIC NOVEL, *The Grapes of Wrath*, John Steinbeck holds corporate greed responsible for the dispossession of the southern yeoman farmer. Historians have been generally more discerning, offering a complex narrative in which soil depletion, cotton dependency, land usage patterns, currency shortages, racism, international prices, government policy, and mechanization, as well as Steinbeck's banks and corporations, all play important roles in a decades-long process. However, with the exception of the "white-hot emotions of a protest movement" fomented by the Southern Farmers' Alliance at the end of the nineteenth century, the yeomen themselves have been portrayed as the passive victims of dispossession. Indeed, the Alliance and the People's Party offered the only widespread, articulated, organized expression of yeoman discontent. Though lack of formalized political expression does not, in itself, indicate either passivity or acceptance, it does make the historian's job more difficult. Economic and political resistance, often in the form of violent public behavior, has to be dissected for meaning, and a text created where none originally existed.[1]

{ 220 }

In the early years of the twentieth century, one factor contributing to the dispossession of yeoman farmers was the eradication of the cattle tick, which carried and transmitted to cattle a disease called Texas fever. The tick was eradicated by a series of operations so onerous and expensive that small-scale farmers were effectively barred from stock ownership, eliminating part of their household production. Recognizing the economic threat of the eradication program and lacking a political voice, yeoman farmers responded with violence, dynamiting cattle-dipping vats and even killing federal agents. Ultimately, science and government triumphed, and the tick was extirpated from the southern United States—but, in the process, countless southern farmers were deprived of an important source of livelihood.

Tracing the story of the cattle tick and its eradication from the perspective of the small-scale farmer forces the historian to search the interstices of history for hidden discourses. Attention has been paid to the resistance of large-scale southwestern ranchers to northern quarantines intended to protect northern herds from infection. But little has been written on the yeomen and tenants who opposed, sometimes violently, federal attempts to eradicate disease borne by the cattle tick. These farmers did not triumph, and, in order to write a progressive narrative, many historians have either accepted the reactionary label applied to them by the agricultural scientists or ignored their story altogether.[2]

To fully explore this resistance requires working from the assumption that irrational violence was not the norm and that such a reaction was provoked by cogent socioeconomic grievances. The opposition of farmers to the eradication of Texas fever embodied valid questions regarding the nature of scientific authority and the cost/benefit ratio of destroying the disease. Eradication ultimately benefited only farmers who raised stock as a cash crop. Small-scale farmers with cattle for personal use or local sale found the expense of enforced disease eradication so high that many were forced to abandon their livestock holdings altogether.[3]

The problem posed by Texas fever represented a symbiosis between natural and social environments. The disease probably arrived in North America in the seventeenth century carried on cattle brought by Spanish colonists from the West Indies. It was transmitted by the cattle tick, which, like cotton plants, generally required two hundred or more frost-free days per year for survival. Consequently, the spatial boundaries of the tick in the United States matched (with some exceptions such as Kentucky) the cultural boundaries of the region known as the South. Traditional southern land-use practices—particularly allowing livestock to range freely—encouraged the spread of the insect, and the disease quickly became endemic.

Initially, southerners showed little concern about Texas fever. Cattle raising was rarely of primary importance in the southern United States, though southern farmers usually maintained some stock, if only for subsistence purposes. Most southern cattle contracted the Texas fever while young, and it rarely proved fatal, although it diminished weight gain and milk production. Southern stock was noted for its scrawny appearance, but the disease attracted little attention or scientific investigation. Agricultural scientists in the South focused on maximizing the production of cash crops, especially cotton. Cattle, used primarily for subsistence by farmers who looked elsewhere for capital income, were adequate for domestic needs.[4]

Antebellum Texas was the exception in the South; it dominated the national cattle industry. Texas had been used as cattle country by the original Spanish settlers, a practice fostered in the early nineteenth century by liberal land grants to American settlers. In the 1850s Texans drove their cattle to markets as far away as New Orleans, California, and Chicago. By 1861 Texas led the nation in beef cattle with 2,934,000 head, a number that is an accurate count of commercial stock but does not include feral and subsistence animals. After the Civil War, the cattle industry in Texas continued to thrive with the consolidation and expansion of old, individual holdings and the emergence of corporate ranches. Other areas of the South, such as the Wiregrass region of Georgia, also developed a cattle industry.[5]

Texas fever was closely associated with the commercial cattle industry. In the South the disease was endemic and debilitating but generally not fatal. Above a certain latitude its incidence was considerably less than it was farther south, but, when cattle contracted it, mortality rates could reach 90 percent. The trailing of Texas cattle to market in the 1850s, and the resulting epidemic infections of northern herds with Texas fever, first brought the attention of agricultural educators to the disease.[6]

Initially, northern resistance to southern cattle trails materialized at the grassroots level. In the 1850s bands of farmers in Missouri turned back cattle drives from Texas for fear of the fever infecting their herds. In 1866 groups of armed men met drovers at the southern borders of Kansas and Missouri and blocked entry into their states, assaulting and even killing some of the cowboys. The herds of those who persisted with their drives were sometimes stampeded and shot. By 1868 farmers in some localities in Illinois had organized to prevent the unloading of Texas cattle from trains in order to avoid the scourge that had caused huge losses in the local herds. However, southern cattle did not always meet northern opposition. A number of towns, such as Dodge City, Kansas, both thrived from the trailing industry and raised little stock themselves, and thus objected to attempts to stop the herds.[7]

Eventually, individual northern states intervened to protect their herds, instituting quarantine laws against southern cattle. Kansas passed legislation in the 1860s that prohibited cattle drives through certain areas of the state. As the state's population grew after the Civil War, the number of susceptible herds increased, and broader legislation became necessary. In 1885 the state legislature passed a law preventing any cattle from below the thirty-fourth parallel being trailed through the state between March 1 and December 1, because observation had shown that the disease was not transmitted during colder weather. The law carried penalties of a two thousand-dollar fine and/or imprisonment for up to a year and damages to farmers who had incurred losses from the disease. By the end of the year, Arizona, Colorado, Montana, Nebraska, New Mexico, and Wyoming had all passed similar legislation, which dealt a serious blow to the trailing industry and the movement of herds to northern ranges. Thus, the first state-level public policy toward Texas fever was containment and was mirrored in action taken by the federal government.[8]

In 1892 the federal government delineated a quarantine line that followed the known northern border of permanent fever infestation. The accompanying regulations stated that cattle could be moved to markets north of the quarantine line only by rail or boat, not on foot, between January 15 and November 15. During this same period, cattle moved north could not be held for fattening but had to be slaughtered immediately. These measures considerably reduced the price that southern beef fetched in the North, which was already low because beef from Texas cattle was tough and stringy.[9]

The curtailment of southern trailing herds led to increased scientific interest in Texas fever. Disease identification and treatment followed, initiated for the most part by southern agricultural experiment stations, with later help from the United States Department of Agriculture (USDA). The agricultural scientists involved in identifying and treating the disease met resistance from some farmers, usually small-scale yeomen, whom they categorized in official literature as reactionary and ill-informed. Financial losses from Texas fever and northern quarantines were not evenly distributed among southern cattle owners. Many small-scale farmers raised cattle for subsistence, running one or two head. These yeomen were affected by the slow weight gain and low milk production of diseased cattle, but their losses were difficult to quantify. The yeoman farmers did not suffer as a result of lower prices for southern cattle on northern markets because, if they sold their animals at all, it was at local markets. Throughout the nation, agricultural scientists paid little attention to yeomen, focusing instead on capital-intensive tick eradication programs that were impossible for small-scale farmers to implement. Southern yeomen, like their counterparts elsewhere, did not have money to invest in updating their operations. At this stage, however, the action taken on state and national levels to contain Texas fever affected only those farmers with large, national livestock businesses. Small-scale farmers, raising cattle for their own purposes, were not affected by the quarantine laws.[10]

In the 1890s agricultural scientists became more interested in eradicating Texas fever. As the boll weevil devastated cotton crops throughout the South, regional agricultural colleges and their experts increasingly emphasized the diversification of farm operations—using arable land for purposes other than cotton culture including commercial livestock operations.[11]

Southern attempts to improve breeding stock by buying from northern herds met with disaster, as 60 to 75 percent of the imported cattle died from Texas fever. The high rate of death made stock improvement prohibitively expensive. Texas fever also prevented southern cattle breeders from exhibiting at national stock or dairy fairs. These disadvantages affected only farmers with sufficient capital to be concerned with upgrading their stock and scientists interested in promoting the diversification of the South's commercial agricultural base.[12]

Scientists increasingly viewed Texas fever as a major hindrance to the modernization of southern agriculture. Their attempts to cure, identify, contain, and finally eradicate the disease increased proportionately. Throughout the second half of the nineteenth century, individual stock owners had investigated the disease on an amateur basis, but in the 1890s the agricultural experiment stations assumed the responsibility of combating Texas fever. As the onus shifted from individual gentleman farmers to scientific experts, theories regarding the cause of Texas fever proliferated. These included the notions that the feet of infected cattle and/or their saliva transmitted the disease and that southern cattle carried the germ of the disease in their feces and urine, spreading it via these excretions.[13] In 1893 the Bureau of Animal Industry, an agency of the USDA, hopped on the scientific bandwagon with yet another theory as to the cause of the disease. That year the bureau published its first bulletin, which was written by Theobald Smith and F. L. Kilborne, who asserted that the villain of the piece was a parasitical protozoan that they called *Pyrosoma bigeminum*. This parasite, they determined, had two hosts: cattle and the cattle tick, *Boophilus bovis*. Once injected into the cattle's blood by the tick, the protozoan infected the animal, causing the well-known symptoms of Texas fever. Kilborne and Smith's work had far-reaching implications. They were the first to prove the cycle of transmission of a disease via a vector from one host animal to another. The discovery had broad medical significance, creating a paradigm that was later applied to human diseases such as malaria and yellow fever.[14]

Kilborne and Smith's discovery of the cause of Texas fever stood the test of time and allowed state agricultural scientists to turn their attention to combating the cattle tick. Tackling Texas fever presented researchers the ideal vehicle for persuading farmers to apply modern, scientific principles to their operations. Scientists could, and did, claim authority in solving the puzzle of the cause and transmission of a disease, and they mobilized the power of law to impose their authority and to solidify government-funded science as the locus of agricultural expertise.

The attack on Texas fever had ramifications beyond science and veterinary medicine. Scientists on the state and federal levels had three main objectives: to find an effective treatment for the disease and to minimize its debilitation; to develop immunization against the fever; and to eradicate the cattle tick in southern pastures. The first two objectives were relatively conservative: they focused on adapting southern cattle to their entomological environment. The third goal was radical: eradicating the tick would fundamentally change the natural environment of the South, necessarily affecting the human environment.

Researchers were unable to find a cure for infected cattle despite attempts to treat the symptoms using existing knowledge. By the twentieth century a number of scientists at experiment stations advocated using quinine to control the fever because of its efficacy in treating malaria, but it was not effective against Texas fever. Scientists also recommended that farmers alleviate fever-induced constipation with a drench of Epsom salts, ground ginger, and other additions including salt and syrup. Farmers were advised to force-feed animals that refused food with a high-protein mixture of eggs and milk. Experts prescribed tonics to revitalize the animal after the fever dropped, including sulfate of iron, powdered gentian root, nux vomica (strychnine), and common salt. All these remedies called for the frequent use of whiskey as a temperature reducer, a restorative, and a nutrient. More significantly, they all required time, fenced space, and money, and so only the wealthier stock owners could seriously pursue the various cures advocated.[15]

In the decade after 1893 southern experiment stations focused primarily on immunizing cattle. The premise was that the fever should be introduced to the stock in a controlled manner when they were at the best age to survive it (twelve to eighteen months of age). The disease could then be treated, and the cattle would recover and remain immune.[16]

The emphasis on immunization stemmed from the opinion of many agricultural scientists that tick eradication was impossible and that such efforts were likely to have consequences that would harm local stock owners. This view was especially prevalent in states, such as Florida and Alabama, that had an infested state between them and the federal quarantine line. The agricultural experts realized that exterminating the tick in all, or a portion, of their states placed stock at high risk when being driven to market through infected regions. Thus to focus on tick eradication in these areas would effectively mean the destruction of any commercial potential in stock raising because their cattle would sicken or die when driven to market. State experiment stations understood the potential benefit of tick eradication but sensibly saw it as a process that should work from the quarantine line south, rather than in the opposite direction.[17]

Thus state scientists investigated various ways of immunizing cattle. They recommended that farmers palpate the inner thighs and dewlaps of local cattle before purchase and buy only animals bearing the marks of previous tick infestations. This careful observation would ensure that new stock had been exposed to the disease and had developed an immunity.[18] Northern cattle could not be checked this way, because their tick marks would come from northern, non-disease-bearing insects. For northern animals, the scientists recommended two basic methods of immunization, the natural method and inoculation. The natural method involved penning calves in a tick-free environment and then infecting the animals with a controlled number of ticks, gradually increasing the number to induce immunity. When the cattle were deemed sufficiently immune they were released into ticky pastures.[19]

As with the cures recommended by experts, only the farming elite could utilize this method of immunization. It required sufficient land to maintain a tick-free quarantine pen for calves. Few southern farmers had the acreage available for such specialized, non-income-producing use. Indeed, most southern farmers who owned cattle did not devote any of their own land to their stock; instead, they turned cattle out to forage under the free-range laws. Also, cattle being immunized often had to be hand-fed because they were penned. Hand-feeding the penned cattle and capturing and breeding ticks for immunization made the process of natural immunization labor-intensive, although it did prove effective.[20]

The inoculation method of immunization involved vaccinating the cattle in order to induce a controlled fever. The experiment stations tried a variety of vaccines. Arkansas scientists investigated three possible vaccines: pulverized tick eggs, larval ticks, and blood removed from engorged ticks. The results were, at best, inconclusive, and researchers realized that these methods were intricate and therefore infeasible on a large scale.[21] Other researchers tried inoculating calves with infected cattle blood. Blood inoculation, while effective to some degree, was difficult and unreliable. The removal of infected blood required surgical techniques that were difficult to perform in the farm environment, and the fever that followed the injection could not be regulated to a fine enough degree.[22]

Researchers attempted to isolate a sterile serum from the blood of immune cattle. They hoped that an injection with such serum would enable cattle to avoid the acute fever brought about by regular inoculation and by immunization using tick infestation. Also, serum would be easier to ship and store and would be free of the complications of coagulation, loss of infectiousness, and septicemia, all of which reduced the usefulness of infected blood as an injectant. However, the blood serum obtained from immune cattle proved ineffective in immunizing others.[23]

All of the methods of immunizing cattle offered by the southern experiment stations—and on which the agricultural scientists spent vast amounts of time—were aimed at capital-intensive, commercial farming. The goal was to inoculate imported northern cattle, which most small-scale farmers could not afford to purchase. The methods required considerable labor, fenced pasturage, shelter for sick animals, special feed, and, in the case of blood inoculation, expensive veterinary equipment. As with the various cures promoted by the experiment stations, immunization appealed only to the established stock farmer who had the wherewithal for its implementation. This bias in favor of large-scale farmers on the part of the USDA and the state experiment stations became more pronounced with the increasing stress on tick eradication.

Although researchers at experiment stations had begun work on eradicating the tick as early as 1898, they soon recognized that their efforts would not be successful unless orchestrated on a national level. Effective eradication had to progress systematically through the entire infected South using an overall plan, which required a unity of purpose not present among postbellum southern farmers. Acknowledging this, the scientists generally only advised immunizing cattle, ridding them of ticks for northern transportation, and perhaps maintaining some tick-free pasture for newly bought calves or a northern stud bull prior to immunization.[24]

In 1906 the federal government assumed responsibility for coordinating tick eradication. Congress appropriated $82,500, enabling the Secretary of Agriculture to work with state authorities in extirpating the cattle tick. For work to begin, each state required laws allowing local officials to inspect herds, enforce quarantines and animal disinfections, and control livestock movement, and allowing federal officials to enforce state laws in these matters. Only seven of the fifteen infested states had passed the necessary legislation—Virginia, North Carolina, Georgia, Kentucky, Tennessee, Oklahoma, and California—and work began in these areas. Federal agents inspected herds and assessed tick presence, educated farmers about the necessity and methods of tick eradication, and helped establish centers for dipping and spraying cattle. In all of this, the government worked closely with state boards of agriculture and state university personnel. In 1907 the federal appropriation increased to $150,000 and in 1908 to $250,000, where it plateaued for the duration of the eradication program. By 1910 South Carolina, Alabama, Mississippi, and Arkansas had passed the necessary legislation to participate in the federal program, while Missouri, Florida, Texas, and Louisiana continued to work on tick eradication independent of the federal government with varying degrees of success.[25]

This national plan bolstered scientific expertise with federal funds and enforced it with state legislation. Not surprisingly, after the appropriation of 1906, state experiment stations focused their energies on promoting tick eradication and abandoned efforts to cure or immunize against Texas fever. This resulted in a narrowing of public options. Farmers could exterminate the cattle tick three ways: on the cattle, in pastures, or both simultaneously. Ultimately all three methods proved integral to success, with attention being paid to the life cycle of the tick to prevent re-infestation.[26]

The pasture rotation system presented the easiest and cheapest way to disinfect a farm. It also complemented nicely the agricultural experiment stations' efforts to encourage the southern farmers to practice diversified agriculture. Entomologist H. A. Morgan, director of the Agricultural Experiment Station in Tennessee, devised the basic system while working at the Louisiana Experiment Station in Baton Rouge. Basing his work on the life cycle of the tick, Morgan suggested that the cattle be placed in a pasture until all the ticks had dropped off them. Before these ticks could lay their eggs and re-infest the herd, the cattle were moved to a pasture previously cleared of ticks (it had long been established that the absence of cattle from a given pasture for a year or more, preferably in conjunction with the plowing or burning of the land, would rid the pasture of its ticks). The cattle were not moved back to the infested pasture until it, too, had been artificially cleaned by fire, or until the ticks had died of starvation. Different experiment stations devised various methods of crop rotation, which dovetailed with Morgan's research, enabling them to push the general notion of diversifying agriculture while simultaneously maximizing farm usage and destroying the cattle tick. This method assumed that farmers had enough land to leave pasture unused and enough money to fence pasture against stray, tick-infested stock.[27]

Morgan also established a process, known as the feed-lot system, by which to eradicate the ticks from cattle. This provided the optimum method for farmers with tick-free farms who wanted to buy an infested herd or for farmers who sold cattle and wanted to increase their price by offering tick-free stock. The system involved cattle being placed in one feed lot for twenty days and then moved to another for twenty days. Twenty days allowed the ticks to drop from the cattle but did not give time for re-infestation to occur. At the end of the forty days the cattle would be tick-free and ready to be placed in clean pasture or to be sold. If the farmer plowed up his entire acreage, including pastures, while the cattle were contained on feed lots, this system could clear the whole farm of ticks.[28]

The pasture rotation and feed-lot methods were efficacious only in a farming situation with fenced livestock. On a ranch, with stock wandering over open ground, pasture clearance proved impossible. For the stock raisers who still utilized the open range or who maintained massive tracts of fenced land, the solutions advocated were not feasible. Any poor or middling farmer who wished to eradicate the tick using these methods also faced difficulties. Owning or farming less than fifty acres, usually devoted to a cash crop, they had insufficient acreage for pasture and little spare money for feed or fences.[29] Moreover, most small-scale farmers did not see the need to eradicate the tick because their native-born cattle developed a natural immunity—the cattle did not die but had a slower weight gain and less milk production—to the disease and were largely used for home consumption or local sale. Thus, the cultural environment of free-range laws that had fostered the spread of the tick presented an obstacle to eradication. Successfully redrawing the entomological boundaries required changing long-held social customs.

In ranching and smallholding, the two extremes of cattle raising in the South, the only effective means of eradicating the tick was regular treatment of cattle. Killing ticks on the stock at two-week intervals throughout the year destroyed the infestation. Exterminating ticks could be done in a number of ways, all of which, as with curing and immunization, were expensive in terms of money, land, or manpower. Several of the earlier bulletins from state agricultural experiment stations recommended curry-combing and handpicking the ticks off the cattle, which was effective but time-consuming and made financial sense only when used to minimize the initial tick infestation on a newly purchased animal.[30]

Another method frequently advocated by experiment stations was spraying or washing the animals. By 1907 and 1908 many experiment stations recognized and recommended this method, proposing the application of crude oil or kerosene. Scientists stressed the importance of complete coverage of each animal and prescribed caution if stock were covered with oil in hot weather, recommending that shade be provided for the treated cattle. Spraying, like hand picking, cost little, but was labor intensive and impractical for large range herds.[31]

In 1894 Mark Francis of the Texas Agricultural Experiment Station started to experiment with the use of dipping vats to kill ticks on cattle. Initially, scientists recommended dipping cattle in crude oil of varying depths floated on a base of water. Oil dips posed two problems: the expense of the oil and the considerable mortality often suffered by the herd. Nevertheless, crude oil remained the federally recommended dip until 1910. Before this, however, some states, such as Oklahoma, experimented with arsenical dips, which were adopted nationally in the 1910s. Arsenic had the advantage of being cheap and easy to use. It did not cling to the cattle and thus adversely affect their health or appearance; on the contrary, it gave the coat a glossy appearance. Caution had to be taken in handling the arsenic and in ensuring that the solution was not too strong. Furthermore, cattle needed to be watered before being dipped to prevent them from drinking the arsenic solution. Some farmers also contended that the arsenic contaminated the stock's milk and reduced dairy yield.[32]

Dipping offered an effective way to eradicate the tick; however, it required the construction of expensive dipping vats. Construction of vats, enforcement of local quarantines, inspection of herds, and treatment of all stock in a given area called for a high level of cooperation among federal and state governments, local organizations, and farmers—cooperation that did not always exist.[33]

Redefining the geographical boundaries of the tick required significant societal change throughout the South. The forces of authority had to focus on destroying the sympathetic cultural environment that had fostered the spread of the tick as well as on control of the insect. Participation in other programs to treat Texas fever had been voluntary and had often hinged on the resources of the individual farmer. However, tick eradication was geographically dependent; for the program to be effective, all cattle in a given area had to be treated. When mandatory participation was implemented, active resistance to the policies of the experiment stations and

USDA emerged. Small-scale and middling farmers resented being required to expend money and effort to treat their cattle for no perceived advantage and some very obvious disadvantages.

The ensuing struggle was part of a broader contest over where agricultural expertise lay. The ultimate victory of the agricultural researchers by means of science and law led to the eradication of Texas fever. It also contributed to the dispossession of many small-scale southern farmers, joining other forces pushing them into a cash economy and cotton peonage. Through their victory, scientists gained authority, not only in implementing their goals but also in fashioning the history of these endeavors. Resistant farmers are portrayed as stubborn and difficult to convince and are deprived of their voice as well as their livelihood.[34]

The first challenge the researchers faced in eradicating the cattle tick was convincing farmers that ticks actually caused Texas fever. The agency of the tick as a parasitical carrier presented a new and complex idea in scientific thought that was difficult to explain and promote to laymen. Additionally, it was the latest in a long line of explanations of the causes of the disease, and many farmers, justifiably skeptical, refused to believe it. To persuade farmers that cattle ticks carried disease, experiment stations such as those in Virginia and Louisiana published entomological bulletins detailing the differences among the various ticks commonly found in local pastures. The life cycle of the cattle tick and the method of infection were also repeatedly explained. Scientists even started referring to the disease as "Tick fever" in their bulletins to highlight causality.

This method of education relied on farmers acquiring and reading bulletins, but while these could be obtained free of charge from agricultural experiment stations, there were few requests for such literature. The other method of disseminating information in the 1900s and 1910s was farm visits. The agricultural agents who undertook these tended to focus on the larger, capital-intensive farmers, partly because they had the money to implement change. Hence, information about the tick and methods of combating Texas fever spread slowly and unevenly. In the 1920s the USDA made some attempts to reach a wider farm audience, issuing a three-reel movie that demonstrated "that only selfishness and prejudice oppose the useful work of tick eradication," thus revealing as much about official assumptions as about farmer bias. Federal officials took the film to southern communities, but the overall impact of this form of propaganda was slight.[35]

The scientists also had to convince farmers that Texas fever reduced their income substantially. Assessments of the monetary loss suffered by southern cattle raisers at northern markets due to imposed quarantines varied. In 1908 R. R. Dinwiddie at the Arkansas Agricultural Experiment Station stated that the market price for a prime northern animal was $7.25 per hundred pounds compared with $6.50 for one from the South. By the end of the decade the discrepancy had increased, according to the Oklahoma State Board of Agriculture, which stated that cattle above the federal quarantine line were worth $3 to $5 more per head than those below. Scientists at both state and national levels made attempts to assess the total loss of southern income due to Texas fever. At Clemson Agricultural College in South Carolina, experts quantified the annual loss to the state's cattle owners at $122,946.30 in 1902. In Georgia two years later, C. L. Willoughby from the state experiment station reported annual state losses of between $400,000 and $600,000. The federal Bureau of Animal Industry estimated total annual losses in 1910 from tick fever of $40 million to $200 million.[36]

Significantly, figures for southern losses from Texas fever and from the federal quarantine come from agricultural scientists who, by the early twentieth century, were pushing farmers toward mandated eradication of the disease rather than mere containment or voluntary treatment. Figures proving the disadvantages inherent in quarantined containment strengthened the case for eradication. Less quantifiable, but perhaps more persuasive, were testimonials in newspapers by prominent local farmers who had directly experienced the benefits of dipping their cattle. However, these elite landowners, raising cattle in quantity for market, operated on an economy of scale in which the construction of private dipping vats paid for itself. Thus, advocacy by these neighbors was as alien to the yeomen as scientific numbers.[37]

Farmers who accepted the tick's role in spreading cattle fever, and hence the economic need to eradicate the parasite, were bombarded with conflicting information on how to address the problem. Drenching their stock with melted lard, injecting them with crushed tick eggs, immunizing them with infected blood, rotating them through various pastures, currycombing them, and spraying them with kerosene were all promoted with the same degree of absolute authority and supposed efficacy. All of these methods cost money and time; some even worked. In the face of a great deal of advice, much of it conflicting, farmers remained suspicious of agricultural experts. Furthermore, if cattle owners found an effective method of eradication, they were sometimes unwilling to try another method.

The method finally adopted by the federal government to eradicate the cattle tick throughout the South required that all farmers dip cattle on a regular basis in cooperation with local, state, and federal agencies. The dipping process varied from state to state. The states that qualified for federal monies used federal, state, and county funds to build dipping vats and pay local veterinarians. Focus areas were established either voluntarily or as determined by state boards of agriculture. The focus area usually adjoined the federal quarantine line and was surrounded by a state quarantine line to ensure against re-infestation.[38]

This state quarantine line, while essential to eradication, hindered cattle farming. It restricted local movement of stock, already seriously circumscribed with respect to long-distance trade. In some instances, the quarantine line was so specific that stock could not be moved from a farm for one to two years, or until officials judged that farm tick-free. Farmers resented these restrictions, and, by 1910, the Bureau of Animal Industry recommended that areas delineated within a state be as large as possible to maximize stock movement. Maximization of quarantine areas was of little consequence in areas such as Texas, where the main trade was out of state. Farmers also faced the re-infestation of their cattle, which in some areas happened repeatedly, resulting in indefinite quarantine.[39]

Counties exercised considerable control over eradication in their locality. Federal and state appropriations invariably proved insufficient; therefore, before a county could be included in an eradication district, local funds had to be raised to pay for the construction of dipping vats and the salaries of local inspectors. Localities raised this money in various ways. In some states voluntary contributions initiated the process of local tick eradication, in others county courts determined funding. Without such help, eradication could not progress. Other states, such as Arkansas, established a method of financing requiring cattle in the counties being treated to be taxed at five cents per head. Usually, the main burden of finance for tick eradication fell on the federal government and the counties being treated. In 1910 Tennessee counties paid $24,235.66 toward the process compared to $23,552.61 from the national government and $2,271.60 from the state. Therefore, local governments possessed considerable financial power to hinder the eradication process if they chose, by restricting their financial contributions.[40]

In addition to financing, counties also controlled eradication through personnel. Local officials were responsible for inspecting farms in a given area to determine infection levels. The laws required that all farmers treat their cattle regularly through at least one season, usually at public dipping vats. These were built, often by local labor, at prominent locations designed to be no more than three miles from any farmer (in some states, such as Oklahoma, treatment was administered on the farm). Farmers had to round up their cattle and drive them to the local dips eight or ten times in a summer. The local, state, and federal inspectors worked to ensure that farmers did indeed dip their cattle and that they understood the need for tick eradication and the benefits that would ensue. These federal agents also regularly inspected herds in order to release them from quarantine as soon as possible.[41]

The dependence of tick eradication on county cooperation made it impossible to implement a program without substantial support from local farmers and various levels of government. Opposition materialized in varied ways. Some counties refused to cooperate with the state and federal governments on any level. This effectively prevented local eradication. Other local governments cooperated but did not prosecute farmers who refused to participate in the program. In some cases, local governments turned a blind eye to considerable violence. In Lowndes and Echols Counties, Georgia, in 1922, the federal tick eradication program was met with dynamited vats and burned cattle pens while state and federal officials were beaten and at least one was murdered. The counties took no action to capture or prosecute the offenders, so the federal government defended its agents and dipping vats by mounting Browning machine guns for use against farmer opposition.[42]

A major obstacle to eradication was the South's historical land use patterns. One of the main reasons for the ubiquity of the cattle tick in the South was the lack of fence laws requiring the enclosure of stock. In free-range areas, where the cattle could roam at large, tick eradication was impossible, and attempts proved ineffective until the county passed stock laws. Thus a county could effectively prevent federal and state intervention by refusing to pass fence laws. Even in counties with stock laws, the farmers often turned their cattle out to graze during the winter after the crops had been gathered. In these counties, resistance to tick eradication did not materialize until farmers realized that the process would circumscribe their free winter grazing.

The promotion of tick eradication and fencing reflected a clear class bias. Most resistance to fencing came from small-scale farmers, raising cattle for subsistence and local sale and reliant on the benefits inherent in free grazing. The tradition of free range was under threat from other forces in the postbellum South. After the Civil War, with an increased focus on the production of cotton for market, the rights to subsistence livestock appeared less salient. Additionally, the presence of a vast body of economically marginal freedmen, often in debt to landlords and/or furnishing merchants, placed wandering livestock at risk of being stolen. The railroads, too, which played a significant role in the development of the postbellum South, objected to the open-range laws, as the companies were required to pay for stock killed by their trains. The farming elite and southern corporations attacked the tradition of open range, while yeomen and tenant farmers supported it.[43]

Despite pressures to implement stock laws, the open range in the South did not completely vanish until the 1970s. Small-scale, white independent farmers, raising cattle for home or local consumption, violently resisted the idea that they should enclose their stock. These farmers—usually living in sparsely populated, largely white counties that were not cotton dominated—did not have the pasture land to fence and so, if forced to enclose their animals, would have to abandon stock raising. Far from being reactionary, these farmers clearly recognized the economic implications of fencing on their farming operations.[44]

These inarticulate and violent men resisted the scientific community's efforts to eradicate Texas fever. Not intending their cattle for sale outside the state, they did not stand to benefit from the lifting of the national quarantine, which would permit year-round cattle sales in the North. The defendants charged with assaulting government officials in Echols County, Georgia, argued that "no showing had been made that the cattle involved were the subject-matter of interstate commerce and liable to supervision by the Secretary of Agriculture." As well as reflecting contested jurisdiction, the case also mirrored the plight of small-scale farmers for whom tick eradication was unnecessary and prohibitively expensive. Yeomen simply could not afford to implement an eradication process based on the construction of fences and dipping vats. These farmers were not ignorant of the benefits of tick eradication, instead they were well aware of the dangers the program posed to their livelihood.[45]

Regional customs sometimes brought yeomen unexpected allies in their opposition to tick eradication. Large stock raisers, especially in dry regions where access to water was a critical factor, had already started to fence their stock using barbed wire that had first appeared on the market in 1874. On the other hand, large stock raisers in the Wiregrass region of Georgia still relied on the open range and joined the yeomen in their protests.[46]

In Texas the opposition of small-scale farmers to fencing was compounded by resistance to the expense inherent in the dipping program. Additionally, a number of large stock raisers opposed the federal policy because of the indefinite and absolute quarantine it placed on cattle. Prior quarantines and exclusions from northern markets had been limiting but not comprehensive. As a result, Texas refused to cooperate with the federal program until 1917. Some localities had displayed interest in eradication earlier, and the federal government had released seven counties and parts of five others from quarantine by 1910. Only when the influential Texas and Southwestern Cattle Raisers' Association placed itself officially behind eradication did the state pass the laws necessary for federal compliance.[47]

Opposition to eradication remained high, however, especially in eastern Texas where small-scale farmers predominated. In Shelby County alone farmers dynamited sixty-seven dipping vats in a single night. Yeomen also resisted dipping their cattle in Brown County in central Texas. These farmers had violently opposed the fencing of public lands by wealthy stock raisers in the mid-1880s. In addition to opposing fencing, Texan yeomen argued against the eradication program on other, equally economic, grounds. According to Robert E. Igo writing for *Farm and Ranch* in 1918, "Many of the small speculators are disposing of their herds, protesting that it is too much worry and trouble to round up and drive twice each month till winter, as it takes one day in most cases to dip and get through, and generally takes from two to three hands, which all claim comes at some time when their labor on the farms would be worth from $5 to $20 per day to them."[48] Yeomen perceived tick eradication as another attempt to undermine their livelihood, and violence reemerged in 1919, with vats being dynamited throughout Brown County.[49]

In addition to encountering violent opposition to stock laws, USDA officials faced the hostility of the South to "a bunch of Federal dictators at Washington, D.C.," an attitude that did not begin to change until the New Deal.[50] Most farmers viewed the USDA's eradication program with considerable suspicion, which was exacerbated by the inexperience and ignorance of federal officials. After four years of the federal program, the Bureau of Animal Industry addressed this issue, stating that its agents had improved greatly through experience, yet the problem of ignorance seemed to persist. The annual report of the Oklahoma State Board of Agriculture for 1916 laid great stress on the incompetence of federal agents, who had caused a number of cattle to be burned in too-strong dipping solutions. Individual farmers requested compensation for their substantial financial losses ($36,000) from Congress, while the state of Oklahoma refused further cooperation with the federal government's tick eradication program.[51]

Tick eradication progressed slowly as a consequence of this resistance by individual farmers, counties, and states. By 1910 only one-fifth of the infected area throughout the South had been cleared, and re-infestation was common. Farmers changed their perspective only with confirmation of eradication benefits from trusted and relevant sources. As officials removed areas from federal quarantine, as owners marketed animals more profitably, and as herds improved through breeding, the benefits of eradication became increasingly apparent to stock raisers. The opposition of the small-scale, subsistence farmers became ineffective as the larger owners, who maintained local political dominance, became convinced of the efficacy of eradication.[52]

Throughout the 1920s work progressed, although the number of experiment station publications on the tick decreased. Causation and prevention had been established, and eradication would eventually follow. By 1933 the tick was controlled to the extent that federal quarantine remained only in parts of Texas, Louisiana, Florida, and Arkansas. This was the last year the federal government considered the disease significant enough to mention it in the USDA yearbook. In the 1940s the disease remained only in specific areas such as the Seminole reservation in Florida and the counties of Texas near the Mexican border, where it continues to be an issue today.[53]

The work of the southern experiment stations to destroy the cattle tick and promote diversification did not increase the number of cattle raised in the South during the first quarter of the twentieth century. In 1906 the state auditor assessed the value of cattle in Arkansas at $8,294,089, whereas the gross income produced by the state's cotton crop for the same year was over $50 million. Ten years later in South Carolina, after considerable attempts by governmental and educational organizations to persuade the farmers to diversify, the cotton crop sold for $104,585,000, while the total value of cattle in the state was assessed at just over $9.8 million.[54]

Gains were made, however, in the number of cattle raised for market. The number of northern pure-bred stock imported for breeding rose dramatically in some states, such as Alabama, after 1910, and by 1914 interested owners were founding baby beef clubs for boys aged ten to eighteen. Although the increase was not as great as researchers wished, the grain-dairy-livestock business grew throughout the South, especially in Virginia, Kentucky, and Tennessee, where relatively large farms (140-plus acres) were the rule.[55]

The rise of the southern cattle business, taken in conjunction with no overall sectional increase in numbers of cattle, indicates an absolute decline in subsistence cattle ownership. The expense and labor involved in the required treatment partially accounts for this decline, but of more significance was the elimination of free grazing through the implementation of stock laws. Examining statistics on a more localized basis illustrates this trend. Between 1890 and 1920, for example, in yeoman regions of Georgia, there was a decrease in the number of cattle, except in the Wiregrass area that was known for its large commercial herds. This trend is attributed to the decline of free range. By the second quarter of the century, the dominance of cattle as a cash crop was evident, with the cash farm income of Georgia cattle and calves rising from five million dollars a year in 1924 to forty million in 1948.[56]

Thus the enforced eradication of Texas fever in the South did not benefit tenants and small-scale farmers. Their violent opposition to this program was founded in sound economic reasoning. Lacking the money to improve and expand their herds for commercial purposes, these farmers had long utilized the free range to supplement their limited family economy. Eradication cost them money and labor and also required a fundamental alteration in their cultural environment through the abandonment of free-range laws. The loss of household meat and milk production helped enmesh farmers further in crop peonage and cotton dependency or forced them out of the rural South altogether.[57]

The progressive historical narrative of tick eradication, compiled through the documentation of dominant actors, correlates scientific advancement with improvement of human life. Texas fever hindered southern commercial stock raising, and science, in the guise of Theobald Smith and F. L. Kilborne, discovered the vectorship of the tick. In response, all levels of government poured funds and manpower into tick eradication, the program succeeded, and the South developed into a cattle-raising area. This narrative leaves no place for rational opposition, so yeoman violence toward the program of tick eradication is either not mentioned or dismissed as a reactionary response born out of ignorance or stupidity.[58]

Probing the interstices of history for the lost voice of yeoman farmers adds depth and complexity to the story. While the progressive narrative is not invalidated, subtleties, contradictions, and options emerge. Far from lacking understanding, the yeoman farmers correctly perceived the tick eradication program as a threat to their livelihood. What they did lack was political power to resist this program effectively. Their violence, therefore, was not a reflection of ignorance but represented the frustration and political expression of the marginalized.

Notes

1. Robert C. McMath Jr., *American Populism: A Social History, 1877–1898* (New York, N.Y.: Hill & Wang, 1993), 179 (quotation). For discussion of the dispossession of the southern yeoman, see Jack Temple Kirby, *Rural Worlds Lost: The American South, 1920–1960* (Baton Rouge: LSU Press, 1987); Gilbert C. Fite, *Cotton Fields No More: Southern Agriculture, 1865–1980* (Lexington: University of Kentucky Press, 1984); Pete Daniel, *Breaking the Land: The Transformation of Cotton, Tobacco, and Rice Cultures Since 1880* (Urbana: University of Illinois Press, 1985); and Steven Hahn, *The Roots of Southern Populism: Yeoman Farmers and the Transformation of the Georgia Upcountry, 1850–1890* (New York, N.Y.: Oxford University Press, 1983).

2. Ernest Staples Osgood, *The Day of the Cattleman* (Minneapolis: University of Minnesota Press, 1929), 169–72; Lewis Nordyke, *Great Roundup: The Story of Texas and Southwestern Cowmen* (New York, N.Y.: Morrow, 1955), 206–10; and Mary Whatley Clarke, *A Century of Cow Business: A History of the Texas and Southwestern Cattle Raisers Association* (Fort Worth: Texas and Southwestern Cattle Raisers Association, 1976), 65–66.

3. For discussion of the Southern Farmers' Alliance and the yeomen's political opposition, see, for example, McMath, *American Populism;* Lawrence Goodwyn, *The*

Populist Moment: A Short History of the Agrarian Revolt in America (New York, N.Y.: Oxford University Press, 1978); Gene Clanton, *Populism: The Humane Preference, 1890–1900* (Boston, Mass.: Twayne, 1991); Peter H. Argersinger, "Populists in Power: Public Policy and Legislative Behavior," *Journal of Interdisciplinary History*, XVIII (Summer 1987), 81–105; Gene Clanton, "'Hayseed Socialism' on the Hill: Congressional Populism, 1891–1895," *Western Historical Quarterly*, XV (April 1984), 139–63; James Turner, "Understanding the Populists," *Journal of American History*, LXVII (September 1980), 354–73. For alternative research techniques that can be applied to the study of other marginalized groups, see Nell Irvin Painter, "Sojourner Truth in Life and Memory: Writing the Biography of an American Exotic," *Gender and History*, 2, 1 (Spring 1990), 3–16; Gyan Prakash, "Subaltern Studies as Postcolonial Criticism," *American Historical Review*, XCIX (December 1994), 1475–90; Gaytari Chakravorty Spivak, "Can the Subaltern Speak?" in Cary Nelson and Lawrence Grossberg, eds., *Marxism and the Interpretation of Culture* (Urbana, Ill.: University of Illinois Press, 1988), 271–313; and Lata Mani, "Contentious Traditions: The Debate on *Sati* in Colonial India," in Kurnkum Sangari and Sudesh Vaid, eds., *Recasting Women: Essays in Indian Colonial History* (New Brunswick, N.J.: Rutgers University Press, 1990), 88–126.

4. J. Crawford King Jr., "The Closing of the Southern Range: An Exploratory Study," *Journal of Southern History*, XLVIII (February 1982), 63; Sam Bowers Hilliard, *Hog Meat and Hoecake: Food Supply in the Old South* (Carbondale, Ill.: Southern Illinois University Press, 1972), 38–40; and Fite, *Cotton Fields No More*, 8, 20, and 77.

5. Edward Everett Dale, *The Range Cattle Industry: Ranching on the Great Plains from 1865 to 1925* (rev. ed.; Norman: University of Oklahoma Press, 1960), 3–10; and Hahn, *Roots of Southern Populism*, 244.

6. Julius Rubin, "The Limits of Agricultural Progress in the Nineteenth-Century South," *Agricultural History*, XLIX (April 1975), 366; L. L. Lewis, "Texas Fever," Oklahoma Agricultural Experiment Station, *Bulletin 81* (June 1908), 31–32; R. M. Gow, "Tick Eradication in Arkansas," University of Arkansas Experiment Station, *Bulletin 119* (July 1914), 3; and Tamara Miner Haygood, "Cows, Ticks, and Disease: A Medical Interpretation of the Southern Cattle Industry," *Journal of Southern History*, LII (November 1986), 553.

7. Jimmy M. Skaggs, *The Cattle-Trailing Industry: Between Supply and Demand, 1866–1890* (Lawrence: University Press of Kansas, 1973), 92; and Cecil Kirk Hutson, "Texas Fever in Kansas, 1866–1930," *Agricultural History*, LXVIII (Winter 1994), 77.

8. Skaggs, *Cattle-Trailing Industry*, 114.

9. E. C. Cotton, "The North American Fever Tick," Agricultural Experiment Station, University of Tennessee, *Bulletin 113* (March 1915), 33; H. A. Morgan, "Texas Fever Cattle Tick: Pasture Methods of Eradication," Agricultural Experiment Station of Tennessee, *Bulletin 71* (January 1905), 4; and W. H. Dalrymple, H. A. Morgan, and W. R. Dodson, "Cattle Tick and Texas Fever," Agricultural Experiment Station, Louisiana State University and A. & M. College, *Bulletin 51* (1898), 232. See maps of the quarantine line in W. M. MacKellar, "Cattle Tick Fever," *Yearbook of Agriculture*,

1942 (Washington, 1942), 575; and Dalrymple, Morgan, and Dodson, "Cattle Tick and Texas Fever," 233.

10. David Danbom, *The Resisted Revolution: Urban America and the Industrialization of Agriculture, 1900–1930* (Ames: Iowa State University Press, 1979), 86–90.

11. Fite, *Cotton Fields No More*, 80–84.

12. C. L. Willoughby, "Cattle Ticks and Texas Fever; Immunizing Experiments in Georgia," Georgia Experimental Station, *Bulletin 64* (August 1904): 145–46.

13. Ibid., 167; L. L. Lewis, "Texas Fever," Oklahoma Agricultural Experiment Station, *Bulletin 39* (May 1899), 1–2; *Second Annual Report of the Arkansas Agricultural Experiment Station at Arkansas Industrial University* (Little Rock, 1890), 121; *Third Annual Report of the Arkansas Agricultural Experiment Station at Arkansas Industrial University* (Little Rock, 1891), 99–101; and Haygood, "Cows, Ticks, and Disease," 551–64.

14. Theobald Smith and F. L. Kilborne, "Investigations into the Nature, Causation, and Prevention of Texas or Southern Cattle Fever," U.S. Department of Agriculture (USDA), Bureau of Animal Industry, *Bulletin 1* (Washington, 1893); and Clarke, *Century of Cow Business*, 64. The name of the cattle tick and its accompanying parasite has varied over time. The two other commonly used names are *Boophilus annulatus* (Willoughby, "Cattle Ticks and Texas Fever," 145) and *Margaropus annulatus* (S. F. Nelson, "The Passing of the Cattle Tick in Oklahoma," in *Oklahoma State Board of Agriculture: History, Achievements, Services* [January 1929], 27). According to modern nomenclature the tick is *Boophilus annulatus* (G. W. Krantz, *A Manual of Acarology* [Corvallis: OSU Book Stores, 1978], 214). The parasite also is cited as *Piroplasma bigeminum* and *Pyrosoma bigeminum*. The former is the currently accepted term today.

15. J. C. Robert, "Texas Fever," Mississippi Agricultural Experiment Station, *Bulletin 69* (November 1901), 12–13; J. C. Robert, "Tick Fever or Murrain in Southern Cattle," Mississippi Agricultural Experiment Station, *Bulletin 73* (July 1902), 23–24 and 41; Charles F. Dawson, "Texas Cattle Fever and Salt-Sick," Florida Agricultural Experiment Station, *Bulletin 64* (October 1902), 544–45.

16. Robert, "Texas Fever," 11–14.

17. C. A. Cary, "Texas or Acclimation Fever," Alabama Agricultural Experiment Station, *Bulletin 116* (September 1901), 239–42; and Dawson, "Texas Cattle Fever and Salt-Sick," 538.

18. Dawson, "Texas Cattle Fever and Salt-Sick," 539.

19. Ibid., 539–40.

20. Ibid., 536 and 539–40; Charles McCulloch, "The Prevention of Texas Cattle Fever and the Amended Laws Controlling Contagious and Infectious Diseases," Virginia Agricultural Experiment Station, *Bulletin 104* (September 1899), 169–70; and M. Francis and J. W. Connaway, "Texas Fever," Texas Agricultural Experiment Station, *Bulletin 53* (October 1899), 61–65.

21. R. R. Dinwiddie and W. Lenton, "Notes on the Cattle Tick and Tick Fever of Cattle. Tick Eradication in Arkansas in 1907," Arkansas Agricultural Experiment Station, *Bulletin 101* (1908), 197–99.

22. Ibid., 199–200. For more on the blood inoculation process, see G. E. Nesom, "Texas Fever: Part II, Inoculation," South Carolina Agricultural Experiment Station, Clemson College, *Bulletin 90* (July 1904), 5–9 and 12–16; W. H. Dalrymple, W. R. Dodson, and H. A. Morgan, "Immunization Against Texas Fever by Blood Inoculation," Agricultural Experiment Station of Louisiana State University and A. & M. College, *Bulletin 57* (1899), 147 and 170–72; Francis and Connaway, "Texas Fever," 72–74; and Willoughby, "Cattle Ticks and Texas Fever," 159–60.

23. W. H. Dalrymple, "Texas Fever: Being a General Summary of Our Knowledge of the Subject to Date," Agricultural Experiment Station, Louisiana State University and A. & M. College, *Bulletin 84* (October 1905), 15; and Francis and Connaway, "Texas Fever," 56–58.

24. Dalrymple, Dodson, and Morgan, "Cattle Tick and Texas Fever," 146 and 251–53.

25. *Yearbook of the United States Department of Agriculture: 1906* (Washington, D.C.: G.P.O., 1907), 29–32; and Cooper Curtice, "Progress and Prospects of Tick Eradication," in *Twenty-Seventh Annual Report of the Bureau of Animal Industry for the Year 1910* (Washington, D.C.: G.P.O., 1912), 255–57.

26. E. C. Cotton, "Tick Eradication: The Life-History and Habits of the North American Fever Tick with Special Reference to Eradication," Agricultural Experiment Station, University of Tennessee, *Bulletin 81* (December 1908), 58–62.

27. H. A. Morgan, "The Texas Fever Cattle Tick Situation and the Eradication of the Tick by a Pasture Rotation System," Agricultural Experiment Station, Louisiana State University and A. & M. College, *Bulletin 82* (1905), 10–11; and Dalrymple, Morgan, and Dodson, "Cattle Tick and Texas Fever," 275.

28. Morgan, "Texas Fever Cattle Tick Situation," 12.

29. Fite, *Cotton Fields No More*, 19–20.

30. G. E. Nesom, "Texas Fever: Part I," South Carolina Agricultural Experiment Station, Clemson College, *Bulletin 72* (June 1902), 17; and R. R. Dinwiddie, "Animal Parasitism. Some Texas Fever Experiments," Agricultural Experiment Station, Arkansas Industrial University, *Bulletin 20* (November 1892), 11–14.

31. Willoughby, "Cattle Ticks and Texas Fever," 151; Louis A. Klein, "Methods of Eradicating Cattle Ticks," South Carolina Agricultural Experiment Station, Clemson College, *Bulletin 30* (May 1907), 10–12; Lewis, "Texas Fever," 14–15; and Cotton, "Tick Eradication," 64.

32. Henry C. Dethloff, "Mark Francis and Veterinary Medicine in Texas, 1880–1936," *Journal of the West*, XXVII (January 1988), 42; John R. Mohler, "Texas Fever (Otherwise Known as Tick Fever, Splenetic Fever, or Southern Cattle Fever), With Methods for Its Prevention," USDA, Bureau of Animal Industry, *Bulletin 78* (1905), 30–32; *Second Biennial Report of the Oklahoma State Board of Agriculture to the Legislature of the State for the Years 1909 and 1910* (Guthrie, Okla., 1910), 43; Gow, "Tick Eradication in Arkansas," 10–13; and Samuel Lee Evans, "Texas Agriculture, 1880–1930" (PhD dissertation, University of Texas at Austin, 1960), 238.

33. J. A. Kiernan, "Cattle Tick Eradication," in *Proceedings of the Fifth Meeting: Texas State Farmers' Institute, 1915*, Texas Department of Agriculture, *Bulletin 48* (Austin, Tex., 1916), 46.

34. For struggles over the location of agricultural expertise, see Danbom, *Resisted Revolution*; Alan I. Marcus, *Agricultural Science and the Quest for Legitimacy* (Ames: Iowa State University Press, 1985); and Claire Strom, "Unattainable Edens: James J. Hill, the Great Northern Railway, and Changing Notions of Agricultural Expertise" (PhD dissertation, Iowa State University, 1998). For negative comments on farmers, see Lewis, "Texas Fever," 3; Dawson, "Texas Cattle Fever and Salt-Sick," 536; and Dinwiddie and Lenton, "Notes on the Cattle Tick," 216. For the problems of hidden historical voices, see Karlene Faith, *Unruly Women: The Politics of Confinement and Resistance* (Vancouver, Canada: Press Gang Publishers, 1993), 1–12.

35. H. A. Morgan, "Ticks and Texas Fever," Agricultural Experiment Station, Louisiana State University and A. & M. College, *Bulletin 56* (1899), 128–39; E. P. Niles, "The Cattle Tick in Virginia," Virginia Agricultural Experiment Station, *Bulletin 76* (May 1897), 45–50; Fite, *Cotton Fields No More*, 79–81; Roy V. Scott, *The Reluctant Farmer: The Rise of Agricultural Extension to 1914* (Urbana, Ill.: University of Illinois Press, 1970), 140; John B. Boles, *The South Through Time: A History of an American Region* (Englewood Cliffs, N.J.: Prentice Hall, 1995), 413; and USDA, *Yearbook of Agriculture, 1926* (Washington, D.C.: G.P.O., 1927), 534 (quotation).

36. Nesom, "Texas Fever: Part I," 7; Willoughby, "Cattle Ticks and Texas Fever," 145; Curtice, "Progress and Prospects," in *Annual Report of the Bureau of Animal Industry* (1910), 255; Dinwiddie and Lenton, "Notes on the Cattle Tick," 212–13; and *Third Biennial Report of the Oklahoma State Board of Agriculture to the Legislature of the State for the Years 1910 and 1911* (Oklahoma City, 1912), 4.

37. Valdosta (Ga.) *Daily Times*, May 14, 1915, 5; June 4, 1915, 5; and July 28, 1915, 5.

38. *First Biennial Report of the Oklahoma State Board of Agriculture to the Legislature. . . . for the Years 1907 and 1908* (Guthrie, Okla., 1908), Part IV, 5–7; *Biennial Report of the [Tennessee] Department of Agriculture, 1909–1910* (Nashville, 191 I), 10–12; Gow, "Tick Eradication in Arkansas," 6–9; R. M. Gow, "Tick Eradication Laws and Regulations of the State of Arkansas," Arkansas Agricultural Experiment Station, *Bulletin 130* (1917), 23–25.

39. Curtice, "Progress and Prospects," in *Annual Report of the Bureau of Animal Industry* (1910), 262; and Kiernan, "Cattle Tick Eradication," 49.

40. *First Biennial Report of the Oklahoma State Board of Agriculture, Part IV, 6*; *Biennial Report of the [Tennessee] Department of Agriculture, 1909–1910*, 10–13; Gow, "Tick Eradication Laws," 23–25; *Annual Report of the Oklahoma State Board of Agriculture, 1916*, 18; and Valdosta (Ga.) *Daily Times*, April 28, 1915, 5, and May 4, 1915, 8.

41. Gow, "Tick Eradication in Arkansas," 10; and *First Biennial Report of the Oklahoma State Board of Agriculture*, Part IV, 6.

42. Curtice, "Progress and Prospects," in *Annual Report of the Bureau of Animal Industry* (1910), 260–62; Willard Range, *A Century of Georgia Agriculture, 1850–1950*

(Athens: University of Georgia Press, 1954), 202; *Farm and Ranch*, December 16, 1922; and *Atlanta Constitution*, July 21, 1922.

43. King, "Closing of the Southern Range," 62; and Valdosta *Daily Times*, July 8, 1915, 3. See also Hahn, *Roots of Southern Populism*; Shawn Everett Kantor and J. Morgan Kousser, "Common Sense or Commonwealth? The Fence Law and Institutional Change in the Postbellum South," *Journal of Southern History*, LIX (May 1993), 201–42; Steven Hahn, "A Response: Common Cents or Historical Sense?' *Journal of Southern History*, LIX (May 1993), 243–58; and Kantor and Kousser, "A Rejoinder: Two Visions of History," *Journal of Southern History*, LIX (May 1993), 259–66.

44. King, "Closing of the Southern Range," 53–70.

45. *Yearbook of Agriculture, 1926*, 482, quoting *Thornton v. United States*, 46 U.S. 585.

46. Niles, "Cattle Tick in Virginia," 48; Curtice, "Progress and Prospects," in *Annual Report of the Bureau of Animal Industry* (1910), 259–62; Dale, *Range Cattle Industry*, 109; and Hahn, *Roots of Southern Populism*, 244.

47. Evans, "Texas Agriculture, 1880–1930," 229–39; Clarke, *Century of Cow Business*, 66; and Curtice, "Progress and Prospects," in *Annual Report of the Bureau of Animal Industry* (1910), 256–59.

48. Robert E. Igo, "Stamping Out the Fever Tick," *Farm and Ranch*, September 7, 1918, 7.

49. Clarke, *Century of Cow Business*, 65–66; Kiernan, "Cattle Tick Eradication," 46; and Thomas Robert Havins, "The History of Brown County" (MA thesis, University of Texas, 1931), 141–42.

50. *Farm and Ranch*, January 31, 1925.

51. Igo, "Stamping Out the Fever Tick"; Scott, *Reluctant Farmer*, 221; Boles, *South Through Time*, 415–18; Curtice, "Progress and Prospects," in *Annual Report of the Bureau of Animal Industry* (1910), 262; and *Annual Report of the Oklahoma State Board of Agriculture, 1916*, 14–15.

52. Curtice, "Progress and Prospects," in *Annual Report of the Bureau of Animal Industry* (1910), 263.

53. USDA, *Yearbook of Agriculture, 1933* (Washington, D.C., 1933), 76–77; and "Eradicating Cattle Tick, Seminole Indian Reservation, Fla.," Hearing before the Committee on Indian Affairs, House of Representatives, Seventy-Seventh Congress, November 1941–February 1942, 1–170.

54. W. Lenton, "Live Stock Sanitary Laws of the State of Arkansas," Arkansas Agricultural Experiment Station, *Bulletin 106* (1910), 351; Harry B. Brown and Jacob O. Ware, *Cotton* (3rd ed.; New York, Toronto, and London, 1958), 543; Gilbeart H. Collings, *The Production of Cotton* (New York and London, 1926), 220–21; and *Thirteenth Annual Report of the Commissioner of Agriculture, Commerce, and Industries of the State of South Carolina* (Columbia, 1917), 49 and 55.

55. *The Second Annual Report of the State Veterinarian of Alabama, 1908* (Montgomery, 1909), 17; *The Eleventh Annual Report of the State Veterinarian of Alabama,*

1917 (Montgomery, 1918), 35; F. W. Farley, "Growth of the Beef-Cattle Industry in the South," *Yearbook of the United States Department of Agriculture, 1917* (Washington, 1918), 327–40.

56. Farley, "Growth of the Beef-Cattle Industry," 328; *United States Census of Agriculture, 1925: Part II: The Southern States* (Washington, 1927), 125, 267, 355, 403, 537, 595, 779, 841, 913, 981, and 1109; Roland M. Halper, "Development of Agriculture in Lower Georgia from 1890 to 1920 with a Summary for the Whole State, 1850 to 1920," *Georgia Historical Quarterly*, VI (December 1922), 327–28; Georgia Crop Reporting Service, "Georgia Agricultural Facts,1900–1956," *Bulletin 511*, College of Agriculture, University of Georgia (Athens, 1957), 186.

57. Fite, *Cotton Fields No More*, 80–83, 96–98; Kirby, *Rural Worlds Lost*, 40; and King, "Closing of the Southern Range," 68.

58. Clarke, *Century of Cow Business*; and Nordyke, *Great Roundup*.

RALPH H. LUTTS

Like Manna from God

The American Chestnut Trade in Southwestern Virginia

Chestnut Trees grow very tall and thick, mostly, however,
in mountainous regions and high land. Its wood is very
lasting, and its fruit exceptionally sweet.
WILLIAM BYRD (1737)[1]

THE YEAR 2004 marks the centennial of the arrival of the chestnut blight and the onset of the greatest ecological disaster to strike the forests of North America in historical times. In less than fifty years the blight
wiped out a dominant tree of the eastern forest, the American chestnut
(*Castanea dentata*). The disease killed an estimated 3.5 billion trees, the
equivalent of over 9 million acres of pure chestnut stand. The disappearance of the chestnut led to the collapse of wildlife populations that were
dependent upon its nuts as a food source, including bear, squirrel, and
turkey. The replacement of the chestnut by other tree species led to the
restructuring of forest communities.[2]

The arrival of the chestnut blight was followed by other exotic diseases
and insect infestations. The beetle-borne Dutch elm disease destroyed one
of the nation's great shade trees. Today, flowering dogwood is under attack
by anthracnose fungus, hemlocks by woolly adelgid insects, and oaks and
other trees by the gypsy moth. Other species are under similar stress as the
Columbian exchange continues to introduce new organisms to the continent and internal threats also arise.[3] But the American chestnut blight has

a special place in the history of American forests. Not only did it create a rapid and large-scale ecological disaster, it also created a social and economic disaster for mountain communities.

The loss of the American chestnut was a tragedy for poor mountain residents in the southern Appalachian region. The nuts were a vital source of food for their families, autumn forage for their animals, and a commodity for barter and sale. Many people relied upon the seasonal crop of nuts and the natural abundance that they represented. As one mountaineer put it, "chestnuts were like the manna that God sent to feed the Israelites." A mountain woman remarked, "A grove of chestnuts is a better provider than a man—easier to have around, too."[4]

A great deal is known about the biology of the blight and its ecological effects.[5] However, the social and economic roles of the chestnut and the effects of the blight on the people who depended upon the tree have received relatively little study. (Indeed, one of the most detailed studies to date was conducted by high school students and published in one of the *Foxfire* books.)[6] The people who participated in the trade and experienced the economic and social effects of the blight are now elderly and memory of these matters is passing with them. Local records of rural commerce are disappearing as they are lost or discarded. This is unfortunate, because the story of the chestnut trade is an important part of the history of the people and forests of the southern Appalachian Mountains.

What follows is an examination of the social and economic roles of the chestnuts in the southern Appalachians. This essay examines the nature and scale of the chestnut trade—including its growth and collapse in southwestern Virginia—and provides new insights into the chestnuts as a foraging commons, the poorly understood practice of managing forest stands of chestnuts as orchards, and the close of the commons in this region. Finally, it reveals the local diversity in the trade that can be discovered through small-scale and comparative studies.

The nuts were an abundant communal resource. Farmers' hogs and turkeys foraged the chestnut commons of mountain forests without regard to property lines. Farm families also foraged for nuts to eat themselves and, once the chestnut trade began, to sell or barter. With improvements in transportation this trade became particularly important to the poorest folks, because it was one of their few sources of cash and store credit. This trade was much larger than is generally realized. In some counties residents collected tens of thousands of pounds, sometimes well over 100,000 pounds for shipment to urban areas.

Exploitation of the chestnut commons boomed in the early twentieth century, only to go bust a few decades later. The boom-and-bust cycle is a well-known feature of resource commons: they are over-exploited, collapse, and (sometimes) recover. The bust of the chestnut trade had nothing to do with over-exploitation, however, nor was the closure of the commons associated with industrialization or class conflict. The tree was killed, the trade stopped, and the chestnut commons closed by a fungal disease.

Most accounts of the role of chestnuts in mountain culture and economy are quite general in nature and none use a comparative approach. As a result, they tell a story that implies a uniformity of experience and practice throughout the southern Appalachian region. This study, however, finds that the scale of the chestnut trade varied widely among neighboring counties in the Blue Ridge of southwestern Virginia, depending upon local transportation systems and economic circumstances. It demonstrates the importance of small-scale comparative studies to an understanding of the trade and the role chestnuts played in mountain culture and economy.[7]

This article focuses on the period of 1900–1930 and the five southwestern Virginia Blue Ridge counties that extend southwest of Roanoke: Franklin, Floyd, Patrick, Carroll, and Grayson. Floyd, Carroll, and Grayson counties are part of the core region of Appalachia as defined by John Alexander Williams.[8] The Blue Ridge portions of Franklin and Patrick counties are topographically and culturally similar to the other three. During that time, the economy of this region was based largely on agriculture, although Grayson County also was involved in a timber boom at the beginning of the century.

Information about the chestnut trade in these counties is limited largely to oral histories and memoirs. Quantitative data are difficult to find, but some country store records from this period help to confirm informants' memories and add greater depth to our understanding. Published material addressing the trade in the larger southern Appalachian region also helps to flesh out this story. If this account sometimes offers more questions than answers, it nevertheless helps to bring new understanding to this important, largely overlooked thread in American environmental history.

The American Chestnut

At the beginning of the twentieth century, the American chestnut ranged from southern Maine, New Hampshire, and Vermont southward along the Appalachian Mountains to Georgia and Alabama. Westward, its range extended to Ohio, Kentucky, Tennessee, and the northeastern corner of Mississippi. In the southern Appalachians the tree often reached 120 feet in height and 7 feet in diameter and sometimes exceeded this size. Common at altitudes above 2,000 feet, chestnuts grew best in moist hollows above 3,000 feet.[9] Chestnuts commonly comprised up to 20 percent or more of the forest trees and locally they could account for 50 percent or more. A member of the beech family, the chestnut tree usually bore dark brown nuts enclosed two or three together within a two- to three-inch spherical burr protected by extraordinarily sharp spines. No one collected chestnuts barefoot.

It is difficult to imagine the oak-chestnut forests before the ravages of the chestnut blight. One person described how the "light, cream-colored blossoms, and a big tree that grew up a hundred feet high would have a spread at the top of it a hundred feet wide, maybe. You could see them sticking up out of the woods, and it was just like big, potted flowers standing up all over the mountain. It was a sight to see." The nature writer Donald Peattie described the trees viewed from a mountaintop in the Great Smoky Mountains, "the great forest below waving with creamy white chestnut blossoms in the crowns of the ancient trees, so that it looks like a sea of white combers plowing across its surface." Another writer remembered the tree's "great domes of yellow, arched up above the lane, and lying like great piles of pollen here and there over the wooded hills. Its perfume is everywhere, not honey-sweet like the locust's, but with a saving tang of acrid, of a kind, but of a differing savor, with that of buckwheat. Is there . . . another woods-tree with bloom so beautiful?"[10]

Native Americans of the eastern woodlands used the nuts as a source of food, eaten raw, boiled, or ground into flour. They sometimes used chestnut bark to cover their shelters and chestnut wood to make canoes. Chestnuts were known to Europeans before they invaded North America. The European chestnut *Castanea sativa* was used as food from ancient times to the present. It was boiled, roasted, made into flour, and included in bread, cake, pudding, and porridge. Historically, it has been an important staple food of the poorest classes.[11] European settlers in America quickly discovered the value of the American chestnut. The nuts, which were much sweeter than those of the European chestnut, were valued highly. "There are also chestnuts here, like those of the Netherlands, which are spread over the woods," Adriaen van der Donck wrote in his account of the New Netherlands, in the present-day New York and New Jersey region, during a visit in the 1640s. "Chestnuts would be plentier if it were not for the Indians, who destroy the trees by stripping off the bark for covering for their houses. They, and the Netherlanders also, cut down the trees in the chestnut season, and cut off the limbs to gather the nuts, which also lessens the trees."[12] Other settlers found it more convenient simply to wait for the nuts to fall, which they often did in great quantity.

American chestnut wood was light, strong, easily split and worked, and remarkably resistant to decay. These qualities led to its use in log houses and other structures, furniture, interior trim, musical instruments, coffins, and cooperage, and also for shingles, mine timbers, railroad ties, telephone poles, and fence posts and rails. The abundance of rail fences in the southern Appalachians attested to the ease with which the wood split. (As one mountaineer said, to make a fence rail, just "cut off what length your rails you wanted . . . you could stick a wedge in it an' it'd jus' pop open.") The wood was used as a veneer and as the core upon which other wood veneers were applied. Once a method was developed to extract the tannin from the wood, chestnut also became important to the tanning industry. Virginia had nine chestnut extract plants in 1914. The leaves were used in folk medicine to treat whooping cough, burns, swelling, and snakebite.[13]

The nuts were important to people living in the southern Appalachian Mountains and, as in Europe, they were especially important to the poorer residents. When the nuts matured and fell from the trees in September and October, the ground often was covered inches deep with them. People gathered them and either ate them immediately or stored them after setting the nuts in the sun to dry. When dry nuts were stored, steps had to be taken to prevent weevil damage, because their larvae commonly infested the nuts. The nuts might be heated in boiling water, or preserved with salt.[14] They were eaten fresh, boiled, roasted, baked, or ground into flour.[15] Partially dried nuts were particularly appreciated, because of their increased sweetness.

The task of collecting the nuts was often a delight to children, who remembered it fondly in their elder years. A Grayson County, Virginia, woman remembered:

> On a windy night, we'd fall asleep dreaming of the ground covered with chestnuts which wind-shaken trees had let go. The next morning, breakfast was gulped down as we hurriedly put on old coats, caps and everyday shoes, grabbed buckets or baskets and headed for the closest big chestnut trees, calling back to remind our father to be sure to write an excuse for tardiness at school. Many of the nuts had already fallen out of open burrs and were hiding under masses of brown frostbitten leaves. Some were still inside of very prickly outside burrs but partly open revealing the velvet inside lining. Sometimes we had to use a foot to squash a burr to give up its fruit.[16]

To get the nuts, people often had to compete with animals, including domestic animals. "There was another chore that had to be taken care of on the farm," wrote a Floyd County, Virginia, resident, "the picking up of chestnuts. You gathered the chestnuts, every one that you could get. If you didn't have turkeys, you could get a pretty good supply. But you had to beat the turkeys to the chestnut tree in the morning if you were to get very many." Another Blue Ridge resident recalled his impoverished childhood: "There was a time of year when we had food. That was in late fall after the gusty winds of a chestnut storm left the ground strewed with nuts. Pa and Ma would take us out by lantern light to beat the hogs to them."[17]

More affluent folks enjoyed nutting as recreation. One author recalled "certain city folk in whom the country heart is still alive and whom memories of boyhood drive to take the night trolleys to the country on blowing October dawns." One morning in rural Pennsylvania, for example, he met a gatherer who was "the proud possessor of a long stocking stuffed full, [who] told me that he must hurry back, as he had to be at his optician's bench in the city by eight o'clock." Urban and suburban families ventured to the countryside to gather chestnuts. Boys would go "clubbing," throwing sticks high into the trees to knock the nuts down. They would often weight the sticks with pieces of metal, sometimes with nuts removed from the bolts that joined sections of railroad track. In the autumn, railroad track-walkers carried extra metal nuts with them to replace those that were missing.[18]

For mountain folk, chestnuts were more than a source of food for themselves. The nuts also fattened their hogs, which foraged freely throughout the local forest. In addition, the chestnuts were a source of income. They were sold at the local general store, or exchanged for merchandise or store credit. Each autumn, many children exchanged nuts for shoes, clothes, and schoolbooks. "A small little kid could pick up chestnuts," recalled a Georgia man. "We'd get up before breakfast and go to these trees where a lot of chestnuts had fallen overnight, beat the hogs there, and pick them up. Take them to market, sell them, and get shoes, clothes, or other things with them." A woman recalled that when she was a girl, "I'd pick them up and get the money for 'em, and I was glad to get to pick 'em up 'cause I'd get the money for 'em. And I was stingy with 'em as I could be, I'll just tell you the truth! When I was little I thought *every* chestnut I picked up had to be sold."[19]

Another Georgia man recalled seeing folks come out of the mountains to trade chestnuts at the store:

> We'd hardly ever see these people at all, except when they came out to go to the store, and in the fall we could see 'em coming, maybe the parents and three or four kids coming down the trail. The old man would have a big coffee sack full of chestnuts on his back, and the little fellers would have smaller sacks, and even the mother would have a small sack of chestnuts caught up on her hip. They'd all trek to the store and they'd swap that for coffee and sugar and flour and things that they had to buy to live on through the winter. That's the way they made their living.[20]

What did the storekeeper do with all these the nuts? Trying to sell them to local customers was like bringing coals to Newcastle. Chestnuts were abundant and free for the taking, so why would anyone pay money for them? Herein lies a tale.

The Chestnut Trade

In the southern Appalachian Mountains, chestnuts had little or no cash value until it was possible to ship them to areas outside the chestnut's range. The nuts acquired cash value as the transportation system improved.

In the early 1860s, chestnuts from Sandy Valley of Appalachian Kentucky were shipped by steamboat. The later development of the road system allowed residents in the Cades Cove community in eastern Tennessee's Great Smoky Mountains to sell chestnuts in Maryville and Knoxville. Southwestern Virginia's Blue Ridge counties depended largely on the railroad to ship theirs, although some surely were shipped by wagons before the railroad arrived. With improvements in transportation, the trade in chestnuts grew. In 1910, a man visited a cabin in the Smokies with a "hundred bushels of chestnuts, piled up there, and about four men packing off, every day." It is no wonder that a 1902 U.S. Department of Agriculture study of the southern Appalachian forests reported that "the collection of nuts forms an important industry."[21]

Throughout the nineteenth century, the economy of Virginia's southwestern Blue Ridge communities was largely subsistence or semi-subsistence in nature. This continued into the twentieth century, although on a lesser scale. These were not classless communities. There was an economic elite that dealt largely in cash, as well as people of lesser means, many of whom had little access to cash and depended to varying degrees upon the fruits of their labor and barter. The country store, also called a general merchandise store or simply a general store, was at the center of this economy. It sold its merchandise for cash, bartered it for locally produced goods and services, or exchanged it for credit against the customer's store account. Much of what it received in trade was shipped for sale outside the region, which brought the owner a cash return. Each day a store owner might find any number of items crossing his counter in exchange for merchandise: from eggs, butter, and dried apples to hams, beef, and animal hides, from live cows, pigs, and chickens, to a hay stack, firewood, and roof repairs.[22] What the owner could not sell locally had to be sold elsewhere. This was the case with chestnuts.

People collected nuts in quantity and their surplus was sold or bartered. A Patrick County, Virginia, resident recalled gathering fifteen to twenty pounds at a time. Another recalled picking up nearly one hundred pounds in a day following a storm. Still another told of how his father would "take the wagon to Jones Mountain and come in loaded." Josie Thomas recalled that her family often gathered nuts. She remembered being a child sitting on a bag of chestnuts behind her father as they rode his horse to the store. They would deliver a bushel of nuts and by the time they returned the family had gathered another bushel. She recalled making three trips a day. Ezra Martin of Carroll County recalled that he could "pick up over a bushel of chestnuts from under a tree on almost any morning in the Fall of the year."[23]

A 1914 Virginia Department of Agriculture publication stated that "the income from the commercial nut crop goes largely to the women and children in the mountainous sections of the state."[24] This may be true, particularly with small-scale gathering, but men and boys also collected and traded in nuts. This was especially the case in large-scale collecting for the trade, which often involved a family effort. Country store account books obscure this fact, because they most often list a family under the name of the head of the household, generally a man. Gender roles in the chestnut trade have not been studied, but it is interesting to note that it was Josie Thomas's father who took the nuts to the store while, presumably, his wife and the other children did the foraging.

The price that people received for nuts was high when the season began and declined later in the autumn as nuts flooded the market. One Patrick County resident recalled that the stores initially paid ten cents a pound and the price decreased to two cents as the market filled with nuts. Another recalled the price began as five or six cents, declining to two or three cents. Still another recalled that chestnuts were worth as much by the bushel as corn. A 1909 store accounts book shows that customers received two or three cents per pound at the beginning of October.[25]

Not all people traded their nuts at the local store. Some acted as dealers, hauling their nuts to a railroad station and shipping them to a wholesale house on their own. Others dealt with hucksters, peddlers who accepted chestnuts and other goods in exchange for merchandise. A Floyd Country resident recalled:

> The chestnuts sold from three to five cents a pound. We gathered lots and lots, but we didn't usually take them to the general store. The huckster came by and got them. Our huckster was Mr. Sam Vest, our neighbor, who usually came in the late afternoon on Wednesday, or early Thursday morning. He was driving his load to Roanoke to sell for the weekend. He would take all the odds and ends that we had to sell, the butter and eggs that you hadn't sent to the grocery store or as we knew it, the general merchandise store.[26]

In southwestern Virginia and elsewhere, when people brought nuts to a store, they had three options for compensation. They could receive cash, exchange them for merchandise, or have the value of the nuts credited to their store account to pay off past or future debts. If they received cash, they were usually paid in cardboard or metal tokens called "due bills," or the amount received was written on a slip of paper called "scrip." These were good only for exchange at the issuing store, so customers actually received store credit, rather than cash. If a store owner had a good reputation for trustworthiness, the store's due bills and scrip might be exchanged in transactions among local people before they were eventually cashed in at the store. In effect, each country store minted its own money.[27]

Store owners kept two different kinds of records. The first, called the day book, was a detailed running record of transactions with customers. This was recorded at the time of the exchange. Some of this information was later transferred to a customer accounts book. This book did not record even-exchange or paid-in-full transactions. The accounts book recorded debt and credit, with a page for each customer. The left column of the page was a record of the customer's debt, of merchandise taken without immediate or full payment. The right column was a record of credit, of payments in cash or barter made against the debt. Thus, the day books provide a full record of the chestnut trade at a country store. This is not true of the customer accounts books, but they provide a clearer understanding of who engaged in the trade and their economic standing. Those who paid off their debts in cash, those who were relatively well off economically, rarely offered nuts against their accounts. In the autumn, those who offered barter against their debt often offered chestnuts. (They sometimes also offered small quantities of chinquapin nuts and, rarely, walnuts.) Some customers, presumably the poorest, paid their debt entirely in chestnuts when they were in season.

Once merchants received chestnuts, they had to ship them to a market outside their region. They bagged the nuts in cloth sacks and hauled them to the railroad station. This was not an easy trip. Although roads in the region had improved by the early twentieth century, they were still dirt roads and travel often was difficult. (Most Blue Ridge communities did not see a paved road until the arrival of the Blue Ridge Parkway in the 1930s, after the chestnut trade had died.) James D. Hopkins, a Patrick County store owner, would haul two thousand pounds of nuts at a time to the railroad station in his horse-drawn wagon. Alternatively, if a supplier brought goods to a store, the merchant might ship the nuts back to town in the supplier's otherwise empty wagon. People recalled wagon loads of nuts traveling daily from the Patrick County Blue Ridge communities of Vesta and Meadows of Dan to the railroad station in Stuart, the county seat. It took two days to make the round trip by wagon to Stuart, a total distance of about thirty-five miles. Murphy Thompson hauled nuts, often two wagon loads at a time, from Floyd County to the railroad station in Franklin County's town of Ferrum. Nuts from other parts of Floyd County and from Carroll County, which also had no railroad, might have been hauled to Radford or Pulaski.[28]

The scale of the chestnut trade is difficult to determine. Published accounts differ. The 1914 Virginia Department of Agriculture publication placed the statewide annual value of the nut crop at $200,000. (At a return of ten cents a pound, this amounted to 2,000,000 pounds of nuts.)[29] On the other hand, a Virginia Writers Project history of Floyd County placed the value of that county's annual nut harvest alone at $100,000 (1,000,000 pounds). A 1937 University of Virginia economic study of Patrick County stated that "Patrick's chestnut crop, at one time, was a greater source of revenue than cattle." The author did not mention a dollar value, but he did note that after a twenty-year decline in the size of the herd (a drop of 2,416 head), the "7,143 cattle reported in 1930 were valued at $336,260. Dairy products sold totaled $52,164." That was the equivalent of over 520,000 pounds of nuts.[30] The 1914 figure of $200,000 for the annual statewide value of the chestnut harvest may be an underestimate, or more likely the trade grew significantly in the years following 1914.

Country store record books provide much more accurate information, but they are difficult to find, especially day books. Records of hucksters' business and personal shipments are virtually nonexistent. There are, though, other clues. A set of Mayberry General Store shipping receipts from the Southern Express Company provide revealing details of the trade of one business. The store, which is located in the Patrick County Blue Ridge community of Mayberry, near the border of Floyd and Carroll counties, shipped its nuts through Stuart. The store shipped at least 9,156 pounds of nuts in 1914, and another 6,560 pounds in 1915, with a total estimated wholesale value of $872, or about six cents per pound. (This store sometimes actually realized nine to eleven cents per pound.)[31] Although some nuts went to wholesalers in Richmond and Norfolk, Virginia, most went to Baltimore, Philadelphia, and New York City. The local trade in chestnuts linked even the poorest folks, who seldom if ever used cash, to the national economy despite the often-encountered myth that these mountain people lived in isolation. The roasted chestnuts sold by vendors on the streets of New York, or stuffed into turkeys in urban and suburban areas throughout the Northeast, may have been gathered by poor children and adults in the Blue Ridge of southwestern Virginia.

Shipments from Stuart moved on the Danville & Western (D&W) railroad, which reached Patrick County, Virginia, in 1884. The narrow-gauge track began in Danville and extended westward to its terminus in Stuart, the county seat. Affectionately called the "Dick & Willie" by county residents, the D&W was upgraded to standard gauge by 1903. The arrival of the D&W expanded economic opportunities for the county and especially for the chestnut trade. The son of a station master recalled that the best money his father made was from shipping chestnuts. He also was an express agent and earned commissions on the shipments. The nuts were shipped at the higher rate for perishables. "His express commissions," his son recalled, "were just fantastic." His father told him that "during the harvest time of chestnuts you could hardly find a place to put the bags of chestnuts down, because everyone was a chestnut dealer, just about. They harvested the chestnuts and brought them and shipped them to the big cities."[32]

Some nuts shipped out of Stuart may have come from bordering North Carolina, but enormous quantities originated within Patrick County. In October 1915, the county newspaper reported, "About thirty wagon loads of chestnuts were brought to Stuart from the Meadows of Dan Saturday and Monday for shipment. The D. & W. Ry. has been taking away a car of chestnuts every day for some time." This was a lot of chestnuts, especially when we realize that the nuts arriving from Meadows of Dan and other Blue Ridge communities often were hauled in horse-drawn Conestoga wagons capable of carrying about two thousand pounds each. Even if the average wagon load was half that amount, this adds up to about 30,000 pounds of nuts shipped in two days.[33]

Despite the romantic tales of children collecting chestnuts to buy new shoes for school, the chestnut trade was not necessarily small; in some areas it was a large industry. The U.S. Agricultural Census of 1910 shows that Patrick County, Virginia, accounted for nearly 160,000 pounds of nuts. This is a high figure, but it is not unique; a single railroad station in West Virginia shipped 155,000 pounds of wild nuts in autumn 1911.[34] These figures probably do not include all of the nuts harvested in these counties. For example, census figures account only for those reported, and the West Virginia figure does not account for nuts that may have been shipped by other means. The newspaper report of what was shipped from Stuart in a single weekend suggests the magnitude of the trade—at the peak of the season the train departed almost every day with a car laden with chestnuts.

The U.S. Agriculture Census figures for 1910 show that Grayson, Carroll, Patrick, Floyd, and Franklin counties produced 360,384 pounds of nuts. This amounted to 43 percent of the entire production of all nuts in Virginia that year. Patrick County produced more nuts than any other county in the state. Although the census figure is for "nuts," with no distinction regarding the kinds of nuts produced, nearly all of the nuts shipped in this region were chestnuts. (These figures may have included limited quantity of chinquapins and, perhaps, a few walnuts.) This conclusion is supported by the fact that twenty years later, after the ravages of the chestnut blight, these five counties together produced a mere 640 pounds of nuts, including only 170 pounds of chestnuts.[35]

It is quite likely that the trade continued to grow rapidly between 1910 and 1920. With an estimated return of ten cents per pound to the merchants, the value of the 1910 crop in Patrick and Floyd counties was only $15,985 and $4,879, respectively.[36] The value of the trade in all five counties would be a mere $36,038. This does not come close to the later estimated annual value of Patrick's crop as over $52,164 ("a greater source of revenue than cattle"), or Floyd's crop as $100,000. It even falls far short at double or triple of the price per pound. If the estimates are correct, the annual trade may have grown in the succeeding decade or more to something approaching 500,000 to 1,000,000 pounds a year in the most productive of these five counties.

There was certainly a small chestnut trade in the late nineteenth century and the Agriculture Census of 1900 showing only 914 bushels of nuts from 891 trees probably underreported the crop.[37] Nevertheless, it is reasonable to assume that the trade at the beginning of the century was modest. In 1910, however, the census reported total production in these counties to be 360,384 pounds from 36,222 trees. In just ten years the production of chestnuts skyrocketed, and it likely continued to grow in the following decade, only to plummet as the blight reached southwestern Virginia. It was a boom-and-bust trade that spanned the arrival of the railroad and the death of the trees.

The wildly varying reported rates of production per tree (from 0.7 to 3.5 bushels in 1900 and from 6.2 to 43.4 pounds in 1910) suggest that the census figures were based on rough estimates. After all, maintaining accurate counts when foraging in the wild is difficult, despite the federal government's demand for accuracy.

Though much of the trade came from foraging, the image of people wandering through the forest to gather nuts only captures part of the story. Some people maintained what they called "chestnut orchards." Although some may have been planted, most of these orchards were conveniently located natural stands of chestnut trees.[38] Why plant orchards when there was an abundance of chestnut trees growing all by themselves? It appears that some of these groves were managed to encourage chestnut trees and make it easier to gather nuts.

Why was there such variation in nut production from county to county? South of Roanoke, the Blue Ridge widens, changing from a range of mountains to a plateau that becomes nearly fifty miles wide at the border of Virginia and North Carolina. Grayson, Carroll, and Floyd counties are on this plateau. (Still farther southward, the Great Smoky Mountains rise from this plateau.) Most of the land area of Patrick and Franklin counties falls within the Piedmont lowlands, rather than the Blue Ridge. Since the American chestnut did not grow on the Piedmont in the twentieth century, it is surprising that Patrick and Franklin counties produced the majority of chestnuts, twice as many pounds of nuts as the other three counties combined. One reason was that railroads entered these counties, providing residents relatively easy access to transportation to ship their nuts. In addition, Patrick and Franklin counties, the largest producers, had the poorest farms of all Virginia counties measured by the value of all farm property per farm, $1,526 and $1,593, respectively. Grayson, Carroll, and Floyd county farms had values of $3,183, $2,192, and $2,928. (The average value of all property per farm in Virginia was $3,397.)[39] Poverty was a good motivation to gather and trade in chestnuts.

Grayson County, the lowest producer, also had the highest farm property value and the lowest number of tenant farms. Its forests were heavily cut during the timber boom of the late nineteenth and early twentieth centuries; virtually the entire county was cut over.[40] The timber industry provided a significant addition to local income during the boom. The industry did not place a high value on chestnut timber, so plenty of nuts were available and local residents gathered them for their own use. The county has some of the most mountainous terrain in the state, including Virginia's highest mountain peaks, which made transportation difficult. However, at the beginning of the twentieth century a railroad from Abingdon, Virginia, to North Carolina was established to serve the timber industry. The Virginia-Carolina (V&C) Railroad, popularly known as the "Virginia Creeper," passed through the western edge of Grayson County and a spur entered the county to haul lumber and supplies. Although the V&C also provided service to the general populace, the chestnut trade did not flourish. The brief prosperity that accompanied the timber economy provided little incentive to trade in nuts. By the time the timber boom ended and the railroad closed, the chestnuts were gone.[41]

It is difficult to make simple generalizations based on the size of the trade in one county and expect them accurately to describe the trade in another.

Chestnut Commons and Chestnut Orchards

Animals such as hogs, turkeys, and cattle were allowed to range freely in these Blue Ridge counties without regard to property lines until well into the twentieth century. They grazed, foraged, and watered wherever they wandered. The free-range agricultural tradition was widely practiced in the South from colonial times and was strongly supported in the mountains, where farmers often owned large tracts of unimproved land. This practice was particularly beneficial to slaves, small land holders, renters, share croppers, and the poor who did not own enough land to support their animals.[42] This open range tradition was upheld in 1900 by the Virginia Supreme Court of Appeals, which declared that "the rule of the common law which requires the owner of animals to keep them on his own land or within enclosures is not in force in [Virginia] . . . and the owner of animals, being under no obligation to restrain them, is not liable for damage done in consequence of their straying on the unenclosed lands of another, unless he drives them there."

If an animal damaged a neighbor's crops, there were few grounds for legal action unless that animal had broken through a fence. People were required to fence their neighbors' animals out, rather than fence their own animals in. A county board of supervisors had the local option to pass an ordinance requiring owners to keep their animals on their own land. However, at the beginning of the twentieth century, only one Virginia county, Accomac, required residents to fence in their animals. The Blue Ridge counties of southwestern Virginia did not begin to require this until long after the blight wiped out the American chestnut.[43]

Much of the unfenced rural landscape of this region thus was a grazing and foraging commons. The ubiquitous rail fences that surrounded household gardens and farm crops bore witness to this. Although individuals owned the land, their unimproved acreage was a communal resource open to everyone's animals. The owners of the animals gained the benefit from the grazing and forage, but the owners of the land bore their effects. Garrett Hardin argued that these circumstances inevitably led to overexploitation and ecological collapse of the commons, because animal owners had no incentive to conserve the resource. This, he argued, was the "tragedy of the commons."[44]

Natural resource commons and the social and ecological impacts associated with their loss have received a good deal of study by ecologists and resource managers. They also have been studied by environmental historians. Marine fisheries provide a good example of the ecological disaster that an unregulated or underregulated commons can experience. There are, though, other examples that are more directly related to the inland rural circumstances of the chestnut commons. Brian Donahue wrote about the loss of community grazing meadowlands when they were flooded by rising waters behind dams; John Cumbler studied the social conflicts leading to the loss of communal fisheries when dam construction blocked passage of migratory fishes; and Jennifer Price described the transformation of passenger pigeons into market commodities that were hunted to extinction.[45] In these examples, the traditional commons were closed in the nineteenth century when industry and economic elites co-opted and gained control of a region's natural resources, or when the resource was overexploited and the commons collapsed.

The seasonal abundance associated with the arrival of migratory fish and with the unpredictable appearance of barely imaginable numbers of pigeons in the sky became social and even celebratory events as rural residents reaped the natural bounty. The seasonal harvest of the chestnut crop was also of great social as well as economic significance. But the collapse of the chestnut commons involves a different story. The abundance of the resource exceeded the demands placed upon it. There were plenty of chestnuts for animals and people alike. In addition, although the commons collapsed in a time of modernization and economic transition in the region, this was not the result of industrialization or competition for control of the resource. The chestnut commons collapsed because of the blight. The trees died and there were no nuts left to harvest.

Despite Hardin's pessimistic assessment of the fate of commons, communities often find formal or informal ways to manage communal natural resources.[46] Did rural Appalachian residents find ways to regulate the chestnut commons? There is little information to help us answer this question. Given the abundance of the nuts, there may have been little incentive to regulate foraging. There were, though, efforts to assert property rights within the commons and, apparently, to remove some trees from the commons.

Cattle, hogs, and domesticated turkeys foraged through unfenced pasture and forest. In the autumn, hogs and turkeys fattened on the bounty of acorns and chestnuts. Hogs were important because their meat could be salted and stored through the winter by people who lacked refrigeration. Although the animals foraged across property lines, there was great respect for ownership of the animals. Owners of hogs and cattle could be identified by unique patterns of notches and holes cut in the animals' ears. The marks were sometimes registered at the local court house. An unmarked young hog born in the woods, however, could be claimed by the first person to find it. Farmers who lived at a lower elevation or had few chestnuts nearby sometimes fattened their hogs by hauling or driving them to more desirable locations to forage on chestnuts. Abraham Helms recalled, for example, that his father would take his hogs to Patrick County's Jones Mountain to fatten them.[47]

Like their animals, people living in the Blue Ridge also were able to hunt and forage without regard to property lines. There is, though, little information about the mountain folks' chestnut foraging strategies, or the extent to which specific families or individuals may have laid claim to specific stands of trees. Would, for example, Helms' father have released his hogs on someone else's land without first receiving permission from the property owner? As the Virginia Supreme Court stated, he would be liable for damages caused by his hogs if he intentionally drove them onto another person's property without the owner's approval. While incidental collecting for personal use may have been free ranging, was this the case when nuts were gathered by the wagon load?

Chestnut orchards provide an interesting case that has not been studied. These orchards, sometimes called groves, were common and are often mentioned in interviews and memoirs. "The chestnut groves were about as valuable to us in those days as other orchards," wrote Pedro Sloan of Franklin County. One Great Smoky Mountains informant recalled that "just about every farm on Fines Creek and Crabtree had a chestnut orchard even though chestnut trees grew wild everywhere."[48] Yet little is known about the orchards. In many cases they were natural forest stands that were managed to favor chestnuts. Louise McNeill, who served as West Virginia's Poet Laureate, recalled one example: "We had always called Uncle Dan'l's trees 'the chestnut orchard,' just across our line fence on the flat knoll of his part of Old Tom's farm. Forty or fifty big American chestnut trees stood there together, as the old men had saved them from the first clearing back in the Indian times, and for generations they had been the neighborhood nutting ground."[49]

One Patrick County resident explained that chestnut orchards were natural stands cleared of underbrush. Farmers kept the ground within the orchards clean to make it easier to find and gather the nuts. Early Hopkins, who lived in the county's Blue Ridge foothills, told an interviewer: "I believe there was more people on top of the mountain had the chestnut orchards, cleaned out all of the undergrowth, than they did down here. But some of them down here you know, they'd go through and cut all their undergrowth, and there was little fine grass come up under that, made it easy to get the chestnuts." Max Thomas, a respected Floyd County elder, local folklorist, and former biology teacher, reported that "people years ago had cleared the woods of everything except chestnut trees, which they lined up in rows about fifty feet apart."[50]

These chestnut orchards began as natural forest stands. Other tree species were weeded out, which opened the grove's canopy and promoted chestnut growth. Hogs and other farm animals foraging in the woods also had a great impact upon the undergrowth and forest regeneration. Perhaps fire also was used to manage the undergrowth, though only one bit of evidence suggests that: a newspaper article, circa 1900, recorded that "Wilber Phipps, a farmer of Freeling, had his barn destroyed by catching fire from some burning leaves about his chestnut orchard."[51] Perhaps Phipps was burning the undergrowth in his orchard.

If fire was used as a management tool, did European colonists learn this method from the natives? Native Americans used fire to manage vegetation near their villages, and some scholars speculate that they also managed forests to encourage nut bearing trees, including chestnut. Indirect evidence of this may be the occurrence of nearly pure stands of American chestnut in some forests: early in the twentieth century, researchers found 82.5 percent chestnuts in a Nantahala National Forest plot in North Carolina; 84.6 percent at Mountain Lake, Virginia; and 81.2 percent in a Maryland plot.[52] Such concentrations of a single species suggest human management. However, these areas might have been abandoned chestnut orchards originally managed by European-American settlers.

In any event, it appears that at least some chestnut orchards were natural stands of trees that, through the labor of individual farmers and their families, were culturally redefined as objects of agriculture. Given the effort that farmers must have devoted to maintaining the orchards, it is reasonable to assume that they tried to control access to them. If so, the chestnut orchards were removed, to some extent, from the foraging commons.

The West Virginia chestnut orchard that Louise McNeill described was used by the neighborhood, so it still was a communal resource to some extent. However, there is an intriguing tale from Cumberland County, Kentucky, that suggests that some people were very possessive of their orchards. According to folklorist William Lynwood Montell, the African American community of Coe Ridge had "a large chestnut orchard," which became contested ground: "Friction between the races was intensified by some of the white boys who made it a habit to go to the ridge and freely partake of the abundant chestnut supply. The Negro boys and girls, who picked up the chestnuts and sold them for cash, resented the intrusion on their personal property. On one occasion, a fight over chestnuts broke out between the races. 'That's what started all of the killing,' claimed Tim Coe."[53]

In this incident and the ensuing feud, issues of racial conflict overshadowed those related to the resource commons. Nevertheless, the incident raises questions about the right of access to the resource, individually and communally. It also introduces race as a framework within which the chestnut commons and trade need to be studied.

Chestnut Blight and the Close of the Commons

The American chestnut was in trouble in its southern range long before the blight arrived. The U.S. Commissioner of Agriculture's 1878 *Report Upon Forestry* noted that the American chestnut was dying out in the Piedmont region of North Carolina. "The chestnut was formerly abundant in the Piedmont region down to the country between the Catawba and Yadkin Rivers," the North Carolina state geologist reported, "but within the last thirty years they have mostly perished." Chestnuts in Virginia experienced a similar fate. "Throughout the Piedmont section of Virginia, especially in the lower portions," reported one observer in 1914, "there has been for thirty years or more a gradual dying or recession of the chestnut toward the mountains." This was not the result of chestnut blight, he argued, but of "either unfavorable soil conditions or root-rot." It turned out that the problem was caused by a root fungus, *Phytophthora cinnamomi*. As a result of this root rot the southern and southeastern range of the tree was already shrinking when the chestnut blight arrived.[54]

However, this disease had little or no impact upon the chestnut trade in the southern Appalachians. In the southwestern Virginia Blue Ridge, the trade grew and flourished well into the early twentieth century. The slow death of the chestnuts in the lower Piedmont regions was quickly surmounted by the rapid destruction of the tree throughout its range by the chestnut blight.

The chestnut blight, caused by the fungus *Cryphonectria parasitica* (formerly known as *Endothia parasitica*), was first noticed in the United States at the New York Zoological Park in 1904. The fungus probably was introduced with nursery stock from Asia. Through their long association with the fungus, oriental species of *Castanea* evolved a resistance to the disease. This was not true of North American and European species. Within a year the blight infected an estimated 98 percent of the American chestnuts in the Bronx, the New York borough in which the park was located.[55] The infection spread rapidly by airborne sexual spores, and by sticky asexual spores that adhered to, and were transported by, insects, birds, and other animals.

By 1908, the blight had reached Massachusetts, Connecticut, New Jersey, and Pennsylvania. By the 1940s, the pandemic had spread throughout the tree's natural range. The blight also infected chinquapins (also of the genus *Castanea*) and some species of oak, especially post oak, *Quercus stella*. It has since spread to Europe. It reached Italy in 1938, infecting the European chestnut *Castanea sativa*, and subsequently reached England, Switzerland, Spain, France, Yugoslavia, Greece, Turkey, and elsewhere.[56]

Blight spores entered the tree through wounds and breaks in the bark and began to grow in the cambium, the thin layer of living tissue between the tree's bark and trunk wood. Eventually, the fungal tissue grew all the way around the tree, girdling it and killing the cambium above the fungal mass. As a result, the above-ground portion of the chestnut died, but not its roots. Over the years the roots kept putting up new shoots, which sometimes grew large enough to bear nuts for a short time. Eventually, though, the shoots were re-infected with blight and died, only to be replaced by new ones in a tragic cycle. This process has continued to the present. It is not uncommon to see living American chestnut saplings growing amidst dead poles in varying stages of decay. The American chestnut did not really disappear from the eastern forests—it ceased to be a part of the forest canopy and is now a part of the shrub understory.

Virginia experienced an outbreak of cicadas in 1911 and millions of these insects opened avenues for blight infection by piercing tree bark with their mouthparts. This hastened the spread of the disease. The blight reached Virginia around 1912 and by 1914 it was found in eighteen counties. It spread at breakneck speed, with the infection rate increasing at a reported rate of 600 percent per year in areas that had experienced the cicada outbreak. By 1914, one hundred infected trees were found in Bedford County, located just northeast of Franklin County. This was an isolated outbreak ahead of the main infestation. The Bedford trees were destroyed and the advance of the infection halted in the county, but this was a temporary reprieve. Nearly all American chestnut trees throughout Virginia were infected by 1920.[57]

Memories of how quickly the trees died vary. Chester and Erma McKenzie of Patrick County recalled that they died gradually, but Abraham and Eula Helms recalled that the trees died quickly. In any event, they died out in Virginia's southwestern Blue Ridge by the end of the 1920s. Sam and Sally Slate recalled that Patrick County's chestnuts finally died out in 1926, the year they were married. Coy Lee Yeatts recalled that he last collected chestnuts on June 19, 1928, the day before his sister died of appendicitis. The blight continued to spread, reaching the southern end of the Blue Ridge in the 1930s. Ninety-nine percent of Great Smoky Mountains trees were infected by 1929 and nearly 85 percent of them were dead when the park was dedicated in 1940. By the mid-1930s, the blight also was found in California, Washington, and British Columbia, killing groves of chestnut trees planted by settlers who had carried the cherished nuts with them on their westward journey.[58]

The death of the chestnut was a terrible blow to the Appalachian forests. In Georgia, at the southern end of the Blue Ridge, one man remarked that "after the blight hit, the bark went to falling off of 'em. Two or three years after that the trunks began to [weaken] and a windstorm'd come up and it'd be awful hearing them trees 'a fallin' in the chestnut belt." Another man described the devastation in 1926 at Fishers Gap in the Blue Ridge of central Virginia:

I passed through a scene impressive in its aspect of desolation, and almost a tribute to the destructive power of the chestnut blight. This section must at one time have been entirely a pure chestnut grove. Now every tree was dead. All the trees had been uprooted and lay on the ground. The rains and the snow had washed away the dead bark and bleached the trunks a grayish white. No underbrush of any sort grew there. The area was as free from tree growth as are some of the western plains. These chestnuts were of tremendous size—a foot or two or three feet in diameter. Now it is a graveyard of giant trees. . . . The area was easily two square miles.

It is no wonder that a man who experienced the blight said, "I thought the whole world was going to die."[59]

As the trees died, chestnuts became increasingly scarce, valuable, and sought after. Suddenly there were not enough nuts to meet the demand and people had to complete over a limited and rapidly dwindling resource. In the early 1930s Mel Jones was shot to death in Ashe County, North Carolina. "They killed him over chestnuts," Clara Daugherty recalled nearly 60 years later.

They shot him with two different guns on a Sunday morning. They's lots of people up there camping out, going to pick up chestnuts on Sunday and it rained all night. Just before good daylight, somebody killed him. . . . Some people wanted the chestnuts so bad that people would move out and camp just to pick them on anybody's land. . . . They put six of them in jail the next day or two. But they never did prove it on any of them. Then they were from everywhere, people from everywhere up there camping out waiting to pick up chestnuts that morning. Well, when they shot him, the chestnut picking up was over.[60]

The forests went through a period of great ecological change as other tree species filled the enormous gaps left by the chestnut. In the southern Blue Ridge, the chestnut was replaced largely by oaks and hickories, and also by yellow-poplar, maple, hemlock, and other species, depending on local conditions. These vegetative changes also brought changes in understory vegetation and animal populations.[61]

Salvage logging by individuals and timber companies became a major enterprise in an effort to recover some economic value from the dead trees. Cutting still-living trees may have hastened the end of the chestnut trade in some areas, but its days were numbered in any event. The dead chestnuts needed to be cut within a few years of their death if they were to be used for lumber. Otherwise, insects, decay, and checking (cracking as the wood dried) destroyed their value. Much of the chestnut timber from the southwestern Virginia Blue Ridge was sold to furniture companies for use as core stock in veneers. The companies wanted high quality wood and refused to accept lumber with worm holes. A lot of wormy chestnut was left to rot in the forest or fed into wood stoves to heat homes before it became a prized wood. Chipped chestnut wood and bark also were used as a source of tannin for the leather industry. For a while, this became the major source of tannin in the United States.[62]

For urban and suburban residents in the Northeast and other areas outside the Appalachians, the loss of the chestnut meant little more than the loss of a seasonal treat. They neither witnessed the dying forest, nor depended on the chestnuts for their livelihood.[63] For many mountain people, however, the loss of the tree brought economic hardship or devastation. The tree and its nuts failed just as the Great Depression arrived, which compounded their economic problems. The loss of the nuts was a double blow. The best sources of cash for the poorest in the southwestern Blue Ridge counties were chestnuts, hogs, moonshine, and, perhaps, dried apples. The blight ended the chestnut trade and the loss of the nuts brought an end to the hogs. Allowing hogs to forage for chestnuts was both the best and cheapest way to fatten them for slaughter. Acorns were not sufficient and most farmers could not afford to raise or purchase hog feed.

The closure of the commons in southwestern Virginia Blue Ridge counties, and perhaps in other Appalachian mountain counties, followed a very different path from that of much of the South. Following the Civil War, many interests worked to close the commons. People who wanted to constrain the liberties of formerly enslaved African Americans, large landowners who wanted to protect their property rights, mercantile interests, and even railroad companies concerned about liability when trains killed livestock tried to pass laws requiring farmers to fence in their livestock. They encountered considerable resistance on the part of small farmers and others, particularly in mountain communities. However, through persistence, political skill, and skullduggery they often succeeded.[64]

They did not succeed in southwestern Virginia. Fence-in ordinances were not passed until late in the twentieth century, if at all. Floyd County, Virginia, did not pass an ordinance requiring owners to fence in their animals until 1975. Patrick County did not pass a similar ordinance until 1977. Franklin passed an ordinance requiring people to fence in their livestock in 1997.[65] According to local folklore, Grayson County had two of its four districts governed by fence-in laws and the two by fence-out laws. However, there is no documentation to confirm this, so all four districts were legally fence-out. The county established a committee to examine the matter, which in 2004 recommended to continue as fence-out throughout the county, thus preserving the open range. Carroll County has yet to pass a fence ordinance, so it has been and continues to be a fence-out county.[66]

These issues are now only related to liability. The practice of free-range grazing was abandoned long ago. Although the commons was not legally closed earlier in the century, it informally passed out of use after the chestnuts died. Farmers simply stopped free ranging their animals. After the loss of the chestnuts there was not enough forage to fatten hogs, and free ranging other animals ended as new agricultural practices were adopted.

The loss of the nuts ended a way of life and brought economic hardship to many. "The blight was hard on people," Max Thomas wrote, "for chestnuts were used as money at the stores." He continued:

Many people started to move to the cotton mills at Fieldale, Spray, and Draper. People will tell you that these people moved because the [Prohibition] law got too tough but that was not right. Making liquor worked a family to death raising corn, and if there was any profit, the man drank it up. It was the chestnuts that kept the family going. Any way you looked at it, liquor was a drawback. Where there had been three cabins on a branch [creek], there were none now. The population decreased to less than half.[67]

Thomas was not alone in his belief that the death of the chestnuts helped to destroy a semi-subsistence economy and forced many mountain residents to find wage labor. Others shared his perception.

While many people did leave, census figures for the region provide a much more complex picture. Floyd County's population already was dropping before the chestnut blight arrived. Between 1910 and 1920, it dropped by 7 percent. It dropped another 11 percent during the decade of the blight, 1920 to 1930. During the same decades, Patrick County also suffered population declines of 2 percent and 6 percent, respectively. Franklin County's population displayed virtually no decline between 1910 and 1920, but dropped by 8 percent in the following decade. During the same periods, the population in Grayson and Carroll counties actually increased by small amounts. Population increases during the Depression years of the 1930s included in-migration of former residents who left the economic trials of urban areas and returned to their agricultural roots.

In the first decades of the twentieth century, many Blue Ridge residents left to find jobs in Piedmont mills in nearby Fieldale and Danville (Virginia), Spray and Draper (North Carolina), and elsewhere. The timber and coal industries attracted others. Jobs in cities in Ohio and other urban areas also attracted Appalachian residents. As available Blue Ridge land became scarce and good agricultural land still scarcer, some families left to find better farming opportunities. Enough Patrick countians moved to Amelia County, located southwest of Richmond, to establish the "Little Patrick" community. One descendant recalled "trying to raise a family by share cropping on hilly red land. All the land that was tenable was taken by former generations and not for sale. When they heard of this land now Little Patrick, in Amelia for sale that was much more level, they too, decided to take the plunge." Other Little Patrick residents tell a similar family story.[68]

The population decline in Patrick, Floyd, and Franklin counties accelerated during the blight years of the 1920s. It is likely that out-migration in response to the loss of the chestnut was a significant contributing factor. Some residents recall a greater population decline than the census figures show and this may well be the case. Of course, it also may be that people's memories conflated the earlier out-migration and that associated with the blight. Nevertheless, a number of factors mask the true scale of movements in and out of the region. For example, births within the counties replaced many who left. In addition, it was not uncommon for people to leave for temporary employment between growing seasons. Others left for longer periods, but later returned. The Patrick and Franklin county figures are confounded by the fact that only a portion of their land areas are in the Blue Ridge. Population figures for their Piedmont areas may obscure more severe drops in their Blue Ridge regions.

Memories of the chestnut loom large for many elderly residents of southern Appalachia. They remember it fondly and mourn its loss.[69] These feelings of loss also may encompass the loss of a way of life that the chestnut has come to symbolize. The first decades of the twentieth century marked a period of enormous social and economic change in the region. Within a few decades, the region experienced the timber boom, the upheaval of World War I, industrialization, the shift from a barter to a cash economy, the chestnut blight and loss of the chestnut trade and hogs, out-migration and the loss of friends and loved ones, the Great Depression, and the construction of the Blue Ridge Parkway and the arrival of tourism. It may be that the gut-wrenching experience of the death of the American chestnut stands in memory for an entire framework of social and economic change.

For generations, the extraordinary abundance of chestnuts provided food for natives and settlers alike, but this seasonal wealth did not gain economic value until the arrival of better transportation. The region's trade exploded in the early twentieth century, growing from a trickle of nuts in the first years to a torrent at the end of the first decade that provided a new source of income for the region, especially the poorest of its residents. The tree and its nuts acquired a new cultural significance. It was transformed from a forest tree to an agricultural crop, from food to an export commodity. With the death of the trees and the bust of the chestnut trade in the late 1920s, the nuts became a memory recalled with a fondness that belies the great labor involved in collecting them and hauling them to the railroad. It is, though, a memory of abundance—of manna that dropped from the forest canopy.

Notes

1. Richmond Croom Beatty and William J. Mulloy, eds., *William Byrd's Natural History of Virginia, or The Newly Discovered Eden* (Richmond, Va.: Dietz Press, 1940), 31.

2. "Chestnut Blight and Resistant Chestnuts," U.S. Department of Agriculture, Farmer's Bulletin No. 2068, 1, 2; Martha K. Roane, Gary J. Griffin, and John Rush Elkins, *Chestnut Blight, Other Endothia Diseases, and the Genus Endothia* (St. Paul, Minn.: APS Press, 1986), 2. For general discussions of the history of the American chestnut, see Susan Freinkel, *American Chestnut: The Life, Death, and Rebirth of a Perfect Tree* (Berkeley: University of California Press, 2007) and Chris Bolgiano, ed., *Mighty Giants: An American Chestnut Anthology* (Bennington, Vt.: American Chestnut Foundation/Images from the Past, 2007).

3. Thomas J. Campanella, *Republic of Shade: New England and the American Elm* (New Haven, Conn.: Yale University Press, 2003); Charles E. Little, *The Dying of the Trees: The Pandemic in America's Forests* (New York, N.Y.: Viking, 1995).

4. Richard C. Davis, *The Man Who Moved a Mountain* (Philadelphia, Pa.: Fortress Press, 1970), 17, 5.

5. See Herman S. Forest, Richard J. Cook, and Charles N. Bebee, *The American Chestnut: A Bibliography*, Bibliographies and Literature of Agriculture No. 103 (Beltsville, Md.: National Agricultural Library, 1990); William L. MacDonald et al., eds., *Proceedings of the American Chestnut Symposium* (Morgantown, W. Va.: West Virginia University Books), 1978; and Roane, *Chestnut Blight*.

6. "Memories of the American Chestnut," in *Foxfire 6*, ed. Eliot Wigginton (New York, N.Y.: Doubleday/Anchor, 1980), 397–421. See also Robert L. Youngs, "'A Right Smart Little Jolt': The Loss of the Chestnut and a Way of Life," *Journal of Forestry* 98 (February 2000): 17–21.

7. This is in keeping with the results of small community studies by Appalachian studies scholars that revealed the social and economic diversity within the region. See Dwight Billings, Mary Beth Pudup, and Altina Waller, "Taking Exception with Exceptionalism: The Emergence and Transformation of Historical Studies in Appalachia," in *Appalachia in the Making: The Mountain South in the Nineteenth Century*, ed. Pudup, Billings, and Waller (Chapel Hill: University of North Carolina Press, 1995), 10–14.

8. John Alexander Williams, *Appalachia: A History* (Chapel Hill: University of North Carolina Press, 2002), 8–14.

9. Emily W. B. Russell, "Pre-blight Distribution of *Castanea dentata* (March) Borkh," *Bulletin of the Torrey Botanical Club* 114 (1987): 183–90. See range map on 184; also, see map on p. 1 of Roane, *Chestnut Blight. Message from the President of the United States, Transmitting a Report of the Secretary of Agriculture in Relation to the Forests,*

Rivers, and Mountains of the Southern Appalachian Region (Washington, D.C.: U.S. Government Printing Office, 1902).

10. Wigginton, *Foxfire 6*, 403; Donald Peattie, *A Natural History of Trees of Eastern and Central North America*, 2nd ed. (New York, N.Y.: Bonanza Books, 1966), 189; Cornelius Weygandt, *A Passing America: Considerations of Things of Yesterday Fast Fading from Our World* (New York, N.Y.: Henry Holt, 1932), 184.

11. Howard S. Russell, *Indian New England Before the Mayflower* (Hanover, N.H.: University Press of New England, 1980), 77, 78, 53, 197–98; U. P. Hedrick, ed., *Sturtevant's Edible Plants of the World* (1919; reprint, New York, N.Y.: Dover, 1972), 153; Kenneth F. Kiple and Kriemhild Conee Ornelas, "Chestnuts," *Cambridge World History of Food*, http://www.cup.org/books/kiple/chestnuts.htm (accessed 25 January 2004).

12. Andriaen van der Donck, *A Description of the New Netherlands* (New York, N.Y.: Syracuse University Press, 1968), 22.

13. P. L. Buttrick, "Commercial Uses of Chestnut," *American Forestry* 21 (October 1915): 960–67; Albert F. Hill, *Economic Botany*, 2nd ed. (New York, N.Y.: McGraw-Hill, 1952), 70–74, 99, 121; interview of Jim Dillon by Jim Gale, 19 July 1975, "Oral History Transcripts for Rock Castle Gorge, 1975–1977" (hereafter cited as RCG), National Park Service, Blue Ridge Parkway Archives, Asheville, N.C., J22 (a set of these transcripts also is located at the NPS Blue Ridge Parkway Rocky Knob Office, Plateau District, Floyd, Va.); Flippo Gravatt, "The Chestnut Blight in Virginia," Virginia Department of Agriculture and Immigration (1 January 1914), 13. Medicinal uses: Eliot Wigginton, ed., *The Foxfire Book* (New York, N.Y.: Doubleday/Anchor, 1972), 232; Wigginton, *Foxfire 6*, 406; Wigginton, *Foxfire 9* (New York, N.Y.: Doubleday/Anchor, 1986), 71; Kay K. Moss, *Southern Folk Medicine, 1750–1820* (Columbia: University of South Carolina Press, 1999), 127, 178. See also the description of chestnut and its uses in George B. Emerson, *Report on the Trees and Shrubs Growing Naturally in the Forests of Massachusetts* (Boston, Mass.: Dutton & Wentworth, 1846), 166–70.

14. Wigginton, *Foxfire 6*, 402, 401–2; Zetta Barker Hamby, *Memoirs of Grassy Creek: Growing Up in the Mountains on the Virginia-North Carolina Line* (Jefferson, N.C.: McFarland, 1998), 194.

15. Robert L. Blue Sr., *Little Boy Blue: The Childhood and Teenage Years of Robert L. Blue Sr., in the Blue Ridge Mountains of Virginia* (Privately printed, 1999), 83; transcript of interview with Earley and Beulah Hopkins, 1 December 1980, 69, Patrick County Project, Special Collection, Newman Library, Virginia Polytechnical Institute and State University, Blacksburg, Va. (hereafter cited as PCP).

16. Hamby, *Memoirs of Grassy Creek*, 194.

17. Effie King Brown, "A Farm Year in Floyd County: Early 1900s, Locust Grove," *Journal of the New River Historical Society* 7 (1994): 3; Davis, *The Man Who Moved a Mountain*, 17.

18. Weygandt, *A Passing America*, 179–82; see also Arthur Stupka, *Great Smoky Mountains National Park*, National Park Service, Natural History Handbook Series No. 5 (Washington, D.C.: U.S. Government Printing Office, 1960), 24.

19. Wigginton, *Foxfire 6*, 401, 407. Memoirs often give the impression that the nuts were gathered primarily by children. Keep in mind, though, these are the recorded chestnut memories of people who were children at that time and that they tend to give us a child's perception of the trade.

20. Wigginton, *Foxfire 6*, 403–4.

21. Mary Beth Pedup, "Town and Country in the Transformation of Appalachian Kentucky," in *Appalachia in the Making*, 280; Durwood Dunn, *Cades Cove: The Life and Death of A Southern Appalachian Community, 1818–1937* (Knoxville: University of Tennessee Press, 1988), 26 (see pp. 63–97 for a discussion of the development of roads and the market economy in that region); Donald Edward Davis, *Where There Are Mountains: An Environmental History of the Southern Appalachians* (Athens: University of Georgia Press, 2000), 195; *Message from the President*, 97.

22. In 1909, the following items were accepted in barter by a general store in the Blue Ridge community of Vesta (Patrick County), Va.: eggs, live chickens, cows, hogs, rabbits, sheep, butter, corn, wheat, rye, oats, millet, beans, hams, bacon, beef, fresh apples, dried apples, chestnuts, chinquapins, yarn, hides (cow, raccoon, opossum), onions, potatoes, a hay stack, fodder, strawberries, honey, firewood, ginseng, lumber, sacks, boxes, a buggy, a watch, 5 days work roofing, mowing, buggy repairs, and general "work." The most frequently accepted service was "hauling," which may have been used to get much of this stuff to the railroad station. Larkin G. Cockram Store (Vesta, Va.) accounts book, 1903–1912, Patrick County Historical Society Museum, Stuart, Va. (hereafter cited as Cockram Store Accounts Book). See also Elvin Hatch, "Delivering the Goods: Cash, Subsistence Farms, and Identity in a Blue Ridge County in the 1930s," *Journal of Appalachian Studies* 9 (Spring 2003): 6–48.

23. Maron Allen Edwards interview, PCP, Tape 1, Side 1, 324/260; Elder [Oscar] and Mrs. Oscar A. Harris interview, PCP, Tape 1, Side 2, 200; Abraham and Eula Helms interview, PCP, Tape 1, Side 2, 196/163; Josie G. Thomas interview, PCP, Tape 1, Side 2, 154/191; Tommy Largen, "Sawmilling in Carroll County, Virginia as Recalled by Ezra Martin," photocopied typescript, Carroll County Public Library, Hillsville, Va., 12.

24. Gravatt, "The Chestnut Blight in Virginia," 13.

25. Josie G. Thomas interview, PCP, Tape 1, Side 2, 154/91; Helms interview, -/175; Robert Samuel and Sally Slate interview, PCP, Tape 3, Side 1, 200/166. Cockram Store Accounts Book: 30 pounds accepted for $0.90 credit, 30 September 30, 1909; 64 pounds accepted for $1.28 credit, 2 October 1909.

26. Brown, "A Farm Year in Floyd County," 4.

27. See Joseph E. Morse, *Virginia's Country Stores: A Quiet Passing* (Manassas, Va.: E. M. Press, 1996), 13–25, photo of due bills on 14. See Eliot Wigginton and Margie Bennett, eds., "The General Store," *Foxfire 9* (New York, N.Y.: Doubleday/Anchor, 1986), 83–206.

28. Earley and Beulah Hopkins interview, PCP, Tape 1, Side 1, -/202; Gino Williams, Floyd County, personal communication, 19 May 2004; Elder and Mrs. Oscar A. Harris interview, PCP, Tape 1, Side 2, -/162.

29. Ten cents per pound is a rough estimate of the resale value of the nuts to the general store owner before the costs of shipping and the wholesaler's commission are deducted. (See note 31 for the source of this figure.)

30. Gravatt, "The Chestnut Blight in Virginia," 13; Gertrude Blair, "Brief History of Floyd County," Virginia Writers Project, typescript, Montgomery-Floyd Regional Library, Floyd, Va., 5 ; Maynard Calvin Conner and William K. Bing, *An Economic and Social Survey of Patrick County*, University of Virginia Record Extension Series, 11 (January 1937): 69, 66.

31. Southern Express Company shipping receipts (bills of lading) for chestnuts from Mayberry General Store, courtesy of Coy Lee Yeatts and Dale Yeatts, Meadows of Dan, Va. These records recently were transferred to the Albert and Shirley Small Special Collections Library, University of Virginia, Charlottesville. Statements from a New York wholesaler, Parker & Allison, indicate that eight bags sold for a total of $36.16 and nine bags for $34.50. With an average weight per bag in 1914 and 1915 of 42.8 pounds, the merchant received about $0.11 and $0.09 per pound, respectively. (After the expense of shipping and commissions were deducted, Mayberry General Store received $27.92 and $21.83, or $0.08 and $0.06 per pound for these shipments.) Statements from Park & Allison Wholesale Commission Merchants dated 9 October and 28 October, Mayberry General Store, courtesy of Coy Lee and Dale Yeatts, Meadows of Dan, Va. No year was noted, but these lots correspond with the store's shipments of 20 September and 21 October 1915. A 1907 letter from a Philadelphia wholesaler to a resident of Pennick, Va., complained of the failing crop in the northeast and promises $11.00–$15.00 per bushel of chestnuts. E. R. Redfield & Co. to J. S. Elliott, 30 September 1907, Bedford County Historical Society Museum.

32. *History of Patrick County, Virginia* (Stuart, Va.: Patrick County Historical Society, 1999), 359; "Railroads in Patrick County," in *Patrick County, Virginia, Heritage Book, Vol. 1: 1791–1999* (Patrick County Heritage Book Committee, n.d.), 4–6. W. Curtis Carter interview, PCP, Tape 1, Side 1, 436/329; Carter, statement made at Reynold Homestead Continuing Education Center, Patrick Co., 13 May 2003.

33. "Personal Mention," *The Enterprise* (Stuart, Va.), 7 October 1915, 1; Hopkins interview, PCP, Tape 1, Side 1, 218/164.

34. U.S. Census of Agriculture, 1910, Virginia, Table 4; N. J. Giddings, [West Virginia Report], *The Conference Called by the Governor of Pennsylvania to Consider Ways and Means for Preventing the Spread of the Chestnut Tree Bark Disease* (Harrisburg, Pa.: Aughinbaugh, 1912), 26.

35. U.S. Census of Agriculture, 1910, Virginia, Table 4; U.S. Census of Agriculture, 1930, Virginia, Table 8. Census reporting of nuts is not consistent from decade to decade. The 1900 census listed major orchard trees and then lumped all other nuts, including chestnut, under "Miscellaneous." The 1910 census lumped all nuts within a single figure. The 1920 census lumped nuts and fruits together, which makes the figure useless for this study, because these counties also produced apples and peaches. The 1930 census provided figures broken down by kind of nut, including chestnut.

36. See note 29.

37. U.S. Census of Agriculture, 1900, Virginia, Table 7, F. It is likely that these figures underreport the trade given the traditional suspicion of the government held by mountain residents.

38. For a description of a commercial chestnut orchard in Pennsylvania, see Nelson F. Davis, "Chestnut Culture," in *The Conference*, 83–99.

39. U.S. Census of Agriculture, 1910, Virginia, Table 1.

40. See the Land Classification Map, Plate 37, in H. B. Ayers and W. W. Ashe, *The Southern Appalachian Forests*, U.S.G.S. Professional Paper No. 37 (Washington, D.C.: U.S. Government Printing Office, 1905).

41. Ronald D. Eller, *Miners, Millhands, and Mountaineers: Industrialization of the Appalachian South, 1880–1930* (Knoxville: University of Tennessee Press, 1982), 96–99; Edward H. Davis and Edward B. Morgan, *The Virginia Creeper Trail Companion: Nature and History along Southwest Virginia's National Recreation Trail* (Johnson City, Tenn.: Overmountain Press, 1997), 47–68.

42. Steven Hahn, *The Roots of Southern Populism: Yeoman Farmers and the Transformation of the Georgia Upcountry, 1850–1890* (New York, N.Y.: Oxford University Press, 1983), 58–69; Ted Steinberg, *Down to Earth: Nature's Role in American History* (New York, N.Y.: Oxford University Press, 2002), 104–6; *Poindexter v. May*, 98 Va. 143, 34 S.E. 971.

43. Code of Virginia of 1924, 790–91; Code of Virginia of 1924, Sec. 3547; *Poindexter v. May*, 98 Va. 143, 34 S.E. 971.

44. Garrett Hardin, "The Tragedy of the Commons," *Science* 162 (1968): 1243–48; Hardin, "An Operational Analysis of 'Responsibility,'" in *Managing the Commons*, ed. Garrett Hardin and John Baden (San Francisco, Calif.: W. H. Freeman, 1977), 66–75.

45. Arthur F. McEvoy, *The Fisherman's Problem: Ecology and Law in the California Fisheries, 1850–1980* (New York, N.Y.: Cambridge University Press, 1986); Brian Donahue, "'Damned at Both Ends and Cursed in the Middle': The 'Flowage' at the Concord River Meadows, 1798–1862," *Environmental Review* 13 (Fall/Winter 1989): 47–67; John T. Cumbler, "The Early Making of an Environmental Consciousness: Fish, Fisheries, Fisheries Commissions and the Connecticut River," *Environmental History Review* 15 (Winter 1991): 73–91; Jennifer Price, *Flight Maps: Adventures With Nature in Modern America* (New York, N.Y.: Basic Books, 1999), 1–55.

46. David Feeney et al., "The Tragedy of the Commons: Twenty-Two Years Later," *Human Ecology* 18 (1990): 1–19; Thomas Dietz, Elinor Ostrom, and Paul C. Stern, "The Struggle to Govern the Commons," *Science* 302 (2003): 1907–12. See also Bonnie J. McCay and James M. Acheson, eds., *The Question of the Commons: The Culture and Ecology of Communal Resources* (Tucson: University of Arizona Press, 1987); Elinor Ostrom et al., eds., *The Drama of the Commons* (Washington, D.C.: National Academy Press, 2002).

47. *History of Patrick County, Virginia*, 43–44; Marshall Wingfield, *Franklin County Virginia: A History* (Berryville, Va.: Chesapeake Book Co., 1964), 28; Helms interview, PCP, Tape 1, Side 2, -/172.

48. Pedro Sloan, *The Way of Life in Turner's Creek Valley Sixty Years Ago* (1943 typescript; reprinted, Virginia: Franklin County Historical Society, 2004), 11; Michael B. Montgomery and Joseph S. Hall, *Dictionary of Smoky Mountain English* (Knoxville: University of Tennessee Press, 2004), 125.

49. Louise McNeill, *The Milkweed Ladies* (Pittsburgh, Pa.: University of Pittsburgh Press, 1988), 103.

50. Chester and Erma McKenzie interview, PCP, Tape 5, Side 1, 373/320; Hopkins interview, PCP, Tape 7, Side 1, -/114; Max S. Thomas, *Walnut Knob: A Story of Mountain Life and My Heritage in Song* (Radford, Va.: Commonwealth Press, 1977), 47.

51. Louise Vanover Vore, "Dickenson County Va—Newspaper Articles, 1890–1900s," http://ftp.rootsweb.com/pub/usgenweb/va/dickenson/newspapers/1890-001.txt, [13] (accessed 21 October 2003).

52. Emily W. B. Russell, "Indian-set Fires in the Forests of the Northeastern United States," *Ecology* 64 (1983): 78–88; William A. Patterson III and Kenneth E. Sassaman, "Indian Fires in the Prehistory of New England," in *Holocene Human Ecology in Northeastern North America*, ed. George P. Nicholas (New York, N.Y.: Plenum Press, 1988), 105–35; Davis, *Where There Are Mountains*, 28–31; Brian Donahue, *Reclaiming the Commons: Community Farms and Forests in a New England Town* (New Haven, Conn.: Yale University Press, 1999), 212; Jeffrey Kirwan, Forestry Department, Virginia Polytechnic Institute, personal communication, 30 March 2004; E. Lucy Braun, *Deciduous Forests of Eastern North America* (1950 reprint, New York, N.Y.: Free Press, 1974), 219, 232, 246.

53. William Lynwood Montell, *The Saga of Coe Ridge: A Study in Oral History* (Knoxville: University of Tennessee Press, 1970), 94. This racial feud began in 1888; see 91, 96.

54. Franklin B. Hough, *Report Upon Forestry* (Washington, D.C.: U.S. Government Printing Office, 1878), 470; Gravatt, "The Chestnut Blight in Virginia," 6; Russell, "Pre-blight Distribution," 185; B. S. Crandall, G. F. Gravatt, and M. M. Ryan, "Root disease of *Castanea* Species and Some Coniferous and Broadleaf Nursery Stocks, Caused by *Phytophthora cinnamomi*," *Phytopathology* 25 (1945): 162–80.

55. Hermann W. Merkel, "A Deadly Fungus on the American Chestnut," *New York Zoological Society Tenth Annual Report* (1906), 97–103. For general accounts of the chestnut and blight, see Davis, *Where There Are Mountains*, 192–98; Youngs, "'A Right Smart Little Jolt'"; David O. Smith, "American Chestnut: Ill-fated Monarch of the Eastern Hardwood Forest," *Journal of Forestry* 98 (February 2000): 12–15; George H. Hepting, "Death of the American Chestnut," *Journal of Forest History* 18 (July 1974): 61–67; Amanda Ulm, "Remember the Chestnut!" *American Forests* 54 (April 1948): 156–59, 190, 192.

56. Roane, *Chestnut Blight*, 1–2; Joseph R. Newhouse, "Chestnut Blight," *Scientific American* 262 (July 1990): 106–11; G. F. and D. E. Gravatt, "Introduced Tree Diseases and Insects," in *Trees: The Yearbook of Agriculture* (Washington, D.C.: U.S. Government Printing Office, 1949), 447; "Chestnut Blight Caused by the Fungus *Endothia*

parasitica," Forestry Commission Booklet No. 3 (London: Her Majesty's Stationery Office, 1950), inside front cover.

57. Gravatt, "Chestnut Blight in Virginia," 3, 7–9; Berlin Eye, "Forests of Warren County," in *An Economic and Social History of Warren County*, ed. Elliot Clarke Haley et al. (Charlottesville: University of Virginia, 1943), 45.

58. Chester and Erma McKenzie interview, PCP, Tape 5, Side 1, 373/320; Helms interview, PCP, Tape 1, Side 2, 196/163; Robert Samuel Slate and Sally Slate interview, PCP, Tape 3, Side 1, 200/166; Freinkel, *American Chestnut*, 73; Margaret Lynn Brown, *The Wild East: A Biography of the Great Smoky Mountains* (Gainesville: University Press of Florida, 2000), 99; Stupka, *Great Smoky Mountains National Park*, 23; Ulm, "Remember the Chestnut!" 192.

59. Wigginton, *Foxfire 6*, 409; Carolyn and Jack Reeder, *Shenandoah Secrets: The Story of the Park's Hidden Past*, rev. ed. (Vienna, Va.: Potomac Appalachian Trail Club, 1998), 136; Davis, *Where There Are Mountains*, 196.

60. Leland R. Cooper and Mary Lee Cooper, *The Pond Mountain Chronicle* (Jefferson, N.C.: McFarland, 1998), 29.

61. Catherine Keever, "Present Composition of Some Stands of the Former Oak-Chestnut Forest in the Southern Blue Ridge Mountains," *Ecology* 34 (June 1953): 44–54; Thomas C. Nelson, "Chestnut Replacement in the Southern Highlands," *Ecology* 36 (April 1955): 352–53; Frank W. Woods and Royal E. Shanks, "Natural Replacement of Chestnut by Other Species in the Great Smoky Mountains National Park," *Ecology* 40 (July 1959): 349–61; J. Frank McCormick and Robert B. Platt, "Recovery of an Appalachian Forest Following the Chestnut Blight, or Catherine Keever—You Were Right!" *American Midland Naturalist* 104 (October 1980): 264–73; Stupka, *Great Smoky Mountains National Park*, 24–26.

62. Gravatt, "Chestnut Blight in Virginia," 13; R. L Humbert et al., *Industrial Survey of Floyd County* (Blacksburg, Va.: Engineering Extension Division, Virginia Polytechnical Institute, May 1930), 27; Ward Compton interview, RCG, F5; Harris interview, PCP, Tape 1, Side 2, 630/159; Alfred J. Stamm, "Chemicals From Wood," in *Trees*, 640; Gravatt, "Introduced Tree Diseases and Insects," 447.

63. Campanella, *Republic of Shade*, 151.

64. Hahn, *The Roots of Southern Populism*, 239–68; Steinberg, *Down to Earth*, 106–10.

65. Judge Gino Williams, Floyd County, personal communication, 19 May 2004; Floyd County, Virginia, Board of Supervisors minutes, 11 August 1975; Floyd County Code Sec. 10-5; Patrick County, Virginia, Supervisors Order Book No. 9, 348; Franklin County, Virginia, Code 4.1 (ordinance approved 21 October 1997).

66. Donald G. Young, county administrator, Grayson County, Virginia, personal communication, 14 May 2004, 21 June 2004; Ronald L. Newman, acting county administrator, Carroll County, Virginia, personal communications, 29 January 2004, 21 May 2004.

67. Thomas, *Walnut Knob*, 47.

68. Williams, *Appalachia*, 312–14; Thomas E. Wagner, Phillip J. Obermiller, and Bruce Tucker, "Introduction," in *Appalachian Odyssey: Historical Perspectives on the Great Migration*, ed. Obermiller, Wagner, and Tucker (Westport, Conn.: Praeger, 2000), xi–xiii; Ruby Faries Arrington, *From the Mountains They Came—The Story of "Little Patrick"* (Privately published, 1994, copy in Blue Ridge Regional Library, Historical Center, Bassett, Va.), 56.

69. This is an early example of "ecological grief." See Phyllis Windle, "The Ecology of Grief," in *Ecopsychology: Restoring the Earth, Healing the Mind*, ed. Theodore Roszak, Mary E. Gomes, and Allen D. Kanner (San Francisco, Calif.: Sierra Club Books, 1995), 136–45.

ALBERT G. WAY

Burned to Be Wild

Herbert Stoddard and the Roots of Ecological

Conservation in the Southern Longleaf

Pine Forest

AS HE DID most every day while visiting the Red Hills region of south Georgia and north Florida, Henry Beadel—the son of a northern industrialist—was out quail hunting with his brother, Gerald, and their African-American driver, Charley. It was a chilly afternoon in February, late 1890s. Upon reaching their shooting grounds, Beadel witnessed the unthinkable: "we saw the whole country on fire, which within a few minutes left the ground black and bare except for scattered clumps of bushes." An area that only the day before stood as an idyllic scene of grand pine woodlands interspersed with small, almost meadow-like agricultural fields, now appeared before them as a fire-blackened hell-on-earth. Unbeknownst to Beadel, the local African-American sharecroppers had "put the fire out" that afternoon, ridding field and forest of a year's worth of accumulated growth. Beadel was not amused. "The country looked to us irretrievably ruined, and the quail *doomed*."[1]

Charley soon set Beadel's mind at ease. He "informed us that this burning took place regularly every spring as far back as his great-grandpapa could remember." Relieved, yet still a bit incredulous, Beadel took "a few calmer squints through the smoke [to see] all the trees still standing, and we even found that we could walk behind the flames without scorching our boots." After a little sleuthing, he discovered that locals "took the practice as much for granted that it had not occurred to them to mention it to us."[2] Setting fires was one of the many local land management practices that mimicked historical ecological disturbance in the South's longleaf-grassland environment—practices that would soon be repeatedly attacked and defended by a bevy of scientific experts.

Almost three decades later, it did not take such a revelatory experience for Herbert Stoddard to realize fire had an essential place in the South's coastal plain ecology. Despite the anti-fire dogma that infused the region in the 1920s, he already understood before arriving in the Red Hills that the stability of the region's longleaf pine-grassland system depended on routine fire. Stoddard came to the Red Hills in 1924 as the leader of a study, sponsored by wealthy landowners and carried out through the U.S. Bureau of Biological Survey, to examine the life history and preferred habitat of the bobwhite quail, and to develop a management scheme to reverse population declines. He had no formal education, but his experience as a young boy in the flatwoods of central Florida, his professional growth in the Midwest, and his profound respect for local people who had long experience with their environment gave him the confidence to proclaim early in the study that "fire is unquestionably a controlling factor in determining the types of woodland in any given area in this region, as well as in the regulation of the ground vegetation."[3] Innocuous as it might seem at first glance, this statement would have enormous implications for the conservation of the longleaf system, and for the now decades-long reconsideration of fire's ecological role. But Stoddard's recommendation came at a time when the prevailing, and practically unwavering, thought on the issue of fire in the South was clear: it should be suppressed at all costs.

Environmental historians have been slow to appreciate the conservation work of Herbert Stoddard.[4] Some recognize his study of the bobwhite quail as the first real field study in wildlife management, but usually defer to Aldo Leopold on matters of intellectual heft. Indeed, like most conservationists of the day, Stoddard deferred to Leopold as well. They were close friends and intellectual kin, but Stoddard recognized Leopold's superiority with the pen. Leopold was the voice for countless conservation professionals, and his writings provided many of the intellectual underpinnings for a future environmental movement.[5] Stoddard's influence was a bit more pedestrian, though in many ways just as important. His writings were extensive, and they remain a crucial resource for understanding his legacy, but his real influence can be gauged in the land he worked. Quite simply, his management was responsible for the survival of the most ecologically sound longleaf-grassland environments remaining.

This essay assesses Herbert Stoddard's early professional work in the context of a regional and national conservation movement. It is part of a larger study on the Red Hills that will probe how this landscape of both wealth and poverty came to be what many now see as a template for conservation in the longleaf-grassland region. As a federal employee, Stoddard struggled to correct deeply misinformed ecological knowledge about the southern coastal plain, especially the role of fire. When the opportunity arose, he fled the federal government's departmental bureaucracy. As a private consultant and researcher, he combined forestry, agriculture, and wildlife management to arrive at a system of land management that stressed the importance of healthy ecological habitat, instead of the dominant production-oriented model so common to the twentieth-century South's fields and forests. His early work was informed and supported by a newly centralized conservation state, but he was best known for using his practical experience in the field to challenge accepted conservation wisdom.

Stoddard's most prolific years on the national level were 1924–1941. While the rest of the South underwent a dramatic transformation toward industrialized agriculture and forestry, Stoddard attempted to push those fields in a different direction through a concern for wildlife habitat. He drew on his early experience in ornithological fieldwork, as well as an older body of local knowledge embedded in the South's system of tenantry. He realized that, as a landscape historically shaped by both natural and human disturbance, the longleaf-grassland environment was distinctly suited to the low-level disturbance patterns of tenantry. The small scale, non-mechanized agriculture, the large blocks of open woodland, and the connecting thread of fire all worked together to maintain the system's historical ecological diversity. Within this landscape of disturbance, Stoddard achieved three major accomplishments during these years in the natural resources field: he helped to create the new profession of wildlife management with his landmark publication, *The Bobwhite Quail*; he reinserted fire into the landscape, beginning a management revolution that is still playing out; and he was among the first to advocate the preservation of working, cultural landscapes as vital reservoirs of ecological diversity. All of these accomplishments foreshadow Stoddard's post–World War II efforts to develop an integrated land management system that mirrors what we call today ecosystem management.

Another purpose here is to place the South within the broader context of environmental history. The West's role in the national conservation movement is beyond reproach, and the Northeast has recently received more attention, but we usually view the South as a conservation backwater.[6] Mart A. Stewart has done much to explain the South's blip on the environmental historian's radar. He argues there was no southern wilderness in the classical sense—that wide open, uninhabited space of frontier legend. The South was an agrarian land, and even in the wilder areas, it never developed "an indigenous notion of 'wilderness' as unoccupied or relatively undisturbed nature."[7] What, then, did southern conservation look like in the first half of the twentieth century, when most of the nation's attention turned toward the public lands of the West? Herbert Stoddard provides a clue. Stoddard was well-connected to the national conservation establishment. More important, his work exemplified the public-private cooperation and conflict that was so common to many aspects of life in the South. In a region deeply entrenched in the values of private landownership and dominated by the geography of agriculture, there was little reason, or possibility, for a state preservation intervention, except in some scenic areas of the mountains and coasts.[8] Stoddard, whose own experience limited notions about pristine nature, was more interested in working within the context that he lived than setting aside wild areas to let nature take its course. In so doing, he was among the first to recognize the potential ecological value of a southern landscape that contained a good deal of agriculture.

Unlike the large federal and state projects of the West and Northeast, this effort was not seen on public maps. The preserve owners used state capacity and expertise to develop local policy, but expertise on the quail preserves developed far from the centralized control of a federal bureaucracy; it was not imposed by a centralized directive, but instead came from knowledge gained in the field, on the local level. Shortly after his arrival, Stoddard, and eventually his followers, began to couch the management choices of private landowners in ecological terms, and they did so largely from outside of the state and academic apparatus. In a region where agricultural and timber interests continued to transform native longleaf ecosystems wholesale, this private network created a land ethic that nourished the historical environment. This southern story not only offers a new variation on how conservation played out locally and regionally, but it also forces us to more fully portray the local elements of national conservation policy.

Beadel's revelation illustrates that Stoddard could not practice conservation in a vacuum. This was a working landscape, and it is impossible to separate the results of Stoddard's career path from the historical and ecological context of the longleaf-grassland ecoregion, and of the Red Hills in particular. Historically, the Red Hills was part of a 90 million acre fire-dependent longleaf-grassland ecoregion that stretched across the southern coastal plain from southern Virginia to east Texas. It was one of North America's largest pre-contact natural communities, and today there is very little of it left. The longleaf-grassland community, though it dominated the coastal plain, was not an ecological monolith; it was part of a diverse mosaic of hardwood bottomlands, upland forests, and transitional areas, all overlapping and intermingling, gradually giving way from one to the other. The well-drained upland longleaf forest—which usually contained an understory of highly combustible wiregrass (*Aristida stricta*)—was the region's most prominent ecological feature, but even its compositional make-up varied across space and time as a result of soil quality, fire patterns, disturbance histories, human land use practices, and other factors. The most prominent disturbance event, and the single most important natural element that held the longleaf-grassland system together, was, and still is, fire. Though forest ecologists have long moved beyond the climax ecology of Frederic Clements, they still call this system a fire-climax community; not only are the species in this ecosystem resistant to fire, but their very existence is dependent on it.[9]

That such a naturally diverse, dynamic landscape was a product of both natural and human history is also crucial to this story. Though on the surface this looks like a familiar conservation story—decline, recognition, preservation—in some important ways it bucks the traditional conservation narrative. This was no static system in a state of climax at the time of human contact. In fact, most agree it was a system of Holocene origin that never existed absent a human presence. Native Americans had arrived in the coastal plain region while the system was taking shape, and there is considerable evidence that their land use practices shaped the forests that Europeans and Africans found thousands of years later.[10] When those latter groups did move in, between 1600 and the late 1800s, they co-existed tenuously with the longleaf-grassland ecosystem, altering it and substantially degrading it in places, but never threatening its existence. By the turn of the twentieth century, it was a system in various stages of ecological development that was simultaneously threatened to the point of destruction by human action and dependent on human maintenance in order to survive.

After many millennia of low-level if accelerating human interaction with the longleaf forests, its two greatest threats emerged at the same moment in time—the late nineteenth century—and they were intimately connected. One threat, the increasing interest in fire suppression among a growing community of professional foresters, arose from the ashes of the other, the turn of the century timber boom. In the 1880s, large timber companies turned their focus from the Great Lakes states to the South, where there remained a substantial amount of timber in the public domain. When Congress retreated from the lofty goals of Reconstruction and repealed the Southern Homestead Act—designed to offer small plots from the public domain to both freedmen and poor whites—public land sales were no longer limited to 80 acres.[11] Timber companies and other speculators proceeded to amass huge tracts of land and construct rail lines into the coastal plain's interior; by the 1920s they had cut the high-grade timber out of millions of acres of longleaf forest and left much of the land in ruins.[12]

Across the upland coastal plain, less fire tolerant pine species such as loblolly and slash replaced the cutover longleaf, and when foresters saw debris-fueled fires sweep through the region, killing these early successional pines, they assumed fire made *all* pine propagation impossible. As it turned out, they were wrong, at least if their goal was to regenerate longleaf forests. Most timber companies operated a high-grade cut; that is, they sought the oldest, straightest trees and left many smaller trees behind, effectively providing the seed stock for the next longleaf forest. In these disturbed longleaf landscapes, fire was necessary to expose the bare mineral soil needed for seeds to germinate, and to suppress early successional pines such as loblolly and slash pine, as well as hardwoods, so the longleaf seed stock could establish its dominance. But without fire these seeds rarely had a chance. Through its destructive cutting, the timber industry deeply wounded the original longleaf forest, and fire suppression deprived this dominant southern ecosystem of a critical source of life support.

Although this environmental transformation occurred across the southern coastal plain, there were pockets of territory that escaped both the timber industry and state-sponsored fire suppression. The Red Hills was such a place, thanks in no small part to the work of Herbert Stoddard and the historical factors that brought him there. The region in which Stoddard landed was, and still is, a unique one.[13] Topographically, the area consists of gently rolling upland hills, transitional bogs, streams, sinks, and bottomlands around the larger rivers. The soils of the uplands are of the Orangeburg-Dothan-Faceville series, a well-drained, clayey type that is rich in fertility. Undisturbed, these rich soils grow a complex mix of plant communities. One study counts as many as twenty-four natural communities within a portion of the Red Hills, with the fire-maintained upland pine forest as the most common.[14]

But this distinct environment did not act alone to make the Red Hills that Herbert Stoddard entered unique. Several important historical trends following the Civil War set the scene for the development of Stoddard's land management system. Unlike many other longleaf areas on the coastal plain, the Red Hills was a large plantation district. In one respect, the region followed the lead of most other plantation districts throughout the postbellum South: landowners and former slaves adopted the crop-lien system and former slave families dispersed over the land as tenants and sharecroppers. Planters struggled to come to economic terms with losing their major source of wealth—slave labor—and croppers entered a crushing debt cycle that required an increasing reliance on cash crops. Left there, the Red Hills might have continued along the path of other plantation districts. The cotton economy would have increased its stranglehold on planters and tenants; landowners would have turned to other economic interests, selling out to industrial timber or agricultural interests, or subdividing and selling plantations in smaller tracts; tenants might have hung on for a while until New Deal programs, World War II, or the Sunbelt boom made them look to the cities to fill the need for industrial labor.[15] To a certain extent, these things did happen in the counties of Thomas, Grady, Leon, and Jefferson. But another trend complicated that narrative.

The fluorescence of the health and tourist trade following the Civil War pointed much of the region in a different direction. During the late 1800s, health seekers headed into many natural environments in search of cures for all sorts of physical and psychological maladies, including tuberculosis, hay fever, and what was then called neurasthenia. Along with hot springs and mountainous regions, physicians and health seekers set upon the piney woods of the South as particularly salubrious. Northerners began visiting Thomasville in the 1870s as a layover stop on their way to winter in Florida, and it gained therapeutic legitimacy when Dr. Thomas S. Hopkins, founder of the South Georgia Medical Association, wrote widely on the restorative qualities of the piney woods, especially for lung disorders such as tuberculosis. As happened in many places that dealt in the health trade, the local commercial elite expanded their publicity efforts beyond the sick, and soon began attracting wealthy northerners who were seeking healthful outdoor exercise and a respite from cold northern winters.[16] In this former landscape of production, wealthy northerners found a landscape of health. Like historian Gregg Mitman's hay-fever tourists in the White Mountains, these visitors to the Red Hills "may have been outsiders to the local community, but their wealth, patronage, and illness combined to make them a powerful force in regional development and land use."[17] The elixir offered up by the Red Hills came in the form of natural beauty and the bobwhite quail—two things that would soon require a conservation intervention for their maintenance.

This convergence of events—the transformation of plantation agriculture and the burgeoning tourist trade—re-created much of the Red Hills into something new altogether. Between 1870 and 1900 the number of individual farms (not landholdings) increased from just over 600 to more than 3,000 in Thomas County alone.[18] This type of small-scale agriculture created a diverse habitat for all sorts of wildlife, the bobwhite quail being the most important to this story. There were small, working fields that were usually just a few acres in size and others of similar size in various stages of old-field succession; there were brushy edge environments; and, perhaps most importantly, there remained substantial, fire-maintained longleaf pine woodlands. The rolling terrain of the Red Hills prevented planters from completely clearing the land for agriculture, and the timber industry stayed away because the region's good soils made it a firmly entrenched plantation district with land prices higher than those in the public domain. The resulting mosaic of open pine forests interspersed with small agricultural fields, reverting old fields, and brushy margins created habitat conditions that were ideal for quail and quail hunting. Herbert Stoddard came to recognize that early twentieth-century quail abundance—a big part of what made this landscape attractive to wealthy northerners seeking recreation in nature—was as much a cultural phenomenon as it was an environmental one.

Soon, northerners not only visited the Red Hills, they started purchasing large plantations and piecing together smaller ones to use as seasonal hunting lands and residences. As modern medical theories challenged claims about the landscape's curative power, quail hunting became a greater lure to upper-class urbanites looking for a rugged, masculine experience in the outdoors. By 1930, non-resident northerners held well over 250,000 acres as hunting preserves in the Red Hills, with other regions scattered across the South also absorbing this new seasonal migration and system of land tenure. The Red Hills contained the oldest game preserves, but as the Depression tightened its grip on southern farmers, real estate agents and insurance companies also began to piece together farms in the Dougherty Plain region surrounding Albany, Georgia, as well as in the coastal and piedmont areas of the Carolinas and old farming districts of Alabama and Mississippi. In assembling large landholdings as game preserves, these people of privilege—in many cases the beneficiaries of the same industries that made the destruction of longleaf forests possible—stepped in at a crucial moment and set the table for modern longleaf conservation.[19] But they also disrupted a complex tapestry of ecological processes and human land uses in ways that ended up threatening their very interests in the region.

As Henry Beadel's remarks indicate, these wealthy new landowners were not accustomed to setting the woods and fields on fire, and most were not as trusting of the locals and their traditions as Beadel came to be. When presented with a choice of whom to trust, they invariably went with the new cadre of professional foresters who moved into the region to deal with the problem of cutover lands, and who pathologized such folk burning practices. As preserve owners curtailed traditional burning over the first two decades of the twentieth century, they soon noticed a drastic decline in quail numbers. As Stoddard put it, this "ecological upset, caused largely by the efforts of well-meaning but uninformed professional foresters, had brought about serious conditions, among them a decline in quail."[20] It became clear to the preserve owners that the question of wildlife habitat was not a pressing issue for state and federal foresters, so they turned to another government organization for help—the Bureau of Biological Survey. With preserve owners Arthur Lapsley, Charles Chapin, and L. S. Thompson in the lead, they approached the Bureau about the possibility of conducting a systematic study of the bobwhite quail, and they soon welcomed Herbert Stoddard as the lead investigator of a jointly-funded venture between the Bureau and a private group of preserve owners.

Herbert Stoddard's appointment to the Bureau of Biological Survey in 1924 marked the culmination of an informal training in natural history that began when he was a youngster in the piney woods of central Florida, and continued in Illinois and Wisconsin when he was an apprentice taxidermist, trapper, and ornithologist. Stoddard was born and lived the first few years of his life in the upper Midwest, a region to which he would return as an adolescent, but it was during the seven years that he spent in Florida that he came of age. He experienced Florida's longleaf forests before the timber industry arrived; he worked for cattlemen, who routinely set fire to the woods; and upon reflection he was "convinced that no schooling or advantages could have been more valuable to me . . . in my later years as ornithologist, ecologist, and wildlife researcher and manager."[21] These early years gave him a body of informal knowledge about the longleaf-grassland forest to fall back on years later, but his return to the Midwest—one of the cradles of the modern conservation movement—got his foot through the professional door.

Upon his family's return to Rockford, Illinois, in 1900, young Herb continued to cultivate an interest in natural history, but a lack of patience with formal education led him to quit high school and move to his uncle's farm in Prairie du Sac, Wisconsin, to work as a farm hand. There he met Ed Ochsner, a local taxidermist, woodsman, and field contact for the Milwaukee Public Museum (MPM), who came to be an important influence. Over the next several years, Stoddard worked on the farm during the growing season and with Ochsner during the winter, learning taxidermy as well as trapping and collecting methods. Like the cattlemen with whom he ran in Florida, Ochsner was a prototype for the knowledgeable land manager that Stoddard would become, but the perquisite of this apprenticeship was that Ochsner had contacts. Stoddard's professional break came in 1910 on a trip with Ochsner to Baraboo, Wisconsin, the winter home of the Ringling Brothers Circus. Alfred Ringling had a dead hippopotamus on his hands. He summoned Ochsner, who decided it should go to the MPM if they could skin and pack it for travel. The head taxidermist for the museum, George Shrosbree, came to Baraboo immediately, and Stoddard stayed on to assist in preparing the skin. Seeing the skills of an enthusiastic young

Stoddard, Shrosbree offered him the job of assistant taxidermist in March 1910. In a professional world that was still taking shape, the informality of such an offer was not all that unusual. But it did give a budding amateur naturalist entrée into the newly developed, insular world of expert-driven, scientific conservation.[22] For the next fourteen years, Stoddard worked in the museum field, for both the Milwaukee Public Museum and the Field Museum of Natural History in Chicago, as taxidermist, field collector, and ornithologist.[23]

Stoddard's experience as a museum field man and taxidermist led to a deepening involvement in the ornithological community, where he made connections critical to his return to the Southeast. He first heard of a possible southern quail investigation at the 1922 meeting of the American Ornithologist's Union, where he helped to found the Inland Bird Banding Association along with legendary bird-bander, S. Prentiss Baldwin. Baldwin had banded thousands of birds at his summer home outside of Cleveland and at his winter get-away in Thomasville, Georgia, and was an early promoter of the technique for tracking bird movements.[24] Stoddard was among the first to follow Baldwin's lead into banding. In 1923, he wrote in the *Yearbook of the Public Museum of the City of Milwaukee* that bird banding "bids fair to revolutionize bird study."[25] He banded birds throughout his travels for the MPM and began publishing accounts of his field experience in journals such as *The Auk* and *The Wilson Bulletin*, drawing the attention of a wider audience.[26] Baldwin, along with W. L. McAtee, head of food habits research in the Biological Survey, soon took note of Stoddard's field work for the Museum and the Inland Bird Banding Association, and kept him in mind for a possible job in the Red Hills.

Meanwhile, on April 25, 1923, a small group of preserve owners from the Red Hills met with a representative of the Biological Survey at the exclusive Links Club in New York City. There, they discussed the possibility of an investigation into the life history of the bobwhite quail in the Southeast. It was not unusual for sportsmen to call on the Biological Survey for help with game management problems, but this particular request was typically the domain of ornithology. The "life history" concept arose from ornithologists frustrated with simply collecting specimens or tracking movements, and not actually recording the habits of birds in the wild. Several researchers in the egg-collecting branch of ornithology (oology) attempted life history studies around the turn of the century, but not until the 1910s did they gain wider acceptance.[27] Prentiss Baldwin was among the earliest voices calling for a life history of the bobwhite. With a foot in the world of both sportsmen and ornithologists, he recognized the two interests could converge to push the concept beyond its limited role as a descriptive addition to ornithological taxonomy. The life history could be a prescriptive conservation tool designed to produce applicable results, that is, practical solutions for land managers in the field. The major thrust of the proposed quail study was to explain the recent quail decline, to discover what natural conditions best suited quail, and then to make management recommendations based on such discoveries. Ultimately, the preserve owners and the Biological Survey would create the framework for the most thorough and innovative life history of an animal species up to that point.

Within a year of the Links Club meeting an agreement was signed between the preserve owners and the Biological Survey. Baldwin and McAtee quickly agreed that Stoddard had "the qualities we think are desirable for the position combined in one man."[28] Those qualities apparently did not include a high school diploma, or any real experience conducting what promised to be a thorough scientific study. But more than a trained and educated scientist, the Cooperative Quail Investigation needed a self-starter who would be able to improvise in the field and work efficiently under a mere skeleton of centralized directives, qualities that S. A. Barrett, Director of the MPM, had already instilled in Stoddard: "The conditions which you encounter in the field must govern your actions and your own judgment is about the only thing that can count for much when it comes to field work . . . we do not wish to dictate from the office just what you shall do."[29] It was just such ability to handle the intangibles that ultimately recommended Stoddard to the Biological Survey. As in so many early federal projects in the field, no one really knew what this one would look like; as Biological Survey chief, E. W. Nelson, put it to Stoddard in the job offer, "the success or failure of the investigation will rest in your hands, and the initiative will rest largely with you as to how the work is carried on and the results obtained." Stoddard immediately accepted the challenge.[30]

The Red Hills landscape allayed any reluctance Stoddard may have felt about leaving the Midwest. Early in 1924, he embarked on a week-long surveillance trip to Thomasville, where he "was delighted to see blocks of virgin longleaf pine that had been preserved on some of the plantations, and the impressive stands of second-growth pine that covered well over half the total preserve acreage."[31] He returned in March 1924 to begin the quail work in earnest. He and his wife, Ada—whom he had married in Milwaukee in 1915—set up residence at L. S. Thompson's 1,000 acre satellite plantation in Grady County, Georgia. Known as "The Hall," and later called Sherwood Plantation, this piece of land served as the investigation's research base along with Thompson's 15,000 acre Sunny Hill Plantation. Stoddard hired an assistant, Charles O. Handley, and began examining the Red Hills environment, trapping and banding quail; observing breeding behavior, nest sites, and daily behavior; examining anatomy; and observing predator-prey relations. These early stages of the study also allowed him to cultivate respect from both locals and preserve owners. His own status as a field agent of the Biological Survey gave him ready legitimacy in the eyes of preserve owners, and unlike many agents of the nascent conservation state, he was not seen as an outsider by locals. Stoddard's rearing more closely approximated that of the local preserve managers and laborers, and his practical approach to research readily co-opted local land management traditions. Instead of forcing an unwieldy cultural landscape to fit an abstract set of scientific principles, he set out to mold a system of management from the region's cultural and environmental past.

For the science of game management, the Cooperative Quail Investigation was a landmark study. It helped to propagate and define the field of game management—later renamed wildlife management to reflect a growing interest in non-game species—and helped make it one of the most important among a growing number of natural resource professions. The book that resulted from Stoddard's investigations, *The Bobwhite Quail: Its Habits, Preservation and Increase* (1931), is often overlooked by environmental historians today, but conservation advocates of the day regarded it as the premier document on wildlife management of any species in any region. Indeed, while Aldo Leopold is often considered the founder of game management as a field, Leopold himself considered that honor to be Stoddard's. Leopold's biographer, Curt Meine, notes that Stoddard was "the first to examine a game species in detail and to utilize that information in a restoration effort. While Leopold was evolving an abstract framework for the science, Stoddard was providing its first concrete example."[32] And Leopold himself later noted that "Herbert Stoddard, in Georgia, started the first management of wildlife based on research."[33] *The Bobwhite Quail* was thus a seminal text, and Stoddard a pioneering figure, in the growth of wildlife ecology and management.[34]

Whereas previous efforts at wildlife management meant little more than setting state hunting regulations, eradicating predators, or artificially propagating game birds, this was one of the first attempts to understand and regulate natural processes. Stoddard's primary concern in *The Bobwhite Quail* was the creation and maintenance of wildlife habitat, a proposition that would bridge several professional fields, including agriculture and forestry. His management ran counter to the progressive science underway in both fields in the 1920s and 1930s. His recommendations to maintain a cultural landscape rooted in the past ignored the new teachings of progressive agriculturalists who felt the only sure path for southern farming was intensive, "clean" agriculture. For foresters, his maintenance of old-growth forests seemed decadent and his insistence on fire downright destructive. Both foresters and agriculturalists were out to produce the maximum of one product. Stoddard and his peers in wildlife management were as well, but through their focus on a single game species, they came to see the wisdom of restrained productivity, which in turn opened up the study of all natural ecological processes.

The use of fire as a strategy to restore quail numbers was perhaps the most significant, and certainly the most controversial, result of the quail study. Trumpeting the use of fire would ultimately help to define Stoddard's legacy in the southeastern forests, but when reports filtered out of the South in 1925 that fire might benefit wildlife, the nation's foresters grew uneasy. As government and industrial forestry organizations attempted to secure administrative control over local resources, practices like woodsburning became anathema to good management. The U.S. Forest Service and the American Forestry Association (AFA), with the cooperation of newly formed state forestry commissions and industry-oriented associations, carried out a propaganda project that reached far and wide into the southern woods. The most effective effort was the AFA's "Dixie Crusader" campaign. Beginning in 1928, they sent scores of young foresters into the South to preach against the sins of woodsburners. By the time *The Bobwhite Quail* hit the market in 1931, fire was by far the most common topic of conversation in land management circles, and few dared to speak of its propriety.[35]

It is a wonder *The Bobwhite Quail* saw the light of day as a government-sponsored monograph. As an agent of the Biological Survey, Stoddard had to measure his enthusiasm for fire so as not to cause undue strain with the Forest Service. As early as June 1926, the chief of the Forest Service, William Greeley, questioned the legitimacy of the Biological Survey in matters of the forest, in terms both biological and sylvan. He asked E. W. Nelson to rein in his charge, writing, "It is to be hoped that . . . Mr. Stoddard will be very guarded in the matter of fire and woods burning so as to guard as fully as possible against any possibility of the public misconstruing his statements to make it appear that the Federal Government advocates burning the woods in order to improve conditions for quail." On the contrary, Greeley contended that the "common practice of yearly burning the woods is effective in large measure in the depletion of game animals and birds. This is one of the standard reasons advanced by State and Federal foresters for preventing woods fires."[36] In other words, the Forest Service had ultimate authority in the woods, and it didn't need a rogue federal agent instilling doubt in the minds of locals. Nelson was quick to defend Stoddard, making it clear that fire suppression "renders great areas absolutely worthless for quail."[37] But he also urged Stoddard to make plain "in your letters talks, or publications" that the need for fire "is due wholly to local conditions and not for general application."[38]

To a certain extent, Nelson was right in his caution. The subtleties of burning depend almost entirely on local conditions, and locals were not always subtle in their practices. But the Forest Service was not one for subtleties either; it had waged a strong and indiscriminate campaign against any sort of forest fires, and Stoddard's recommendations clearly threatened to challenge that orthodoxy. In the end, Stoddard had to qualify his recommendations. He tempered the chapter on fire in *The Bobwhite Quail* with many remarks on the dangers of uncontrolled fire and the localized nature of his own study. Shortly after the book's publication, he confided to one friend that "as this had to go through the Survey editorial office . . . it is by no means as strong as I feel on the subject."[39] Nevertheless, the chapter's opening line remained, leaving little room for misinterpretation of Stoddard's view: "The bobwhite of the Southeastern United States was undoubtedly evolved in an environment that was always subject to occasional burning over."[40] This statement alone shows a fairly sophisticated knowledge of the region's evolutionary ecology, but, Stoddard had to make clear, it was not to be "used to embarrass the forester in his attempts to protect forest growth over the region at large."[41] Despite being watered-down, Stoddard's ideas on fire turned heads throughout the natural resource professions, and helped to spark a thorough reconsideration of fire.

The region at large, of course, was full of pyrophobic professional foresters, and immediately after the book's publication Stoddard was no longer much concerned with their feelings. He left the confines of the Biological Survey and became a private consultant to hunting preserves throughout the South, where he hoped to spread the word about the beneficial role of fire.[42] The forestry interests, however, ratcheted up their calls for woods-burning to be criminalized. Such appeals caused Stoddard to worry that "landowners would not be permitted to do necessary burning, even when every precaution was taken to confine the fires to their own property, and when they had very definite ideas as to just what they wanted to accomplish."[43] The long-term goal was to reestablish fire across the coastal plain, but his immediate concern was over the legal right to burn. Fortunately, he was not alone.

As early as 1913, botanist Roland Harper recognized the longleaf forest to be fire-dependent.[44] In 1918, Henry Hardtner, head of Urania Lumber Company in Louisiana, suggested "'controlled burnings' should be practiced in every forest as an aid to successful forestry."[45] The year before, Hardtner had offered the use of the Urania Experimental Forest to H. H. Chapman, an influential forester at Yale. Chapman conducted fire experiments at Urania and published a series of important articles in the 1920s and 1930s on the role of fire in the longleaf ecosystem.[46] At about the same time, a U.S. Department of Agriculture (USDA) Animal Industry Division field agent, S. W. Greene of the McNeill Experiment Station in Mississippi, declared burned over lands to yield more nutritious cattle feed than lands kept in the rough. The master link in all of this research was the southern coastal plain's longleaf-grassland environment. In later years, the fire research that came from the South would deeply influence a national, and even global, re-examination of fire as a natural ecosystem process, as well as a tool of ecological management.[47]

In the early 1930s, however, these voices came together with Stoddard's simply to counter the prevailing notions about fire in their own region. Of interest here is the actual lack of consensus among these renegades on how they might use fire on the ground level. These internal spats reveal the developmental nature of a new field of science that bridges many biological disciplines. Fire did not respect the disciplinary boundaries of wildlife management, forestry, range management, or agriculture, and those who wanted to harness it wanted fire to work expressly for their interests, which created a certain amount of volatility even among such an agreeable group. Greene was the most vocal of the bunch. He fired off a volley of letters to the AFA's publication, *American Forests*, in 1931, lambasting the "travesties in truth published in AMERICAN FORESTS for a number of years."[48] His caustic tone got the attention of Ovid Butler, executive secretary of the AFA and editor of *American Forests*, who, to his credit, allowed Greene a voice in the October 1931 issue of the magazine. "The Forests that Fire Made" was probably the first article for popular publication that redressed the South's anti-fire propaganda. In it he drew on natural history, Native American land use, and his own research to show the natural range of the longleaf depended entirely on fire.

Stoddard was enthusiastic in his support of Greene's efforts, but Hardtner and Chapman had reservations. They agreed with Greene's general arguments, but were in no hurry to broadcast them to the public. Before the publication, Chapman wrote Greene, saying, "Unless we can properly control and hedge the propaganda regarding fire so that an average southern white farmer can understand what we are talking about . . . I would prefer to have very little said about the use of fire . . . Personally I have no intention of bursting into print until the conclusion of certain experiments."[49] Chapman's longleaf research did reach print, and it was indeed groundbreaking. His academic outlets, however, were not likely to reach many southerners. In Chapman's mind, Greene was engaging in a dangerous campaign. Discussions on controlled burning among the experts were all well and good, but Greene wanted to broadcast generalizations about fire that would reinforce generations of "miscreant" behavior in the South. Chapman told Hardtner that he would be "exceedingly sorry if Mr. Greene or any other agency became responsible through their statements for the publication of misleading, false, and mischievous statements regarding the promiscuous use of fire."[50]

Greene's *American Forests* piece did, in fact, lack the usual cautionary statements about uncontrolled fire, and even implied that local woods-burners were the true experts in the field, a proposition that made Chapman recoil. As a scientist firmly rooted in the forestry establishment,

Chapman wanted to route a resolution through the scientific apparatus. He felt "much sympathy with the state foresters and the American Forestry Association in their warfare against the habit of indiscriminate and uncontrolled burning," and a public airing threatened to "cause confusion and loss in their effort to create a fire consciousness in the minds of the southern people."[51] There's little doubt that southerners had a fire consciousness, just not in the way Chapman wanted. His professional concern was with growing trees, and if fire might aid in that goal, he thought, then we should subject it to the scrutiny of the scientific method. Indeed, Stoddard and Greene were establishing a science of fire as well, only from a different perspective. The understory was foremost in their minds, regardless of the forest type it harbored. Stoddard attempted to ease Chapman's mind about burning in different forest types, writing in a friendly, but pointed letter that "we do a great deal of burning both of loblolly and long-leaf lands . . . We have found that if the burning is carried on carefully at night when the dew is falling we can run fires through loblolly after it is a few years of age with little damage to the trees . . . We have found that there are all kinds of fire and that a person can use any kind he desires, from extremely light to very severe."[52] This raises an important distinction in Stoddard's experience with fire. First, he recognized "the rural populations . . . know a great deal [about fire] and are not the ignoramuses" they were made out to be.[53] Second, as a wildlife manager, he was concerned with more than trees. He understood that fire could take on certain characteristics depending on environmental conditions, and a low-level fire in a loblolly, shortleaf, or mixed forest could create an understory habitat beneficial to a variety of wildlife, and still not harm the trees. He, too, was interested in creating a science of fire, but it was one based in what we would call today applied ecology, not forestry. Indeed, Stoddard would go on to later develop an informal fire taxonomy that was crucial to its application in the field.[54]

The 1935 meeting of the Society of American Foresters was the real coming-out party for prescribed fire. Stoddard, Hardtner, Chapman, and Greene, along with long-time southern foresters Austin Cary and Inman Eldridge, put aside their differences to hold a panel on the beneficial role of fire that was largely greeted with acceptance. As happened in other conservation circles, long-time assumptions were being turned on their heads in the forestry profession as well. There was still a concern "of the public not understanding our methods or plans," but Hardtner conceded that "the people who live in the forest . . . are forest minded and are actually acquainted with the very problems" of controlled fire.[55] When Stoddard returned from the conference, he wrote to Aldo Leopold, expressing a deep sense of relief: "If you are interested in the Southeastern fire question, you will find the papers and discussions of the last afternoon well worth careful perusal, as much of a revolutionary nature was brought out. For the first time in ten years I had a feeling that perhaps I was not a 'public enemy' after all."[56] Although the costs and benefits of fire continued to be debated for years (and still are today), at least it was a subject recognized as being worthy of debate.

Again, the primary difference between Stoddard and the other panelists was their professional proclivities. Wildlife management and forestry were intimately connected from the beginning, but being concerned with wildlife habitat meant dabbling in many pools of expertise. A quail covey's range, after all, was not cordoned off at the forest's edge. They went where their habitat took them, which included the many fields and edge environments that covered the South. With that in mind, Stoddard had to look beyond the questions of forest and fire to examine the history and management of the South's peculiar system of agriculture. *The Bobwhite Quail*, then, not only helps us understand the forestry profession's reconsideration of fire in the longleaf, it also provides indispensable documentation of the region's early twentieth-century eco-cultural landscape. His study was rooted in quantitative science, but some of the most important findings were based on the assumption that the environment could not be treated outside of its social, cultural, and economic context. Of quail and their living conditions, Stoddard wrote, "it is becoming a difficult matter in the Eastern United States to find areas where quail are living under natural conditions, unaffected by man and his works."[57] Indeed, quail and their habitat were contingent on the qualitative actions of humans on the land, and Stoddard's book sought to direct those actions as much as possible. Stoddard, in other words, was not simply advocating the conservation of a natural environment; he was among the first to call for the preservation and maintenance of the biological diversity found in a cultural landscape.

   During and after the years of the quail study, American agriculture, and southern agriculture in particular, was experiencing dramatic changes. Across the country, mechanization and consolidation allowed farmers to do a more thorough job of clearing and cultivating fields with less labor. In the South, the threat of the boll weevil kept farmers in a constant state of anxiety, and encouraged a cleaner, more manicured farmscape. Boll weevils over-wintered in the protective brush at field edges, and many agricultural experts argued that the elimination of such habitat was crucial to boll weevil control. At the same time, sharecropping and tenancy were on the wane, to be replaced with a more efficient tractor-driven agriculture, with the land-owner becoming more directly involved in daily farm operations through the direction of a handful of wage laborers. As a result, the southern plantation environment underwent a massive transformation throughout the first half of the twentieth century. Farmers abandoned many of their less productive fields, allowing them to move through successional stages from broomsedge to old field pine and eventually to a dense tangle of hardwood and pine. Meanwhile, the region's best soils were farmed with increasing intensity, leaving few of the edge habitats upon which quail relied.[58]

Many saw these as progressive steps toward a more modern agriculture. Stoddard, somewhat aloof to the social dimensions of this transformation, was mainly wary of its ecological effects: "As the 'red hills' are mostly good agricultural ground, cultivation in some sections here, as elsewhere, has become too intensive for quail. If more cover were left between the fields, even the most intensively farmed sections could continue to produce surplus quail. The tendency, however, to clean up all sheltering thicket cover with a view to destroying possible hibernating places of the cotton boll weevil and creating an appearance of neatness is proving disastrous to quail. Thousands of acres are classed as 'shot out' by the misinformed, where bobwhites could not exist under any system of protection or restocking, simply because the environment no longer suits their requirements."[59] For Stoddard, agriculture did not necessarily mean ecological barrenness; in fact, if farms were managed in certain ways, they could promote diverse plant and animal species. Indeed, Stoddard joined with Aldo Leopold in pointing out that some of the gravest threats to wildlife and biological diversity during the 1930s were occurring on the nation's agricultural lands, this at a moment when most conservation attention was focused on the nation's public domain and its various management regimes. Of Leopold's 1939 essay "The Farmer as a Conservationist," which encouraged farmers to rehabilitate depleted wildlife habitat, Stoddard thought it "one of the best articles I ever read & I wish every American with brains could read and ponder it."[60] Stoddard shared with Leopold the hope that, with a bit more attention to the details of wildlife habitat and a bit less enthusiasm for modernization at all costs, the nation's farmers might continue to protect vital biotic reservoirs from becoming monocultural barrens.[61]

The South's landscape of tenantry offered the ideal biotic reservoir. For quail to thrive, Stoddard revealed, they needed two essentials: food and cover. Successional seed plants—more likely known as weeds to progressive farmers—grew vigorously in the highly disturbed tenant landscape. Ragweed, beggarweed, pigweed, rough button-weed, Mexican clover, and bull grass, among many others, sprouted after a field was "laid by," and occupied field edges and open woodlands throughout the growing season. A variety of tree and shrub masts also contributed to make the landscape a quail haven. Stoddard advised farmers that "quail are fond of, and more or less dependent upon a wide variety of small wild fruits, and the 'mast' from trees for their living," especially wild black cherry, dewberries, sassafras, blackberries, wild plum, huckleberries, and mulberries, "which are often abundant on not too intensively cultivated farm lands." He added that "it is well to remember their value to quail, wild turkeys and other birds when considering the cutting of wild cherry for fence posts, and brushing out around fields and along fence lines, roadsides and so forth, for the destruction of such food and shelter producing vegetation may be the means of reducing the number of quail on the farm."[62]

The other key to the functional quail landscape was cover. Many of the same plants that provided food also gave quick cover from predators; "thickets and vine tangles around field borders, on fence lines and roadsides, and here and there in open woodlands" were essential requirements for quail. Stoddard identified the "blue-darter" hawks (Cooper's and Sharp-shinned) as the only troublesome winged predators, and unlike many land managers of the day, recommended leaving these coverts as a substitute to predator eradication.[63] Again, the older landscape of tenantry had all of these measures built-in, but "where farmers cut out such refuge cover to give their farms an air of 'neatness,' . . . a decline in the numbers of quail and other thicket-loving birds is inevitable."[64] Such neatness threatened the traditional wildness of southern farms, and on lands outside of his control, there was little Stoddard could do about the trend beyond recommending otherwise. On the quail preserves, however, his word carried a great deal of weight and much of his advice was carried out to the letter.

In the nomenclature of the time, Stoddard called tenantry a "primitive" or "crude" system of agriculture, but he was unequivocal about its ecological superiority to modern systems. In his chapter in *The Bobwhite Quail* titled "Preserve Development and Management," he advised that the best "situations in which to establish new preserves, consist of ground of medium or low price, land that is, or has recently been, under a system of crude agriculture." "*Where fields are small and well distributed,*" he continued, "with small open woodlands between, and thicket cover is plentiful, the all-important matter of environment is favorable to start with and the food supply in most cases can be built up quickly."[65] His preference for small scale agriculture was practical; it had little to do with a romantic primitivism in the face of modernization. Nor did it have much to do with the preservation of untouched nature. Stoddard's advocacy was for the wealth of plant and animal diversity found in working, cultural landscapes—a diversity that would likely disappear if left to nature.

Stoddard was not particularly keen to the social and racial injustices of the tenant system, but he did recognize one of its environmental paradoxes. It could create a wealth of ecological diversity, but it also created a very real potential for ecological destructiveness. Tenantry, especially on hilly land, has long been associated with soil erosion and infertility.[66] Much like the Piedmont sections to the north, the soil of the Red Hills gave way on countless hillsides, and was leached out on others. One of many consequences was a detrimental effect on wildlife habitat. Indeed, he used part of the quail study to rail against cotton monoculture and its leaching of the soil. "The methods used in cotton raising are highly detrimental to quail," Stoddard argued. "Not only are cotton fields an unfavorable quail environment, but the planting of the crop year after year in the same fields, without rotation, has put hundreds of thousands of acres into an unproductive condition."[67] He cautioned those interested in developing lands for quail to closely consider past land use, for worn out lands would take time to replenish. Land where "the fertility of the soil has been exhausted to a point where it can not produce a vigorous growth of weeds and leguminous plants will not support quail in abundance."[68] It is this attention to habitat in an eco-cultural landscape, and not merely his innovative thinking on fire, that gave Stoddard's monograph such ecological breadth. Quail were undoubtedly its main concern, but this life history of a single species led Stoddard to a broader interrogation of coastal plain ecology in all of its diversity.

Like the birth of many conservation regimes, this early history of southern quail management was rife with social inequality.[69] In Leopold's Midwestern context, it was relatively uncomplicated to celebrate traditional non-intensive agriculture as protective of biological diversity. In Herbert Stoddard's region of interest, however, the farm and forest habitats of the coastal plain came packaged within a socioeconomic system that made such retrospective claims of ecological beneficence tricky at best. Stoddard was not particularly interested in critically assessing the region's attachment to tenantry, but he was interested in directing the actions of those tenants who remained on quail lands. There was no shortage of potentially good quail land in the Depression-era South, and virtually all of it purchased for quail management had tenants spread throughout. On land with tenants, Stoddard wrote, "it is undoubtedly best to keep all who respond to fair treatment and cooperate with the owner in special matters."[70] Tenants continued most of their traditional patterns of land use, like cultivating small fields and gardens and hunting small mammals, but the "special matters" to which Stoddard referred were not inconsequential. He made it clear that managing this environment would also involve managing the tenants remaining on it. The most significant management change recommended by the quail report was the elimination of free-ranging cattle, poultry, cats, and dogs. Cattle competed for quail food plants, and trampled much of the nesting range, while free-ranging chickens may have transferred diseases to quail. Stoddard recognized that controlling tenants' domestic animals was a ticklish matter, and he provided special counsel on dealing with roaming cats and dogs: "As the greater portion of these animals belong to the tenants living on the land, tact and diplomacy rather than force have to be relied upon in handling the delicate problem of the restriction in number, control or disposal of these pests."[71] Clearly, not all tenant behavior was beneficial from an ecological standpoint. Stoddard celebrated the unruliness of the tenant landscape, but he also sought to manage the very tenants whose behavior had helped produce it.

Beyond his hope for tact and diplomacy, Stoddard left little record of what he personally thought of the region's economic and racial disparities, but it is apparent that neither he nor the preserve owners sought to

overturn deeply entrenched patterns of power in the South. Racial patronage and concerns over a dwindling labor supply were as common for
the preserve-owning industrialists as they were for the southern planter
classes.[72] It is significant, though, that conservation on the quail preserves
did not mean general expulsion from the land like it did in so many other
contexts. Contrary to what happened on other conservation landscapes,
the partition and control of the quail preserves actually created a local,
or more precisely, a private commons for the residents of the properties.
The lands were posted to outsiders from early on, to be sure; but, outside
of the "special matters," those who lived and worked on the preserves had
free range over the preserve environment.[73] In other words, conservation
on the quail preserves did not entail the imposition of a simplified version
of non-human nature. Instead, it involved the discovery and regulation of
what made the longleaf-grassland environment in the first place: a mixture
of natural and human disturbance. Stoddard borrowed from the region's
cultural and environmental past to build a system that managed land to
be wild.

World War II signified a loss of momentum for Stoddard's wildlife
work. With wealthy landowners cutting back on non-essential services,
and expanding government wildlife programs offering free management
advice before and after the War, the privately-funded Cooperative Quail
Study Association fast became an anachronism. Stoddard turned his energies to preserve development and forestry work, and began to work out an
even more complex system of ecological management. As the cultural and
environmental landscapes of agriculture and forestry continued to change
dramatically, Stoddard took an even more active role on the quail preserves
by directly managing timber resources to produce a conservative return
from the forests while maintaining and enhancing overall landscape diversity. His system came to be known as the Stoddard/Neel method of land
management when his young apprentice, Leon Neel, took over the work
in the 1950s and 1960s to let Stoddard focus on his first love of ornithology.
Stoddard died in 1970, but his system of ecological management continues
as a vital link to the region's environmental and cultural past.[74]

In the end, perhaps the best qualified voice to speak to the broad ap-
plicability of Stoddard's land ethic, besides Stoddard himself, is Aldo Leopold. When asked for his opinion of Stoddard's work by a large timberland
owner in south Georgia, Leopold was emphatic in his praise: "I have just

spent several days with Stoddard and came away with a conviction that he has been too modest about the conservation methods he has worked out for the Southeast. They are commonly regarded as applicable only to game preserves, but in my opinion he has developed principles which are equally applicable to lumber company holdings, national forests, and all other owners of coastal plain longleaf . . . I of course am biased, for he is one of my closest personal friends. I am lecturing to my students Monday on the Stoddard method of handling Southeastern pine lands."[75]

The lessons that Leopold shared in his Midwestern classroom are still useful today. At its root, this story is about a system of land management that was responsible for the most ecologically diverse pockets of the longleaf-grassland environments remaining on the southern coastal plain today. Stoddard accomplished so much by responding to the region's environmental, cultural, and historical context. First, he understood the ecological problems caused by fire suppression in the longleaf-grassland system. In the face of heavy opposition, he helped to make legitimate the centuries-old practice of burning the South's fields and forests. Second, he suggested that working landscapes could have ecological value. This was a historically peopled landscape, and there was not much chance of changing that. Human land use helped to create the preserve environment, and with guidance, it would help maintain it. Furthermore, this disturbance-prone, fragmented landscape required close management of human and environmental resources; management was not only possible, but necessary, for the maintenance of the natural system. In this private, and distinctly southern, world, the wilderness model of preservation—setting land aside to let nature take its course—simply never made sense. Stoddard's model is a useful reminder that the creation of wild land often has as much to do with culture as it does nature.

Notes

1. Henry Beadel, "Fire Impressions," Tall Timbers Fire Ecology Conference, *Proceedings*, vol. 1 (Tallahassee, Fla.: Tall Timbers Research Station, 1962), 2–3.

2. Ibid.

3. Herbert Stoddard, "Report on Cooperative Quail Investigation: 1925–1926" (Committee of the Quail Study Fund For Southern Georgia and Northern Florida; U.S. Biological Survey), 56.

4. Stoddard has received some attention from environmental historians, but he has not been the subject of extensive research. See Ashley Schiff, *Fire and Water: Scientific Heresy in the Forest Service* (Cambridge, Mass.: Harvard University Press, 1962); Susan Flader, *Thinking Like a Mountain: Aldo Leopold and the Evolution of an Ecological Attitude Toward Deer, Wolves, and Forests* (Madison: University of Wisconsin Press, 1974); Steven J. Pyne, *Fire in America: A Cultural History of Wildland and Rural Fire* (Princeton, N.J.: Princeton University Press, 1982); Curt Meine, *Aldo Leopold: His Life and Work* (Madison: University of Wisconsin Press, 1988); Thomas R. Dunlap, *Saving America's Wildlife* (Princeton, N.J.: Princeton University Press, 1988); Jonathon Blu Buhs, *The Fire Ant Wars: Nature, Science and Public Policy in Twentieth-Century America* (Chicago, Ill.: University of Chicago Press, 2004).

5. The scholarship on Leopold is vast. See Meine, *Aldo Leopold*; Flader, *Thinking Like a Mountain*; Aldo Leopold, *The River of the Mother of God and Other Essays by Aldo Leopold*, ed. Susan L. Flader and J. Baird Callicott (Madison: University of Wisconsin Press, 1991); Paul S. Sutter, *Driven Wild: How the Fight Against Automobiles Launched the Modern Wilderness Movement* (Seattle: University of Washington Press, 2002).

6. There is too much scholarship on the West to cite here. For an older overview, see Richard White, "American Environmental History: The Development of a New Historical Field," *Pacific Historical Review* (August 1985): 297–335; on the Northeast, see Richard Judd, *Common Lands, Common People: The Origins of Conservation in Northern New England* (Cambridge, Mass.: Harvard University Press, 1997); Karl Jacoby, *Crimes Against Nature: Squatters, Poachers, Thieves, and the Hidden History of American Conservation* (Berkeley: University of California Press, 2001). On the South, see Albert E. Cowdrey, *This Land, This South: An Environmental History* (Lexington: University of Kentucky Press, 1983); Tim Silver, *A New Face on the Countryside: Indians, Colonists, and Slaves in South Atlantic Forests, 1500–1800* (New York, N.Y.: Cambridge University Press, 1990); Jack Temple Kirby, *Poquosin: A Study of Rural Landscape and Society* (Chapel Hill: University of North Carolina, 1995); Mart A. Stewart, *"What Nature Suffers to Groe": Life, Labor, and Landscape on the Georgia Coast, 1680–1920* (Athens: University of Georgia Press, 1996).

7. Mart Stewart, "If John Muir Had Been an Agrarian: American Environmental History West and South," *Environment and History* 11 (2005): 139–62, quote from 147.

8. On the importation of western notions about wildland preservation into the South, see Margaret Lynn Brown, *The Wild East: A Biography of the Great Smoky Mountains* (Gainesville: University Press of Florida, 2000).

9. On the ecology of the longleaf-grassland system, see Bruce Means, "Longleaf Pine: Going, Going. . .," in Mary Byrd Davis, ed., *Eastern Old-Growth Forest: Prospects for Rediscovery and Recovery* (Washington, D.C.: Island Press, 1996), 210–29; Lawrence S. Early, *Looking For Longleaf: The Fall and Rise of an American Forest* (Chapel Hill: University of North Carolina Press, 2004); W. G. Wahlenberg, *Longleaf Pine: Its Use, Ecology, Regeneration, Protection, Growth, and Management* (Washington D.C.: U.S. Forest Service, U.S. Department of Agriculture, 1946); Janisse Ray, *Ecology of a Cracker Childhood* (Minneapolis, Minn.: Milkweed Press, 1999).

10. On Native American and colonial land use in the longleaf, see Silver, *New Face on the Countryside*; Sheperd Krech III, *The Ecological Indian: Myth and History* (New York, N.Y.: Norton, 1999); Robbie Etheridge, *Creek Country: The Creek Indians and Their World* (Chapel Hill: University of North Carolina Press, 2003).

11. Michael L. Lanza, *Agrarianism and Reconstruction Politics: The Southern Homestead Act* (Baton Rouge: Louisiana State University Press, 1990).

12. Michael Williams, *Americans and Their Forests: A Historical Geography* (New York, N.Y.: Cambridge University Press, 1989); Tycho de Boer, "The Corporate Forest: Capitalism and Environmental Change in Southeastern North Carolina's Longleaf Pine Belt, 1790–1940" (PhD dissertation, Vanderbilt University, 2002).

13. The Red Hills region makes up portions of four counties: Thomas and Grady in Georgia, and Jefferson and Leon in Florida. Thomasville, Georgia, and Tallahassee, Florida, are the urban centers. See William Warren Rogers, *Thomas County 1865–1900* (Tallahassee: Florida State University Press, 1973); William Warren Rogers, *Transition to the Twentieth Century: Thomas County, Georgia, 1900–1920* (Tallahassee: Sentry Press, 2002); Clifton Paisley, *From Cotton to Quail: An Agricultural Chronicle of Leon County, Florida, 1860–1967* (Gainesville: University of Florida Press, 1968); Clifton Paisley, *The Red Hills of Florida: 1528–1865* (Tuscaloosa: University of Alabama Press, 1989). Also see Edward E. Baptist, *Creating an Old South: Middle Florida's Plantation Frontier Before the Civil War* (Chapel Hill: University of North Carolina Press, 2002).

14. Steve Gatewood et al., *A Comprehensive Study of a Portion of the Red Hills Region of Georgia* (Thomasville, Ga.: The Thomas College Press, 1994).

15. See Gavin Wright, *Old South, New South: Revolutions in the Southern Economy Since the Civil War* (Baton Rouge: Louisiana State University Press, 1986); Pete Daniel, *Breaking the Land: The Transformation of Cotton, Tobacco, and Rice Cultures Since 1880* (Urbana, Ill.: University of Illinois Press, 1985); Jack Temple Kirby, *Rural Worlds Lost: The American South, 1920–1960* (Baton Rouge: Louisiana State University Press, 1987); James C. Cobb, *The Most Southern Place on Earth: The Mississippi Delta and the Roots of Regional Identity* (New York, N.Y.: Oxford University Press, 1992).

16. The literature on health and the environment has grown considerably in recent years. See Conevery Bolten Valencius, *The Health of the Country: How American Settlers Understood Themselves and Their Land* (New York, N.Y.: Basic Books, 2002); Linda Nash, "Finishing Nature: Harmonizing Bodies and Environments in Late-Nineteenth Century California," *Environmental History* 8, 1 (2003): 25–52; Gregg Mitman, "Hay Fever Holiday: Health, Leisure, and Place in Glided-Age America," *Bulletin of the History of Medicine* 77 (2003): 600–635; Gregg Mitman, "In Search of Health: Landscape and Disease in American Environmental History," *Environmental History* 10, 2 (2005); Kenneth Thompson, "Trees as a Theme in Medical Geography and Public Health," *Bulletin of the New York Academy of Medicine* 54 (1978): 517–31.

17. Mitman, "In Search of Health," 198.

18. Rogers, *Thomas County*, 27.

19. On the quail plantation families, see William R. Brueckheimer, "The Quail Plantations of the Thomasville-Tallahassee-Albany Regions," in *Proceedings, Tall Timbers*

Ecology and Management Conference, February 22–24, 1979, 141–65; and Brueckheimer, "Leon County Hunting Plantations: An Historical and Architectural Survey, Volume I" (Tallahassee, Fla.: The Historic Tallahassee Preservation Board, 1988).

20. Herbert Stoddard, *Memoirs of a Naturalist* (Norman: University of Oklahoma Press, 1969), 194.

21. Ibid., 58.

22. See Samuel P. Hays, *Conservation and the Gospel of Efficiency: The Progressive Conservation Movement, 1890–1920* (Cambridge, Mass.: Harvard University Press, 1959); Robert Weibe, *The Search for Order, 1877–1920* (New York, N.Y.: Hill and Wang, 1967); Brian Balogh, "Scientific Forestry and the Roots of the Modern American State: Gifford Pinchot's Path to Progressive Reform," *Environmental History* 7(2) (2002): 198–225.

23. On taxidermy and its place within natural history, see Donna Haraway, *Primate Visions: Gender, Race, and Nature in the World of Modern Science* (New York, N.Y.: Routledge, 1989), 26–58.

24. On the advent of bird-banding, see Mark V. Barrow Jr., *A Passion for Birds: American Ornithology After Audubon* (Princeton, N.J.: Princeton University Press, 1998).

25. Herbert Stoddard, "Bird Banding in Milwaukee and Vicinity," *Yearbook of the Public Museum of the City of Milwaukee*, vol. III, 1923, 117.

26. Between 1916 and 1923 Stoddard published ten articles in *The Auk* and three in *The Wilson Bulletin*. For a full bibliography, see Stoddard, *Memoirs of a Naturalist*, 285–88.

27. See Barrow, *A Passion for Birds*, 172–75.

28. W. L. McAtee to Herbert L. Stoddard, January 2, 1924, W. L. McAtee Papers, Box 10, Stoddard Correspondence, Manuscripts Division, Library of Congress.

29. S. A. Barrett to Herbert Stoddard, March 23, 1922, Taxidermy Correspondence, 1921–1925, Milwaukee Public Museum Manuscripts.

30. E. W. Nelson to Herbert L. Stoddard, February 5, 1924, Herbert L. Stoddard Papers, Quail Investigation Correspondence, Archives of Tall Timbers Research Station.

31. Stoddard, *Memoirs of a Naturalist*, 179.

32. Meine, *Aldo Leopold*, 264.

33. Aldo Leopold, "The Outlook for Farm Wildlife," in Callicott and Flader, eds., *The River of the Mother of God and Other Essays by Aldo Leopold*, 323.

34. Five years after publication of *The Bobwhite Quail*, Stoddard was named special counselor, along with Leopold, in the founding of The Wildlife Society, the first professional organization for wildlife managers.

35. See Schiff, *Fire and Water: Scientific Heresy in the Forest Service* (Cambridge, Mass.: Harvard University Press, 1962); Stephen Pyne, *Fire in America: A Cultural History of Wildland and Rural Fire* (Princeton, N.J.: Princeton University Press, 1982).

36. W. B. Greeley to E. W. Nelson, June 10, 1926, Stoddard Papers, Fire Correspondence, TTRS (hereafter SPFC).

37. E. W. Nelson to W. B. Greeley, June 17, 1926, SPFC.

38. E. W. Nelson to Herbert Stoddard, June 18, 1926, ibid.

39. Herbert Stoddard to S. W. Greene, May 8, 1931, ibid.

40. Herbert L. Stoddard, *The Bobwhite Quail: Its Habits, Preservation and Increase* (New York, N.Y.: Charles Scribner's Sons, 1931), 401.

41. Ibid., 403.

42. See Herbert L. Stoddard, Henry L. Beadel, and E. V. Komarek, "The Cooperative Quail Study Association, July 1, 1934–April 15, 1943" (Tallahassee, Fla.: Tall Timbers Research Station, Miscellaneous Publication no. 1, 1961).

43. Herbert Stoddard to H. H. Chapman, October 7, 1931, SPFC.

44. Roland Harper, *Geological Survey of Alabama*, monograph no. 8, 1913.

45. Henry E. Hardtner, "Henry E. Hardtner, Urania Lumber Company, Urania, La., Discusses Reforestation and Controlled Burnings," *Lumber Trade Journal*, vol. 74 (November 18, 1918), 35.

46. H. H. Chapman, "Factors Determining Natural Reproduction of Longleaf Pine on Cut-over Lands in La Salle Parish, La.," *Yale University School of Forestry Bulletin* 16 (1926); "Some Further Relations of Fire to Longleaf Pine," *Journal of Forestry*, 30 (1932): 602–4; "Is The Longleaf Type a Climax?" *Ecology* 13 (January, 1932): 328–34.

47. See *Tall Timbers Fire Ecology Conference, Proceedings*, vols. 1–16 (Tallahassee, Fla.: Tall Timbers Research Station); and Pyne, *Fire in America*.

48. S. W. Greene to Ovid Butler, September 14, 1931, SPFC.

49. H. H Chapman to S. W. Greene, September 10, 1931, ibid.

50. H. H. Chapman to Henry Hardtner, September 10, 1931, ibid.

51. H. H. Chapman to Henry Hardtner, September 10, 1931, ibid.

52. Ibid.

53. Herbert Stoddard to Lucien Harris, March 27, 1944, ibid.

54. Herbert L. Stoddard, "Use of Fire on Southeastern Game Lands," in "The Cooperative Quail Study Association, July 1, 1934 to April 15, 1943" (Tallahassee, Fla.: Tall Timbers Research Station, 1961).

55. Henry Hardtner, "A Tale of Root," *Journal of Forestry* 33 (March 1935): 357; for the entire panel presentation see the same issue, 320–60.

56. Herbert Stoddard to Aldo Leopold, February 18, 1935, Aldo Leopold Papers, Series 9/25/10-1, Box 3—Stoddard Correspondence, University of Wisconsin, Madison Archives.

57. Stoddard, *The Bobwhite Quail*, 342.

58. Daniel, *Breaking the Land*; Kirby, *Rural Worlds Lost*; James Conrad Giesen, "The South's Greatest Enemy?: The Cotton Boll Weevil and Its Lost Revolution, 1892–1930 (PhD dissertation, University of Georgia, 2004).

59. Stoddard, *The Bobwhite Quail*, 6.

60. Hand-written note accompanying article, in private collection of Leon Neel.

61. On the development of Leopold's views on agricultural lands, see Sutter, *Driven Wild*, 89–98; Curt Meine, *Correction Lines: Essays on Land, Leopold, and Conservation* (Washington, D.C.: Island Press, 2004); and Aldo Leopold, *For the Health of the Land: Previously Unpublished Essays and Other Writings*, ed. J. Baird Callicott and Eric T. Freyfogle (Washington, D.C.: Island Press, 1999).

62. Herbert L. Stoddard, "The Bobwhite Quail: Its Propagation, Preservation, and Increase on Georgia Farms" (Atlanta, Ga.: State Department of Game and Fish, 1933), 365–67, in Stoddard, Beadel, and Komarek, "The Cooperative Quail Study Association."

63. Stoddard was among the first to call for environmental management of predators, and contributed important research, along with Paul Errington, to the national debate over predator control. See *The Bobwhite Quail*, 415–38; and Herbert L. Stoddard and Paul Errington, "Modifications in Predation Theory Suggested by Ecological Studies of the Bobwhite Quail," in *Transactions of the Third North American Wildlife Conference* (Washington, D.C.: American Wildlife Institute, 1938), 736–40.

64. Stoddard, "The Bobwhite Quail . . . On Georgia Farms," 357.

65. Stoddard, *The Bobwhite Quail*, 362, emphasis in original.

66. See Stanley W. Trimble, *Man-Induced Soil Erosion on the Southern Piedmont, 1700–1970* (Ankeny, Iowa: Soil Conservation Society of America, 1974); Stanley W. Trimble, "Perspectives on the History of Soil Erosion Control in the Eastern United States," *Agricultural History* 59 (1985): 162–80; John Fraser Hart, "Loss and Abandonment of Cleared Farm Land in the Eastern United States," *Annals of the Association of American Geographers* 58 (1968): 417–40.

67. Stoddard, *The Bobwhite Quail*, 350–51.

68. Ibid., 351.

69. See Louis S. Warren, *The Hunter's Game: Poachers and Conservationists in Twentieth-Century America* (New Haven, Conn.: Yale University Press, 1997); Jacoby, *Crimes Against Nature*; Mark Spence, *Dispossessing the Wilderness: Indian Removal and the Making of the National Parks* (New York, N.Y.: Oxford University Press, 1999); Steven Hahn, "Hunting, Fishing, and Foraging: Common Rights and Class Relations in the Postbellum South," *Radical History Review* 26 (1982): 36–64.

70. Stoddard, *The Bobwhite Quail*, 367.

71. Ibid., 421.

72. Among the more condescending treatments of African-American life on a Red Hills hunting preserve is Lillian Britt Heinsohn, *Southern Plantation: The Story of Labrah Including Some of Its Treasured Recipes* (New York, N.Y.: Bonanza Books, 1962).

73. *African-American Life on the Southern Hunting Plantation*, compiled by Titus Brown and James "Jack" Hadley (Charleston, S.C.: Arcadia Publishing, 2000).

74. Stoddard went on to found Tall Timbers Research Station in 1958, an important private institution that promoted fire research not only locally, but globally. In recent years, Leon Neel has continued his work in ecological management as a member of the Scientific Advisory Committee of the Joseph W. Jones Ecological Research Center at Ichauway, an important research station in Albany, Georgia.

75. Aldo Leopold to Daniel Hebard, October 20, 1939, Aldo Leopold Papers, 9/25/10-2, Box 4, File 10.

WILLIAM BOYD

Making Meat

Science, Technology, and American Poultry Production

IN HIS 1948 CLASSIC, *Mechanization Takes Command*, Siegfried
Giedion posed the following question: "What happens when mechanization encounters organic substance?"[1] Well aware of the application of
mass-production techniques to agriculture and of the role of genetics
in facilitating "the structural alteration of plants and animals," Giedion
nevertheless held to a basic distinction between "living substance" and
mechanization. The idea of nature as technics, of biophysical systems as
technological systems, would have seemed inappropriate in his framework.
For Giedion, interventions in the organic growth process were qualita-
tively different from efforts to subject other aspects of modern life to the
dictates of the machine.

In the half century since Giedion posed this question, numerous scholars have explored the relationship between nature and technology in a
variety of areas, emphasizing the difficulty of making hard and fast distinctions. Environmental historians such as Donald Worster, William Cronon,
and Richard White have interrogated some of the ways in which nature is
incorporated into technological and political-economic systems.[2]

Historians of science such as Robert Kohler have explored how experimental creatures (drosophila in his case) arc constructed as research instruments and technologies.[3] And several historians and social scientists have
investigated the role of science and technology in the industrialization of
agricultural systems. Jack Kloppenburg and Deborah Fitzgerald, for example, have both demonstrated how a particular biological organism (hybrid

corn) has been refashioned as an agricultural commodity and a vehicle for capital accumulation.[4]

Following these leads, this article focuses on another organism, the broiler, or young meat-type chicken, asking how science and technology have subordinated its biology to the dictates of industrial production. By looking explicitly at those technoscientific practices involved in making the industrial chicken, it offers a perspective on the course of technological change in agriculture that further blurs the distinction between nature and technology.[5]

A product of key innovations in the areas of environmental control, genetics, nutrition, and disease management, the industrial broiler emerged during the middle decades of the twentieth century as a very efficient vehicle for transforming feed grains into higher-value meat products. By the 1960s the broiler had become one of the most intensively researched commodities in U.S. agriculture, while complementary changes in the structure, financing, and organization of leading firms created an institutional framework for rapidly translating research into commercial gain. The resulting increases in productivity and efficiency led to falling real prices, despite growing demand, and successfully brought chicken to the center of the plate for many Americans.

Like hybrid corn, the story of the industrial chicken must be seen as part of a larger process of agro-industrialization, which not only transformed the social practices of agriculture, food production, and diet in twentieth-century America but also facilitated a profound restructuring of the relationship between nature and technology. This article explores the various and ongoing efforts to intensify and accelerate the biological productivity of the chicken—asking how nature has been made to act as a force of production. Like Jack Kloppenburg's analysis of how capital intervenes in and circulates through nature in the case of plant breeding and biotechnology, the following story focuses quite specifically on the role of science and technology in incorporating biological systems into the circuits of industrial capital.[6]

Yet where Kloppenburg offers an institutional analysis of how the "commodification of the seed" serves as an accumulation strategy, this essay focuses more broadly on a variety of technologies involved in accelerating biological productivity. While breeding and genetic improvement were clearly central vectors of technological change in making the industrial chicken, they were by no means the only ones. Intensive confinement, improved nutrition and feeding practices, and the widespread use of antibiotics and other drugs also represented important aspects of a larger technology platform aimed at subordinating avian biology to the dictates of industrial production.

Given the unpredictable nature and emergent properties of biological systems, however, any program aimed at the systematic intensification of biological productivity will almost inevitably be confronted with new sources of risk and vulnerability. Efforts to accelerate biological productivity must confront the vagaries of nature and the unintended consequences of attempts to simplify and incorporate biological processes into industrial systems. New vulnerabilities associated with genetic monocultures, the emergence of new pathogens, the spread of antibiotic-resistant bacteria, and related problems of food safety are just a few of the unintended consequences of the industrialization of broiler biology. Although some of these new risks and vulnerabilities create new business opportunities (in the animal health industry, for example), they also pose considerable threats to the continued viability of the industry. As Rachel Carson put it almost forty years ago: "Nature fights back."[7]

A Chicken in Every Pot

By any economic standard, the success of the U.S. broiler industry during the post–World War II period has been remarkable. Between 1950 and 1999 U.S. production increased at an average rate of 7 percent per year to over forty billion pounds, while real prices declined by almost a third.[8] Today the average American consumes over eighty pounds of chicken a year, more than beef, pork, or any other animal flesh protein. Annual revenues for the industry exceed fifteen billion dollars, and many of the largest firms are moving aggressively into the export market.[9] Industry giant Tyson Foods now produces roughly 140 million pounds of chicken per week, almost three times as much as its nearest competitor and more than any other entity outside of the United States except China and Brazil. Tyson, which has led the industry into fast food, further processing, and, more recently, the export market, now refers to chicken as "a global protein" around which the company "speaks many languages."[10]

At the heart of the postwar success of the U.S. broiler industry have been systematic innovation, massive increases in productivity, and a relentless development of new products and new markets, all facilitated by an institutional transformation that has made the industry one of the most advanced systems of food production in the world—the very definition of agribusiness.[11] Since the early 1960s, integrated firms have controlled as much as 90 percent of broiler production in the United States. These firms, known as integrators, own their own hatcheries, feed mills, and processing operations while contracting out live production, or "grow-out" operations, to small farmers.

Paralleling vertical integration has been an equally pronounced process of geographic concentration in the American South. Since the 1960s, more than four-fifths of all broilers produced in the United States have come from the South, despite the fact that it remains a feed deficit region. The modern integrated broiler industry, in short, has possessed a distinctive southern accent since its inception. The reasons for this are many and varied, but include most prominently the changing structure of southern agriculture, deeply embedded merchant-farmer relationships, and the availability of surplus rural labor to service the processing plants. Though a full discussion of these factors is obviously well beyond the scope of this essay, it should be emphasized that the emergence of the modern broiler industry, with its extensive reliance on contract farming and low-wage labor markets, was very much a product of the South's distinctive post–New Deal agrarian transition.[12]

For the purposes of this article, the critical point regarding the institutional sophistication of the broiler industry has been its ability to capture the gains associated with rapid technical advance—a fact that clearly presupposes the existence of a system of research and development capable of generating innovations in the first place. This system of innovation emerged out of a complex mix of public research, private science, and business enterprise during the first half of the twentieth century. As they did with other agricultural commodities, publicly supported scientists affiliated with the land-grant university complex performed much of the early basic research on the principles of poultry genetics, nutrition, and health, while private actors effectively assimilated this research and applied it for commercial gain. Indeed, by the time the commercial broiler industry emerged in the 1930s, one of the most important elements of this innovation system—the field of applied poultry science—was already well established.

Unlike most other animal sciences, which did not emerge as well-defined fields of research until the 1940s, poultry science flourished during the 1910s and 1920s.[13] Emerging from the relatively ill-defined field of poultry husbandry in the agricultural experiment stations and agricultural colleges, poultry science quickly became the focus of a "cluster of subsciences" that included bacteriology, biochemistry, and the economics of egg and meat production.[14] This transformation of "husbandry" into "science" was largely a response to the new problems associated with the growing demand for healthy poultry products stimulated by the growth of urban markets, the changing American diet, and the rise of refrigeration.[15] It also reflected the fact that chickens were far more versatile as laboratory animals than other commercial livestock species and were regularly used for early research in nutrition, genetics, and health. Given the shorter biological time lags involved in chicken reproduction and growth, for example, breeding experiments and genetic improvement could proceed much faster in chickens than in other farm animals. Equally significant, the autonomy of chicken embryogenesis (that is, the fact that chicken embryos develop in eggs outside the hen rather than in the womb) combined with the early use of artificial incubation facilitated the rapid multiplication of chickens for both experimental and commercial purposes. Consequently, knowledge of chicken genetics, nutrition, and physiology accumulated rapidly during the first half of the twentieth century, putting poultry in the vanguard of animal improvement efforts.

Beginning in the interwar years and accelerating rapidly after World War II, advances in nutrition, health, and genetics translated into massive increases in the biological productivity of broilers. Such gains facilitated and were in turn reinforced by the subsequent integration of the industry. By accentuating the problems of coordination between different segments of the industry, rapid advances in productivity and throughput added to the incentive to integrate.[16] At the same time, the incorporation of hatcheries, feed mills, contract grow-out operations, and processing plants within a single firm provided an institutional vehicle for further rationalizing the production system in order to capture productivity gains. As the industry grew in size and sophistication, moreover, there was a clear shift in the locus of research and innovation from the public to the private sphere.[17]

By the early 1960s, integrated firms, primary breeders, and animal health companies had become the drivers of innovation in the industry, transforming the lowly chicken into one of the more thoroughly industrialized commodities in American agriculture.

The overall trend has been a phenomenal increase in biological productivity. Between 1935 and 1995 the average market weight of commercial broilers increased by roughly 65 percent while the time required to reach market weight declined by more than 60 percent and the amount of feed required to produce a pound of broiler meat declined by 57 percent. In short, a commercial broiler from the 1990s grew to almost twice the weight in less than half the time and on less than half the feed than a broiler from the 1930s.

As in other agro-food sectors, this process of biological intensification depended upon a cluster of innovations, with advances in one area often calling forth or even requiring advances in other areas. Through technologies of confinement and continuous flow, nutrition and growth promotion, and breeding and genetic improvement, the barnyard chicken was made over into a highly efficient machine for converting feed grains into cheap animal-flesh protein.

Confinement and Continuous Flow

Intensive confinement was a critical first step in the process of industrialization. The ability to raise broilers in a confined environment provided for a kind of biological time-space compression, creating a platform upon which intensification efforts in nutrition and breeding could proceed. Yet attempts to fully adapt chickens to laboratory conditions and, more important, to confine them for commercial purposes met with only limited success during the early twentieth century. Due to a nutritional deficiency among chickens known as "leg weakness," which occurred in the absence of ultraviolet light, chickens could only be confined for relatively short periods of time. Until this problem could be solved, industrial broiler production remained a distant prospect.

Working at the University of Wisconsin in the early 1920s, researchers discovered that vitamin D, when added to a chicken's diet, prevented leg weakness.[18] Cod-liver oil, which was rich in the vitamin, quickly became a universally applied supplement in poultry feed.[19] Hens could now be kept inside year round, and chicks could be "carried to maturity under strict confinement."[20] This was of tremendous importance to the poultry industry, in that it overcame one of the first major biological obstacles to industrial, continuous-flow production. As one researcher from the Ohio Agricultural Experiment Station noted in 1928: "No specialist could fully succeed in raising the large numbers of chicks required for quantity production . . . without brooding them in confinement, where temperature, ventilation and sanitation can be kept under positive control."[21] Thirty years later, a leading poultry nutritionist reflected that "without it [the discovery and use of vitamin D] the present day poultry industry would not have developed."[22]

Confinement also received a substantial technological boost from the growing availability of electric power. Completed in the 1940s and 1950s, rural electrification proved instrumental in the proliferation of chicken houses, particularly in the up-country South. Electric brooders, feeders, and other devices allowed for more precisely controlled growing environments and huge increases in labor productivity. In 1940 an average of two hundred and fifty man-hours were required to raise one thousand birds to maturity; by 1955 the required time had dropped to forty-eight hours. Electrification thus allowed for significant increases in the scale of poultry farming. What had once been a small-scale operation, with a single family producing several hundred chickens per year, became a mass-production affair, with single families producing several thousand chickens per year.[23]

Successful confinement operations, however, required a continuous supply of high-quality chicks, a technical challenge met in part by the widespread adoption of artificial incubation and improved environmental control in hatcheries during the 1920s and 1930s. Given the autonomy of chicken embryogenesis and the increased availability of reliable energy in the form of electricity, thermostatically regulated incubators substituted for the brooding hen, allowing large numbers of newly hatched chicks to be produced on demand. American commercial hatchery operations expanded dramatically, growing in number from two hundred and fifty in 1918 to more than ten thousand in 1927. By 1934, roughly half of all chickens raised in the United States were hatched in artificial incubators, with state-of-the-art hatcheries operating as "veritable chick factories" capable of producing more than one million chicks per year.[24]

Yet intensive confinement still faced considerable obstacles during the 1920s and 1930s. Most significantly, contagious diseases threatened to wipe out early broiler operations. Pullorum disease, for example, destroyed as much as half of the flock on the Delmarva Peninsula between the Chesapeake and Delaware Bays during this period and was endemic in many commercial hatchery operations.[25] Because the disease spread vertically from infected hens to chicks, halting it necessitated the removal of infected birds from the population—an undertaking that required an unprecedented degree of cooperation between commercial hatcheries, growers, and government agencies.

Without effective disease control, confinement operations were doomed. In the absence of uniform quality standards, moreover, growers hesitated to purchase baby chicks, unable to determine that they were buying birds of a specific breed that had been inspected and certified as disease free. Although several states attempted to institute programs to deal with such concerns, only a coordinated national program would effectively meet the challenge.

In 1935, the federal government responded with the National Poultry Improvement Plan (NPIP), a unique partnership between government and industry operating at both federal and state levels. In essence, the plan sought to reduce the mortality of chicks from pullorum and other diseases and to improve the production and breeding qualities of poultry through research and the development of uniform standards. The U.S. Department of Agriculture's Bureau of Animal Industry assumed responsibility for administration and coordination of individual state efforts, while designated state agencies performed selection, testing, and inspection tasks on breeding flocks and hatcheries. Based on performance records and systematic testing, breeding and disease control classifications were established to provide for uniformity and reliability in chicks and hatching eggs. In the process, an institutional infrastructure at state, regional, and national levels emerged to coordinate industry-wide responses to disease problems and to establish uniform quality standards for poultry breeders.[26] By the 1950s, poultry breeders and hatcheries throughout the country were testing for the disease on a regular basis and nearly all had adopted uniform national standards. Two decades later, pullorum had been virtually eliminated from the commercial poultry industry in the United States.[27]

Viral diseases, which tend to spread horizontally, also resulted in periodic epidemics among poultry populations, often proving quite difficult to control.[28] Marek's disease, a particularly destructive virus that causes cancer in chickens, emerged in the 1960s, leading to condemnations of as many as one-fifth of the broiler flocks in the United States. Another virus, Newcastle disease, pushed mortality rates as high as 90 percent in England during the 1960s and 1970s. An outbreak of avian influenza in Pennsylvania forced the destruction of millions of birds during the early 1980s. More recently, a highly pathogenic strain of avian influenza emerged in Mexico, where mortality rates in affected areas were as high as 70 percent. And, in the winter of 1997, yet another highly pathogenic strain of avian influenza emerged in Hong Kong, leading to the deaths of at least four people (this was the first case of a poultry disease jumping species to infect humans) and the destruction of more than a million chickens.[29]

Efforts to combat poultry viruses have proceeded apace, benefiting, in part, from the important role that chickens have played in virology and vaccine development. Indeed, since Pasteur first used them in experiments on inoculations against cholera in the 1870s and 1880s, chickens have remained a favorite experimental creature. During the late 1920s and early 1930s, for example, Ernest W. Goodpasture and Alice M. Woodruff developed a method of using chick embryos to cultivate live viruses and produce commercial vaccines. Although this research fed most directly into the development of vaccines to fight human diseases, it also led to the development and use of a commercial vaccine for fowl pox in poultry. Since that time, numerous other poultry vaccines have been developed. Of particular importance was the work done by researchers during the 1970s to develop a vaccine for Marek's disease—the world's first licensed vaccine for fighting a viral cancer. As with other viral diseases, however, new strains of Marek's disease have since emerged that render previously effective vaccines obsolete.[30]

Still, the challenges of managing disease within the poultry industry have hardly diminished. As soon as one problem is solved, others emerge. Intensive confinement, geographic concentration, and the increased genetic uniformity of broiler flocks have created a fertile environment for the emergence and spread of infectious diseases. As of 1997, estimated losses from disease cost the U.S. poultry industry approximately $1.6 billion per year. Not surprisingly, much of the applied research in university poultry science departments has been devoted to understanding and dealing with the complexities of various diseases. So far mortality rates have been reduced to manageable and, more important, predictable levels.[31] In effect, disease risks have been quantified and incorporated into the economic calculus of the industry. By simplifying and standardizing the vagaries of nature, disease management and intensive confinement have provided a basis for further investments in nutrition and breeding to proceed.

At the same time, intensive confinement combined with the increasing scale and geographic concentration of the industry has created a host of new environmental problems.[32] In a number of high-production areas, the volume of poultry waste now exceeds the absorptive capacity of local and regional ecosystems, impairing the quality of surrounding waterways. On the Delmarva Peninsula, which produces more than six hundred million chickens annually, the regional environment must contend with some 1.5 billion pounds of manure every year—more than the waste load from a city of four million people.[33] Traditional waste management practices of spreading poultry manure on surrounding crop and pasture lands—a practice that proved to be a great boon to efforts in some parts of the American South to restore and rejuvenate eroded crop and pasture lands—can no longer keep up with the growing volume of waste; surrounding lands simply cannot absorb all of the nutrients. As a result, excess nitrogen and phosphorous are washing into local waterways, feeding algal blooms, which in turn deprive the waterways of the dissolved oxygen needed by other species. Some of the affected aquatic ecosystems are literally dying of asphyxiation. In some cases, moreover, toxic algae and microorganisms, such as the mysterious dinoflagellate *Pfiesteria piscicida*, have emerged out of the altered ecology of these streams and waterways, causing massive fish kills and threatening human health.[34] The new industrial ecology created by intensive confinement has ramifications far beyond the chicken house.

Nutrition and Growth Promotion

As confinement techniques became more effective, efforts to understand and improve the diets of chickens emerged as a key component in the effort to accelerate growth rates and increase metabolic efficiency. While such efforts have a long history, the "scientific" approach to poultry nutrition can be traced to the turn of the twentieth century and the emergence of a more general science of nutrition. Christiaan Eijkman's pioneering research on beriberi, for example, was based on his observations of variations in the diets of fowls. Because of the chicken's utility as a laboratory animal and its commercial potential, moreover, academic researchers used chickens extensively in early nutrition studies. Thus, chickens were the first animals to be used in experimental vitamin B studies and, along with other livestock species, were important subjects in elucidating the physiological functions of essential nutrients.[35]

This is hardly surprising. Scientists working at agricultural experiment stations performed some of the principal work in American nutrition research, particularly with vitamins. With general support for practical nutrition research and an institutional context fostering cooperation between biologists and chemists, the American agricultural research complex provided fertile ground for developing basic principles of nutrition and applying them to animal husbandry. In the case of poultry nutrition, knowledge accumulated rapidly and was quickly translated into commercial applications. By the beginning of World War II, the nutrient requirements of chickens were known more precisely than those of any other commercial animal species.[36]

In addition to early work on vitamins, research on carbohydrate and protein needs also proved instrumental in the industrialization of the chicken diet and the wholesale adoption of formula feeding in the industry. During the 1930s and 1940s, for example, researchers at Cornell University in Ithaca, New York, found that better growth and improved feed-conversion efficiency could be obtained by feeding chickens low-fiber, high-energy rations. Corn, which contained the highest metabolizable energy value of the cereal grains, was an obvious choice for such rations. Meanwhile, in the early 1940s, researchers at the University of California began identifying the essential amino acids needed for protein synthesis in chickens. Because amino acid deficiency translated directly into reduced growth rates, protein supplements could be used to boost performance. With wartime supplies of animal protein running short, these researchers turned their attention to the soybean—a virtual protein pill, high in crude digestible protein and low in fiber, which proved highly suitable for meeting the particular requirements of chickens.[37] Together, corn and soybean meal provided an almost ideal combination for the high-energy, high-protein commercial poultry rations that came into widespread use during the 1950s. None of this could have happened, of course, without larger changes in U.S. agriculture. In particular, dramatic increases in corn yields proved central to the rise of a commercial feed manufacturing industry. Between 1930 and 1965 the volume of U.S. corn production increased by 2.3 billion bushels, despite a reduction in total harvested acreage of some 30 million acres.[38] As the American corn belt was also ideal for growing soybeans, this decline in corn acreage, along with declines in the amount of farmland devoted to oats, hay, and pasture, created significant room for the expansion of soybean production.[39] With the adoption of solvent extraction methods in soybean processing during the 1950s, moreover, soybean meal could be produced much more cheaply and on a much larger scale than before.[40] These two developments, combined with the growing demand for soybean meal for livestock and poultry feed, spurred a dramatic increase in soybean production during the postwar period. Between 1941 and 1966, soybean acreage increased by more than 500 percent, while production increased almost 800 percent.[41] Taken together, these increases in the supply of corn and soybeans underwrote the growth of intensive animal agriculture, establishing some of the key economic and ecological linkages that have structured the postwar American agro-industrial complex. In effect, as the chicken was made over into a more efficient machine for converting corn and soybeans into animal flesh protein, the broiler industry became a vehicle for channeling the increased throughput of Midwestern corn and soybeans into higher-value food products for retail supermarkets.

These new poultry rations were not cheap, however. Because feed accounted for the largest overall share of live production costs, faster growth rates and precise calibration of nutrients to the metabolic requirements of the grow-out cycle became economic imperatives.[42] More rapid growth rates meant less time to market and less feed wasted on the maintenance of bodily functions. Reducing turnover time emerged as the over-riding concern for integrated firms as they sought to capture the added value associated with the transformation of feed grains into chicken meat. The critical advances in this respect were found in breeding and genetic improvement, which will be discussed in the following section, and in the widespread use of antibiotics and other antibacterials as growth promoters.

Few developments have had a more dramatic impact on animal agriculture than the use of antibiotics to promote growth. During the late 1940s and early 1950s, experiments with chicks at American Cyanamid laboratories found that antibiotics administered in feed increased the weight gain of chicks by 10 percent or more. Subsequent experiments also noted increases in feed-conversion efficiency and improved disease control. The livestock industry changed virtually overnight. By 1951, the U.S. Food and Drug Administration (FDA) had approved the use of penicillin and chlortetracycline as feed additives. Two years later, oxytetracycline was approved. Large pharmaceutical and chemical firms quickly ramped up production capacity to mass produce antibiotics for use in animal agriculture. Penicillin and tetracycline (either as chlortetracycline or oxytetracycline) were widely deployed in poultry and livestock feeding programs.[43] Antibiotics became cheap growth enhancers for the livestock industry.

Their use in animal feeds skyrocketed. In 1954, 2 million pounds of antibiotics were produced in the United States, of which some 490,000 pounds were used in livestock feed. By 1960, American farmers were feeding commercial livestock and poultry 1.2 million pounds of antibiotics per year. By the late 1990s, out of the total estimated U.S. production of 50 million pounds, roughly 25 million pounds were dedicated to livestock, most mixed into feed to promote growth.[44]

Although antibiotics are used in all farm animals, the poultry industry has employed them most extensively. By the 1970s, according to the U.S. Office of Technology Assessment, 100 percent of the commercial poultry raised in the United States received antibacterial supplements in their feed.[45] By the late 1990s, poultry producers were using an estimated 10.5 million pounds of antimicrobials annually, more than the amounts used for either hogs or cattle.[46] Beneficial effects included disease prevention, more uniform growth, improved weight gain, and enhanced feed-conversion efficiency. As for quantitative gains in field performance, which have been somewhat difficult to measure, various experiments for poultry conducted in the late 1970s found weight gain and feed-conversion efficiency increases of 5 percent or more, depending on the antibiotic used. Estimates of production losses that would occur if antibiotics were banned from use in animal feeds ranged between 8 and 20 percent.[47] According to one 1981 study, this translated into a "savings" of some $3.5 billion per year in lower prices for the American consumer.[48]

In short, even though debate continues as to exactly how these drugs promote growth when administered at "subtherapeutic levels," the use of antibiotics in livestock and poultry feed has had significant implications for productivity growth in the industry.[49] Proponents argue that improved disease control associated with these drugs has increased the viability of confinement operations, while enhanced feed-conversion efficiency combined with greater and more uniform growth has led to increased material economies and more precise and standardized integration between live production and processing operations.[50]

Antibiotic use in industrial animal production has become increasingly controversial, however. Critics argue that such practices have exacerbated the problem of antibiotic resistance and created serious public health risks. Indeed, not long after the widespread use of antibiotics in animal feeding began, public health officials and others began raising questions about the proliferation of antibiotic-resistant bacteria and the potential long-term consequences associated with extensive use of antibacterials in animal feeds.[51] Since the 1970s, government researchers in the United States have studied the issue extensively, and a host of private interest groups have weighed in on the pros and cons of regulating or even banning the subtherapeutic use of antibiotics in animal feed. The FDA and the Office of Technology Assessment looked into the issue during the 1970s, and though both voiced concern over the public health implications, neither discovered strong evidence that directly linked animal feeding practices to instances of human illness. In 1980 the National Academy of Sciences reached similar conclusions. In recent years the FDA has revisited the issue; hearings have been held and advisory committees assembled. The National Research Council and the Institute of Medicine have taken up the question, concluding in a 1998 report that although there are problems and legitimate public health concerns, the overall incidence of human disease that can be traced to the use of antimicrobials in animal agriculture is very low. Major policy recommendations included more study and stronger regulatory oversight of the development and use of new drugs.[52]

Critics have argued in response that even when definitive epidemiological data linking antibiotic use in animal agriculture to human health become available (and the evidence is accumulating) the key issue will still be the spread of resistant bacteria among animal and human populations and the overall potential for reducing the effectiveness of antibiotics. The primary concern, in other words, is not the incidence or prevalence of diseases resulting from pathogens in the food supply but the undeniable fact of increased resistance and what this means for the capacity to treat infectious diseases (whatever their origins) over the long term.[53]

Notwithstanding such criticism, supporters of intensive animal agriculture continue to defend antibiotics as necessary components of modern industrial food production.[54] Proponents suggest that the real issue is one of food hygiene.[55] While establishing links between resistant bacteria and food-borne illness is not easy, industry arguments appear to rest on increasingly shaky foundations. A growing mass of evidence from countries all over the world is beginning to demonstrate a definitive link between food-borne illnesses and resistant bacteria of animal origin.[56] And although the dangers associated with food-borne pathogens can be mitigated to some extent by improvements in food hygiene, the proliferation of resistant bacteria will most certainly not decline until the use of antibiotics is curbed. Efforts to contain the spread of resistant bacteria are not likely to succeed either. As Stuart Levy, of the Center for Adaptation Genetics and Drug Resistance at Tufts University School of Medicine in Massachusetts, notes: "Microbes circulate everywhere, and there is a continual exchange among the human, animal and agricultural hosts." The issue, Levy contends, represents one of society's "gravest public health problems."[57]

In addition to these very serious public health concerns, the continued use of antibiotics in animal feed also has important implications for the viability of poultry and livestock populations and for those who earn their livelihoods in animal agriculture. Given the current dependency on animal drugs, substantial losses would likely result from any ban on the subtherapeutic use of antibiotics. At the same time, however, the continued use of antibiotics in animal feed might be creating the potential for even more serious vulnerabilities and losses in the future. As early as 1979, an Office of Technology Assessment report noted that "such widespread use [of antibiotics in animal feed] poses an identical threat to the health of livestock and poultry and may even occur earlier and more visibly than the threat to human health. Present production is concentrated in high-volume, crowded, stressful environments, made possible in part by the routine use of antibacterials in feed. Thus the current dependency on low-level use of antibacterials to increase or maintain production, while of immediate benefit, also could be the Achilles' heel of present production methods."[58]

The tradeoff, of course, is between immediate economic benefit and longer-term risks. Obviously, animal monocultures are highly vulnerable to pathogenic bacteria. Antibiotics, at both therapeutic and subtherapeutic doses, have certainly provided protection from pathogens in the past. By altering the ecological balance between resistant and sensitive bacteria, however, antibiotics are creating very accommodating niches for resistant bacteria that infect but do not necessarily kill the population. In the process, the likelihood of chronic, low-level losses (as well as acute, epidemic losses) increases. The most common pathogen now affecting chickens, for example, is *E. coli*, which is also highly resistant to broad spectrum antibiotics such as the tetracyclines. To date, most of the strains affecting chickens have only been weakly pathogenic and thus have resulted primarily in low-level losses. The potential that a highly pathogenic strain might emerge and acquire resistance, however, increases in proportion to the amount of resistant bacteria in circulation. Such a strain could easily wreak havoc in poultry populations and has obvious implications for food safety. The U.S. poultry industry's widespread dependence on antibiotics is thus very much a double-edged sword. Although it has allowed for major improvements in quality control and huge expansions in productivity, the new ecological imbalances and interdependencies it has created raise the specter of serious problems down the road.

Breeding and Genetic Improvement

If confinement provided the foundation for subordinating broiler biology to the dictates of industrial production, and if advances in nutrition and growth promotion marked the first step in the process of biological intensification, breeding and genetic improvement proved to be the primary drivers in the effort to accelerate biological productivity. As with poultry nutrition, systematic research on poultry inheritance began around the turn of the twentieth century. Stimulated by the rediscovery of Gregor Mendel's work, European and American researchers used chickens extensively in early studies of heredity. William Bateson, considered by some the founder of modern genetics and a major force in the spread of Mendelism during the first decade of the twentieth century, started conducting experiments with poultry in 1898. Four years later, with support from the evolution committee of the Royal Society, Bateson published the first scientific paper on poultry inheritance, demonstrating Mendelian segregation in animals.[59]

While Bateson and his colleagues focused largely on the pure science of poultry genetics, early American researchers, most of whom were associated with the agricultural experiment stations of Maine, Massachusetts, Rhode Island, and Kansas, sought to use their understanding of poultry genetics and breeding to select for valuable economic traits.[60] Many of these researchers participated in the American Breeders' Association (ABA), an organization established in 1903 by members of the American Association of Agricultural Colleges and Experiment Stations. Composed of commercial breeders, scientists from agricultural colleges and experiment stations, Department of Agriculture researchers, and other groups interested in inheritance and scientific breeding, the ABA proved to be a very receptive audience for Mendel's work.[61] Members involved in plant and animal breeding appreciated the predictive value of Mendelian ratios and set to work on applying the "fundamental laws of breeding" to agricultural improvement. Willet M. Hays, a professor of agriculture at the University of Minnesota and the first secretary of the ABA, spoke of bringing together scientists and practical breeders "in a grand cooperative effort to improve those great staple crops and magnificent species of animals." Only on the basis of such cooperation between "the breeders and the students of heredity," Hays argued, could the "wonderful potencies" of heredity be harnessed and "placed under the control and direction of man, as are the great physical forces of nature."[62]

Papers on animal and poultry inheritance published by the ABA provided details on breeding experiments demonstrating the application of Mendel's "laws" and offered suggestions for future improvement efforts.[63] Among others, Charles B. Davenport, who would later become a major figure in American eugenics, presented a number of papers on poultry inheritance based on experimental research at his Cold Spring Harbor laboratory in New York and was directly involved with the work of the ABA's poultry committee. In a paper delivered to the third annual ABA meeting in 1907, for example, Davenport spoke of the "exceptional interest" that fowls held for the "student of heredity" because of their great variety, fecundity, and diversity of characteristics. These features, according to Davenport, provided a wealth of opportunities for those interested in hybridization as a method of improvement. Using language that anticipated his later enthusiasm for eugenics, Davenport suggested that poultry breeding efforts should focus on racial "purification" as a step toward creating "a new race which shall combine various desirable characteristics found in two or more races."[64]

For early poultry breeders, however, it soon became clear that the commercially desirable characteristics of poultry (egg and meat production, fertility, growth rate, and so forth) were complex characters that could not be reduced to sharply defined Mendelian factors. The existence of so-called continuous or quantitative variation in traits such as size and color had been noted by Mendel, Bateson, Davenport, Castle, and others. What was unclear was the implication of continuous variation for Mendelism and, by extension, for future efforts in plant and animal improvement. On this matter, the work of T. H. Morgan and his colleagues on the genetics of drosophila proved decisive in demonstrating that certain aspects of the phenotype were controlled by multiple genes at different locations on the chromosomes. This confirmation that "multiple-factor inheritance," or polygeny, was responsible for continuous variation and thus consistent with Mendelian principles cleared the way for the development and application of quantitative genetics to breeding.[65]

Such findings, of course, did not make the task of the commercial poultry breeder any easier. Indeed, the realization that most economically valuable traits were controlled by multiple genes (not to mention the vagaries of environment) dashed the initial hopes of poultry breeders that simple Mendelian analysis could be used to achieve prompt improvements. As a result, most commercial poultry breeders continued their practices of selective improvement, albeit with a bit more Mendelian sensitivity. Despite the fact that two famous American geneticists could claim in 1927 that "more is known specifically about Mendelian inheritance in poultry than in any other farm animal," the practice of commercial poultry breeding during this time looked more like an art than a science.[66]

The advent of population genetics in the 1930s and 1940s offered new tools for rationalizing commercial poultry breeding. On the basis of heritability data and the mating systems analysis pioneered by Sewall Wright, poultry breeders could make more informed predictions about the potential improvements from selection and the relative gains attainable from different combinations. Given the multiple objectives of poultry breeding programs and the polygenic character of most commercial traits, quantitative genetics offered a means for developing selection indexes to identify the monetary value of particular qualities and the tradeoffs involved in particular breeding programs. Efforts to enhance valuable traits through intensive selection and inbreeding could now proceed on the basis of statistical analysis. Greater calculability, it was hoped, would bring accelerated improvement. By the 1940s, poultry breeders began applying the principles of quantitative genetics on a systematic basis.[67]

Meanwhile, the successful development and widespread adoption of hybrid corn created considerable enthusiasm among poultry breeders about the potential for heterosis, or hybrid vigor. Many saw the success of the corn breeder in developing pure inbred lines and combining them into superior hybrids as an important model for the poultry industry.[68] As in the case of hybrid corn, moreover, interest in using the techniques of hybridization with poultry shifted the locus of innovation further to the private sector. Indeed, some of the earliest efforts to develop hybrid poultry breeds were direct spin-offs of private ventures with hybrid corn.[69]

The real watershed in the push for hybridization among commercial chicken breeders, however, came with the "Chicken of Tomorrow" contests of 1948 and 1951. Sponsored by the Great Atlantic and Pacific Tea Company, these contests had the explicit aim of stimulating interest in the breeding of broad-breasted, "meat-type" chickens.[70] As early examples of retailer power in product design, they reflected the emergence of new self-service supermarkets in the United States, where chicken could be sold in various prepackaged cuts. Both contests were won by a crossbreed developed by Charles Vantress of California. With instant national publicity, Vantress and the other prize winners quickly captured large market shares for male and female birds, causing a rapid shakeout of smaller firms.[71] By the early 1950s more than two-thirds of all commercial broilers raised in the United States "carried the blood lines of Chicken of Tomorrow prize winners."[72]

With control of substantial market share, the larger commercial breeders stepped up their efforts to develop hybrids during the 1950s.[73] The Arbor Acres breeding firm, a second-place Chicken of Tomorrow winner, introduced its first hybrid female broiler in 1959 after spending the better part of the decade inbreeding and testing its purebred lines. The company gambled on hybridization despite the fact that it did not expect to attain the productivity gains possible from fine-tuning its purebred bird for at least five years.[74] The key advantage of hybrids lay in the so-called biological lock of hybridization. Because only the first cross of two distinct parent lines would produce the high-yielding uniform hybrids, any effort to subsequently cross these hybrids with one another would create populations that lacked uniformity and varied considerably in yield. In the case of hybrid corn, this made it economically impossible for farmers to save seed for replanting, forcing them to go back and repurchase hybrid corn seed every year.[75] Similarly, if the hybrid birds developed by Arbor Acres or other primary breeding companies were subsequently bred by hatcheries or farmers, "the pedigrees would genetically self-destruct." For these firms, "hybridization secured, through the laws of nature rather than through the laws of man, an intellectual property right."[76] Thus, as in the case of hybrid corn, these new hybrid poultry breeds, with their unique, biological form of property protection, quickly became the genetic foundation of the industry. Primary breeders focused on fine-tuning their pedigrees to meet the growing demands for genetic uniformity and high performance. Their assets, their reputations, and ultimately their profits came to be embodied in these highly valued pedigrees.[77]

By the end of the 1950s, then, the era of the designer chicken had arrived. With improved nutrition, increased survivability, and better environmental control, broiler firms now had added incentive to pay a premium for chicken breeds with superior genetic potential. Surveying the field of poultry breeding in 1958, one poultry geneticist remarked that "the outstanding example of the contribution of breeding work is to be found in the broiler industry since here stocks have virtually been made to order to meet the needs of the meat industry."[78] But poultry breeding was not an easy business. Given the high-volume, mass-production nature of the broiler industry, breeders typically operated on very thin margins. In addition, long capital-intensive research cycles and the various biological risks associated with breeding translated into structural rigidities and considerable exposure to market risk. If a particular breed turned out to have a proclivity for a certain disease or did not meet the specific needs of customers, a breeder firm could lose market share very rapidly. Because of the long biological time lags involved in breeding cycles (at least five years), only the very largest firms would be able to sustain such a miscalculation. As a result of such pressures, the primary breeding industry concentrated rapidly during the 1960s and 1970s, with most primary breeders specializing in either male or female lines.[79] By the early 1980s, fewer than fifteen primary breeders supplied the breeding stock for the 3.7 billion chickens produced annually in the United States, and two companies, Peterson and Arbor Acres, together controlled more than 60 percent of the breeding stock.[80]

Meanwhile, as the center of broiler industry shifted to the American South, primary breeders also began to establish operations in the region. In the early 1950s, Arbor Acres moved some of its grandparent flocks to Georgia and Mississippi and established a research facility in Alabama to support the southern broiler industry. In 1956, Charles Vantress moved his whole operation from California to Duluth, Georgia.[81] Such moves signified the emerging networks and alliances developing between primary breeders and the integrated broiler firms in the American South.[82]

By the early 1970s, the advent of the so-called new biotechnologies stimulated considerable interest in the broiler breeding industry. Hoping to use the new techniques of genetic engineering to develop breeds that could serve as effective vehicles for selling proprietary animal health products, several large pharmaceutical firms purchased breeder firms.[83] With the U.S. Supreme Court's *Chakrabarty* decision of 1980, poultry breeders also began exploring the possibility of creating transgenic chickens that would be subject to patent protection and thus provide an alternative to the conventional approach of trade secrets and hybridization.[84]

The transgenic manipulation of chickens, however, has faced certain obstacles not present with mammalian systems. In particular, specific features of the reproductive system of the hen render the earliest stages of chick-embryo development relatively inaccessible, inhibiting the direct application of methods used in the production of transgenic mammals. Still, successful techniques have been developed. In 1992, Amgen and Arbor Acres received a patent on a process for transferring nucleic acid sequences into avian germ cells. More recently, researchers at the Roslin Institute in Great Britain, home of Dolly the cloned sheep, reported on the development of a new, more efficient method of transferring DNA into the chicken germ line.[85]

Pending the isolation of desirable genes and the further development of transgenic techniques, the production of genetically engineered chickens is thus very much a technological possibility.[86] Given the current furor over genetically modified crops, however, it is not at all clear if and when it will be politically and economically feasible.

Efforts to map the chicken genome represent another area in which the new genetic technologies could have a major impact on commercial breeding ventures. As in other sectors of the emerging life sciences industry, the development of genomics holds great promise for those interested in further manipulating the chicken genetic program. Although the first linkage map for chickens was developed more than six decades ago, only in recent years has the notion of a comprehensive molecular genetic map become a real possibility.[87] Given the relatively small size of its genome and the fact that its DNA can be isolated from nucleated red blood cells (in contrast to mammalian species), the chicken is well suited to genetic mapping, and it has become the focus of an international collaborative mapping effort involving several foreign and American universities, the U.S. Department of Agriculture, and a number of other governmental and nongovernmental institutions.[88] By identifying, isolating, and sequencing particular genes and developing detailed linkage maps based on DNA markers, researchers hope to dissect the genetic component of the various quantitative or polygenic traits that are of commercial interest to breeders.[89] This would effectively allow selective improvement to proceed on the basis of genotype rather than phenotype, representing a very significant expansion in "breeding power."

That said, although breeding efforts have succeeded in extending the biological potential of the chicken, tradeoffs between genetic susceptibilities and the performance of breeds geared to particular product mixes have become increasingly apparent.[90] Ongoing efforts to increase breast-meat yield, for example, have created a higher propensity for musculoskeletal problems, metabolic disease, immunodeficiency, and male infertility, primarily because the extra protein going to breast muscle production comes at the expense of internal organ development.[91] In recent experiments comparing breeding stock from 1957 and 1991, mortality rates for the 1991 breed were found to be up to three times higher than those of the 1957 breed.[92] To date, feed restriction programs, increased use of drugs, and improved sanitation have all been used in attempts to compensate for these increased genetic susceptibilities. Such management adjustments, however, will not solve the problem. As one poultry geneticist remarked: "We are severely changing the way these animals grow . . . I believe the time is rapidly approaching when management alone won't be able to overcome the genetic problems because of the metabolic stresses that are being put on these birds."[93] In effect, breeding programs have attained higher breast-meat yields at the expense of increased susceptibility to various diseases and increased mortality—a situation that appears even more serious when viewed in the context of increasing concentrations of broiler operations in specific geographic areas, the proliferation of antibiotic-resistant bacteria, and the threat of emerging diseases.

Intensification and the Problem of Nature

The story of the industrial chicken illustrates a number of more general tendencies manifest in the industrialization of agricultural systems. Based upon the precise coordination of a package of high-quality inputs—genetics, feed, medication—and ever more careful grow-out management, avian biology was (and continues to be) pressed into the service of industry and made to operate as a productive force.[94] But the manipulation and acceleration of biological productivity via the systematic application of science and technology was and is only part of a much larger story involving substantial changes in agrarian structure, the agricultural labor process, and the relation of farm-level production to various input and output sectors. Indeed, the story of biological intensification in the broiler industry has been intimately bound up with the rise of vertically integrated agribusiness firms, the spread of contract farming, and the concentration of production in the American South. To adequately treat these aspects of the larger history of the American broiler industry would require far more space than is available here. Instead, by focusing exclusively on the technologies of intensification, this article has sought to develop a perspective on technological change in agriculture that tries to capture the varied and variable ways in which nature is incorporated into agro-industrial systems.

Such a perspective points unambiguously to the sobering conclusion that any program of biological intensification will generate its own set of unintended consequences. If pushed too far, efforts to subordinate biological systems to the dictates of industrial production have a tendency to undermine their own biological foundations and facilitate various forms of ecological disruption. Of course, there is nothing novel in (and no lack of supporting evidence for) the claim that technological change carries with it all sorts of risks and produces all sorts of unintended consequences. The history of industrial agriculture contains numerous examples of the unforeseen and often disruptive effects of technological development—the failures of monocropping, the spread of pest resistance, genetic erosion, and soil degradation, to name a few. As James Scott notes, "cultivation is simplification," and simplification implies loss of resiliency and increased vulnerability.[95] By ramping up technological change, the industrialization of agriculture can increase the scale and scope of simplification and, as a result, the associated disruptions and vulnerabilities.

The broiler industry is paradigmatic in this regard. Indeed, virtually every effort to further industrialize broiler biology has resulted in the emergence of new risks and vulnerabilities. Intensive confinement combined with increased genetic uniformity has created new opportunities for the spread of pathogens. Increased breast-meat yield has come at the expense of increased immunodeficiency. And, of course, widespread recourse to antibiotics has created a niche for the proliferation of resistant bacteria. Since most of these risks affect the live production sector most directly, it is hardly surprising that integrated firms prefer to outsource grow-out operations to small contract farmers.[96]

Many of these problems also have ramifications farther down the food chain. In particular, concerns over food safety have achieved a very high level of national and international prominence in recent years, raising serious questions about the sustainability of the prevailing model of industrial livestock production in the United States and other industrialized countries. Growing numbers of food-borne illnesses, the spread of antibiotic-resistant bacteria in chicken, beef, pork, and other foods, and the growing animal waste problem associated with intensive confinement have led some to suggest that the inherent contradictions of industrial livestock production are beginning to manifest themselves—the proverbial chickens come home to roost. "Modern meat," to borrow the title of Orville Schell's 1978 book on the subject, may not only be creating some very serious public health problems but may also be undermining its own biological foundations.[97] The problem of nature, previously considered as a set of obstacles to be overcome via the industrialization of avian biology, has reemerged as a question of ecological risks and vulnerabilities.

Notes

1. Siegfried Giedion, *Mechanization Takes Command: A Contribution to Anonymous History* (New York, N.Y.: Oxford University Press, 1948), 6.

2. See, for example, Donald Worster, *Rivers of Empire: Water, Aridity, and the Growth of the American West* (New York, N.Y.: Pantheon Books, 1985); William Cronon, *Nature's Metropolis: Chicago and the Great West* (New York, N.Y.: W. W. Norton, 1991); and Richard White, *The Organic Machine* (New York, N.Y.: Hill and Wang, 1995). See also Jeffrey K. Stine and Joel Tarr, "At the Intersection of Histories: Technology and the Environment," *Technology and Culture* 39 (1998): 601–40.

3. Robert E. Kohler, *Lords of the Fly: Drosophila Genetics and the Experimental Life* (Chicago, Ill.: University of Chicago Press, 1994).

4. Jack Ralph Kloppenburg Jr., *First the Seed: The Political Economy of Plant Biotechnology, 1492–2000* (New York, N.Y.: Cambridge University Press, 1988); Deborah Fitzgerald, *The Business of Breeding: Hybrid Corn in Illinois, 1890–1940* (Ithaca, N.Y.: Cornell University Press, 1990), and "Beyond Tractors: The History of Technology in American Agriculture," *Technology and Culture* 32 (1991): 114–26. On the historical development of agricultural science and the U.S. agricultural research system, see Margaret Rossiter, "The Organization of the Agricultural Sciences," in *The Organization of Knowledge in Modern America, 1860–1920*, ed. A. Oleson and J. Voss (Baltimore, Md.: Johns Hopkins University Press, 1979), and Charles E. Rosenberg, *No Other Gods: On Science and American Social Thought* (Baltimore, Md.: Johns Hopkins University Press, 1997), chaps. 8–12.

5. On the history of breeding and intellectual property in the American chicken industry, see Glenn E. Bugos, "Intellectual Property Protection in the American Chicken-Breeding Industry," *Business History Review* 66 (1992): 127–68. For the relation between the "science of genetics" and the "art of breeding" in Raymond Pearl's research on egg production, see Kathy J. Cooke, "From Science to Practice, or Practice to Science? Chickens and Eggs in Raymond Pearl's Agricultural Breeding Research, 1907–1916," *Isis* 88 (1997): 62–86.

6. Kloppenburg; Edward Yoxen, "Life as a Productive Force: Capitalizing the Science and Technology of Molecular Biology," in *Science, Technology, and the Labour Process*, vol. 1, ed. Les Ledivow and Bob Young (London, 1981); David Goodman and Michael Redclift, *Refashioning Nature: Food, Ecology and Culture* (New York, N.Y.: Routledge, 1991), 169.

7. Rachel Carson, *Silent Spring* (New York, N.Y.: Houghton Mifflin, 1962), chap. 15.

8. Price trends are since 1960. See U.S. Department of Agriculture (USDA), *Poultry Yearbook* (Washington, D.C.: Economic Research Service, 1995) and *Poultry—Production and Value, 1999 Summary* (Washington, D.C., 2000).

9. USDA, *Poultry—Production and Value, 1999 Summary*; Gary Thornton, "Nation's Broiler Industry," *Broiler Industry* 61 (1998).

10. Tyson Foods Inc., *Fact Book* (February 2000) and *1997 Annual Report*, available at www.tyson.com/investorrel/publications.

11. J. H. Davis and R. A. Goldberg, *A Concept of Agribusiness* (Cambridge, Mass.: Harvard University Press, 1957); B. W. Marion and H. B. Arthur, *Dynamic Factors in Vertical Commodity Systems: A Case Study of the Broiler System* (Wooster: Ohio Agricultural Research and Development Center, 1973).

12. William Boyd and Michael Watts, "Agro-Industrial Just-in-Time: The Chicken Industry and Postwar American Capitalism," in *Globalising Food: Agrarian Questions and Global Restructuring*, ed. David Goodman and Michael Watts (New York, N.Y.: Routledge, 1997), 192–225. See also Jack Temple Kirby, *Rural Worlds Lost: The American South, 1920–1960* (Baton Rouge: Louisiana State University, 1987), 355–60.

13. Dairy science had also been established by this time; see Rossiter (n. 4 above).

14. Professional associations both grew out of and facilitated these developments. The American Poultry Science Association was formed at Cornell University in Ithaca, New York, in 1908, and launched its own journal in 1914; Rossiter (n. 4 above), 228–30. See also Rosenberg (n. 4 above), chaps. 8–12; Lawrence Busch and William B. Lacy, *Science, Agriculture, and the Politics of Research* (Boulder, Colo.: Westview Press, 1983); and W. E. Huffman and R. E. Evenson, *Science for Agriculture: A Long-Term Perspective* (Ames: Iowa State University Press, 1993), 17.

15. Rossiter, 229–30.

16. On this broad question, see Alfred D. Chandler Jr., *The Visible Hand: The Managerial Revolution in American Business* (Cambridge, Mass.: Belknap Press, 1977).

17. Busch and Lacy, 33, and S. L. Pardue, "Educational Opportunities and Challenges in Poultry Science: Impact of Resource Allocation and Industry Needs," *Poultry Science* 76 (1997): 938–43.

18. See the following articles in the *Journal of Biological Chemistry*: E. B. Hart, J. G. Halpin, and H. Steenbock, "Use of Synthetic Diets in the Growth of Baby Chicks: A Study of Leg Weakness in Chickens," 43 (1920): 421–41; E. B. Hart, J. G. Halpin, and H. Steenbock, "The Nutritional Requirements of Baby Chicks II: Further Study of Leg Weakness in Chickens," 52 (1922): 379–86; E. B. Hart, H. Steenbock, S. Lepkovsky, and J. G. Halpin, "The Nutritional Requirements of Baby Chicks III: The Relation of Light to the Growth of the Chicken," 58 (1923): 33–40.

19. Thomas H. Jukes, "Review: Recent Studies of Vitamins Required by Chicks," *Journal of Nutrition* 13 (1937): 376–82.

20. Hart et al., "Nutritional Requirements III," 34.

21. D. C. Kennard, "The Trend toward Confinement in Poultry Management," *Poultry Science* 8 (1928): 23.

22. L. C. Norris, "The Significant Advances of the Past Fifty Years in Poultry Nutrition," *Poultry Science* 37 (1958): 259.

23. The U.S. Rural Electrification Administration, the Tennessee Valley Authority, and the Electric Farm and Home Authority were vigorous in their efforts to push electric poultry farming among small farmers. See, for example, U.S. Rural Electrification Administration, *More Power to Your Poultry Raising* (Washington, D.C., 1945). For a discussion of the impacts of electrification on poultry farming (and agriculture more generally) in the South, see D. Clayton Brown, "Rural Electrification in the South,

1920–1955" (PhD diss., University of California at Los Angeles, 1971), 280–90. Labor productivity figures are taken from USDA, Packers and Stockyards Administration, *The Broiler Industry: An Economic Study of Structure, Practices and Problems* (Washington, D.C.: U.S. G.P.O., 1967), 15.

24. See Walter Landauer, *The Hatchability of Chicken Eggs as Influenced by Environment and Heredity* (Storrs, Conn.: University of Connecticut, Agricultural Experiment Station, 1961), 44; Gordon Sawyer, *The Agribusiness Poultry Industry: A History of Its Development* (New York, N.Y.: Exposition Press, 1971), 28; and E. L. Warren and M. T. Wermel, *An Economic Survey of the Baby Chick Hatchery Industry* (Washington, D.C.: U.S. G.P.O., 1935), 7, 27. This rapid growth of commercial hatcheries was reinforced by the explosion of mail order sales of baby chicks. See Warren and Wermel, 26–27; Sawyer, 29–32.

25. See Richard E. Austic and Malden C. Nesheim, *Poultry Production*, 13th ed. (Philadelphia, Pa.: Lea & Febiger, 1990), 245–47; H. J. Stafseth, "Advances in the Knowledge of Poultry Diseases over the Past Fifty Years," *Poultry Science* 37 (1958): 741, and Sawyer, 57.

26. USDA, *The National Poultry Improvement Plan* (Washington, D.C.: U.S. Dept. of Agriculture, 1938), 16, and *Improving Poultry through the National Poultry Improvement Plan* (Washington, D.C.: U.S. Dept. of Agriculture, 1938), 2; U.S. Agricultural Research Service, *Facts About the National Poultry Improvement Plan* (Washington, D.C., 1957). Under the NPIP program, poultry-producing states moved quickly to eliminate pullorum. See Sawyer, 60, and George Winn, "Poultry Improvement Focus of Ga. Group," *Georgia Farmers and Consumers Market Bulletin* 79 (1996).

27. By 1975 only 0.0008 percent of chickens tested contained antibodies specific to pullorum; Austic and Nesheim, 246–47. Pullorum was only one of several diseases that threatened the expanding broiler industry. Another bacterial disease, fowl typhoid, wreaked havoc in broiler flocks during the 1940s. See Austic and Nesheim.

28. Among the major viral diseases are Newcastle disease, Marek's disease, laryngotracheitis, avian leukosis, and avian influenza. Vaccines have been developed for many of these. See Stafseth; Austic and Nesheim, 229–58.

29. K. Rudd, "Poultry Reality Check Needed," *Poultry Digest* 54 (1995): 12; T. Horimoto and E. Rivera, "Origin and Molecular Changes Associated with Emergence of a Highly Pathogenic H5N2 Influenza Virus in Mexico," *Virology* no. 213 (1995): 223–30; K. Subbarao and A. Klimov, "Characterization of an Avian Influenza A (H5N1) Virus Isolated from a Child with a Fatal Respiratory Illness," *Science*, 16 January 1998, 393–96; C. Beard, "Assessment of H5N1," *Broiler Industry* 61 (1998); and D. E. Swayne and J. R. Beck, "Efficacy of Recombinant Fowl Pox Virus Vaccine in Protecting Chickens against a Highly Pathogenic Mexican-origin H5N2 Avian Influenza Virus," *Avian Diseases* 41(1997): 910–22.

30. A. M. Woodruff and E.W. Goodpasture, "The Susceptibility of the Chorioallantoic Membrane of Chick Embryos to Infection with Fowl Pox Virus," *American Journal of Pathology* 7 (1931): 209–22; Margaret A. Liu, "Vaccine Developments," *Nature Medicine* 4 (1998): 515; Stafseth, 749; Maurice R. Hilleman, "Six Decades of

Vaccine Development—A Personal History," *Nature Medicine* 4 (1998): 510. For historical context, see Greer Williams, *Virus Hunters* (New York, N.Y.: Knopf, 1959), 135–53. To date, most of the vaccines used by the poultry industry are "biologicals," that is, killed viruses or modified live viruses. More recently, recombinant vaccines have come into use; see Rudd, 12–13.

31. B. S. Pomeroy, "Poultry Disease Guide," *Feedstuffs Reference Issue* 70 (1998): 114–20.

32. See S. T. Rice, *Interregional Competition in the Commercial Broiler Industry* (Newark, Del.: University of Delaware Agricultural Experiment Station, 1951); W. W. Harper, *Marketing Georgia Broilers*, Georgia Experiment Station Bulletin 281 (n.p., 1953); USDA, Packers and Stockyards Administration (n. 26 above), 13; Marion and Arthur (n. 11 above), 21; and Boyd and Watts (n. 12 above), 209.

33. Georgia and Arkansas each produce over one billion chickens per year, with production concentrated in northern Georgia and northwestern Arkansas; see USDA, *Poultry—Production and Value* (n. 9 above). For a report on the animal waste problem in the poultry and livestock industries, see U.S. Senate Committee on Agriculture, *Nutrition, and Forestry, Animal Waste Pollution in America: An Emerging National Problem* (Washington, D.C.: U.S. G.P.O., 1997). See also U.S. General Accounting Office, *Animal Agriculture: Information on Waste Management and Water Quality Issues* (Washington, D.C.: G.A.O., 1995). For a discussion of the Delmarva waste problem, see Peter S. Goodman, "An Unsavory Byproduct: Runoff and Pollution," *Washington Post*, 1 August 1999.

34. Michael A. Mallin, "Impacts of Industrial Animal Production on Rivers and Estuaries," *American Scientist*, January–February 2000, 26–37; Thomas C. Malone et al., "Nutrient Loadings to Surface Waters: Chesapeake Bay Case Study," in *Keeping Pace with Science and Engineering: Case Studies in Environmental Regulation*, ed. Myron F. Uman (Washington, D.C.: National Academy Press, 1993), 8–38; Robert H. Boyle, "Phantom: The Tenacious Scientist and the Elusive Fish Killer," *Natural History*, February/March 1996, 17–19; Colin Macilwain, "Scientists Close in on 'Cell from Hell' Lurking in Chesapeake Bay," *Nature*, September 1997; and Eugene Buck et al., *Pfiesteria and Related Harmful Blooms: Natural Resource and Human Health Concerns* (Washington, D.C.: Congressional Research Service, Library of Congress, 1997).

35. Norris (n. 22 above), 256. See also Elmer Verner McCollum, *A History of Nutrition: The Sequence of Ideas in Nutrition Investigations* (Boston, Mass.: Houghton Mifflin, 1957), 216, and Jukes (n. 19 above), 376.

36. Rosenberg (n. 4 above), 202 and chap. 12. See also Austic and Nesheim (n. 25 above), chap. 7, and Norris.

37. Norris, 266–68; G. E. Heuser, "Protein in Poultry Nutrition—A Review," *Poultry Science* 20 (1941): 362–68; and John C. Hammond and Harry W. Titus, "The Use of Soybean Meal in the Diet of Growing Chicks," *Poultry Science* 23 (1944): 49–57. See also James P. Houk, Mary E. Ryan, and Abraham Subotnik, *Soybeans and Their Products: Markets, Models, and Policy* (Minneapolis: University of Minnesota Press, 1972), 40.

38. Kloppenburg (n. 4 above), 91.

39. Ray A. Goldberg, *Agribusiness Coordination: A Systems Approach to the Wheat, Soybean, and Florida Orange Economies* (Boston, Mass.: Harvard University, 1968), 101–47.

40. Houk, Ryan, and Subotnik, 44–45; James Schaub et al., *The U.S. Soybean Industry* (Washington, D.C.: U.S.D.A., Economic Research Service, 1989), 31.

41. Goldberg, 103.

42. See Heuser, 363; Austic and Nesheim, 222–28; U.S. Agricultural Research Service, *A Least-Cost Broiler Feed Formula Method of Derivation* (Washington, D.C.: U.S.D.A., 1958); Park W. Waldroup, "Dietary Nutrient Allowances for Chickens and Turkeys," *Feedstuffs Reference Issue* 70 (1998): 66–77.

43. Office of Technology Assessment (OTA), *Drugs in Livestock Feed*, vol. 1, Technical Report (Washington, D.C.: U.S. G.P.O., 1979), 29. The first study to demonstrate the growth-promoting effects of antibiotics in chickens was P. R. Moore et al., "Use of Sulfasuxidine, Streptothricin, and Strepotomycin in Nutritional Studies with the Chick," *Journal of Biological Chemistry* no. 165 (1946): 437–41. For subsequent research, see E. L. R. Stokstad et al., "The Multiple Nature of the Animal Protein Factor," *Journal of Biological Chemistry* no. 180 (1949); 647–54; E. L. R. Stokstad and T. H. Jukes, "Further Observations on the 'Animal Protein Factor,'" *Proceedings of the Society for Experimental Biology and Medicine* 73 (1950): 523–28, and "Effects of Various Levels of Vitamin B12 upon Growth Response Produced by Aureomycin in Chicks," *Proceedings of the Society for Experimental Biology and Medicine* 76 (1951): 73–76; A. C. Groschke and R. J. Evans, "Effect of Antibiotics, Synthetic Vitamins, Vitamin B12, and an APF Supplement on Chick Growth," *Poultry Science* 29 (1950): 616–19; L. J. Machlin et al., "Effect of Dietary Antibiotic Upon Feed Efficiency and Protein Requirement of Growing Chickens," *Poultry Science* 31 (1952): 106–9; M. E. Coates et al., "A Mode of Action of Antibiotics in Chick Nutrition," *Journal of the Science of Food and Agriculture* 3 (1959): 43–48; and Norris (n. 22 above), 263–64. See also H. R. Bird, "Biological Basis for the Use of Antibiotics in Poultry Feeds," in *The Use of Drugs in Animal Feeds* (Washington, D.C., 1969), 31–41. On the use of specific drugs and regulatory approval, see OTA, *Drugs in Livestock Feed*, 22–23, and Animal Health Institute, *Summary of the Antibiotic Resistance Issue* (n.p., 1996).

44. Margaret Mellon, Charles Benbrook, and Karen Lutz Benbrook, *Hogging It: Estimates of Antimicrobial Abuse in Livestock* (Washington, D.C.: n.p., 2001). See also Orville Schell, *Modern Meat* (New York, N.Y.: Random House, 1984), 23, and Stuart Levy, "The Challenge of Antibiotic Resistance," *Scientific American*, March 1998, 50–51.

45. This compared to about 90 percent of swine and veal calves and 60 percent of cattle; OTA, *Drugs in Livestock Feed*, 3.

46. See Mellon, Benbrook, and Benbrook, 42.

47. OTA, *Drugs in Livestock Feed*, 29–36.

48. Council for Agricultural Science and Technology, *Antibiotics in Animal Feeds*, cited in Richard H. Gustafson, "Antibiotics Use in Agriculture: An Overview," in

Agricultural Uses of Antibiotics, ed. William A. Moats (Washington, D.C.: American Chemical Society, 1986), 5.

49. OTA, *Drugs in Livestock Feed* (n. 43 above), 29. See also Virgil W. Hays, "Biological Basis for the Use of Antibiotics in Livestock Production," in *The Use of Drugs in Animal Feeds* (Washington, D.C.: National Academy of Sciences, 1969), 11–30; Austic and Nesheim (n. 25 above), 192; Levy (n. 44 above), 51.

50. Widespread recourse to antibiotics as feed additives also fueled the growth of the animal health industry during the postwar period. See Animal Health Institute, *Summary of the Antibiotic Resistance Issue* (n. 43 above).

51. Stuart Levy, "Antibiotic Resistance: An Ecological Imbalance," in *Antibiotic Resistance: Origins, Evolution, Spread*, ed. D. J. Chadwick and J. Goode (Chichester, N.Y.: Wiley, 1997), 2. For early discussion of antibiotic resistance, see OTA, *Drugs in Livestock Feed* (n. 43 above), 42, and Schell (n. 44 above) 24–27. For more recent assessments of the issue, see the essays in Chadwick and Goode; National Research Council (NRC), *The Use of Drugs in Food Animals: Benefits and Risks* (Washington, D.C.: National Academy Press, 1998); Dan Ferber, "Superbugs on the Hoof?" *Science*, 5 May 2000, 792–94; and Mellon, Benbrook, and Benbrook (n. 44 above).

52. NRC, *The Use of Drugs in Food Animals*, 1–10.

53. Schell, 113–15; Levy, "Challenge of Antibiotic Resistance" (n. 47 above) and "Antibiotic Resistance: An Ecological Imbalance."

54. See T. H. Jukes, "Discussion," in *The Use of Drugs in Animal Feeds*, 60.

55. See Richard Carnevale, "Industry Viewpoint on Antimicrobial Use in Food Animals" (paper presented at the American Academy of Veterinary Pharmacology and Therapeutics Symposium, "The Role of Veterinary Therapeutics in Bacterial Resistance Development: Animal and Public Health Perspectives," College Park, Maryland, 20–22 January 1998).

56. For a review of recent studies, see Mellon, Benbrook, and Benbrook, 1–5, and Ferber. On the annual incidence in the United States of salmonellosis and campylobacteriosis (the two major forms of bacterial food-borne illness from poultry), see F. L. Bryan and M. P. Doyle, "Health Risks and Consequences of *Salmonella* and *Campylobacter jejuni* in Raw Poultry," *Journal of Food Protection* 58 (1995): 326–44.

57. Levy, "Antibiotic Resistance: An Ecological Imbalance" (n. 51 above), 2.

58. OTA, *Drugs in Livestock Feed* (n. 43 above), 41.

59. D. C. Warren, "A Half Century of Advances in the Genetics and Breeding Improvement of Poultry," *Poultry Science* 37 (1958): 5–6. Bateson coined the term "genetics" in 1906. See W. E. Castle, "The Beginnings of Mendelism in America," in *Genetics in the Twentieth Century: Essays on the Progress of Genetics During Its First Fifty Years*, ed. L. C. Dunn (New York, N.Y.: Macmillan, 1951), 60. See also Ernst Mayr, *The Growth of Biological Thought: Diversity, Evolution, and Inheritance* (Cambridge, Mass.: Belknap Press, 1982), chaps. 16–17. Between 1902 and 1909, Bateson, along with E. R. Saunders, R. C. Punnett, and C. C. Hurst, presented the results of their experiments on poultry heredity in the *Report to the Evolution Committee of the Royal Society*. See, in particular, W. Bateson and E. R. Saunders, "Experiments with Poultry," in vol.

1 (London, 1902); W. Bateson, E. R. Saunders, and R. C. Punnett, "Experimental Studies in the Physiology of Heredity," and C. C. Hurst, "Experiments with Poultry," in vol. 2 (1905); W. Bateson, E. R. Saunders, and R. C. Punnett, "Poultry," in vol. 3 (1906); and W. Bateson, E. R. Saunders, and R. C. Punnett, "Experimental Studies in the Physiology of Heredity," in vol. 4 (1908). See also William Bateson, "The Progress of Genetics Since the Rediscovery of Mendel's Papers," *Progressus Rei Botanica* 1 (1906): 378–80; Mendel's *Principles of Heredity* (Cambridge, Mass.: University Press, 1913); L. C. Dunn, *A Short History of Genetics* (New York, N.Y.: McGraw-Hill, 1965): 66; and Castle, 59–76.

60. See D. C. Warren, "A Half Century of Advances," 3–4; Oscar Kempthorne, "The International Conference of Quantitative Genetics: Introduction," and A. W. Nordskog, "Introductory Statement: Poultry," in *Proceedings of the International Conference on Quantitative Genetics*, ed. E. Pollak, O. Kempthorne, and T. B. Bailey Jr. (Ames: Iowa State University Press, 1977).

61. For a historical treatment of the ABA and its relation to genetics and eugenics in the United States, see Barbara A. Kimmelman, "The American Breeders' Association: Genetics and Eugenics in an Agricultural Context, 1903–1913," *Social Studies of Science* 13 (1983): 163–204. Rosenberg (n. 4 above), 211–24, compares the reception of Mendel's work among plant and animal breeders in the United States with its reception among biologists and members of the medical profession. See also Diane B. Paul and Barbara A. Kimmelman, "Mendel in America: Theory and Practice, 1900–1919," in *The American Development of Biology*, ed. Ronald Rainger, Keith R. Benson, and Jane Maieschein (Philadelphia: University of Pennsylvania Press, 1988), 281–310.

62. Willet M. Hays, "Address to the First Meeting of the American Breeders' Association," in *Proceedings of the American Breeders' Association*, vol. 1 (Washington, D.C., 1905), 9–10. See also Willet M. Hays, "American Work in Breeding Plants and Animals," in *Proceedings of the American Breeders' Association*, vol. 2 (Washington, D.C.: n.p., 1906), 158; and the editorial "Heredity: Creative Energy," *American Breeders Magazine* 1 (1910): 79 (Hays was the editor of the magazine). For more on Hays and his role in the ABA, see Kimmelman, "The American Breeders' Association," and Paul and Kimmelman, "Mendel in America."

63. On animal breeding in general, see W. E. Castle, "Recent Discoveries in Heredity and Their Bearings on Animal Breeding," and W. J. Spillman, "Mendel's Law in Relation to Animal Breeding," both in *Proceedings of the American Breeders' Association*, vol. 1 (Washington, D.C.: n.p., 1905). See also the yearly reports of the Committee on Animal Hybridizing, in *Proceedings of the American Breeders' Association*, vols. 1–4 (Washington, D.C.: n.p., 1905–9). On poultry breeding, see C. D. Woods, "Investigations Relating to Breeding for Increasing Egg Production in Hens," in *Proceedings of the American Breeders' Association*, vol. 1 (Washington, D.C.: n.p., 1905), 127–31, and the yearly reports of the Committee on Breeding Poultry, in *Proceedings of the American Breeders' Association*, vols. 1–4 (Washington, D.C.: n.p., 1905–9).

64. C. B. Davenport, "Inheritance in Pedigree Breeding of Poultry," in *Proceedings of the American Breeders' Association*, vol. 3 (Washington, D.C.: n.p., 1907), 26–33, esp.

33. See also C. B. Davenport, "Recent Advances in the Theory of Heredity," in *Proceedings of the American Breeders' Association*, vol. 4 (Washington, D.C.: n.p., 1908), 355–57; "A Suggestion as to the Organization of the Committee on Breeding Poultry" and "The Factor Hypothesis in Its Relation to Plumage Color," both in *Proceedings of the American Breeders' Association*, vol. 5 (Washington, D.C.: n.p., 1909), 379–80, 382–83; and C. B. Davenport, "Eugenics, A Subject for Investigation Rather than Instruction," *American Breeders Magazine*, no. 1 (1910), 68. On Davenport and his relation to American eugenics, see Kimmelman, "The American Breeders' Association," and Rosenberg, 89–97.

65. Mayr (n. 59 above), 790–94, characterizes this as a debate between biometricians and Mendelians. See also Garland Allen, *Life Science in the Twentieth Century* (New York, N.Y.: Wiley, 1975), 56–72, esp. 70, and "The Transformation of a Science: T. H. Morgan and the Emergence of a New American Biology," in Oleson and Voss, 173–210, esp. 200–201. For a discussion of the implications of polygeny and Morgan's work on linkage for poultry breeding, see M. A. Jull, "The Selection of Breeding Stock in Relation to the Inheritance of Form and Function in the Domestic Fowl," *Poultry Science* 5 (1925): 1–19.

66. Ernest Brown Babcock and Roy Elwood Clausen, *Genetics in Relation to Agriculture*, 2d ed. (New York, N.Y.: McGraw-Hill Book Company, 1927 [1918]), 496–97.

67. D. C. Warren, "A Half Century of Advances" (n. 59 above), 16. For an early attempt to develop a selection index for poultry, see I. M. Lerner, V. S. Asmundson, and D. M. Cruden, "The Improvement of New Hampshire Fryers," *Poultry Science* 26 (1947): 515–24. See also Jay L. Lush, "Genetics and Animal Breeding," in Dunn, *Genetics in the Twentieth Century* (n. 59 above), 493–525, and Nordskog (n. 60 above), 47.

68. D. C. Warren, "Hybrid Vigor in Poultry," *Poultry Science* 7 (1927): 1–8. For discussion of some of the difficulties involved in applying the methods developed for hybrid corn to poultry, see D. C. Warren, "Techniques of Hybridization of Poultry," *Poultry Science* 29 (1950): 59–63; A. E. Bell et al., "Systems of Breeding Designed to Utilize Heterosis in the Domestic Fowl," *Poultry Science* 31 (1952): 11–22; and A. W. Nordskog and F. J. Ghostley, "Heterosis in Poultry," *Poultry Science* 33 (1954): 704–15.

69. See D. C. Warren, "A Half Century of Advances" (n. 59 above), 14.

70. H. L. Shrader, "The Chicken-of-Tomorrow Program: Its Influence on 'Meat-Type' Poultry Production," *Poultry Science* 31 (1952): 3–10.

71. Shrader, 6; Bugos (n. 5 above), 139–40; B. F. Tobin and H. B. Arthur, *Dynamics of Adjustment in the Broiler Industry* (Cambridge, Mass.: Harvard University Press, 1964), 31–35.

72. Shrader, 9–10.

73. See Bell et al. (n. 68 above), 11, for a discussion of the costs associated with the development and maintenance of inbred lines and the testing necessary to develop commercial hybrids in poultry.

74. Bugos (n. 5 above).

75. Kloppenburg (n. 4 above), 91–129.

76. Bugos (n. 5 above), 143–44.

77. For an interesting discussion of these issues, see Bugos (n. 5 above).

78. D. C. Warren, "A Half Century of Advances" (n. 59 above), 16.

79. See Bugos (n. 5 above), 145.

80. OTA, *Impacts of Applied Genetics: Micro-Organisms, Plants, and Animals* (Washington, D.C.: U.S. G.P.O., 1981), 170; Bugos (n. 5 above), 162.

81. D. Amey, "Arbor Acres Farm, Inc.: New Products, Changing Philosophy," *Broiler Industry* 55 (1992); Bugos (n. 5 above), 146.

82. On the changing ownership structure of the primary breeding industry in the 1960s and their move into international markets, see Bugos, 152–53, 161; W. van der Sluis, "We Believe in One Bird for All Markets: Profile of Cobb-Vantress," *World Poultry* 10 (1994).

83. In 1974, Upjohn bought the Cobb Breeding Company, Merck Pharmaceuticals bought Hubbard, and Pfizer Chemical bought H&N Breeders; Bugos (n. 5 above), 161.

84. *Diamond v Chakrabarty*, 447 U.S. 303 (1980), in which the court held that a live, human-made microorganism is patentable subject matter under U.S. patent law. See Bugos, 162–68; Daniel J. Kevles, "*Diamond v Chakrabarty* and Beyond: The Political Economy of Patenting Life," in *Private Science: Biotechnology and the Rise of the Molecular Sciences*, ed. Arnold Thackray (Philadelphia: University of Pennsylvania Press, 1998), 65–79. As used here, the term "transgenic" refers to an organism (plant or animal) into which genetic material from some other sexually incompatible organism has been inserted.

85. Helen Sang, "Transgenic Chickens—Methods and Potential Applications," *Trends in Biotechnology* 12 (1994): 415–20. The Roslin Institute work is discussed in A. Sherman et al., "Transposition of the Drosophila Element Mariner into the Chicken Germ Line," *Nature Biotechnology* 16 (1998): 1050–53.

86. Most commercial breeders would likely agree with Hubbard Farms geneticist Ira Carte's recent prognosis that the industry is still "many years away from having transgenic poultry available for commercial production"; "Poultry Breeding and Genetic Engineering," *Poultry International*, October 1995, 17.

87. David W. Burt et al., "Chicken Genome Mapping: A New Era in Avian Genetics," *Trends in Genetics* 11 (1995): 190. See also M. A. M. Groenen et al., "A Comprehensive Microsatellite Linkage Map of the Chicken Genome," *Genomics* 49 (1998): 265–74.

88. Hans H. Cheng, "The Chicken Genetic Map: A Tool for the Future," *Poultry Digest* 53 (1994): 24–28. A public database has been established at the Roslin Institute in Edinburgh to provide access to a summary of chicken genome mapping data. See Burt et al., 193.

89. Burt et al., 193–94.

90. T. J. Martin, "Industry Efficiency: A Changing Paradigm," *Broiler Industry* 59 (1996): 26.

91. Gary Thornton, "High Yielding Broiler Production: The Big Trade-Off," *Broiler Industry* 59 (1996): 18–22.

92. G. B. Havenstein et al., "Growth, Livability, and Feed Conversion of 1957 vs. 1991 Broilers When Fed 'Typical' 1957 and 1991 Broiler Diets," *Poultry Science* 73 (1994): 1785–94.

93. Quoted in Thornton, 22.

94. On the question of the relative contribution of genetic improvement to broiler performance (versus nutrition, disease control, etc.), see Havenstein et al.

95. James C. Scott, *Seeing Like a State: How Certain Schemes to Improve the Human Condition Have Failed* (New Haven, Conn.: Yale University Press, 1998), 264.

96. On the outsourcing of grow-out operations, see Boyd and Watts (n. 12 above).

97. Schell (n. 44 above). For a more recent popular account of food safety issues, see Nicols Fox, *Spoiled: The Dangerous Truth about a Food Chain Gone Haywire* (New York, N.Y.: Basic Books, 1997).

JOSHUA BLU BUHS

The Fire Ant Wars

Nature and Science in the Pesticide

Controversies of the Late Twentieth Century

IN HER 1962 BESTSELLER *Silent Spring*, Rachel Carson attacked the profligate use of pesticides, arguing that the chemicals did little to control insects, but were deadly to wildlife, livestock, and humans. She pointed to the federal campaign to eradicate the imported fire ants from the American South as evidence. The ants had arrived in Mobile, Alabama, in the late 1910s. By the 1950s, they had spread across the South and suddenly there was a roar of complaints: the ants reportedly attacked crops, killed wildlife, worried livestock, built large earthen mounds that interfered with farm machinery, and stung painfully. Carson suspected that the United States Department of Agriculture (USDA) had fabricated the claims to justify a huge program to eradicate the insects and increase its bureaucratic strength. In the process, the department killed quail and rabbits, cows and pigs, and threatened human health. Carson called the USDA's program "an outstanding example of an ill-conceived, badly executed, and thoroughly detrimental experiment in the mass control of insects." Hers was not the only voice raised in protest. Concerned citizens, entomologists, hunters, nascent environmental groups, and wildlife biologists urged the department to end the eradication program. Complaints continued into the late 1970s, when the Environmental Protection Agency (EPA) finally banned the chemicals used to eradicate the insects. Carson's philippic was one salvo in a conflict that would last twenty years, a conflict so intense it was dubbed the fire ant wars.[1]

This essay explores the interaction of nature and science in the fire ant wars by combining methodologies from the history of science and environmental history. Over the past quarter century, historians of science have staked out a constructivist approach that focuses on the way that social processes are implicated in the manufacture of all natural knowledge. While not necessarily opposed to examining the role of the material world in the construction of scientific ideas, earlier constructivist analyses focused on the social machinery of science, ignoring nature.[2] More recently, there have been a number of experiments to broaden constructivism by making the natural world an actor in historical narratives.[3] This essay attempts something by importing techniques from environmental history. Environmental historians take as their central endeavor the study of the interactions between humans and nature at different times and in different places. William Cronon has argued that to fulfill this agenda historians need to answer three intertwined questions: How does nature work in the time and place being studied? How do humans view this world and create ideas about nature? And, how do those ideas, transformed into action, affect the natural world?[4] The second question is the question asked by constructivist historians of science. The first and the third investigate the role of the natural world. As these three questions are answered, and connections are drawn between the answers, the integral place of the material world in histories of science is revealed.

Nature in this essay is embodied by the fire ants. The insects are opportunistic organisms, adapted to disruption, exploiting the changing ecology of the mid-twentieth-century American South. Neither the USDA's entomologists nor their opponents focused on the cause of the irruption, though. The federal employees, excited by the power of the new insecticides that had been introduced after World War II and worried that the ants threatened agricultural production, thought only of finding the most efficient methods to kill the bugs. Carson, her allies, and descendants, on the contrary, saw the insects as ecological innocents, not exploiters of the South's ecology but organisms fitting into the North American ecology. The real threat, they said, was posed by bureaucrats who intervened in natural processes, disrupting nature and chipping away at personal liberties. Both sides expressed their views using a vocabulary borrowed from debates over the structure of American democracy during the Cold War. Simultaneously reflecting alternative interpretations of the relationship between nature, science, and the state and a powerfully persuasive rhetorical tool, the Cold War imagery gave the fire ant wars their form and their urgency: the imagined ends of the Cold War came to stand for the imagined ends of the fire ant wars, the resolution answering both how to properly respond to the insects and how to properly structure the American democratic system.[5] The two sides alternated in seeing their ideas realized, first the USDA attempting to eradicate the ants, and then, in the 1970s, the agency's opponents successfully banning the insecticides used to kill the ants, allowing the insects to integrate into the southern ecology. The ideas, however, were not simply imposed on a passive nature. The biology of the ants and the actions of the two groups interacted in unexpected ways, with repercussions for the insects and the world that they inhabited as well as for the humans who claimed to understand the insects.

The Natural History of the Imported Fire Ants

Fire ants belong to the subgenus *Solenopsis*, a diverse group of ants that originated in South America about sixty-five million years ago. All *Solenopsis* possess a sting that gives the group its common name. The insects at the heart of the fire ant wars were actually two closely related species from this assemblage, *Solenopsis richteri*, a brown or black ant with a yellow stripe across its gaster, and *S. invicta*, a red species. Entomologists noted the color differences early on, but since the insects are otherwise hard to distinguish they lumped the two under the name *Solenopsis saevissima richteri*, most savage fire ant. They were considered the same species that the English naturalist Henry Walter Bates had seen attacking the village of Aveyros in the Amazon River Basin. "A greater plague than all other [insects] put together," he had called them, eating everything in sight and attacking "people out of sheer malice."[6]

The two species inhabit different parts of the world's largest wetland, an expanse of marshy land that follows the Río Paraguay and Río Parana through Brazil, Paraguay, and northern Argentina to their confluence with the Río de La Plata and ultimately into the Atlantic Ocean. The area is characterized by frequent disturbances. During the dry season, thick grasses clog the riverbeds; when the rains come, the water is forced to cut new channels, eventually overflowing and flooding the landscape. The river's vagrancy has created a wealth of microclimates and the area is dominated by a rich array of plants. In 1929, a geographer noted, "The most striking feature in the natural vegetation is its lack of uniformity." The ants have adapted to this situation by exploiting the disturbances. They are opportunistic—one entomologist calls them weeds—infiltrating disrupted areas, growing quickly—a single queen gives birth to 250,000 workers in three years—and forced out when the ecology matures.[7]

Solenopsis richteri was the first of the two species to break from the wetland and travel north. In the late nineteenth and early twentieth centuries, Argentina's cattle industry flourished and international trade was brisk.[8] The ants, living near major points of distribution, stowed away on one or several ships, reaching Mobile, Alabama, around 1918. The world the insects faced was climatically similar to South America, but ecologically very different. "Extensive timberlands and swamps, almost quite impenetrable," surrounded Mobile.[9] Approximately 80 percent of the land within a one hundred mile radius of the port city was thick forest.[10] The rest of the southern coastal plain was equally uninviting, devoted to fields often left fallow by sharecroppers and groves of trees allowed to grow dense.[11] With nowhere to go, the ants settled into the Government Street Loop, a run-down section of Mobile where the trolleys turned around.[12] Some two decades later, after the cattle industry reached deeper into the South American interior where *S. invicta* lived, the red ants reached the same city. As they arrived, the South was on a brink of a revolution that would alter the ecology of the region, opening vast new spaces for the ants to colonize.

Beginning in the 1930s the USDA began to modernize the South, making it more efficient, more like the Midwest. Tractors, harvesters, and combines replaced field hands and farms grew in size, doubling in Alabama and tripling in Georgia, Louisiana, and Mississippi between 1920 and 1969. Wastelands were plowed under, groves of trees felled, and fields seeded from fencepost to fencepost. New crops were cultivated, soybeans and cattle, especially. During World War II, military contracts were sent south, absorbing the idle workforce and pulling rural citizens into urban areas. Cities sprawled "with little attention to urban planning and zoning," and suburbs suddenly appeared. The southern historian C. Vann Woodward called these interlocking changes "the bulldozer revolution."

The revolution would last into the 1970s, transforming the South into the Sunbelt.[13]

The spread of *S. invicta* was an unexpected consequence of this modernization process. Thriving in disturbed areas, the ants were presented with a vast extent of disrupted habitats to exploit. Humans also unwittingly provided a means of transport out of Mobile and across the South. For decades southern nurseries had struggled against discriminatory railroad rates that favored the North. With the post-War economic boom, roads grew, the trucking industry introduced cheap transport, and nurseries bloomed. Mobile became the nation's fifth largest horticultural center. The ants found their way into the nursery stock, were shipped across the region, and were deposited in the disrupted sites—suburban developments, highway rights of way—that the insects preferred. The late-arriving red ants were not as restricted in their distribution as their congeners and so were better prepared to take advantages of the changing southern ecology. *Solenopsis richteri* languished, reaching only parts of northern Alabama and northern Mississippi. *Solenopsis invicta* spread widely.[14]

By the mid-1950s, the red ants could be found in nine southern states. The ants are omnivorous, preferring insects but taking what food is available. As their population increased, they could not always find favored foods and turned to other caloric sources that brought them to the attention of southerners. The ants ate seeds and crops and even young quail, which caused consternation since the birds were the South's most important game animals. The insects colonized lawns and the open spaces of the newly built military bases, where they came into intimate contact with humans. In 1955, a boy in New Orleans died after being stung three times. Two years later, ant stings sent three soldiers from Maxwell Air Force Base to the hospital. The imported fire ants especially favored cow pastures, the fields open and constantly disrupted by the big beasts.[15]

It might have been possible to ignore many of these problems—even the boy's death was a rare occurrence, and the ants killed far fewer people than bees and wasps—except that the spread of the ants was so dramatic and so intense that ignoring the formicids was difficult. Traveling to North America, the ants had left behind predators and parasites; the bulldozer revolution diminished competition. Freed from constraints, the ants' population exploded, the insects sometimes building one hundred mounds on a single acre of land. The hundreds of thousands of workers in each nest scurried from the colony, looking for food, stinging gardeners and soldiers. Landowners could not use their tractors to mow pastures without breaking blades or kicking the angry insects onto their backs. Laborers refused to harvest heavily infested fields.[16]

Many introduced organisms undergo similarly dramatic increases in their population and density. The increase is usually followed by an equally dramatic crash, as parasites and predators attack the newcomers, the ecology of the area stabilizes, and the imported organisms compete with themselves over increasingly scarce resources.[17] The imported fire ants followed this pattern, as both their number and population density declined in the years after introduction, but there were also significant deviations in the pattern. The bulldozer revolution accounts for some of the deviation. The revolution assured that there were always new areas to exploit as suburbs sprawled, old areas were razed, and new roads were built. Looking at the course of invasion over a single patch of ground, southern Alabama, say, reveals the familiar rise-and-fall pattern. On a regional scale, however, the irruption did not crash, but continued, the ants finding their way to more and more parts of the South. By 1957, they had spread from Mobile to cover twenty million acres.

The rest of the deviation is accounted for by a biological quirk. In their homeland, *S. invicta* populations live in two social forms: monogynous and polygynous colonies. Monogynous colonies have only a single queen that mates in aerial swarms and founds her colony independently; polygynous colonies contain several, sometimes several hundred, queens, most of which mate within the nest and form new colonies by adopting workers from the mother colony, walking to a likely, nearby area, and building a new nest. Both forms arrived in America. Bigger and stronger, the monogynous queens initially predominated. They could spread widely and colonize the many disturbed habitats quickly. But, as the environment became saturated with ants, the polygynous colonies came to dominate. Young queens were protected in the nest and were subsidized by the mother colony when founding their own nests. The increasing prevalence of polygyny allowed more and more ants to be packed into the same area, softening the expected crash in the fire ants' population. In the 1990s, some fields in Texas sagged under the weight of over 400 imported fire ant mounds per acre.[18]

Ideas about Nature: The Fire Ants in a Cold War

The spread of the fire ants occurred in a post-War America optimistic about the future and confident it could use its natural resources, science and technology, and democratic institutions to solve any problem. The economy hummed, domestic problems seemingly obliterated by the power of mass consumption. Antibiotics had a death-grip on disease. The federal government was in the capable hands of affable Dwight Eisenhower. But, beneath this optimism was a dark layer of concern. Science brought not only antibiotics, but also the bomb, radioactive fallout, and pollution. Conformity was not only the root of the good economy, but also the root of totalitarianism. And democratic institutions not only guaranteed Americans were the freest people on earth, but also could be perverted to squash individual liberties in the name of defending those liberties. How best to live in nature, how to use science and technology, and how to bring nature, science, and technology to bear on the maintenance of democratic traditions—these were the questions that would become intertwined with the fire ant wars.[19]

Control entomologists and their administrative allies within the USDA shared a vision of how nature, science, and democracy related. Nature, they thought, was imperfect: insects destroy crops, diseases kill livestock, and weather is foe as often as friend. Survival is a struggle, achieved only by the correct application of scientific ideas to hold the forces of nature at bay and protect civilization. One entomologist wrote, "To clothe and feed this vastly increased population, man must maintain his position of dominance, and our agricultural production must continue to increase even at the expense of the further displacement of native plants and animals."[20] By the time that the fire ants had spread across the South, the USDA had adopted insecticides as a principal weapon in the struggle against nature. Control entomologists who supported the use of the chemicals had elbowed aside other insect biologists (often called research entomologists) who employed tools such as biological and cultural control to manage insect outbreaks. DDT was safer than the arsenic and cyanide solutions that had been used by earlier generations of entomologists and had been used in World War II to protect American soldiers from Typhus and malaria, the control entomologists pointed out. Now, that insecticide and its chemical relatives could be used to protect public health and agricultural production and entomologists need not be limited to only controlling insects—that was the mark of old-fashioned entomology—but could eradicate them completely. The chemicals, they admitted, might kill wildlife and other desirable animals, but the gain in farming efficiency was worth more than the cost. One farmer made the calculus explicit, noting, "I believe I have been as much for conserving our wildlife as the next one and have spent a great deal of effort and money to see wildlife increase but if one of us should be hurt by treating the land for fire ants I do not believe it should be the man who owns the land and pays taxes on the same, especially when it means the survival of himself and family."[21]

Using science to control the ants did more than preserve public health and increase agricultural production, the federal entomologists contended. The insecticides helped the nation in its struggle with the Soviet Union. It was an article of faith at the USDA that American democracy grew from the soil: agriculture was a Cold War weapon. Byron Shaw, head of the USDA's Agricultural Research Service, for example, said in 1958, "I think the times were described rather aptly a year or so ago, when a Soviet premier told an American television audience that communism would win its contest with capitalism when the Soviet's per-capita production of meat, milk and butter surpassed that of the United States. He was really saying that a nation is as strong as its agriculture." Eradicating the ants would allow the United States to increase its productivity and win the Cold War. If, on the contrary, the ants were left to spread, agricultural output would plummet, dissatisfaction would increase, and the seeds of revolution would be sown.[22]

The Department of Agriculture had reason to believe that the imported fire ants represented an especially dire threat to the modernizing South. In the late 1940s, the state of Alabama had tapped E. O. Wilson, then an undergraduate at the University of Alabama, to study the insects. Wilson and a classmate determined that the ants significantly damaged the state's agriculture. More foreboding, he concluded that the red ants were newly evolved mutants that were better adapted to life in North America and more aggressive than their black counterparts. The taxonomic decision explained the chronology of the ants' irruption without reference to the bulldozer revolution: the ants, Wilson argued, had remained unremarkable until the mutation appeared sometime around the end of World War II allowing the insects to spread across the South. Wilson's ideas made the ants even more threatening, unpredictable—a constantly evolving pest.

Thus, C. C. Fancher, head of the USDA's fire ant program, could say without irony that the eradication of the insects would protect "the American way of life" and provide a "service for mankind."[23]

In popular culture more broadly, other connections were drawn between the ants and communist subversives. The insects lived in a hierarchically arranged social system that extinguished individualism—"regimented automatons, driven, dutiful in their prescribed pointless doing." The ants undermined the concept of private property, building their mounds without respect to landlines and making capitalist production difficult. They also perverted gender roles, the males reduced to mere bearers of sperm that died after mating and the females ruling the colony, just as communists promised to abolish sexual hierarchies, another perversion. As the fire ants impinged on southern life, the connections between the insects and communists were made quickly and easily. One newspaper labeled the insects "the red peril" and "fifth columnists," while a hunting magazine noted, "This ferocious little ant . . . has carried communism to the ultimate, and its actions suggest a certain cold-blooded intelligence."[24]

Military metaphors permeate the history of insect control and Americans have a long tradition of drawing parallels between insects and ostracized humans. But despite the triteness of the language (or maybe because of it), the analogy was useful to the USDA.[25] To eradicate the ants, the federal agency needed to spread insecticides on all land, "without regard to location, land use, or ownership."[26] If any land was left untreated, some ants might survive and spread, threatening American agriculture. Broad support was necessary to ensure that all land could be sprayed. Using the shared Cold War imagery, the USDA generated the needed mandate. A department press release, for example, noted, "Uncle Sam is ready to use a fleet of 60 planes to go to war against the dreaded fire ant . . . Only the modern airplane, dropping insecticides on twenty million acres in the critical area, can hope to stop the menace." The word "menace," of course, had deeper connotations, linking with concerns over the Red Menace.[27] Congressional testimony favoring the eradication program drew upon the same lexicon. One southerner testified, "The government should be building as big a defense against the fire ants as they are against the Russians. The ants have already invaded."[28] The rhetoric proved persuasive and in late 1957 Congress gave the agency $2.4 million to initiate the program. The USDA took the money and transformed their ideas into action, spreading chemical insecticides onto one million acres in the South the first year and millions more before the fire ant wars ended.

As the USDA entomologists worked to put their ideas into practice, a loosely federated group of biologists, citizens, early environmentalists, and hunters offered an alternative vision of how nature, science, and democracy fit together and an alternative response to the ants. To varying extents, the members of this group saw nature not as imperfect but as finely tuned and integrated. Over the course of the previous two decades, wildlife biologists had shown how animal populations kept each other in balance.[29] For an even longer time, many entomologists, before they had been elbowed aside by the upstarts promising to use insecticides to eradicate insects, had studied insects as part of an ecological community.[30] The job of the scientist was not to battle nature, but to elucidate natural processes and find ways to accommodate human life to the rhythms of nature. This view of the relationship between science and nature was seen to serve democracy in several different ways. Some saw the protection of nature as the promotion of spiritual values above economic ones, and thus a means for creating a better citizenry.[31] Some felt that wildlife was one of the nation's most important natural resources and thus its conservation was a way of maintaining the country's strength.[32] Others felt that living in accord with nature proved the vitality of democratic institutions. If insecticides, say, were used without regulation, killing wildlife, that meant that agricultural agencies had gained too much power and warped the political process, silencing those who voiced concern for wildlife. A rich, varied natural world was evidence of a strong democracy, in which policies were set to appease competing factions. The USDA's favoring of agriculture over wildlife in the fire ant wars represented a threat to American democracy.[33]

Entomological research and early studies on the effects program provided evidence for these views. Done mostly by university entomologists, this research examined the invasion not as a regional phenomenon, but instead studied insects in limited locations that the insects had inhabited for some time—places where the irruption was dying and the damage done by the insects less intense. Kirby Hays, for example, an entomologist at the Alabama Polytechnic Institute (renamed Auburn in 1960), visited South America in early 1957 and was told by local scientists that the ants were considered beneficial for preying on other insects. Research on the insects' behavior in Alabama by his brother, Sydney, a graduate student at Auburn,

substantiated these opinions. The younger Hays tested the feeding preference of laboratory-reared imported fire ants, finding that they ate only insects, becoming cannibalistic rather than consume plant material. Another
Auburn graduate student showed that the ants only consumed 4 percent
of young quail and research in Louisiana showed that the ants were major
pests of sugar cane borers and, perhaps, boll weevils. In 1958, a report by
the Alabama state forester that had been written at the time of Wilson's
survey re-appeared. The ants, it claimed, were not pests.[34]

These reports became the basis of Carson's discussion of the ants in *Silent
Spring*. While writing the book, Carson had corresponded with Wilson and
learned that he considered reports of the ants' beneficial traits exaggerated,
but she ignored his conclusions and concentrated on the positive aspects
of the ants' biology. Carson reinterpreted the meaning of their nests, for
example, not seeing them as impediments to agricultural production, but
as necessary to the ecology of the earth. "Their mound-building activities,"
she wrote, "serve a useful purpose in aerating and draining the soil."[35] The
weight of her book, she concluded, "thoroughly documented that the fire
ant has never been a menace to agriculture and that the facts concerning it
have been completely misrepresented."[36] Ignoring the distinctions between
the two species (or mutants) and the role that humans had played in the
irruption, Carson argued that for most of the ants' time in North America,
they had been inconsequential: the sudden interest resulted from USDA
propaganda, not biology; the ants were actually well-behaved parts of the
ecosystem. In the late 1930s, Carson had written an essay about the starling, a bird imported into America that many considered a pest but that
she thought was becoming a necessary part of the American ecological order. She argued that it was time to give citizenship papers to the starling.[37]
Twenty years later, she was working to naturalize another immigrant, the
imported fire ants.[38]

The insecticides, by contrast, remained outside the American ecological
order, a true threat. Biologists monitoring the effect of the fire ant program found dead wildlife at every spot that they checked. The Alabama
Department of Conservation, for example, found sixty-two dead animals
on a one-hundred acre plot of land while biologists with the U.S. Fish and
Wildlife Service, scouting a two acre sample plot in Georgia, found six
dead quail, seven dead rabbits, twenty dead songbirds, three dead rodents,
and one dead cat, all with enough insecticide in their bodies to account for

their deaths; two months after the application, they could not find a single live bird. Quail populations plummeted by almost 90 percent. Livestock, as well, frequently died and the chemicals were seeping into the milk supply, and, possibly, into the bodies of children. The USDA was not working with nature, but against it. The application of the insecticides, Carson wrote, "follow[ed] the impetuous, heedless pace of man, not the deliberate pace of nature."[39]

The eradication program was more than a threat to wildlife. It was a threat to democracy, the USDA's opponents said, turning the federal agency's rhetoric on its head. The critique of the fire ant program had raised a serious question. If the insects were not pests and the insecticides were so deadly, why would the USDA undertake to eradicate the ants? To answer these questions, the USDA's opponents called on a traditional American distrust of centralized governmental control. Anti-statism has a long history in America, but it took on a particularly keen intensity during the Cold War. As historian Michael Hogan has shown, there was a widespread fear that in building a national security system against communism, the United States would take on the traits of its enemy. National defense required centralized control and secrecy and conformity, all characteristics of the Soviet Union. The Cold War, many feared, would transform the United States into a garrison state. The USDA had already defined itself as part of the national security system, and the agency's marriage to the eradication ideal demanded centralized control. Carson and others drew on this imagery to attack the USDA. Why would the USDA spread deadly chemicals against a pest that was not a pest? Because the agency was drunk on its own power and beyond democratic accountability.[40]

In *Silent Spring*, Carson wrote, "Who has decided—who has the *right* to decide—for the countless legions of people who were not consulted that the supreme value is a world without insects, even though it be also a sterile world ungraced by the curving wing of a bird in flight? The decision is that of the authoritarián temporarily entrusted with power." Others followed the same line of reasoning. The wildlife biologist Clarence Cottam, for example, wrote, "I am convinced some of the philosophies expressed and actions taken by the pest control arm of our Federal Department of Agriculture strike at the very heart of American democracy. The problems, therefore, far transcend the control program or any entomological considerations." He urged others to agitate against eradication campaigns and avoid becoming "numbered pawns of the state." This form of critique was so powerful that it drew to wildlife groups those who opposed the growth of bureaucracies but had little interest in wildlife. The Mobile nursery owner J. Lloyd Abbot, for instance, joined the Alabama Wildlife Federation explicitly to stop the imported fire ant program not because he worried about the danger of insecticides but because "the threat to the continued existence of our Democracy, and whether or not we are going to be taken over by *internal* bureaucracies, could not be more clearly illustrated than it is by this whole reprehensible situation."[41]

The USDA's opponents had more difficulties putting their vision of the relationship between nature, science, and democracy into practice than the department. The agricultural agency was one of the most powerful federal bureaucracies and control entomologists had embedded themselves deeply within a network of relationships with powerful allies.[42] No attempts to stop pesticide use gained much political traction in the 1960s, but the protest against the imported fire ant program seemed the least likely to succeed. Just as *Silent Spring* was published in 1962, the USDA introduced a new insecticide for eradicating the ants, Mirex, which nullified the objections of the department's opponents. Billed as the perfect pesticide, Mirex was less harmful to vertebrates than its predecessors and was used at the incredibly low dose of one-seventh of an ounce per acre. With little to object to and little power, the USDA's opponents turned their attention to other issues. When Carson died in 1965, the fire ant wars seemed to be over.[43]

By the 1970s, however, the situation had changed: Mirex was seen as dangerous and the environmentalists were on the ascendancy. Richard Nixon, wanting to co-opt a Democratic constituency, created the Environmental Protection Agency (EPA) and charged it with regulating the introduction of chemicals into the environment.[44] An increasingly self-conscious environmental movement allied with the EPA to ban dozens of insecticides, most famously DDT, institutionalizing their ideas about the proper relationship between nature and science and endeavoring to create what they considered a more democratic nation.[45] In 1973, the agency, prompted by the Environmental Defense Fund, initiated a court case over the fate of the fire ant eradication program.[46] In the years since it had been called the perfect pesticide, Mirex had been shown to accumulate in the fat of fish, kill shrimp and crabs, and, possibly, cause cancer.[47] The ants, on the contrary, were even more firmly established as non-threatening. In the late 1960s, some of E. O. Wilson's older contemporaries, feeling overshadowed by the young man's rapid ascent, revisited his taxonomic work—"*Someone has to do the niddy-griddies to check out Wilson's theories while he continues onward and upward to still greater and greater glories*"—and determined that the red and black forms were not mutants, but separate species, and that the red form was not as dangerous as Wilson had implied.[48] Others suggested that the ants were a key part of the southern ecosystem that should not be removed.[49] Even Wilson had changed his mind, calling the eradication program "The Vietnam of Entomology": a battle with inchoate goals and no clear winners, only loss.[50]

The power of the EPA and the environmental movement slowly overwhelmed those promoting the eradication of the fire ants. The court case over the fire ant program and Mirex did not definitively settle the matter, but it made the cost of continuing too high for Allied Chemical, the maker of the insecticide. In 1976, Allied dropped out of the proceedings, selling its plant to the state of Mississippi for one dollar. Mississippi's waxing was short-lived, however. Two years later, the EPA determined that Mirex and its by-products caused cancer and that the chemical could be found in the bodies of almost one in every two Mississippians. The use of Mirex was phased out.[51] In the years since it had been established, the EPA had also banned all other chemicals used to eradicate the imported fire ants. By the end of the 1970s, the fire ant wars were over and a new idea was being put into practice. The ants were left to accommodate themselves to life in North America, safe from the chemical barrage.

Ideas into Actions: The Effect of the Fire Ant Wars

The USDA and its opponents had focused on different aspects of the natural history of the imported fire ants and generalized those traits into the essence of the animal—like the five blind wise men who touched different parts of an elephant and divined the essence of the pachyderm from those parts, one touching the tail and deciding an elephant was like a rope and another feeling the ear and deciding the beast was like parchment. Committed to protecting American agriculture and confronting the ants on a regional scale, the federal entomologists focused on the negative aspects of the insects. The dissenters, on the contrary, looking at the invasion on a smaller scale and, wedded to the belief that nature was integrated, studied the places where the irruption was dying and saw that the ants were no longer pests. They pointed to the opportunistic ants preying on other insects as evidence of their beneficence and their acceptance into the American ecological order. Both sets of ideas, however, were simplifications of a more complicated natural history. When the ideas were transformed into action and applied through American agricultural and environmental policy, the friction between the ideas and the reality created situations that no one expected.

The USDA entomologists believed that nature could be remade without consequence and so applied the insecticides fully expecting to eradicate the ants. The insecticides, however, were broad-spectrum poisons, killing huge numbers of insects and game animals. When they were applied, the insecticides disrupted an area, much as the rivers of South America did. Imported fire ants invaded the poisoned parcels of land, mocking the eradication ideal. In 1957, for example, Arkansas was declared ant-free after 12,000 acres were sprayed. In 1958, however, the ants occupied 10,000 acres, many of them the same ones that had been treated previously. And in 1959, the ants could be found on 25,000 acres.[52] By 1960, the USDA noticed the re-invasion problem on a regional scale. One disappointed entomologist complained, "It is probable that the acreage being reinfested plus the expansion into new areas each year is as great as the acreage that can be treated with presently available funds. The program can hardly be termed an eradication program if there is no net gain in acreage free from ants."[53] Over the course of the fire ant wars, the USDA tried a number of different insecticides and a number of different rates of application, but all failed.[54]

With the failure of eradication came a fading belief in the professional competency of control entomologists. Control entomologists had bet their scientific legitimacy on eradication, C. C. Fancher announcing at the beginning of the fire ant program, "It would be a disgrace to entomologists of this country to permit the imported fire ant to become established."[55] As the fire ant program progressed, though, the dream faded. The ants continued to spread, as did other insects targeted by the USDA—bark beetles, gypsy moths, Japanese beetles.

By the 1960s, the embarrassment was acute, and it would only get worse. Even with the introduction of the perfect pesticide, many entomologists in the USDA doubted whether eradication was possible.[56] Their backbone stiffened in 1969 when Nixon appointed J. Phil Campbell to the USDA. A former commissioner of agriculture in Georgia, Campbell had built his career battling the ants—reportedly diverting money for eradication into a slush fund—and demanded that the agency renew its commitment to eradication.[57] Campbell's enthusiasm, though, could not stem the spread of the insects. In 1978, deciding that the battle against the ants could not be won, the USDA shifted all funding for the program away from control entomologists and to insect biologists who hewed to older traditions in entomology, investigating insect natural history and employing biological and cultural control. Study of parasites and predators increased and in 1995 the agency began releasing flies that decapitate the ants into the wild. The goal now was control, not eradication. A sign of how far acceptance of the control entomologists' terms had fallen, the Jackson, Mississippi, *Clarion-Ledger* reported, "'Eradication' is a dirty word among the small corps of fire ant researchers."[58]

Environmental policy created similar, if less severe, professional problems, and for the same reason: the unexpected outcomes of mixing human practices and the biology of the ants. In her rehabilitation of the ants, Carson had excluded any consideration of the role humans played in creating the fire ant irruption. This exclusion was part of Carson's more general tendency to see humans as separate from the natural world, a habit of thought that was taken up by later environmental groups and institutionalized by the EPA. The perspective removed human responsibility for the fire ant problem and led to solutions that failed to address the root cause of the spread of the fire ants. The insecticides were banned, but the bulldozer revolution continued and the ants continued to spread, covering another one hundred million acres by the century's end. They reached western Texas, New Mexico, Arizona, Nevada, and California. Wherever they appeared, their population exploded, the ants wreaking havoc.[59] By separating humans and nature, the critical importance of interaction between the two was obscured.

Many felt vulnerable without a way to stop the spread. Several commercial insecticides were available, but these were for individual use, not widespread spraying, and they could not stop the introduction of the ants into a new area, only ameliorate the danger once the insects were ensconced. Meanwhile, alternative control techniques were slow in coming. The USDA took twenty years to initiate a biological control program on a wide scale and there remains no measure of its effectiveness. The EPA, for its part, blocked the introduction of other alternative techniques. In the early 1970s, the biotechnology company Zoecon developed an analogue of a fire ant hormone, a chemical that would prevent ant larvae from developing into adults. The insect growth regulator, as it was called, was expensive to develop and had a smaller market than DDT and other such chemicals, since the hormone analogue could be used only against the imported fire ants. The EPA, however, following in Carson's tradition, was leery about introducing chemicals into the environment and required that the analogue undergo the same battery of tests applied to a broad-spectrum pesticide; and when Zoecon's president pleaded for grants to help fund the necessary studies, the EPA refused. The cost was prohibitive and the insect growth regulator did not make it to market. Other species-specific chemicals, lacking support from the EPA, experienced similar fates.[60]

The EPA, then, had banned the chemicals perceived to control the ants, prevented the development of alternative forms of control, and left the ants to spread. Now it was the EPA—not the USDA—that seemed staffed with bureaucrats unconcerned with civil liberties. The president of Zoecon made this point when he noted that the Soviet Union had asked his company to develop new pest control methods. The most communist country on earth recognized the innovative possibilities of his company, but an American bureaucracy could not see it. The USDA also exploited the growing resentment toward the EPA in an attempt to win back some of the power it had lost to the agency.[61] Here, too, was one of the roots that would develop into the Reagan-era backlash against environmentalism and the EPA, when the agency went into a decade long dormancy.[62] Exterminator-cum-House Whip Tom Delay, exercised at the ban on Mirex, charged the EPA with stifling necessary insect control operations under a pile of red tape. Texas Senator Phil Gramm also attacked the EPA's policy on the fire ant, both legislators looking for an excuse to eviscerate the regulatory bureaucracy.[63]

The EPA's loss of status was not as stark as it was for the control entomologists—the EPA remains the nation's largest regulatory body—nor was its failure as great—the EPA did take carcinogenic chemicals from the market—but the decline in legitimacy stemmed from the same cause. The biology of the ants and the human activities interacted in unexpected ways. The ants were not ecological innocents, ready to become well-behaved citizens. They were opportunists, exploiting the disruption of the bulldozer revolution and the constant building in the irrigated West. Failing to deal with the causes of the fire ant irruption, the EPA and environmental community saw their predictions founder and their legitimacy weaken.

Conclusion

In 1976, when Mississippi purchased the Mirex manufacturing plant, environmentalists believed that their prophecies had come true. The ideology of eradication had led to American socialism: a state owned a business. Journalists sympathetic to the anti-insecticide crusade labeled it "Magnolia-Scented Socialism." One newspaper wrote, "A losing effort to conquer a tiny, unconquerable insect has brought a strange and costly species of socialism to the Deep South. Today, the final citadel of this socialism is to be found, of all places, in Mississippi, whose politicians for decades urged the voters to resist any hint of socialism wherever it seemed to be nibbling at the woodwork of free enterprise."[64]

The situation, though, was not so easy to interpret. The imagined ends of the Cold War—victory, capitulation, or transformation—that had come to stand for the imagined ends of the fire ant wars were too restrictive: Magnolia-Scented Socialism collapsed. There was neither victory nor capitulation nor transformation as the ants continued to spread and entomologists continued to battle them in a country that continued to favor relatively weak bureaucratic governance. When it became clear that these imaginings were inadequate, a new view emerged, one less dedicated to castigating or praising the imported fire ants. A Texas entomologist encapsulated this new view when he wrote in the late 1970s that imported fire ants do not wear a white hat, nor a black one, but a gray hat. The insects do damage crops and they do attack young quail, but they also consume boll weevils.[65] This new, ambiguous ant is celebrated on the first Saturday of October each year in Marshall, Texas, when the city puts on a Fire Ant Festival. Participants are encouraged to vent their aggression toward the insects by tearing apart a stuffed ant. But they also choose a Miss Fire Ant in a beauty pageant, compete in a fire ant mating call contest, and judge a chili cook-off, in which each pot must contain at least one fire ant.[66] The environmentalist and singer-songwriter Bill Oliver has captured this image in song:

You who live in cities, you who live in neighborhoods
Fire ants, it's understood, may come and take their stand
The males that die in nuptials, the queens that come in multiples,
The fire ant, combustible, is hard to understand.[67]

The combined tools of the history of science and environmental history, however, make the story of the ants less hard to understand. Environmental history teaches the need to pay attention to the natural world and the effects humans have on it. History of science teaches the need to look at the social processes that are constitutive parts of scientific thought and work. Put together, these techniques reveal intricate and important interconnections between nature and science. The biology of the fire ants mattered, the insects misunderstood by both the USDA and its opponents: the ants were neither specially adapted mutants nor invented bogeymen, but opportunists following the bulldozer across the South. The social history of the groups mattered, too, for the fire ant wars were not about Rachel Carson speaking truth to power but about the clash of two different visions of nature, science, and the state.

The interaction of the humans and the fire ants mattered as well. The legitimacy of the USDA control entomologists and their various opponents rested on this interaction, reliant on a nature that did not always behave as predicted, responding instead to a combination of its own rhythms and the actions of humans. Over the past three decades, historians of science have shown how scientists gain and maintain cultural authority through rhetorical techniques and political machinations. A focus on nature adds a new category of analysis to this familiar repertoire: cultural authority depends, also, on interactions with nature, on making the material world perform in particular, specified ways. Historians of science need ways to integrate the natural world into their accounts to make sense of this—and other—aspects of science. Environmental history offers such tools, opening new paths in the field that build on the hard won victories of past generations and provide for even fuller historical narratives.

Notes

1. Rachel Carson, *Silent Spring* (Boston, Mass.: Houghton-Mifflin, 1962), 162. For histories of the fire ant wars, see Harrison Wellford, *Sowing the Wind* (New York, N.Y.: Grossman Publishers, 1972), 286–309; Phillip M. Boffey, *The Brain Bank of America: An Inquiry into the Politics of Science* (New York, N.Y.: McGraw-Hill Book Company, 1975), 200–226; Thomas R. Dunlap and Christopher J. Bosso, *Pesticides and Politics: The Life Cycle of a Public Issue* (Pittsburgh, Pa.: University of Pittsburgh Press, 1987), 85–90; Pete Daniel, "A Rogue Bureaucracy: The USDA Fire Ant Campaign of the Late 1950s," *Agricultural History* 64 (1990): 99–114; Elizabeth F. Shores, "The Red Imported Fire Ant: Mythology and Public Policy," *Arkansas Historical Quarterly* 53 (1994): 320–39; Pete Daniel, *Lost Revolutions: The South in the 1950s* (Chapel Hill: University of North Carolina Press, 2000), 78–87.

2. For an overview, see Jan Golinski, *Making Natural Knowledge: Constructivism and the History of Science* (New York, N.Y.: Cambridge University Press, 1998).

3. For examples of the integration of nature into narratives in the history of science, see Bruno Latour, *The Pasteurization of France*, trans. A. Sheridan and J. Law (Cambridge, Mass.: Harvard University Press, 1988); Robert Kohler, *Lords of the Fly: Drosophila Genetics and the Experimental Life* (Chicago, Ill.: University of Chicago Press, 1994); and Angela N. H. Creager, *The Life of a Virus: Tobacco Mosaic Virus as an Experimental Model, 1930–1965* (Chicago, Ill.: University of Chicago Press, 2002).

4. William Cronon, "The Uses of Environmental History," *Environmental History Review* 17 (1993): 1–22.

5. On this point, see Steven Shapin and Simon Schaffer, *Leviathan and the Air-Pump: Hobbes, Boyle, and the Experimental Life* (Princeton, N.J.: Princeton University Press, 1985), 15.

6. Henry Walter Bates, *The Naturalist on the River Amazons* (London, England: John Murray, [1863] 1892), 227. (The imported fire ants are no longer believed to be the same species as Bates saw.) Fire ant biology is reviewed in Stephen Welton Taber, *Fire Ants* (College Station: Texas A & M Press, 2000). For a fuller look at a more complicated taxonomic history, see chapter 2 of my dissertation, Joshua Blu Buhs, "The Fire Ant Wars: *Solenopsis* and the Nature of the American State, 1918–1982" (PhD diss., University of Pennsylvania, 2001).

7. The ecology of the region is from E. W. Shanahan, *South America: An Economic and Regional Geography with an Historical Chapter* (London: Methuen & Co., Ltd., 1927) (quote, p. 90) and A. A. Bonettos and I. R. Wais, "Southern South American Streams and Rivers," in *River and Stream Ecosystems*, ed. C. E. Cushing, K. W. Cummins, and G. W. Minshall, vol. 22 of *Ecosystems of the World*, ed. David W. Goodall (Amsterdam: Elsevier, 1995), 257–93. The comparison of the ants to weeds is from Walter Tschinkel, "The Ecological Nature of the Fire Ant: Some Aspects of Colony Function and Some Unanswered Questions," in *Fire Ants and Leaf-Cutting Ants: Biology and Management*, ed. C. S. Lofgren and R. K. Vander Meer (Boulder, Colo.: Westview, 1986), 72–87.

8. Ysabel F. Rennie, *The Argentine Republic* (Westport, Conn.: Greenwood Press, 1945), 142–50. For the migration of the ants, see F. E. Lennartz, "Modes of Dispersal of *Solenopsis invicta* from Brazil into the Continental United States—A Study in Spatial Diffusion" (master's thesis, University of Florida, 1973) and James C. Trager, "A Revision of the Fire Ants *Solenopsis geminata* Group (Hymenoptera: Formicidae: Myrmicinae)," *Journal of the New York Entomological Society* 99 (1991): 141–98.

9. A. H. Howell, "Physiography, 1908," Box 1, Folder 17, Fish and Wildlife Service, USDI Field Reports, 1887–1961, Series I, Record Group 7176, Smithsonian Institution Archives.

10. Edward L. Ullman, "Mobile: Industrial Seaport and Trade Center" (PhD diss., University of Chicago, 1942), 46.

11. On the natural history of the area, see Ecological Society of America, Committee on the Preservation of Natural Conditions, *Naturalist's Guide to the Americas*, ed. Victor E. Shelford (Baltimore, Md.: Williams and Wilkins, 1926); Merle J. Prunty, "The Renaissance of the Southern Plantation," *Geographical Review* 45 (1955): 459–91.

12. William Steel Creighton to Murray S. Blum, 22 April 1968, William Steel Creighton papers, an unprocessed box of material incorporated in the uncatalogued E. O. Wilson papers, Library of Congress (hereafter Creighton papers).

13. The first quotation is from Pete Daniel, *Standing at the Crossroads: Southern Life in the Twentieth Century* (New York, N.Y.: Hill and Wang, 1986), 136–37, the second from C. Vann Woodward, *The Burden of Southern History*, 3rd ed. (Baton Rouge: Louisiana State University Press, 1993), 6. The changes are documented in Pete Daniel, *Breaking the Land: The Transformation of Cotton, Tobacco, and Rice Cultures since 1880* (Urbana: University of Illinois Press, 1985); Jack Temple Kirby, *Rural Worlds Lost: The American South, 1920–1960* (Baton Rouge: Louisiana State University Press, 1987); Albert E. Cowdrey, *This Land, This South: An Environmental History* (Lexington: University Press of Kentucky, 1996).

14. Edward O. Wilson and William L. Brown, "Recent Changes in the Population of the Fire Ant *Solenopsis saevissima* (Fr. Smith)," *Evolution* 12 (1958): 211–18; William F. Buren et al., "Zoogeography of the Imported Fire Ants," *Journal of the New York Entomological Society* 82 (1974): 113–24; Henry W. Lawrence, "The Geography of the U.S. Nursery Industry: Locational Change and Regional Specialization in the Production of Woody Ornamental Plants" (PhD diss., University of Oregon, 1985).

15. "Fire Ants Spread as Pastures Shrink," *Montgomery Advertiser*, 17 February 1957, and "Maxwell Reports Plague of Fire Ants; 3 in Hospital," 14 March 1957, box 62, fire ants—news items, Plant Pest Control Division papers, RG 463, 86/6/3, National Archives and Records Administration, College Park, Maryland (hereafter PPC papers).

16. Undated notes and W. G. Bruce, H. T. Vanderford, and A. L. Smith, "Survey of the Imported Fire Ant *Solenopsis saevissima* var. *richteri* Forel," Special Report S-6, 19 November 1948, in early fire ant records file, E. O. Wilson papers, unprocessed, Library of Congress (hereafter Wilson papers); Edward O. Wilson and James H. Eads Jr., "A Preliminary Report on the Fire Ant Survey," Alabama Department of Conservation, SG 9977, Alabama Department of Archives and History, Montgomery, Alabama

(hereafter ALDoC papers); Sanford D. Porter et al., "Intercontinental Differences in the Abundance of Solenopsis Fire Ants (Hymenoptera: Formicidae): Escape from Natural Enemies?" *Environmental Entomology* 26 (1997): 373–84.

17. On the ecology of invasions, see Charles S. Elton, *The Ecology of Invasions by Animals and Plants* (London: Chapman and Hall, [1958], 1977); R. Groves and J. Burdon, eds., *Ecology of Biological Invasions* (Cambridge: Cambridge University Press, 1984).

18. Sanford D. Porter and D. A. Savignano, "Invasion of Polygyne Fire Ants Decimates Native Ants and Disrupts Arthropod Community," *Ecology* 71 (1990): 2095–2106; Rodger Lyle Brown, "Fire Ants: Buggy Battalions Beating Mere Mortals," *Atlanta Journal-Constitution*, 21 June 1992, M/02; Kenneth G. Ross and Laurent Keller, "Ecology and Evolution of Social Organization: Insights from Fire Ants and Other Highly Eusocial Insects," *Annual Review of Ecology and Systematics* 26 (1995): 631–56.

19. This interpretation of the 1950s is based on Paul A. Carter, *Another Part of the Fifties* (New York, N.Y.: Columbia University Press, 1983) and Michael Sherry, *In the Shadow of War: The United States Since the 1930s* (New Haven, Conn.: Yale University Press, 1995).

20. George C. Decker, "Pesticides Relationship to Conservation Programs," *National Agricultural Chemicals Association News and Pesticide Review*, May 1959: 4–7, 13–14, quotation on 7; John L. George, *The Program to Eradicate the Imported Fire Ant: Preliminary Observations* (New York, N.Y.: The Conservation Foundation, 1958); W. L. Popham and David G. Hall, "Insect Eradication Programs," *Annual Review of Entomology* 3 (1958): 335–54; "Conservation Through Pest Control," 3 June 1958, box 82, information—speeches file and Woodrow O. Owen to Spears, 13 June 1960, box 128, fire ant-wildlife file, PPC papers.

21. O. G. McBeath to E. D. Burgess, 17 December 1958, box 197, fire ant file, PPC papers. For more on the distinction between control and research entomologists and the rise of the eradication ideal, see John H. Perkins, *Insects, Experts, and the Insecticide Crisis: The Quest for New Pest Management Strategies* (New York, N.Y.: Plenum Press, 1982).

22. Byron T. Shaw, "Development of Research Facilities and the Role of Regional Laboratories in State and Federal Programs," 10 November 1958, box 34, speeches file, Entomology Research Division: General Correspondence, 1954–1958, 5 (UD), Agricultural Research Service Papers, RG 310, NARA (hereafter ARS papers).

23. C. C. Fancher to E. D. Burgess, 27 June 1958, box 198, fire ant-wildlife losses file, and Fancher to J. F. Spears, 7 June 1960, fire ant—1 file (1960), both in PPC papers. On Wilson's work, see Edward O. Wilson, "Invader of the South," *Natural History* 68 (1959): 276–81; *idem*, "The Fire Ant," *Scientific American* 198 (1958): 36–41, 160. On the importance of calling the insects mutants, see portion of a letter to J. Lloyd Abbot, 27 June 1957, box 62, fire ant file; Wilson to Robert L. Burlap, 11 January 1959; Wilson to Clifford Lofgren, 11 February 1959; and Wilson to E. D. Burgess, 11 February 1959, box 213, fire ant file; Wilson to Philip Charam, 14 July 1964, box 247, imported fire ant—10 file, all in PPC papers.

24. "Of Ants and Men," *The Christian Century* 74 (13 November 1957): 1339 (first quotation); "Fire Ants Sting Congress into Action," *Dayton Daily News*, box 62, fire ant—news items file, PPC papers (second quotation); John Foster, "Secrets of the Fire Ant," *Mississippi Game & Fish* 19 (July 1957): 4–5 (third quotation). See also Greg Mitman, "Defining the Organism in the Welfare State: The Politics of Individuality in American Culture, 1890–1950," in *Biology as Society, Society as Biology*, ed. Sabine Maasen, Everett Mendelsohn, and Peter Weingart (Dordrecht and Boston, Mass.: Kluwer Academic Publishers, 1995), 249–78.

25. Gary Alan Fine and Lazaros Christoforides, "Dirty Birds, Filthy Immigrants, and the English Sparrow War: Metaphorical Linkage in Constructing Social Problems," *Symbolic Interaction* 14 (1991): 375–93; Edmund P. Russell, *War and Nature: Fighting Humans and Insects with Chemicals from World War I to Silent Spring* (New York, N.Y.: Cambridge University Press, 2001).

26. The phrase was ubiquitous in the USDA, but for one example, see W. L. Popham to Lister Hill, 18 January 1957, box 752, regulatory crops-1-–fire ants file, General Correspondence, 1954–1966, 1 (UD), ARS papers.

27. The story was widely printed. For an example, see box 62, fire ant—news clippings file, PPC papers.

28. John Devlin, "Fire Ant Alarms South," *New York Times*, 19 March 1957, 40.

29. Susan Flader, *Thinking Like a Mountain: Aldo Leopold and the Evolution of an Ecological Attitude Toward Deer, Wolves, and Forests* (Madison: University of Wisconsin Press, 1974); Thomas R. Dunlap, *Saving America's Wildlife: Ecology and the American Mind, 1850–1990* (Princeton, N.J.: Princeton University Press, 1988).

30. W. Conner Sorenson, *Brethren of the Net: American Entomology, 1840–1880* (Tuscaloosa: University of Alabama Press, 1995).

31. Paul B. Sears, "The Road Ahead in Conservation," *Audubon* 58 (March–April 1956): 58–59, 80; Alfred G. Etter, "A Protest against Spraying," *Audubon* 61 (July–August 1959): 153; Robert Rudd, "The Indirect Effects of Chemicals in Nature," in "The Effects of Toxic Pesticides on Wildlife," p. 16, box 35, file 583, Rachel Carson papers, YCAL 46, Beinecke Rare Book Library, Yale University (hereafter Carson papers); *idem*, "The Irresponsible Poisoners," *The Nation* 188 (1959): 496–97; Samuel P. Hays, *Beauty, Health, and Permanence: Environmental Politics in the United States, 1955–1985* (New York, N.Y.: Cambridge University Press, 1987).

32. Clarence Cottam, "A Conservationist's Views on the New Insecticides," in *Biological Problems in Water Pollution*, ed. C. M. Tarzwell (Washington, D.C.: U.S. Department of Health, Education, and Welfare, 1960), 42–45; John L. George, "The Pesticide Problem: Wildlife—The Community of Living Things," May–June 1960, box 135, folder 221 file, Paul B. Sears papers, 663, Manuscripts and Archives, Yale University.

33. Willhelmine Kirby Waller, "Poison on the Land," *Audubon* 60 (March–April 1958): 68–70; Bill Ziebach, "Fire Ant Problem," *Mobile Press-Register*, 22 June 1958, 6B; "Farmers Protest Fire Ant Control Program 'Throat-Ramming,'" *Conservation News* 23

(15 August 1958): 4–5; "Experiments of USDA Violate Individual Rights," 11 February 1961, box 94, fire ant—8 file, PPC papers.

34. Research at Auburn is covered in Frank S. Arant, Kirby L. Hays, and Dan W. Speake, "Facts about the Imported Fire Ant," *Highlights of Agricultural Research* 5 (1958): 12–13; "The Present Status of the Imported Fire Ant, *Solenopsis saevissima richteri* Forel, in Argentina," Report to the Governor, 16 June 1958; Gene Stevenson, press release, 21 February 1958; and Kenneth B. Roy, press release, 24 April 1958, all in box 2, Ralph B. Draughon papers, RG 107, Auburn University Archives (hereafter Draughon papers); Albert S. Johnson, "Antagonistic Relationships between Ants and Wildlife with Special Reference to Imported Fire Ants and Bobwhite Quail in the Southeast," *Proceedings of the Annual Conference of the Southeastern Association of Game and Fish Commissioners* 15 (1961): 88–107. Other research can be tracked in S. D. Hensley et al., "Effects of Insecticides on the Predaceous Arthropod Fauna of Louisiana Sugarcane Fields," *Journal of Economic Entomology* 54 (1961): 146–49; Leo Dale Newsom to Philip Charam, 17 July 1964, box 247, imported fire ant—10 file, PPC papers.

35. Wilson to Carson, 14 May 1959, and Wilson to Carson, 23 October 1958, both in box 44, folder 841, Carson papers; Carson, *Silent Spring*, 163.

36. Carson to J. Lloyd Abbot, 6 October 1961, folder 1586, Carson papers.

37. Rachel Carson, "How about Citizenship Papers for the Starling?" *Nature Magazine* 32 (June–July 1939): 317–19.

38. E. O. Wilson, then at Harvard University, and the USDA entomologists both dismissed the discoveries. See portion of a letter to J. Lloyd Abbot, 27 June 1957, box 62, fire ant file; E. O. Wilson to Philip Charam, 14 July 1964, box 247, imported fire ant—10 file, both in PPC papers.

39. Carson, *Silent Spring*, 7; Ralph H. Allen Jr., "The Fire Ant Eradication Program and its Effect on Fish and Wildlife," fire ant file, Alabama Department of Conservation papers, 1943–1951, ALDoC papers, SG 17018; Daniel H. Janzen, "Effects of the Fire Ant Eradication Program upon Wildlife," 25 May 1958, in box 30, fire ant file, Entomology Research Division: General Correspondence, 1954–1958, 5 (UD), ARS papers; Walter Rosene, "Whistling-Cock Counts of Bobwhite Quail on Areas Treated with Insecticides and Untreated Areas, Decatur County, Georgia," *Proceedings of the Southeastern Association of Game and Fish Commissioners* 12 (1958): 240–44.

40. Michael Hogan, *A Cross of Iron: Harry S. Truman and the Origins of the National Security State, 1945–1954* (New York, N.Y.: Cambridge University Press, 1998).

41. Carson, *Silent Spring*, 127, emphasis in original. Clarence Cottam, "Pesticides and Wildlife," 21–23 February 1960, Carson papers, box 35, file 581; Abbot to Members of the Board of Directors—Alabama Wildlife Federation, 24 June 1959, box 1, Abbot file; Correspondence of Assistant Secretary for Fish and Wildlife Ross L. Leffler, 790 (AI), Secretary of Interior papers, RG 48, National Archives and Records Administration II, College Park, Maryland (hereafter USDI papers), emphasis in original.

42. Margaret W. Rossiter, "The Organization of Agricultural Sciences," in *The Organization of Knowledge in Modern America*, ed. John Voss and Alexandra Oleson (Baltimore, Md.: Johns Hopkins University Press, 1979), 211–48.

43. Maurice F. Baker, "New Fire Ant Bait," 1963, box 165, fire ant file—5—coopera-tion file; Jamie L. Whitten, *That We May Live* (Princeton, N.J.: Van Nostrand Press, 1966), 115; Harrison Wellford, "Pesticides," in *Nixon and the Environment: The Politics of Devastation*, ed. James Rathelsberger (New York: Taurus Communications, 1972), 146–62.

44. J. Brooks Flippen, *Nixon and the Environment* (Albuquerque: University of New Mexico Press, 2000).

45. "Toxic Substances: EPA and OSHA Are Reluctant Regulators," *Science* 203 (1979): 28–32; Dunlap, *DDT.*

46. William A. Butler to Executive Committee and Executive Director, 11 May 1973, box 68, correspondence (from July 1, 1971) file and Lee Rogers to Charlie Wurster, 29 May 1973, box 71, correspondence, internal file, both in Environmental Defense Fund papers, MS 232, State University of New York, Stony Brook (hereafter EDF papers).

47. Deborah Shapley, "Mirex and the Fire Ant: Declines in the Fortune of a 'Perfect' Pesticide," *Science* 172 (1971): 358–60; K. L. E. Kaiser, "The Rise and Fall of Mirex," *Environmental Science and Technology* 12 (1978): 520–28. On the EPA's preoccupation with cancer, see Edmund P. Russell, "Lost among the Parts Per Billion: Ecological Protection at the United States Environmental Protection Agency, 1970–1993," *Environmental History* 2 (1997): 29–51.

48. William F. Buren to Creighton, 24 April 1972, Creighton papers (quote, em-phasis in original); William F. Buren, "Revisionary Studies on the Taxonomy of the Imported Fire Ants," *Journal of the Georgia Entomological Society* 7 (1972): 1–26; Joshua Blu Buhs, "Building on Bedrock: William Steel Creighton and the Reformation of Ant Systematics, 1925–1970," *Journal of the History of Biology* 33 (2000): 27–70.

49. William L. Brown to W. Wallace Harrington, 7 May 1973, and "Environmen-tal Defense Fund Response to 1972 Environmental Impact Statement," 17 February 1973, both in *Miscellaneous Publications and Unpublished Documents Relating to the Use of Mirex to Control the Imported Fire Ant in the USA*, Comstock Library, Cornell University.

50. "Fire Ant War Lost by U.S.," 29 September 1975, box 73, Mirex—press releases file, EDF papers, and "Fire Ants: Vietnam of Entomology," news clippings, MDAC pa-pers.

51. Shapley, "Mirex and the Fire Ant," 359; "South Still Fights Its Longest War, Learns to Live with Surly Fire Ants," 28 June 1976, news reports file, MDAC papers; Wil-liam A. Banks et al., "An Improved Mirex Bait Formulation for Control of Imported Fire Ants," *Environmental Entomology* 2 (1973): 182–85; "Human Tissue Shows Mirex," 16 July 1976, and "Mirex Found in Bodies Fuels Pesticide Controversy," 8 July 1976, both in box b194, Mirex file, NAS papers; "Mirex Found in 44 per cent of Mississippi-ans," 25 August 1976, box 73, Mirex—press releases file, EDF papers; "Mississippi Back in Mirex Business," n.d.; "State Asks EPA to Ban Mirex Use in Two Years," n.d.; and "Mirex's Phase out," n.d., all in news reports file, MDAC papers.

52. Lamar J. Padget to E. D. Burgess, 11 March 1959, and Padget to W. E. Blasin-game, 29 June 1959, box 213, fire ant file, PPC papers.

53. "Appraisal Survey of the Cooperative Fire Ant Program, September, 1960, Summary and Comments," 12 October 1960, fire ant file, 1960, PPC papers.

54. "Fire Ant Control," report no. 62 (Ames, Iowa: Council for Agricultural Science and Technology, 1976); and Anne-Marie A. Callcott and Homer L. Collins, "Invasion and Range Expansion of Imported Fire Ants (Hymenoptera: Formicidae) in North America from 1918–1995," *Florida Entomologist* 79 (1996): 238–51.

55. Fancher to E. D. Burgess, 20 May 1958, box 197, fire ant—Southern region file, PPC papers.

56. Shepherd to F. J. Mulhern, 5 May 1969, box 260, file 8, PPC papers; John A. Schmittker to George Mehren et al., 27 October 1967, box 4679, insects (October) file, SOA papers.

57. Wellford, *Sowing the Wind*, 302–3.

58. "Fire Ants: The Experts Throw up Their hands," *U.S. News and World Report*, 17 January 1977, 79; Alan Huffman, "Environment May Pay the Price in Fire Ant War," *Clarion-Ledger*, 4 November 1988; Sanford D. Porter, David F. Williams, and R. S. Patterson, "Rearing the Decapitating Fly *Pseudacteon tricuspis* (Diptera: Phoridae) in Imported Fire Ants (Hymenoptera: Formicidae) from the United States," *Journal of Economic Entomology* 90 (1997): 135–38.

59. William P. Mackay and Richard Fagerlund, "Range Expansion of the Red Imported Fire Ant, *Solenopsis invicta* Buren (Hymenoptera: Formicidae), into New Mexico and Extreme Western Texas," *Proceedings of the Entomological Society of Washington* 99 (1997): 757–58; Deborah Schoch, "Fire-Ant Fear on the March in Western States," *Los Angeles Times*, Orange County Edition, 7 February 1999.

60. Gene Bylinsky, "Zoecon Turns Bugs against Themselves," *Fortune* 88 (August 1973): 94–103; Carl Djerassi to Robert Long, 12 November 1973, box 5855, insects, April 19 to July 16 file, and Carl Djerassi, Christina Shih Coleman, and John Diekman, "Operational and Policy Aspects of Future Insect Control Methods," 12 February 1974, box 5855, insects, April 19 to July 16 file, both in SOA papers; "John Diekman, Direct Testimony," 21 February 1974, box 68, summaries file, EDF papers; Carl Djerassi to Paul A. Vander Myde, 14 May 1974, box 5855, insects, April 19 to July 16 file, SOA papers. For similar complaints against the EPA, see Marc K. Lansy, Marc J. Roberts, Mark K. Landy, and Stephen R. Thomas, *The Environmental Protection Agency: Asking the Wrong Questions from Nixon to Clinton*, expanded ed. (New York, N.Y.: Oxford University Press, 1994), and Mark Winston, *Nature Wars: People vs. Pests* (Cambridge, Mass.: Harvard University Press, 1997), 158–59.

61. Carl Djerassi to Robert Long, 14 February 1974, box 5855, insects, April 19 to July 16 file, SOA papers; U.S. Congress, Subcommittee on Department Operations, Investigations and Oversights, Committee on Agriculture, *Fire Ant Eradication Program*, 94-1, 1975; "The Year of Insects," editorial, *The Wall Street Journal*, 15 August 1978.

62. Hays, *Beauty, Health, and Permanence*, 491–526.

63. Nancy Mathis, "EPA under House Siege; DeLay Plans to Lead Assault for Changes in Environmental Policy, Agency Funding," *Houston Chronicle*, STAR edition,

8 October 1995, 13A; Scott Norvell, "Force of Nature," *The Washington Post* Magazine, 23 June 1996, 14.

64. "Mississippi to Make Pesticide," 12 May 1976, box 71, correspondence, internal file, EDF papers; "'Magnolia-Scented Socialism' Invades Mississippi," news reports file, MDAC papers; "Solenopsis the Unconquerable," July–August 1976, box 73, Mirex—press releases file, EDF papers.

65. W. L. Sterling, "Imported Fire Ant . . . May Wear a Grey Hat," *Texas Agricultural Progress* 24 (1978): 19–20.

66. Suzanne Gamboa, "Fire Ant Festival Offers a Chance for Revenge: 45,000 Expected at Marshall's Weekend Party," *Dallas Morning News*, 3 October 1988; Richard Conniff, "You Never Know What the Fire Ant Is Going to Do Next," *Smithsonian*, July 1990, 48–57.

67. Bill Oliver and the Otter Space Band, "Queen Invicta (Fireant Invincible)" on "Have to Have a Habitat" (Texas Deck Music, BMI, 1995).

EILEEN MAURA MCGURTY

From NIMBY to Civil Rights

The Origins of the Environmental

Justice Movement

IN THE SUMMER of 1978, Robert Burns and his two sons drove liquid tanker trucks along rural roads in thirteen North Carolina counties and through remote sections of the Fort Bragg Military Reservation. Driving at night to avoid detection, they opened the bottom valve of the tankers and discharged liquid contaminated with polychlorinated biphenyls (PCBs) removed from the Ward Transformer Company in Raleigh onto the soil along the road shoulders. This violation of the Toxic Substance Control Act (TSCA) continued for nearly two weeks until 240 miles of road shoulders were contaminated. Robert Ward had hired the Burnses to illegally dispose of the contaminated liquid in an attempt to avoid the escalating cost of disposal that was due, in part, to increasing regulation of hazardous waste.[1] Since the contamination occurred on state-owned property, North Carolina was responsible for remediation. Within a few months after detecting the contamination, the state devised a plan calling for the construction of a landfill in Warren County, a rural area in northeastern North Carolina with a majority of poor, African-American residents. Warren County also suffered the most contamination of any of the thirteen counties affected by the illegal disposal. A farmer in the small community of Afton, facing a foreclosure and bankruptcy, sold his property to the state for use as a final resting place for the contaminated soil.[2]

The announcement of this disposal site sparked intense resistance from county residents concerned with the possible contamination of their groundwater and the potential threat to local economic development from

{ 372 }

the stigma of a hazardous waste facility. After three years of legal battles unsuccessfully waged by Warren County against North Carolina and the U.S. Environmental Protection Agency (EPA), the state was permitted to begin construction of the landfill in the summer of 1982. When it became apparent that the standard processes of recourse would not stop the forty thousand cubic yards of soil from being buried at the site, citizens of Warren County changed their oppositional strategy to disruptive collective action. In the process of planning for the protest events, they also shifted their primary rationale for opposing the site. While threats to groundwater and the local economy were still worries for the citizens, the disruptive action focused on environmental racism. Protesters argued that Warren County was chosen, in part, because the residents were primarily poor and African-American. As one activist put it, "The community was politically and economically unempowered; that was the reason for the siting. They took advantage of poor people and people of color."[3] The citizens garnered support from regional and national civil rights leaders and organized protest events daily during the six-week period while soil was delivered to the landfill. The unrelenting protests resulted in a delay and disruption of the land-filling project, with nearly five hundred arrests and significant state and national media coverage, but they failed to stop the landfill.

Despite the failure of the protests to reach the immediate objective, the controversy over the Warren County landfill had a major impact on contemporary environmental activism and the environmental policy agenda. The events in Warren County are proclaimed by activists and policymakers alike as the birth of the environmental justice movement.[4] Environmental justice activists argue that the inequitable distribution of environmental degradation and systematic exclusion of the poor and people of color from environmental decision making is perpetuated by traditional environmental organizations, also known as mainstream environmentalism, and by environmental regulatory agencies.[5] The topic seemed to explode overnight, creating the perception that environmental justice has shaped an original challenge to the contemporary environmental discussion. In reality, potential negative social impacts of both environmental degradation and regulatory policies have been at the core of environmental discussions since the onset of the modern environmental era. Charges of racism, exclusion, elitism, and regressive policies had been leveled against mainstream environmentalists and regulatory agencies prior to the emergence of the activism identified as "environmental justice."

These conflicts first emerged between 1968 and 1975, a period of heightened environmental and social activism. Within this context, the conflict in Warren County transformed the relationship between mainstream environmentalists and the civil rights movement. Civil rights leaders incorporated an environmental aspect into the civil rights agenda, motivated by the nature of the toxic contamination, the national and local political landscape, and the direct conflict with government agencies responsible for environmentally related decisions. As civil rights leaders with influence among African-Americans and within the established political system integrated the new notion of environmental racism into their program, the cause gained legitimacy and strength. In addition to the transformation of the African-American agenda, the local, primarily white residents working against the landfill incorporated civil rights claims as part of their environmental cause in order to keep their opposition alive with the help of experienced civil rights activists. Although the bulwark between civil rights and environmentalism began to weaken, the conflicts of the period from 1968 to 1975 did not completely disappear with the emergence of the contemporary environmental justice movement. The well-established, mainstream environmental organizations did not have any part in either the embrace of environmentalism by civil rights activists or the embrace of a civil rights agenda by local environmentalists. As a result, the "marriage of social justice with environmentalism" remains a rocky union between ambivalent partners.

The Conflicts Erupt, 1968–1975

Although specific cases vary, evidence indicates that the processes of environmental degradation and social marginalization are interwoven in various cultural and historical contexts.[6] In the United States, discussions about the disproportionate impact of environmental degradation and environmental reform on the poor and people of color occurred in full force in the late 1960s when "environmentalist" became a meaningful identity and part of the public discourse. The ideological clashes between "those who seek environmental quality" and "those who seek social justice" emerged as a concrete conflict over the exclusive membership and staff of major environmental organizations and the regressive impacts of certain environmental policies.[7]

Soon after the 1970 Earth Day euphoria, many claimed that environmentalism had been a fad and was now on the way out. To counter this attack, environmentalists tried to demonstrate that environmentalism appealed to a broad constituency. Common speculation held that environmental organizations had an elite membership and staff. This supposition led to one of two conclusions. Either environmental organizations explicitly excluded the poor and people of color or the environmental agenda simply was not relevant to their lives. These suspicions of elitism were confirmed in 1973 when the EPA commissioned the National Center for Voluntary Action (NCVA) to examine environmental volunteerism with the goal of strengthening the movement. The study found that newly formed groups, as well as older "conservation" organizations that had recently changed their priorities and approaches, were staffed primarily by "middle-class, professional, white, married men in their thirties."[8]

The NCVA realized that this narrow base of support was a potential obstacle for the environmental movement and strongly encouraged organizations to consider the needs of the poor, especially poor minorities in urban areas; however, the report only addressed these concerns in one of its twenty-eight recommendations. The NCVA wanted Volunteers in Service to America (VISTA) to include volunteers for work on environmental issues. Anticipating the argument that such work might divert funds from other social projects, its leaders suggested a separate and independent arm for environmental volunteers. By separating the two programs, the recommendation gave credence to the view that environmental degradation and poverty should be seen as isolated issues with different solutions.

The lack of diversity in the membership of environmental organizations was a concern even before the findings of the NCVA were published. In 1972, Tom Bradley, an African-American member of the Los Angeles City Council and future mayor, asked members of the Sierra Club why "to many of our nation's 20 million blacks, the conservation movement has as much appeal as a segregated bus," especially since "the problems of poverty and environmental quality are inextricably interrelated."[9] A few months later, the Sierra Club conducted a survey of its members to determine which general direction the membership wanted the organization to take. In light of the ongoing claims of elitism, the surveyors also felt compelled to document the socioeconomic backgrounds of their members. The average club member fit the predicted profile exactly.[10] The club responded with the assertion that, while all social groups were not represented in the membership, the actions of the organization were taken on behalf of everyone. The simpler and less destructive style of outdoor recreation advocated and practiced by club members enabled more people to enjoy the outdoors. The issue of access was not addressed. Instead, the club urged members to boost recruitment efforts among minorities and immediately enroll anyone who thought the Sierra Club had restrictive membership policies. Despite these efforts, when the members were asked "Should the Club concern itself with the conservation problems of such special groups as the urban poor and ethnic minorities?" the majority of members, 58 percent of respondents, did not agree. Posing the question in terms of "special groups" contradicted the idea that Sierra Club activities would benefit everyone, regardless of their association with the organization. While actions to improve outdoor recreation opportunities or increase wilderness acreage were seen as a benefit to all, ameliorating urban environmental decay was not identified with the betterment of all, only select "special groups." The environmental problems of the "urban poor and ethnic minorities" belonged to them, not to everyone.

With the survey results seemingly confirming charges of elitism, the club found a glimmer of hope in younger members, who were more likely to agree that the organization should be involved in issues of concern to the urban poor. Another survey supported the club's hope that attitudes about the relationship between poverty and environmentalism were changing. Eighty-eight percent of black high school seniors polled in 1971 wanted to see increased federal involvement in controlling pollution. Concern for pollution among these students outranked "eliminating poverty" (76 percent) or achieving school desegregation (73 percent). This survey did not indicate decreasing elitism among conservationists; instead, it indicated that environmental degradation impacted the daily lives of people of color and that actions to improve environmental conditions were not adequate.

The Audubon Society also felt compelled to ward off claims of elitism, but it employed a different strategy. Although environmental action, especially action in the courts, was taken on behalf of all, the society acknowledged that environmental activists were elite in one sense: "Naturally the well-to-do are often best equipped to press these issues because [it] take[s] time, know-how and money. But this does not make the results less applicable to the people as a whole."[11] The suggestion that mainstream environmental organizations would act as a "van guard" was a controversial proposition at best. Mobilizing resources—technical and political knowledge, time, and money—might be seen as the underlying problem facing social movements, but the solution did not necessarily lie in an elite leadership. Another approach might entail nurturing leadership among the poor and people of color, as well as empowering them to mobilize the necessary resources themselves.

The popular press highlighted the divide between white and black activists. In August 1970, just months after the first Earth Day, *Time* covered "The Rise of Anti-ecology."[12] While the article described a political backlash from both the left and the right, the piece mainly argued that "blacks are the most vocal opponents of all." First, a "black militant" was quoted: "I don't give a good goddam about ecology!" Next, the article quoted two influential black leaders, Carl Stokes, mayor of Cleveland, and Richard Hatcher, mayor of Gary, Indiana. Stokes argued that housing and food for the hungry should be priorities over clean air and water, and Hatcher echoed this sentiment: "The nation's concern with environment has done what George Wallace was unable to do: distract the nation from the human problems of black and brown Americans."[13] This "trade-off" perspective posed economic survival and environmental amelioration as separate problems rather than focusing on the connections between economic deprivation and environmental degradation, as Tom Bradley had proposed to members of the Sierra Club, and it begged a serious question: Who would pay for the cost of pollution control and cleanup? In particular, when the Nixon administration estimated that such an operation would require $2.4 billion, public outcries arose against tax increases and higher consumer prices. These impacts from environmental regulation appeared regressive and disproportionately harmful to the poor and people of color.[14]

Warren County and the Emergence of Environmental Justice, 1978–1983

During the six weeks of protests in Warren County, North Carolina, in the autumn of 1982, white land owners joined together with black residents and civil rights activists to produce a significant disruptive collective action. The process of coming together transformed the two parties in the coalition and loosened the strict boundaries between environmental and civil rights causes. Civil rights activists embraced an environmental perspective as a result of a toxic threat to the daily lives of African-Americans and through their direct conflict with government agencies responsible for environmental decisions. Local whites, who began their opposition with the narrow focus of keeping hazardous waste out of their community, expanded their resistance to include a concern for inadvertent racist ramifications of some environmental policies. The political landscape for African-Americans at the local and national levels, the emerging toxic construct, and the economic instability of the county all contributed to the transformative moment. This new movement for environmental justice emerged from the lived experience of the residents of this rural, poor county in North Carolina and their connections to powerful African-Americans, not from mainstream environmental groups. This union of two causes which emerged from the Warren County events was partly in conflict with the traditional environmental organizations involved in the case. The conflict is still reflected in the ongoing tension between the two causes as they seek common ground.

The Remediation Process: Expediency and Uncertainty

The Toxic Substance Control Act of 1976 banned the manufacture of PCBs and regulated the disposal of PCB-contaminated soil in landfills. Within these federal constraints, there were still several options available to North Carolina in its effort to clean up the 240 miles of contaminated soil. The soil could be moved to an approved hazardous waste landfill. With the nearest site located in Emelle, Alabama, this option was assumed to be too expensive. Since the contamination was spread throughout thirteen counties, the state could have constructed multiple landfills. The logistic complications and probable expense deemed this option unfeasible as well, forcing the state to find one site. Government officials examined state-owned property within the central counties and issued a plea to citizens and local governments to volunteer tracts of land. Over ninety sites were examined as potential locations.[15]

Within a few months, the choices were limited to two sites. One of these was the Afton site in Warren County owned by Carter and Linda Pope. As early as October 1978, the Division of State Property began negotiations with the Popes and signed an option to buy on December 1, 1978.[16] The second site was a six-acre section of the Chatham County sanitary landfill. Since the Chatham County site was publicly owned, final approval to sell the property was subject to input by county residents. At a public hearing on December 11, 1978, they voiced strong opposition to the plan to sell part of the landfill to the state. The following day, the county commissioners withdrew their offer, and the state submitted its request to the EPA for a permit to construct the landfill on the Popes' farm.[17]

The choice of the Warren County site was shaped by the state's need to immediately deal with the contamination and uncertainty over how to pay for this remediation. The drive for expediency emerged in part from concerns about a potential public health crisis and the possibility of a significant loss to the agriculturally dependent communities adjacent to the contaminated roads. These two issues, coupled with a desire to avoid a public relations debacle, motivated the state to move as quickly as possible.[18] The Comprehensive Emergency Response, Compensation, and Liability Act of 1980, popularly known as Superfund, had not yet been conceived, although the North Carolina contamination catastrophe added to the impetus for its eventual passage in 1980. In 1978, there was no federal assistance available, but by the time the landfill was actually constructed in 1982, the North Carolina roadways had been placed on the "National Priority List" of contaminated sites in need of remediation, making their cleanup eligible for 90 percent funding through Superfund. Four years earlier, when the state was searching for answers, no one could have foreseen this complete transformation in environmental policy.

The Popes' land was available and relatively inexpensive, and the sale was not subject to public review. Purchase of the property also helped the state avoid the sticky problem of using eminent domain. While it was important to state officials that the landfill be located in a sparsely populated area, finding a location with little potential for resistance was not a major concern. Expediency was vital, but in 1978 there was not much reason to expect that public outcry would significantly delay the project. Based on the experience of hazardous waste management in the 1970s, waste facility siting faced only limited obstacles from local residents and had not encountered a major difficulty.[19] While Warren County was one of five counties in North Carolina with a majority of African-American residents, it was also among the poorest and agriculturally least productive. Given the agricultural downturn and economic recession of the 1970s and the already problematic economic situation in the county, it was not surprising that a farmer in Warren County was willing to sell his property to the state in an effort to regain financial security.

The Popes' property was a quick answer to a difficult problem, but it was not necessarily the best place to put a landfill. Without any idea of how to pay for remediation, the state tried to keep the costs as low as possible. As a result, the permit application requested waivers for three out of five regulations governing landfill construction: the distance to groundwater, the underliner leachate collection, and the artificial liner. The state asked for the exemptions on the premise that the extremely low permeability of the clay would amply protect the groundwater.[20] Eventually, through the court case and the environmental impact statement, the design was changed, and the landfill was built with a plastic liner and a double leachate collection system, one above the liner and one below. The landfill was also redesigned to include a plastic and clay liner on the sides and the top.

The Initial Opposition: "Not In My Backyard!"

The initial protest in Warren County began typically, as a narrowly defined, self-interested response to a local threat: "We don't want that facility in our backyards." Residents were primarily concerned with public health repercussions from potential groundwater contamination and negative economic impacts of a waste facility near their homes. The fear of contamination was fueled by the timing of the North Carolina incident: the dumping of the PCB-contaminated liquid occurred exactly at the same time when hazardous waste became a household word as a result of the Love Canal catastrophe in August 1978. In Love Canal, New York, a community just southeast of Niagara Falls, a housing subdivision and public school were built adjacent to an area used by the Hooker Chemical Company to dispose of over forty-three million pounds of industrial wastes. By the 1970s, this toxic material had seeped into the homes and the school, creating significant health problems for residents, including asthma, lethargy, cancer, miscarriages, and birth defects. In August 1978, New York officials decided to evacuate 240 families from the area. Television news coverage of these events showed how toxic contamination had destroyed normal suburban life by financially destroying families and creating significant social disorder.[21] One week after Love Canal first appeared in the national media, North Carolina learned of the illegal dumping along the road shoulders. During the following week, network television news covered both Love Canal and the North Carolina roadways in the same segments.[22]

The infusion of the hazardous waste issue into public discourse through the Love Canal news coverage had two impacts. First, the toxic threat itself was always lurking in the background; no one had immunity from the silent killer, not whites, not blacks, not the wealthy, not the poor. Second, the government was implicated in the victimization of citizens by toxic materials. Distrust of the agency with the official environmental label became the rallying cry for the new activists. The direct connection of the North Carolina contamination with the Love Canal catastrophe reinforced both of these notions. The already strong connection between the two cases of contamination increased when PCBs were identified as part of the toxins at Love Canal. In December 1978, when county residents read in the newspaper that the state had submitted a permit application for a landfill site in Warren County, they responded based on these newly formed constructs and vehemently resisted the plan.

Warren County Citizens Concerned about PCBs (Concerned Citizens) became one of many local groups opposed to the hazardous waste facility, countering "facts" from the state and the EPA with their own data showing the flaws in the state's plan. In this way, they were like numerous other opponents of locally unwanted land uses, worried that a hazardous waste facility would ruin the natural resources upon which they depended and destroy their already shaky economy. The post–Love Canal activism also created an aggregate of resistance groups that developed a new synergy. On regional and national levels, networks sprang up quickly to put local activists in touch with each other and to disseminate the most up-to-date information about the emerging field of hazardous waste management and remediation. These groups had access to information and also had experience in organizing against toxic contamination. Concerned Citizens were in need of both, and the emerging activist networks provided the necessary information for them to organize significant resistance.[23]

The "not in my back yard" (NIMBY) response diagnosed the problem as a technical issue: Where best to put the soil? Citizens pressed for alternative solutions based on technical information they could trust from experts who were not affiliated with state or federal agencies. The technical arguments against the Warren County site presumed that a suitable site did exist someplace else; the unacceptable properties of the Afton site were often compared to the properties of other locations, both real and hypothetical:

> We think that the site chosen for the PCBs should be safe beyond any reasonable doubt whatsoever. In as much as there appear to be sites elsewhere in the state of North Carolina that can handle PCBs, we feel that it is only reasonable that the state would look at those sites and reject the Pope site.[24]

Better yet, according to citizens, why not truck the contaminated soil to the chemical waste landfill in Emelle, Alabama? The site had been approved by the EPA, had already been built, and had been operating successfully. In January 1979, Chemical Waste Management (CWM), owners of the Emelle landfill, estimated that shipment and disposal of the contaminated soil would cost $8.8 million.[25] It seemed to citizens that the only reason for not using the Alabama site was the high cost involved. Citizens were outraged that the state would jeopardize their health, the health of future generations, and the shaky economy in order to save money. How could the state put a price tag on the value of lives in Warren County? In 1979, shipment to Alabama, no matter what the cost, became the official position of Concerned Citizens. Ken Ferrucio, the leader of the group, made this clear at an EPA-sponsored public hearing: "PCB on the shoulders and PCB in temporary storage [should] be sent to Alabama, one of the three legal national dumping sites where I understand every precaution has been taken, unlike the situation here in Warren County."[26]

Residents of Warren County traveled to the landfill in Alabama to see if it was an acceptable place for the contaminated soil and found it suitable: "They buried this stuff 70 feet deep with 630 feet of clay under that."[27]

The technical arguments were clearly an "anywhere but here" discussion. Once the county entered the judiciary system with its civil suit against the state and the EPA, it was forced to continue in this vein, arguing over technical problems with the site and flaws in the design of the landfill. If the county did not agree that a safe disposal method was possible, as was presumed under the federal regulations, then what would the state do to remediate the problem? There had to be a solution; it was unthinkable that this situation could not be fixed with the application of sound science. As a result, once the court ruled that the design improvements transformed the Warren County property into an acceptable site, the county was forced to accept the landfill. In the spring of 1982, the county withdrew its suit after securing the design changes and gaining the deed to the 120 acres of the Pope farm which was not to be used for the landfill. The court lifted the injunction, and the state began construction of the landfill in June, with the contaminated soil scheduled to begin arriving at the site in September.[28]

The Coalition Is Formed

Late in the summer of 1982, with the soil delivery looming, the citizens made a drastic shift in their strategy by moving toward disruptive collective action. Protests were not generally a part of the cultural experience of the white members of the group, and when faced with the reality of organizing a direct action, Concerned Citizens realized that it lacked expertise. In fact, demonstrations in the South were typically associated with black civil rights activism often leveled against local whites. During the tumultuous 1960s in Warren County, many confrontations between black and white residents occurred in the middle of Warrenton on Main Street. Prior to its association with black civil rights groups, Concerned Citizens reached out to both Ronald Reagan and Jesse Helms; Helms had reportedly helped the group to secure a meeting with the Office of Toxic Substances at EPA headquarters in 1979. Also, in their last minute effort to halt the disposal of the soil, the group attempted, in vain, to recruit Reagan and Helms as allies by writing to both and asking for help, which never materialized. The willingness of Concerned Citizens to ally with Reagan and Helms, two major opponents of civil rights activists, demonstrated that local whites did not easily engage in an analysis of racial politics.[29]

Given the long history of racial discrimination and tension, it was most astonishing that a largely white opposition group in a rural southern county would reach out to black protest leaders for help and advice to revive their movement. It was even more astonishing that many whites, although not all, stayed and participated in the meetings, marches, and acts of civil disobedience. The nature of toxic contamination, the political climate in the county, and the tenacity and coalition-building skills of opposition leaders made these unlikely partners collaborate.

The white land owners involved in Concerned Citizens were distressed over the potential contamination of groundwater and the destruction of economic development plans. More importantly, Warren County residents were angry that a decision about the use of county land had been made without their input. Anger about the loss of local control over land use decisions was a powerful mobilizing factor.[30] This central issue in hazardous waste policy became the key to transforming the Warren County case from just another NIMBY resistance to a defining moment for the environmental justice movement. Fear of losing control over a local decision motivated Concerned Citizens to change their strategy to direct action and to build a coalition with civil rights activists.

Neither the state nor the EPA was willing to conduct genuine and sincere public involvement, as evidenced by the highly technical public meeting held in January 1979. The usurpation of local decision making was epitomized in the alleged comments of David Kelly, special assistant to the secretary of crime control and public safety and the official in charge of the state's remediation program. Citizens were distraught over his remark that the landfill would be sited in Warren County "regardless of public sentiment." Although no one could recall the original source of the comment, residents were adamant that Kelly had expressed total disregard for their opinions and that his words symbolized a government out of control.

In addition to anger over losing control of a local land use decision, the longstanding animosity between black residents and the white county board also played a significant role in building the coalition. When the county board settled the case with the state, the 1982 elections were only a few months away. The court settlement gave blacks in the county another reason to vote against the largely white political establishment. Black residents had struggled to gain equal representation in county decision making since the passage of the Voting Rights Act of 1965, which removed prerequisites for registering and voting.[31] After 1965, there was a significant increase in the number of blacks registered to vote in the county, and by 1976 an equal number of blacks and whites were registered. It was not until 1978 that there were enough black votes to elect an African-American, George Shearin, to the county board. In 1981 and 1982, as part of the extensive campaign throughout the South to garner congressional support for an extension of the Voting Rights Act, renewed efforts were made at voter registration among African-Americans in the county. The same African-Americans who led the voter registration campaign in the county played key roles in the direct action protests at the landfill during the autumn of 1982, and the two issues of black political power and landfill opposition were inextricably linked.[32] In the time between the county's withdrawal of the suit and the general election of 1982, the overall number of voters registered in Warren County increased by 30 percent; 65 percent of the overall increase came from nonwhite registrants.[33] Since race still determined the outcome of elections, the huge increase of black registered voters changed the political landscape. In November 1982, African-Americans won a majority of offices in the county, including a majority of seats on the county board, the sheriff, the registrar of deeds, and the state assembly representative. After the election results, the *Durham Herald* proclaimed the county "Free at Last!"[34]

In the summer of 1982, while Concerned Citizens were building a coalition with local civil rights activists familiar with direct action campaigns, the local chapter of the National Association for the Advancement of Colored People (NAACP) brought another suit against the state, arguing that the high percentage of minority residents was one factor influencing the decision to site the landfill in Warren County. Given that there were nearly eight hundred thousand acres of land with clay soils less permeable than those in Warren County and that the state had to request three waivers to qualify for a permit for the Warren County site, the NAACP argued that there must have been other than technical reasons for choosing the site in Afton. The plaintiffs argued that the large black population in Warren County was the other reason for the state's decision, but the court did not agree:

> There is not one shred of evidence that race has at any time been a motivating factor for any decision taken by any official—State, federal or

local—in this long saga. . . . Although population *density* was understand-ably a criterion in the selection process, absolutely nothing indicates that the racial makeup of the population influenced the decision. Failure of the plaintiffs to raise any question of race throughout the laborious process of public hearings and earlier lawsuits leads to the conclusion that its injec-tion at this late hour is a last-ditch effort to forestall or prevent the project from being completed.[35]

In fact, the issue had been raised by Warren County residents at the 1979 EPA hearing and in public statements by the local NAACP chapter, but no one on either side of the controversy was ready to delve into its impli-cations. The state did not take these sentiments seriously enough to even dispute them, nor did Warren County attempt to marshal evidence in sup-port of the claims. Instead, black and white citizens supported the official stance of the county board who were pursuing the case in court. As the county became more immersed in the court cases and the environmental impact statement, the discussion became more centered on the technical merits of the site and the quality of the landfill design. Out of necessity, landfill opponents engaged more fully in the language of environmental law. There was no room in that language for the larger social issue of en-vironmental racism. In July 1982 when they attempted to raise the issue of discrimination, the court easily dismissed it for lack of any earlier serious discussion on the topic.

In addition to the factors motivating white members of Concerned Citizens and African-Americans in the county to join forces, participants and bystanders attributed the success of the coalition to Ken and Deborah Ferruccio, two well-educated and tenacious individuals who had moved to North Carolina from Ohio in 1975 in hopes of raising their children in a peaceful, rural setting.[36] When it was time to contact civil rights leaders for assistance, neither Ferruccio had any direct ties to black leaders. They drew on their association, through Concerned Citizens, with the pastor of the nearby black Baptist church to make the initial contact with the powerful and influential United Church of Christ Commission on Racial Justice (UCC). Reverend Luther Brown of Coley Springs Baptist Church was not a politically active pastor; he did not believe that the spiritual well-being of his congregation depended on fundamental political and social change. In early 1979, concerned for the health of his parishioners,

Reverend Brown met with the Ferruccios and several other Concerned Citizens. Although this type of action was unfamiliar to Reverend Brown, he continued to follow the activities of the group. Reverend Brown and Ken Ferruccio eventually contacted Reverend Leon White, the director of the North Carolina office of the UCC; while Brown did not know Reverend White well, his position as a black pastor proved essential in linking the two organizations.[37]

Leon White, who had orchestrated much of the voter registration drive in Warren County, had many years of experience in organizing civil rights demonstrations and had the institutional support of the UCC behind him. One of the most significant impacts from the involvement of White was his connection with the Reverend Benjamin Chavis, the renowned leader of the "Wilmington Ten."[38] As a member of White's UCC congregation located in Warren County, Chavis became an important symbolic leader for local blacks involved in the protests. He delivered a motivational speech to the group, and on the third day of the protests he was arrested while leading a group of activists in blocking Department of Transportation trucks.[39]

Chavis evoked respect from African-Americans, caution from law enforcement, and intense interest from the media. Locals felt that participation from Chavis meant he was still connected to his roots in northeastern North Carolina. Because he had a national reputation, it also meant that their local struggle was meaningful in a larger arena. Although law enforcement officials were not surprised by his participation nor taken off guard by it, Chavis gave the action a serious connotation, with a potential for extreme disruption, and perhaps even violence. His position also gave the newly embraced environmental issue legitimacy among African-Americans. After his brief experience with the Warren County residents, Chavis became the chief crusader among civil rights leaders combating what he called "environmental racism." Several years later, he convinced the UCC to fund extensive study of the relationship between the location of toxic waste and the racial composition of the surrounding community. The result, Toxic Waste and Race, became a cornerstone of the environmental justice movement. The participation of Chavis, his influential position with African-Americans, his influence in national policy arenas, and his dynamic personality catapulted the new linkage between environmentalism and civil rights into the minds and hearts of a multitude of Americans—blacks, whites, civil rights activists, and environmentalists.[40]

In addition to expertise from the UCC, local opponents received support from the Southern Christian Leadership Conference (SCLC), the organization associated with Martin Luther King Jr. and the nonviolent civil rights actions of the 1950s and 1960s. The initial involvement of the SCLC led to the arrest of Walter E. Fauntroy, a nonvoting member of Congress from the District of Columbia, and increased media attention associated with this unusual occurrence.[41] When Fauntroy returned to Washington, he initiated the first government-sponsored inquiry into the correlation of race and income with landfill sites. The subsequent General Accounting Office (GAO) study influenced Chavis to support the more extensive Toxic Waste and Race and started the drive toward documenting discrimination in siting and in environmental hazards. Although questions remain about the validity of the results and the use of the conclusions for forming public policy, the GAO study has had a large impact on the development of the environmental justice movement and on the resulting changes in policy.[42] Because an influential black political leader like Fauntroy was in a position to marshal government resources on behalf of Warren County activists, the environmental justice movement took its first step toward documenting its central claim.

With the assistance of experienced civil rights organizers, a direct action campaign against the landfill was waged from September 15 through October 12, 1982. The number of participants ranged from a handful to several hundred, and the protest successfully disrupted the orderly and efficient completion of the landfill. Tensions were high in the county, particularly in late August after an unknown vandal slashed the landfill's plastic liner with a knife. This vandalism, coupled with the organizing support from well-known, even feared and notorious, civil rights leaders, convinced the state that the potential for violence was high; more than two hundred state patrol officers were posted at the scene and a battalion of the National Guard was placed on alert.[43]

The power of the protests came from the repertoire of actions honed by civil rights activists two decades earlier.[44] Observers saw the similarities immediately:

The whole thing was a revival of the whole civil rights stuff—the tone, the look, the cants, the point. It was more like a civil rights protest than any

NIMBY with all kinds of technical stuff about why not near them. There was some of that [in Warren County] but the tone of the marches was more "you are doing this to us because we're poor and black."[45]

Participants were familiar with the pattern for activism and could easily fall into its rhythm. Although not all whites in the county were willing to join, the actions of the civil rights movement were familiar to both blacks and whites. Meetings at the local black Baptist church (located less than two miles from the landfill site), the high visibility of well-known African-American activists, the incorporation of prayer into all the protests, and the long distance march—from Warrenton to Raleigh—were all part of an established program of civil rights activism familiar to both county residents and activists from other places who joined the locals.

The landfill situation also presented an opportunity for dramatic action. When the Department of Transportation trucks brought the contaminated soil from the road shoulders to the landfill, the protesters lay down on the road in front of the oncoming vehicles. None of the Warren County residents participating in the protests had ever "put their bodies on the line" in such a literal sense. This tactic of symbolically blocking the source of the contamination delayed the project and raised the visibility of the events, inviting more extensive media coverage and encouraging others to join the protests.[46]

Environmental Racism:
Not In African-American Backyards!

African-Americans saw the hazardous waste landfill as an environmental problem for their county, but they did not align this environmentalism with their perception of traditional, mainstream environmentalism. As one participant explained, trying to distance herself from mainstream environmentalism, "African-Americans are not concerned with endangered species because we are an endangered species." The concern of the local activists seemed more closely aligned with public health, with threats to the places where people live, work, and play. The concept of contamination by synthetic chemicals enabled the addition of an environmental aspect to the civil rights framework, especially fears of both groundwater contamination and potential economic devastation from the stigma of the landfill. These two issues resonated with past experiences of African-Americans in the county: blacks had been victims of past transgressions at the hands of whites in power, resulting in excessive poverty, physical suffering, and even death. The landfill was the latest manifestation of their experience for the past several centuries. One participant, a local civil rights activist since the early 1960s, stated the case bluntly: "They use black people as guinea pigs. Anytime there is something that is going to kill, we'll put it in the black area to find out if it kills and how many. They don't care. They don't value a black person's life."[47]

Changing discriminatory land use decisions had been part of an earlier civil rights agenda, but the civil rights framing of the Warren County case added environmental, social, economic, and political dimensions to the problem. The contamination was thrust upon the community by the state and federal governments. Since government had failed many times in the recent past to protect blacks, it was not difficult to believe that another failure was imminent. Civil rights activists adopted an environmental perspective to protect African-Americans, their health, and the resources upon which they depended. This environmental viewpoint was in opposition to the government agencies that were charged with taking protective action, but did not protect all citizens equally.[48]

Offenses against black residents of the county occurred at all three levels of government. State environmental agencies chose the Warren County site; the EPA approved the state's request, including waivers of key regulations; and the county government settled with the state, adopting a compromise position. Because the county government had very little power to change the situation once it settled the suit, it would have been futile for activists to wage a campaign at that level. In fact, the campaign was better waged in the voting booth, where African-American residents now had a chance to win elections because of the recent push for voter registration. This narrowed the conflict to two antagonists, the EPA and the state environmental agencies. This was the first time that national-level civil rights organizations defined the EPA and other agencies responsible for implementing environmental regulations as their opponents. In addition to the threat to drinking water that framed the hazardous waste landfill as an environmental issue, defining the enemy as government agencies responsible for environmentally related decisions forced civil rights organizations to engage in environmental analysis.

At the onset of the controversy in December 1978, the state and federal structures for managing hazardous waste were insubstantial. Although the disposal of PCBs was legislated under TSCA, the practical regulatory issues fell under the hazardous waste program of the Resource Conservation and Recovery Act of 1976 (RCRA). Although RCRA emerged from Congress with little controversy as opposed to TSCA, the implementation of the act was constrained by the low priority accorded it by the Carter administration. As a result, partial regulations were issued in 1980, two years after the statutory deadline. These regulations omitted the technical standards for treatment, storage, and disposal facilities. Permits were easily obtained based on interim, and very loose, standards. According to the General Accounting Office's review, the standards were ineffective at protecting public health and the environment.[49]

By 1982, the regulations had become slightly more firm, but the EPA was even more vulnerable as a result of Superfund-related scandals. Although Superfund was intended to remediate sites whether or not a responsible party could be identified and held liable, the Reagan administration gave priority to sites where cleanup costs could more readily be recovered. In the North Carolina case, arrests had been made and criminal prosecution was well under way by the time the National Priority List was first issued in October 1981. Since the EPA under Administrator Anne Gorsuch was under severe attack from critics, North Carolina was a perfect case to push because of its high media profile and the clear identification of responsible parties.[50] Once the civil rights organizations proclaimed that an environmental problem had relevance to the daily lives of African-Americans, they looked for the source of the problem and found a vulnerable government agency. From this, they concluded that the opponents of the landfill were the true protectors of public health and the surrounding resources, not government agencies mired in political muck.

The civil rights agenda extended itself to include an environmental agenda based on how activists redefined what constituted an environmental problem and who their opponents were. Alliances with traditional environmental organizations were not part of the extension into the environmental arena. When African-Americans spoke about the involvement of environmental organizations in the controversy, they only referred to the government agencies that made environmentally related decisions, especially the EPA. The "Group of Ten," the largest mainstream environmental policy group in the nation, did not fit the definition of an "environmental organization" for blacks and did not touch the lives of the Warren County protesters with the same force as the EPA. Civil rights leaders depended on the information provided by the antitoxic organizers, but in 1982 these activists hardly had the same power and authority that the mainstream environmental organizations had in the environmental policy arena.[51]

Although not central to the landfill opposition, two mainstream environmental organizations did play a very small role in the landfill siting controversy: the state chapter of the Sierra Club and the Conservation Council of North Carolina, an influential organization started in 1969 by scientists, lawyers, and academics. While both groups offered suggestions to state officials about how to handle the cleanup and how to design the landfill, neither organization participated extensively, and both distanced themselves from the Warren County citizens once the protests began.

If an environmental perspective meant being against the environmental agencies and having a focus on hazards that threaten public health, then alliances with the mainstream environmental organizations were not necessary for the joining of civil rights with environmentalism. In fact, the tactics advocated by landfill opponents did not sit well with the traditional environmentalists in the state. They were uncomfortable with emphasizing the social dimensions of environmental issues over the technical and legal dimensions, and they were unwilling to engage in direct action.[52] The Sierra Club and the Conservation Council stayed on the sidelines, trying to work with the state and the EPA to find a resolution to this very difficult problem. While mainstream environmentalists focused on technical problems and eschewed direct action, environmentalism was transformed by the collective actions in Warren County. As a result, mainstreamers emerged as "outsiders" to the environmental justice movement, not setting the agenda, but responding to the agenda established by civil rights activists who embraced an environmental perspective through the actions in Warren County.

As the diagnosis of the problem began to include discriminatory siting based on race, the problem grew into something larger than Warren County's landfill. There were many Warren Counties out there, and perhaps many of these poor, predominantly black communities were host to hazardous waste facilities. As Golden Frinks, an experienced organizer, explained:

> I did not know anything about it, so I did a little research. I called Atlanta and told Albert [Love] what I was involved in and wanted him to put it in the ear of Lowery. That I thought it was a good movement and thought he should become involved. I also wanted him to find out if there were other toxic waste dumps in black communities. They found it in South Carolina.[53]

This new definition of the problem had an important implication for Warren County: the shipment of the contaminated soil to Emelle, Alabama, was no longer a viable option. As it turned out, the largest hazardous waste facility in the nation had major compliance and regulatory problems and was also located in a poor town with a predominantly African-American population.[54] Environmental racism cemented the problem within a victimization framework, where the injustices done impacted a class of victims beyond the local residents, enabling these residents to downplay the NIMBY aspect of their resistance. For white activists, poverty and ruralism marked residents as among the politically powerless. Environmental racism was the catalyst to a more comprehensive framework, but it was also the cause of a major chasm in the environmental justice movement, which became entrenched in trying to determine which factor, race or class, was a better indicator of the location of environmental hazards. This ongoing conflict within environmental justice began in Warren County.[55]

Environmentalism Transformed:
The Impact of Environmental Justice

The rising problem of hazardous waste management, the emergence of antitoxic activism, and the shifting politics of civil rights merged together in a place where the deteriorating economic condition of African-Americans was severe. Warren County, like many rural southern counties, was hit particularly hard by the recession of the early 1980s. Warren was attempting to make the transition from an agriculturally based economy to a mixed economy and was on the verge of some success at the time the landfill was proposed. The landfill threatened any hope for economic development in this largely black southern county. Growing difficulties with hazardous waste management and its emerging regulatory structure emphasized the impacts of environmental hazards on the daily lives of citizens. The inadequate implementation of hazardous waste reform provided opportunities for intensified political action, and this burgeoning activism helped to shape the fledgling Warren County opposition movement.

The political landscape for African-Americans was also changing. The election of Ronald Reagan created a significant increase in political action among African-Americans, especially in regard to the 1981 reauthorization of the Voting Rights Act of 1965. When the act was reauthorized and strengthened, African-American residents in Warren County seized this opportunity to change the county political structure to more closely resemble its racial demographics. The increased electoral activities among African-Americans in Warren County helped define the issue of the landfill as one of racial discrimination.

The heritage of civil rights activism in the county impacted the organizing of the landfill opposition. Warren County activists were able to link with powerful African-American elites by renewing associations with earlier civil rights activism. Through reforms resulting from this activism, these individuals had gained access to official political institutions. These positions of power enabled the fledgling movement to raise a new issue— distributive justice of environmental hazards—in public policy debates. As these African-American elites rallied behind a cause that linked environmental integrity and economic justice, they embraced the notion that Tom Bradley had articulated a decade earlier: "The problems of poverty and environmental quality are inextricably intertwined."

Actions on behalf of environmental quality were not necessarily "distractions from the problems of black and brown Americans," but were instead an integral part of making daily life healthy, safe, and economically secure. Such a notion helped to blur the distinction between environmentalism and social justice causes. While this transformation did not eliminate elitism in the mainstream organizations or the potential regressive impacts from several environmental reforms advocated by these groups, challenges are now made by activists who have incorporated an environmental awareness into their cause and who can envision alternatives. Warren County and the unlikely coalition that formed there began the process of overcoming these limitations of the environmental movement.

Notes

1. Robert Burns and his two sons were found guilty of violating TSCA. Al Hanke, telephone interview by author, 15 March 1995; William Meyer, interview by author, tape recording, Raleigh, N.C., 25 May 1994.

2. The Toxic Substances Control Act of 1976 banned the manufacture of PCBs and regulated their disposal. On the properties of PCBs, see Marshall Lee Miller, "Toxic Substances," *Environmental Law Handbook*, 7th ed., ed. J. Gordon Arbuckle (Rockville, Md.: Government Institute, Inc., 1983).

3. Dollie Burvell, interview by author, Warren County, N.C., 22 May 1994.

4. See Robert D. Bullard, "Environmental Justice for All," in *Unequal Protection: Environmental Justice and Communities of Color*, ed. R. D. Bullard (San Francisco, Calif.: Sierra Club Books, 1994), 5–6; Benjamin Chavis, foreword to *Confronting Environmental Racism: Voices from the Grassroots*, ed. Robert D. Bullard (Boston, Mass.: South End Press, 1993), 3; U.S. Environmental Protection Agency, *Environmental Equity: Reducing Risks for All Communities*, vol. 1, EPA 230-R-92-008 (Washington, D.C.: G.P.O., 1992), 6.

5. See Robert Gottlieb, *Forcing the Spring: The Transformation of the American Environmental Movement* (Washington, D.C.: Island Press, 1993).

6. For examples, see Donald Worster, *Dust Bowl: The Southern Plains in the 1930s* (New York, N.Y.: Oxford University Press, 1979); Andrew Hurley, *Environmental Inequalities: Race, Class, and Industrial Pollution in Gary, Indiana, 1945–1980* (Chapel Hill: University of North Carolina Press, 1995); and Richard White, *The Organic Machine: The Remaking of the Columbia River* (New York, N.Y.: Hill and Wang, 1995).

7. James Noel Smith, ed., *Environmental Quality and Social Justice in Urban America* (Washington, D.C.: The Conservation Foundation, 1974).

8. Clem L. Zinger, *Environmental Volunteers in America* (Washington, D.C.: National Center for Voluntary Action, 1973), 17.

9. Thomas Bradley, "Minorities and Conservation," *Sierra Club Bulletin*, April 1972, 21.

10. Don Combs, "The Club Looks at Itself," *Sierra Club Bulletin*, July/August 1972, 35–39.

11. "The Environmental Cause is No Cop-out for the Affluent," *Audubon*, November 1971, 35–39.

12. *Time*, 3, 4 August 1970, 42.

13. See Hurley, *Environmental Inequalities*, 111–53.

14. Daniel Zwerdling, "Poverty and Pollution," *The Progressive*, April 1971, 25–29; "The Coalition of the Clean," *Commonweal*, 20 February 1970, 549; "Where Pollution Control is Slowing Industrial Growth," *U.S. News and World Report*, 23 April 1971, 47–50; Henry Wallack, "Paying for the Clean-up," *Newsweek*, 26 January 1970, 72.

15. Department of Crime Control and Public Safety, "Final Environmental Impact Statement," 13 November 1982, RC-CCPS, File 236, Division of Records, State of North Carolina Archives, Raleigh, N.C.

16. J. K. Sherron, Negotiating Diary for PCB Storage Site, 1978, and J. K. Sherron to Carl Pope, 28 November 1978, RC-AG, File 2363, Division of Records, State of North Carolina Archives, Raleigh, N.C.

17. County of Chatham, Public Hearing Before County Commissioners, 11 December 1978, tape recording, RC-CCPS, File 236, Division of Records, State of North Carolina Archives, Raleigh, N.C.; Department of Crime Control and Public Safety, "Final Environmental Impact Statement."

18. Department of Crime Control and Public Safety, "Application for Cooperative Agreement between the U.S. Environmental Protection Agency and the State of North Carolina for the Construction of PCB Landfill and the Clean-up of PCB Contaminated Soil Along N.C. Roadways Using CERCLA or Superfunds," April 1982, RCCCPS, File 697, Division of Records, State of North Carolina Archives, Raleigh, N.C.; David Levy, interview by author, tape recording, Washington, D.C., 16 December 1994; Meyer, interview; C. Gregory Smith, interview by author, Raleigh, N.C., 24 May 1994; John Moore to Dr. Martin Hines, 15 August 1978, RC-CCPS, File 697, Division of Records, State of North Carolina Archives, Raleigh, N.C.

19. On limited resistance to hazardous waste facilities before Love Canal, see Andrew Szasz, *Ecopopulism: Toxic Waste and the Movement for Environmental Justice* (Minneapolis: University of Minnesota Press, 1994). For a historical perspective on NIMBY, see William B. Meyer, "NIMBY Then and Now: Land-Use Conflict in Worcester, Massachusetts, 1876–1900," *Professional Geographer* 47 (1995): 298–308.

20. U.S. Environmental Protection Agency, "Public Hearing before the Environmental Protection Agency on the Matter of the Application to Dispose of Soil Contaminated with PCB's at a Selected Site in Warren County, North Carolina," January 1979, RG-CCPS, File 697, Division of Records, State of North Carolina Archives, Raleigh, N.C., 19–25, 54–66; *Warren County v. State of North Carolina*, Civil Action No. 79-560-CIV-5, U.S. District Court, Eastern District of North Carolina, Raleigh Division, RC-AG, File 2363, Division of Records, State of North Carolina Archives, Raleigh, N.C.

21. For extensive analysis of the Love Canal media coverage, see Szasz, *Ecopopulism*, 38–68.

22. *Television News Abstracts and Index*, 1978, Vanderbilt Television News Archive, Nashville, Tenn.

23. Keri Ferruccio, interview by author, tape recording, Warrenton, N.C., 24 May 1994; *Warren (N.C.) Record*, "Mass Arrests Made by Patrol," 22 September 1982, 1.

24. U.S. Environmental Protection Agency, "Public Hearing," 154.

25. Herbert L. Hyde to Governor James B. Hunt, memorandum, 23 January 1979, RGCCPS, File 697, Division of Records, State of North Carolina Archives, Raleigh, N.C.

26. U.S. Environmental Protection Agency, "Public Hearing," 100.

27. Ibid., 149.

28. *Warren County v. State of North Carolina*.

29. Warren County Citizens Concerned About PCB to President Ronald Reagan, 14 August 1982, and Letter to Senator Jesse Helms, February 1979, Warren County File, Division of Solid Waste Management File Room, Department of Environment, Health and Natural Resources, State of North Carolina, Raleigh, N.C.

30. N. Freudenberg, *Not in Our Backyards! Community Action for Health and the Environment* (New York, N.Y.: Monthly Review Press, 1984); Michael R. Greenberg and Richard F. Anderson, *Hazardous Waste Sites: The Credibility Gap* (New Brunswick, N.J.: Center for Urban Policy Research, 1984); Kent Portney, *Siting Hazardous Waste Treatment Facilities: The nimby Syndrome* (New York, N.Y.: Auburn House, 1991); Frank J. Popper, "The Environmentalists and the LULUs," in *Resolving Locational Conflict*, ed. Robert Lake (New Brunswick, N.J.: Center for Urban Policy Research, 1987).

31. For background on the Voting Rights Act, see U.S. Commission on Civil Rights, *The Voting Rights Act: Unfulfilled Goals* (Washington, D.C.: U.S. Commission on Civil Rights, 1981).

32. Burwell, interview; Charles Lee, interview by author, tape recording, New York, 8 February 1995; Mary Guy Harris, interview by author, tape recording, Red Hill, N.C., 2 September 1994; Florence and Edward Somerville, interview by author, tape recording, Afton, N.C., 30 August 1994; Leon White, interview by author, Warren County, N.C., 22 May 1994.

33. Voter Registration Records file, Board of Election Office, County of Warren, Warrenton, N.C.

34. "Free at Last," *Durham Herald*, 8 December 1982, 1.

35. *National Association for the Advancement of Colored People of Warren County, et. al. v. Anne Gorsuch, et. al.*, Civil Action No. 82-768-CIV-5, U.S. District Court, Eastern District of North Carolina, Raleigh Division, RC-AG, File 2363, Division of Records, State of North Carolina Archives, Raleigh, N.C., 9–10.

36. Golden Frinks, interview by author, tape recording, Edenton, N.C., 19 January 1995; Luther Brown, interview by author, tape recording, Soul City, N.C., 8 June 1994; Frank Ballance, interview by author, tape recording, Warrenton, N.C., 29 August 1994; Richard Hart, interview by author, tape recording, Chapel Hill, N.C., 18 January 1995; Jane Sharpe, interview by author, tape recording, Chapel Hill, N.C., 20 January 1995; Jack Harris, interview by author, tape recording, Warrenton, N.C., 16 June 1994; Mary Guy Harris, interview; White, interview.

37. Brown, interview; Ferruccio, interview; White, interview.

38. For details on Chavis and his political battles, see Lennox S. Hinds, *Illusions of Justice: Human Rights Violations in the United States* (Iowa City, Iowa: School of Social Work, University of Iowa, 1978), and "Chavis Battling Reagan Policies," *Raleigh News and Observer*, 4 April 1982, 3:D.

39. His home was in Oxford, North Carolina, in a county adjacent to Warren and about twenty miles from the proposed landfill. By February 1997, Chavis had left the UCC and become a member of the Nation of Islam.

40. Chavis is often credited with coining the term "environmental racism." For examples of his statements about environmental justice, see forewords in Bullard, *Confronting Environmental Racism*, and United Church of Christ, Commission for Racial Justice, *Toxic Waste and Race in the United States: A National Report on the Racial and Socioeconomic Characteristics of Communities Surrounding Hazardous Waste Sites* (New York, N.Y.: United Church of Christ, 1987); Charles Lee, ed., *Proceedings: The First People of Color Environmental Leadership Summit* (New York, N.Y.: United Church of Christ, 1992); House Committee on the Judiciary, Subcommittee on Civil and Constitutional Rights, *Environmental Justice: Hearings*, 103d Cong., 1st Sess., 1993, 11–14.

41. Marguerite Ross Barnett, "The Congressional Black Caucus: Illusions and Realities of Power," in *The New Black Politics: The Search for Political Power*, ed. Michael B. Preston, L. J. Henderson Jr., and Paul Puryear (New York, N.Y.: Longman, 1982), 28–54; Walter E. Fauntroy, interview by author, tape recording, Washington, D.C., 14 December 1994.

42. Sylvia N. Tesh and Bruce A. Williams, "Science, Identity Politics and Environmental Racism," unpublished manuscript, n.d., Department of Urban and Regional Planning, University of Illinois at Urbana-Champaign, 10–13 (author's personal file). The GAO attempted to overcome some of these shortfalls with an updated study, *Hazardous and Nonhazardous Waste: Demographics of People Living Near Waste Facilities*, GAO/RCED-95-84, June 1995. For a complete discussion of design and methodology for studies of the correlation between race and location, see Rae Zimmerman, "Issues of Classification in Environmental Equity: How We Manage is How We Measure," *Fordham Urban Law Journal* 21 (1994): 633–69.

43. "Special Incident Report: PCB Incident," Warren County, N.C., 1982, North Carolina State Highway Patrol, Department of Crime Control and Public Safety (author's personal file).

44. Don Griffin, interview by author, tape recording, Charlotte, N.C., 19 January 1995; Jack Harris, interview; Jane Sharpe, interview.

45. Hart, interview.

46. Ferruccio, interview; Burwell, interview; Mary Guy Harris, interview.

47. Mary Guy Harris, interview.

48. Ballance, interview; Brown, interview; Burwell, interview; Somerville, interview; White, interview.

49. Szasz, *Ecopopulism*, 11–37.

50. Hugh Kaufman, interview by author, Washington, D.C., 15 December 1994; Samuel Epstein, Lester Brown, and Carl Pope, *Hazardous Waste in America* (San Francisco, Calif.: Sierra Club Books, 1982), 248–56.

51. Gottlieb, *Forcing the Spring*, passim.

52. Levy, interview; Sharpe, interview.

53. Frinks, interview.

54. Connor Baily, Charles E. Faupel, and James H. Gundlach, "Environmental Politics in Alabama's Blackbelt," in *Confronting Environmental Racism: Voices from the Grassroots*, ed. Robert D. Bullard (Boston, Mass.: South End Press, 1993), 107–22.

55. A recent GAO report indicates that "minorities and low-income people were not over represented near the majority of nonhazardous municipal landfills." *Hazardous and Non Hazardous Waste*, 4. For a strong argument against the existence of environmental racism, see Vicki Been, "Locally Unwanted Land Uses in Minority Neighborhoods: Disproportionate Siting or Market Dynamics?" *Yale Law Journal* 103 (1994): 1383–1422.

TED STEINBERG

Do-It-Yourself Deathscape

The Unnatural History of Natural Disaster in South Florida

IN THE AFTERMATH of Hurricane Andrew, with the wheels of federal relief turning ever so slowly, President George H. W. Bush arrived in Florida and told people that it was a bad idea to "play the blame game." In one respect, *Newsweek* reported, everyone could agree with the president. "Andrew was what the insurance companies call 'an act of God,' a happening for which no mere human can be held to account." And yet the blame game continued, with angry politicians demanding more and faster federal relief aid, second-guessing the level of community preparedness, and intimating that someone should have forecast the hurricane earlier. Unable to stomach any more finger-pointing, the author Glenn Garvin of Coral Gables wrote in an op-ed piece for the *New York Times* that "the hysterical hunt for the guilty in the wake of a natural disaster seems to be a peculiarly American phenomenon."[1] This statement implied that it would be better to adopt a calmer approach to the disaster, to take it in stride, perhaps to see it as an act of God or nature. In such a view, there is no need to play the blame game because no one could be held responsible for the disaster. Yet the question persists: Who or what was really responsible for the 1992 hurricane disaster in south Florida? Was it all or mostly the fault of nature or God?

Obviously, the hurricane itself, which triggered the destruction, was a natural event. Or was it? *Newsweek*, as indicated above, declared the hurricane "an act of God." But in a brief sidebar, the magazine noted that human-induced global warming may have helped to increase the intensity of the storm. Evidently, Andrew was a postmodern disaster, without any single, definitive cause. Still, given the relative positioning of the two articles and the way the magazine underscored the storm as an act of God, the editors were clearly more impressed with the naturalness of the event.[2]

The opinions of *Newsweek*'s editors aside, there is no questioning the role that human social and economic forces—poorly enforced building codes, low federal standards for mobile homes, eviscerated zoning laws—played in the calamity. Most students of natural disaster would agree that events like Hurricane Andrew are not entirely natural, but human complicity in such calamities has been slighted. In the domain of natural hazards research, paltry sums support inquiries into the human dimensions of disaster, while vast amounts are reserved to study its physical aspects. Such a lopsided approach resulted because the dominant scientific view of calamity—still subscribed to by many in the natural hazards field—tends to see nature as the main force behind disaster. According to geographer Kenneth Hewitt, believers in the dominant view of natural disaster interpret these events as chiefly the "result of 'extremes' in geophysical processes." In other words, "the initiative in calamity is seen to be with nature." Natural disasters, in this paradigm, are "chance recurrences of natural extremes, modified in detail but fortuitously by human circumstances."[3] Given the tendency to naturalize, to depoliticize these events, it might not be such a bad idea to play the blame game.

What follows is a venture into the unnatural history of natural calamity. The goal is to expose human complicity in these phenomena by looking closely at the making of south Florida's high-risk environment. How do risky manscapes come to be? What are the central forces that help to create them? Who benefits from their construction? When disaster does strike, how is the human dimension of calamity obscured and denied in order to foster more economic growth and land development?

In answering such questions, the role that natural forces play in explaining Florida's vulnerability to hurricane disaster must not be overlooked. The incidence of hurricanes in the Sunshine State is high; 36 percent of all hurricanes make landfall there. But it is also true that vast numbers of people and large quantities of highly developed property lie in the path of danger. This is no accident. The counties of Dade, Broward, and Palm Beach are home to four million people, a population exceeding that of twenty-nine states. As of 1993, the value of insured property in Florida's coastal counties surpassed $971 billion, more than the combined amount of insured property in all coastal counties from Texas to Delaware.[4]

To see just how risky a proposition south Florida is, compare the city of Miami with other hurricane-prone cities, such as Mobile, Alabama, and Galveston, Texas. All three cities have a 50 percent chance of experiencing an intense hurricane sometime within the next thirteen years. But with a population of almost two million and more than $160 billion in insured property (1993), Miami contains more than three times the number of people and amount of property as Galveston and Mobile combined. That explains why some analysts estimated $65 billion in damages had Hurricane Andrew made landfall just slightly to the north.[5]

South Florida is a disaster waiting to happen, mainly because private developers have sought to maximize the land's tourist and agricultural potential by building in areas susceptible to hurricanes and flooding. In their quest to maximize profits, developers have had help from the state. Until at least the 1950s, the state of Florida raced to give away land and natural resources to private interests, providing a tremendous subsidy to developers who gobbled up the state's scenic but risk-prone barrier islands and other places prone to inundation. And yet, at the same time that economic development driven by private property interests helped to sow the seeds of future destruction, Florida's commercial community sought to deny the very real risks of that development, and where possible, to blame nature for disaster when it did occur. Natural disaster has a very shadowy history in south Florida, rooted in years of denial for the sake of profit. This study probes the sources of that denial and explores the unnatural history of natural disaster in a state where, despite the wishes of the tourist industry, the sun does not always shine.

Making of a Manscape

Miami Beach was once just a thin spit of sand, two hundred feet wide, with a low ridge of dunes running down it. West of the dunes toward the bay, weeds gave way to a dense swamp of red mangroves, a species with dense roots and stems. A swamp crisscrossed by mangrove and buzzing with mosquitoes and sandflies was hardly conducive to the kind of tropical paradise that would attract sun-starved northerners. So developers launched a makeover of the landscape that made the area into something it was not.

The man largely responsible for initiating this makeover was Carl Fisher, an automobile magnate best known for building the Indianapolis Speedway and the first cross-country highway. Fisher was a daring man, not at all shy about taking risks, and evidently not a big fan of mangrove swamps. He avidly raced bicycles, boats, and cars, and once staged a promotional stunt in which he donned a padded suit and rode a bicycle across a tightrope stretched twelve stories off the ground. On another occasion he sailed over Indianapolis in a car that hung from a balloon. Will Rogers, in a generous moment, said that Fisher had done more "novel things" than anyone he had ever met. Desperate for adventure and risk, Fisher first came to Miami on vacation in 1910 and several years later purchased two hundred acres of land on what would eventually become Miami Beach from John Collins, a New Jersey investor who used the cash to finish building a bridge to his remaining property.[6]

In the summer of 1913, Fisher and several other investors with land on the beach hired the First Clark Dredging Company of Baltimore to clear away one thousand acres of mangrove swamp and replace it with six million cubic yards of bay bottom land. The company employed African-American laborers for the brutal, insect-ridden task of slashing through the tangle of mangroves. After the bay front was bulkheaded and bay bottom pumped up to neatly cover the shore, soil from the Everglades was shipped in and the land divided into lots and planted with shrubs. "In this manner," writes Polly Redford in *Billion-Dollar Sandbar*, "the original landscape was erased as if it had never been and a more salable one built in its place."[7] Although more salable, the landscape was also more risk-prone now that the mangroves, which provide natural protection to coastal areas from hurricane-induced storm surges, were destroyed.

Fisher's genius was to anticipate the extraordinary premium that investors would soon place on waterfront property. In a promotional tract published in 1926, *Florida in the Making*, the authors observed a "mania for water frontage." "There is nothing mysterious or deep about this buying. It simply means that in people's minds the ocean, the gulf and the lakes are Florida; and aside from the farmers, the buyers do not care so much for property that has no water frontage." By bulkheading the swamp at Miami Beach and paving it over, Fisher soon realized huge profits in land sales. In

1925 alone, he and his business associates sold property on Miami Beach totaling more than $23 million.[8]

Bulkheading became something of an obsession for Fisher. Not content to simply dredge and fill along the barrier beach itself, Fisher turned his attention in 1917 to creating artificial islands in the middle of Biscayne Bay. Star Island, which was later converted into a yacht club, was his first such venture. Purchasing the bay bottom from the state for roughly seventeen thousand dollars, Fisher bulkheaded an area half a mile in length and a quarter of a mile in width. He then pumped sand in to create the island. Later he helped to subsidize a county bond that led to the building of the County (now MacArthur) Causeway, linking Star Island with the mainland. Eventually he sold the property for two hundred dollars per waterfront foot. The success of Fisher's Star Island venture did not go unnoticed by other developers, who subsequently engaged in more island-building. In the early 1920s, developers bulkheaded and filled the Venetian Islands, linking them to the mainland via the Venetian Causeway (which replaced the Collins Bridge) at a cost of more than $2.5 million. By 1931, some six thousand acres of land had risen from the depths of Biscayne Bay.[9]

One may wonder how the bottom of Biscayne Bay—a navigable waterway supposedly held by the state in trust for the public under the common-law—wound up in private hands. Even Florida's Supreme Court recognized as late as 1909 that the disposal of a vast amount of bottom land in a navigable waterway would violate the so-called "public trust" doctrine. But ironically, this doctrine's common-law roots meant that it could be modified by the Florida legislature.[10]

Florida has a long history of giving away the state's natural resources to private enterprise. Of the approximately thirty-five million acres of land and water in the state, more than twenty-three million were controlled by the Trustees of the State Internal Improvement Fund, the board responsible for caring for state-owned lands, and all but a mere three million acres had been deposited in private hands by the turn of the century. By the 1950s, almost all the land in the fund had disappeared. Various pieces of legislation dating from the mid-nineteenth century helped to fuel this monstrous shift of public resources into the pockets of private entrepreneurs. The legislature became even more accommodating to real estate developers in the early twentieth century as the value of waterfront property in southern Florida became increasingly clear. A 1913 law encouraged the development of property in the middle of bays by vesting title in many submerged lands in the Internal Improvement Board and allowing it to dispose of this public resource to private interests. Carl Fisher and other developers in the Miami area availed themselves of precisely this key piece of legislation to help turn Biscayne Bay into a miniature Venice.[11]

If there is something to be said for creating increasing amounts of waterfront property, either from a developer's or tourist's perspective, it is also true that this practice placed increasing numbers of people and their property in harm's way. In 1915, property in Miami Beach was assessed at approximately one-quarter of a million dollars. A decade later that number had increased to $44 million. By 1926, Miami Beach, once an undeveloped barrier spit, had been transformed into a real estate theme park complete with 56 hotels, 178 apartment houses, and 858 private homes. But for those who chose to notice them, signs abounded that all this property stood on an extremely dynamic piece of land. As early as 1918, before the land boom of the 1920s, enough evidence of serious erosion existed to necessitate the installation of two 60-foot jetties in front of the Roman Pools, a bathing pavilion and casino, which had been built, like most of the hotels along the ocean, far too close to the water.[12]

Despite evidence of these and other more life-threatening risks, developers just could not get close enough to the sea. In the spring of 1926, only months before one of southeastern Florida's most destructive hurricanes came ashore, a group of land promoters was under fire for planning to turn a set of coral reefs south of Cape Florida into artificial islands, a suicidal idea that would certainly have led to death and damage had the scheme gone forward. Major opposition scuttled the plan, which presented a threat to real estate interests throughout Biscayne Bay. Typically the majority of deaths from hurricanes result from storm surges, which happen when low pressure causes a large dome of water to swell over the land. If a landmass is convex, the impact of the storm surge tends to fan out and dissipate. But Biscayne Bay is concave and enclosed by offshore islands. As those opposed to the real estate venture explained, let the plan to build more islands on the coral reefs proceed, preventing water from returning quickly back to the ocean, and the effects of the storm surge would surely be felt more intensely.[13]

That some land-hungry souls seriously entertained the idea of building on the extremely vulnerable reefs is testament to the reckless abandon that characterized real estate development in this period. John Kenneth Galbraith observed that the Florida land boom was founded on a craving for instant gratification, "an inordinate desire to get rich quickly with a minimum of physical effort."[14] Evidently for some, the yen for quick riches was accompanied by another form of fantasy—a death wish.

Smile

The Miami real estate boom went on under fair skies. By 1926, two decades had passed since the last intense hurricane had made landfall in the Miami area. Even the 1906 storm, which caused considerable damage and loss of life, did the vast bulk of its destruction south of the city in the lower Keys. This apparent immunity from violent weather and the rush to cash in on the red-hot real estate market resulted in a profusion of hastily and poorly built structures. Many homes constructed during the 1920s boom had little or no bracing and were designed without regard to wind pressure and hurricanes. One newspaper reported that "real estate buyers who inquired about the menace of tropical storms were laughed at."[15]

One could still hear the laughter as late as July 1926, when a hurricane bore down on the city. After the storm ended, traffic ground to a halt on the County Causeway as curiosity seekers tried to catch a glimpse of what the strong winds did to Miami Beach, though the real damage was done farther north in Palm Beach, which experienced millions of dollars in losses. No lives were lost in Florida (although some 150 died in the Bahamas), leading the *Miami Herald* to conclude that fearful as hurricanes may be, "there is more risk to life in venturing across a busy street." Before scarcely a week had passed, meteorologist R. W. Gray of the U.S. Weather Bureau told members of the local Kiwanis Club that Miamians need not fear serious damage from a hurricane.[16]

Events soon proved otherwise. On September 18, 1926, an extremely powerful storm with winds close to 140 miles per hour battered Miami, causing the deaths of 115 people there. In the midst of the raging storm, Philip London, a Miami businessman with a cameraman in tow, set off to film the disaster for the benefit of moviegoers in New York. Threading their way through debris-clogged streets, they made it to Miami Beach and then forged their way up the coast as far as Fort Lauderdale, filming the grisly horror of the storm. "Life was following its happy, careless course in Miami on Friday last," explained London upon his arrival in New York City. Morning newspapers, he continued, had carried reports of a hurricane; afternoon papers denied the possibility. "We dismissed the thought." London slipped into bed only to be awakened at 2:30 a.m. by a jolt and a loud roar as wind and rain shook the house. Then the lights went out. Later in the morning, London peered outside and saw a tangle of telephone poles and wires. The Halcyon Hotel was missing its roof. A big electric sign on top of the Olympic Theater had been broken in two. A little before noon, the winds let up and the rain stopped, allowing people to venture outside. "Everybody tried to smile and appear happy," London reported. The owner of a downtown store hung out a sign: "Start the day with a smile!"[17]

Twenty-five thousand people were left homeless after the hurricane, but it did not take long—scarcely two weeks—for the *Miami Herald* to declare that things were back to normal in the city:

> The normalcy that has come is in the minds of the people. They are still just a little bit dazed, but they are sane—there is an absence of any of the hectic outbreaks that nearly always accompany disaster. . . . Miami has not yielded to the emotional temptations that come in such a time as has been experienced here. Mental normalcy means the most rapid rehabilitation of the city that is humanly possible.

The *Herald*, launched in 1910 to support the pro-development intentions of the railroad builder Henry M. Flagler, had a long record of downplaying events that shed a negative light on Miami. When the Associated Press estimated that the city experienced $100 million in damage, the *Herald*'s managing editor, Olin Kennedy, directed his subordinates in the newsroom to divide the figure by ten. Ultimately the paper printed the absurdly low figure of $13 million in damages, playing down the disaster in the hope that people would stay calm, and even better, forget that disaster had ever struck. "By January 1," predicted the *Miami Herald*, "we will have ceased to think or talk of the hurricane. It will have written its story in the history of the city, but Miami will be looking forward, not backward." Forward, that is, to a society that saw disaster as normal, as part of the price for developing land in disaster-prone locales.[18]

Little about the disaster remained in popular memory thanks to efforts by city boosters to downplay the situation. "It has become a habit in resort regions to minimize or even suppress news of disasters that might frighten away tourists and investors," observed *Literary Digest*. Nowhere was this more true than in Florida. Mayor E. C. Romfh of Miami sent a telegram to mayors of all the major U.S. cities thanking them for their offers of assistance. But, he continued, "after inspection of the damaged region, I find the situation not as bad as reported. Will call on you if the need arises." He never called. Romfh believed that a very exaggerated sense of the situation prevailed in the country, and to some extent this may have been the case immediately after the disaster. Truth was in very short supply. The *New York Times* reported that some journalists in Miami had seen 175 bodies in temporary morgues on the Monday after the storm, while city officials counted only 115. In tallying these numbers, however, officials admitted that "the names of negroes were not always included." For his part, Governor John Martin also downplayed the extent of the damage and even went so far as to refuse to call a special session of the legislature to appropriate relief funds.[19] Perhaps the most revealing example of the twisted logic employed by the minimizers came from Peter O. Knight, owner of the *Tampa Tribune* and a major figure in Florida boosterism, who was upset that many saw the hurricane as a "Florida" disaster:

> When San Francisco was visited by an earthquake, the press of the country did not talk about the California disaster. When Chicago had its great fire, the press of the country did not talk about the Illinois disaster. When Galveston was destroyed, no one spoke of the Texas disaster. . . . And now when but a small portion of Florida has been affected by the hurricane, the country refers to this as the great Florida disaster.[20]

The logic behind all this disaster nosology apparently eluded Knight, who never seems to have considered that a disaster responsible for several hundred deaths and major damage throughout a huge part of southern Florida could appropriately be called the "Florida" disaster.

If such efforts to minimize the hurricane had any effect, it was on the Red Cross; for the first time in its history, the organization failed to solicit the requisite amount of money necessary to relieve the suffering. As of mid-October, only $3 million of the $5 million in needed funds had been subscribed. The shortfall led John Barton Payne, chairman of the

Red Cross, to accuse state and city officials of placing real estate interests ahead of the needs of storm victims: "The disaster in Florida is really much greater than the interests there would have us believe, and there is going on in Florida a conflict between the humanitarian efforts of some on the one side and the selfishness of business interests on the other." The end result of this policy, explained the Homestead Enterprise, was that Florida bore increasing resemblance to, of all places, feudal England: "England in feudal times had food and comfort and pleasures for the wealthy, while outside the gates the peasants starved. Florida in this day can handle all the tourists that she did before—and then some, while another class of people are living from hand to mouth, dazed and bewildered at the change that has taken place."[21] In fact, the state bore a much stronger resemblance to the United States under early twentieth-century capitalism.

Surface Damage

If the Red Cross's failure to meet its $5 million goal hurt anyone, it was the people of Moore Haven, a small town on the southwestern shore of Lake Okeechobee that had been almost completely annihilated as the 1926 hurricane tracked northwest from Miami. With the storm raging in the middle of the night, Moore Haven residents stumbled out of bed to reinforce the dike that protected the town, breaking their backs to add two feet to its height. The effort proved futile, not to mention self-destructive. By morning, the dike began to break up and the all-night vigil to add to its height only served to increase the force with which the water eventually rushed forth into the town. Exactly how many died in the flooding is unclear. The official count was 150, but a very knowledgeable local source claimed that 300 died, in a town with a total population of just twelve hundred.[22]

Howard Sharp, for one, was not surprised. The editor of the *Everglades News*, published in nearby Canal Point, he virtually predicted the disaster in what is surely one of the most accurate prophecies of doom on record. A full understanding of his prediction requires a little history and an appreciation for the stakes involved in settling this part of south Florida. Early in the twentieth century, Napoleon Bonaparte Broward sought to reclaim the Everglades; under his leadership, the state embarked on a decades-long drainage project. By 1929, close to $18 million had been spent to build 40 miles of canals and levees with but one purpose in mind: to transform the rich muck lands of the Everglades into valuable farmland. By the late 1910s and early 1920s, as railroads forged their way to the south shore of the lake, small frontier towns—Pahokee, Belle Glade, Clewiston, and Moore Haven—began to sprout. To say the least, it was not an entirely safe place to live, although it may well have seemed risk free to many at the time.[23]

During the 1910s, as development near Lake Okeechobee proceeded apace, there were no hurricanes or floods to speak of. Then in 1922, prolonged, heavy rains caused Lake Okeechobee to rise roughly four and one-half feet, flooding Clewiston and Moore Haven and inspiring residents to build a muck dike along the lake's southern shore. Two years later, another period of intense storm activity raised the level of the lake, causing more flooding.[24] Finally, in the summer of 1926, before the September hurricane, heavy rains again raised the level of the lake, causing Howard Sharp to beg state drainage officials to take the necessary steps to lower the water. "The lake is truly at a level so high as to make a perilous situation in the event of a storm," he wrote in an editorial.[25]

Not surprisingly, no one wanted to take responsibility for the death and destruction at Moore Haven. State officials like attorney general J. B. Johnson blamed nonhuman forces: "The storm caused the loss and damage. . . . It is not humanly possible to guard against the unknown and against the forces of nature when loosed." Governor John Martin agreed, explaining that nobody could "ever guarantee that the hand of Providence that sends winds and earthquakes and rains will have no effect, more or less, on this area, and the public is advised that now and for all times the Everglades area is subject to the same rules of Providence, and is under the same guiding hand that other lands of the earth are, namely, that of God Almighty."[26] The fact that the state had subsidized and encouraged settlement around Lake Okeechobee seemed not to cross the mind of either elected official.

Two years later, disaster struck again. On September 16, 1928, a powerful storm with a barometric low of 27.43—even lower than that recorded at Miami in 1926—swept ashore near Palm Beach. It is impossible to say how many died. The Red Cross estimated 1,770, virtually all of them drowned in the towns along the southeastern shore of Lake Okeechobee as the strong wind sent a wall of water crashing over the dikes.[27] Most of the dead were black migrant workers who had come to the Everglades just a short time before for the planting season. Governor Martin toured the devastated area and described the human toll:

> In six miles between Pahokee and Belle Glade I counted twenty-seven corpses in water or on the roadside but not taken from the water. Total dead on roadside and not buried and counted but not in plank coffins was one hundred and twenty-six. In six additional miles more than five hundred and thirty-seven bodies were already interred. Fifty-seven additional bodies were hauled out of this area today in trucks and tonight four truck loads of bodies were brought from adjoining areas by boat, loaded and sent to West Palm Beach for burial.[28]

Sightseers, brimming with morbid curiosity, filed into the Okeechobee region to see the mounds of swollen, rotting corpses firsthand. According to one report, "the visitor would stare for moments entranced, then invariably turn aside to vomit." Bodies were still being found more than a month after the disaster, when any further searching was called off for lack of funds.[29]

In an editorial following the calamity, the *Wall Street Journal* educated its readers: "Cyclone or hurricane damage is essentially surface damage. It has every element of the spectacular and it always looks several times as bad as it really is." The best way to deal with the disaster was to remain calm and sympathetic. As the *Journal* put it in a subsequent editorial, "there is every need for sympathy but no need for hysteria." At a distance of some twelve hundred miles from the smell of rotting flesh, it was perhaps easy to counsel restraint. Meanwhile, Peter Knight, no doubt eager to label this anything but the "Second Florida Disaster," was similarly unruffled by the tragedy. He purportedly told a syndicated columnist that the hurricane was "trivial."[30]

Howard Sharp did not agree. Again, he seemed remarkably prescient on the matter of calamity, writing a week before the storm that those who advocated a high water level in Lake Okeechobee were taking "a terrible responsibility on themselves."[31] In truth, it was almost an impossible task for state authorities to manage the lake's water level to everyone's satisfaction. Commercial fishermen and those who used the lake for irrigation or transportation purposes wanted the water level high; farmers, especially those near the lake shore, wanted it low to guard against flooding.

After more than twenty years of Everglades drainage work, the problem of managing the region's water remained, spurring the state to seek the help of the federal government. In a 1929 congressional hearing, Florida attorney general Fred Davis tried to explain the state's almost criminal neglect of flood control in the area near Lake Okeechobee. He pointed out that most residents of southern Florida came from outside the state. Yet it was the people of northern Florida settled much earlier than the flood-prone southern part who dominated state politics. When it came right down to it, Davis told the congressional committee, given that most Everglades residents came from outside Florida, "it is mighty hard to get people in other parts of the State interested in whether they perish or not."[32] And perish they did.

Lipstick Traces

Barometrically speaking, the most intense hurricane in the history of the United States occurred in Florida in September 1935, with the eye of the storm passing directly over the Florida Keys. The storm left the *Dixie* stranded at sea, its passengers forced to don life vests. Aboard ship was passenger Sol J. Lupoff, who offered some observations of life during the calamity. What struck him most was the rather odd behavior on the part of the women passengers, who, in the midst of this life-threatening situation, apparently took time out to put on lipstick and rouge. The *Miami Herald*, a longtime foe of hysteria in times of disaster, took heart in the women's actions. Such behavior, noted the paper, "may indicate strong nerves and calmness in a crisis."[33]

Actually, the women's behavior, if accurately reported, more likely reflected the "other-directed" anxieties of a consumer culture, where one did not want to be caught looking bad in an unguarded moment. In any case, the *Herald* was more concerned that people in south Florida remain calm so that the fallout from the calamity could be contained. Again, some raised the question of whether this hurricane constituted another "Florida" disaster. The paper lamented that the state had experienced some devastating hurricanes over the previous decade: "These tempests are thrust onto the front pages when they hit Florida, and thus they become Florida hurricanes." But there was no use trying to disabuse people of the fact that the hurricanes did not really originate in Florida, "because the less said the better." The paper concluded that "people forget rather quickly. It is wiser to let them do so."[34]

Only it was not going be easy to forget the four hundred people who died in the disaster, most of them impoverished war veterans who had been sent down to the Keys by the Federal Emergency Relief Administration (FERA) to fill in gaps in the highway between the mainland of Florida and Key West. Historian Gary Dean Best notes that while the story of the unemployed veterans' 1932 March on Washington and their demand for relief is familiar to many, few are aware of the veterans who died in the tragedy during the 1935 Florida Keys storm. In their haste to rid Washington of these so-called "bonus marchers," the Roosevelt administration had not given "consideration to the conditions under which the veterans were being housed and cared for on the keys."[35] The housing provided for the workers was flimsy and dismal and certainly no match for the hurricane-force winds that accompanied the most intense storm in U.S. history. Nor were there adequate plans for evacuating the veterans in the event of a storm, despite the fact that the risk of hurricanes was well-known both in and outside of government.

When the hurricane hit, a storm surge estimated from fifteen to twenty feet in height swept over the veterans' camps, which were located barely above sea level. The blame game began almost immediately. Some indicted the U.S. Weather Bureau for failing to offer an accurate storm forecast, but without more advanced weather-tracking technology, which only became available after the World War II, precise forecasts were difficult.[36] Others blamed the federal government for not having an adequate evacuation plan, which was true enough. By the time officials dispatched a train to the Keys, it was already too late—the train was derailed by the high winds and water. For their part, FERA and the Veterans Administration, charged with investigating the disaster, concluded in their official report that "the catastrophe must be characterized as an act of God and was by its very nature beyond the power of man."[37]

Clearly, those officials charged with overseeing the welfare of the veterans demonstrated administrative incompetence; no question exists that a more accurate weather forecast may well have helped to lessen or even avert the disaster. But in all the efforts to fix responsibility for the calamity, it seems amazing that no one pointed the finger at the most fundamental reason for the death and destruction: economic development driven by private property interests and the accompanying pro-growth attitude that opened the hurricane-prone Florida Keys to settlement in the first place.

Railroad magnate Henry Flagler led the way in clearing the Keys for human habitation. Having constructed a railroad that spanned all the way from Jacksonville to Miami by the late nineteenth century, he began working on a project in 1905 that would prove to be one of the more daring episodes in railroad history. Flagler planned to extend his Florida East Coast Railway all the way from Homestead to Key West—a deep-water port—in the hope of capitalizing on the anticipated increase in trade from the Panama Canal. The track would span roughly 130 miles, crossing forty-three stretches of water or tidal marsh, the longest of which was seven miles in length. It was an extraordinarily ambitious—some would say suicidal—venture, and Flagler could find only one contractor willing to even discuss the project. The railroad took seven years to build, cost $20 million, and employed 40,000 workers, seven hundred of whom drowned in hurricanes while on the job.[38]

The demise of so many workers should come as no surprise. No less than three hurricanes—in 1906, 1909, and 1910—struck the low-lying Keys while the railway project progressed. In the fall of 1906, about 175 workers constructing the Long Key viaduct were living aboard a sizable wooden barge that was totally destroyed during the storm. According to the chief engineer on the project, William J. Sanders, some of the men on the barge went "wild with panic" and simply resigned themselves to death, drinking laudanum and going to sleep on tables, their pockets filled with the heaviest objects they could find. But Flagler remained undeterred by the hurricane disasters. Legend holds that after each storm he telegraphed just two words to his men: "Keep going." Completed in 1912, the railroad helped to fuel the 1920s land boom in the Keys.[39]

Not only was it dangerous to build in such a hurricane-prone locale, but the construction of the railroad track actually increased the danger. Flagler spent huge sums to build seventeen miles of steel bridges and concrete viaducts. To cut down on the need for any additional water-spanning structures, twenty miles of filled causeways were built, closing off the many gaps between the Keys. As a result, the causeways were then able to dam up hurricane tides, increasing the potential for death and destruction, precisely what happened during the 1935 hurricane. Longtime residents of the Keys criticized the causeways, arguing that they had bottled up the water between the Keys and mainland, increasing the intensity of the destruction and ultimately washing hundreds of people out to sea.[40]

Such criticism aside, by 1935 no amount of death and destruction could apparently stop south Florida's boosters in their quest to deny the dangerous reality of living in this area. Just two months after the September 1935 disaster, another hurricane descended on Miami. Only a handful of people died, although several million dollars of damage resulted. The *Miami Daily News,* not always as fierce in its pro-growth proclivities as the *Herald,* but a city booster nonetheless, declared that Miami had withstood the storm's test. More people die in traffic accidents in a single day than died in the storm, it pointed out, arguing that "the chief suffering from any hurricane is caused by hysteria." Instead of retreating, people should go back to work rebuilding in precisely the same risk-prone locales.[41] Evidently, disaster in southern Florida was nothing that some lipstick and a smile couldn't handle.

Bulking Up

The 1935 Great Labor Day Hurricane was the last massively deadly storm to strike Florida. Since then, hurricanes have killed far fewer people, generally less—far less—than one hundred per occurrence. Even the most intense storms to hit the state in the last sixty years—the Pompano Beach hurricane in 1947, Hurricane Donna in 1960, and Hurricane Andrew in 1992, all category 4 storms—caused just fifty or fewer deaths each. Otherwise, death figures from the other twenty-eight hurricanes that have made landfall in the state have numbered in the single digits. A combination of factors, the most important being improved warning and evacuation plans, explains the decline.[42]

But as deaths have fallen, property damage has risen. Prior to 1960, only the 1926 hurricane caused damages amounting to more than $1 billion (in 1990 dollars). Between 1960 and 1975 alone, four hurricanes topped the $1 billion mark: hurricanes Donna (1960), Dora (1964), Betsy (1965), and Eloise (1975). Untrammeled desire for waterfront and other low-lying property explains in part why damages have soared.[43]

Consider Miami Beach. Further growth of tourism in the 1930s caused the hotel business to boom. Ten hotels went up in the city in 1935, followed by 38 more the next year. By 1940, there were 239 hotels in the city, forming a concrete wall right on the edge of the ocean. In the decade after World War II another hotel building boom consumed the city. In 1946, the Martinique went up with 137 rooms. The Sherry Frontenac followed in 1947 with 250 rooms. The glamorous Saxony Hotel rose in 1948, a year which saw the construction of 17 new hotels with 1,500 new rooms. Then came the Sans Souci and the Casablanca, the Empress, the massive DiLido, and finally Ben Novack's world-famous Fontainebleau with 545 rooms. Fifty-five new hotels were added to the city during the decade after the war, creating almost 7,000 new rooms. By the late 1950s, more than 150 hotels lined Miami Beach's oceanfront. The hotel boom was followed by a surge in high-rise apartments in the 1960s the Seacoast Towers, Manhattan Towers, Regency Tower, Surfside Tower, and others filled in the waterfront even more. By the mid-1960s, oceanfront lots were virtually nonexistent, and by 1968 the price of oceanfront property had been driven up to five thousand dollars per front foot. All of this expensive oceanfront real estate was naturally prone to inundation and wind damage from hurricanes.[44]

Development in Miami Beach paralleled what was happening throughout Dade County, which also experienced sustained development during the 1920s and after World War II. Some of the new land developments, such as Coral Gables, were laid out on the Atlantic coastal ridge, an elevated area generally protected from inundation. But other municipalities, such as Miami Springs and Hialeah, were built atop areas that had once been little more than saw grass marsh. In the 1940s, Hialeah Gardens, Medley, and Pennsuco were established—despite the fact that these areas had hardly any population at the time of incorporation—creating three new municipalities west of the coastal ridge in areas that were subject to severe flooding. These shotgun incorporations were approved simply to satisfy the desires of promoters for cheap land on which to build, placing increasing amounts of property in the path of danger in the process.[45]

Nowhere were the pro-growth intentions of local government more obvious than in Miami Beach, where the city council had long been cavalier about the risk of natural disaster. In an attempt to encourage further development of waterfront property in 1948, the council extended the bulkhead line seventy-five feet seaward. This move served the interests of beachfront property owners; by moving the line which marked the eastern most extent of private property farther seaward, property owners could now construct a bulkhead and gain additional land. The ordinances extending the bulkhead line amounted to a series of enclosure acts, reminiscent of what happened to common lands in Britain during the eighteenth century. The extension of the bulkhead line allowed hotels to expand the size of their lots by enclosing the foreshore—the area of land between the ordinary high and low water mark, title to which was vested in the state in trust for the public—thereby turning it into private property for the exclusive use of hotel guests.[46]

This extraordinary giveaway of public land to benefit private interests did not go unchallenged. The state of Florida and others sued the city of Miami Beach and various hotel owners, seeking an injunction forbidding the city from issuing permits for the building of structures on the foreshore. The injunction was granted in 1953, reasserting public ownership over the foreshore.[47] But the ruling came too late to stop the hotels' land grab, with one report noting that "virtually every ocean front hotel had already run bulkheads, lines of cabanas or groins which fenced in their beaches."[48] Allowing the hotels to build right up to the water's edge not only closed off public access to the beaches, but also increased the amount of property in harm's way.

Embracing Disaster

Beginning in the 1930s and accelerating after World War II, the federal government joined the state in subsidizing private development on barrier islands by helping to bear the costs of constructing causeways, bridges, and water supply systems, and by providing disaster relief and flood insurance. As a result, private development and population growth surged as the public sector bore the costs of both building infrastructure and recovering from disaster.

In the Florida Keys, public funds were used as early as the 1930s to help bolster growth and development. In 1934, the governor declared a state of emergency in Key West, then suffering the ravages of the Depression. This action opened the door to funds from the FERA, which sought to turn the city into a resort town. One year later, the Great Labor Day Hurricane obliterated much of the Overseas Railroad and so demoralized the Florida East Coast Railway that the company sold its right of way and bridges to the state. The Monroe County Toll Commission, with help from the Works Progress Administration, set about building a highway from Florida City to Key West, which opened in 1938, providing better access to the Keys and smoothing the way for increased population growth and development. After the war, the highway was widened and repaved to accommodate modern automobile travel. The U.S. Navy and the Florida Keys Aqueduct Commission collaborated on a pipeline for shipping water from the mainland to the Keys. Opened in 1942, the pipeline offered residents a steady supply of water for the first time, after years of trucking it into the area. The federal government also helped provide reliable electric service to the Keys through the Federal Rural Electrification Administration. The combination of adequate access, water supply, and electricity helped to boost private development and population growth. Not including Key West, almost fourteen thousand people lived on the hurricane-endangered Keys by the 1960s, an increase of 296 percent over the population in 1950.[49]

The rise in population and development that occurred in south Florida after the war coincided with a period of relative calm in terms of hurricane activity, but when disaster struck the region in the 1960s, federal legislation was already in place for helping Floridians rebuild. Legislation enacted in 1950, for instance, allowed the president to authorize disaster relief for the rebuilding of public facilities without seeking congressional approval. The federal government wove its disaster safety net even tighter three years later with legislation authorizing the Small Business Administration (SBA) to make low-interest loans available during disasters.[50]

Florida reaped the rewards of government subsidy beginning with Hurricane Donna in 1960. President Eisenhower declared the Florida Keys a disaster area following the storm, opening the way for millions of dollars to pour into the area to help rebuild bridges, highways, and water lines in this hurricane-prone area. The SBA offered homeowners and businesses low-interest loans. Federal funds continued to flow into south Florida in the aftermath of hurricanes Cleo (1964) and Betsy (1965). Hurricane Betsy, in particular, helped to further open the pocketbooks of taxpayers. After the hurricane, Congress passed legislation allowing the SBA to cancel as much as eighteen hundred dollars per loan, the first time that "forgiveness" was granted. The hurricane also led to legislation mandating that the Department of Housing and Urban Development (HUD) study the issue of federal flood insurance; ultimately, HUD recommended passage of a federal flood insurance program, a policy that increasingly subsidized development in risky locales throughout the nation.[51]

Federal largesse, for all its merits, did have a downside. For decades, boosters throughout Florida tried to eschew any mention of the word "disaster" in the wake of hurricanes, but to receive federal aid it was necessary to admit the obvious: that a *disaster* had in fact taken place. This label upset some of south Florida's growth advocates. In an editorial written after Hurricane Cleo, the *Miami Herald*, historically a major force behind increased land development and tourism, lamented that the disaster label was necessary to secure federal funds. Such disaster talk, the paper mused, might give the rest of the nation the mistaken impression that "Florida's Visitorland has been clubbed to its knees. . . . 'Disaster' talk is inaccurate, and it is injurious." Similarly, Clark Ash, the associate editor of the rival *Miami News*, felt it unfortunate that for the sake of some federal funds "a region which depends primarily on the tourist business must be publicized all over the nation as a major disaster area."[52] While south Florida's tourist-based business community might tolerate the disaster label in return for federal money, other strings attached to these funds were harder to accept.

Zero Beach

A bather needed swimming trunks, a towel, and, most important, a ladder to swim in the ocean in front of Miami Beach's Singapore Hotel in 1959, since no beach remained there and climbing was the only way down to the water. Miami Beach had become by the 1950s a gigantic misnomer—there was no beach. The protective dune and sandy beach that had once defined the area's identity had been destroyed, partly as a result of erosion caused by intense storms. The problem of beach erosion developed as early as the 1910s and intensified after the 1926 hurricane. The city installed groins to trap sand and save the beach; so many had been built by the 1970s that the beach looked like "a military obstacle course." But mainly, it was the building of hotels and other structures too close to the water that caused the beach to disappear. The extension of the bulkhead line in 1948 allowed hotels such as the San Souci, Cadillac, and Saxony to build cement pools and cabana decks right across the foreshore. Even after the 1953 legal decision forbidding such construction across public land, hotel owners continued to build right up to the sea. In 1956, the Americana Hotel in Bal Harbour constructed the foundations of its hotel just fifteen feet from the ocean. A sea wall in front of the hotel only added to the problem as waves lashed the wall and removed the sand in front of it.[53]

In 1964, the U.S. Army Corps of Engineers provided Miami Beach with a plan to restore the now nonexistent beach. The idea was to dredge sand from the continental shelf and pump it onto the beach, widening the stretch from Haulover Beach ten miles south to Government Cut. Apart from restoring the recreational value of the beach, the plan also provided hurricane protection by restoring the beach's original protective dune. By absorbing some of a hurricane tide's total energy, the dune would help to lessen the impact farther inland. The Corps planned to design the dune to withstand a 70-year storm, but required Dade County to inform residents of Miami Beach that the restoration project would not provide total protection against a storm tide similar to the one that struck the city in 1926.[54] The total cost of the project was estimated at $10 million, of which the federal government would pay a little less than half. The project enjoyed the support of many officials, including Miami Beach's mayor in the late 1960s, Jay Dermer, but it was not implemented until 1977, mostly because of opposition from Miami Beach's hotel owners.

Why would the hotel owners fight against a proposal designed to improve the tourist value of beaches as well as mitigate hurricanes? The answer stems from money and land ownership. The Corps was willing to contribute substantially more money toward the project if the newly created beach was deemed public property. This proviso angered hotel owners, who by the 1950s had transformed the bulk of the beach—7.5 out of a total of 10 miles—into their own exclusive, private domain. "Miami Beach was built and became the World's No. 1 resort because of private beach ownership," explained Edwin Dean, executive director of the Southern Florida Hotel and Motel Association.[55] His group, which spoke for most of the hotels on the beach, vigorously opposed the Corps' restoration plan. "We do not need beaches. We have plenty of beaches," Dean told reporters in 1969.[56] Besides being untrue, Dean's statement was also contradicted by the fact that the hotels had advanced their own plan to restore the area's dwindling beaches as early as 1967 by repairing the many storm-damaged groins.[57] But as Mayor Dermer pointed out, the hotel owners' plan offered no hurricane protection, and any further delay in implementing the Corps' plan could prove disastrous in the event of an intense storm.

Natural disaster was probably one of the last things on the minds of owners such as Ben Novack of the Fontainebleau, although he did have visions of the Corps' beach nourishment plan causing sandstorms and driving tourists for cover.[58] The hotel owners were mainly concerned that their private beaches be maintained. "Anybody who spends big money for an oceanfront room is entitled to a private beach," Novack remarked.[59] The thought of nonregistered guests venturing along the beach at the city's expense drove him wild. "Do we want a Coney Island here?" Novack fumed. "Maybe he's Coney Island merchandise," Novack said of Mayor Dermer. The hotel owner, who had spent millions to make the Fontainebleau into a private luxury resort, would never tolerate public access to his premises: "Beaches are necessary to the people of this city, and we have them. We don't have the type of beaches they have in some native areas where there is no advancement or progress. We're not that type of place where you can walk along the beach." As far as hurricane protection was concerned, the logic of the Corps' plan eluded him. "Those sand dunes won't stand up under hurricanes," Novack pointed out. "The sand will go into hotel lobbies, and we'll have to shovel it out."[60]

Eventually, the hotel owners changed their minds. Their turnabout on the issue resulted in part from the outcome of a lawsuit which determined that restoration of a new beach in front of hotel property would not harm the hotels or cause them any monetary damages, and probably from the dawning realization that they could not bear the costs of improving the beach on their own.[61] In any case, their decision to support the Corps' beach nourishment plan certainly did not grow out of any deep seated concern for protecting the city from hurricanes or opening its beaches to the public.

The $68 million Dade County Beach Erosion and Hurricane Protection project, as the Corps' plan was called, began in 1977 and lasted four years. Fourteen million cubic yards of sand—four times the amount of construction material used in Egypt's Great Pyramids—were dredged up from offshore and spewed on to the beach. By most accounts the project is a success. Today, storm-induced waves must first crash into the restored protective dune, helping to protect Miami from inundation. But even the Corps admits that the restored beach will not last forever. Erosion of a restored beach is estimated to occur ten times more quickly than on a natural shore, and with the beach in constant need of replenishment, the offshore sand is going to run out. By the early 1990s, officials in Dade and Broward counties, concerned about the dwindling sand supply, floated a plan to ship sand in from the Bahamas. But there are obstacles to such a plan. First, the cost of mining such sand would be extremely high; second, there are federal import rules to consider; and third, there is concern that since the Bahamian sand is mostly limestone, mixing it with the quartz-based Florida sand and subjecting it to the region's heavy rains might turn the material into cement.[62]

Built to Sell

After Hurricane Betsy in 1965, south Florida went almost three decades without experiencing a major hurricane. In the Miami area, the freedom from destructive storms was even more dramatic. The city had not been directly hit by a major hurricane since 1950, making for forty-two years of quiescence before Hurricane Andrew delivered its vicious blow. The lull in storm activity, coupled with population growth and development, especially during the 1980s, paralleled the evisceration of south Florida's building code. Prior to World War II, the municipalities of Miami, Miami Beach, and Coral Gables each had their own building codes. But in 1957, the Miami area's building interests put pressure on public officials to rationalize this complex set of codes in an effort to save them money. The resulting South Florida Building Code, which applies to all municipalities in Dade County, has long been considered one of the most stringent in the country. Its rules require that buildings be able to withstand winds of up to 120 miles per hour. Ironically, the code actually may have contributed to a decline in building quality. Prior to its passage, builders were extremely conscientious about building quality structures. The passage of the code may simply have lowered standards to a common denominator. Whether this was the case or not, no question exists that the code, whatever its merits, was laxly enforced. This became especially evident after hurricanes Donna and Betsy, when studies commissioned by the state showed evidence of complacency among builders. The studies were roundly ignored.[63]

Even worse, the building code itself was slowly watered down, starting in the late 1960s, coinciding precisely with the lull in hurricane activity. A study conducted by the *Miami Herald* reviewed the minutes of the Board of Rules and Appeal, which interprets the building code for Dade County. The *Herald* found that the board, most of whose members came from the building industry, had "repeatedly given in to a construction industry looking for cheaper, quicker ways to build." In 1968, the board recommended that the county sue Coral Gables because the municipality refused to abide by the less rigorous standards of the South Florida Building Code. Two years later, the board allowed builders to use Masonite siding on exterior walls of homes, without any plywood backing. In 1972, the idea of including workmanship standards in the code was first broached, yet it took twenty years for the board to revise the code so that there would be some quality assurance.[64]

In the 1980s, a decade of unbridled capitalist optimism and deregulation, the code was eviscerated still further, especially as poor refugees in need of housing poured into Dade County, spurring the construction industry to build as cheaply and as quickly as possible. In 1983 and 1984, the board was informed that the staples it allowed to secure roofs were not holding; it did nothing until after Hurricane Andrew. In 1984, the board permitted builders to use waferboard instead of plywood on roofs; after Andrew the waferboard was banned.[65] The loosening of regulations spurred builders on as they expanded development farther south and west in Dade County. "The sad thing is that in a hurricane-prone community like this, the builder should know he needs to be careful," said one Dade County civil engineer. "Alarm bells should go off in his head. People were just oblivious to things, as if they thought we never were going to have a hurricane in this area."[66]

Not covered under the gradually weakened South Florida Building Code were mobile homes. Nothing demonstrates better the failure of public responsibility regarding hurricanes than mobile home regulation. During the 1980s, the number of mobile homes in south Florida increased by one-third. By the early 1990s, more than 100,000 people in Dade, Broward, and Palm Beach counties lived in this form of housing, despite its extreme vulnerability to wind.[67] The primary appeal of manufactured housing is its low price, making it affordable for many low-income and elderly people; in Dade and Broward counties, the median household income of mobile homes is one-third less than that of those households occupying conventionally built homes.[68] Mobile home sales representatives repeatedly told these people that their trailers were "hurricane resistive," able to withstand a wind of 110 miles per hour. That turned out to be an unabashed lie.

Mobile homes in Florida, as in all states, are regulated by federal legislation passed in 1973 and administered by HUD, which asked the National Bureau of Standards to come up with two sets of rules designed to protect mobile homes, one for 70 mile per hour winds and the other for 90 mile per hour winds. The latter standard was to be applied in hurricane-prone locales. The bureau issued a report that HUD largely ignored. Indeed, both HUD officials and manufacturers made the absolutely disingenuous claim that the mobile homes were safe even in winds as high as 110 miles per hour. Not surprisingly, the congressional subcommittee established to review mobile construction standards has long been packed with legislators who eagerly accept money from the mobile home industry. In 1989 and 1990, twenty-nine of the subcommittee's forty-four members collected donations from mobile home political action committees.[69] In truth, mobile homes under the HUD design rules are only able to withstand winds of 80 miles per hour or less, a fact demonstrated in 1989 by two engineers, James McDonald and John Mehnert.[70] In Florida, this was public knowledge as early as 1983, when a state-commissioned study found that "housing constructed under the Southern Building Code is more wind-resistant than a mobile home built under the HUD code. "[71]

Any doubts about the safety of mobile homes were dispelled by Hurricane Andrew's violent winds. The storm destroyed approximately 90 percent of the 10,593 mobile homes in Dade County.[72] Four people died in mobile homes, while seven perished in conventional homes, even though almost fifty times as many people lived in the latter form of housing.[73] Yet even in the face of such carnage, Ken Cashin, the president of the Florida Manufactured Housing Association, insisted that the mobile homes were built to withstand winds of 110 miles per hour. In his opinion, Andrew was simply not a typical hurricane, packing winds of 140 miles per hour, with gusts as high as 175 miles per hour. "After surveying the damage, meteorologists now believe some areas received gusts of nearly 200 miles an hour," Cashin told a congressional committee after the disaster. Edward Hussey of Liberty Homes told the same committee that press reports claiming that "manufactured homes in particular were destroyed by only modest winds generated by Hurricane Andrew is dangerous and misleading. . . . There is not a single building code anywhere in the United States today which requires structures to be designed to withstand sustained winds ranging from 140 to 200 miles an hour."[74] In fact, most reputable meteorologists and engineers agree that most of Dade County experienced winds of 120 miles per hour or less; the hurricane, despite its enormous devastation, fell within the design standards set by the South Florida Building Code.[75] Mobile homes bore a disproportionate share of the damage simply because they were designed to withstand winds of much lesser force, despite the claims of the mobile home industry. In a rare moment of candor, a mobile home manufacturer admitted the obvious: "We don't build these homes to live in, we build them to sell."[76]

Home Bodies

One of the more shocking statistics surrounding Hurricane Andrew is that almost one-third of those ordered to evacuate their homes failed to do so. With the majority of those living in Dade County having little or no firsthand knowledge of the destructive power of a major hurricane, some three hundred thousand people, out of the one million ordered to leave, stayed on to flirt with disaster. Some, including a group of three hundred European and American tourists, attended hurricane parties in several of Fort Lauderdale's oceanfront hotels. Others seemed to have internalized the decades-old mantra of Miami's commercial community that urged people not to panic. Said one resident of Key West, "I don't really worry about hurricanes. . . . I'm a Key Wester, I don't panic."[77] Indeed, preliminary results of a study done by researcher Carla Prater of Texas A & M University indicated that most residents in the area affected by the storm did not panic.[78]

Psychiatrists argue that it is not uncommon for people in danger to simply deny the risks of their situation. "It's a common defense to use denial to escape the anxiety that realization of the extent of danger will cause," remarked Dr. Laurie Kenfield, a psychiatrist interviewed after Andrew.[79] While denial doubtlessly provided a popular defense mechanism for coping with the anxiety that Andrew produced, historical factors that encouraged such thinking must not be overlooked. Ample evidence exists that from early in the twentieth century until well into the 1960s, south Florida's real estate and tourist interests, sometimes with the help of a complicit press, downplayed the dangers of hurricanes. In addition, both state and federal governments further disguised the true risks of living in south Florida, especially in the years after World War II, to bolster private development in hurricane-prone areas by shifting the cost to the public sector. Downplaying the threat of hurricanes while simultaneously subsidizing further development in risk-prone locales may well have helped to encourage people to settle and sit tight while in the path of danger. It is often extremely difficult to explain collective behavior, but given this particular historical context, the decision of three hundred thousand people to remain in Andrew's path and endure the threat of death and destruction may be quite understandable.

To be sure, the last twenty-five years have seen the emergence of a more balanced approach to hurricane disasters, especially as officials of the National Hurricane Center have tried to reverse the decades-long practice of minimizing the threat. Still, Robert Sheets, director of the center, pointed in 1993 to what he called a "false sense of security," especially among those who weathered Hurricane Andrew at home. He had in mind the many residents of Miami Beach's condominiums who refused to evacuate and yet lived to tell about it. Sheets warned that had the storm made landfall just twenty miles farther north, there would have been hundreds of deaths, many of them as the storm turned beachfront high-rises inside out.[80]

Of course, this tragedy did not occur. Or did it? Could a storm so violent as Andrew have killed just forty people? According to one rumor, the large number of dead bodies found after the storm forced the U.S. Army to commandeer Budweiser trucks to transport them to Homestead Air Force Base, where they were eventually flown out of the state. Many stories circulated about large numbers of dead farm workers, perhaps a reference to the vast number of migrant workers who died in 1926 and 1928; one rumor told of three thousand workers lying dead in a Burger King in Florida

City.[81] While people did not panic in the wake of the storm, rumors persisted that the government was covering up a huge number of casualties in order to protect tourism.

These rumors suggest several conclusions. While the idea of a government cover-up seems farfetched, one must not forget how hard real estate, tourist, and other commercial interests had worked over the years to play down the possibility of hurricane disaster. Still, common people must be given credit for common sense. Residents had good reasons to be anxious about the possibility of large-scale death and destruction in the wake of a powerful storm like Andrew. Finally, with massive casualties a potential reality, one can perhaps imagine a place for such rumor-mongering, at least to the extent that it makes people aware of the risks of life on the edge of disaster. For south Florida, a panic attack may be just what the doctored ordered.

Notes

1. "What Went Wrong?" *Newsweek*, 7 September 1992, 23; "Hunting for Scapegoats in South Florida," *New York Times*, 2 September 1992, A19.

2. "Was Andrew a Freak—Or a Preview of Things to Come?" *Newsweek*, 7 September 1992, 30.

3. Kenneth Hewitt, "The Idea of Calamity in a Technocratic Age," in *Interpretations of Calamity: From the Viewpoint of Human Ecology*, ed. Kenneth Hewitt (Boston, Mass.: Allen and Unwin, 1983), 5; Pamela Sands Showalter, William E. Riebsame, and Mary Fran Myers, "Natural Hazard Trends in the United States: A Preliminary Review for the 1990s," Natural Hazards Research and Applications Information Center, Working Paper No. 83 (Boulder, Colo.: University Press of Colorado, 1993), 37–38.

4. Roger A. Pielke Jr., *Hurricane Andrew in South Florida: Mesoscale Weather and Societal Responses* (n.p., Environmental and Societal Impacts Group, National Center for Atmospheric Research, 1995), 51, 56, 64, 67.

5. Ibid., 6, 51, 53.

6. Luther J. Carter, *The Florida Experience: Land and Water Policy in a Growth State* (Baltimore, Md.: Johns Hopkins University Press, 1974), 74; Polly Redford, *Billion-Dollar Sandbar: A Biography of Miami Beach* (New York, N.Y.: Dutton, 1970), 45, 48.

7. Ruby Leach Carson, "Forty Years of Miami Beach," *Tequesta* 15 (1955): 11; Redford, *Billion-Dollar Sandbar*, 73.

8. Frank Parker Stockbridge and John Holliday Perry, *Florida in the Making* (Jacksonville, Fla.: de Bower Publishing Co., 1926), 289; Redford, *Billion-Dollar Sandbar*, 154.

9. Redford, *Billion-Dollar Sandbar*, 99; Carter, *Florida Experience*, 76; Carson, "Forty Years of Miami Beach," 14, 19; Millicent Todd Bingham, "Miami: A Study in Urban Geography," *Tequesta* 8 (1948): 99.

10. Frank E. Maloney, Sheldon J. Plager, and Fletcher N. Baldwin Jr., *Water Law and Administration: The Florida Experience* (Gainesville: University of Florida Press, 1968), 356.

11. John M. De Grove, "Administrative Problems in the Management of Florida's Tidal Lands," in Per Bruun and John M. De Grove, *Bayfill and Bulkhead Line Problems: Engineering and Management Considerations*, Studies in Public Administration, no. 18 (Gainesville: University of Florida, 1959), 20–22.

12. Carson, "Forty Years of Miami Beach," 20; Redford, *Billion-Dollar Sandbar*, 107, 154.

13. Ralph Middleton Munroe and Vincent Gilpin, *The Commodore's Story* (n.p.: Ives Washburn, 1930), 340–42.

14. John Kenneth Galbraith, *The Great Crash: 1929* (New York, N.Y.: Avon, 1979), 3.

15. "In the Wake of the Hurricane," *Saturday Evening Post*, 27 November 1926, 60; Frank Bowman Sessa, "Real Estate Expansion and Boom in Miami and Its Environs During the 1920s" (PhD diss., University of Pittsburgh, 1950), 332; "Disaster Follows Collapse of Boom," *New York Evening Post*, 20 September 1926.

16. "Causeway Traffic Delayed By Storm," *Miami Herald*, 27 July 1926; editorial, *Miami Herald*, 28 July 1926; "City Well Protected," *Miami Herald*, 31 July 1926.

17. "Miamian Grinds Camera All through Hurricane," *Tampa Morning Tribune*, 22 September 1926.

18. "Flimsy Construction," *Miami Herald*, 30 September 1926; Nixon Smiley, *Knights of the Fourth Estate: The Story of the Miami Herald* (Miami, Fla.: E. A. Seeman, 1974), 27, 30, 81; "Ninety Days Hence," *Miami Herald*, 25 September 1926. See Paul J. Herbert and Robert A. Case, *The Deadliest, Costliest, and Most Intense United States Hurricanes of This Century (And Other Frequently Requested Hurricane Facts)*, NOAA Technical Memorandum, NWS NHC 31 (Springfield, Va.: U.S. Department of Commerce, National Technical Information Service, 1990), 7, 8.

19. "The Row Over Florida Relief," *Literary Digest*, 16 October 1926; "Miamians Criticize Martin," *New York Times*, 2 October 1926; "Governor Refuses Special Session For Relief Work," *Homestead (Fla.) Enterprise*, 1 October 1926.

20. "Florida Damage of Local Import," *Wall Street Journal*, 8 October 1926.

21. "Florida Fund Failure is First For Red Cross," *New York Times*, 15 October 1926; "President Praises Red Cross As Ideal," *New York Times*, 5 October 1926; "Will South Florida Wake Up?" *Homestead Enterprise*, 8 October 1926.

22. Joe Hugh Reese, *Florida's Great Hurricane* (Miami, Fla.: Lysle E. Fesler, 1926), 53, 54, 57.

23. Carter, *Florida Experience*, 68–69, 71, 73.

24. Alfred Jackson Hanna and Kathryn Abbey Hanna, *Lake Okeechobee: Wellspring of the Everglades* (Indianapolis, Ind.: Bobbs-Merrill, 1948), 254–55.

25. "Lower the Lake," *Tampa Tribune*, 28 September 1926.

26. "Apology for the Drainage Board in Press Story," *Homestead Enterprise*, 22 October 1926; "Martin Pleads Lack of Funds," *Miami Daily News*, 28 October 1926.

27. American National Red Cross, *The West Indies Hurricane Disaster, September, 1928: Official Report of Relief Work in Porto Rico, the Virgin Islands and Florida* (Washington, D.C.: American Red Cross, 1929), 53.

28. Lawrence E. Will, *Okeechobee Hurricane and the Hoover Dike* (St. Petersburg, Fla.: Great Outdoors Publishing, 1961), 84.

29. Ibid., 88, 89–90.

30. "A Measurable Disaster," *Wall Street Journal*, 19 September 1928; "A Touch of Hysteria," *Wall Street Journal*, 22 September 1928; Will, *Okeechobee Hurricane*, 83.

31. Will, *Okeechobee Hurricane*, 101.

32. Ibid., 103.

33. "Lipstick First," *Miami Herald*, 12 September 1935.

34. "Naming the Hurricane," *Miami Herald*, 14 September 1935.

35. Gary Dean Best, *FDR and the Bonus Marchers, 1933–1935* (Westport, Conn.: Praeger, 1992), 5.

36. See, for example, "The Whys of Matecumbe," *Miami Daily Tribune*, 5 September 1935, and "What Price Buck Passing?" *Miami Daily Tribune*, 6 September 1935.

37. "Storm Deaths an Act of God Says Williams," *Miami Daily News*, 9 September 1935.

38. See Oliver Griswold, *The Florida Keys and the Coral Reef* (Miami, Fla.: Graywood Press, 1965), 58–59; Carter, *Florida Experience*, 66.

39. Griswold, *Florida Keys*, 60–61.

40. Ibid., 59, 69; "Matecumbe Investigation," *Miami Daily Tribune*, 7 September 1935.

41. "Miami Stands the Test," *Miami Daily News*, 5 November 1935.

42. See Fred Doehring, Iver W. Duedall, and John M. Williams, *Florida Hurricanes and Tropical Storms, 1871–1933: An Historical Survey*, Technical Paper No. 71 (Gainesville: Florida Sea Grant College Program, University of Florida, 1994), 61–67.

43. Ibid., 63–65.

44. Redford, *Billion-Dollar Sandbar*, 204, 216, 255; Carson, "Forty Years of Miami Beach," 23–25; "Let's Go to the Beach—But Where Did It Go?" *Miami News*, 21 September 1958.

45. Carter, *Florida Experience*, 144, 151–52; Edward Sofen, *The Miami Metropolitan Experiment* (Bloomington: Indiana University Press, 1963), 15–16.

46. Melvin J. Richard, "Tidelands and Riparian Rights in Florida," *Miami Law Quarterly* 3 (1949): 349, 359.

47. See *State v. Simberg*, 2 Fla. Supp. 178 (Dade Cty. Cir. Ct. 1952); *State v. Simberg*, 4 Fla. Supp. 85 (Dade Cty. Cir. Ct. 1953).

48. "Despite Court Ruling Against Hotels," *Miami Daily News*, 16 August 1953.

49. Charlton W. Tebeau, *A History of Florida* (Coral Gables, Fla.: University of Miami Press, 1971), 403–4; Griswold, *Florida Keys*, 70–72.

50. Peter J. May, *Recovering From Catastrophes: Federal Disaster Relief Policy and Politics* (Westport, Conn.: Greenwood Press, 1985), 23, 30.

51. Griswold, *Florida Keys*, 121; May, *Recovering From Catastrophes*, 28, 33.

52. "Disaster? Not in Miami," *Miami Herald*, 29 August 1964; "A 'Disaster' to Think About," *Miami Herald*, 31 August 1964.

53. "Beaches Are Washing Away, Golden Foot by Foot," *Miami Daily News*, 9 August 1959; Orin H. Pilkey Jr. et al., *Living With the East Florida Shore* (Durham, N.C.: Duke University Press, 1984), 44, 139; "Public Beach Access 'Eroded' Away," *Miami Herald*, 19 October 1967; "Beaches Are Holes Near the Water Into Which One Pours Money," *Miami Herald (Tropic Magazine)*, 10 July 1977.

54. "Beaches Are Holes."

55. "The Sands of Time Are Running Out for Miami Beach," *New York Times*, 10 May 1970.

56. "Judge Questions Miami Beach's Right in Erosion Suit," *Miami Herald*, 21 December 1969.

57. "Hotels Offer Own Plan to Save Beachfronts," *Miami Herald*, 21 October 1967.

58. Jack Roberts, "A Mayor Covers the Waterfront," *Miami News*, 10 November 1967; "No Beach is Good Beach?" editorial, *Miami Herald*, 4 December 1965.

59. Roberts, "A Mayor Covers the Waterfront."

60. Ben Novack, "It's No Place for Picnics," *Miami Herald*, 29 May 1970.

61. "Hotels OK Plan for 10-Mile Public Beach," *Miami Herald*, 14 October 1971.

62. Pilkey et al., *Living With the East Florida Shore*, 37; "Believe It: S. Florida Short on Sand," *Miami Herald*, 25 October 1993.

63. Sofen, *Miami Metropolitan Experiment*, 20, 26; "Older is Often Better for Dade Homes, Experts Say," *Miami Herald*, 6 September 1992; "Donna's Lessons From 1960 Ignored," *Miami Herald*, 10 September 1992.

64. "Building Code Eroded Over Years," *Miami Herald*, 11 October 1992.

65. Ibid.

66. "Builders' Shortcut to Disaster," *Miami Herald*, 20 December 1992.

67. "Safety Claims for Mobile Homes Called a Dangerous Myth," *Miami Herald*, 7 September 1992.

68. "Despite Storm's Carnage, Mobile Home Sales Are Brisk," *Miami Herald*, 26 September 1992.

69. "Feds Failed to Heed Mobile Home Warnings," *Miami Herald*, 21 September 1992.

70. See James R. McDonald and John F. Mehnert, "Review of Standard Practice for Wind-Resistant Manufactured Housing," *Journal of Aerospace Engineering* 2 (1989): 88–96.

71. "Feds Failed to Heed Mobile Home Warning."

72. Coordinated Hurricane Andrew Recovery Team, *Metropolitan Dade County Hurricane Andrew Recovery Status Report*, comp. Joaquin G. Avino, 18 June 1993, 1. The

number of mobile homes is from Standard and Poors, *Creditweek Municipal*, Special Report, 23 November 1992, 69.

73. "Safety Claims For Mobile Homes Called a Dangerous Myth."

74. U.S. House Committee on Banking, Finance, and Urban Affairs, Subcommittee on Housing and Community Development, *Manufactured Housing*, 102d Cong., 2d sess., 1992, 33, 35.

75. Pielke, *Hurricane Andrew in South Florida*, 137. A small area near the storm's center had winds of 145 miles per hour, with gusts reaching 175 miles per hour.

76. U.S. House Committee on Banking, Finance, and Urban Affairs, *Manufactured Housing*, 127.

77. Pielke, *Hurricane Andrew in South Florida*, 105.

78. "Hurricane Protection Debated," *Miami Herald*, 20 March 1999.

79. "Why Don't People Evacuate? Denial, Turf Worries," *Miami Herald*, 25 August 1992.

80. "Area Not Set for the Next 'Big One,' Expert Says," *Miami Herald*, 22 February 1993.

81. "Rumors of Death," *Miami Herald (Tropic Magazine)*, 20 December 1992.

CRAIG E. COLTEN

Reintroducing Nature to the City
Wetlands in New Orleans

Introduction

FOR MORE THAN two centuries, New Orleans' builders struggled
to expel the soggy wetlands from within their city. Early settlers saw little
value in the swamps after they had harvested the virgin cypress forests and
marshes held no value as urban real estate. The original city grew during
the early 1700s along the natural levee, a narrow band of relatively high
ground deposited by recurring river floods, and several faubourgs gradually extended into the miasmatic backswamps by the end of the colonial
period (1803). Levee construction along the river coupled with canal excavations toward the lakefront were the key colonial public works projects
to drain water from the city and thereby reclaim the swamps and marshes
within the urbanized territory. Only after a viable flood protection barrier
was in place by the mid-nineteenth century and the effective completion
of major drainage systems by the 1930s were developers able to extend
streets and subdivisions across the marsh to the Lake Pontchartrain shore.
In addition to expanding usable real estate, the massive drainage projects
greatly reduced disease threats that had plagued the city for two centuries.
To accommodate post–World War II suburbanization, wetland drainage
pressed westward into adjacent Jefferson Parish, into the marshes east of
New Orleans, and southward beyond the natural levee on the Mississippi's
west bank.[1] By the late 1960s, technical capability and real estate demand
seemed poised to complete the wetland conquest within the city limits.

Yet after more than two centuries, the drive to enlarge the drained territory reversed itself. Fundamental changes in public attitudes toward
the environment in general and wetlands in particular have impeded the

Crescent City's ever-expanding drainage program since about 1970. While the city will not abandon the existing drainage system, it has shelved expansion plans. There has arisen an overwhelming urge to protect marsh and swamp in and near the city, along with programs creating wetlands as relics of Louisiana's natural history. This paper proposes to answer the question of why there was a reversal in this fundamental aspect of urban development in New Orleans. It will consider the abandonment of the belief that the city was no place for a swamp, and its replacement by practices that preserved wetland tracts to satisfy public will. Beyond sentiments about urban uses of wetlands, a second underlying attitude shift was necessary. This involved the adoption of notions about nature as utility. In order to justify the preservation of wetlands, society first had to embrace the concept that these preserves would serve as educational settings and also provide necessary ecological functions. Finally, while social institutions refer to these preserves as nature, they must invest considerable effort to maintain highly modified environments. By considering the forces and ideas behind the creation and maintenance of the Audubon Zoo swamp exhibit, the Louisiana Nature Center, the National Park Service's Barataria Preserve, and the Bayou Sauvage Wildlife Refuge, this paper examines these sites as landscapes that are shaped to resemble pre-urbanized environments, that function in an urban setting as part of an evolving concept of parks and open spaces, and that stand as concrete evidence of public attitudes and environmental policies. Taken as a whole, the forces behind landscape modification and the actual transformation or preservation of wetlands speak to fundamental aspects of human use of urban space that are vastly different than a century ago and are altering urban form in the process.

Nature in the City

At their core, the four examples represent efforts to replicate or set aside parcels of a pre-colonial lower Mississippi River delta environment. Envisioned as places where the public could come in contact with and learn about native flora and fauna or where actual vestiges of nature could survive, they were all post-1970 creations or delineations. In this respect they reflected several obvious trends in public policy toward wetlands and urban open space—that is, wetland preservation and large urban preserves.[2] The impulse to create and preserve wetlands in an urban setting was also part of another process—the management of the non-human world within highly urbanized American cities. Despite extensive discussions about rural wetlands,[3] New Orleans provides a fundamentally different situation because the wetlands were and are within the *direct* reach of urban influences. Although the growth of cities around the turn of the twentieth century prompted drainage efforts, both rural and urban, different processes were at work in the two locales. The city, as a market, propelled rural drainage of floodplains to create farmland in order to feed growing urban immigrant populations in the Midwest and along the eastern seaboard.[4] This was an indirect outreach of urban economic influences into rural hinterlands. Wetlands in the path of expanding cities also underwent drainage to eliminate disease threats and accommodate the direct expansion of urban land uses—the Lake Calumet area in southeast Chicago, for example, became a major industrial district.[5] While also economically inspired, conversion of marsh and swamp within cities fell under the footprint of the urban juggernaut.

In Louisiana, urban wetlands were distinct from their rural counterparts. Long despised as harbors of pestilence and platted as residential and commercial real estate, these lands had an urban imprint applied to them by cartographers before the construction of drainage canals, levees, or streets. Rural wetlands, by contrast, served as locales for hunting and fishing, both commercial and sport, commercial timber removal, and oil extraction. When Louisiana set aside over 200,000 acres of marsh habitat in the early twentieth century, it offered no comparable protection for urban parcels.[6] Hunters, fishermen, and a few tourists ventured out to enjoy the rural swamps and marshes, while urban tracts drew only the attention of developers. Only in the last third of the twentieth century, with the emergence of public concern for wetlands accompanied by chemical control of mosquitoes, did city residents demand wetland creation and preservation within New Orleans.

The Crescent City's residents, as their counterparts in other cities, have not created structural cocoons that completely sever their connections with nature. As historian Ari Kelman eloquently observed, New Orleanians manipulated nature in numerous ways to make a more secure settlement on the banks of the Mississippi River. Nevertheless, the levees and floodways that protect the city from regular inundation have not diminished the river's significance in the city's existence.[7] Likewise the wetlands, long targets of attempted modification by engineers and developers, have remained a critical non-human element in an urbanized setting. The massive engineering works, constructed to rid the city of numerous public health problems and provide more space, placed a huge financial burden on the partly-below-sea-level city because they merely managed water, they did not eliminate the conditions that created wetlands. In addition, the dewatered peaty soils within the flood barriers subsided, causing problems for suburban construction. Nature persisted throughout the urban fabric, and efforts to showcase and preserve segments of the pre-European environment constituted a relatively recent campaign with an urban point of view.[8]

Rutherford Platt traces open-space development in urban America through the romantic, sanitary reform, city beautiful, and garden city periods.[9] Parks developed during these periods endowed cities with lovely open spaces, and provided access to an idealized nature in the city.[10] These parks emulated nature with the use of carefully landscaped terrain, and in the eyes of their creators provided urban residents with spaces for emotional rejuvenation. New Orleans' Audubon Park traces its inception to the romantic period and its full-blown development to the city beautiful period.[11] Since the 1970s, Platt states an entirely different entity has emerged to serve the urban longing for open space. Valued for their climatic, hydrologic, and ecological contributions, expansive reserves comprise the current objective of open-space planners.[12] Their creation reflected efforts by land managers to conform to post-1970 federal environmental laws and a public demand that environmental considerations enter the urban development equation. The Endangered Species Act along with Section 404 of the Clean Water Act dramatically impacted land management, both rural and urban, and they compelled public bodies to protect certain areas. Public support for defending the environment accompanied the passage of these laws, although opposition also emerged. Another aspect of public support commonly rested on the ecological significance of wetlands, and management policy mandated public access to the protected areas—for education and recreation. Efforts, for example, to protect the Lake Calumet and New Jersey wetlands have paralleled the New Orleans situation.[13] Through the act of designation, society has domesticated places viewed as natural areas for public use.[14] Even though the late twentieth-century reserves have received less formal landscaping than traditional parks, the latter open spaces are not just wildlife preserves, but also must satisfy the demands of an urban population.

The founders of the New Orleans areas under consideration here did not see them as pristine. In fact, they were anything but. Indeed, as areas set apart both for wildlife and for humans, they blur the distinction between nature and artifice.[15] They are neither completely of nature nor of the city—more a hybrid landscape. Audubon Zoo's swamp exhibit is a zoological exhibit, crafted by designers and maintained by the staff. The Nature Center's swamp exhibit also is the creation of landscape designers, although it is situated in a wooded tract that appears to some as untouched nature. Both are well within the fully urbanized territory of New Orleans. The two larger reserves, Barataria Preserve and Bayou Sauvage refuge, were wetlands long before European arrival in the lower delta. Nonetheless, prehistoric societies acted upon these latter locales for millennia. Extensive human manipulation continued into the twentieth century as the city grew outward toward these tracts. Designating these properties as preserves did not initiate their preservation. As private property these tracts endured as viable habitat even without government management efforts. Nature was at work and human alterations had not eliminated all potential for wildlife support. Under the auspices of federal natural resource agencies these parcels have come under more thorough management plans than previously, and under such supervision they will continue to provide habitat for wild animals and plants, all the while being made accessible to the public. Wetland preservation in the New Orleans urban area, as much as protecting habitat and wildlife, provides people with physical and intellectual entry to marsh and swamp.

Public Attention to Wetlands

Each of the organizations that created swamp exhibits or set aside wetlands shared a common objective: to introduce the urban public to this endangered habitat and to reveal the connections between the humanized and the non-humanized world. The presentation of wetlands builds on an erratic history of swamp and marsh interest. Victorian-era artists discovered and painted the rural Louisiana swamp, while rugged hunters and fishers sought game in the wetlands. The latter group was instrumental in prompting conservation-oriented efforts to set aside massive wildlife refuges.[16] Distinct from the more recent urban efforts, the early twentieth-century refuges were both spatially and conceptually distant from the city.

It has taken more than a century of popular tourism in the New Orleans area for guides and promoters to make wetlands a destination for urban tourists. Travel literature and sightseeing tours traditionally emphasized the city's cultural landscapes—the French Quarter, the above-ground cemeteries, and lavish mansions—along with nightclubs. Hunters, by contrast, could hire guides to take them into the rural swamp. A nineteenth-century guidebook touted alligator hunting as "a favorite sport," but lamented the decline in game: "There are not as many alligators in the suburbs of New Orleans as there were before the skins of the mighty saurians became commercial commodity . . . You will have no difficulty in finding as many alligators as you want in the innumerable bayous and lakes just back of Algiers."[17] Located outside the city, the hunter's wetland was a place where men could camp in palmetto lodges, like the ones built by native peoples centuries before, and hunt wildlife. This experience was not urban.

Victorian America witnessed a surge of interest in the wetlands as a place to observe sublime and picturesque nature. Longfellow's tale of Evangeline described the cypress swamp as an ancient cathedral[18] and James Hamilton's painting "Bayou in Moonlight" portrayed a swamp that was not just the domain of the rustic hunter, but one of rural beauty. During the 1870s and 1880s, artists gathered in New Orleans and from there ventured into the swamp searching for suitable scenes to paint.[19] Apparently inspired by their romantic images, George Coulon embarked upon a 350-mile voyage through the Atchafalaya Basin—a vast wetland west of New Orleans—in search of "virgin nature."[20] Both visual and narrative presentations of Louisiana's wetlands directed attention to the rural swamps and marshes, but tourism in the early twentieth century relegated such adventures to sportsmen and artists.

The Federal Writers' Project New Orleans guide noted that fishing and hunting remained popular attractions in the bayous and lagoons surrounding the city in the twentieth century. It also suggested several tours through the bayou country to places such as Barataria and Lafitte (both near the modern Barataria Preserve) where one could see oaks and cypress and the "trembling" prairie—a type of marsh.[21] During the 1950s, guide-books continued to point visitors toward routes *through* the rural wetlands where they might view Spanish moss or where men might go fishing and hunting in nearby parishes.[22] While families could observe wetland flora from the highway, only males typically penetrated the swamps in quest of game. Thus the Louisiana wetlands presented to tourists were either a picturesque backdrop of live oaks and cypress trees festooned with moss, or an untrammeled wilderness where males could prey on waterfowl, alligators, or fish. In either instance, it was hardly an urban experience. Rather, to appreciate the wetlands, one had to leave the city—at least this was the case up until the 1960s.

Tentative opportunities for urban tourists to penetrate Louisiana's wetlands began in the early 1960s when the large excursion boats added "bayou trips" to their customary river cruise offerings. Phonebook listings for sightseeing opportunities first included bayou trips offered by the *Steamer President* and the *Voyageur* in 1961.[23] Both multi-deck boats operated from the foot of Canal Street, the heart of the city, and took visitors on junkets along the Intercoastal Canal, a human-made waterway that passed through swampland south of New Orleans. These excursions were on large vessels with restrooms and food service and gave tourists a glimpse of wetlands similar to the one available via auto tours, yet with all the comforts and convenience of an urban river cruise.

From this modest beginning, several related influences sparked additional interest in the wetlands during the 1970s. Louisiana environmental activists made the Atchafalaya River basin their cause celebré as they battled with the Corps of Engineers over its management of the massive wetland. At issue in the Atchafalaya basin was a series of Corps of Engineer proposals to stabilize the engineering works that provided flood protection for the lower Mississippi River valley. In short, these plans would upset the basin's ecology and disrupt both commercial and sport fishing and hunting activities. Traditional fishermen and hunters shared some fundamental objectives with environmental organizations, and they worked to block the more destructive elements of the Corps' plans.[24] Tapping a growing awareness, C. C. Lockwood, a local photographer, further aroused public concern over the Atchafalaya in the 1970s with his colorful images of this territory.[25] National environmental organizations encouraged contact with the bayous and wetlands surrounding New Orleans by promoting tours for those willing to propel themselves in canoes.[26] Such concerns coalesced into efforts to create urban wetlands.

Tour operators also responded to growing public interest in rural swamps. Beginning in 1980 New Orleans directories included advertisements for "swamp tours," and since then the number of swamp tour operators has escalated. By 1990 eight services placed their advertisements in the New Orleans telephone book and by the late 1990s a score of operators advertised in various media.[27] No longer were the tours conducted on large river boats, but the new swamp adventures traveled in single-deck (20–80 passenger) boats that could negotiate smaller bayous and canals. This offered a much more intimate experience. Also, these operators set up bases outside the city, pulling riders away from the tourist bubble into the wetlands at the urban fringe. Indeed, several of the operations have docks near the Barataria Preserve or the Bayou Segnette State Park and one cruises through the Bayou Sauvage Refuge. Increasing access to the rural wetlands both fueled public interest in wetlands and served a growing demand for access.

Exhibiting Wetlands

The compulsion to construct natural enclaves and put them on display in New Orleans emerged over a fifteen- to twenty-year span beginning in the 1970s. At the root was a growing social concern about nature in general and wetlands in particular.[28] At the national level, public articulation of wetlands' environmental significance emerged in a 1956 report. Although largely rural in its orientation, it noted federal apprehension over the vulnerability of wetlands as waterfowl habitat in the Northeast due to urban land-use pressures.[29] Several years later, participants at a national conference deliberated the need to preserve space for outdoor recreation and claimed that "the first task is to provide recreation for the metropolitan areas" because land was the most precious there.[30] At another conference organized to address "nature in the city," one commentator claimed that "nature is rapidly disappearing from our urban environment as an annual 1 million acres of land give way to urbanization."[31] Obviously, the open space and wetlands preservation advocates saw urban land as a key part of the discussion. Even in the South, although long considered lagging in environmental activism, the Atchafalaya River basin sparked one of several regional controversies in the early 1970s.[32] Southern environmentalism remained largely rural, although New Orleans provided expression of an urban impulse in line with national trends. Furthermore, the fact that most open space in south Louisiana is also wetland made swamps and marshes an easy choice for preservation efforts. The initial phase of the Louisiana campaign created two wetland educational exhibits in the city.

Audubon Park Zoo Swamp Exhibit

In New Orleans, it took shame to stir local action with an urban focus. A 1966 account of the whooping crane's perilous situation pointed out that New Orleans' Audubon Zoo housed seven birds that were to be the centerpiece of the Fish and Wildlife Service's captive breeding experiment. Faith McNulty, the gifted nature writer, described the zoo as having a "shabby air of ease."[33] Shortly thereafter, a local journalist used harsher language, referring to the zoo as a "zoological ghetto" and an "animal concentration camp."[34] In addition to the abysmal conditions at the zoo, McNulty argued that "its lack of trained staff or special facilities make it an unlikely site for a crucial experiment in aviculture."[35] Indeed, her remarks were an oblique reference to the sudden death the previous year of the zoo's female half of a successful mating pair. With the whooping cranes' fate in the allegedly incompetent hands of the New Orleans zoo, many in the wildlife conservation movement were troubled.

Publicly humiliated, zoo supporters organized to restore conditions at the municipally supported facility. As a first step in 1971, a local research organization evaluated whether the zoo should be rejuvenated in situ or rebuilt from scratch at a new location. Ultimately, the study advocated that the zoo should continue at the existing site—part of a large city-beautiful era park designed by the Olmsted firm—but with major improvements, namely larger and more naturalistic settings for the animals. In a dramatic departure from traditional zoological park purposes to exhibit the rare and exotic, the researchers called for exhibits "emphasizing the natural resources of Louisiana."[36] At a time when the official state bird, the brown pelican, had virtually disappeared,[37] and the emblematic megafauna of the Louisiana wetlands, the alligator, was under serious threat,[38] the report suggested that local fauna serve as the key attractions. This represented a critical turning point in attitudes toward the local swamps and marshes. Specifically, the new view was that the public had a responsibility to *protect* wetland fauna and flora for its own sake and not just *conserve* it for a sustained yield. Furthermore, this responsibility was an urban imperative; it suggested that hope for wetlands lay with the nation's majority, urban residents, who were woefully unfamiliar with the swamp and marsh that surrounded them.

A schematic plan for the zoo's rehabilitation showed a Louisiana exhibit larger than the entire grounds at the time. Within this area, a swamp exhibit would "include spectacular aquatic birds peculiar to Louisiana together with extensive exhibits of alligators and other appropriate swamp life."[39] A conceptual drawing showed a "tracked" *African Queen*-like launch motoring past the alligators on the banks of an artificial bayou to "increase the excitement" of the zoo exhibit. In order for this exhibit to become a reality, a portion of the natural levee had to be reworked, secure exhibit facilities built, and animals acquired. The plan underwent some alterations from its initial conception, progressing from a Disneyesque ride to a walk-through exhibit that attempted to replicate both the biophysical and cultural landscapes of the Louisiana wetlands.[40] Native plantings and structures modeled after vernacular buildings found in the nearby swamp created the ambiance of the Atchafalaya Basin. Touted as an effort to preserve "a vital part of the state's heritage" when it opened in 1984,[41] planners intended for this exhibit to convince urban residents that they actually had visited a Louisiana swamp. Today, raised walkways allow visitors to see alligators, pelicans, herons, egrets, and a variety of ducks placed in naturalistic settings consisting of ponds surrounded by cypress and other native vegetation. Since its opening, the swamp exhibit has consistently been the zoo's leading attraction.[42] One key impetus for creating this type of nature in the city was to replicate a bit of a rapidly disappearing and increasingly inaccessible swamp. Zoo officials accomplished this purpose without the advantage of pre-existing swamp at the site; consequently the exhibit's creation was not a direct part of the subsequent effort to set aside and preserve wetlands.[43] Nonetheless, it was fundamentally part of that same social impulse and contributed to local concern about wetlands, as did its suburban counterpart, the Louisiana Nature Center.[44]

Louisiana Nature Center

At about the same time as the zoo overhaul, a group of private citizens organized to create a nature education center in 1972. A board consisting of local civic and university leaders secured a two-acre site, buffered by a larger eighty-acre city-owned woodland in rapidly urbanizing eastern New Orleans. The nature center's staff justified its existence with the argument that most city residents had not seen or heard of the marshlands that encircled the metropolis and that they had no appreciation for the ecological and economic significance of these wetlands to the city and the state. They asserted that the center's purpose was to stimulate "an awareness and understanding of our total environment, natural and altered, . . . and to develop a sense of responsibility for the care and wise use of the environment."[45] Like the zoo supporters, the nature center advocates did not think that their small tract would actually preserve nature, but that they would use their tiny wooded setting to illustrate non-human processes within an urban territory and promote understanding of the environment within the city. One of its first major exhibit projects was to create a swamp. On a site that had once been marsh, drained for residential and commercial development, this entailed excavating two ponds, one for catfish and a second for crawfish, along with planting cypress trees and other swamp plants, and erecting a raised walkway through the exhibit.[46] The center's management plan called for planting native species that were not found at the site, while at the same time battling exotic plants and animals within its limited grounds.[47] Although not as thoroughly crafted as the zoo exhibit, the nature center's swamp had to be created, literally, in a location where there had never been a swamp and then maintained through human agency.

Both of the earliest wetland efforts reflected a desire to employ nature and to put it to work in an educational capacity. At the zoo and nature center, exhibits were intended to inform and to enlighten the urban public about the significance of Louisiana's best-known but receding habitat. They both presented wetlands that planners thought urban youth needed to encounter—either through a zoo exhibit or a small woodland in the midst of suburban sprawl. Neither of these projects included plans to acquire large tracts of land or actually to set aside existing wetlands. Although the nature center eventually leased a total of eighty-six acres from the city and participated vigorously in the creation of the Bayou Sauvage wildlife refugee, the center itself did not significantly deflect the conversion of wetland to suburb. The site of the zoo was on the natural levee, some of the highest ground in the city; and the nature center's property occupied former marshland that had been drained by the time of its inception. Neither effort actually preserved wetland, and both had to physically create swamp exhibits.

New Orleans advocates for nature preservation were part of a larger national movement and Louisiana was in synch with the times.[48] A spate of late 1960s and early 1970s federal environmental laws began impeding wholesale wetland development in the New Orleans area. Most notably, Section 404 of the Clean Water Act (1972) prompted court decisions that expanded the protection of wetlands in navigable waters to almost all wetlands.[49] Filling or draining wetlands under this law required permits from the Corps of Engineers, thus providing public groups with a means to question wetland alterations. Armed with legal tools, local wetland protection advocates stalled seemingly relentless development pressures in eastern New Orleans.[50] Protection efforts rested on arguments that wetlands served vital ecological purposes with benefits to humans—flood retention, wildlife habitat, groundwater recharge. In the case of New Orleans, they also served as a vital buffer to coastal erosion processes.[51]

By the mid-1970s public attitudes toward wetlands in New Orleans were undergoing a fundamental shift. Driven by shame surrounding the zoo controversy, near extinction of two emblematic state creatures, and increased public attentiveness to environmental issues, and armed with federal legislation and supporting case law, there emerged sufficient concern with wetlands to begin major programs to reconfigure the geography of wetland management, to set aside islands of nature. Once viewed as an impassable mire that bred disease or provided a livelihood for reclusive "swamp rats," wetlands as habitat and vital ecosystems assumed an entirely different value in public opinion.[52] Socially reconstituted and legally protected, swamps and marshes became desirable locales, worthy of protection, investigation, and recreation—even in urban areas.

Preserving Urban Wetlands

Along the Gulf Coast private land ownership has dominated since colonial times, so any effort to create public reserves required the transfer of titles to a public entity. This was the case when private foundations set aside vast tracts of rural Louisiana marsh as refuges in the early twentieth century.[53] Such efforts, carried out in the 1910s through the 1930s, operated on conservation principles, and principally sought to sustain waterfowl populations for sport hunters. These impulses differed from the late twentieth-century efforts to preserve wetlands for their inherently desirable environmental conditions and for urban users—not a bag limit. In and around New Orleans, the driving motivation was to preserve a disappearing habitat, to maintain ecological and hydrological conditions, and to protect the city from relentless coastal erosion. The rise of public concern for wetlands, plus federal laws that inhibited unrestricted drainage, undercut development schemes that had long targeted the expansive wetlands and thereby created possibilities for wetland protection.

In the early 1970s much of the eastern Orleans Parish remained largely undeveloped marsh. With the exception of a few transportation routes crossing the area and some recreational facilities along the lake and bays, large privately owned marshlands lay ready for the same type of drainage and subdivision that had transformed much of the territory along the Pontchartrain lakefront. The restrictions presented by wetland regulations complicated a once straightforward technical process and also increased development costs. Other complications also arose with marsh development. For example, in the early 1970s subsidence of drained marshlands in Jefferson Parish caused gas pipeline fractures, resulting in several dramatic explosions. Entire subdivisions suffered fractured streets, driveways, and foundations when built on recently drained peaty soils. In some neighborhoods where builders used pilings to stabilize homes, the residences seemingly rose above the earth when the earth around them sank. Owners trucked in fill to raise their lawns and close the gaps between their foundations and the sunken ground. In some areas of Kenner (west of New Orleans), subsidence exceeded ten feet.[54] Such complications prompted local ordinances that added costs to wetland development. When coupled with general economic malaise in the mid-1980s and the regulatory situation, these difficulties effectively blocked further drainage projects in eastern

New Orleans, which also had subsidence-prone subsoils. As development ground to a halt, other options for wetlands entered the public discussion. At the forefront were plans to preserve sprawling urban examples.

Barataria Preserve

Conversations about setting aside a larger wetland tract as National Park property began in the early 1970s. When the National Park Service (NPS) first deliberated the establishment of a park that would include several sites representative of Louisiana's wetland traditions, its personnel expressed concern over a wetlands unit. Most of the potential locations around New Orleans were second-growth cypress swamp, canalized marsh, or landscapes extensively altered by human activity. NPS personnel feared that no potential park-service property would meet the "integrity" standard required of a "nationally significant" natural area. Nonetheless the idea remained afloat under the rubric of a "cultural park," as opposed to a natural area, which would enable the removal of a passable, although not pristine, wetland from development pressures and permit urban residents access to this rapidly disappearing ecosystem.[55] An additional impetus may have come from the NPS's identification of wetlands as an under-represented ecosystem and one prioritized for acquisition. By the late 1970s, discussions about a wetland unit, recast as a preserve,[56] gained momentum.

At 1977 congressional hearings concerning the establishment of an 8,000 acre wetland unit, Louisiana's delegation predicted that it would "preserve" an important environmental setting while providing access for school children. Some local interests, however, saw another side of the picture. The 8,000-acre parcel, to be supplemented with an additional 20,000-acre "protection zone" (or buffer), would constitute a significant shift in property ownership and in their view threaten access and use by local fishermen, hunters, trappers, and oil prospectors. Local governments feared tax revenue losses and federal intrusion into local politics.[57] Louisiana's congressional delegation inserted language in the bill creating the new unit that resolved most concerns and secured the bill's approval in 1978.[58]

As finally passed, the enabling legislation called for acquisition of approximately 20,000 acres for the Barataria Preserve of the Jean Lafitte National Historical Park and Preserve and a buffer or protection zone.[59] The new preserve had a mandate to "preserve for the education, inspiration, and benefit of present and future generations *significant examples of natural and historical resources* and to provide for their interpretation in such a manner as to portray the development of cultural diversity in the region."[60] In terms of the "natural" conditions, the Park Service was to preserve and protect the fresh-water drainage patterns, the vegetative cover, the integrity of the ecological and biological systems, and air and water quality. At the same time, and as a concession to local interests, the Park Service had to allow "traditional uses"—namely commercial fishing, trapping, and oil prospecting—within the service's overall management guidelines. The NPS also had to recognize private rights to some 200 existing "camps," or fishing and hunting cabins. This created a difficult prospect for the Park Service within its mission of providing safe public access and protecting the biological integrity of the preserve. Yet, the highly modified parcel, subject to sewage from neighboring towns, external drainage, tidal manipulations, and exotic species, was not ecologically intact.

The site acquired by the Park Service contained several settings that represented the range of ecological zones found in the lower delta. A transect across the park, which roughly is centered on a former Mississippi River distributary, would pass over the natural levee covered with live oak, down the backslope and its maple forest into the cypress tupelo gum swamp and out into a freshwater marsh. Human activity in the area has been extensive. Native peoples began building shell mounds about 2,000 years ago. Timber removal, both of oaks from the higher natural levees and of cypress from the backswamps, began in the early colonial period and lasted until the 1950s. Commercial cypress removal was most intense between about 1880 and 1925, when skidders used to pull the giant logs to collection points scoured sizable ditches through the wetlands. Land clearing and agriculture brought significant change to the natural levees and relict field ditches still exist in reforested areas. Additionally, land owners built artificial levees along the natural levee crests to protect their crops. Both these agricultural modifications altered the hydrology of the area. More recently oil extraction companies cut larger canals throughout the Louisiana coastal plain, including the Barataria Preserve, and they constructed drilling pads, mounds of fill, which now rise above the surrounding wetland surfaces. Over the course of two millennia, human alteration to both the

CRAIG E. COLTEN

physical topography and moisture-sensitive plant and animal life has been extensive.[61] This is the wetland that the Park Service acquired to manage as a natural and historical preserve.

Situated within an urbanizing region, the Barataria Preserve faced greater external threats than many other parks and consequently had to implement more extensive environmental management plans than its rural counterparts.[62] Of particular importance in the initial land protection plan, park authorities had to contend with flooding resulting from increased runoff in upstream urban areas and also the release of untreated sewage that entered park waterways. Levees constructed within the protection zone to protect neighboring suburbs had accelerated subsidence and thereby altered natural hydrological and ecological conditions. Canals allowed greater saltwater intrusion from the Gulf of Mexico.[63] In response to the dual issues of external threats and pre-existing environmental modifications, the Park Service had to work with numerous agencies to develop management plans that maintained its resources within a larger regional ecosystem. With a mandate to preserve, protect, and interpret the natural values of the unit, the Park Service sought to reestablish the pre-urban conditions—in terms of water quality, levels, and surface flow. This required extensive management to obtain the desired conditions. The services necessary to maintain conditions in the preserve include providing adequate sewage treatment for neighboring communities, diverting storm runoff, and controlling water levels on flood-protection levees.[64] Each of these procedures required actions by other government bodies—which may not have shared objectives with the Park Service.

Recognizing inherent conflicts between "traditional use" and "preservation," the Park Service carefully reviewed its impact on practices predating the creation of the preserve. Despite legislation mandating the toleration of numerous traditional activities, some came under regulatory pressure. The park curtailed annual burns of marsh grasses and also the digging of trenasses by trappers.[65] By outlawing motorized vehicles and by filling trenasses, the Park Service has effectively blocked some traditional trapping activity, without explicitly banning those locally important practices. At the same time it permitted trappers to remove unwanted and non-native nutria from the park territory. During the 1990–91 season, trappers captured over 2,000 nutria[66] which harvest served to protect marsh grasses and ensured better habitat for native species.[67] Wildlife management practices disrupted other traditional practices as well. Protection of native species, such as alligators, reduced sport fishing within the park, while prohibitions against cutting wax myrtle branches—used to catch softshell crabs—reduced this type of commercial fishing.[68]

Within the property acquired, as stipulated in the management plan, human oversight and husbandry of the environment has been a pervasive influence. Human action has become essential for the natural conditions that the Park Service desires to exist. Certainly nature abounds within this manipulated setting, and the NPS sought to minimize influences from the highly altered surrounding territory. Nonetheless, the preserve's managers exerted considerable efforts to protect the property's ecological workings. Similar circumstances prevail at the refuge in New Orleans' eastern extreme.

Bayou Sauvage

After the creation of the Barataria Preserve, nearly another decade passed before Louisiana wetlands advocates could position themselves to make their most significant transfer of marsh from private to public management—in this case creating the Bayou Sauvage Wildlife Refuge. New Orleans East (NOE), a major land development company with over 20,000 acres of marshland within New Orleans' city limits, had struggled, but failed, to obtain approval to develop its sprawling wetland and lapsed into receivership in 1985. Faced with opposition to wetland drainage, Section 404 obstacles, and increasing costs for safely developing the peaty ground, NOE transferred the property to South Point, Inc., a subsidiary of its financier, to manage. In a desperate attempt to get a return on its bad loan and unload the property, South Point began meetings with city, environmental, and federal officials. A proposal that appealed to the investors called for selling the marsh to the federal government as an urban wildlife refuge. This would ensure a fair-market price for the entire tract, thereby securing the developer's investment, plus eliminating the need to "bank" a portion of the wetland under Section 404 and lose revenue on that acreage.[69]

Environmental groups and city officials championed the proposed urban wildlife refuge in testimony before Congress in 1986. They claimed the refuge would help offset the rapid loss of Louisiana wetlands, maintain marshland for educational purposes, and preserve wetlands for their essential ecological functions. Louisiana's congressional delegation pressed hard to establish the refuge, which they hailed as a means to protect the habitat of some 40,000 migratory birds and a nursery for shrimp, crabs, and fish. One advocate argued that the area could only survive with human management, suggesting nature could not sustain this wetland tract without the intervention of humans.[70] The only critical question came from the Fish and Wildlife Service. James Pulliam, the regional director, testified that the Bayou Sauvage area in New Orleans east had not been identified as a critical habitat using the Service's normal prioritization system. While not opposing the designation, the Service simply had not evaluated the site in terms of how important it was in the larger picture of wildlife protection.[71] The Louisiana delegation remained determined to deliver a refuge to the state and whittled away at the Fish and Wildlife Service representative's concerns. Ultimately, refuge advocates prevailed. Legislation passed in 1986 authorized the acquisition of more than 22,000 acres to be placed under federal management.[72]

Like the Barataria Preserve, the newly created Bayou Sauvage Wildlife Refuge was a thoroughly reworked territory due to its urban location. About 60 percent of the acreage was within the hurricane protection levee system and was subject to complete water-level management by the Corps of Engineers. Large lakes occupied huge excavations where crews had excavated fill to raise interstate highway exchanges, and several canals and their spoil mounds traversed the area. Additionally, the Fish and Wildlife Service acquired the largest sanitary landfill in the greater New Orleans area. Within the refuge territory, subsidence was causing marshland to disappear at a rate of over 100 acres per year. Between 1956 and 1988 about half the marsh had sunk below the water table, although controlling water levels within the levee system could reduce that rate.[73] Nonetheless, extensive marshes, used by migratory waterfowl, made up most of the property. The fact that levees and canals were part of the deal simply meant that the infrastructure to manage the environment was already in place.

Among the key goals of the Fish and Wildlife Service's management plan were to (1) preserve, maintain, and restore natural habitat, (2) enhance and maintain wildlife diversity, (3) provide for public access, education, and research, and (4) foster a stewardship ethic. To accomplish these goals in an area already subject to substantial alteration, the Service claimed that extensive management was essential. The master plan set in motion several procedures. The first and perhaps most critical was the control of water levels. Lowering the water levels in spring stimulated emergent vegetation and raising levels in late summer maintained waterfowl feeding areas. Control of nuisance species was a second objective. This included eradication of mosquitoes, plus elimination of non-native species such as water hyacinth by flooding with saltwater and trapping nutria and feral hogs. Further, shoreline stabilization was necessary to prevent excessive coastal erosion. Key elements of this effort included creating wave dampening barriers along with stimulating oyster reefs along the shore outside the levee system.[74] Without human intervention, the wetlands would become a saltwater bay and waterfowl would have to winter elsewhere. Human involvement at Bayou Sauvage was essential to maintain the wetland as it existed when established and to prevent it from being destroyed by non-human processes.

The preserve and the refuge, along with additional restoration projects not mentioned here,[75] represent the latest phase in New Orleans' struggle with its largely wetland site. Faced with restrictive laws, local interests re-calibrated the value of wetlands by touting them as important educational and ecological resources. At the risk of assigning too much importance to the federal laws involved, it must be understood that development costs and other economic issues clouded the potential for full-scale wetland drainage and development. Nonetheless, convincing the federal government to purchase and manage over 40,000 acres of wetlands within easy reach of the downtown New Orleans has provided local and out-of-town visitors with ready access to a once remote environmental setting. In addition to programs offered by the Park Service and the Fish and Wildlife Service, swamp tourism facilities have sprung up in the vicinity of both properties. Both permit entry to an urbanized nature.

Conclusions

After more than two centuries of trying to exclude wetlands from their city, New Orleans citizens took on a grand crusade to reintroduce swamp and protect marshes within the city. Construction of levees and drainage systems had enlarged the territory where the city could stand and elimination of mosquito habitat dramatically reduced the threat of insect-borne disease. Consequently, little fear of the miasmas persisted into the 1970s and few could recall the long-lasting struggle to rid the city of wetlands.

With much of the negative attitude toward wetlands forgotten, preservation proponents first had to create a demand to preserve this ecosystem. National environmental movements provided one impetus by sparking public concern with Louisiana's remaining rural wetlands and the threatened alligators. By literally creating swamp exhibits in the city zoo and nature center, citizens fostered understanding about local environments and wildlife, thereby contributing to public support for subsequent efforts.

The wetlands set aside as nature in New Orleans fit within a broader pattern of open space preservation for biological and hydrological purposes prompted in part by federal laws. Nature, in such situations, must earn its keep by serving socially valued purposes such as maintaining diversity, educating the population, or serving as a flood control reservoir. In New Orleans the additional chore of protecting the city from coastal erosion provides a particularly urgent rationale for preservation.

In seeking to set aside actual swamp and marshland, local advocates found that while wetlands abounded, they were highly altered by human action. Both the proposed Barataria Preserve and the Bayou Sauvage Refuge required considerable management to offset urban influences and internal modifications. Thus, the nature presented to the public is a hybrid, a domesticated breed, made accessible and maintained by human intervention. The National Park Service and the Fish and Wildlife Service worked with the properties they inherited, and they actively managed the environments within their boundaries.

A social desire to reconstitute wetlands in the city has created two exhibits and two large preserves in the New Orleans metropolitan area. While these tracts must perform educational and other ecological functions to earn their keep, they stand as physical evidence of the changing significance of the non-human world in urban territories. Urban dwellers long sought to deny that the city was a place for swamps, and consequently drainage was an essential and all-consuming endeavor in New Orleans. A reversal of attitudes toward urban wetlands acknowledged that nature continues to function in New Orleans and indeed all urban territory and that nature had a place in the city. Despite magnificent engineering works, New Orleans will never be able to completely drain the sponge it rests upon. Likewise, other cities face countless eruptions of hydrologic, geologic, and meteorologic events that are undeniable elements of urban life. We may envision human and non-human environments as separate and draw boundaries that separate the city from wetlands, but the two nonetheless are bound in the larger web of human-nature interaction. At all scales—neighborhood, city, metropolitan, and urban systems—non-human environments have prevailed. As society delineates 100-year floodplains and sets aside green space in urban areas, it deflects other urban land uses, distorts traditional land-use models, and alters property values. Thus non-human processes become ever more important in the process of city building. Recognition of this relationship is fundamental to our understanding and management of urban environments.

Notes

1. An excellent overview of New Orleans' geographic development is Peirce Lewis, *New Orleans: The Making of an Urban Landscape* (Cambridge, Mass.: Ballinger Publishing Company, 1976), esp. 31–66.

2. See John B. Wright, *Rocky Mountain Divide: Selling and Saving the West* (Austin: University of Texas Press, 1993); Anne Matthews, *Wild Nights: Nature Returns to the City* (New York: North Point Press, 2001).

3. Ann Vileisis, *Discovering the Unknown Landscape: A History of America's Wetlands* (Washington, D.C.: Island Press, 1997); Hugh Prince, *Wetlands of the American Midwest: A Historical Geography of Changing Attitudes* (Chicago, Ill.: University of Chicago Press, 1997); Martin Reuss, *Designing the Bayous: The Control of Water in the Atchafalaya Basin, 1800–1995* (Alexandria, Va.: U.S. Army Corps of Engineers, Office of History, 1998); Gay Gomez, *A Wetland Biography: Seasons on Louisiana's Chenier Plain* (Austin: University of Texas Press, 1998); and David McCally, *The Everglades: An Environmental History* (Gainesville: University of Florida Press, 1999).

4. See William Cronon, *Nature's Metropolis: Chicago and The Great West* (New York: W. W. Norton, 1991); Vileisis, chapters 7 and 8; Daniel W. Schneider, "Enclosing the Floodplain: Resource Conflict on the Illinois River, 1880–1920," *Environmental History* 1 (1996): 70–96; and Christopher Meindl, "Past Perceptions of the Great American Wetland: Florida's Everglades during the Early Twentieth Century," *Environmental History* 5 (2000): 378–95; Prince.

5. On the Calumet wetland, see Alfred H. Meyer, "Circulation and Settlement Patterns of the Calumet Region of Northwest Indiana and Northeast Illinois," pt. 1, *Annals of the Association of American Geographers* 44 (1954): 245–74, and pt. 2, 46 (1956): 312–26, and Craig E. Colten, *Industrial Wastes in the Calumet Area, 1869–1970: An Historical Geography* (Champaign, Ill.: Hazardous Waste Research and Information

Center, Research Report 1, 1985); National Park Service, Midwest Regional Office (NPS, MRO), *Calumet Park Ecological Park Feasibility Study* (http://www.lincolnnet.net/environment/feasibility/calumet1.html, 1998).

6. See Gomez, 120–23.

7. Ari Kelman, "A River and Its City: Critical Episodes in the Environmental History of New Orleans" (PhD dissertation, Brown University, 1998), 11–12. See also Blake Gumprecht, *The Los Angeles River: Its Life, Death and Possible Rebirth* (Baltimore, Md.: Johns Hopkins University Press, 1999).

8. See several essays in Craig E. Colten, ed., *Transforming New Orleans and Its Environs: Centuries of Change* (Pittsburgh. Pa.: University of Pittsburgh Press, 2000).

9. Rutherford H. Platt, "From Commons to Commons: Evolving Concepts of Open Space in North American Cities," in *The Ecological City: Preserving and Restoring Urban Biodiversity*, ed. Rutherford H. Platt, Rowan A. Rowntree, and Pamela C. Muick (Amherst: University of Massachusetts Press, 1994), 21–39.

10. Henry W. Lawrence, "The Greening of the Squares of London: Transformation of Urban Landscapes and Ideals," *Annals of the Association of American Geographers* 83 (March 1993): 90–118; Terence Young, "Modern Urban Parks," *Geographical Review* 85 (October 1995): 535–51; Anne Whiston Spirn, "Constructing Nature: The Legacy of Frederick Law Olmsted," in *Uncommon Ground: Toward Reinventing Nature*, ed. William Cronon (New York: W. W. Norton, 1995), 91–113.

11. See L. Ronald Forman and Joseph Logsdon, *Audubon Park: An Urban Eden* (New Orleans: Friends of the Zoo, 1985).

12. Hugh Prince, "A Marshland Chronicle, 1830–1960: From Artificial Drainage to Outdoor Recreation," *Journal of Historical Geography* 21 (1995): 3–22, and Don Davis and Randall Detro, "Louisiana's Marsh as a Recreation Resource," *Geoscience and Man* 12 (1975): 91–98.

13. NPS, MRO, *Calumet Park Ecological Park Feasibility Study* (http://www.lincolnnet.net/environment/feasibility/calumet1.html, 1998), and New Jersey Meadowlands Commission, *Meadowlands Environmental Center* (http://www.hwdc.state.nj.us/ec/environment_center.htm, 2001). See also Lisa Cameron, "Experimental Park Grows on a Landfill," *Public Works* 126 (June 1995): 48–52.

14. William Cronon, "The Trouble with Wilderness; or Getting Back to the Wrong Nature," in *Uncommon Ground*, 80–81.

15. See Platt, "From Commons to Commons," and Julie Tuason, "*Rus in Urbe*: The Spatial Evolution of Urban Parks in the United States," *Historical Geography* 25 (1997): 124–47, esp. 126–27.

16. See Gomez, 120–23.

17. *Historical Sketch Book and Guide to New Orleans and Environs* (1885, New York: W. H. Coleman, 1924), 245.

18. Henry Wadsworth Longfellow, *The Poetical Works of Henry Wadsworth Longfellow*, V. II (New York: AMS Press, 1966), 67.

19. See David C. Miller, *Dark Eden: The Swamp in Nineteenth-Century American Culture* (Cambridge: Cambridge University Press, 1989), 32–33, 57–68.

20. George A. Coulon, *350 Miles in a Skiff through the Louisiana Swamps* (New Orleans: George Coulon, 1888), 1–2.

21. Federal Writers' Project, *The WPA Guide to New Orleans* (New Orleans: Historic New Orleans Collection, 1983 [1938]), 87, 391–92.

22. Stanley Arthur, *Louisiana Tours* (New Orleans: Havmansen, 1950), 55 and 86. See also Oliver Evans, *New Orleans* (New York: Macmillan, 1959), 136–39, and Thomas K. Griffin, *New Orleans: A Guide to America's Most Interesting City* (Garden City, N.Y.: Doubleday, 1961), 93–95.

23. *Southern Bell Telephone Directory: New Orleans, Louisiana* (New Orleans: Southern Bell, 1955–1961).

24. See Martin Reuss, *Designing the Bayous*, esp. chapters 8 and 9.

25. Jack and Anne Rudloe, "Trouble in Bayou Country," *National Geographic* 182 (September 1979): 377–97; C. C. Lockwood, *Atchafalaya: America's Largest River Basin Swamp* (Baton Rouge: Beauregard Press, 1981).

26. See John P. Sevenair, *Guide to Louisiana Wilderness Trails and the Delta Country* (New Orleans: New Orleans Group of the Sierra Club, 1978).

27. *South Central Bell Telephone Directory: Greater New Orleans* (New Orleans: South Central Bell, 1977–1999) and brochures obtained in New Orleans hotel information racks.

28. Samuel P. Hays, *Beauty, Health, and Permanence: Environmental Politics in the United States, 1955–1985* (New York: Cambridge University Press, 1987), and for wetlands in particular, see Vileisis, esp. 211–48.

29. Samuel P. Shaw and C. Gordon Fredine, *Wetlands in the United States* (Washington, D.C.: U.S. Fish and Wildlife Service, Circular 39, 1956), 28.

30. *Outdoor Recreation for America: A Report to the President and Congress* (Washington: Outdoor Recreation Resources Review Commission, 1962), 81.

31. Frank J. Tysen, "Nature and the Urban Dweller," *Man and Nature in the City Symposium* (Washington: U.S. Department of the Interior, Bureau of Sport Fisheries and Wildlife, 1968), 12. See also Adam Rome, *The Bulldozer in the Countryside: Suburban Sprawl and the Rise of Environmentalism* (New York: Cambridge University Press, 2001).

32. James C. Cobb, *Industrialization and Southern Society, 1877–1984* (Chicago: Dorsey Press, 1984). Additional discussions of environmental action in the South appear in Jeffery Stine, *Mixing the Waters: Environmental Politics and the Building of the Tennessee-Tombigbee Waterway* (Akron: University of Akron Press, 1993); Richard Bartlett, *Troubled Waters: Champion International and the Pigeon River Controversy* (Knoxville: University of Tennessee Press, 1995); Reuss; and McCally.

33. Faith McNulty, *The Whooping Crane: The Bird that Defies Extinction* (New York: E. P. Dutton, 1966), 18.

34. Herschel Miller, "The Angry Animals," *New Orleans* 3 (October 1968): 17–20, 38–41.

35. McNulty, *The Whooping Crane*, 18.

36. Bureau of Government Research, *Audubon Park Zoo Study: Part 1, Zoo Improvement Plan* (New Orleans: Bureau of Government Research, 1971), 2.

37. Donald Norman and Robert Purrington, "Demise of the Brown Pelican in Louisiana," *Louisiana Ornithological Society News* 55 (15 August 1970): 3–6, and U.S. Fish and Wildlife Service, Division of Endangered Species, "Brown Pelican," *Endangered and Threatened Species of the Southeastern United States* (http://endangered.fws.gov/i/b/sab2s.html, 1995). Also, Joseph E. Brown, *The Return of the Brown Pelican* (Baton Rouge: Louisiana State University Press, 1983).

38. Gomez, 81.

39. Bureau of Government Research, *Audubon Park Zoo Study: Part 1*, 56.

40. Rick Atkinson, Curator of the Audubon Zoo Swamp Exhibit, interview with author, 21 December 2000.

41. Marjorie Roehl, "Swamp to Open at Zoo," *New Orleans Times Picayune,* 6 April 1984, 15.

42. Rick Atkinson, Curator of the Audubon Zoo Swamp Exhibit, interview with author, 21 December 2000.

43. Kay Anderson, "Culture and Nature at the Adelaide Zoo: At the Frontiers of 'Human Geography,'" *Transactions of the Institute of British Geographers* NS 20 (1995): 275–94.

44. Now operated by the Audubon Institute, the same organization that manages the Audubon Zoo, the nature center acquired a new name in 2000, the Audubon Louisiana Nature Center.

45. *Louisiana Nature Center* (New Orleans: Louisiana Nature Center, 1977), 1–2.

46. "Swamp Scene," *Louisiana Nature Center News* 1 (Winter 1980–1981): 1; Robert Harrison and Walter Kollmorgen, "Drainage Reclamation in the Coastal Marshlands of the Mississippi River Delta," *Louisiana Historical Quarterly* 30 (1947): 654–709; and New Orleans Sewerage and Water Board, *Fortieth Semi-Annual Report* (New Orleans: Sewerage and Water Board, 1919), 77.

47. Louisiana Nature Center, *Concept Master Plan* (New Orleans: Louisiana Nature Center, 1979–1980).

48. Vileisis, esp. chapters 12 and 13; Reuss, esp. chapters 9–10.

49. Two landmark cases that expanded the Clean Water Act's influence over wetlands were *Natural Resources Council v. Calloway*, 392 F. Supp. 685 (1975), and *U.S. v. Riverside Bayview Homes*, 474 U.S. 121 (1985). See Rutherford H. Platt, *Land Use and Society: Geography, Law, and Public Policy* (Washington, D.C.: Island Press, 1996), 436–41.

50. Willie Fontenot, Louisiana Attorney General's Office, personal conversation, January 2001.

51. Sherwood M. Gagliano, Klaus J. Meyer-Arendt, and Karen Wicker, "Land Loss in the Mississippi River Deltaic Plain," in *Transactions: Gulf Coast Association of Geological Societies, Transactions*, 31st meeting (Corpus Christi, Tex.: October 1981), 295–300.

52. Prince, *Wetlands of the American Midwest*, esp. chapter 9. See also Robert Sullivan, *The Meadowlands Wilderness Adventures at the Edge of a City* (New York: Scribner, 1998); Cam Cavanaugh, *Saving the Great Swamp: The People, The Power Brokers, and an Urban Wilderness* (Frenchtown, N.J.: Columbia Publishing, 1978).

53. Gomez, 122–23.

54. J. O. Snowden, W. C. Ward, and J. R. J. Studlick, *Geology of Greater New Orleans: Its Relationship to Land Subsidence and Flooding* (New Orleans: New Orleans Geological Society, 1980).

55. National Park Service (NPS), *Proposed Jean Lafitte National Cultural Park, Louisiana* (Washington: National Park Service, 1972), 60–73.

56. A preserve is an area set aside primarily for its ecological characteristics.

57. U.S. Congress, Senate, Subcommittee on Parks and Recreation of the Committee on Energy and Natural Resources, *Hearings: Jean Lafitte National Park*, 95th Cong., 2nd sess., Publication 95-97, 1978.

58. Jean Lafitte National Historical Park, Public Law 95-625, 1978, 92 Stat. 3534.

59. Jean Lafitte National Historical Park, Public Law 95-625, 1978, 92 Stat. 3534.

60. Jean Lafitte National Historical Park, Public Law 95-625, 1978, 92 Stat. 3534, emphasis added.

61. See Betsy Swanson et al., *Terre Haute de Barataria* (Harahan, La.: Jefferson Parish Historical Commission, Monograph 11, 1991).

62. William Halvorson and Gary Davis, eds., *Science and Ecosystem Management in the National Parks* (Tucson: University of Arizona Press, 1996), and R. Gerald Wright, *Wildlife Research and Management in the National Parks* (Urbana: University of Illinois Press, 1992).

63. NPS, *Jean Lafitte National Historical Park: Land Protection Plan* (New Orleans: National Park Service, 1984).

64. NPS, *Land Protection Plan: Jean Lafitte National Historical Park and Preserve* (New Orleans: National Park Service, 1989), 15–16.

65. Trenasses are small canals dug by trappers for passing through the marsh grass in traditional boats known as pirogues.

66. Jean Lafitte National Heritage Park and Preserve, Barataria Preserve Trapping Season Summary, 1992, Jean Lafitte National Heritage Park and Preserve Collection, University of New Orleans, Archives, MS 294, Box 11, folder 859, New Orleans, Louisiana.

67. NPS, *Jean Lafitte National Heritage Park and Preserve: Amendment to the General Management Plan* (Denver, Colo.: National Park Service, Denver Service Center, 1995).

68. Impact Assessment, Inc., *Traditional Use Study: Barataria Preserve, Final Report* (New Orleans: National Park Service, 1998).

69. U.S. Congress, House of Representatives, Subcommittee on Fisheries and Wildlife, Committee on Merchant Marine and Fisheries, 99th Cong., 2nd sess., *Hearings: Bayou Sauvage Urban National Wildlife Refuge*, Serial 99-55, 1986, esp. testimony

of John A. Hilton, 18–21. See also Todd Shallat, "In the Wake of Hurricane Betsy," in *Transforming New Orleans and Its Environs*, 134–35.

70. Sherwood Gagliano, Testimony, in U.S. Congress, *Hearings: Bayou Sauvage*, 21–24.

71. James Pulliam, Testimony, in U.S. Congress, *Hearings: Bayou Sauvage*, 10–11.

72. Cashio, Cochran, and Torre; Coastal Environments, N-Y Associates, *Bayou Sauvage National Wildlife Refuge: Master Plan* (New Orleans: U.S. Fish and Wildlife Service, 1994), 3.

73. Cashio, Cochran, and Torre; Coastal Environments *Bayou Sauvage National Wildlife Refuge*, 3–9.

74. Cashio, Cochran, and Torre; Coastal Environments, *Bayou Sauvage National Wildlife Refuge*, 38, 83–89.

75. See Coastal Environments, Inc., *Remote-Sensing Survey of the Bayou LaBranche Wetlands Restoration Borrow Area, St. Charles Parish, Louisiana* (New Orleans: U.S. Army Corps of Engineers, New Orleans District, 1993).

JACK TEMPLE KIRBY

Epilogue

Nature Suburbanized, and

Other Southern Spaces

THE WOOD STORKS glide in over the marsh with the rising sun. So very long, slim, and elegant in flight, these great birds, once settled by the big ditch next to Palmetto Road, stand together, slumped, their black under-wing markings hidden, rendering them all white, a bit blimpy, a minor conclave of retired archbishops. We watch them on and off much of the day from east windows and the back balcony. Now they sit, again they rise; a few great white herons have joined them. Ever so deliberately, a great white and a pair of storks wade into the water, filter-feeding. After lunch, they huddle again, the herons standing slightly aside, and the storks lie down.

Storks are hardly ever alone, but fly, rest, wade, and feed at least in pairs, often five or so, sometimes a baker's dozen and beyond. We cherish their company, I must think, because they are elsewhere in summer. Meanwhile, human neighbors drive by, also tradespeople making their calls, and strangers checking the tide at the county boat ramp on the river. All slow, look, admire. A few cars and pickups ease onto the grassy margin for closer, longer looks, adults softly instructing children with them. The wood stork is the only stork native to North America. Aren't they beautiful, odd, approachable, companionable!

Whatever the season, this tidal marsh, its waters rising and falling between suburbs, teems with life and activity. Brown pelicans pass over in formation, back and forth overhead, moving between ocean and river. Ibises sometimes appear; and once there was a single roseate spoonbill, strolling where storks had convened. Much of the year great white herons are joined by lesser whites, great and lesser blues, green and tri-colored herons, and snowy egrets. The belted kingfishers reappear by March, as the storks begin to decide on their departure. Kingfishers feeding here by the marsh are advantaged by utility wires overlooking the big ditch on the south side of Palmetto. Kingfishers perch, staring down, waiting for minnows or tiny crabs to approach the water's surface; then they dive like tiny naval bombers, emitting their rattling attack call. Raptors are common here, too: kestrels, osprey, red-tailed hawks, swallow-tails, and, not infrequently, bald eagles. Florida black vultures and turkey buzzards circle regularly. And at night barred and other owls appear over the marsh from their high homes on suburban oaks. There are not only minnows and tiny crabs down there, but bigger fishes, especially mullet. Wounded birds and other small creatures will not long survive raptors' gazes either. Nor larger animals foolish or desperate enough to leave cover—domestic cats; cute brown marsh rabbits who, when stark-still, seem to consider themselves invisible; raccoons, opossums, rats and mice. Armadillos burrow by marsh banks bordering houses and anywhere else offering soft earth and cozy cover. Night ramblers, armadillos explore and excavate lawns and gardens and much else. Surely owls take interest, but the armored waddlers seem impervious.

They share spaces, or are at least neighbors to, much more subterranean life, however. The marsh and the low ridges on which our houses are built slither with serpents—fat black snakes up to four feet long; skinny black racers that cross driveways and streets in broad daylight, their heads raised for better views, revealing their distinctive white chin-streaks; rough green and garter snakes; and a profusion of rat snakes, who climb trees for birds as well as sneak and burrow for rodents. Here on Anastasia Island, rat snakes are typically a brilliant copper, two or three feet long. Elsewhere they may be yellowish or tan. Yet not long ago, a neighbor hand-clearing a downspout after a big rain, came up with a five-footer wrapped around his arm and staring him in the eye. This rat snake was likely quite old, and not copper but a mottled brown with faint black markings. The big snake's temporary captive—himself once a soldier in snaky southeast Asian jungles—killed the valuable and beautiful creature with the assistance of a couple of neighbors. Not this one, who has made himself aware of the probability of serpent-sightings with every outdoor footstep, every hedge-trimming, every garden-weeding.

A gorgeous young corn snake spent a winter in an outdoor cabinet housing our irrigation pump and controls. Pencil thin and about eighteen inches long, it preferred to lie on the controls box, just under the cabinet lid. I felt compelled to look for it nearly every day, and invited neighbors, especially children, to have a see. Whenever the lid opened the juvenile serpent coiled defiantly, the tip of its tail vibrating soundlessly. We rather miss the little rascal.

There are some real vipers out there, though. Over the years at least two neighbors have confronted (at safe distance) eastern diamondback rattle-snakes. In Marjorie Kinnan Rawlings's *The Yearling*, such a bushwhacker near-fatally struck the novel's hero, Penny Baxter. While tracking a bear, Penny had moved underbrush, very likely saw palmetto, with a bare hand, inadvertently challenging the viper. Rattlers commonly lurk beneath the cover of saw palmetto, and suburban householders are well advised not to install or encourage this plant. South of us, around Crescent Beach, the soils are sandier and more inviting to pygmy rattlers. These are especially notorious for biting the noses of curious, meandering dogs, and humans are advised by the Audubon field guide that pygmies are ever "quick to strike." No one has seen such here, though; and better yet, the salty marsh harbors no cottonmouth moccasins, which are freshwater snakes.

Long as we humans have inhabited this Earth and island, snakes, vipers included, have been here longer. Now Earth and this island have never been more densely peopled, and we have claimed and altered spaces snakes and much else had occupied. Human encroachment brings expanses of pavement and obliterates saw palmetto and much more cover, not to men-tion provender. Surviving snakes, among many wild creatures, have come to our homes to roost, so to speak. Doubtless, all Anastasia Island's wild populations are much reduced since, say, 1945, and especially since 1960, when the vast human migrations to coastal places began in earnest. The extinction of deer is often proclaimed as the island's build-out is being completed. Yet a long-legged yearling appeared in our yard, recently and near mid-day, finishing off our kumquats.

So, as we observe every day, non-human life abounds here in a micro-setting that illustrates both destruction and accommodation. When I first laid eyes on our house and neighborhood, for instance, I assumed that the assemblage was another bulldozer creation, hardly God's. So much of

Florida and the coastal East is constructed on old lowlands mounded up by fill—fill from elsewhere or fill from near-site, creating fake wetlands, ponds and lakes that present water views and elevate real estate values. But being a compulsive peasant-with-spade, I discovered beneath our yard huge stumps of very old oaks and pines. Later, local old-timers confirmed that our housing development, hardly more than two decades old, rests on a low ridge, or hammock, in the Floridian parlance. So, too, is the marsh original and legitimate, a living thing of eons past fed from a creek wandering westward and emptying into Matanzas River.

Except that the marsh has been replumbed, as it were, engineered to provide access from SR AIA—that is, to create Palmetto Road and its parallel raised road that leads to the mouth of the creek and Butler State Park, with its expansive parking and a wide boat landing. Under each road there is a large culvert that conducts the river's and creek's tides, demonstrating that the marsh is not quite flat, but slightly silted downward, north to south. As high tides recede, brackish water gushes with considerable force from the culvert near the park. Engineering includes more, though. Three-feet culverts' flow function hardly equals that of two hundred yards of marsh now diked by fill to support the two roads, nor could builders and prospective buyers be the least confident of the integrities of private properties bordering the marsh. So developers excavated a huge rectangle of ditches—"canals" seems the preferred term—making four right angles (utterly foreign in nature) between the roadways. The canals divert and contain water not passing more forcefully through the constrained culverts. Cord-grasses, needlebrush, and other maritime plants grow alongside and, inevitably, into the canals. Otherwise one might easily put a kayak or canoe into the marsh at high tide, especially one corresponding to a full moon, and paddle about the big rectangle. But other obstacles to such an odd tour materialize, too: on either side of both culverts, the daily motion of detritus-laden silt has created, in the hardly five years that we have watched, little deltas that break the straight lines between right angles—a hazard to would-be navigators and, potentially, to estuarial function. Engineers will probably return, to restore straight lines and right angles.

Worse, recently developers with exceptionally gifted attorneys managed to gain permits to construct a massive condominium complex next to the park road, atop a good part of the little estuary that feeds the essential creek. The complex is named—inevitably—The Estuaries! Another reminder of a sad old anthropologists' joke: kill and/or drive out the Indians, name the new town Indianapolis. The Estuaries was completed in 2006, just before the national real estate collapse, and two years later, early investors have backed away and hardly three buyers have actually occupied condos. Upstream, we wonder if—or more likely, how much—estuarial function has been lost.

Another tiny narrative of landscape occupancy and manipulation on Anastasia, the longer story being one of peace and war, of chaotic change brought by natural disaster and human hubris, of ruin, return, then, usually, change of unexpected new dimensions. For a long time the island was lightly but systematically farmed and fished—this by a people called Seloy who belonged to the Timucuan language group. After the Spanish came to stay, in 1565, the Seloy fed them rather well, voluntarily and otherwise. The Spaniards' mission was military, not the making of civilization, so they farmed not. Soon the Seloy and related inland polities fell victim not only to diseases but to de facto enslavement, via the agency of Franciscan missions; and ironically, the Spanish grew more numerous even as the Timucua declined. On Anastasia Island, meanwhile, diminished Seloy farmers and fishers became miners for the Spanish. Seloy laborers excavated the local soft stone, called coquina, then ferried cut blocks across Matanzas Bay, piled and mortared them as impregnable replacement for the wooden forts that had lamely defended the harbor and St. Augustine. This was the grand Castillo de San Marcos, now a national monument. By the eighteenth century, the serious mining now diminished, the island would become virtually covered with orange groves—finally something for the market. Predictably, the groves ultimately succumbed to freezes, the phenomenon that, over time, drove commercial citrus culture farther and farther down the Floridian peninsula.

Practically the only rural industry that succeeded in all La Florida was the beef business. The Spanish established enormous ranchos between the Matanzas and St. Johns, employing first Seloy and then other natives as their vaqueros. Long after Spain's second and final departure, cattle herding and drives thrived here still; but also near the Gulf Coast, and ultimately into the fringes of the Everglades. Agriculture seemed to maintain continuity only at the provisioning level, for big-scale commodity production with contracted and enslaved labor regularly failed. Young William

Bartram was hardly alone in failing as northern Florida planter, several years before his fabled southern perambulations as flora/fauna collector.

Farther south, a grand scheme to produce indigo on a huge plantation at New Smyrna collapsed also, sending several hundreds of indentured workers streaming north, to St. Augustine. The workers—Greeks, Italians, Spaniards, Portuguese, and others from the northern Mediterranean—had sailed from the Spanish island of Minorca and were known collectively as Minorcans (or Menorcans). Some became farmers, others tradespeople and watermen in and around St. Augustine. Today, indeed, St. Augustine's "Mediterranean" bona fides are arguably more attributable to the Minorcans and their many descendants than to the long-gone Spanish. In addition to the descendants, Minorcan influence on regional culture is best represented in cuisine. This is centered on a particular hot pepper, supposedly brought from the Mediterranean by immigrants, the datl—or datil (rhyming with "that'll"). More likely, a visiting Cuban sent home for this particular Capsicum, a Caribbean native. Datls may flavor many dishes, but they are famously associated with seafood chowders—clam, conch, any shell—or most any fin-fish. Production of datl peppers thrives today, west of the city in rural St. Johns County, whose farmland is also renowned for potatoes, cabbage, other winter greens, and much else. Datl growers sell pepper plants to nurseries and processors, the latter mixing and bottling variations of datl sauces, all sublime.

Today Florida's farms are threatened by housing and commercial development, like farmland in much of the American rural elsewhere. In St. Johns County, long famous for potatoes and datls, the past decade's rising crop has been lawn-grass sod to dress subdivisions-in-progress, many of these on former farmland. A money-crop is a crop and money, after all. Farmers must eat, too—as well as pay taxes and buy trucks and tractors. St. Johns, including its possible agrarian birthplace, Anastasia Island, hardly differs from the vast southern piedmont. The path of present-day Interstate 85—from Richmond and Petersburg, Virginia, down through Greensboro and Charlotte, North Carolina, to Spartanburg and Greenville, South Carolina, Atlanta to Montgomery—was transferred by farmers not only to governments, for rights-of-way, but to developers. Spaces between the cities offer views mostly of what are often mistaken for forests, and supposedly a welcome re-greening of the region after generations of deforestation and soil-mining for cotton and corn. Actually the forests are plantations of another sort, loblollies bound for the mills of an enormous pulp/paper complex. Most of the mills, in turn, are located in tidewater/coastal places, from West Point, Virginia, the South's pioneer paper-maker, on down to Plymouth, North Carolina, Georgetown, South Carolina, St. Marys, Georgia, Jacksonville, Florida, and along the Gulf Coast through Louisiana. Loblollies dominate tidewater landscapes, too; and WestVaCo, a West Virginia paper-maker, illustrates the complex's reach into the mountain South as well.

So, while farming persists broadly, visibly, here and there in the southern today, one must concede that the ancient rural/agrarian dominance—glory and curse—which characterized the region until about 1950 or so, is no more. To rediscover its imprint (other than read some history), one must leave the interstates—85, 95, 20, 10—and step into a tree plantation. There, running parallel, perpendicular, diagonally, or alongside the rows of pine, one may find remnants of older rows—or "hills," as raised furrows were called—of cotton, corn, or tobacco. The sprawling new plantations, meanwhile, demand scant human populations to tend them. Now life and labor are lived and performed in the suburbs, the edge cities, malls, warehouses, truck depots, fuel plazas. The historical paths to these contemporary landscapes were hardly smooth, or paradigmatic in some global narrative of inevitable "progress," or succession. Rather, the South's millennium-long experience with breaking the soil was bumpy, often broken; and northern Florida, once more, illustrates.

As Mart Stewart has so perceptively observed, when John Muir walked from Indianapolis onto the Floridian Gulf Coast in 1867, he had traveled a thousand miles through agrarian landscapes. The lush corn belt surrounding (and especially, south of) Indianapolis had, hardly a generation before, passed from a frontierish family-farming and herding culture to one thoroughly modern and commercial. Below the Ohio, however, war had afflicted (if not ruined) much capitalist agriculture and crippled fatally the open-range pork enterprises of many thousands of ordinary men and women. Plantation manses were torched, and untold miles of crop-field fences, essential to the South's agrarian system of production, were torn down and burned. Penned and range animals alike were consumed by soldiers and starving, refugeeing civilians. The scene in Florida was hardly different, except that Florida, being an old territory but relatively new state, had hardly achieved a stable rural production system before the Civil War, when disorder, uncertainty, and insecurity were imposed by others once more. Black Belt-type cotton plantations had only slowly been established along the Suwanee and down toward Tampa, during the relatively secure years following the Second Seminole War's conclusion, in the early 1840s. A third Indian war broke out just before the Civil War—not so intense and dangerous to whites as the previous uprising, yet enough to remind all Floridians that Euro-civilization there was hardly safer than in parts of Texas and Kansas. Now the remnant Seminoles retreated toward the Everglades, but slavery was abolished, a new labor scheme was not yet quite determined, and credit was scarce. Who knew, but that Florida and much of the rest of the South might once more become abandoned to return to nature wild, at least for a time.

Muir was hardly inspired to wait and see, and having apparently met no congenial neo-Transcendentalists in the Deep South, he turned right, set sail, and finally walked into the High Sierras. This was one odd choice. In 1492 (according to estimates by Shepard Krech and others), the West Coast of what is now the United States had the densest populations. (The South was second in density.) Pacific natives hunted, fished, and farmed, and they lived primarily in towns, like most eastern peoples. In California the Spanish founded missions, subjugated natives, established latifundia—rather as in Florida. Natives perished; Yankees, then Yankee soldiers, came during the 1840s; a gold rush brought forth sudden and enormous new populations and landscape alterations. California, no less than Florida, had been briefly a vast widowed landscape, especially at higher elevations. So it was here, in biblical mountains, that Muir proclaimed pristine wilderness.

Lightly populated (or unpopulated), mostly forested mountains have essential function, of course: snows accumulate and melt; trees and understory slow run-off; and valleys are watered, rivers supplied. No wonder that Muir joined comfortably with Theodore Roosevelt and other conservationists, for a while. Then, as all recall, John Muir, resident of the Bay Area and founder of the Sierra Club, broke with San Franciscan and Rooseveltian conservationists over the issue of supplying the Bay Area with potable water from the Hetch Hetchy Valley in Yosemite. Muir and his followers and admirers had fixed on a historical moment in the West and rendered, or tried to render it, sacred and permanent.

Surely Muir believed that sacred/eternal nature was not applicable to the South, where mountains were not so high and abandoned landscapes were rather promptly reclaimed by new people—even the Everglades. Oftentimes resettlers were farmers who could read old Indian topographies, parsing native associations of tree cover with soil values, and resuming cultivation. Agrarian traditions survived, however ethnically and chronologically discontinuous. On the other hand, different times and places brought different land uses, too—as on Anastasia Island in Florida and many other locales.

But then—and very late—the notion of wilderness finally came to the South, especially to certain mountain ranges, naturally. The enormous cutdown of southern forests by well-mechanized corporations, between ca. 1880 and 1920, did awful mischief in uplands, where destroyed watersheds released mounting spring floods. Reforestation fell to governments—as state and federal preserves where wood-taking and hunting were restricted. The making of a great eastern "nature" preserve, a majestic space to be visited but not lived in, fell to the federal Park Service. Margaret Lynn Brown has brilliantly, sorrowfully described the making of Great Smoky Mountains National Park—the betrayal of old communities within the park-to-be, an absurd "western ranch" tourist site, extensive road-building to accommodate automobiles, cruel (often stupid) manipulations of animal populations, and much else. In the end, this bizarre eastern version of western nature-without-humanity merely elaborates our generalization: the South has ever been chaotically human. So even in the Great Smoky Mountains National Park, where we are forbidden to live, there are traffic jams, especially when drivers halt to meet and treat bears, who for the longest time, along with wolves, represented profound threats to civilization! Daniel Boone, Davy Crockett, and Penny Baxter might, or might not, be amused.

CONTRIBUTORS

VIRGINIA DEJOHN ANDERSON is professor of history at the University of Colorado, Boulder. She has written two books and several articles on early American history; her most recent monograph is *Creatures of Empire: How Domestic Animals Transformed Early America* (2004).

WILLIAM BOYD is an associate professor of law at the University of Colorado, Boulder. Previously, he served as counsel to the Democratic minority staff of the U.S. Senate Committee on Environment and Public Works. He has a PhD from the Energy and Resources Group at UC-Berkeley and a J.D. from Stanford Law School. He is currently completing a book manuscript for Johns Hopkins University Press on the legal, economic, and environmental history of the forest products industry in the post–New Deal American South.

LISA BRADY is an associate professor of history at Boise State University. Her research focuses on the interplay between nature and warfare and has been published in *Environmental History, Diplomatic History*, and *Ohio Valley History*. Her book-length study on the American Civil War is forthcoming from the University of Georgia Press.

JOSHUA BLU BUHS, who received his PhD from the University of Pennsylvania's History and Sociology of Science Department, is an independent scholar. He is the author of *The Fire Ant Wars: Nature, Science, and Public Policy in Twentieth-Century America* (2004) and *Bigfoot: The Life and Times of an American Legend* (2008).

JUDITH CARNEY is professor of geography at the University of California, Los Angeles. She is author of *Black Rice: The African Origins of Rice Cultivation in the Americas* (2001), and she is currently completing a book on the role of African plants in the Atlantic slave trade, *Seeds of Memory: Africa's Botanical Legacy in the Atlantic World* (University of California Press, forthcoming).

JAMES TAYLOR CARSON is an associate dean and professor of history at Queen's University in Kingston, Ontario, Canada. He writes in the field of southern ethnohistory and his recent publications include "American Historians and Indians," *The Historical Journal* 49 (2006): 1–13, and *Making an Atlantic World: Circles, Paths, and Stories from the Colonial South* (2007). He is also executive editor of a new journal, *Native South*.

CRAIG E. COLTEN is the Carl O. Sauer Professor of Geography at Louisiana State University and the editor of *Geographical Review*. His most recent book is *An Unnatural Metropolis: Wresting New Orleans from Nature* (2005).

S. MAX EDELSON is associate professor of history at the University of Illinois at Urbana-Champaign. His recent publications include *Plantation Enterprise in Colonial South Carolina* (2006) and "The Nature of Slavery: Environmental Disorder and Slave Agency in Colonial South Carolina" in Robert Olwell and Alan Tully, eds., *Cultures and Identities in Colonial British America* (2005). His current research examines geography and empire in early America.

JACK TEMPLE KIRBY is W. E. Smith Professor Emeritus of History at Miami University in Oxford, Ohio, and currently lives on Anastasia Island in Florida. He is author or editor of eight books, including *Mockingbird Song: Ecological Landscapes of the South* (2006), for which he won the 2007 Bancroft Prize.

RALPH H. LUTTS is a member of the faculty at Goddard College where he coordinates a graduate concentration in environmental studies. He is author of *The Nature Fakers: Wildlife, Science and Sentiment* and editor of *The Wild Animal Story*. His home is in Patrick County on the Blue Ridge of southwestern Virginia.

CHRISTOPHER J. MANGANIELLO is a PhD candidate at the University of Georgia, where he is at work on a dissertation—tentatively titled "Dam Crazy with Wild Consequences: Artificial Lakes and Natural Rivers in the Savannah River Valley, 1890–1990"—that explores the genesis of the American South's modern waterscape and the consequences for nature and culture.

EILEEN MAURA MCGURTY, associate chair of the graduate program in environmental sciences and policy at Johns Hopkins University, is the author of *Transforming Environmentalism: Warren County, PCBs, and the Origins of Environmental Justice* (2007).

TED STEINBERG is Adeline Barry Davee Distinguished Professor of History and professor of law at Case Western Reserve University. He is the author of five books, including *American Green: The Obsessive Quest for the Perfect Lawn* (2006), *Down to Earth: Nature's Role in American History* (2002), and *Acts of God: The Unnatural History of Natural Disaster in America* (2000).

MART STEWART is a professor in the Department of History and an affiliate professor in the Huxley College of the Environment at Western Washington University. He is the author of *"What Nature Suffers to Groe": Life, Labor, and Landscape on the Georgia Coast, 1680–1920* (1996; updated in 2003), and he is currently completing a book-length manuscript, to be published by the University of North Carolina Press, on the cultural history of climate in America.

CLAIRE STROM is the Rapetti-Trunzo Chair of History at Rollins College and the editor of *Agricultural History*. She is the author of *Profiting from the Plains: The Great Northern Railway and Corporate Development in the American West* (2003) and *"Making Catfish Bait out of Government Boys": Politics, Class, and Environment in the New South* (University of Georgia Press, forthcoming).

PAUL S. SUTTER is an associate professor of history at the University of Georgia. He is the author of *Driven Wild: How the Fight Against Automobiles Launched the Modern Wilderness Movement* (2002), and he edits the University of Georgia Press's "Environmental History and the American South" book series.

HARRY WATSON is a professor of history at the University of North Carolina, Chapel Hill, where he also serves as director of the Center for the Study of the American South and co-editor of its journal, *Southern Cultures*. His most recent book is *Andrew Jackson Versus Henry Clay: Democracy and Development in Antebellum America* (1998), and his *Liberty and Power: The Politics of Jacksonian America* appeared in an updated edition in 2006.

ALBERT G. WAY, currently a postdoctoral fellow in the Institute for Southern Studies at the University of South Carolina, received his PhD in history from the University of Georgia in 2008. His published essays have appeared in *Environmental History, Southern Cultures*, and *Forest History Today*.

INDEX

Mississippian cultures, 5
Mississippi River, 63, 64, 434; delta environment, 433; at New Orleans, 432, 446; at Vicksburg, 176–78
Mississippi Territory, 66, 68, 69
Missouri: cattle tick eradication in, 229; infected cattle rejected in, 222–23
Mitchell, Margaret, 133
Mitman, Gregg, 288
Mobile, Ala., 64, 402; and fire ants, 345, 348–50, 357
mobile homes, 423–25
Monroe County Toll Commission, 418
Montana, cattle tick eradication in, 223
Montell, William Lynwood, 265
Montgomery, Ala., 463
Montgomery County, N.C., 145
Montrie, Chad, 12
Moore Haven, Fla., 409–10
Morgan, H. A., 229
Morgan, Philip, 7, 200
Morgan, T. H., 328
Mountain Lake, Va., 265
Muir, John, 10, 196–97, 200–201, 213, 464–66

Nairne, Thomas, 112
Nantahala National Forest, 265
Nash, Roderick, 173
Nash County, N.C., 142, 143, 144, 145
Natchez Indians, 66
Natchez Weekly Courier, 174
Natchitoches Indians, 65
National Academy of Sciences, 324
National Association for the Advancement of Colored People (NAACP), 385–86
National Bureau of Standards, 424
National Center for Voluntary Action (NCVA), 375
National Poultry Improvement Plan (NPIP), 318

National Priority List, 379, 391
National Research Council, 324
Natural Enemy, Natural Ally (Tucker and Russell), 171
Nebraska, cattle tick eradication in, 223
Neel, Leon, 304
Nelson, E. W., 295
Netherlands, 30, 251
Neuse River, 138, 142, 148
Nevada, 360
Newberry District, S.C., 149
Newcastle, U.K., 253
Newcastle disease, 319. *See also* broiler industry
New Deal, 200, 238, 287, 314
New England, 7, 8, 29, 157; fishermen from, 136
Newfont, Kathy, 12
New Hampshire, 250
New Jersey, 251, 267, 403
New Market, Va., 180
New Mexico, 63; cattle tick eradication in, 223; fire ant in, 360
New Netherlands, 251
New Orleans, La., 432–52; cattle market in, 222; fire ant in, 349; Hurricane Katrina and, 17; maroon community in, 205
New Orleans East (NOE), 448
New Smyrna, Fla., 463
Newsweek, 400
New Western History, 2
New York, 251
New York City, N.Y., 258, 406–7
New York Herald, 182, 183
New York Times, 400, 408
New York Zoological Park, 266
Niagara Falls, N.Y., 381
Nichols, George Ward, 168
Niger River, 82
NIMBY ("Not In My Backyard"), 16, 379–83

Russell, Edmund: *Natural Enemy, Natural Ally* (with Tucker), 171; *War and Nature*, 171, 190
Russia, 212, 353
Rutledge, John, 147

Sabal palmetto, 121. *See also* palmetto tree
Sabine River, 65
Saint Augustine, Fla., 462, 463
Saint Johns County, Fla., 463
Saint Johns River, 90, 138, 462
Saint Marys, Ga., 464
Saluda River, 141, 145, 147
salvage logging, 269
Sanders, William J., 414
Sandford, Robert, 113
Sandy Valley, 254
San Francisco, Calif., 408; Bay Area, 465
San Marcos, Castillo de, 462
Santee River, 119, 138
Sargent, Governor Winthrop, 67, 68
Savannah, Ga., Civil War and, 183–86
Savannah River, 94, 141, 147, 150, 183, 187; maroon community, 205
Savannah River Site, 18
Schell, Orville, 334
Scott, James, 334
Sea Island, 131
Second Massachusetts Volunteers, 185
Second Seminole War, 465
Seloy Indians, 462
Seminole Indians, 465
Seminole Reservation, 238
Senegal, 82
septicemia, 228
Seventh Ohio Cavalry, 174
Seventy-ninth Indiana Infantry, 174
shad, 8, 13, 131–59; impacted by mill-dams, 131–59; life cycle and biology of, 138; petitions to save, 140–45; quality of, 141
Sharp, Howard, 409–11
Shaw, Byron, 352

Shearin, George, 385
Sheets, Robert, 426
Shelby County, Tex., 237
Shenandoah Valley, 9, 169, 179–80, 190
Sheridan, Philip H., 169, 172; in Shenandoah Valley, 179–82, 184, 190; targets agricultural interests, 175, 176, 189
Sherman, William Tecumseh, 10, 168, 169, 170, 172; in Mississippi, 178; targets agricultural interests, 175, 189, 176
Sherman's March to the Sea, 9, 169, 170, 182–88
Sherwood Plantation, 293
shifting cultivation, 9, 10
Sibley, John, 65
Sierra Club, 196, 377, 392, 465; member survey, 375–76
Sierra Leone, 83, 84
Sierra Nevada Mountains, 200, 465
Sigel, Franz, 180
Silent Spring (Carson), 15, 345, 355–57
Silver, Timothy, 6, 107–8
slavery: Civil War and, 187; fishing and, 159; in Florida, 465; plantations and, 8; racialized landscape created by, 200; shifting cultivation and, 9
slaves: Civil War and, 178; environmental knowledge and, 201–5; palmetto trees and, 122; Red Hills agriculture and, 287; South Carolina rice and, 80–82, 88–100
Small Business Administration (SBA), 418, 419
Smith, John, 28
Smith, Robert, 36
Smith, Theobald, 225, 240
Society of American Foresters, 298
soil exhaustion, 208
Solenopsis invicta, 347–50. *See also* fire ants
Solenopsis richteri, 347–49. *See also* fire ants
Solenopsis saevissima richteri, 347. *See also* fire ants

Environmental History and the American South

Lynn A. Nelson
Pharsalia: An Environmental Biography of a Southern Plantation, 1780–1880

Jack E. Davis
An Everglades Providence: Marjory Stoneman Douglas and the American Environmental Century

Shepard Krech III
Spirits of the Air: Birds and American Indians in the South

Paul S. Sutter and Christopher J. Manganiello, eds.
Environmental History and the American South: A Reader

Claire Strom
Making Catfish Bait out of Government Boys: The Fight against Cattle Ticks and the Transformation of the Yeoman South

CPSIA information can be obtained at www.ICGtesting.com
Printed in the USA
LVOW08s1338300716

498417LV00002B/227/P